THE PHILOSOPHY OF ENCHANTMENT

THE PHILOSOPHY OF ENCHANTMENT

Studies in Folktale, Cultural Criticism, and Anthropology

R. G. COLLINGWOOD

Edited by

DAVID BOUCHER,

WENDY JAMES,

and

PHILIP SMALLWOOD

CLARENDON PRESS · OXFORD

This book has been printed digitally and produced in a standard specification
in order to ensure its continuing availability

OXFORD
UNIVERSITY PRESS

Great Clarendon Street, Oxford OX2 6DP
Oxford University Press is a department of the University of Oxford.
It furthers the University's objective of excellence in research, scholarship,
and education by publishing worldwide in
Oxford New York
Auckland Cape Town Dar es Salaam Hong Kong Karachi
Kuala Lumpur Madrid Melbourne Mexico City Nairobi
New Delhi Shanghai Taipei Toronto
With offices in
Argentina Austria Brazil Chile Czech Republic France Greece
Guatemala Hungary Italy Japan South Korea Poland Portugal
Singapore Switzerland Thailand Turkey Ukraine Vietnam

Oxford is a registered trade mark of Oxford University Press
in the UK and in certain other countries
Published in the United States
by Oxford University Press Inc., New York

ISBN 978-0-19-926253-3

To Teresa Smith

NOTE ON ILLUSTRATIONS

Part 1: Frontispiece from *The Life and Death of Cormac the Skald*, translated by W. G. Collingwood and Jon Stefansson, 1902.

Part 2: Frontispiece from *Thorstein of the Mere*, by W. G. Collingwood, 1895.

Part 3: Illustration from *The Story of the Volsungs*, translated by Eirikr Magnusson and William Morris, 1888, edited by H. Halliday Sparling.

ACKNOWLEDGEMENTS

We are grateful for the support of Mrs Teresa Smith, Colling-wood's daughter, who encouraged this project from an early stage, and generously consented to the publication of our selection from her father's unpublished work. Professor David Hopkins of Bristol University and Professor Roger Scruton both assisted us when taking the measure of Collingwood's 'Words and Tune'. Dr John Mullarkey of the Department of Philosophy at the University of Sunderland helped locate Collingwood's manuscript quotations from Bergson. Professor Jack Zipes of the University of Minnesota read through the entire folktale manuscript and gave the editors the benefit of many valuable observations and judgements. The editors are also grateful for the support and encouragement of Professor Donald S. Taylor, Emeritus Professor of English at the University of Oregon and author of the annotated *Bibliography* of Collingwood's unpublished manuscripts. Professor Taylor was one of the first scholars to recognize the value to literary history and theory of Collingwood's unpublished writings on folktale.

Colin Harris and his deputy Oliver House in the Modern Manu-scripts Reading Room of the Bodleian Library have given us expert and tireless support through the process of inspecting and transcri-bing the manuscripts in the Collingwood Papers archive. We are grateful to Naomi van Loo, of the McGowin Library at Pembroke College, to Mr Robin Darwall-Smith, archivist of University College, and to Dr James Connelly of Southampton Institute who shared with us his notes on Collingwood's library and gener-ously assisted in locating reports of Collingwood's lectures on Jane Austen. We would like to thank Marnie Hughes Warrington for her initial work on producing an electronic copy of the folktale manuscript, this kindly funded by William Rieckmann. At Cardiff University Lisa Berni has been extremely generous in devoting time to furthering the project, for which we are again very grateful. We should like to thank staff of the British Library, Will Ryan of the Warburg Institute, Honorary Librarian of the Folklore Soci-ety, and Caroline Oates, Librarian of the Folklore Society, for assistance in locating material. Staff of the Oxford University Press Archives gave us valuable support, and we are in debt to Dr Kathleen Taylor and Dr Gillian Wright for helping with the interpretation of Collingwood's handwritten Greek.

For permission to adapt, as part of our Introduction and apparatus, some material previously published in essay form, we should like to thank the editors of *Collingwood Studies*. Dr Peter Rivière kindly commented on our account of anthropology in the 1930s.

The hospitality and intellectual stimulation of the Visiting Scholarship scheme at St John's College, Oxford—of which Philip Smallwood was a beneficiary in the summer vacation of 2003—has helped us greatly in bringing our editorial work to a conclusion. All three editors have been given sterling support by family over the long gestation of this project.

Finally we should like to thank Peter Momtchiloff of Oxford University Press for his receptiveness to the publication of manuscript material by Collingwood and for his encouragement and advice at every stage. The detailed and expert guidance of the anonymous readers for the Press has proved indispensable in ways too numerous to mention.

January 2005

CONTENTS

ABBREVIATIONS

Citations of the following books by Collingwood, in the apparatus to this edition, are abbreviated as follows:

A   *An Autobiography* (1939)
EM   *An Essay on Metaphysics* (1940; rev. edn. 1998)
EPM   *An Essay on Philosophical Method* (1933)
IH   *The Idea of History* (1946; rev. edn. 1993)
IN   *The Idea of Nature* (1945)
NL   *The New Leviathan* (1942; rev. edn. 1992)
OPA   *Outlines of a Philosophy of Art* (1925)
PA   *The Principles of Art* (1938)
RP   *Religion and Philosophy* (1916)

The folktale manuscript published in this volume is abbreviated as FT1–6. Other manuscripts published in this volume are abbreviated as follows:

AM   'Art and the Machine' (*c.*1936)
ATAP   'Aesthetic Theory and Artistic Practice' (1931)
JA1   'Jane Austen' (1921)
JA2   'Jane Austen' (?1934)
LPA   'Lectures on the Philosophy of Art' (1924)
MGM   'Man Goes Mad' (1936)
OL   'Observations on Language' (n.d.)
WT   'Words and Tune' (1918)

Other abbreviations:

F-L   *Folk-Lore: A Quarterly Review of Myth, Tradition, Institution, and Custom*, incorporating *The Archaeological Review* and *The Folk-Lore Journal*.
FLS   Folk Lore Society.

MR   Maureen E. Rudzik. 'Folklore and History: An Analysis of an Unpublished Manuscript by R. G. Collingwood', Ph.D. thesis (Toronto, 1990).

EDITORS' FOREWORD AND NOTE

DAVID BOUCHER, WENDY JAMES, AND PHILIP SMALLWOOD

Collingwood is probably best known for his posthumously published book *The Idea of History* (1946). This more than any other work on the philosophy of history in the English-speaking world came to be the touchstone for discussions of the intellectual integrity of claims to historical knowledge. It included some of his most controversial theories, such as the claims that all history is the history of thought; that the achievement of historical knowledge entails the re-enactment of past thoughts, and that historical knowledge owes nothing to the methods of natural science. It is the most widely cited of his books and continues to be extensively used to introduce students to the problems of historical inquiry. Collingwood's *The Principles of Art* (1938) similarly remains an important text in aesthetics, articulating the theory that art, instead of being pure imagination as he had previously thought, is the expression of emotion. Art, in other words, was more to do with what the artist expressed, than with the object of art in itself.

During his lifetime, which extended from 1889 to his premature death in 1943, Collingwood was a true virtuoso, a Renaissance man, who saw all human activity as an invitation to interrogate it, and to relate it to the broader scheme of things. In *Speculum Mentis* (1924), for example, this scheme was experience as a whole. He wrote extensively on philosophical method, on metaphysics, the philosophy of history, the philosophy of science, political philosophy, and aesthetics. Correlative with these interests he worked relentlessly on his archaeological projects, specializing for example in the Roman inscriptions of Britain, on which he was the world's leading authority. When he died he left his widow, Kathleen Collingwood, a large quantity of manuscripts; and he left instructions to her and Kenneth Sisam of Oxford University Press that nothing of an ephemeral nature was to be published.

Following his death, T. M. Knox, one of Collingwood's former pupils, was appointed by Oxford University Press (and reluctantly accepted by the Collingwood family) as the editor of a collected volume of his work that was to have contained a memoir. With the publication of *The Idea of Nature* (1945) and *The Idea of History* (1946) Knox declared that there was nothing else of value to publish. Knox was not a sympathetic editor and had very strong views that biased him to the period he artificially constructed, the middle Collingwood of *An Essay on Philosophical Method* (1933). He disregarded Collingwood's own authorization for the publication of *The Principles of History*, and ignored the family's desire to see the folktale manuscript published. Between 1947 and 1989 no new manuscript material written by R. G. Collingwood appeared in print. However, a systematic reassessment of the value of Collingwood's manuscripts has taken place since they became accessible to the public by being placed on deposit in the Bodleian Library, Oxford, in 1979.

The unpublished manuscripts have revealed a wealth of material that demonstrated how Collingwood came to reach the conclusions he did in his mature works, with, for example, numerous reworkings of the lectures on ethics that came to be the basis of the theory articulated in *The New Leviathan* (1942), the last of his books to be published in his lifetime. They also demonstrate, in addition, a wealth of writing, in varying stages of completion, revealing in-depth knowledge of things only intimated in the published works. In the Ashmolean Museum, for instance, there is an almost complete manuscript, fully illustrated by Collingwood himself, on Roman brooches. Among the manuscripts in the Bodleian Library are literary studies and an almost complete draft of a book on folktale and magic, also referred to as the 'Fairy Tales' manuscript. To this field of study Collingwood applies his philosophy of history, and in a manner which may initially seem a surprising departure. The book-length text of the folktale study is comparable in quality to that of *The Principles of History* (1999) edited by W. H. Dray and Jan van der Dussen, and the essays we have chosen to supplement this core text both illuminate its arguments and extend them into broader areas of culture. In other words, true to the spirit of Collingwood's *Speculum Mentis*, our volume aspires to transcend strictly disciplinary barriers and demonstrates how widely applicable Collingwood's arguments are to the humanities and social sciences in general.

This volume thus offers first and foremost an annotated critical edition of what is probably the most significant single and sustained document to be preserved amongst R. G. Collingwood's hitherto unpublished papers. The folktale manuscript may so far have had little attention; yet many decades later it still stands to make a compelling contribution to the study of human culture, deeper and wider than its nominal—and at first sight narrow—'folklorist' focus. Collingwood joined the Folk Lore Society in 1936, chaired two of its meetings in 1937, and was invited to deliver a lecture to the Society in 1938 on 'The Place of Magic in Human Life'. Unfortunately the lecture had to be postponed because of Collingwood's illness, but it is evident that he had developed an interest in this field that went far beyond the immediate needs of the lecture and indeed extended to the conception of a book. We know from papers held at Oxford University Press that Collingwood had often talked to Kenneth Sisam at the Press about a proposed book on the theme of the folktale, and that both Ethel Collingwood and Kate Collingwood were enthusiastic about its possible publication.

Collingwood's writings on folktale and magic belong together as a whole, grafted upon the initial four integrated chapters clearly designed as the heart of a book. But rather than publishing them as a volume in isolation, the value of these manuscripts is greatly enhanced by placing them in the supporting context of other unpublished essays on the central value of literary practices and artistic sensibility in civilized life. The general theme of the chapters on folktale as a genre of narrative is to explore the richness of 'folk' literature and arts, their long lineage, and the debt owed by the sophisticated arts of civilization to these humble roots. A continuity and interconnection of thought and symbolic or emotional response between ourselves and peoples remote from 'us' in time or space, Collingwood argues, can be traced through the transmission of the spoken tale, and this is a surer route than some other kinds of anthropological evidence to an understanding of our underlying affinity with them. There is a tone of nostalgia, even lament, about the onset of those utilitarian practices and values that have cut us off from our roots, and distanced us from an older kind of civilization that integrated human thought and feeling. These are motifs also found in less pronounced form in Collingwood's published writings on art and literature, as they are in his work on modern technology and the politics of nationalism. For these reasons, we have chosen a selection of his unpublished essays on these topics to lead into, and reflect back upon, his ideas about folktale and magic. In Part I, Art and Culture, we include several philosophical but appreciative pieces on language, music, aesthetics, and literature. The main body of the book is presented as Part II, Tales of Enchantment, including the folktale chapters and related shorter pieces. In Part III, The Modern Unease, we conclude the book with two sharply critical essays explicitly mourning the loss of folk practices and those artistic capacities which Collingwood saw as essential nourishment to civilization, a loss consequent upon the advance of the machine in various guises, the power of nations, and the rise of militarism. Our juxtaposition of these pieces with the folktale study conveys Collingwood's vision of the fragility of modern liberal society, and may in this regard be viewed as prophetic tales of *disenchantment*.

The Introduction to the present volume is in three parts. Each consists of a new assessment of the sources, significance, and analogues of Collingwood's folktale study by the respective editors, specialists in distinct but complementary areas. Philip Smallwood analyses its twentieth-century literary, critical, cultural, reader-reception, and translational meanings. Wendy James writes from the perspective of social anthropology as it came to develop from the mid-twentieth century on, a development itself marked by a Collingwood-style shift away from scientific naturalism and functionalism towards a more historical and literary approach. David Boucher considers the folktale study from the viewpoint of historical method and in the light of Collingwood's new definition of cultural archaeology, and offers a defence of Collingwood's philosophy of history against both his critics and friends.

COLLINGWOOD'S TEXTS

In the first part of this volume we offer a set of texts on specifically literary-cultural, critical, and interdisciplinary themes that illuminate what we regard as Collingwood's conception of the deep value of artistic practice to civilized life. Aesthetic and political planes intersect in several of these pieces. The interlocking concepts of reason, emotion, and history are principally articulated by the folktale chapters themselves; but they are also anticipated in the collection of 'early' documents included here. These papers have tended hitherto to be viewed as marginal fragments peripheral to the Collingwood canon. Here we show them to be connected by their complementary opening out to interdisciplinary consideration the analysis of meaning, language, civilization, and history in its artistic and thus emotional, mythological, and aesthetic dimensions. The 1918 paper 'Words and Tune' (25/1)[1] incisively examines the relations between musical and poetical notation, pitch and stress. Collingwood's analysis of the components of song in this paper serves as a prelude to his discussion of the continuities of oral and literary-cultural forms in the folktale manuscript.

Next, Collingwood's few pages entitled 'Observations on Language' (16/13, n.d.) isolate the identity of language in near-Wittgensteinian terms and round out his explorations of what language ultimately is. Collingwood's two lectures on the novels of Jane Austen (17/2 and 17/3, 1921 and c. 1934 respectively) then follow. Both can be appreciated as aspects of Collingwood's larger interdisciplinary and critical project, and in their focus on a single canonical author, the lectures relate Collingwood's analysis of the meaning of human society to fictional, textual, narrative, characterological, sociological, literary, and historical paradigms. Both moreover provide a productive forum for appreciating Collingwood's positive literary taste. In their juxtaposition with the folktale study, the lectures illustrate Collingwood's sense of the continuities between the passions of the putatively 'civilized' mode of 'polite' society found in Austen's novels of courtship, love, and marriage, and what has been taken for an essentially remote, ritualized consciousness of a primitive 'other'. Together the literary comedy of manners and the pre-literary oral forms resolve extremes within an extended conception of human creative nature embodied in the common language of story.

In his 'Lectures on the Philosophy of Art' (25/2) from 1924 we then show Collingwood exploring the philosophical problem of defining art, examining the notion of the 'sublime', and sketching a psychological theory of revolution and change representing

---

[1] The numbers in parentheses make reference to the shelfmark of Collingwood's unpublished MSS in the archive of the Bodleian Library Collingwood Papers, University of Oxford. The first is the box number, and the second is the item number. All MSS have now been microfilmed and the original MSS conserved to avoid deterioration. The originals may be consulted with the permission of Mrs Teresa Smith, Collingwood's daughter and literary executor.

an early statement of a literary-historical 'anxiety of influence'. He here diagnoses the 'error of the Romantic movement' (returned to in the folktale study itself and in the lectures on Austen), and views Romanticism controversially as a denial of the 'primitivism' of art. Then, in 'Aesthetic Theory and Artistic Practice' (25/4) from 1931 Collingwood goes on to discuss general trends in nineteenth-century literature and the influence of naturalism upon them, comments interestingly on literary figures such as Hardy, and articulates a conception of mutual dependence between theory and practice.

In Part II, the core of the volume, the six main folktale chapters are positioned within the frame established above. In general, the structured whole of the folktale study is evidently Collingwood's own achievement and is congruent with the various chapters' implied destination as a published work (he refers to them as a 'book'). Collingwood's lucidity and his thematic control are evident from the opening of the first chapter, 'Fairy Tales' (21/4). This sets the agenda for thinking about the use of tales as non-documentary evidence of the cultural past. Chapter 2, 'Three Methods of Approach: Philological, Functional, Psychological' (21/5), works within the traditions of satirical as well as logical polemic to address the different ways in which the study of the oral narrative tradition has fallen foul of positivistic, pseudo-scientific, xenophobic, and naturalistic modes of enquiry within anthropology. Chapter 3, 'The Historical Method' (21/6), establishes grounds for a new kind of historical, anthropological, and archaeological approach that is more sympathetically inward with its object than the methods rejected in the previous chapter. Chapter 4, 'Magic' (21/7), articulates in ways which recall the prose energies of a D. H. Lawrence the two-way relationship between the supposedly 'primitive' mind implied by the pre-literary forms of the tales and the world of the modern anthropological scholar who studies them. Chapter 5, to which we have given the title 'Excavating *Cinderella* and *King Lear*' (21/10), provides a case study of the new methods and takes up the question of history by reference to multiple versions of one especially influential tale recorded in various parts of the world. Collingwood's treatment here of the archaeological 'strata' of ancient narrative exemplifies in discursive terms the principle of historical re-enactment and illustrates its overlap with the 'high' literary culture of Shakespeare's *King Lear*.

Finally, chapter 6, which we entitle (from Collingwood's first draft) 'The Authorship of Fairy Tales' (21/9), draws away from particular examples in ways which anticipate (but also differ significantly from) both the 'author-function' and the non-referential 'archaeology of knowledge' later made current by Michel Foucault. The transactional link between creators and audience within a system of social relations here focuses the question of authors as original creators, critiques the hypothesis of their individuality and 'privileged' authority, and dissolves the individual creator within a process of cultural and literary transmission. We also present here some fragmentary pieces closely linked to the core of the volume, such as the untitled notes (21/8) and the pages on the issue of the folktales' 'diffusion' versus theories of their independent origin (21/11).

The concluding section, Part III, consists of two essays that open up the gloomy prospect of the future decline and decay of civilization. In 'Art and the Machine' (25/8) Collingwood bristles with annoyance at the invasion of our lives by mechanical forms of amusement such as gramophones (but the argument no doubt goes beyond them) in place of actual musical practice and performance. The more serious piece, 'Man Goes Mad' (24/4), reflects in disturbingly prophetic ways on the political threats to liberal values and civilization as a result of the rise of nationalism and militarization. Collingwood's reflections here not only prefigure his impassioned last book, *The New Leviathan*, but take their bearings explicitly from the erosion of that real art and feeling which he celebrates in the essays presented here, an erosion that in some dark way is linked to the spread of the new dangers.

NOTE ON EDITORIAL PROCEDURE

Throughout the volume, the texts have been carefully edited on the same lines as *The Principles of History*. Footnotes are used throughout to make connections with published and unpublished works. They also complete some of Collingwood's references, point to the intellectual or cultural sources and context of his remarks, and explain obscure allusions. We have tried to present as unimpeded a text as is consistent with the need to convey certain scribal particulars of the manuscripts, and to signal from time to time the stages in the compositional process that took place. Where an amendment is a minor matter of expression, as most often the case, it has usually been silently adopted. Where Collingwood has deleted, or pasted over, a section of text in the manuscript (sometimes with a pencilled amendment, sometimes in ink) we have usually followed the perceptible intentions of the author in printing only genuine second (and prospectively better or better expressed) thoughts in the main text, and have not reproduced the deleted material. At other times, Collingwood's minor deletions or pastings over have appeared to us sufficiently interesting—in that they say something well that is not said elsewhere—to be recorded as notes. Some of his revisions occur not because the material has been rejected as sub-standard, but to shorten a written essay for oral delivery. Minor inconsistencies or errors of punctuation, original manuscript subheadings, and presentational devices that do not alter the sense, have generally been silently amended or standardized, and errors in his quotations have been corrected usually without comment. Ordinal numbers in the main text are rendered in words. In the main text and the footnotes, 'and' appears in place of Collingwood's regular manuscript use of the ampersand, and the text has been standardized throughout using single quotation marks. Folio numbers relating to the manuscripts in the archive of the Bodleian Library Collingwood Papers are inserted in square brackets for ease of reference to the originals.

Compared with the practices common within modern scholarship, Collingwood's footnotes in most of his major writings are fairly light. We have followed the practice of earlier Oxford University Press editions of manuscript material by Collingwood in normally marking his own footnotes, as he marked them himself, with an asterisk. Collingwood's manuscript footnotes are not always accurate or complete. To avoid over-complex notes, or where the particular edition of a text has proved unascertainable, we have sometimes retained Collingwood's original citation, placing certain pagination and other details from the original note in single inverted commas; in all such cases further bibliographical information can be located in our 'Bibliography of Works Cited'. In the main, however, we have silently standardized and amplified names and bibliographical details, within the note, according to the current style of Oxford University Press. Where bibliographical information has been added by us to an abbreviated citation by

Collingwood that does not identify a particular edition, we have in general cited editions that Collingwood could have used rather than modern standard editions; though we have borne in mind that some standard editions available to Collingwood have now been superseded, and that it is sometimes useful for the modern reader to be guided toward modern texts. Except where information has been added simply to complete a bibliographical citation or to identify an author, our extensions to footnotes are enclosed in square brackets. Parenthetical references used by Collingwood have as a rule been reduced to notes keyed into the main text by a superscript numeral; unless we enclose them in inverted commas, they are similarly standardized.

EDITORS' INTRODUCTION

1. THE RE-ENACTMENT OF SELF: PERSPECTIVES FROM LITERATURE, CRITICISM, AND CULTURE

PHILIP SMALLWOOD

Collingwood on Folktale: Subject, Context, and Critical Style

This book is concerned with what human civilization might be, what place art might have in it, and how it can be born, continued, and destroyed. To this end, we have selected as forming the core of Collingwood's 'Philosophy of Enchantment' essays that were composed originally as lectures for the Folk Lore Society in 1936.[1] The motivation of the folktale essays is revealed by Collingwood from the datum of his opening remarks, and is developed within an interdisciplinary framework that is unusually wide, but grasped with confidence. Jan van der Dussen has observed that Collingwood 'did not get very far with his study of this subject' and that his work 'is really a prolegomenon to anthropology' which is 'in essence a transcendental analysis of the subject [of anthropology itself]'.[2] But anthropology, as the reader will see here, is joined to a very distinctive combination of themes in the folktale essays, and constitutes a disciplinary mix that has with certain exceptions not been taken up or discussed at length hitherto;[3] nor has the community of folktale and literary historians outside specialist Colling-

---

[1] Collingwood's election to the Society is recorded in *Folk-Lore: A Quarterly Review of Myth, Tradition, Institution, and Custom*, 47 (1936), 346. The journal announces itself as 'Incorporating *The Archaeological Review* and *The Folk-Lore Journal*'. (Hereafter abbreviated as *F-L.*)

[2] See Jan van der Dussen, *History as a Science: The Philosophy of R. G. Collingwood* (The Hague: Martinus Nijhoff, 1981), 191.

[3] Previous commentaries include Jan van der Dussen's discussion, ibid 231–41; Donald S. Taylor, 'A Bibliography of the Publications and Manuscripts of R. G. Collingwood', *History and Theory*, 24/4 (1985), and *R. G. Collingwood: A Bibliography* (New York and London: Garland Publishing, 1988), 73–7; David Boucher, *The Social and Political Thought of R. G. Collingwood* (Cambridge: Cambridge

wood studies had any substantial opportunity to put the essays
to the test on their own terms, to integrate them into the history
of folktale studies, nor, as I shall suggest below, to consider
their wider relevance to criticism, critical history, and literary
theory. And yet the essays are strikingly pertinent to several active
zones of exchange within these fields—the extensions toward
textuality without writing for example, and the textual politics
of literacy and orality;[4] the philosophical, anthropological,
and historiographical underpinning of 'post-colonial' criticism
(where the 'otherness' of separate national, cultural, and sexual
histories has been sought); the study of non-canonical, non-élite,
or 'marginal' literary forms (in the field of 'popular culture');
the domain of the literary fantastic, and contingent interest in
theories of historical narrative, the enchantment of story, and
literary translation. The interests embedded in the essays synthe-
size a 'traditional' critical humanism and a politically 'radical'
anticipation of 'High Theory'; they reveal the depth and range
of Collingwood's literary and critical commitments as a tem-
porarily lost thread in the history of twentieth-century humanistic
study.[5]

But why should Collingwood—an academic authority on the
history of Roman Britain and the world's leading authority on

University Press, 1989), 196–206, and again in 'Collingwood and Anthropology as
a Philosophical Science', *History of Political Thought*, 23 (2002), 303–25; Maureen
E. Rudzik, 'Folklore and History: An Analysis of an Unpublished Manuscript by
R. G. Collingwood', Ph.D. thesis (Toronto, 1990) (hereafter MR); Sonia Guisti,
'Collingwood's Unpublished Writings on Folklore', in *Storia, antropologia e scienze
de linguaggio*, 8/3 (1993), 23–41; Wendy James, 'Tales of Enchantment: Collingwood, Anthropology, and the "Fairy Tales" Manuscripts', *Collingwood Studies*, 4
(1998), *Variations: Themes from the Manuscripts*, 133–56; and Philip Smallwood,
'Historical Re-Enactment, Literary Transmission, and the Value of R. G. Collingwood', *Translation and Literature*, 9/1 (2000), 3–24.

[4] For an influential and authoritative theoretical study of oral culture, see Walter
J. Ong, *Orality and Literacy: Technologizing of the Word* (London and New York:
Routledge, 1982).

[5] Collingwood's major published writings had been thought pertinent to the
work of literary critics up to the 1970s. Even in 1984 Raman Selden can write of
the development of Collingwood's idea of history in his *Autobiography* (hereafter *A*)
that his 'defence of an independent historical methodology against the realists'
scientism has implications . . . for criticism as a form of knowledge'. See *Criticism
and Objectivity* (London: Allen & Unwin, 1984), 24.

the Roman inscriptions in Britain,[6] a published aesthetician, historiographer, archaeologist, and philosopher of philosophical method—turn to the most fancifully un-philosophic, unhistorical topic of oral tales of wonder in the mid-1930s? One answer that I shall go on to explore in this introductory essay is the extent to which Collingwood's interests and procedures were inflected by the literary and critical consciousness of his time. The enchantment of the oldest stories is an inescapable focus of attention for anyone valuing creative literature and its European varieties and sources; such a tradition is forged in English literature through the mythology of Chaucer (who associates fairies with King Arthur[7]), and through the imagery of Spenser, Shakespeare, Dryden, or Pope. It draws likewise upon the pre-Christian universe of Greek and Roman classical machinery—the magical transformations of Ovid's *Metamorphoses* and the gods of Homer and Virgil—sources from which later English and European poets had gathered so much inspiration, and their materials for literary translation, over hundreds of years.[8]

But Collingwood's interest in fairy tales also has deep roots in his personal experience, the home environment where fairy tales were part of the daily life of the Collingwood family at Lanehead on the shores of Coniston Lake. Collingwood's father, W. G. Collingwood, was a composer and accomplished teller of tales, and R. G.'s enthusiasm for the sagas of ancient societies goes back to the earliest stages in his thinking life. Collingwood recalls in his

[6] Collingwood's collaborative study with John N. L. Myers, *Roman Britain and the English Settlements*, first appeared as vol. i of *The Oxford History of England*, ed. G. N. Clark, in 1936, and in a 2nd edn. (Oxford: Clarendon Press, 1937). Collingwood's *The Roman Inscriptions of Britain* (Oxford: Clarendon Press, 1965), was completed by R. P. Wright.

[7] As Collingwood notes in his summary of Alfred Nutt's Presidential Address on 'The Fairy Mythology of English Literature: Its Origin and Nature', *F-L*, 8/1 (Mar. 1897), 37–8. See Collingwood's 'Bibliographical Notes, Bodl.' (Bodleian Library Collingwood Papers, dep. 21/1–3), 21/1, fo. 10. These 'Bibliographical Notes' are recorded in three exercise books headed 'English Folklore' I, II, and III and run to some 228 pp. For a summary of the contents of the notebooks, see *MR*, appendix IV, 221–7. For a 'Bibliography of Works for the Folklore Manuscript' (drawn in the main from the notebooks) see *MR*, appendix II, 214–17. The scope of the notebooks suggests that Collingwood's scheme may originally have been larger than the essays that it actually generated.

[8] See Graham Anderson, *Fairy Tale in the Ancient World* (London: Routledge, 2000).

Autobiography that 'from an early age I wrote incessantly, in verse and prose, lyrics and fragments of epics, stories of adventure and romance, descriptions of imaginary countries and bogus scientific and archaeological treatises'.[9] The philosophy of Ruskin was pervasive in the 1920s and 1930s in establishing a context for Collingwood's redefinition of the principles of art, and may have encouraged him to expand these interests of his youth. And in the Introduction to an edition of *German Popular Stories* of 1868, reprinted from the brothers Grimm, Ruskin had written more specifically of the 'true historical value' of the fairy tale,[10] a theme which Collingwood develops at length in the essays. In a similar vein, the folklorist E. S. Hartland could suggest in 1890 that 'Custom cannot be studied apart from superstition, nor superstition from tale or song' and could gesture toward the historical value of such study when undertaken in scientific terms: 'In the hands of men like Tylor, McLennan, Lang, and Gomme', he wrote, 'it has taught us more about the real thoughts and practices, not merely of savage tribes, but of our own forefathers, than we ever knew before.'[11] An inspiration more specific to the literary sources supporting Collingwood's reconvened interest is recalled in the first of the folktale chapters. These are the tales, published in 1888, 1892, and 1893 by W. B. Yeats; but this inspiration also reflects in more general terms the penetration of Yeats's poetry by the myths and legends of ancient Ireland.

Such influences were doubtless greatly reinforced by advances in academic folktale scholarship that had appeared nearer the date when Collingwood's essays were composed (many titles in the field being recorded in three manuscript notebooks[12]). They suggest the areas of expertise personal to Collingwood, such as the theory and

---

[9] *A* 3. For an account of life at Lanehead, see Teresa Smith, 'R. G. Collingwood: "This Ring of Thought": Notes on Early Influences', *Collingwood Studies*, 1 (1994), *The Life and Thought of R. G. Collingwood*, 27–43.

[10] John Ruskin, 'Fairy Stories' (1868), in *The Works of John Ruskin*, ed. E. T. Cook and Alexander Wedderburn, 39 vols. (London: George Allen, 1903–12), ixx. 236. The original of *German Popular Stories* was edited by Edgar Taylor (London: John Camden Hotten, 1869).

[11] Edwin Sidney Hartland, *English Fairy and Other Folktales* (London: Walter Scott, 1890), pp. xxiii–xxiv.

[12] Bodleian Library Collingwood Papers, dep. 21/1–3.

practice of archaeology,[13] that continued into, or were developed further within, his later life. Thus Benedetto Croce's introductory essay on the Neapolitan poet and story-teller Giambattista Basile was translated by N. M. Penzer in 1932 and may have helped to define the essays' occasion within the aesthetic and historiographical tradition in which Collingwood's work had matured.[14] The wave of interest in Frazer's *The Golden Bough*, appearing in a long series of volumes from 1890, was encouraged by the contemporary prestige of T. S. Eliot's *Waste Land*, and as the closing pages of *The Principles of Art* will suggest, this interest was undoubtedly shared by Collingwood.[15] The suppositions of Frazer's monumental study are critiqued in chapter 2 of the folktale essays, and the work is a point of reference throughout. Several of the examples used by Collingwood—as that of the king whose weakness and illness leads to the wasting of the land and the failure of the crops—are taken from those selected for symbolic and imaginative purposes by Eliot's poem. Earlier references to the art of primitive communities in company with critiques of contemporary psychology and anthropology appear in Collingwood's early published writings; his analysis of the relations between ritual, religion, and magic in his first published work of philosophy, *Religion and Philosophy* of 1916, can be seen as reworked and reviewed in the essays. But as his detailed references to the journal *Folk-Lore* will suggest within the essays, it is also clear that Collingwood did much new reading and fresh intensive research on folktale scholarship in the 1930s. His citations of the voluminous output of the Finnish school of folklore scholars tell a similar story. The three manuscript exercise books of reading notes on folklore and folktale sketch out many of the arguments of the dense and pointedly written chapters that were later to emerge.[16]

[13] For a discussion of this aspect of Collingwood's inspiration see MR 174–86. Collingwood was engaged in excavating the Westmorland site known as 'King Arthur's Round Table' in 1936 and 1937. For his reports and papers on the subject see Bodleian Library Collingwood Papers, dep. 23/15–18 and dep. 23/23–4.

[14] See *The Pentamerone of Giambattista Basile*, tr. N. M. Penzer, 2 vols. (London: John Lane and the Bodley Head, 1932), i, pp. xvi–lxxv. Section III (pp. xlvii–lxi) deals with '*Lo Cunto de li Cunti* as a Literary Work'.

[15] Collingwood writes that Eliot's poem 'depicts a world where the wholesome flowing water of emotion . . . has dried up'. See *The Principles of Art* (hereafter *PA*), 335.

[16] Bodleian Library Collingwood Papers, dep. 21/1–3.

There is, of course, an urgent and momentous practical and contemporary occasion which Collingwood responds to in and through his essays on folktale and this is reflected in his other work of the mid-to late 1930s. In their discussion of the Grimms' philology and of Max Müller's mythological fantasies of a putative Aryan language and sun-worship themes, the folktale essays reveal how traditional scholarly practices adopted in interpreting the tales were linked to the politics of German nationalism and early nineteenth-century Romanticism. This had profound implications for Collingwood's reflections on the historical moment of 1930s Europe, a crisis of civilization, an act of moral suicide, and a reassertion of barbarism that was soon to be registered in eloquent form in his *Autobiography* (1939) and with a combination of urgency, bleakness, and fierceness in the lean and staccato prose of the *New Leviathan* of 1942.[17]

The myths of a fairy universe in which magical forces preside (as they do in some tales, though magic is mocked in others) seem on the other hand designed to have their readers escape the difficult realities of any single historical moment. In its stead there is a gesture toward the kind of mental and imaginative dream landscape suggested by the fantasies of J. R. R. Tolkein (a Fellow of Pembroke College in Collingwood's day) and of C. S. Lewis (an Oxford contemporary for whom fairy stories could tell truths beyond the conceptual[18]). And in so doing, as well by their familiarity as their strangeness, the tales bring us closer to certain permanent psychological realities that are culturally independent. In this light, Collingwood's emphasis can be seen as consonant with the distinctive *critical-prophetic* atmosphere of the 1930s, a time of revaluation of the literary-critical and literary-historical past and its relevance to present civilization and current human

[17] Extended MS draft fragments of *The New Leviathan* (hereafter *NL*) can be found in the Bodleian Library Collingwood Papers, dep. 24/12. The folktale scholar Jack Zipes laments that very little attention has been paid to fairy tales in attempts 'to grasp the essential features of Weimar and Nazi culture and the crucial links between these two phases of German history'. See *Fairy Tales and the Art of Subversion: The Classical Genre for Children and the Process of Civilization* (1983; New York: Routledge, 1991), 134.

[18] See Lewis's 1940 paper, 'On Stories', in *Of Other Worlds*, ed. Walter Hooper (London: Geoffrey Bles, 1966), 3–21. Lewis wrote that 'The story does what no theorem can quite do. It may not be "like real life" in the superficial sense: but it sets before us an image of what reality may well be like at some more central region' (15).

needs. Such an atmosphere was invigorated by the best of the theoretical essays of T. S. Eliot, a literary hero of Collingwood's and the major poet of the Anglophone world;[19] but it was also encouraged (at different extremes within the paradigm) by the 'culturalization' of literary studies in the wake of Arnold's criticism, the assertion of 'life', of emotional immediacy and of presence in the novels and prose of D. H. Lawrence. There is moreover the esteem of ancient romances in the work of C. S. Lewis, and the revaluative work of contemporary British literary critics within the *Scrutiny* circle.[20] Not only did the chief luminary of this group, the critic F. R. Leavis, refer in later years to Collingwood as 'the true creative mind' (to be placed between Lawrence and Blake),[21] the division between an audience of academic literary scholars and the claims of a cultivated extra-mural readership was being brought into question by Leavis and Eliot in a more general way that Collingwood (in common with Lewis) would find congenial. In the light of Collingwood's interest in the folktale as a means of transmitting culture (preserving ancient values that industrialism renders extinct), one must add the focus on the accompanying translational intelligence of this time. Defined in part, at least, by the work of Ezra Pound, such a focus was also encouraged by the generation of students of Oxford Classical 'Greats' that had come to maturity in the early decades of the twentieth century. The continuities of classical and modern myths and legends would have been deeply familiar to Collingwood from his own university training in classical literature, and, in later life, by his sense of the complex system of accords and contrasts between Roman and British traditions.

[19] Collingwood reviewed books on philosophy for Eliot's *Criterion*, and his own volume, *Religion and Philosophy* (hereafter *RP*) was reviewed therein. Eliot had written a doctoral thesis on F. H. Bradley, the British Idealist philosopher of the generation preceding Collingwood's, and had attended Collingwood's lectures on Aristotle in Oxford.

[20] F. R. Leavis's influential work of literary history and literary evaluation, *Revaluation: Tradition and Development in English Poetry*, was first published by Chatto & Windus in 1936, at about the same time that Collingwood was composing his folktale MS.

[21] F. R. Leavis, *The Living Principle: 'English' as a Discipline of Thought* (London: Chatto & Windus, 1975), 233. Collingwood had cited Blake's 'Listen to the fool's reproach! It is a kingly title' as the epigraph to his draft of *NL*. See Bodleian Library Collingwood Papers, dep. 24/12.

To recur to the literary and critical language of the 1930s is to focus attention on Collingwood's belief that the philosopher's terminology 'must have that expressiveness, that flexibility, that dependence upon context, which are the hall-marks of a literary use of the words as opposed to a technical use of symbols'.[22] There is appropriately an inescapable literary value in Collingwood's expositional manner in the essays—a voice audible as a resonance within his work at its most expressive.[23] Appraised in stylistic terms, Collingwood's essays on folktale are as elegant, forceful, abrasive, or satiric as the best of his published books and are complete and 'finished' in that sense: chapters 1 to 4 unfold in an eloquent sequence. They suggest the dimension of the whole project, and are carefully integrated in reasoning, illustrative digression, and structural control. The principal argument, that folktales can be treated as evidence in the historical study of the human past, develops progressively through the setting forth of initial assumptions, then via the evaluation of existing approaches in philology, psychology, and anthropological functionalism, to an account of Collingwood's personal theory of a cultural past in his central chapters on 'The Historical Method' and on 'Magic'. At this level, moreover, the rhetorical turns of the essays contain some of Collingwood's most pungent satire of fashionable intellectual manners and theories. Thus, in chapter 2, the Romantic mixtures of emotion derived from early nineteenth-century German nationalism, are now 'of interest chiefly because . . . the metaphorical phrases in which they found expression continue to encumber the ground of anthropological discussion, dead blocks of verbiage from which all meaning has flown'.[24]

The tonal quality and imagery of the essays is frequently striking, and is typified by an implicit gesture of intellectual defiance and self-definition. The confusion between race and culture in the Romantic tradition goes, he says, with 'its tendency to project images derived from emotional sources upon the blank screen of

---

[22] *An Essay on Philosophical Method* (hereafter *EPM*), 207.

[23] In 'Life after Life', his review of three new editions of Collingwood's work for the *London Review of Books* (20 Jan. 2000), Jonathan Rée describes Collingwood's *An Essay on Metaphysics* (hereafter *EM*) as 'one of the glories of English philosophical prose—lucid and stern, but also lithe and ironic' (10).

[24] Folktale MS (hereafter *FT*), ch. 2, fo. 2.

the unknown past'.[25] The mythologist Max Müller, writes Collingwood, 'Shutting his eyes to most of the facts, . . . finds himself in a world of shadows, a phantasmagoria in which almost anything can be almost anything else, a twilight in which all cats are grey'.[26] Here and elsewhere, the distinctive literary expressiveness of the folktale essays reinforces the sense that Collingwood is tapping into English traditions of satirical polemic and is composing philosophy in a tradition informed by the resources of literary and literary-critical language. At its best his prose communicates the judgemental economy and brusqueness, the full-outness, the crushing impatience with fools, that is the hallmark of a Leavis or a Lawrence (in *Phoenix* and *Fantasia of the Unconscious*, for example).[27] (Ian Robinson can in the event place Collingwood among *The English Prophets*,[28] as part of the same essential—and coherently English—tradition that includes not only Lawrence and Leavis, but also Coleridge[29] and Arnold.)

Much of Collingwood's philosophical purpose is conveyed by the largeness of his canvas and by this audacity of tone—the irony, for example, he employs to deal with Carl Jung's historically ignorant and pretentious attempt to analyse folktales as the dreams of a people. Jung refers on one occasion to the stories of Proserpina, Deianira, and Europa by saying that 'the capture of women

---

[25] FT2, fo. 5.   [26] FT2, fo. 9.

[27] D. H. Lawrence, *Phoenix: The Posthumous Papers of D. H. Lawrence*, ed. Edward D. McDonald (London: Heinemann, 1936). James Patrick has commented on Collingwood's 'linguistic fluency reminiscent of Wilde or Chesterton' and his 'tone of uncompromisingly adversarial zeal almost imperceptibly brushed with contempt and joined with a frank disregard for popular opinion' in the late 1930s. See 'Fighting in the Daylight: The Penultimate Collingwood', *Collingwood Studies*, 2 (1995), *Perspectives*, 73.

[28] See Ian Robinson, *The English Prophets: A Critical Defence of English Criticism* (Denton: Edgeways, 2001). For an account of Leavis's engagement with Collingwood's ideas, particularly in *The Living Principle*, see Philip Smallwood, ' "The True Creative Mind": R. G. Collingwood's Critical Humanism', *British Journal of Aesthetics*, 41/3 (July 2001), 293–311.

[29] George Watson, *The Literary Critics: A Study of English Descriptive Criticism* (London: Chatto & Windus, 1964), draws attention to resemblances between Coleridge's and Collingwood's distinctions between 'art' and 'craft' (115). For an analysis of Collingwood's 'idealist' relation to Coleridge with regard to historical knowledge, see Christopher Parker, *The English Idea of History from Coleridge to Collingwood* (Aldershot: Ashgate, 2000).

was something general in the lawless prehistoric times'. Collingwood's withering reply is as follows:

Two comments are called for. First, these three stories are based on three
radically different themes. . . . Secondly, what times is he referring to?
The La Tène period or the Hallstatt? The Bronze Age, late, middle, or
early? The Neolithic? The Magelmose or The Mas d'Azil? And what is his
evidence that the period in question was a lawless one? It would be
interesting to know, because, so far, the evidence has not been revealed
to anthropologists and prehistorians, who have found many societies with
many kinds of law, but never a lawless one.[30]

And yet in another sense—when the disparate elements of the
folktale writings are taken together as a single unpartitioned
whole—Collingwood's essays appear clearly unfinished, and towards the end of the sequence of extant manuscripts and fragments, some ragged edges appear. The theme of the essays is not
fully defined at the point when Collingwood set them aside unpublished, partly through illness, and perhaps to focus more completely on *The Principles of Art*. The materials of the reading notes
can offer a highly detailed guide to Collingwood's unrealized intentions here (as Maureen E. Rudzik has shown); but there is no
definitive 'list of contents' for the prospective volume and, with the
exception of chapters 1–4, no absolute guarantee that the final
order that Collingwood *would* have imposed is the one that we
have proposed. The location of chapter 5, for example, is the
editors' decision, and its title is ours. Chapter 6, by contrast, on
'The Authorship of the Fairy-tales' (Collingwood's own phrase),
can be read as having more clearly the air of a concluding statement
in which many of the themes of the foregoing material are combined. Under 'Addenda' we have collected miscellaneous pieces on
the topic of the folktale including the fragments of ostensible
earlier drafts. What we record, then, in this volume, is in some
measure a critical reconstruction of Collingwood's book in the
most readable and logical form we can devise. We hope that it is
both fair to Collingwood's intentions, as they can be inferred, and
satisfying to current intellectual and critical needs. But the basic
structure is Collingwood's.

---

[30] FT2, fos. 48–9. Collingwood had reviewed C. G. Jung's *Psychological Types,
or the Psychology of Individuation* for the *Oxford Magazine*, 41 (1922–3), 425–6.

The experimental, yet wide-ranging and ambitious direction taken by the entirety of the work is suggested by the content of the individual chapters. Thus the central chapter on 'Magic', and its role in the 'savage' mind, is not consistently focused on the attributes of the fairy tale as such. Collingwood is not in these essays attempting a comprehensive contribution to scholarly or historical knowledge of folktale and, despite his detailed research, only a few tales are actually named. Collingwood's reading notes on folktale and folktale scholarship contain many reflections on individual tales, their characteristics, and the connections between them; but the essays themselves do not address in detail the internal motifs and complex international development of the tale of wonder in the mode of a twentieth-century folklorist, and his writings are not on the whole concerned to analyse or historically survey the intricate cross-fertilization of oral and literary forms from the Orient, Italy, France, and Germany that preceded the first edition of Wilhelm and Jacob Grimm's two-volume collection of *Kinder-und Hausmärchen* (Children's and Household Tales) of 1812–15. Collingwood does not trace the emergence of the literary fairy tale (initially as an adult, aristocratic, and feminine, and then as a bourgeois form[31]) out of its origins in oral culture, nor attempt to classify the narrative into its various types, the Sagas, Nursery Tales, Drolls, Apologues, and Cumulative Tales identified by E. S. Hartland—whose work on folklore Collingwood knew.[32]

Collingwood is less interested in all the kinds of fairy tales that exist, that is, than in what Max Lüthi claims is referred to with 'striking unanimity' among folktale scholars as ' "the fairytale proper", the fairytale of magic'.[33] Yet he is also clear that his interest is not with the stories themselves, as works of oral 'literature'—for their generic sake as it were—but with the reworking of their *themes*, and the historical and collective process this reworking suggests.[34]

---

[31] For an excellent discussion of the early literary history of the fairy tale preceding its value as a narrative for children, see Jack Zipes, *Fairy Tale as Myth: Myth as Fairy Tale* (Lexington: University Press of Kentucky, 1994), 17–48.

[32] See Hartland, Introduction to *English Fairy and Other Folk Tales*, p. viii.

[33] Max Lüthi, *The Fairytale as Art Form and Portrait of Man* (Bloomington: Indiana University Press, 1984), 134.

[34] On the topic of history as process, cf. Collingwood's essay, dated Dec. 1935, and entitled 'Reality as History'. The essay is printed in *The Principles of History*, ed. W. H. Dray and W. J. van der Dussen (hereafter *PH*), 170–208.

So, in discussing the interdependence of diffusion and independent invention in the case of the English *Tom Tit Tot* and its German analogue *Rumpelstilzchen*, Collingwood writes that 'it is the origin of the themes, not the origin of the story, which concerns us in this enquiry'.[35] Accordingly, with the exception of the 'Cinderella' narrative in the penultimate chapter (as it is designated here), Collingwood seems relatively little absorbed in cataloguing the artistic and technical attributes of the overlapping and interwoven fairy stories that have intrigued other commentators—the generic mixture of real and unreal elements, the intrinsic literary quality, the repetitions, variations, shocking transitions and tragic ironies, the treatment of characters, children, animals, and heroes, the scenes of isolation and loss, the incidence of happy, inconsequential, and unhappy endings, the homecomings and searchings, the unsettling combinations of the horrific, randomly cruel, affectionate, comic, and the sardonic. For Lüthi, 'the fairytale as a genre offers its hearers a representation of man which transcends the individual story, which reappears time and again in countless narratives',[36] and this conception of the form is very germane to Collingwood's intellectual and interpretive approach in the essays. But where Lüthi saw the reader of the fairy tale as 'first and last interested in the narratives themselves, not in the historical circumstances out of which they developed',[37] Collingwood gestured to the horizons of civilized life and society on which the tales can shed light, and to social structures from the pre-historical to the late feudal and bourgeois. His primary interest is the history of human development; he indicated in chapter 2 of his book that 'fairy tales cannot be considered except in relation to the whole culture in which they arise'.[38]

On these distinctive grounds—inflected by the appeal of an Arnoldian cultural tradition of British criticism prescient of the logic, though not in practice the method, of British and American 'cultural studies' emergent twenty years after their composition—Collingwood's writings on folktale can be contrasted most clearly with Lüthi's scholarly and critical work. When, in addition, they are set against the celebrated structural analyses of Vladimir Propp on plot formation (first published in Russian in

---

[35] FT1, fo. 9.   [36] Lüthi, *Fairytale*, p. ix.   [37] Ibid.
[38] See FT2, 'Three Methods of Approach: Philological, Functional, Psychological', fo. 29.

1928),[39] they appear more substantially concerned with the material of the tales as a means to the ulterior purposes of historical study. Oral narratives are seen as an integral part of primitive civilization in its relationship to the world of modern ritual and of mind. Here Collingwood's central topic, when the various prior disciplinary frameworks are taken away, can be regarded as the modern historical and anthropological mind which surveys and examines the tales. In his chapter on 'Cinderella' Collingwood includes himself, and his own writing and thinking, in this conjunction of subject and object:

The hunter thinks of himself as a wanderer beset with perils, like the beasts of his own chase; born, like them, into a community of his own kind, in which a sufficiency of births, like a sufficiency of births among his quarry, is the object of his anxious care; living like them under the law and custom of his tribe; and dying perhaps—who knows?—like them to feed another life which will be his own life in a new shape. And these thoughts he will express not in philosophical prose, but in a ritual which he devises and performs about as blindly, and about as intelligently, as I write these sentences: not knowing why I write them or whether anyone will read them, not even sure that I am making my thought clear to myself or to anyone else, but knowing that there is in me something that craves expression and knowing that, if I am to express it at all, I must express it through that pen-driving ritual which is the custom of my tribe.[40]

In this emphasis on the ultimate identity of the knower and of the known, the imaginative sympathies of the historical, folkloric, or anthropological researcher and the subject of the research, the essays reveal both continuities and change in Collingwood's own intellectual development and in the emotional temper of his work as it approached its final, most courageous, and most self-conscious phase. Largely in reaction to Freud's arguments from *Totem and Taboo*, for example, there is here a move away from the earlier tendency[41] to adopt without apparent discomfort the term 'savage' in company with its pejorative connotations, and to

[39] Vladimir Propp, *Morphology of the Folktale*, ed. Louis Wagner and Alan Dundes, tr. Laurence Scott, 2nd rev. edn. (Austin, Tex.: University of Texas Press, 1958). Writing in the 1920s, Propp identified thirty-one distinct components (or 'functions') of a tale that control the progress of its action. He goes without mention by Collingwood.

[40] FT5, fo. 26.

[41] See below the discussion of Collingwood's 'Lectures on the Philosophy of Art' (hereafter LPA) in this essay.

abandon the inclination to see the world of savages, madmen, and children as parts of a continuous and connected problem. The folktale manuscript represents a decisive rejection of the idea of the 'savage' as a descriptive term for *other* people,[42] and clearly announces the fundamental distinctions between the primitiveness of childhood rationality, early humanity, and the adult who is mentally ill.[43] Collingwood concentrates throughout the essays on the internality of anthropological inquiry (the mind of the modern cultural historian being, as it were, a part of the consciousness that he or she studies);[44] yet only the chapter on the many versions of the 'Cinderella' story in fact gives sustained attention to the internalized regeneration of any particular tale. (Collingwood uses Marian Roalfe Cox's summaries of its 345 recorded varieties.) And here too, the discussion soon moves off into themes of a more general archaeological or anthropological nature: totemism, primitive religion, cave art, and the relics of Neolithic civilization and of the Bronze Age. The final chapter is by contrast a classic account of the principles of collaborative creation that link oral and literary traditions (the oral folktale and the literary fairy tale for children) and this is duplicated nowhere else in Collingwood's writings.

To recapitulate: the chapters on folktale are stylistically polished, but the material was not completely structured at the time Collingwood abandoned the project of writing a book based on his planned lectures to the Folk Lore Society; what remains represents an exploratory, complex, interlocking *rapprochement* of Collingwood's own making and brings the study of folktale to the centre of a broad humanistic inquiry. The motivation of the essays is often a

[42] 'Every civilization is called uncivilized by every other; and when we have agreed to extend the term civilized to a group of peoples (with ourselves, of course, in the centre) whose civilization is a good deal like our own, we use the word savage as a general name for others outside that charmed circle' (FT2, fo. 30).

[43] The analogizing of these elements has still not been entirely abandoned: e.g. the intuition that fairy tales can be thought suitable for children on the grounds that they share a psychology with 'uncivilized' (adult) peoples. Cf. Norbert Elias, *The Civilizing Process* (New York: Urizen, 1978), p. xiii; quoted by Zipes, *Fairy Tales and Subversion*, 19.

[44] Collingwood's attack on the positivistic study of folklore, and the 'horrid fascination' (FT3, fo. 7) for its traditional subject the 'savage' or 'primitive' society, bears comparison with the critique of '*positional* superiority', as set forth in Edward Said's seminal *Orientalism: Western Conceptions of the Orient* (London: Routledge & Kegan Paul, 1978).

vigorous and engaging critique of contemporary psychology and anthropology that works within the agenda of T. K. Penniman's history of the last one hundred years of anthropology published in 1935. Their purpose is in the main to see folktale narratives in terms of a 'way of knowing'.[45] 'What is Man?', asks Collingwood, echoing in the opening of his *New Leviathan* the famous speech by Shakespeare's Hamlet. Collingwood uses the essays to explore a methodology within the humanities that is intimately connected to the re-enactive philosophy of history he was mapping in lecture form—and to a similar purpose—at about the same time.

In the light of Collingwood's *Idea of History*, there are, however, two immediate difficulties in Collingwood's wish to bring the 'materials' of oral culture, and their exhibition of process, within the orbit of historical study in a way that is available to the literary historian. Both touch with especial relevance on Collingwood's thinking in its relation to the problems of literary history that Donald S. Taylor has explored in his analysis of the parallels between Collingwood's concept of historical re-enactment by the historian proper and the kind of recreation undertaken by the literary historian and literary critic.[46]

The first derives from W. H. Dray's observation that Colling-wood 'has . . . an irritating habit, especially in his earlier work, of calling two things "identical" when all he has really shown is that they are similar in some important respect'.[47] Collingwood sets out in chapter 1 to use fairy tales as evidence of ancient civilization in the way that a fragment of pottery is used by the archaeologist to reconstruct the world from which the survival comes: 'The methods to be used in this kind of excavation', he writes, 'will resemble those used by the archaeologist.'[48] The word 'resemble' is an important *caveat* here, since orally transmitted tales (the kind

---

[45] See e.g. Michael M. Metzgerand and Katharina Mommsen (eds.), *Fairy Tales as Ways of Knowing: Essays on Marchen in Psychology, Society, and Literature* (Berne and Las Vegas: P. Lang, 1981).

[46] See Donald S. Taylor, *R. G. Collingwood: A Bibliography* (New York and London: Garland Publishing, 1988), esp. Introduction § 2 on 'Is Art History Possible?' (24–30) and § 3 'Parallels between Historical Thinking and Artistic Response' (30–8).

[47] W. H. Dray, *History as Re-Enactment: R. G. Collingwood's Idea of History* (Oxford: Oxford University Press, 1995 and 1999), 29.

[48] FT1, fo. 5.

Collingwood is primarily interested in) precisely do not exist as evidence in that kind of material sense. Our knowledge of them has usually evolved from sources which by the same token we cannot retrieve and cannot subject to the interrogation reserved for historical documents—such as Collingwood requires in his *Idea of History*. When ultimately written down (as they were by the great collectors of the nineteenth century) or when (as in Perrault's 1698 collection) they entered literary tradition at an earlier date, the tales record a continuum interesting historically to the extent that it is presumed to have existed orally once upon a time; but in the absence of tapes, compact discs, or other recording devices, this tradition cannot be studied in that form. 'It is extremely difficult to describe what the oral wonder tale was', writes Jack Zipes, 'because our evidence is based on written documents',[49] and many 'oral' narratives, as historians of folktale agree, will often have written precedents or analogues that defy the distinctness of a watertight 'oral' tradition and deflect or inflect it. Hartland had written suggestively of the way that English and Welsh sagas 'have become preserved in the amber of literature', while poets, 'enraptured with their beauty, have rendered many of them imperishable as the mind of man.'[50]

Collingwood's solution to this problem of historical evidence special to the oral tale is to distinguish, in chapter 6, a tradition whose *esse* is, ultimately, its *fieri*. The tradition has 'the impalpable being of a tale which survives only because it is re-told'.[51] From the initial analogy with archaeology in chapter 1, where 'A theme contained in . . . a story is a fragment of ancient custom or belief, very much as a stone implement is a fragment of ancient technical skill',[52] Collingwood moves over the course of the essays toward an accommodation with history closer to T. S. Eliot's sense (in 'Tradition and the Individual Talent' of 1919, reprinted in his *Selected Essays*, 1932) of a constantly evolving literary tradition whose connected materials are available to the present reader as an immediate experience, an artefact communally generated and consumed, and open to endless modifications. He embraces at the

---

[49] Jack Zipes, 'Cross-Cultural Connections and the Contamination of the Classical Fairy Tale', in Zipes (ed.), *The Great Fairy Tale Tradition: From Straparola and Basile to the Brothers Grimm* (New York and London: Norton & Co., 2001), 846.

[50] Hartland, *English Fairy and Other Folktales*, pp. xii–xiii.

[51] FT6, fo. 21.   [52] FT1, fo. 17.

same time the non-determining sense of the literary past embodied in Pound's conception of literary translation as a process of 'making it new'. And he recalls the reworkings of traditional themes by literary cultures such as Collingwood had studied in a juvenile piece on Dante's, Milton's, and Goethe's accounts of the Devil.[53] In another light, Collingwood is in the folktale essays theorizing those parts of his own earlier and later practice as a writer where he is committed to re-enacting major works of the past—Hobbes's *Leviathan* in the *New Leviathan* for example—and is illuminating the process of self-re-enactment (as one might call it) of his *Autobiography*. The effect is to bring 'history' and 'translation' more closely together (as forms or expressions of each other), to charge an empirical method with the concepts of mutability and flux.[54]

A second difficulty, contingent on his emphasis on the magical oral tale, appears when Collingwood depicts the folktale as a medium of emotional canalization to be understood from within our own emotional condition, perspective, or crisis; this topic is given considerable emphasis in *The Principles of Art* (1938), and in the closing pages, Collingwood responds to T. S. Eliot's *Waste Land* in a passionate lament on the 'corruption of consciousness' that afflicts the modern civilization of the industrial West. But just as *The Principles of Art* does not explicitly enter into the theory of diachronic relations between works in different periods (though art from many periods is discussed), so the leaving out of emotion from the subject matter of history has often proved troubling to readers of Collingwood's *Idea of History*. Dray has written that Collingwood may from time to time have talked of emotion as the equivalent of feeling or sensation, but that 'Even as such, he ought to have seen it as belonging to history's subject-matter to the extent that it enters into the explanation of actions.'[55] Collingwood's conception of history is famously a history of thought, the re-enactment of a thinking agent,[56] and as Dray observes, emotions

---

[53] See 'The Devil in Literature—an Essay upon the Mythology of the Evil One . . . Read before "Etanos" 1908', Bodleian Library Collingwood Papers, dep. 1/1. The paper contains substantial quotations from the major authors translated by Collingwood.

[54] For a fuller discussion of this point see Smallwood, 'Historical Re-Enactment, Literary Transmission, and the Value of R. G. Collingwood'.

[55] Dray, *History as Re-Enactment*, 128.   [56] See *IH* 205.

seem in this conception excluded from historical study via historical re-enactment. So too, by extension it seems, is the possibility of a history of art and (if art is what literature is—as pre-eminently it is for Collingwood) the possibility of a history of literature.[57]

One can, according to Collingwood, have a history of artistic *achievements* but not a history of the *problems* of art (a position that appears to eliminate from the history of art the history of its successive philosophies, and from the history of literature a history of its theories).[58] Dray has suggested the several ways in which Collingwood's account of artistic works in the context of their historical development does not square with his general claims about the history of art; but what perhaps he does not suggest strongly enough—in answer to Collingwood's intuition about historical re-enactment and emotion being incompatible—is the gap between *The Idea of History* and the forceful argument from reactivated past emotion in the folktale essays. The theme of emotion is especially strong in Collingwood's chapter on 'Magic'. Collingwood here begins by contrasting the promise of examining the past through the lens of the emotions with the 'rationalistic psychology' by which Tylor 'built up his classical theory of magic as pseudo-science'. Such a theory led to the conclusion that Collingwood could not accept—on the grounds of their many impressively rational accomplishments—that primitive societies were in some sense deranged; in terror of an enemy's treatment of a person's nail-clippings, for example:

Perhaps we shall do better if we seek the source of the idea not in the savage's intellect, but in his emotions. And since we can understand what goes on in the savage's mind only in so far as we can experience the same thing in our own, we must find our clue in emotions to whose reality we can testify in our own persons.[59]

Collingwood goes on suggestively to describe the emotional identity of those things we have made or owned as 'outposts of our personality'. They generate passionate feelings:

We all have a feeling—not an intellectual idea, but an emotional one—of an intimate connexion between ourselves and the things which we have made.

---

[57] Cf., latterly, the analysis of this problem in David Perkins, *Is Literary History Possible?* (Baltimore and London: Johns Hopkins University Press, 1992).
[58] As Taylor notes, *Bibliography*, 27.   [59] FT4, fo. 2.

These things are felt as parts of ourselves, in the sense that an injury to them is felt as an injury to us. If a picture I have drawn, or a letter I have written, or some trifling thing, useful or useless, which I have made, is destroyed by accident, my sense of loss bears no relation to the intrinsic value or merit of what has been destroyed; it is like a wound or blow to myself, as if the destroyed thing had been a deposit or outpost of my personality in the world around me. And if the destruction was malicious, the sense of injury is more severe, as a deliberate blow is harder to bear than an accidental one.[60]

It is in the folktale essays (more emphatically than in any of Collingwood's hitherto published theories) that the emotional life is installed as at the centre of the study of the past. The observation of this centrality achieves here its fullest and most eloquent expression and provides the documentary support for Donald S. Taylor's argued claims for an accommodation of *The Idea of History* to *The Principles of Art*. Since fairy stories are based upon the operations of magic, Collingwood seems here to insist, they give us a point of entry into the life of the emotions as a cause of action. To the extent that fairy stories are subject to re-enactment (critical recreation by each successive generation of tellers) they conform to, and hold together, Collingwood's conception of a common artistic and historical procedure. And whereas the tenet that 'all history is a history of thought' has led to the conclusion that Collingwood wished to exclude emotion, the dictum appears in a significantly different form in chapter 1 of the folktale essays. Now, we are told, 'All historical knowledge involves the recreation in the historian's mind of the past experience which he is trying to study.'[61] In the movement from 'thought' to 'experience' (as potentially including emotion) the subject matter of history has opened up.

Collingwood's chapters on folktale thus analyse in ways ultimately consistent with the translational literary modernisms of Eliot and Pound—these joined to the urgent call for a restoration of the emotional life in both Eliot and Lawrence[62]—the nature of continuity and change in the historical and cultural transmission of the

---

[60] FT4, fo. 2.   [61] FT1, fo. 18.

[62] Lawrence writes in 'A Propos of *Lady Chatterley's Lover*' (1930) that we are 'creatures whose active emotional self has no real existence, but is all reflected downwards from the mind'. See *Phoenix II: Uncollected, Unpublished and Other Prose Works by D. H. Lawrence*, ed. Warren Roberts and Harry T. Moore (London: Heinemann, 1968), 493.

tales; their evolutionary condition reflects and prophetically asserts a collaborative enterprise (influenced, quite deeply it seems,
in Collingwood's account, by Cecil J. Sharp's analysis of the common authoriality of the folk-song).[63] By their narrative metamorphosis, the tales produce a political critique of authorial
individualism that is recognized as such by Collingwood, and
that looks forward to the poststructuralism of Barthes and Foucault but is not eclipsed by them.[64] In his 'poststructuralist' study,
the *Archaeology of Knowledge*, Foucault was to take the opportunity for verbal play with the term 'archaeology' in order to abolish
the distinction between an intermediary 'discourse' and the realities of history to which this discourse referred.[65] The 'textual' is
the *only* reality in this conception. Collingwood is by contrast
concerned in the folktale essays with the transfer of a Baconian
method (described in his *Autobiography* as a 'logic of question and
answer') to the understanding of the forms of human life behind
the narrative artefacts and their mediate, documentary, record:

> Like all archaeology . . . [the study of folktale] aims at reconstructing the
> past of mankind from the evidence of things he has made which are still
> with us. . . . . But whereas archaeology in the ordinary sense studies the
> fragments of his industry and manufacture, this new kind studies frag-
> ments of his customs and beliefs handed down in traditional stories.[66]

In denoting his work 'archaeological', Collingwood appears here
committed to a conception of historical reference that poststructuralism rejects.

There is in other respects, nonetheless, an anticipation of Foucault. In his essay 'What is an Author?' Foucault was also to ask
'what is a "work?" ', and thus suggests a current theoretical sympathy which builds a connecting bridge to Collingwood's thought

---

[63] Cecil J. Sharp, *English Folk-Song: Some Conclusions* (London: Novello & Co.,
1907). Collingwood draws attention to this volume in FT1. Paul Thom, writing of
the indeterminate nature of folk-songs passed on in oral tradition, notes that: 'The
specifications for singing the song are not precisely specifiable. They are not fixed
by the existence of an authoritative score. The music is not thought of as definitive,
but as open to indefinitely many versions.' 'The Intepretation of Music in Performance', *British Journal of Aesthetics*, 43/2 (Apr. 2003), 129.

[64] Both Maureen Rudzik and Wendy James have suggested anticipations of
continental poststructuralism in the folktale essays.

[65] Michel Foucault, *The Archaeology of Knowledge* (London: Routledge, 1972).

[66] FT1, fo. 19.

from the present day. Foucault wrote that the 'author' does not 'precede the works', but rather 'he is a certain functional principle by which, in our culture, one limits, excludes, and chooses; in short, by which one impedes the free circulation, the free manipulation, the free composition, decomposition, and recomposition of fiction'.[67] In his essay on 'The Death of the Author' Barthes had in a similar vein seemed to tilt at the notion of the Author as one thought 'to *nourish* the book, which is to say that he exists before it, thinks, suffers, lives for it, is in the same relation of antecedence to his work as a father to his child'.[68] For Collingwood oral narratives are passed down the generations through decomposition and recomposition; and whereas 'modern novels are invented . . . [,] folktales are not':[69] they escape the finitude of a written text interpreted as the work of an author.[70] And this, Collingwood intimates, is the way with all works of art in some important respect. In the implication that the folktale essays give an equity of cultural significance to oral and written forms (in worlds equally penetrated by rationality and magic), Collingwood stands with Barthes and Foucault. He resists a history where (as in the terms of Foucault) 'literary discourses came to be accepted only when endowed with the author function'.[71] He insists that the written text is subject to 'corruption', while for the oral narrative, there is no text to corrupt; but Collingwood's achievement is also to have closed the gap between civilizations with and without writing. The stories Collingwood considers in these essays exist in their endless becoming; the process of cultural decomposition and recomposition makes them available without our having to know first-hand the versions from which they began.

[67] Michel Foucault, 'What is an Author?', in *The Foucault Reader*, ed. Paul Rabinow (London: Penguin, 1984), 118–19.

[68] Roland Barthes, 'The Death of the Author', ('La Mort de l'auteur' (1968)), in *Image Music Text*, tr. Stephen Heath (London: HarperCollins, 1977), 145.

[69] See Collingwood's notes on A. M. Hocart, *Psychology and Ethnology*, 'English Folklore I', Bodleian Library Collingwood Papers, dep. 21/1, fo. 70.

[70] Collingwood was not alone in qualifying the authority of originating authoriality in favour of a context of reception, but his comments in the folktale essays should not be seen as entirely accordant with the theory or politics of authoriality that has *since* tended to emerge, as e.g. in European structuralist and poststructuralist schools of critical thought.

[71] *Foucault Reader*, 109.

Collingwood thus does more than his poststructuralist successors to reconnect the arts and rituals of civilized society with the
world of 'primitive' magic in which we all in fact live. And although Collingwood nowhere writes explicitly of the theory of
literary history (a topic subsumed under the rubric of 'reception
aesthetics' and developed at length by his European successors
Gadamer[72] and Jauss[73] and by R. S. Crane,[74] Paul Ricoeur,[75]
and Donald S. Taylor[76] in the USA), the essays thereby round
out Collingwood's 'idea of history' by reference to an experience of
the literary, and do so to a fuller extent than has been recognized
hitherto.[77] They focus Collingwood's conception of 'civilization',
and they explore his definition of art in ways that seem to bring the
emotional life that is so prominent in *The Principles of Art* to centre
stage in the study of the past. As Wendy James points out in this
volume (in the next section of the Introduction), the impetus of the
essays is to redefine the future humanistic direction that anthropology might take, and its integration with historical study and
artistic expression alike. In this they recall Collingwood's analysis
of philosophy itself, and the emphasis there—in his *Essay on Philosophical Method* of 1933—on the philosopher's use of a poetical
language.[78] It is within this literary and critical orientation that the

[72] Hans-Georg Gadamer, author of *Truth and Method*, was to write the Introduction to the German translation of Collingwood's *Autobiography*.

[73] Hans Robert Jauss, 'Literary History as a Challenge to Literary Theory',
Toward an Aesthetic of Reception, tr. Timothy Bahti (Minneapolis: University of
Minnesota Press, 1982), 3–45. This essay draws explicitly on Collingwood.

[74] See, in particular, R. S. Crane's 'On Writing the History of Criticism in
England, 1650–1800' and 'Critical and Historical Principles of Literary History'.
Both are reprinted in *The Idea of the Humanities and Other Essays*, 2 vols. (Chicago:
University of Chicago Press, 1968), ii. 45–175.

[75] In vol. 1 of *Temps et Récit* (Paris: editions du Seuil, 1983), 179, 183, Ricoeur
appeals to, and in effect adopts, Collingwood's ideas on narrative causality from
EM, and in vol. iii, *Le Temps Raconté* (1985), he cites *IH* on the distinction between
history and evolutionary change (136).

[76] Taylor, *Bibliography*.

[77] The conception of history *as itself* a literary structure (comic, ironic, or tragic)
is found in the work of Hayden White. See e.g. 'Interpretation in History', *Tropics
of Discourse: Essays in Cultural Criticism* (Baltimore: Johns Hopkins University
Press, 1978), 51–80.

[78] The critic William Empson refers to *An Essay on Philosophical Method* as 'a
grand exposure of philosophy from the inside'. See *The Structure of Complex Words*
(London: Chatto & Windus, 1951), 320 n.

folktale essays gather meaning from the context of other works by Collingwood on cultural production, music, fiction, language, art, and nature that appear for the first time in this volume, and it is to Collingwood's unpublished work on these topics that we can now turn.

Essays on Music, Fiction, Language, and Art

In one of his earliest essays, 'Words and Tune' of 1918,[79] Collingwood focuses on a theme in philosophical aesthetics that he was to return to on a number of occasions in his later career; but even at this stage Collingwood is already exploring a special case of collaborative creation that was to emerge both in the folktale essays and in *The Principles of Art*. Such a notion evolves here from his examination of the complex and mysterious relation between the literary (the words) and the musical sounds (the tune). In his analysis of the problem of putting music *to* words, Collingwood begins by evaluating the basis of several existing theories of literary and musical expression. First by outlining, and then opening to criticism, the theory of 'musico-literary parallelism', Collingwood argues that, while it is true that the songwriter must work independently as a composer, within his own melodic constraints (using the musical scale, the components of pitch, stress, duration, and intensity of sound), he must also collaborate with the words. Good vocal composers find an emphasis in the words of a poet; they then invent a tune that combines with this emphasis, brings out the meaning of the words and reinforces them. But amongst the questions raised by this short theoretical essay must be asked what happens to the musical experience when the quality of the poetry set by the composer is not good? And such questions are ones that Collingwood cannot examine in detail. Doubtless, his framing of the issue in terms of 'tunes' as distinct from harmonies leads to certain conclusions rather than others; and the essay is perhaps weakened by dismissive judgements of Bach, Mozart, Brahms, Schubert, and Schumann, such as are not consistent with estimates that he formulates elsewhere. 'Words and Tune' suggests in this connection the iconoclastic stance which Collingwood

---

[79] In introducing this essay I am particularly grateful for the advice of Professors David Hopkins and Roger Scruton.

never fully transcended. In asking what music *adds* to the meaning of a poetical text, and by supposing that the meaning of the poetry exists independently of the music, Collingwood appears to be begging the question of what the musical element in written language actually is.

Yet in the process of exploring how words and tune are related, Collingwood suggests much that is independently of value to the understanding of poetical language. He draws attention to poetry's distinctive articulatory mode—one of imagined or orally rendered patterns of sound and intonation; and he analyses aspects of the problem of representation in 'programme music',[80] and in the practice of 'pseudo-copying'. In the latter event, the musical notation attempts to simulate on the musical page such natural occurrences as the waves as they roll on the shore or the zig-zag flashes of lightning. The success of the good poem, Collingwood concludes, is that it sings its own song; and the success of the good song is then a re-enactment—not a parallelism but an internalized recreation within a different medium—of the original inspiration of the words. The writer of songs is after all not *adding* music to poetry so much as *discovering* within the words a beauty or felicity already there as an unlocked potential.

A fascination with the permeable bounds of form and matter runs likewise through the short, undated piece headed 'Observations on Language', a document that is no more than a series of notes, but reinforces Collingwood's linguistic paradigm in *The Principles of Art* (chapters 11, 'Language', and 12, 'Art as Language'), and where the whole nature of language is understood not as a system of referential equivalents but from language in use.

More substantial, however, and next only to the folktale essays in importance, are the two intact manuscript drafts of a lecture on the novels of Jane Austen,[81] the first dated 1921, the second

---

[80] His inspiration is probably Ernest Newman's essay on 'Programme Music', which he quotes, and which was printed in his *Musical Studies* (London: Bodley Head, 1905), a book that Collingwood had received as a school prize for harmony.

[81] The many references to poets, novelists, and dramatists in Collingwood's folktale essays, as in *PA*, tend to be made as the tip of a vast pyramid of literary experience, while the strictly literary material in the unpublished papers (that on Shakespeare, Kyd, Racine, and Greek tragedy) is of the somewhat preliminary or *ad hoc* kind.

probably composed in or shortly before 1934.[82] We see here Collingwood's evolving aesthetic philosophy harnessed to the critical needs of the literary audience for a single novelist's œuvre and to the elucidatory requirements of the language of English narrative fiction at its best. The value accorded to Jane Austen's novels, alongside other fiction, is extremely similar in the two versions, and extremely high; but one lecture is not a 'draft' of the other in the sense of being the same essay in a more obviously primitive state.[83] We can experience more of the trenchant muscularity and (Hobbesian?) directness of Collingwood's writing at its most wittily forceful in the 1921 essay:

It is not enough, as Meredith's philosophy would have us believe, that a man should laugh. The comic spirit in itself has no special value over and above any other privilege of humanity, such as the possession of four incisors in each jaw. You must discriminate between laughter and laughter: the cracked laughter of the maniac, the boor's guffaw, the vacant giggle of the idiot, the snarl of the misanthrope, and so on. It is by this test that we begin to see the true greatness of Jane Austen.[84]

In writing of this kind, where the distinctions are drawn with an almost anthropological starkness, Collingwood can distinguish Jane Austen's 'aesthetic vision of life' from that of the satirist, who is 'a flagellator, not an artist' and who 'lives at the very opposite pole of thought',[85] and he pointedly does not define her

[82] In introducing the Jane Austen lectures here, I draw on my essay 'From Illusion to Reality: R. G. Collingwood and the Fictional Art of Jane Austen', *Collingwood Studies*, 4 (1998), *Themes from the Manuscripts*, 71–100.

[83] I am inclined to disagree with Donald S. Taylor's judgment that '[t]he undated manuscript [on Austen] seems to be a source for the more polished 1921 manuscript'. See Taylor, *Bibliography*, 53. From the three reports of the lectures' delivery contained in the minute books of the Pembroke Beaumont and Johnson Societies, the 'more polished 1921 manuscript' was given in 1923 and 1924, the 'undated' one ten years later in 1934. (For details see the final note to the text of the 1921 lecture, below.) In terms of transitional continuities the 'undated' MS used in 1934 seems the smoother and more 'polished' of the two. In 1921 Collingwood wrongly refers to Jane Austen's mother as a 'daughter of the then Master of Balliol' (1921, fo. 8); in 1934, she is correctly referred to as his 'niece' (1934, fo. 5). He gives different ages at point of death for Jane Austen's admiral brothers—73 and 92 in 1921 (fo. 9), 75 and 90 in 1934 (fo. 6). The correct ages are 73 (Charles) and 91 (Francis).

[84] 'Jane Austen—Johnson Society Nov. 27. 1921' (hereafter JA1), fo. 5. Collingwood is apparently referring to George Meredith's essay 'On the Idea of Comedy and of the Uses of the Comic Spirit', first printed in the *New Quarterly Magazine*, 8 (June–July 1877), 1–40.

[85] JA1, fo. 6.

success in terms which condone the fashionable doctrine of 'art for art's sake'.[86] While the 'world' that Collingwood refers to in 1921 resembles the philosopher's 'world' in the sense that he uses the term in *The Idea of History*,[87] Collingwood seems also to be contributing to the *literary* context of his terms at the same point. Collingwood is speaking to a community of literary critics when he dissolves the false dichotomy between 'realism' and what T. S. Eliot called 'good writing for its own sake',[88] between art as the mirror or copy of nature, and art as a purely imagined, mentally generated reality:

I do not mean that her work was what is nowadays called realistic.[89] When an unimaginative person records the misunderstood facts which he half-sees, he calls it realism: what Jane Austen did was not to write down the way in which she saw her parents and friends behaving, but to see in their behaviour a whole world of subtle meanings and to make that world her home.[90]

'Life' is what makes Jane Austen's novels 'great art', and Jane Austen herself, as F. R. Leavis was later to determine, 'the inaugurator of the great tradition of the English novel'.[91] Together, the lectures on Austen are in this fashion integral both to critical tradition and to the body of Collingwood's work, just as the earlier lecture[92] anticipates the mesh between the creative psychology of the artist and child psychology developed in the folktale essays.

In the progress of literary and cultural history, Collingwood—sharing Ruskin's view of the novel—places Jane Austen firmly on

[86] Or e.g. A. C. Bradley's 'Poetry for Poetry's Sake' (1901), where the poem has 'intrinsic value', and the experience of it is 'an end in itself'. See *Oxford Lectures on Poetry* (London: Macmillan, 1909), 4.

[87] See, in particular, the passages in the chapter of *IH* on 'Scientific History' in England where Collingwood is summarizing (in approving terms) Oakeshott's theory of history: 'History is not a series but a world: which means its various parts bear upon one another, criticize one another, make one another intelligible' (153).

[88] T. S. Eliot, 'Johnson as Critic and Poet' (1944), in *On Poetry and Poets* (London: Faber & Faber, 1957), 191.

[89] Collingwood took up the general question in *Speculum Mentis or, the Map of Knowledge* (hereafter *SM*): 'The artist as such does not know what the word reality means. . . . What he imagines is simply those fantasies which compose the work of art' (63).

[90] JA1, fo. 7.

[91] F. R. Leavis, *The Great Tradition* (London: Chatto & Windus, 1948), 16.

[92] JA1, fo. 10.

the anti-romantic, anti-mystical side of the moral and aesthetic divide.[93] There is no 'romantic revolution' in literary fiction for him to endorse in the lectures, and the times do not, ultimately, explain Jane Austen's achievement. To conceive Jane Austen's significance in the historical mode is to delve into the consciousness of the present. Collingwood thus shows how *Pride and Prejudice* sheds light on what 'civility' means at the deeper levels of consciousness and conduct, and suggests a standard for the relations of duty within a society. And thus does the critical occasion of his response to Austen anticipate interests that were to develop into a political-philosophical analysis of human 'civilization' (as antidote to human barbarity) in *The New Leviathan*, in the unpublished essay of 1936 'Man Goes Mad' (printed in Part III of this volume), and in other pieces. But if later theorists have called into question the boundaries of the 'literary' by an explicitly political criticism, Collingwood, at his date, can exalt Jane Austen's literary work for its 'purely literary qualities'. He defines her literary quality in terms of a moral problem that writers such as Dickens and Arnold Bennett ('snobs and sentimentalists') are not able to face.[94] It is the problem that from first to last runs through Collingwood's own philosophy, as it does through the whole history of philosophy as Collingwood conceives it:

The problem in all her books is the problem of knowing one's own mind. Every one of her heroines is placed in a situation where a resolute and fearless facing of her own motives is demanded of her. The catastrophes are one and all caused by failure to distinguish one's real thoughts and desires from those which one idly supposes oneself to have;[95] and the happy endings take place invariably by a moral crisis in which these illusions are swept away and the heroine is left face to face with her real self. This crisis, tragic as in *Emma*, or comic as in *Northanger Abbey*, is the turning-point of all the books, whose common theme is thus the conversion of the soul, as Plato would call it, from illusion to reality.[96]

[93] B. C. Southam has pointed out that 'While Ruskin had no objection to novels as such, he deplored the effect of their "overwrought interest": "The best romance becomes dangerous, if by its excitement, it renders the ordinary course of life uninteresting" '. See Southam (ed.), *Jane Austen: The Critical Heritage*, ii. *1870–1940* (London and New York: Routledge & Kegan Paul, 1987), 8.

[94] 'Jane Austen' (?1934) (hereafter abbreviated as JA2), fo. 18.

[95] Cf. D. H. Lawrence's distinction between 'real feelings' and 'mental feelings' in 'A Propos of *Lady Chatterley's Lover*', 493.

[96] JA2, fo. 18.

It is this conception of a 'civilization' based on the priority of self-knowledge that most seems to connect the study of an oral popular narrative with the themes of Austen's novels, and suggests the continuum between the oral tales and the canonical literary forms.[97] It is such narratives we need, Collingwood seems to suggest, and have always needed, to comprehend the relations between the surface of life and its depths. In such narratives we see ourselves as we are.

Where the Austen lectures analyse works of literary art in the particular case, the two remaining pieces published in Part I of our selection subsume literary expression within a general definition of art. Collingwood's 'Lectures on the Philosophy of Art' (1924) stands with the folktale material as generating later thinking on the cultural, political, and social relations of art. The lectures pervade the whole plan, substantive content, and logical order of the *Outlines of a Philosophy of Art*, completed in August of 1924 and published in 1925; they are absorbed into chapter 3 of *Speculum Mentis*, into the idea of 'art-as-imagination' that is the central doctrine of *The Principles of Art*, and into those parts of the folktale material which deal with the relations between the art of the primitive and the art of the civilized. The initial effort to define art as 'imagination', divisible into inspiration, sublimity, and Nature, here recalls other works where Collingwood asserts the total indifference of art to the real existence of the things it evokes or depicts, and where his stress falls on the reality of art's imaginative existence: 'The imagined object may be real: but to imagine it is to pay no attention to the question whether it is real.'[98] Collingwood was to write in *Speculum Mentis* that 'The aesthetic experience cares nothing for the reality or unreality of its object',[99] and in *The Principles of Art* he is subsequently to claim that 'Imagination is indifferent to the distinctions between the real and the unreal.'[100]

The essay is divided into three broad sections, unequal in length—on 'The General Nature of Art', on its 'Dialectic', and on 'The Place of Art in the Life of the Spirit', where Collingwood examines art in its relation to religion, science, and morality (the

[97] See e.g. Huang Mei, *Transforming the Cinderella Dream: From Francis Burney to Charlotte Brontë* (New Brunswick, NJ, and London: Rutgers University Press, 1990).
[98] LPA, fo. 4.   [99] *SM* 60.
[100] *PA* 136.

terms, in fact, in which Arnold, Eliot, or Leavis conceive the external relations of literature). Here, the 'Lectures' subdivide into chapters 5 and 6 of the *Outlines* ('The Life of Art' and 'Art and the Life of the Spirit'), while the sections of the *Outlines* concerned with 'Genius and Taste: the Classics' (23), and on 'The Revolt against the Classics' (24), substantially echo the 'Lectures'. In the number of primary and secondary divisions that are transplanted, expanded, shifted, recombined, recycled, or otherwise replaced in the *Outlines*, the 'Lectures' thus enable us to appreciate, once again, the detailed, restless, and persistent process of thinking, rethinking, drafting, and redrafting, by which Collingwood's aesthetic thought has evolved. In this they sketch with respect to art not so much the 'position' or theoretical identity of Collingwood at any particular time ('realist', 'anti-realist', 'idealist', etc.), but the ambitiousness of his intellectual journey, his own process of thought, his tendency at every point to establish connections between disciplines, to beat the bounds of his subjects, and to engage several aspects of his intellectual nature at once.

In the remainder of his 'Lectures' Collingwood speculates on the value of natural beauty as distinct from a beauty that is made by man, on the fragility of the English countryside and its destruction by modern urbanization and post-industrial taste.[101] A further discussion concerns the role of technique, and the place of the education of the artist as child in making the transition from imitation to free creation. But the most compelling evocation of the laws of cultural and literary transformation (as being reminiscent of the folktale essays) is the collective psychology behind an age's revolt against its established 'classics'. Collingwood sees this as essentially a revolt of the mind against the part of itself that feels under others' oppressive control. The passage is revised for the *Outlines*, but it is in its original form additionally fluent, direct, and less burdened by cumbersome detail. Collingwood is inward with the collective psychological processes of literary and critical history. He suggests that our attitude to any literary or critical classic,

---

[101] In common with his polemic on the collapse of artistic value in 'Art and the Machine' (hereafter AM; see Part III of this volume). Collingwood's position on this issue resembles F. R. Leavis's call for the reconstitution of a declined 'organic community' of English life. See F. R. Leavis and Denys Thompson, *Culture and Environment: The Training of Critical Awareness* (London: Chatto & Windus, 1933).

as of any classic of art, is a complex combination of attractions and repulsions, of love and of hate, of loathing of others and of self-loathing. It is above all a highly emotional as distinct from a purely intellectual matter, a reflection on our perpetual idolization and canonization of the classics of culture:

Rebellion is simply the negative phase which is inherent in all activity: because activity must, by its very nature, go forward, it must destroy what it has created and wipe out its past achievement, on pain of stagnation.

When this phase of rebellion has burnt itself out, in a revolt against the spirit of revolt itself, what is left behind is not just nothing but a new frame of mind, namely the attitude of combatants who because they have fought their battle to a finish can be friends again. We return not to the blind worship of our first attitude but to a discriminating enjoyment of works of art, which we can now enjoy the better for being able to praise as equals and to keep our admiration on this side of idolatry. We now no longer, like children, call any work of art either good or bad without qualification, but we can discuss each work on its merits and point out its strong and weak sides impartially.[102]

What Collingwood has to say in this passage about reactions to the classics might as aptly apply to the narrative archetypes used by literary history, and to the reactions of the Romantics against their eighteenth-century critical and poetic forebears—as Collingwood justly points out. Today, his words might on the same principle also apply to literary-critical rebellions against reason itself.

In common both with the 'Lectures on the Philosophy of Art', and with various parts of the folktale material, 'Aesthetic Theory and Artistic Practice' of 1931 also feeds into *The Principles of Art*; and it is in substantial ways a working through of recurrent issues that occur as independent arguments at this point.[103] The manuscript was originally drafted as an essay of some 12,000 words, but was then reduced, perhaps in a longer and a shorter version, for lecture delivery. In ways that look forward to the opening sections of *The Principles of Art*, Collingwood explores

---

[102] LPA, fo. 36.

[103] Between *Outlines of a Philosophy of Art* (1925) (hereafter *OPA*) and *PA* Collingwood had also published a paper on 'Aesthetic' in R. J. S. McDowall (ed.), *The Mind* (London: Longmans & Co., 1927), and based on a series of lectures delivered at King's College, London. The essay is reprinted with an introduction by James Connelly as 'Aesthetic and the Mind', *Collingwood Studies*, 3 (1996), *Letters from Iceland and Other Essays*, 194–215.

the relationship between aesthetic theory and artistic practice under the aspect of normative and descriptive accounts of art, and sets forth the function of an aesthetic philosophy. Can a better theory of art make practice better, Collingwood asks; or is the philosophy of art merely descriptive, independent of practice, and not meant for this use? Should the philosopher and the artist mind their own business? In order to exemplify the ideal reciprocity of theory and practice, Collingwood discusses the trend towards naturalistic copying in mid-nineteenth-century art that is derived from the theory of Ruskin, who in turn was influenced by the practice of Wordsworth; in this trend artists, and particularly landscape artists, forsook design in order to imitate the beauty of nature. As he moves between the media of painting and poetry, Collingwood identifies a parallel development in nineteenth-century literature and describes the effects of naturalism upon it. Commenting on Hardy's fiction as a drama of mind, he concludes that theory and practice are mutually necessary; that the artist must at some level hold a theory of art if he is to know what he is trying to do (without which he is doing nothing), just as the philosopher of art, in the absence of art, has no material to work with.[104]

'External criticism is valueless', Collingwood had written in *Speculum Mentis* (1924): 'the true critic is one who can place himself at the point of view criticized, and in his own person live out its consequences to the bitter end'.[105] In that they enable us to apply Collingwood's thinking to the history of literature, to 'critical' thought, and more importantly to critical performance, the inferences we can draw together from work published for the first time in this volume will suggest an 'idea of history' which illuminates the literary past. Through the patterns of cultural transmission evinced in the folktale essays Collingwood helps to redefine the notion of 'civilization' as constructed by art. We may note the frequent 'translational' ramifications of these and his other essays on cultural themes, their contemporary inspiration, their presiding intellectual confidence, their practical engagement with others'

[104] Cf. *PA* 3: 'Philosopher-aestheticians are trained to do well just the thing that artist-aestheticians do badly'.

[105] *SM* 45. Cf. Collingwood's definition of the criticism of philosophy in *EPM* that: 'Criticism does not begin until the reader has . . . submitted to the discipline of following the author's thought and reconstructing in himself the point of view from which it proceeds' (219).

texts, and the satire which is part of their meaning. Together they amplify the principle accorded to 'criticism' in *Speculum Mentis*—that it is 'a vindication of the very experiences which it refutes, for it exhibits them not as strange and inexplicable perversions of the mind, morbid types of thought indulged by the foolish and depraved, but as stages through which the critic has himself passed, and which he can confess without forfeiting his claim to rationality'.[106]

The folktale and other manuscripts on cultural themes give then a personal dimension—a sense of rootedness in his own intellectual and emotional experience—to Collingwood's conception of re-enactment; and they reveal the pertinence of literary and cultural thought to his development. Collingwood's is a voice that may have been partially drowned out hitherto, and the essays we print here for the first time suggest the interconnectedness of all of his work along the axis of the cultural. There is the link (along with its correspondingly developed distinction) between the literary, the oral, and the musical performance, between sound and written text, between the language of song, of literature, of pictorial naturalism, the worship of nature, and the telling of realistic or miraculous tales, between the question 'what is art?' and the answers available within a chronological and formal range, between the elements of the question 'what is civilization?'—a challenge that does not come to published expression until *The New Leviathan*—and the formulation of art as magic, or as Collingwood insists, as itself. Within a conception whose reverse face is the profound *dis*enchantment of 'Man Goes Mad', Collingwood can explore art at once through the earliest formalizations and symbolizations of human emotion, in the tales of enchantment and romance, and in the modern social rituals, comical, satirical, rational, and vividly realist, of a Jane Austen novel. In this there is a vision that is not resolved into a philosophical *system* as such (an expectation Collingwood had seemed to invite in *Speculum Mentis*). Rather, the essays published here for the first time typically take us behind the scenes of a restlessly sceptical mind as it lives through its experiences 'to the bitter end' (as it were), but 'without forfeiting . . . [its] claims to rationality'. Perhaps, it has been suggested, Collingwood's thinking is always provisional and unsettled, his

---

[106] *SM* 45.

views strident and overstated, polluted by a lonely pugnacity;[107] but the energy of revision, the ceaseless recasting of old themes in new forms and according to new intellectual occasions, the untiring experiments with intellectual range, its elements in different combinations, the blending of the philosophy with the living, the living with the philosophy, bring a moving openness to Collingwood's work that will guarantee its survival when conclusive 'systems' of thought are defunct. We turn now, then, from their contexts in literary criticism and aesthetics to the implications of Collingwood's chapters on folktale for the history of one of its major themes—social and cultural anthropology itself.

---

[107] T. M. Knox's article on Collingwood in the *Dictionary of National Biography 1941–1950*, ed. L. G. Wickham Legg and E. T. Williams (Oxford: Oxford University Press, 1959), 168–70, charges his later writings with 'febrility and a sense of strain' (169). Compare the more sympathetic treatment by Stefan Collini and Bernard Williams in the new edition of the *Dictionary of National Biography* (Oxford: Oxford University Press, 2004).

2. A FIELDWORKER'S PHILOSOPHER: PERSPECTIVES FROM ANTHROPOLOGY

WENDY JAMES

In the early summer of 1936, R. G. Collingwood delivered two talks which at first glance were on the same topic: the first, in June, posed the question 'Who was King Arthur?' and was read to a literary society in Oxford.[1] The second was delivered on 8 July in the open air, to a party of the Cumberland and Westmorland Antiquarian and Archaeological Society, visiting a site known as 'King Arthur's Round Table', near Penrith in the present county of Cumbria. There is not much to see there, except the remains of an unadorned earthwork damaged by modern roads and development (nearby Mayborough, however, still displays a large standing stone, which the party also visited, among other places of interest). Collingwood's theories about the Round Table site were in fact very little to do with the post-Roman legend of Arthur; he was interested in the possibility of its very great antiquity, going back to the Bronze Age, on account of the parallels with other known sites of this period. He suggested to his listeners that we might have here 'a miniature Avebury'.[2] The following year, he led a careful excavation on behalf of the Society specifically to test this hypothesis, and found a submerged level at which there had once plausibly been a wooden ceremonial structure confirming his suspicion.[3] Such a site could well have been associated with nobility or ritual chiefship, though the legendary association with Arthur was the product of much later historical developments.

Sites connected with Arthur are of course found all over Britain, and if Collingwood's suggestion (which still commands respect)

[1] ' "Who was King Arthur?" (paper read to the *Martlets*, Univ. Coll. Oxon., June 1936)', Bodleian Library Collingwood Papers, dep. 23/15.

[2] 'King Arthur's Round Table and Mayborough: A Report of the Excursion', *Transactions of the Cumberland and Westmorland Antiquarian and Archaeological Society*, NS 37 (1937), 190–1. Cf. ' "Mayborough and King Arthur's Round Table", a paper read 8 July 1936', Bodleian Library Collingwood Papers, dep. 23/16.

[3] 'King Arthur's Round Table: Interim Report on the Excavations of 1937', *Transactions of the Cumberland and Westmorland Antiquarian and Archaeological Society*, NS 38 (1938), 1–31. For a recent commentary, see Stein Helgeby and Grace Simpson, 'King Arthur's Round Table and Collingwood's Archaeology', *Collingwood Studies*, 2 (1995), 1–11.

that he was a fifth-century Romano-British leader who managed to reassemble a heavy cavalry force in the Roman manner and make use of the Roman road network against the Saxons, this is not surprising. Was Arthur a historical figure or a myth? Collingwood had argued in print as follows:

The fact that his name in later ages was a magnet drawing to itself all manner of folk-lore and fable, and that an Arthurian cycle grew up composed partly of events transferred from other contexts, no more proves him a fictitious character than similar fables prove it of Alexander or Aristotle. . . . It tends rather to prove the opposite. The place which the name of Arthur occupies in Celtic legend is easiest to explain on the hypothesis that he really lived, and was a great champion of the British people.[4]

A champion, though not necessarily a king—his noble origin having been added later. A view of 'sites' as actually attracting layers of legendary elements grafting themselves on each other over time raises the possibility of 'excavating' stories as one might a long-occupied site. It also opens up the possibility that some British folk stories might have sketchy links going back thousands, rather than hundreds, of years.

Such an extended perspective invites us to contemplate some of the key questions of anthropology, that is, the general study of our habits and the shaping of our skills as a species over space and time; a philosophical region indeed rather beyond the domain of orthodox history or even archaeology.[5] In her unpublished thesis, Maureen Rudzik has shown how Collingwood saw the study of folktales as a way of extending the horizons of history to link up with the kind of questions that anthropology had made its own, and to find new ways of dealing with them.[6] Collingwood had long been interested in anthropology, and touched on it in some of his earliest publications. There are general references to it, for example, in his *Religion and Philosophy* of 1916.[7] The authors he

---

[4] R. G. Collingwood and J. N. L. Myers, *Roman Britain and the English Settlements* (Oxford: Clarendon Press, 1936), 321. Cf. also 322–4.

[5] An overview of the discipline and some aspects of its history is offered in Wendy James, *The Ceremonial Animal: A New Portrait of Anthropology* (Oxford: Oxford University Press, 2003).

[6] See MR, ch. 6, which discusses the Arthurian legend and archaeology.

[7] He was here critical of the 'anti-intellectual' stance of those anthropologists (unnamed) who give ritual, rather than belief, primacy in understanding early

was loosely indicating here shared a curiosity about long-term human history, but almost always cast their enquiries in a general 'evolutionary' framework set primarily in the processes of an un-thinking nature. We can perhaps detect, even at this time, an embryonic scepticism in Collingwood's response. In the first of his pieces we have included in Part I, on 'Words and Tune' written in 1918, he refers in passing to the ideas of Herbert Spencer about the origins of song and comments on 'the stupidity of the evolu-tionary philosopher'.[8] His alertness to the antiquity of some extra-ordinary works of art, and thus to the undeniable sophistication of early humankind, was also clear in his early years; in his 'Lectures on the Philosophy of Art' below, he emphasizes in a very positive way the *'primitiveness of art'* (his italics; we might today say *pri-macy*) both in human history and in the life of the individual (something that few evolutionary anthropologists then consid-ered). 'Man in the Reindeer age had little that could be called religion, and still less that could be called science, but he had an art of extraordinary richness and power.'[9] In an unpublished note of 1933 on the idea of 'primitive mind', he treats the anthropolo-gists rather cursorily and devotes more thought to the psycholo-gists.[10] In later writings too he was often dismissive of the mistaken naturalism of well-known mainstream anthropological writings. In the recently published collection *The Principles of History* we read, for example, that like classical economics, which describes 'a certain set of transient historical conditions under the belief that it was stating eternal truths', anthropology is 'crypto-history'. 'A number of different historical complexes are lumped together under the name of "primitive life" or something like that: and their characteristics . . . are thus by a fiction abstracted from these contexts and treated as a kind of matrix . . . within which

religion (*RP* 4–7, 24). Cf. also 'Comparative religion is the classification and comparison of different religions or different forms of the same religion. It is therefore on the one hand anthropological, . . . and on the other psychological, as determining the religious beliefs of this or that individual considered as a member of a certain class, sect, or nation. Comparative religion or religious anthropology is therefore not really to be distinguished from the Psychology of Religion' (*RP* 39).

[8] WT, fo. 13.   [9] LPA, fo. 37.
[10] 'Outline of a Theory of Primitive Mind', Bodleian Library Collingwood Papers, dep. 16/8.

historical formations arise.'[11] Several references can be found in
The Idea of History, where anthropology is opposed, as 'a kind
of natural history of man', to history.[12] 'Herder is thus the father
of anthropology', he writes, in distinguishing the variation of
human physical types and the range of manners and customs
supposedly linked with them, but Herder's conception was not a
genuinely historical one. 'There is still no conception of a people's
character as having been made what it is by that people's historical
experience', and against the racism of Herder he suggests that
following the work of modern anthropologists, 'We know that
physical anthropology and cultural anthropology are different
studies.'[13]

What did Collingwood mean to signify by emphasizing this? We
know that he did not mean to endorse any fundamental dichotomy,
whether between the physical and the mental sides of human life or
in the study of humanity. We know that he regarded such dichoto-
mies as inappropriate in the domain of concepts bearing on
human life and language, where, as he explained in his *Essay on
Philosophical Method*, the sharp either/or logic of the sciences was
unsuitable. Rather, there was overlap as well as discrimination
between concepts, in what he called a 'scale of forms'.[14] Clearly,
for him, the evolutionary anthropologists had discriminated
too strongly between the primitive and the civilized, and, moreover, had set the nature/culture boundary too close to modern
times.

In the mid-1930s Collingwood was certainly seeking to explore,
and spell out, the connections of his philosophical with his historical and archaeological work, especially after his appointment in
1935 to the Waynflete Chair of Metaphysical Philosophy, and his
release from a heavy teaching load. In the lecture 'Method and
Metaphysics' which he gave to the Jowett Society in the same year,
for example, he includes explanation and discussion of the 'scale of
forms' and other ideas from the *Essay on Philosophical Method*,
arguing for example the need to go beyond the existence of classificatory forms as such, to their historical context. The lecture
also indicates as a matter of importance the fact that 'mind' has
come into existence in a world which was once a world of mere

[11] 'Notes on Historiography', in *PH* 244.   [12] *IH* 79.
[13] *IH* 91–2.   [14] *EPM*, ch. 3.

body.[15] This has the feel of an 'anthropological' question, one of a longer term and more philosophical kind about the nature of consciousness than one can pursue through normal historical sources or even through the discipline of field archaeology. Had it become a part of Collingwood's intention at this time to apply the philosophical methods of his 1933 book, and in particular the notion of the 'scale of forms', to human history in the widest sense, and, as a part of this project, to turn to what the folklorists and anthropologists had been investigating?

Collingwood's philosophy had never been set exclusively in the abstractions of the mind, nor of that discipline's written texts. It was an exploration of the human world as it is lived, and as it has been lived. Not all his philosophical readers have understood this, nor have all his archaeological readers appreciated the fact that he did represent the literal unearthing of the human past as a metaphysical enquiry. His genius lay in seeing how these endeavours were related; but few of his contemporaries appreciated this vision, rarely focusing their eyes beyond the apparent certainties of the printed word—in the philosopher's case—or the gritty turf and stones laid bare by the excavator's pick in the other. Even now, as there is a rising interest in Collingwood's work among the philosophers, few go up to Cumbria and take into account its connection with the practical business of digging up the earth to see who built which bits of a Roman road, when, and why, and how they lived and felt. The past of north-western Britain, and indeed northwestern Europe, was a part of the imaginative world of the family home Collingwood had been brought up in, not only through archaeological digs but also through painting, textual scholarship, and the writing of historical novels.[16] The folktale manuscript illustrates very clearly the inner connection between the two

---

[15] ' "Method and Metaphysics"—Paper read before the Jowett Society, 19 June 1935', Bodleian Library Collingwood Papers, dep. 19/3, 5. Cf. Collingwood's evocation of the 'scale of forms' in countering Hegel's dialectic of Nature and Spirit in history: 'Notes towards a Metaphysic' in *PH* 126.

[16] See e.g. the first two articles in *Collingwood Studies*, 1 (1994), *The Life and Thought of R.G. Collingwood*: Douglas H. Johnson, 'W. G. Collingwood and the Beginnings of *The Idea of History*', 1–26; and Teresa Smith, 'R. G. Collingwood: "This Ring of Thought"': Notes on Early Influences', 27–43. On tracing roads, see e.g. R. G. Collingwood, 'Two Roman Mountain-Roads', *Transactions of the Cumberland and Westmorland Antiquarian and Archaeological Society*, NS 37 (1937), 1–12.

sides of Collingwood's outlook in this respect: he was above all a fieldworker's philosopher.

Collingwood's premises were thus very different from the naturalistic approach of the armchair evolutionary anthropologists whose work was available to him. Not only did he take as his starting point the *irreducibly cultural* character of the worlds in which human beings have always lived and have created civilization, but also their historicity in the fullest sense. For Collingwood, as we know, the specific forms of language, literature, art, music, and the shared emotional understanding built into action have always defined human history, and thus 'mind', as far back as we can trace any evidence, and our attitude to that evidence must therefore start from this point. Moreover, perhaps unlike most of the earlier anthropologists, he did not take for granted that the human condition was generally on an upward curve. Civilization was not always a matter of robust progress; that engagement of sensibility and creativity which, on his account, has been integral to the real achievements of human history is a fragile phenomenon. It had already (that is, even from the viewpoint of the mid-1930s) been damaged by the advent of large-scale industry and technology, and further threats from the advancing technology of war and associated nationalism—a kind of 'new barbarism'—he feared might undermine the essential qualities of civilized human life itself.

This latter theme came to dominate some of Collingwood's later writings, evident already in the piece 'Man Goes Mad' with which we conclude this volume, and which itself is a prelude to his wartime book *The New Leviathan*.[17] The sense of human loss and the damage inflicted by modern industrial progress and militarism is conveyed powerfully in these works. Regret for the way that the modern era was eroding evidence of the sophistication of the lived past was perhaps always with Collingwood, something possibly built in to the mind-set of archaeologists everywhere. It is expressed rather elegantly in his lament over the decline of the home-based arts and the rise of such mechanical entertainments as art reproductions, the gramophone, and the radio in his sketch 'Art and the Machine'. We have included this piece as a curtain-raiser in our Part III to introduce the darker tone of the longer essay. In

---

[17] *NL*, published in 1942; revised edn., 1992.

'Man Goes Mad' the quiet nostalgia has disappeared, and we are confronted with a sharp anger. The piece was begun at the end of August 1936. In retrospect, we can perhaps guess that this blast against the evils of war and destruction, and the accompanying threat to civilized life and values, had led Collingwood to ponder more exactly what it was that was under threat; what of qualitative value in civilization had been lost to the point where modern thought failed even to recognize a kinship with the past. If this were the kind of question in his mind at that time, when he was also pondering the very practical matter of unearthing evidence possibly pointing back to ceremonial structures of the Bronze Age in Cumbria, it is entirely understandable that he decided to turn to the literature of anthropology and folklore, and to embark on an intensive quest, through this literature, for the nature of those continuities that could be discerned in civilization over the long term.

We know that it must have been in September or early October of 1936 that Collingwood wrote off proposing himself to the Folk Lore Society in London, for he was admitted as a member (unusually, without a sponsor) at their Council meeting on 21 October.[18] As soon as that term's teaching in Oxford was over, he wrote to ask if he might use the Society's library, and spent several days in London reading there.[19] During this visit, and possibly further periods reading in London and Oxford, he made notes on what he found interesting in the Society's journal and a range of other

[18] From the Minutes of the FLS we learn that 'Professor P. G. Collingwood' [sic] was admitted as a new member among a list of others on 21 October 1936. FLS Archives, 'Minutes of Evening and General Meetings, 1936–59'.

[19] On 5 Dec. Collingwood wrote to the Secretary of the FLS: 'Dear Sir, / I want to come and do some reading in the Folk-lore Society's Library this week. I understand that the Library is open to members on notice being given to yourself, and I believe it is at 52 Upper Bedford Place. I propose to come up to London on Tuesday and spend the rest of the week in town. On getting to town on Tuesday (at 11.10) I shall, unless I have already heard from you, come to 52 Upper Bedford Place and inquire for you or for a message from you. / Yours faithfully . . . ' A week later, on 12 Dec., he wrote again: 'Dear Sir, / Thank you for your letter of the 8th. Miss Martindale very kindly put me in touch with Mr Johnson, who welcomed me most hospitably and put University College at my disposal. I spent 5 very profitable days there and enjoyed myself thoroughly. I shall very likely go back from time to time as need and opportunity arise, for we have nothing in Oxford that can compare with the Society's collections. / It is good of you to suggest that I should read the Society a paper. I think the Society's meetings are on Wednesdays, when I regularly

specialist studies published over the previous few decades.[20] It was on the basis of this work that Collingwood began to draft, presumably over the Christmas vacation of 1936 and the first months of 1937, the series of chapters on folktale and magic that we are offering as the core of the present volume. He designed this project explicitly as a critical contribution to the debates in anthropology current at the time. Beyond that, however, his polemics can be read as a kind of elegy for a lost enchantment: a magic sensibility that modern humanity has almost forgotten among the urgencies of self-definition in a world of increasingly utilitarian values and national striving. He does not refer, except very indirectly, to the currently rising levels of worry over war that are clearly indicated in 'Man Goes Mad'; but in our view Collingwood's passionate search in the folktale study for evidences about the roots of human civilization was driven partly by that consciousness, and his findings even as contained in the unfinished book are absolutely central to his whole philosophical purpose. It was known to various parties that he intended to publish a book on this topic, and the Oxford University Press exchanged some correspondence with the family about the manuscript shortly after his death, but there was no follow-up.[21]

What was the state of anthropology, as Collingwood found it and conducted his own excavation of it, in the mid-1930s? With few exceptions, according to him at least, it was guilty of scientism, false naturalism, and a parochial utilitarianism in distancing 'primitive' humanity from 'ourselves' and from what we claimed

hold an evening class here; but I could see whether that could be moved in another year. I will bear it in mind. / Yours sincerely . . . ' FLS Archives, 'FLS Corres.' box for 1935.

[20] See Bodleian Library Collingwood Papers, dep. 21/1–3 and 21/12–13.

[21] Kenneth Sisam of the Oxford University Press wrote to Mrs Kate Collingwood on 24 Feb. 1944: 'I should like to enquire about . . . his Lectures to the Folk Lore Society in which he dealt with Fairy Tales. He often talked to me about a proposed book on Fairy Tales, and I should be personally interested to see the Lectures if they survive, though I do not expect they are suitable for publication to his standards.' Mrs Collingwood replied: 'I shall send you the fairy tale manuscript . . . in a few days. I am nervous about publishing the fairy tale book; it's off Robin's usual beat, and I don't think he would have offered it to you without very careful rewriting.' Mrs Kate Collingwood to Kenneth Sisam, 28 Feb. 1944. See the Oxford University Press Archives (filed as OP 2395/17613).

as our 'advanced' civilization.[22] We can find plenty to endorse this view by glancing, for example, at the journals of the Royal Anthropological Institute for this period, whose coverage extended across the anthropological and archaeological spectrum in a systematic endeavour to place new discoveries on record, classify new findings, and put forward explanatory theories of customs, practices, and beliefs across the world. Although the label 'social anthropology' was established at Oxford as early as 1910 with the title of R. R. Marett's Readership, Collingwood did not often use it, possibly feeling uncomfortable with the 'scientific' aims claimed for it by Marett and shared by most of the discipline's professionals in the inter-war period. At an international meeting he had helped sponsor in 1934, Marett made his view of anthropology as a natural science clear to his colleagues: 'I welcome the assembling of this, the first Congress of the Anthropological Sciences, because it foreshadows closer cooperation in the future between those students of all nations who seek to understand human development in terms of natural law.'[23] In his turn, Radcliffe-Brown, following Marett as the first Professor of Social Anthropology at

---

[22] *IH* 224.

[23] R. R. Marett, 'The Growth and Tendency of Anthropology and Ethnological studies', Plenary Address in the *Proceedings of the International Congress of Anthropological and Ethnological Studies* (London: Royal Anthropological Institute, 1934), 39–40. This address is summarized in *Man*, 34, 162 (1934), 141–2. Marett further wrote, for example, in recommending the Polynesian concept *mana* as a general category for the comparison of religious ideas, 'Now any historical science that adopts the comparative method stands committed to the postulate that human nature is sufficiently homogeneous and uniform to warrant us in classifying its tendencies under formulae coextensive with the whole broad field of anthropological research. Though the conditions of their occurrence cause our data to appear highly disconnected, we claim, even if we cannot yet wholly make good, the right to bind them together into a single system of reference by means of certain general principles.' See Marett, 'The Conception of Mana' in *The Threshold of Religion* (1909), 2nd edn. (London: Methuen, 1914), 101. Cf. 'We shall try to examine the elemental stuff of primitive religion by an analytic or piecemeal method. Proceeding in such a way as is appropriate to what after all is a biological, not a chemical, investigation, we shall do our best as it were to vivisect this highly complex form of experience, which, though organic with the rest of our nature, is yet so basic and central as almost to amount to a living thing on its own account.' See Marett, *Faith, Hope and Charity in Primitive Religion* (Oxford: Clarendon Press, 1932), 16. Collingwood does occasionally use the phrase 'social anthropology', e.g. in FT2, fo. 42; but it was yet to acquire the more humanistic sense bestowed by scholars like Evans-Pritchard from the 1950s on.

Oxford from 1937, and evoking Durkheim from the start, later campaigned for his discipline to be recognized as 'the theoretical natural science of human society', which could stand on its own by focusing on the 'ethnographic present' without reference to history.[24] Against this and perhaps significantly, Collingwood writes below that 'Darwin was a great naturalist, but he lived and wrote before social anthropology had begun.'[25] Collingwood had clearly been more comfortable with 'cultural' anthropology, a broader category well-established in America and already associated in Britain with the work of Edward B. Tylor and with the world of museum archaeology and ethnology. T. K. Penniman, later to become curator of the Pitt Rivers Museum, had classed 'social' anthropology as a subdivision of the 'cultural' variety, implying its close sympathy with the particularities of history and archaeology.[26] In chapter 2 of his study, Collingwood referred explicitly to the current state of anthropological theory, and associated himself with the reforming efforts of his contemporaries:

A reader may ask why I say nothing of the controversies and inquiries which are occupying the minds of anthropologists today: the diffusionist controversy, for example, or the attempt to blend the functional and psychological methods into a new synthesis. If I ignore these it is not because I doubt their importance. It is because the cross-currents of a 'critical period', as the present age of anthropological studies has been called . . . are of interest not for what they have achieved but for what may come of them. . . . What I have to say is rather a contribution to the work of this critical period than an estimate of it.[27]

Marett had identified the contemporary era for anthropology a 'critical period' at the Congress of 1934, and the phrase was adopted as a chapter title in Penniman's overview.[28] The 1930s were felt generally to be a time of assessment and reflection on the

[24] A. R. Radcliffe-Brown, 'On Social Structure', Presidential Address to the Royal Anthropological Institute, 1940, in *Journal of the Royal Anthropological Institute*, 70 (1940), 1–12; reprinted as ch. 10 in *Structure and Function in Primitive Society, Essays and Addresses* (London: Cohen & West, 1952), 188–204.

[25] FT2, fo. 42.

[26] T. K. Penniman, *A Hundred Years of Anthropology* (London: Duckworth, 1935), 15.

[27] FT2, fos. 1–2.

[28] Marett, 'Growth and Tendency', 51. Cf. Penniman, *Hundred Years*, 21–2, ch. 5, 'The Critical Period, 1900–1935', 242–344.

human predicament, not least in literature and philosophy, and Frazer's *Golden Bough* had opened up a store-house of rich material for such reflection. Frazer's sense of nostalgia for a lost integrity and the treasures of earlier times was echoed not only in Eliot's poetry but in many general writings and in the public ethos. Some of the points made by Collingwood in his critique of early anthropology are mirrored in Wittgenstein's almost contemporary notes made on the *Golden Bough*, also little known and most fully published only in 1993.[29]

Collingwood attended a number of meetings of the Folk Lore Society in London (which shared an address with the Royal Anthropological Institute), chairing at least two of their lectures and on occasion dining with them.[30] The Society's meetings were evidently very lively at this time; for example, Jomo Kenyatta (then studying at the London School of Economics) had signed in as a guest on 17 January 1934, and again on 16 October 1935, when Audrey Richards spoke of 'Divination Rites in North Eastern Rhodesia'. Malinowski was present on this occasion, and there was an 'animated discussion' in which Mr Kenyatta is listed as taking part.[31] Collingwood gladly accepted an invitation in May 1937 to address the Society himself, writing in reply:

[29] Ludwig Wittgenstein, 'Remarks on Frazer's *Golden Bough*', in James Klagge and Alfred Nordmann (eds.), *Philosophical Occasions 1912–1951* (Indianapolis and Cambridge: Hackett, 1993), 115–55.

[30] A letter from Collingwood to the Secretary of the Society, 15 May 1937, accepts an invitation to dine on 19 May 1937, and one from Mrs Ethel Collingwood, 8 Feb. 1938, apologizes for his not being able to accept the invitation for 16 February. See the FLS Archives, 'FLS Corres.' boxes for 1937 and 1938. At the meeting on 21 Apr. 1937, Collingwood chaired a talk given by Mr John Fletcher on 'Folk Pastimes: the Survival and Revival of Folk Art'; and the minutes for the next meeting, on 19 May 1937, are signed by him. On this occasion, a paper was read by Adrian N. Newell on 'Celtic Religious Sculpture in Roman Gaul'. Various people took part in the discussion, 'the chairman having dealt with several points in the paper'. On 15 June 1938, 'Professor Hooke expressed the sympathy of the Society for Professor Collingwood in his long illness and the regret that it had been necessary on that account to postpone the hearing of his paper.' John Layard was a distinguished anthropologist, also based in Oxford, who occasionally appeared among those present in the late 1930s, as did R. R. Marett, who made arrangements for several meetings of the Society to be held in Oxford, some at Exeter College, during the war. Meetings continued at the college even after Marett's death in 1943. See the FLS Archives, 'Minutes of Evening and General Meetings, 1936–59'.

[31] FLS Archives, 'Minutes of Evening and General Meetings, 1936–59'.

I should like to read a paper to the Society: but I am in doubt whether the kind of thing I could contribute to its counsels would be of very much interest to it. I have no field-work to report; but in my business as a philosopher I have to think over the general significance in human life of the facts which the Society deals with; and the time seems to me ripe for a revolt against the orthodox Tylor–Frazer theory of magic and the statement of a new one. I have worked out such a theory, and could easily state it in a paper, called something like 'The Place of Magic in Human Life'. But would this be too philosophical for the Society?[32]

Unfortunately, illness prevented him from actually giving the paper, and the event was postponed more than once. We assume that chapter 4 below corresponds to the paper in question.

We can see today that Collingwood's criticisms of naïve evolutionism, as applied to human mentality and social life, resonate with those of a rising generation of anthropologists and others in the 1930s who were endeavouring in their own way, especially through first-hand fieldwork, to overcome the us/them divide, and to move beyond the stereotypes of 'primitive man'. Of particular importance here was the growing voice of E. E. Evans-Pritchard, though he came to be really influential only after the war, when he helped move 'British social anthropology' away from scientism and towards a more sympathetic engagement with the humanities and with history. I return to Evans-Pritchard's work, and its implicit and explicit connections with Collingwood's, below. First, we should sketch in some details of the Oxford anthropology scene in the 1920s and 1930s.[33]

Marett's Circle at Exeter College, and other Oxford Anthropologists

R. R. Marett had originally attended lectures on anthropology by Tylor at the Pitt Rivers Museum. He subsequently helped establish a Diploma in Anthropology in 1905 and founded the Oxford University Anthropological Society (still extant) in 1908. Following his appointment to a University Readership in 1910, his seminars at Exeter College became something of a centre for anthropological

[32] From the letter of 15 May 1937, mentioned above. FLS Archives, 'FLS Corres.' box for 1937.

[33] In what follows I develop parts of the discussion in my paper 'Tales of Enchantment: Collingwood, Anthropology, and the "Fairy Tales" Manuscripts', *Collingwood Studies*, 4 (1998), *Variations: Themes from the Manuscripts*, 133–56.

studies for the next three decades, as he has himself described in his autobiography *A Jerseyman at Oxford*.[34]

Marett was assiduous in promoting the public profile of anthropology, making contacts and bringing anthropologists from all over the world together, often at the college. He was also a prolific writer, as the bibliography prepared by T. K. Penniman for his *festschrift* indicates.[35] No one in Oxford with the slightest interest in anthropology or allied subjects could have failed to be aware of Marett's confidently presented views on primitive man, his society, and his psychology, nor of his ambition to lay the foundations of a science of comparative religion. He regularly published reviews of books in anthropology and archaeology across a wide range of journals, including the *TLS* and even the *Oxford Magazine*, right through the 1920s and 1930s. The subject had indeed gained a definite momentum over this period through the keen popular reception of major works, especially Frazer's *Golden Bough*, and the world of scholarship began to respond.

Dorothy Emmet (who was later, as Professor of Philosophy in Manchester, to draw not only upon Collingwood but also upon social anthropology in her own work) was a student in the 1930s. She was one of those who attended lectures both by Marett and by Collingwood, and has left a record of this, though she did not compare them directly. She has told us 'My first introduction to Social Anthropology was a course of lectures on 'Primitive Morality' by R. R. Marett which I attended as an undergraduate. . . . He had the charismatic quality Weber attributes to the "gifted pirate chief" '.[36] At about the same time Collingwood was introducing a new mix of references, and of ideas, into his Oxford lectures. His lectures were (perhaps for this reason) very popular with the undergraduates; eyewitnesses have told me that students *flocked* to them, that people ('apart from a few Americans') were so fascinated they forgot to take notes; word got around that Collingwood's lectures were the only ones in Oxford where you would hear any reference to the novels of Dorothy L. Sayers. Dorothy Emmet has recorded: 'He was one of the spell-binders of my own

---

[34] R. R. Marett, *A Jerseyman at Oxford* (London: Oxford University Press, 1941).

[35] Dudley Buxton, *Custom is King* (London: Hutchinson, 1936), 303–25.

[36] Dorothy Emmet, *Function, Purpose and Powers: Some Concepts in the Study of Individuals and Societies* (London: Macmillan, 1958), 237–8.

undergraduate days at Oxford; and for some of us our delight in his lectures was spiced by knowing that our tutors disapproved of him.[37]

Evans-Pritchard also found himself attracted, as a young man, both to the lively scholarship of Collingwood and to the anthropological scene organized by Marett. He was officially reading Modern History as an undergraduate at Exeter College, from 1921 to 1924. In an autobiographical note he has told us, however, how he moved away from this kind of history, and has explained why:

My tutor at Oxford, C. T. Atkinson, was a complete philistine, the narrowest of military historians, and though he was a good man, I got little inspiration from him. On the other hand Exeter College was then the home of Oxford anthropology. Dr. Marett, that genial boaster, later the Rector, gave an anthropological tone to the College. . . . In that climate I began to vary the tedium of the History School, so I then regarded it, by taking an interest in books like Tylor's Primitive Culture and Frazer's Golden Bough; and thus I became a social anthropologist in embryo.

He commented that there was, however, nobody at Oxford who had engaged in field research—'I had had enough of Oxford anyway'—so he went to London to study under Professor Seligman. Malinowski started teaching there in the same year, 1924, and Evans-Pritchard adds 'I learnt more from him than from anyone.'[38]

In his own autobiographical account, Marett mentions Evans-Pritchard and A. M. Hocart among contributors to his *festschrift*, who 'though they had not actually taken our Diploma Course, were Exeter men whom I had known from their youth up'.[39] The book is a fulsome survey of all his closer and more distant friendships and contacts, and looking back it is curious that there is not a single reference to Collingwood (though we know that Colling-

[37] Dorothy Emmet, *Rules, Roles and Relations* (London: Macmillan, 1963), 371.
[38] The same passage also mentions that 'Henry Balfour, Curator of the (ethnology) Pitt Rivers Museum, and Dudley Buxton, Reader in Physical Anthropology, were members of Common Room; and various other anthropologists, such as Rattray, had a close association with Marett. Also I came to be a close friend of the archaeologist Francis Turville-Petre, then reading anthropology at Oxford (at Exeter College)'. In London 'I used to see quite a lot of Haddon, Elliot Smith and Perry'. See E. E. Evans-Pritchard, 'Genesis of a Social Anthropologist: An Autobiographical Note', *The New Diffusionist*, 3/10 (1973), 18–19.
[39] *Jerseyman at Oxford*, 267–8.

wood did visit the college, for example to give a talk on 'The Good, the Right, and the Useful' to the Exeter College Dialectical Society, on 3 March 1930).[40]

There is as yet no evidence that Evans-Pritchard met Collingwood socially; but a later colleague of his, Godfrey Lienhardt, thought it very likely that he had attended some of Collingwood's lectures when he was a student. We know for certain, however, from his enthusiastic 1932 review of the second edition of *Roman Britain*, that Evans-Pritchard was an admirer of Collingwood. He commended the book to ethnologists, pointing out that the data of archaeologists are concrete and objective, and 'contrast in these characteristics with much of the loose data of ethnology that are so often a product of introspection followed by projection into savage behaviour'.[41] He also pointed out Collingwood's emphasis on the blending of cultural elements in history, as against their 'diffusion', which was a current preoccupation of the ethnologists. Reading between the lines, there is an unspoken affinity between these independent thinkers and committed fieldworkers, each of whom evidently shared many interests with Marett but maintained a distance from his court at Exeter. Both men developed critical views of the earlier orthodoxies in anthropology, partly as they were represented in Marett's somewhat hidebound views, and later formulated creative responses which have much in common. Evans-Pritchard's work on these questions, from the early 1930s onward, is mostly published and is well known.[42] Collingwood's contemporary responses to anthropology are embedded, almost buried, in many of his later works, especially *The Principles of Art* and *An Essay on Metaphysics*: but they are lucidly laid out for us in the folktale manuscript, around which we have arranged the present volume.

Before commenting further on the text itself, it is worth taking notice of the preparation Collingwood undertook for this project. Following his admittance to the Folk Lore Society in late 1936, Collingwood recorded his initial responses to the literature of anthropology and folklore in three notebooks full of close observation and comment. He covered works by several of the standard

---

[40] Bodleian Library Collingwood Papers, dep. 6/5.

[41] E. E. Evans-Pritchard, Review of *Roman Britain* by R. G. Collingwood, new enlarged edn. (Oxford: Clarendon Press, 1932), in *Man*, 32 (Sept 1932), 220–1.

[42] See T. O. Beidelman, *E. E. Evans-Pritchard: A Bibliography* (London: Tavistock, 1974).

folklorists such as Hartland and Joseph Jacobs besides Frazer; several by Freud and Jung; and several by key anthropologists such as Tylor, Hocart, Seligman, Marett, and Malinowski.[43] Collingwood made various critical comments in his notes: for example, an article by Frazer on 'Popular superstititions of the Ancients' is castigated as a 'bad example of the comparative method' and 'the method run mad'.[44] Freud's *Totem and Taboo* is 'an inconceivable muddle'; we should ditch the term 'savage'.[45] Commenting on Tylor's *Primitive Culture* he criticizes the concept of a 'low intellectual condition' as applying to anyone; 'the people who invented such things as the plough or axe, metallurgy or stone-cutting, were gigantic intellects'.[46] Collingwood seems to have admired the works of Hocart, for example referring to *The Progress of Man* as a 'good book'[47] and to an article of his on myth as 'an admirable analysis'.[48] Among others we would identify today primarily as social anthropologists, Collingwood makes notes on particular articles by Marett and by Brenda Seligman, and detailed observations on Malinowski's *Crime and Custom in Savage Society*, as well as referring to an article of his distinguishing three kinds of stories.[49] Mention is made in passing of Durkheim, in the context of an article by Clodd on 'Magic in Names',[50] an easily identifiable source for some of his discussion of this topic in chapter 4 below. Where we have been able clearly to identify sources of this kind for Collingwood's arguments and evidence in the folktale study we have done so in footnotes to the main text. Most of the implicit references are to works which appear in the three notebooks mentioned, but there are other sources which Collingwood had at his disposal and occasionally mentioned specifically (for example, T. K. Penniman's 1935 overview).[51] We also know that he would have been aware of contemporary works in ethnography and anthropology, especially those published by the Clarendon Press, of which he had been made a delegate in 1928. In the surviving part of his library still in the care of Teresa Smith, we

---

[43] For a summary of the works mentioned in the notebooks see MR, appendices II and IV.

[44] 'English Folklore I–III', Bodleian Library Collingwood Papers, dep. 21/1, fos. 15–16.

[45] Ibid., fos. 78, 85.   [46] Ibid., fo. 56.   [47] Ibid., fos. 14–22.

[48] Ibid., fos. 70–2.   [49] Ibid., fo. 73; 21/2, fo. 49; 21/3, fos. 6–10, fo. 48.

[50] Ibid., dep. 21/2, fo. 12.   [51] *Hundred Years*.

find, for example, alongside books of relevant date specifically on folklore (one of which was given to him by a student),[52] two substantial works on the peoples of northern Nigeria by Meek, two important books by Rattray on the Ashanti kingdom of what is now Ghana, and an ethnography of the Orokaiva by Williams.[53] His copy of Margaret Murray's *The Witch-Cult in Western Europe* is annotated with scathing comments.[54] We are fairly safe in guessing that Collingwood would have had advance information about (and perhaps even read in manuscript) Evans-Pritchard's first book, *Witchcraft, Oracles and Magic among the Azande* (published in 1937, but originally submitted to the Press in February 1935).[55]

To his survey of the anthropological literature and what he judged its misuses by philology and psychology, Collingwood brought insights from a literary sensibility, from that side of his personality and intellectual skills emphasized by Philip Smallwood in the opening section of this Introduction, and illustrated by our selection of his writings in Part I. In characterizing this sensibility, beyond the well-known emphasis on 're-enactment' through an exercise of historical imagination, we could add his recognition of *social and cultural form* as the context of individual experience and expression. Tylor in his evocation of the thinking of 'early man' had in mind *an individual* who reflected, using his (sic) internal powers of reason, on such phenomena as dreams; in proposing continuities of a cultural kind Tylor also tended to identify *individual* traits and practices as 'survivals' from the past. There is, however, a great difference between the thoughts of an individual, or the 'survival' of odd items of culture, on the one hand, and the

---

[52] A. H. Krappe, *The Science of Folk-Lore* (London: Methuen, 1930); this is initialled 'R. G. C. 1936'.

[53] C. K. Meek, *The Northern Tribes of Nigeria* (Oxford: Clarendon Press, 1925) and *Law and Authority in a Nigerian Tribe* (Oxford: Clarendon Press, 1937); R. S. Rattray, *Ashanti Law and Constitution* (Oxford: Clarendon Press, 1929) and *The Tribes of the Ashanti Hinterland* (Oxford: Clarendon Press, 1932); see also F. E. Williams, *Orokaiva Society* (Oxford: Clarendon Press, 1930). I am indebted to James Connelly for sharing with me his notes on Collingwood's surviving library, and also to Mrs Teresa Smith for giving me the opportunity to browse there.

[54] M. Murray, *The Witch-Cult in Western Europe* (Oxford: Clarendon Press, 1921).

[55] E. E. Evans-Pritchard, *Witchcraft, Oracles, and Magic among the Azande* (Oxford: Clarendon Press, 1937); an abridged paperback version was published in 1976 (Oxford: Clarendon Press).

Collingwoodian notion of the *composed* quality of thought within a particular cultural setting and the social processes of *recomposition* which are fundamental to the transmission (as against the passive 'survival') of any cultural practice. Folktales, he emphasizes, are a 'social institution'.[56] We can see clearly in Collingwood's work the presumption that the patterns in art, or music, or literature, or activities, are shared forms, part of the social milieu which shapes our personal thought and experience. In the early essay 'Words and Tune' which opens our selection of his writings, we are invited to see how individual sounds, of language or of a musical instrument, are meaningless on their own, but only in relation to each other—as *organized* within a composition. The theme is taken up vigorously in 'Aesthetic Theory and Artistic Practice', where the 'composed' quality of even 'naturalistic' schools of painting is emphasized. He returns again and again to the notion of underlying patterns of 'composition', not only in the making of works of art, but in the phenomena of social action as well, which are similarly subject to moral judgement, as well done or poorly done, according to the local criteria. Even battle strategies or road building, as Collingwood's regular analyses of life in Roman Britain showed, also required the rechoreographing of traditional forms in co-ordinated action. Collingwood's practical investigations of the past, perhaps even more clearly than his theoretical work, took for granted the essentially *social* nature of consciousness and action. Past thoughts and actions were carried out not simply by individuals on a priori grounds, but in the social context of the day. Re-enactment of past thought thus surely entails the re-enactment, in the imagination, not just of one person's outlook but of scenes from a social world in movement, and the principles of their 'composition'.

The project of the historian (or anthropologist, we can now add) thus comes very close to the project of translation from one language and artistic style to another, and of course translation from the classics and from modern European languages was an everyday practice for Collingwood. Moreover, the interpretation of any text or other evidence of thought necessarily entails some effort at 'translating' the underlying premisses of a social world.[57] There

---

[56] FTI, fo. 2.
[57] Cf. Philip Smallwood, 'Historical Re-enactment, Literary Transmission, and the Value of R. G. Collingwood', *Translation and Literature*, 9/1 (2000), 3–24.

is in this sense a distinctly sociological cast to Collingwood's interpretations of literature and folktales. In the opening pages of his folktale study he criticizes the claim that 'fairy-tale themes' arise directly from the unconscious mind, pointing out that, while such themes are widely diffused, they are not more so than weapons or implements, 'and not more widely than the forms of social life to which, on the view I am here putting forward, tales and implements are alike organic'.[58] And yet he was keen to criticize the claims of academic sociology: in 'Reality as History', written in late 1935, he pointed out that the historian thinks of facts 'in their concrete actuality', and 'cannot tolerate the substitution for any one fact another more or less like it' in the generalizing principles of Comtian sociology—itself a testimony to the 'dominance of the scientific spirit and the precarious position of historical thought in the world'.[59] The 'sociological sciences' are useful to the historian, but the relation should not be inverted—they cannot be allowed to 'represent themselves as the end to which historical thought is the means'.[60]

These are some of the basic attitudes which guided Collingwood in his critical reflections on anthropology, increasingly distancing itself at the time from naturalistic evolutionary models but moving rather towards 'Comtian sociology' as reformulated by Durkheim and applied explicitly by him and his colleagues to the evidence of the ethnographic record. Collingwood clearly regarded the literature of anthropology and folklore studies as useful resources in his wider campaign to reposition the claims of 'historical method' in relation to the understanding of those primary philosophical questions about humanity which the anthropologists kept asking but had not yet approached in the proper way. Even they stubbornly misunderstood such things as belief in magic, widely reported from—even diagnostic of—'savage peoples', but something very prominent also in the fairies and miraculous events of folktales still current and closer to home. Collingwood saw a kind of integrity in the way these stories were composed, more true to the past of our own peasantry in Britain, even to the remote past before conventional history began, than was recognized in most professional ethnographic reports of 'magical' beliefs in today's faraway places.

---

[58] FT1, fo. 5.   [59] 'Reality as History', in *PH*, 180.
[60] Ibid. 180–1.

Beyond the often incidental reports of odd customs and rituals observed by passing ethnographers, and different also from Tylor's somewhat fragmentary conception of 'survivals' from the past, folktales retain something of an intellectual and imaginative coherence. While they do indeed get modifed and transformed, they are not completely broken into fragments. They are *recomposed* with new relevance as they are transmitted across the world, and even down the generations to ourselves. They are a living link, over time, as against poorly reported items of tribal belief or the remnants of potsherds and axes buried in the ground. Internal to them are evocations of emotional experience to which we can respond from our own lives.

Collingwood on 'Fairy Tales', Reason, and Magic

Some existing commentaries on the folktale manuscript (see n. 3 to Philip Smallwood's section of this Introduction above) consider this work mainly as a contribution to 'folklore' studies as such, a subject which has more of a constituency among lay readers even today than it has in the universities and among academic anthropologists. And yet Collingwood's writings, in retrospect, can be regarded not only as a remarkable (if then unknown) intervention in debates going on in the anthropology of his time, but will be found lively and pertinent by today's generation of professionals and students in anthropology and neighbouring 'fieldworking' disciplines (especially archaeology, social history, and the cognitive side of the human sciences). These almost prophetic essays in the archaeology of reason, poetry, and life's magic in fact address the modern humanities and social sciences as a whole. Stereotypes of tribal peoples, weird foreign mentalities, and cultural relativism still pervade academic work, not to mention the pervasive utilitarian outlook that Collingwood so hated. The alternative of seeking knowledge of others through the 'historical method', which he recommends in his well-known existing published work, is here presented in a particularly persuasive way. This method, as David Boucher explains more fully below, involves more than a documentation of facts about the human world external to ourselves, because we are members of that world too. People living even in the most remote fringes of that world (as it seems to us moderns) in time or in space, where we have perhaps little or no conventional historical evidence, are in fact equally members of it. Moreover, there is more evidence around us than might at first be thought, which together with judicious use of the resources of our own experience we can use to recognize the world of those remote periods and places as part of a fully shared heritage. Folktales, along with the better kinds of ethnography, are prime examples of the kind of evidence which we can use more creatively than has been done before. Collingwood's commentaries, as explained above, consist of four integrated chapters, two substantial but incomplete essays, and some fragments, all of which we have grouped as a reconstructed book, 'Tales of Enchantment', in Part II.

Collingwood opens his first chapter, initially entitled 'Fairy Tales "A"', with a discussion of the mixed historical sources of English culture. It is quite clear that he is enquiring into the folk arts not simply for their own sake, but because of their long continuity and their links with high civilization, a continuity now partly broken and under severe threat. He surveys the various kinds of evidence available to the historian for the era before written materials were produced. These have included the artefacts of the archaeologist, but an important and qualitatively different category includes 'fairy tales'—or what scholars of today would call 'oral literature' or folk narratives, of the kind first collected in Europe especially from the mid-nineteenth century and later from around the world. These tales have qualities in common; they are 'not necessarily about fairies', but they do have magical and ritual themes, they are about 'faëry . . . fays' work or enchantment'.[61] This may make them difficult to credit today, and so the general attitude of scholarship has been to displace them back into the supposedly more credulous past, especially that of the rural peasantry or of an imagined tribal ur-world. Collingwood emphasizes on the contrary the continuing life in these tales. They belonged to past 'forms of social life' to which they were organically connected, as much as were tools and implements, but have continually been transformed and recreated in a way that artefacts are not.[62] We can attempt to 'excavate' their history, and that of the people who produced and transmitted them; here Collingwood proposes a 'new kind of archaeology'.[63] This is to be more than simply placing stories in the context of the

---

[61] FTI, fo. 1.   [62] FTI, fo. 5.   [63] FTI, fo. 19.

past, for they are with us today, and while we can immediately see
the way they have nourished the work of playwrights and artists,
we do not easily see how they touch our lives in more unexpected
ways. We dismiss the 'magical' element in such tales, for example,
because of the pre-eminence we give our modern, rationalistic way
of thinking. He points out that 'the laws of the fairy-tale country,
in so far as they are based on what we call magic, are certainly very
different from the laws of natural science'.[64] But, the question
implicitly follows, how far do we really live in accordance with
such laws? Ethnologists have usually exaggerated the difference
between 'ourselves' and those peoples who live with magic in their
daily lives.

In the next chapter on 'Three Methods of Approach: Philological, Functional, Psychological', Collingwood develops his argument that the ethnological evidence, including folktales, used by
leading theorists from the mid-nineteenth century on, was being
misunderstood through lack of a proper historical sympathy with
the peoples concerned. Their customs were distanced from the
present by assumptions of a clear evolutionary divide between
the primitive and the civilized. He launches specific and very
detailed cases against the Grimm brothers and Max Müller,
founders of modern folklore collection on the one hand and its
use as a tool to look into the human psyche on the other. His
commentary speaks for itself; it reads strikingly like the account a
critic might produce today.[65] The next targets are the founders of
anthropological comparison in the field of religious belief and
human thought, Tylor and Frazer. Tylor had helped to put anthropology 'on the map' in the 1880s; it came to be known in
Oxford as 'Mr. Tylor's science'.[66] Collingwood was more comfortable perhaps with Tylor's empathic recreations of early human
experience, particularly his diagnosis of the intellectual sources of
animism, than with Frazer's grand generalizations about the stages
of human mental and civilizational evolution, though Frazer is the
one who made extensive use of folktales—or rather, what he distinguished and elevated particularly (having a background in the

[64] FT1, fo. 16.   [65] For more discussion and context, see MR 66–72.
[66] See Godfrey Lienhardt, 'Edward Tylor (1832–1917)', in Timothy Raison
(ed.), *The Founding Fathers of Social Science*, a series from *New Society* (Harmondsworth: Penguin, 1969), 84–91.

classics) as myth. Again, it would be difficult to fault Collingwood's critique by modern standards; and what he has to say is
remarkably close to commentaries which have been accepted
since.[67] With reference to these main founding figures of anthropology, Collingwood castigates what he terms the 'functional' or
naturalistic school of anthropology, which he dates to the period
1870–1910. I should make the point that he has adopted the term
'functional' here in what might look today an idiosyncratic way: it
was certainly current in the 1930s, but was in the process of being
reinvented, mainly by Malinowski, to mark a distinction between
the community-based field studies he advocated and the library-
based studies of Tylor, Frazer, and Marett. Collingwood was
however using the term in the sense he found explained in Penniman's overview, where it marked a break from the textual scholars
and the philologists on the one hand, and those on the other who
sought to place 'myths' in the context of ethnographic evidence
about local ritual practice, religious or magical beliefs, and indeed
everyday custom.

The final part of this chapter is directed with some energy at
Freud, especially his speculations in *Totem and Taboo* about early
social and family organization, and to a lesser extent at Jung. There
were indeed intense debates among anthropologists over the nature of the human family and of kinship patterns. This is a field of
study which social anthropology has made particularly its own,
and even today provokes passionate argument over questions of the
naturalness of the nuclear family or of male dominance, the rights
of women to have their own children, even through assisted
methods of reproduction, the disciplining of sexuality, or the inheritance of property. Serious anthropological studies in the early
twentieth century examined family structure and limits upon mar-
riageability between kin, essentially in order to speculate on original forms, and it is this literature which Collingwood dipped
into in order to mount his critique of Freud. But few anthropologists, let alone archaeologists or philosophers, have ever thought it
worth taking seriously Freud's tangled reconstructions of the origins of incest prohibitions and father figures, and certainly no one
to my knowledge has justified them. The reasons are plain in

[67] See e.g. E. E. Evans-Pritchard, *Theories of Primitive Religion* (Oxford: Clarendon Press, 1965), esp. ch. 2.

Collingwood's critique here. Freud otherwise had the respect and serious interest of Collingwood, but as the account here shows, his fancyings about the beginnings of family life and the regulation of sexuality are flimsy constructions and do not relate to real-world ethnography or plausible theory.[68]

In responding to such large-scale generalizations of one kind or another seeking to 'explain' strange customs and their origin, Collingwood begins to recommend his own alternative lines of interpretation: here we find lucid expression of many of the characteristic themes which run through his already well-known writings. For example, 'In anthropological science man is trying to understand man; and to man his fellow-man is never a mere external object, something to be observed and described, but something to be sympathized with, to be studied by penetrating into his thoughts and re-enacting those thoughts for oneself. Anthropology—I refer to cultural, not physical, anthropology—is an historical science.' He uses the example of mathematics; Greek or Egyptian geometry may be a crude and primitive thing, but if we are to study historically we must think again for ourselves the thoughts of those early geometers.

There is no difference of principle between this and any other case in which an attempt is made to study the early history of human ideas. The universal rule in every such case is to reconstruct for oneself and in oneself the ideas whose history one is trying to study. If one cannot do this, one may speak with the tongues of men and of angels, but the result is not anthropology.[69]

This effort required a reorientation of the anthropologist in relation to his materials, a kind of Copernican revolution.[70] It is to this end that Collingwood devoted his efforts in preparing his arguments, explicitly at book length, dealing nimbly and effectively with a large range of existing literature, and with the tangled technical terminology of debates over exogamy, endogamy, incest, totemism, taboo, and magic. To an average reader, questions in this area may not look like 'history', but of course Collingwood

---

[68] Bronislaw Malinowski came closest to a serious evaluation of Freud, though a very critical one, in his second ethnography of the Trobriand Islanders, *The Sexual Life of Savages in North-West Melanesia* (London: Kegan Paul, 1927) and his general critiques such as *Sex and Repression in Savage Society* (London: Kegan Paul, 1927).

[69] FT2, fo. 26.   [70] FT2, fo. 12.

is not limiting himself to the orthodox notion of what history might be.

Let us now turn to the third chapter of the book manuscript, 'The Historical Method', which might well surprise an orthodox historian (Evans-Pritchard's comment on his college tutor comes to mind), because indeed it seems to be more about anthropology than history, and merges into the topic of chapter 4, 'Magic'. Collingwood praises the much improved methods of the modern fieldworker, but implies that empirical reporting as such does not make for understanding such matters as belief in 'magic'. This can only be approached with the further engagement of the inner capacity of the scholar for feelings of recognition based upon their own experience. Despite the emotional aridity of modern, utility-obsessed life and scholarship, this capacity is present in everyone and should be allowed its place in the study of remote times and places. This is a very engagingly written chapter, evoking the fragility of what we may take to be European civilization in its best sense, the 'waste-land' of its modern collapse (a purposeful reference to T. S. Eliot's co-option of Frazer[71]) and a highly personal appeal to the reader's own sense of a feeling self. This sense is what Collingwood invokes in his discourse on 'our' experiences of the everyday rituals of dress or cleanliness; of the satisfaction of using powerful machines like vacuum cleaners, or even controlling other people; of the joy of shaping and giving life to fine instruments like sailing boats; of creating art, and being linked intimately with the works of art we have created. Our sense of personality extends into the world, to things we or others have made or done, and on many occasions—very obviously the condensed ceremonial times of bereavement, for example—we treat 'things' almost as extensions of people. Common reports of 'magical' action being taken against people through their nail-clippings is not necessarily different from the decision to scuttle King George V's yacht on his death, rather than put it on the market. Modern utilitarianism, which Collingwood condemns as permeating the anthropology of his time, cannot give an account of such feelings, nor their pervasive presence in the world.

[71] See R. Angus Downie, *Frazer and 'The Golden Bough'* (London: Gollancz, 1970), with references to Eliot at 21, 60–1; and Brian V. Street, *The Savage in Literature: Representations of 'Primitive' Society in English Fiction 1858–1920* (London: Routledge & Kegan Paul, 1975), 177–9.

Chapter 4 includes significant reference to art. It is in this section of the manuscript that Collingwood formulated some of the ideas and arguments later to be published in *The Principles of Art*. There he makes explicit reference to the Azande, and in the chapter 'Art as Magic' writes that he is trying to rescue the word 'magic' from its degradation by earlier anthropologists of 'two generations ago', who sought the explanation of magical acts in the terms of a prevailing positivistic philosophy, labelling them as false science, and thus bringing into contempt civilizations different from our own.[72] Collingwood's argument in chapter 4 below is a more sustained and elaborate discussion than in its later published form. Here he explains and more fully illustrates his point that we must understand 'the nature of magic' not by defining the term, which is merely a convenient label, the investigation of which would only tell us about 'the minds of anthropologists'. What we should rather do is to understand the beliefs and customs to which the label has been applied, and this requires becoming aware of the emotional side of our own experiences. His eloquent evocations of why people in 1930s North Oxford wear certain kinds of clothes, keep themselves clean, and so on is very readable and speaks for itself; it also addresses questions which have since surfaced explicitly in academic anthropology concerning the social organization of practices concerning purity and propriety.[73] He may have overdone his claims for magic *tout court*. Perhaps by recognizing the 'glorious' feeling of sailing a fine boat before the wind, or even gaining power over other people—with or without the aid of machinery—we are not necessarily able to make all manner of 'magic' phenomena, such as the contents of fairy tales, more intelligible. Nevertheless, Collingwood convincingly evokes felt power in a way we can grasp, and through sport, ritual, art, and poetry indeed we celebrate. Magical action in this sense is a part of the way we engage with the world and with others; as a kind of 'felt power', magical acts including song and art do accompany social projects like going to war, and we can empathize with that in ourselves.

Collingwood's championing of the 'magical' element in life will read to some in a slightly whimsical way today, when even the

---

[72] *PA* 57–61.

[73] See e.g. Mary Douglas, *Purity and Danger: An Analysis of Concepts of Pollution and Taboo* (London: Routledge & Regan Paul, 1966).

buttoned-up English are wearing their emotions on their coat-sleeves. By suggesting that there is 'magic' in our lives too, Colling-wood was of course intending to shock his 1930s readers a little. The idea of 'magic' has a kind of quirky appeal in popular culture today (as in the magic of scary films, fashion, or football stars). But as a serious category *of everyday life* it looks a little uncertain, perhaps still too odd a combination of the weird occult and the antiquarian. Of course one of the main reasons why it carries this implication is that many scholars in the past have castigated it as a phenomenon counter to religion and enlightened civilization. The main scholarly approach to magic in the West has been the story of its marginaliza-tion by the growth of the Church.[74] From the mid-nineteenth cen-tury on, there has been a series of attempts by humanists and anthropologists to place it within the broad evolutionary frame of one theory or another of the growth of reason. 'Magic' in scholarly interpretations, if not even in social life itself, has thus often been cast in opposition to orthodoxy and authority. Marcel Mauss and Henri Hubert characterized it in a classic essay of 1904 as essentially subversive ritual practice, as something pursued by individuals against the dominant collective interests of society.[75]

Arguments about 'magic' became highly technical among an-thropologists of the early twentieth century. Evans-Pritchard led the way in formulating a critique of theories about the evolution of the mind from a state closer to nature when 'magical' ideas for one reason or another were only to be expected. He prepared a series of lectures while teaching in the University of Cairo in 1932–3, on existing anthropological theories of religion, magic, and 'primitive mentality'.[76] The first of these contained criticisms of Tylor and

---

[74] See e.g. Keith Thomas, *Religion and the Decline of Magic* (Harmondsworth: Penguin, 1972).

[75] Marcel Mauss, with Henri Hubert, *A General Theory of Magic* (1904), R. Brain (London: Cohen & West, 1972). Republished in Routledge Classics, 2001.

[76] See E. E. Evans-Pritchard, 'The Intellectualist (English) Interpretation of Magic', *Bulletin of the Faculty of Arts*, University of Cairo, 1/2 (1933), 1–21; 'Lévy-Bruhl's Theory of Primitive Mentality', *Bulletin of the Faculty of Arts*, University of Cairo, 2/2 (1934), 1–26, reprinted in the *Journal of the Anthropo-logical Society of Oxford*, 1 (1970), 39–60; 'Science and Sentiment: An Exposition and Criticism of the Writings of Pareto', *Bulletin of the Faculty of Arts*, University of Cairo, 3/2 (1936), 163–92. See also, for edited excerpts from the above, E. E. Evans-Pritchard, *A History of Anthropological Thought*, ed. A. Singer (London: Faber & Faber, 1981), chs. 10–13.

Frazer while deploying some of his own Zande field data in his arguments for the intelligibility of 'witchcraft' beliefs, the general human capacity for clever argument, and the historically enduring character of basic cultural axioms. This first paper, and the second which dealt in a subtle and appreciative way, if a critical one, with Lévy-Bruhl's theory of primitive mentality, were written while he was already drafting his first major book, *Witchcraft, Oracles, and Magic among the Azande*, and it is clear from some of his later commentaries that the book was designed in part as an answer, from the field, to the theories of the latter.[77] Evans-Pritchard had come back to Oxford to join Marett, as a Research Lecturer in African Sociology, in 1935, and Marett is the person who wrote a letter to the Oxford University Press recommending the publication of his book.[78] Marett would surely have been given a copy of Evans-Pritchard's Cairo lectures, and while it is tempting to suppose that Evans-Pritchard might even have sent a copy to Collingwood (whose *Roman Britain* he had just reviewed, as I have mentioned above), we do not have direct evidence of this. Nevertheless, the parallels between the content of the first three Cairo lectures, and Collingwood's chapter on 'Magic', are striking. There are also significant differences of emphasis.

Evans-Pritchard, in a sense, found himself arguing on his opponents' grounds when he shaped his Cairo lectures and his book on Azande beliefs into a justification of their intellectual rationality, even about the supposed mumbo-jumbo of witchcraft and magic. Intent on undermining the stereotype of the primitive as lacking reason and always swayed by emotion, he perhaps avoided giving the affective aspects of witchcraft and magic, or even of the motivations of jealousy, vengeance, and punishment, their due. He based his argument on very specific definitions of his key terms, keeping close to the way that the Zande language differentiates, for example, between involuntary 'witchcraft', deliberate 'sorcery', and the 'magic' of spells and medicines used to counteract these. Collingwood, similarly motivated in defence of the intelligibility of 'primitive' thought, used the English 'magic' in a much more

[77] Evans-Pritchard, *Witchcraft, Oracles, and Magic*. Cf. his *Theories of Primitive Religion*.

[78] R. R. Marett, letter of 11 Feb. 1935. Oxford University Press Archives, LB 7652.

diffuse and general way, drawing on some of its older layers of use in European history and literature. Unlike many terms now obsolete (especially the anthropological jargon of 'totemism', 'taboo', etc.), this particular term is very much alive; it has had a long and complex history, and there are residues of meaning which Collingwood persuasively evokes. This was part of his broader effort to give more space to emotional experience and the felt power of human agency in an account of social life and history, and there is no reason why we should not respond to his appeal. He has certainly made a strong case for restoring a language which recognizes those 'irrational' feelings, indeed those elements of passion, especially the arts of managing other people, which enliven so much of our everyday behaviour.

The text we have included as chapter 5 is a draft analysis of the Cinderella story-cycle. It is a less finished piece, and was not integrated as it stood into the manuscript of Collingwood's book on folktale and magic, but was clearly intended as a case study to illustrate, even to test, his insights and his methods.[79] 'Cinderella' is a complicated essay, though engaging and readable if one pursues the main line of argument and mentally brackets off, at least for a first reading, those passages which offer the detailed justifications. The piece is a concentrated study based on a book produced by Miss Marian Cox in 1893, which analysed 345 variants of the tale. These stories are found all over Europe and in many parts of Asia including Japan, and a few are found in Africa and the New World (though these may represent relatively recent transmission). Collingwood explains how Miss Cox arranged the stories in three main classes:

1. *Cinderella 'proper'*: a girl is ill-treated by her stepmother, receives magical help, usually from an animal, so she can go to a gathering where a young man falls in love, follows her, picks up a shoe by which he recognizes and marries her.

2. *Catskin*: the heroine leaves home in order to escape her father, who has fallen in love with her. She becomes a servant in a great house, attends a gathering, but is recognized [though

---

[79] There are also several manuscript pages of tables analysing the elements of the story from different versions, which we have not selected for publication here. See 'English Folklore III', Bodleian Library Collingwood Papers, dep. 21/3.

sometimes disguised in a catskin] by the food she cooks for her lover.

3. *Cap o'Rushes [or King Lear]*. This resembles *Catskin* except in the opening: here, the girl is driven from home by her father, angry because she does not express her love for him warmly enough; she often says in these stories that she loves him like salt. She later marries, and makes a saltless meal to convince her father of the value of salt.

Apart from Maureen Rudzik's contribution emphasizing its innovatory character,[80] Collingwood's essay on Cinderella has scarcely been discussed by scholars and is, I believe, virtually unknown among folklorists of the present day. It is not referred to, for example, in Dundes's compilation of old and new essays on the Cinderella story.[81] However, it has some distinctive aspects. The early twentieth-century folklorists tended to seek out primary source areas, and original, authentic versions of tales. Collingwood follows the 'historical' method he has advocated, in treating all variants in a cycle as viable, and as representing the continuing creativity of 'tradition'. He pursues an 'excavation' of the modern Cinderella, revealing possible connections and patterns of change in the way elements of the story and its cognates have been combined and recombined since the medieval period. He draws attention particularly to the way in which European variants recombined elements which probably came from Asia in the first place and were then shaped by medieval European traditions, on the one hand of romantic love culminating in marriage (giving our Cinderella); and, on the other, of Christian motifs of threatened virgins and violence done to chastity—medieval story-tellers 'piling on the agony' to yield, for example, the story of a father's injustice in *King Lear*. The modern paradoxes of social morality are reconstructed from the materials of an older juxtaposition of marvellous elements. We should note today that interested uses (or misuses) of the Cinderella story are very much with us; it was recently selected, for example, by neo-Darwinian sociologists as evidence that humankind, along with the other creatures, favour fully genetic kin over non-kin (our popularly known Cinderella is a

---

[80] MR 107, 114–24.
[81] Alan Dundes, *Cindrella: A Casebook* (Madison: University of Wisconsin Press, 1982).

step-daughter, and that is why she was treated badly). Collingwood, we need you still![82]

The discussion moves on to the role of wild animals, and the
interaction of human and animal, in many variants of the Cinderella cycle. Collingwood suggests in a tentative way that there is no
reason why we may not assume some kind of continuity with the
Bronze Age, and even the cave art of the Upper Paleolithic. He is
undeniably here on more questionable ground, invoking 'totemism' as a supposed early form, even though this kind of method is
what he has criticized in the folktale study itself. Nevertheless, it is
true that there is today a growing sensitivity to the natural world,
and to philosophical ideas about human/animal interaction, which
have been dubbed a new kind of totemism, and such recognition is
arguably part of the thrust of Collingwood's argument.[83]

Leaving this speculation aside, the comparison of myths across
the Indo-European region has remained an important area of study
within anthropology.[84] Collingwood's work could also now be seen
to foreshadow aspects of Lévi-Strauss's structural analysis of myth
(mainly for the native peoples of the Americas, but also for the
Oedipus story from classical Greece up to the time of Freud), a
method designed to reveal basic principles of the formal relationship between motifs in a mass of narratives. What are generally
seen as the most effective of Lévi-Strauss's applications of the
method also reveal their connection with social form.[85] More
recent work in this vein has tended to concentrate, as Collingwood
himself did, less on abstract pattern than on the historicity of
specific variations and transformations in the way that oral literature and myth are recreated in the course of their transmission.

---

[82] Martin Daly and Margo Wilson, *The Truth about Cinderella: A Darwinian View of Parental Love* (London: Weidenfeld & Nicolson, 1998). This attractively presented little book is one of a series 'Darwinism Today', ed. Helena Cronin and Oliver Curry. For critical comment, see James, *Ceremonial Animal*, 24–5.

[83] See e.g. R. G. Willis, *Signifying Animals: Human Meaning in the Natural World* (London: Allen & Unwin, 1990), esp. pp. xx–xxv, 5–7.

[84] See e.g. some of the recent essays by N. J. Allen, in *Categories and Classifications: Maussian Reflections on the Social* (Oxford and New York: Berghahn, 2000).

[85] Claude Lévi-Strauss, 'The Structural Study of Myth', in *Structural Anthropology*, i (1958; London: Allen Lane, 1963); *The Raw and the Cooked: Introduction to a Science of Mythology*, i (1964), tr. J. and D. Weightman (London; Jonathan Cape, 1970) and further volumes in this series; 'The Story of Asdiwal' in *Structural Anthropology*, ii (1973; London: Allen Lane, 1977), esp. 152–8.

The related manuscripts of Collingwood include a few further pieces, discussed in the first part of this Introduction, of which the most substantial and polished is entitled 'The Authorship of Fairy Tales', included here as chapter 6 and together with some shorter pieces concludes our reconstruction of what his book might have been.

The exercise on Cinderella was not fully brought into line with Collingwood's major arguments about the 'magical' side of life today. But it had clearly been a serious exercise. Whether or not one is comfortable today with the details of this attempt to rescue the enchanted side of our experience, his arguments are likely to appeal to today's readers, familiar as they are with ideas stemming from phenomenology and less confident over their own rationality than were Collingwood's contemporaries. To separate out the utilitarian from the felt, the poetic, and the enchanted in the way we live our lives does not aid our self-understanding. Today, we could say that Collingwood's mode of approaching the classic topic of magic in anthropology is somewhat prophetic; it strikes a chord with us more effectively perhaps than does the dogged rationalism of Evans-Pritchard's Azande. Of course Evans-Pritchard had his reasons for writing the book the way he did, and there is much there besides his passionate advocacy of Zande intellect. Evans-Pritchard presumably remained quite in the dark as to Collingwood's efforts in anthropology, which were forgotten about until quite recently. I believe that, had the material been published, Evans-Pritchard would have recognized a kinship tie even stronger than that he had clearly become aware of as early as 1932. He himself, with younger colleagues, launched a series of volumes in the 1960s on the oral literature of Africa, his own contribution being specifically on the Zande 'trickster' or magician in folktales.[86] Conversely, Collingwood's own later publications came to emphasize the role of 'logic' and reason in the way that both regular conversation and research enquiries were conducted: that is, the well-known logic of 'question and answer'.[87] It is regarded as likely by several commentators that Collingwood drew on Evans-Pritchard's first and famous Zande book in the very precise formulation he

[86] E. E. Evans-Pritchard, *The Zande Trickster*, Oxford Library of African Literature (Oxford: Clarendon Press, 1967).
[87] *A, EPM*.

came to give to this procedural logic: for this is explicitly how the
Azande test the validity of their oracles, and thus come to know the
truth about witchcraft.[88]

Collingwood and Today's Anthropology: A Note

The most obvious relevance of Collingwood's work to anthropology today, in general and in the present volume in particular, is
that anthropology itself, like its younger sibling cultural studies,
has generally turned to history, and is even taught in several
universities today alongside Collingwood's specific practical discipline of archaeology. But there are further points to make. The
varieties of the 'natural science' approach in anthropology are still
with us: especially the new biological sciences which advocate the
genetic conditioning of behaviour, and 'rational choice' theories in
philosophy, politics, economics, and sociology which give primal
importance to utility and the individual drive to maximize wealth
or power. These have to be accepted in their totality, or countered,
as Collingwood attempted to counter their earlier forms. We can
learn a good deal from his example. We are sensitive in new ways
today to the powers of language, metaphor, image, and poetic or
religious forms in social life, as well as to those of non-verbal
language, music, dance, and performance. We are rehabilitating
ideas of magic, ritual, art, and the generally ceremonial character of
language and action, including political action, even within the
broad framework of what still views itself as 'utilitarian' civilization. We also try to read works of philosophy and write papers and
books about language and emotion, or the pluralities and ambigu-
ities of personal identity. A few pioneers are trying to bring back
into fashion notions of animism and magic in the way we relate to
the world of art and artefacts.[89] In respect of these current trends,
Collingwood's folktale study and related manuscripts are directly
illuminating. Finally, we should note that mass media, the technology of entertainment, public behaviour, global communications,

---

[88] Evans-Pritchard, *Witchcraft, Oracles, and Magic*, chs. 8 and 9. Cf. James,
'Tales of Enchantment', 138–9; James Connelly, 'Natural Science, History and
Christianity: The Origins of Collingwood's Later Metaphysics', *Collingwood Stud-
ies*, 4 (1998), *Variations: Themes from the Manuscripts*, 101–32; see esp. 124–8.

[89] e.g. Alfred Gell, *Art and Agency: An Anthropological Theory* (Oxford: Clarendon Press, 1998).

and so on have also become objects of anthropological scrutiny. Despite Collingwood's proclamations, it is possible to argue, as many modern anthropologists do, that beyond the negative side of mechanical production, communication, and entertainment, cultural transformations of factory-made forms are surprisingly vital, and that art may yet survive the machine.[90] Current studies of violence and of war are less sanguine. Collingwood's last work *The New Leviathan*, first published in 1942 shortly before his death, seems to foreshadow some current anxieties in today's anthropological thought and practice, in particular over human vulnerability to power and violence, and the problematic place of the scholar, especially the fieldworking scholar, in the face of gathering clouds of war. This book has been little referred to by comparison with the rest of his publications, but it is possible that here too, Collingwood has a great deal to offer, of a rather different kind from his earlier work which is now becoming well known. There has been a rash of Collingwood references in anthropology books and journals, easily visible in a sort of spreading epidemic of footnotes— particularly striking among those trained in the Evans-Pritchard tradition.[91]

Talal Asad is one of those anthropologists who has specifically drawn attention to the significance, for this discipline, of Collingwood's discussions of the connectedness of thought and emotion, and the relevance of this connection for analysing religion. In a critical essay Asad refers his readers to *The Principles of Art* for 'a discussion of the integral connection between thought and emotion, where it is argued that there is no such thing as a universal emotional function . . . . If this view is valid, then the notion of a generalized religious emotion (or mood) may be questioned'.[92] He interestingly castigates Evans-Pritchard for not having made even more of Collingwood than he did, specifically on the mutual implication of private emotion and public ritual. Evans-Pritchard had tended to draw a clear line between social institutions and private

---

[90] See e.g. the varied collection in Marcus Banks and Howard Morphy (eds.), *Rethinking Visual Anthropology* (New Haven and London: Yale University Press, 1997).

[91] I hope to document this elsewhere.

[92] Talal Asad, *Genealogies of Religion: Disciplines and Reasons of Power in Christianity and Islam* (Baltimore and London: Johns Hopkins University Press, 1993), 31 n. 5.

emotional states; by contrast with Collingwood's argument that
when sensations are captured in thought (that is, language) they
cease to be fleeting and private. 'Collingwood's writings were
admired and occasionally cited by Evans-Pritchard, so it is surprising to find that neither he nor his followers at Oxford ever
engaged Collingwood's views on emotions and thought.'[93] In relation to the connections between meanings and feelings in the
discipline of religious traditions, Asad further discusses Collingwood's views on the link with the nature of language itself: in its
widest sense, language for him was simply 'bodily expression of
emotion, dominated by thought in its [logically] primitive form as
consciousness. Verbal language was not the only, nor yet the "most
developed" kind of language; there were several (aural, visual,
gestural—and within each, again different kinds)' and Asad concludes: 'According to Collingwood, there can be feelings (sensations) without language, but no language without feelings
(emotions). . . . He argued in effect that the existence of specific
vocabularies of emotion was a precondition for the existence of
specific emotions, and that emotions could be learnt and cultivated
through discourse.'[94]

'Discourse', like 'archaeology' itself, is a term which has, of
course, acquired more layers of meaning since the works of Foucault than it had in the 1930s. But modern uses have something of
a Collingwoodian echo. Mark Hobart refers regularly to Collingwood's books in his work. He has criticized 'loony relativists'[95] and
comments, using Collingwood, 'Not only can cultures or discourses incorporate new information about the world, but previous
knowledge is continually being reworked in the light of experience.
So knowledge is partly both archaeological and contextual. The
resultant dialectic has been called a "Scale of Forms" '. He points
out that discourses overlap, as in the world of modern Bali in the
face of tourism. 'As we come to know more about the Balinese, we
are also learning more about ourselves, or understand ourselves in

[93] Asad, *Genealogies of Religion*, 74 n. 19.
[94] Ibid. 130–1 n. 6.
[95] Mark Hobart, 'Summer Days and Salad Days: The Coming of Age of Anthropology', in Ladislav Holy (ed.), *Comparative Anthropology* (Oxford: Blackwell,
1987), 43.

different ways. The Balinese, of course, are doing something similar from a different starting point. The process is a kind of mutual,
if incommensurable, critical ethnography of people in one culture
on people in another.'[96]
    This surely echoes what Collingwood himself would have said
about Bali, one of the few places he did visit outside Europe, on his
voyage of 1939. In a late essay in which he explicitly applies the
'scale' idea to the history of civilization he observes: 'An American
lady whom I met in Bali, on first seeing the mud walled and grass
villages of that country, asked me "How long do you think it would
take to civilize these people?" but a few hours later when she had
heard a Balinese orchestra and seen Balinese dancing, was sorry
she had spoken.'[97] Collingwood's own version of the overlapping
of 'discourses' had been worked out for the history of art in Roman
Britain, and in particular the recovery of Celtic art after the period
of Roman imperial rule. This period of history in Britain, what
came after and what might have come before, was the stimulus to
much of his thought about the past. The philosophy which he
developed, and which is so closely related to his concept of 'the
historical method', is presented in the following section by David
Boucher. It is a philosophy which embraces anthropology as properly integral to history, and the way Collingwood approached the
study of folktales is a lucid and still relevant demonstration of his
vision.

---

[96] Ibid. 44.
[97] R. G. Collingwood, 'What "Civilization" Means', published for the first time
as appendix 2 to the revised edn. of *The New Leviathan: or Man, Society, Civilization and Barbarism*, ed. David Boucher (Oxford: Clarendon Press, 1992), 480–511.

3. IN DEFENCE OF COLLINGWOOD: PERSPECTIVES FROM PHILOSOPHY AND THE HISTORY OF IDEAS

DAVID BOUCHER

The publication for the first time of Collingwood's folktale manuscript and related material provides the opportunity to review his philosophy of history in the light of current claims to be beneficiaries of his anti-positivist legacy, and to defend his position against theorists who reject his ideas on behalf of what has been called the return, or revenge, of literature. In Collingwood's view anthropology, like archaeology and history in general, is capable of facilitating greater historical understanding by using as evidence folktales expressive of a society's cultural practices, including myths and magic, developed and modified over time. Collingwood's conclusions are not merely of antiquarian interest because the problems he identified and to which he gave answers still persist in modern debates on historical interpretation. As an archaeologist, and the world's principal authority on the Roman inscriptions in Britain, Collingwood concluded that evidence for the cultural practices, history, and thought of a people extended far beyond traditional and largely written sources. Traces of everyday life, such as terracotta tiles, jewellery, and industrial and commercial artefacts were used by the archaeologists of the nineteenth century as evidence of the activities of societies that left no, or very few, written records.[1] Archaeological study had led to a vast enlargement in historical knowledge. A further enlargement could be effected, he thought, by the development of a new kind of archaeology which takes myths, customs, and fairy tales, handed down in traditional stories, as fragments of the historical life of societies. He maintained, for example, that: 'A theme contained in such a story is a fragment of ancient custom or belief, very much as a stone implement is a fragment of ancient technical skill. In each case the historian uses the fragment by reconstructing in his mind the life and thought of the people who have left him this sample

---

[1] Besides his many other archaeological studies e.g. he began a full-length study of Roman brooches, beautifully illustrated, but never finished. See the W. P. Wright papers, Ashmolean Library, Oxford. There is a brief discussion of brooches in the metalwork section of *Roman Britain* (Oxford: Oxford University Press, 1932), 104–8, and a chapter in *The Archaeology of Roman Britain* (London: Methuen, 1930).

of their work.'[2] In other words, Collingwood was suggesting that the oral tradition of folktale constituted valuable evidence for the expansion of historical knowledge and that changes over time were equivalent to different archaeological strata. The fairy tale story must be excavated, carefully removing modern debris, in order to uncover the earliest stratum.

The principal features of Collingwood's precepts for the study of history, namely the necessity of identifying the questions to which authors addressed themselves, and the need to recover the intentions of those authors constitute the distinctive features of a particular manner of studying the history of ideas in the Anglophone world, particularly in the United Kingdom, North America, and Australasia. The most prominent member of this school of historians calls it the 'Collingwoodian approach'.[3] I want first to identify the characteristics of this approach from the point of view of those who claim to be following Collingwood's lead. I want then to look at the contemporary reaction to this approach, what has been called 'The Return of Literature' or 'The Revenge of Literature',[4] and examine the claims that it cannot deliver on the promise of recovering authorial intentions. Does this literary turn really undermine a Collingwoodian approach, and is Collingwood really a Collingwoodian? I want to suggest that on both sides of the fence

[2] FT1, fo. 17.

[3] Quentin Skinner, 'The Rise of, Challenge to and Prospects for a Collingwoodian Approach to the History of Political Thought', in Dario Castiglione and Iain Hampsher-Monk (eds.), *The History of Political Thought in National Context* (Cambridge: Cambridge University Press, 2001), 175–88. Skinner has latterly come to call the approach to the history of ideas advocated by the 'Cambridge School' Collingwoodian. Among such followers are Peter Laslett, Stefan Collini, John Dunn, J. G. A. Pocock, James Tully, Richard Tuck, and Geoffrey Hawthorn. For an assessment of the extent to which they follow a common line see my 'New Histories of Political Thought for Old', *Political Studies*, 31 (1983), 112–21. Also see David A. Hollinger, 'The Return of the Prodigal: The Persistence of Historical Knowing', *American Historical Review*, 94 (1989), 612, who stresses the importance of the 'Collingwoodian' principle of determining the questions an argument was meant to answer.

[4] For the attack on intellectual history see David Harlan, 'Intellectual History and the Return of History', *American Historical Review*, 94 (1989), 581–609; and Linda Orr, 'The Revenge of Literature: A History of History', in Ralph Cohen (ed.), *Studies in Historical Change*, (Charlottesville, Va., and London: University of Virginia Press, 1992), 84–108.

only a literal interpretation of some of Collingwood's statements, which were all too often overstatements subject to severe qualification, stands him squarely against the literary turn and firmly in the 'Collingwoodian' camp. In essence I want to defend Collingwood against both his friends and critics. Both camps reject what Collingwood regarded as the most crucial aspect of his philosophy of history, namely, the belief that historical knowledge is unattainable without re-enacting the thoughts of those we seek to understand. It is, however, absolutely crucial for Collingwood in overcoming the general Idealist problem of a dichotomy between the mind and its objects.

I want further to argue that the so-called 'Collingwoodian' approach needs itself to be contextualized in the broader concerns of Collingwood's philosophy. I would go as far as to say that the contextualists have failed to contextualize the elements of Collingwood's thought that they found conducive. I go on to argue that the methodological precepts to be gleaned from *An Essay on Philosophical Method* and *An Essay on Metaphysics* need to supplement those that are said to constitute a Collingwoodian approach to history. In conclusion I will show how this broader context is brought to bear on the argument to be found in his writings on folktales and anthropology.

Commandeering Collingwood: The Elements of a Collingwoodian Approach

The so-called 'historical revolution' in the history of political thought, and the history of ideas is self-confessedly 'Collingwoodian'.[5] Referring to himself, J. G. A. Pocock, and John Dunn, Quentin Skinner maintains that: 'all three of us have in turn acknowledged the influence which R. G. Collingwood has exercised over our methodological studies'.[6] What are the features of this Collingwoodian approach? First, Collingwood is credited with emphasizing the importance of discerning the question to which a

---

[5] Robert Wokler called it a historical revolution in 'The Professoriate of Political Thought in England since 1914: A Tale of Three Chairs', in Castiglione and Hampsher-Monk (eds.), *History of Political Thought*, 155.

[6] Quentin Skinner, 'Some Problems in the Analysis of Political Thought and Action', in James Tully (ed.), *Meaning and Context: Quentin Skinner and his Critics* (Cambridge: Polity Press, 1988), 103. See also 'A Reply to My Critics', ibid. 234.

text is meant to be an answer.[7] In other words, we have to aim to retrieve the precise questions that particular philosophical texts address.[8] Second, the contextual nature of understanding is emphasized by the argument that there are no perennial problems in history, only individual answers to individual questions.[9] Collingwood argues, for example, that when Plato and Hobbes talked about the state they were asking themselves very different questions. We cannot assume that they were giving answers to the same question because ancient Athens was a very different social and political setting from seventeenth-century England. Third, history is not about discovering covering laws.[10] Collingwood was one of the leading anti-positivist philosophers in England.[11] He argued that historical facts were themselves an achievement established on historical principles and that nothing more could be learnt about them by demonstrating that similar things happened elsewhere. Fourth, Collingwood like Dilthey, and for that matter Gentile, saw utterances, including complex philosophical arguments, as aspects of the history of action.[12] In other words, like Austin after him, Collingwood was well aware that in using words people are performing complex social actions. Fifth, Collingwood is seen as a representative of the *verstehen* school in England, with his emphasis upon understanding rather than explanation.[13] Sixth, Skinner is said to offer ingenious support to Collingwood's dictum that all history is the history of ideas.[14] What Collingwood means by this dictum is that all human artefacts, from Stone Age arrow-heads, or triangular terracotta loom weights to complex

[7] Quentin Skinner, 'Meaning and Understanding in the History of Ideas' and 'Interpretation and the Understanding of Speech Acts', in *Visions of Politics*, i. *Regarding Method* (Cambridge: Cambridge University Press, 2002), 83 and 103–4 respectively.

[8] Skinner, 'Collingwoodian Approach', 177.

[9] Skinner, 'Meaning and Understanding', 88.

[10] Quentin Skinner, ' "Social Meaning" and the Explanation of Social Action' in Skinner, *Regarding Method*, 130.

[11] Skinner, 'Some Problems in the Analysis of Political Thought and Action', in Tully (ed.), *Meaning and Context*, 103.

[12] Richard Tuck, 'History', in Robert E. Goodin and Philip Pettit (eds.), *A Companion to Contemporary Political Philosophy* (Oxford: Blackwell, 1993), 82.

[13] James Tully, 'The Pen is a Mighty Sword', in Tully (ed.), *Meaning and Context*, 8.

[14] Martin Hollis, 'Say it with Flowers', in Tully (ed.), *Meaning and Context*, 139.

philosophical texts, are expressive of thought, and embody purposive activity.

The Revenge of Literature

What has been called 'The Revenge of Literature' is a direct attack
on the 'Collingwoodian' approach to the history of ideas. David
Harlan claims that intellectual historians, by which he largely
means contextualist historians influenced by Collingwood, of the
Skinner, Pocock, and Dunn type, in recent times have somewhat
credulously come to believe that they have exorcised the ghost of
literature and placed history on a firm foundation of objective
method and rational argument.[15] Linda Orr suggests that modern
history in detaching itself from literature has tried to emulate the
social sciences, especially the more quantitative aspects.[16] Keith
Jenkins contends that adequate answers to the question 'What is
History?' are no longer to be found in the standard texts of G. R.
Elton and E. H. Carr. They are at once old-fashioned and modernist in a postmodernist and postmodern age in which the text is
the thing and where the possible meanings are endless.[17] Hermeneutic and postmodern theorists tell us that texts dislodge themselves from their authors and from their contexts, a process that
Gadamer and Ricoeur call 'distanciation'. The signifier has escaped the signified, freeing the signs that purportedly unified
them, namely the words, to undergo meaning transformations
independent of authorial intention. Authorial meaning is elusive
and never determinate. It is in the nature of interpretation that
each time it takes place it is a reinterpretation, a different configuration of meaning, and perhaps even an instance of authorship
itself. The deconstructionists, such as Derrida, Foucault, and Paul
de Man further undermined contextualism by announcing the
death of the author, the vanishing text, the disappearing knowing
subject, the illusion of the historical agent, the absence of the
author, and finally the dissolution of the interconnected network

---

[15] Harlan, 'Intellectual History', 581. See also Hollinger, 'Return of the Prodigal'.

[16] Orr, 'Revenge of Literature', 84.

[17] Keith Jenkins, *On What is History?* (London: Routledge, 1995), esp. 1–42.

of intellectual discourse.[18] The past itself is constituted rather than recovered, evidentially imagined rather than discovered, and cannot, because it no longer exists, act as a criterion against which to measure different interpretations.[19]

Given that locating the text in its historical context in order to expose its primary intentions is an impossibility according to such thinkers as Gadamer, Ricoeur, Derrida, Foucault, Paul de Man, and Rorty, Harlan recommends that we should do the sort of thing that Chomsky did in his *Cartesian Linguistics* or that Walzer did in *Exodus and Revolution*. Both abjured the search for contextual authorial intentions, and instead abstracted those aspects of the text relevant to their present and pressing interests.[20] In other words, contemporary relevance is the criterion of selection and meaning. We are asked to embrace once again a form of Whig history about which Herbert Butterfield so vehemently complained, and about which Michael Oakeshott remarked that it was like looking at the past through the wrong end of the telescope. The suggestion of Harlan is in effect a plea to return to the good old days prior to the methodological turn of the 'Cambridge School' and prior to 'The Return of Literature'. Both positions have in fact cancelled themselves out. Elsewhere he puts his recommendation succinctly: 'I wanted to point out that, by discrediting contextualism, recent developments in literary criticism and the philosophy of language make it possible for intellectual historians to return to an *earlier* understanding of their discipline: intellectual history as a conversation with the dead about things we value'.[21] In order to appreciate Chomsky's and Walzer's practically oriented history there seems little reason to pass through the scenic route of poststructuralism and deconstructionism.[22] We are left, in practical terms, with the Machiavellian view of history and

---

[18] Cf. Joyce Appleby, 'One Good Turn Deserves Another: Moving beyond the Linguistic: A Response to David Harlan', *American Historical Review*, 94 (1989), 1327.

[19] See e.g. Jenkins, *On What is History?*, 10.

[20] Noam Chomsky, *Cartesian Linguistics* (New York and London: Harper Row, 1966) and Michael Walzer, *Exodus and Revolution* (New York: HarperCollins, 1985).

[21] David Harlan, 'Reply to David Hollinger', *American Historical Review*, 94 (1989), 625.

[22] Cf. Hollinger, 'Return of the Prodigal', 618.

we should all don our togas and converse with the ancients in order to learn, or indeed fabricate (after the example of *The Florentine History*) some useful lessons about statecraft. In theoretical terms we are left with something like the Crocean position, without it being attributed, and without it being so eloquently articulated. Croce famously told us that all history is contemporary history. He meant by this that history without passion, without the resonance of contemporary concerns animating one's interest in the past, history becomes mere chronicle.[23]

Harlan tells us that there are two lessons to be learnt from the return of literature. First, contextualists should stop berating their colleagues for presentism. John Keane argues that history invites us to apply the Baconian principle of putting evidence on the rack, forcing it to reveal answers to *our* questions. Orr, in fact, approvingly invokes Collingwood in her endorsement of this point. She claims that Collingwood 'describes the historical method as "torture". The inquisitor gets the answer he wants and the witch forever escapes as she is burned. The historian kills the past he claims to resurrect; he is the detective of the crime he himself commits.'[24] Harlan uses Rorty's comparison of historians with anthropologists to consolidate his case against the contextualists. Rorty contends that:

The anthropologist is not doing his job if he merely offers to teach us how to bicker with his favourite tribe, how to be initiated into their rituals, etc. What we want to be told is whether that tribe has anything interesting to tell us—interesting to *our* lights, answering to *our* concerns, informative about what we *know* to exist. Any anthropologist who rejected this assignment on the grounds that filtering and paraphrase would distort and betray the integrity of the tribe's culture would no longer be an anthropologist, but a sort of cultist. He is, after all, working for *us*, not for *them*. Similarly, the historian of X, where X is something we know to be real and important, is working for those of us who share that knowledge, not for our unfortunate ancestors who did not.[25]

---

[23] Benedetto Croce, *Theory and History of Historiography*, tr. Douglas Ainslie (London: Harrap, 1921), esp. 12, 19, and 134.

[24] Orr, 'Revenge of Literature', 101. She cites *IH* 269.

[25] Richard Rorty, J. B. Schneewind, and Quentin Skinner (eds.), *Philosophy in History: Essays on the Historiography of Philosophy* (Cambridge: Cambridge University Press, 1984), 6–7.

The second lesson Harlan extrapolates is that, given the recent developments in literary criticism and the philosophy of language, with the consequent undermining of a belief in 'a stable and determinable past' and the possibility of recovering authorial intentions, contextually minded historians should desist from insisting that every historian follow their misguided example.[26] John Keane, for example, criticizes the 'new history' for trying to revive Collingwood, and unsuccessfully establish the centrality of authorial intentions. Keane argues that: 'interpretation cannot be conceived as a reproductive act, which rehabilitates a primal or original past' because every age must 'understand a transmitted text in its own way'.[27]

This gives rise to three sets of questions in relation to Collingwood. First, did he, like Harlan, think that the Baconian method was applicable to the questioning of historical evidence, and did this entail, in conformity with the view of Linda Orr, murdering the past? By implication was he denying John Keane's claim that each generation has to reinterpret the past for itself? Second, did he believe that there was 'a stable and determinable past', given his emphasis upon the recovery, by means of re-enactment, of authorial purposes and intentions? And third, to what extent is Rorty's view of the role of the anthropologist an endorsement of Harlan's implicit criticism of Collingwood's contextualism? Historians do not simply repeat what authorities tell them. Testimony is not history and therefore the historian formulates questions that the evidence is forced to answer. Collingwood calls this 'Baconian' or scientific history. The historian constantly asks questions of the evidence that participants or authors did not ask themselves. The Baconian historian decides what he or she wants to know or learn from a text in putting it to the question.[28]

In archaeology this method is most obviously evident. An archaeologist does not merely describe what he or she finds. It is almost impossible to give an account of one's findings without implicitly attributing purposes in the act of interpretation. Such terms as 'wall', 'pottery', 'implement', and 'hearth' all imply

---

[26] Harlan, 'Intellectual History', 608.
[27] John Keane, 'More Theses on the Philosophy of History', in Tully (ed.), *Meaning and Context*, 211 and 212.
[28] *III* 269–70.

purposive activity.[29] It is perfectly legitimate, then, to ask of a text what answer is implied in relation to entirely different questions from those the author asked.[30] Does this entail, as Orr suggests, murdering the past?

For Collingwood the past is certainly not dead. The historical process differs from a natural process in that the former lives on in the present. The various stages of a natural process are distinct and separate and therefore not continuous.[31] Each phase in a natural process leaves behind what it supersedes and therefore they stand outside of each other. It is a process of change in which one form is abolished in the creation of another.[32] Natural processes, as Collingwood tells us in *An Essay on Philosophical Method*, do not, unlike philosophical concepts, constitute series of overlapping forms. Mind, as opposed to Nature, is a continuous process. History is its self-knowledge. At each stage of its development the process retains something of its past. The phases in a historical process are inextricably related and do not fall outside one another. 'Mind', it is suggested, 'in becoming something new, also continues to be what it was; the stages of its development interpenetrate one another.'[33]

A historical process is further distinguished from a natural process in that it makes a distinction between the inside and outside of an event. The outside of an event designates those characteristics that are its observable physical properties. The inside of an event is the process of thought that becomes manifest in the outside. A human action entails both the inside and outside of an event and is the subject matter of history. The historian's work often begins with discovering the outside of the event, but quickly proceeds to the main task of rethinking the thoughts which comprise its inside. For the scientist the event is a spectacle discerned by perception and explained by assigning it to a category or class of such occurrences, which stand in a law-like or causal relation to a different class of occurrences. For the historian it is

---

[29] *A* 133.   [30] *PH* 24.

[31] One of the main purposes of *EPM* is to show that the scientific concept and the philosophical concept are quite different in character.

[32] *IH* 225. Cf. 217.

[33] R. G. Collingwood, ' "Human Nature and Human History"—March 1936'. First draft of paper rewritten May 1936 and sent up for publication by the British Academy, Bodleian Library Collingwood Papers, dep. 12/11, fo. 16.

not the event itself, but the thought expressed in it, which has to be discovered. Identifying and understanding the thought is, for Collingwood, the same thing.[34]

A historical process, in becoming historically known, lives in the present, and does so because it is capable of being re-enacted. It is this element of re-enactment that is explicitly denied by the self-styled Collingwoodian historians, and without which, for Collingwood, historical knowledge is not possible.[35] Collingwood links the mind of the author, or authors, with the meaning of the text. Of this there can be little doubt. His theory of re-enactment, which the modern 'Collingwoodians' ignore, is meant to be the key to the retrieval of authorial meaning. In this respect he is linked to the hermeneutic tradition associated with Wilhelm Dilthey, and against which both Hans-Georg Gadamer and Paul Ricoeur have rebelled. Dilthey, they maintain, placed undue emphasis upon authorial intentions, and failed to see the extent to which a text takes on a life of its own, carrying with it a surplus of meaning open to interpretative exploitation.[36]

Those who subscribe to the revenge of literature thesis and the contextualists themselves misunderstand Collingwood in the same way. They understand the theory of re-enactment in too literal a fashion. Skinner's understanding of Collingwood, for example, follows early discussions by such philosophers as W. H. Walsh, W. B. Gallie, and Patrick Gardiner, and prominent historians such as Geoffrey Elton and Geoffrey Barraclough. They thought Collingwood was offering methodological prescriptions, and accused the theory of being intuitionist. They believed that Collingwood thought that historians in some way had a direct empathetic link with the minds of the persons they studied. More recently Quentin Skinner writes as if Collingwood thought that empathetic understanding allowed direct access to the past as it really was. Skinner

---

[34] *IH* 214.

[35] See e.g. Skinner, 'Interpretation and Understanding of Speech Acts', 120; and, Skinner, 'Collingwoodian Approach', 185.

[36] See Hans-Georg Gadamer, *Truth and Method* (1960), tr. Joel Weinsheimer and Donald G. Marshall, 2nd rev. edn. (London: Sheed & Ward, 1989); Paul Ricoeur, *Hermeneutics and the Human Sciences*, ed. and tr. John B. Thompson (Cambridge: Cambridge University Press, 1981); and Paul Ricoeur, *Interpretation Theory: Discourse and the Surplus of Meaning* (Fort Worth, Tex: Texas Christian University Press, 1976).

contends that: 'we can surely never hope to abolish the historical distance between ourselves and our forebears, speaking as though we can spirit away the influence of everything that has intervened, empathetically reliving their experience and retelling it as it was lived'.[37] Elsewhere Skinner explicitly rejects the idea that his methodological prescriptions imply anything like re-enacting or re-experiencing past thoughts.[38]

Those who regard Collingwood as an intuitionist have suggested that the distinction between the inside and the outside of an event implied that mind is suspended in some non-spatial vacuum into which the historian mystically projects his or her mind. History was not inferential, barely evidential, non-criteriological, and permissive of imaginative flights of fancy, and impossible to corroborate with evidence. They argue that historical knowledge for Collingwood was immediate and intuitive rather than inferential and discursive. Patrick Gardiner, for example, suggests that Collingwood strongly intimated that some sort of telepathic communication with past thoughts was possible, and that the criterion of knowledge offered is the acquaintance theory of truth, where knowing something is equated with being acquainted with it.[39]

The intuitionist interpretation of Collingwood is at variance with the Baconian principle that Collingwood recommends, which affirms as the condition of historical knowledge a non-intuitionist, evidential manner of inferential reasoning. The intuitionist interpretation of Collingwood does not at all conform to what he has to say in the two most important sections of *The Idea of History* (§ 3 'Historical Evidence' (1939) and § 4 'History as Re-enactment of Past Experience' (1936)), *An Autobiography* (1939), and *The Principles of History* (written in 1939). He is emphatic that historical knowledge is inferential reasoning based on evidence, and has nothing to do with observation. In *An Autobiography* Collingwood maintains that survivals from the past have to be interpreted as purposive. The historian must determine what a particular object was for, and whether it was successful, not by

[37] Skinner, 'Collingwoodian Approach', 185.
[38] Skinner, 'Interpretation, Rationality and Truth', *Regarding Method*, 47.
[39] Patrick Gardiner, *The Nature of Historical Explanation* (1952; London: Oxford University Press, 1961), 36 and 39.

guesswork, but on the basis of evidence. The answer he or she gives must be what the evidence demands or is able to sustain.[40]

Collingwood's stress upon the autonomy of the historian does not give support to the intuitionist interpretation. Autonomy does not imply that the historian is independent of evidence. The historian is autonomous in being independent of testimony or authority. The historian's thought is autonomous, not requiring any other authority but his or her own in that independent thought is required in making inferences from evidence, thinking the thoughts of the people studied and criticizing those thoughts in the context of his or her own thoughts.[41] There are various ways in which this autonomy is manifest. First, the act of selection is the simplest level at which this autonomy is expressed. Historians do not merely reproduce authorities. They have to be selective. Second, the historian is responsible for what goes into his or her history and not the authorities. Authorities may point to certain phases in an historical process, but often do not account for the intermediate or missing links. Employing his or her own methodological principles, and criteria of relevance, through a process of inferential reasoning, the historian fills in the gaps left by authorities. This is what Collingwood calls the *a priori imagination*.[42] The historian constitutes himself, or herself, as his or her own authority, and what for scissors-and-paste historians were authorities become evidence for the scientific historian.[43] Third, the autonomy of the historian is more clearly demonstrated in the act of criticism. The authorities are interrogated and perhaps dismissed as unreliable. Predecessors may be convicted of too credulously accepting at face value what has now been exposed as an unreliable authority. The a priori imagination is the criterion by which the historian evaluates and criticizes sources and pronounces them consistent, or inconsistent, with the coherence of the picture imaginatively constructed. The a priori imagination is an absolute presupposition of history. Without it the practice of history could not proceed. It is therefore not questioned, merely absolutely presupposed.[44] Does this theory invite the charge of being radically subjectivist?[45]

[40] *A* 128.   [41] *IH* 236. Cf. *IH* 274.   [42] *IH* 240–1.
[43] *IH* 237.
[44] Louis O. Mink, *Mind History and Dialectic* (Bloomington: Indiana University Press, 1969), 183–6; and, Lionel Rubinoff, *Collingwood and the Reform of Metaphysic* (Toronto: University of Toronto Press, 1970), 275.
[45] Rex Martin, *Historical Explanation* (Ithaca, NY: Cornell University Press, 1977), 63–5.

In *The Idea of History*, part V, § 3, 'Historical Evidence', which was originally chapter 1 of *The Principles of History*, Collingwood argues that scientific history transforms authorities into sources. Historians do not ask whether the sources are right or wrong, instead they want to know what they mean;[46] not what the person who made the statement means, but what the evidence means in the light of the questions posed to it by the autonomous historian.[47] Collingwood extended this discussion in *The Principles of History* in arguing that the relics that comprise evidence are not important in themselves: they are important because of what they say and because of their relation to what they mean.[48]

History begins not with the evidence itself, but with what the historian, familiar with the language, understands it to mean. He or she makes his or her own autonomous statement of the fact that a statement has been made. The historian's judgement comes into play in saying that I read this evidence to be saying this rather than that, and it is in this respect that the historian is autonomous in relation to the evidence. Collingwood argues in *The Principles of History* that 'this is why it could be insisted in the foregoing chapter [which was the only chapter published in *The Idea of History*] that in respect of his evidence the historian was autonomous or dependent upon his own authority: for, as we can now see, his evidence is always an experience of his own'.[49] Interpreting evidence is for Collingwood always a personal experience, 'an act which [the historian] . . . has performed by his own powers and is conscious of having performed by his own powers: the aesthetic act of reading a certain text in a language he knows, and assigning to it a certain sense'.[50] Historians, then, make their own evidence in their own minds. It is their minds that interpret what the evidence says and what it means. Analogously, food *per se* does not nourish us. It is our bodies that convert food into a form of energy. The body and not the food creates the energy. This does not mean that any substance can be selected or manufactured without regard for its value in the overall process, and if the digestive system is defective, no matter how wholesome the food, the end result will be perverted. In the same way only pertinent sources, of which the

[46] *IH* 260.   [47] *IH* 275.   [48] *PH* 39.   [49] *PH* 54.
[50] *PH* 54.

historian is the judge, serve as evidence for the well attuned historical consciousness.

Rewriting History

When Collingwood is understood to reject the intuitionist and acquaintance theories of historical knowledge he appears nothing like as rigid on issues such as the question of an objective unchanging past, or the possibility of attaining certainty in interpretation, as the critics and proponents of contextualism think. Thought can be re-enacted not because there is immediate telepathic communication, but because evidence of past thought survives in the present. The distinction between the inside and outside of an event is really a metaphor and Collingwood was adamant that the thought and its objectifications are inextricable.

If the doctrine of re-enactment is understood not as a method, but as a condition of historical knowledge, the view that each generation rewrites the past is not so difficult to reconcile with it. Contrary to the view that a literal interpretation of re-enactment generates, Collingwood believed that historical interpretation is constantly changing, and none is ever a final achievement. This is not only because of the obvious reason that evidence changes as methods become more refined and competence increases, but also because the principles of interpretation change. Interpretation entails the bringing to bear upon a problem of one's whole experience, knowledge of history, nature, life, philosophy, and mathematics, but also habits of thought and mental furniture of all kinds. These elements change, and with them our view of the past. Scales of value become transformed, often very slowly, but with each change history is viewed through a different prism and what was once considered good may in the light of a different scale of values appear the opposite.[51] An obvious example would be a modern-day account of the democratic ideals of the Levellers or of the Chartists in comparison with near contemporary historical assessments. Each generation writes history anew in the light of its changing values and experience. Each historian is not content to offer new answers to old questions, but reformulates the questions themselves, and in true Baconian fashion puts the evidence to the

[51] 'Can Historians be Impartial?' In *PH* 218.

torture.[52] During the course of a single historian's career, the historical past changes as a result of the historical process itself continuing to move on, a process of which he or she is a part. Collingwood to some extent agrees with Heidegger and Gadamer in believing that the historian is historically situated, and that this situatedness cannot help but colour how the historical past is reconstructed from one age to another. This does not make historical thinking irrational or arbitrary. Collingwood argues in the recently published *Principles of History*, the work he strove all his life to complete, that:

> because we are historical individuals having our own place in the historical process, the varying endowments which that process has conferred upon us make it inevitable that we should envisage that process itself each from his own point of view. This is why every generation and every people must rewrite history in its own fashion and can never be content with second-hand historical knowledge.[53]

Certainty

The implication of much of the work of the likes of Gadamer, Ricoeur, and Derrida is that we cannot know for certain what meanings an author intended his or her text to convey. In the absence of certainty we should give up searching for authorial meanings.[54] Jenkins too thinks that historians tarred with the modernist brush were in pursuit of certainties in talking of objectivity, disinterestedness, 'facts', and the truth. He calls them 'certainist historians'.[55] Did we really need postmodernism to tell us what some of the most arch-empiricists have been telling us in their different ways for years? Hume, and later Russell, and later still the logical positivists were sceptical about certainty, and even Popper's falsification criterion posits certainty only where refutation is concerned. Hume contended that serious reflection about knowledge eventually generates a sceptical attitude to certainty.[56] Russell opens *The Problems of Philosophy* by suggesting that the question of certainty is the most difficult problem in philosophy.

[52] *IH* 248.   [53] *PH* 165: Cf. *IH* 248.
[54] Cf. Skinner, 'Collingwoodian Approach', 181.
[55] Jenkins, *On What is History?*, 7 and 38.
[56] See Preface to Linda Martin Alcoff (ed.), *Epistemology: The Big Questions* (Oxford: Blackwells, 1998), p. ix.

Following Hume, who pointed out quite forcefully the problem of induction, Russell argues that no amount of observation could conclusively verify a proposition.[57] We can only deny beliefs on the basis of other beliefs. We consider which among them is more likely, and hence subscribe to something like degrees of certainty, and 'though the possibility of error remains, its likelihood is diminished by the interrelation of the parts and by the critical scrutiny which has preceded acquiescence'.[58] Ayer does not recognize the problem of induction as a problem at all, because there is no way to solve it. We cannot prove that certain empirical generalizations based on past experience will continue to hold in the future.[59] This is because a generalization based on a finite number of observations cannot be logically extended to cover an infinite number of observations. The statement that all men are mortal refers not only to all men we have known up until now, but to all men *per se*. This does not mean that it is irrational to believe empirical propositions. Indeed, it would be irrational if we sought certainty where certainty is not possible.[60] Rationality simply means for Ayer the adoption of beliefs arrived at by methods that we now regard as reliable. We have confidence in the methods of modern science because they have been successful in practice. Should we lose confidence in those methods it would be irrational to continue to hold the beliefs we do.[61] All truths of science and of common sense are empirical hypotheses that cannot be absolutely verified. What this means for Ayer is that even the observations we make to verify propositions are themselves tentative hypotheses subject to further testing by sense experience. There are, then, no final propositions.[62]

Only the most arrogant of intellectual historians would claim to have arrived at a definitive interpretation of what an author hoped to convey. Most would, in Oakeshottian terms, claim no more than that the interpretation they offer is what the evidence obliges us to believe. It is a provisional understanding, subject to change in the face of a more convincing interpretation or configuration of

---

[57] Bertrand Russell, *The Problems of Philosophy* (1912; Oxford: Oxford University Press, 1974), chs. 1 and 6.

[58] Ibid. 12.

[59] A. J. Ayer, *Language Truth and Logic*, with an introduction by Ben Rogers (1936; London: Penguin, 2001), 34.

[60] Ibid. 65.   [61] Ibid. 101.   [62] Ibid. 92.

evidence, or if new evidence comes to light that has implications for the whole. Skinner, for example, argues that all historical conclusions are tentative and offered by way of hypothesis. Whereas we may never be able to prove conclusively an interpretation correct, we may be able to refute it categorically.[63]

We have already seen that for Collingwood no historical account is a final achievement, and all interpretations are subject to change. Collingwood argues that we cannot ever hope to have absolute certainty in historical interpretation.[64] Any interpretation of evidence can be improved upon, and the only certainty there is in historical thinking is the knowledge of improving upon previous theories. The aim is not to know the past as it really was, because that is a vain hope, but to solve with accuracy, and with as great a degree of certainty as can be attained, on the basis of available evidence, the problems that present themselves to particular historians.[65] It is only in relation to this that Collingwood's overstatement that the conclusions of history can be as certain as those of mathematics can be understood.[66] It is not certainty about the past as such, but certainty about evidence providing specific answers to specific questions that the historian has formulated and tortured the evidence to yield.

Bringing Collingwood Back in

A truly Collingwoodian approach would entail more than bringing back in the idea of re-enactment. In *An Essay on Philosophical Method* Collingwood discusses the features of a philosophical judgement, namely quality and quantity. Qualitative judgements are distinguished into affirmative and negative. In philosophical judgements the affirmative and negative overlap. In every philosophical statement negation implies affirmation. In what is being denied, or negated, something positive is being affirmed. This is what he calls the 'principle of concrete negation', and its neglect he calls 'the fallacy of abstract negation'. There are also corresponding

---

[63] Skinner, 'Collingwoodian Approach', 187. Cf. Karl Popper, *Unended Quest: An Intellectual Biography* (London: Routledge, 1992), 78–90.

[64] *IH* 73.

[65] Collingwood, 'Lectures on the Philosophy of History', in *IH* 392, and 'Outlines of a Philosophy of History', in *IH* 427 and 487.

[66] *IH* 262; and *PH* 18.

principles of concrete affirmation and abstract affirmation.[67] The
implication is that in one's own thought it is necessary in what you
are asserting to be clear about what is being denied, and in the study
of another person's thought you should not be content with asking
what is being affirmed without at the same time asking what is being
denied. In the study of great philosophers, for example, their views
have often come down to us having been formulated in criticism of
other contentions, without these other views themselves surviving,
'except so far as we can reconstruct them from these same criticisms'.[68] If we are not able to discern what is being denied we
cannot fully grasp what is being asserted.[69] In this volume, the
central section of which offers a conception of anthropology and
the use of folktale as anthropological evidence, in affirming that
anthropology is a historical science, Collingwood denies that it can
be assimilated to the natural sciences. He launches a full-scale
attack on positivism in the human sciences which resurfaces in his
discussion of art as magic and the neglect and suppression of the
emotions in *The Principles of Art*; in the discussion of psychology,
and of Ayer's criticism of metaphysics in *An Essay on Metaphysics*;
and throughout the posthumously published *Idea of History*
(compiled by T. M. Knox), and *The Principles of History*, that
Collingwood himself authorized for publication, but which Knox
suppressed.

What all of these texts have in common is that they assert the
criteriological nature of their subject matter. That is, they conceive
of human beings as purposive, and able to formulate their own
intentions in terms of criteria of success and failure. The natural
sciences on the contrary, including psychology, ignore and deny
the relevance of such factors in explaining human conduct. In
Collingwood's view understanding human action entails, at least
partially, the extent to which human beings succeed in what they
set out to do. Philosophy is normative in that it articulates the
ideals and criteria by which a man or woman can judge his or her
conduct successful or unsuccessful.[70] A 'text', in the broadest

---

[67] *EPM* 106.   [68] *EPM* 109.

[69] Joseph Levenson explicitly draws upon the methodological precepts Collingwood recommends in *EPM*. It is more usually the case that *IH* and *EM* provide the
inspiration for historians of ideas. See Joseph R. Levenson, *Confucian China and its
Modern Fate*, 3 vols. (London: Routledge & Kegan Paul, 1958–65).

[70] *EM* 109.

conceivable sense of the word, including archaeological fragments and strata of folktale, is evidence of purposive human thought. We do not start in absolute ignorance and end with absolute knowledge. The aim is to understand better something that is already understood, and to understand an author better than he, or she, understood himself, or herself. Collingwood assumes, with Vico and Dilthey, that we are at home everywhere in this mind-created and historically understood world and that there is no meaning in it apart from that to be discerned in the activities of the actors in their interrelations with each other.

More than any single philosopher in the English-speaking world R. G. Collingwood attempted to circumvent the claim of positivism that scientific knowledge, whether analytic or inductive, was the only valid form of knowledge. Against this claim he countered that history was not only a valid form of knowledge, but was in fact the only valid form of knowledge for the human sciences. During the course of developing his defence A. J. Ayer confronted Collingwood with an immensely influential and engaging restatement of the ideas of the Vienna circle for English consumption. Ayer's *Language, Truth and Logic* constituted a challenge to all forms of traditional philosophy. 'Philosophy' seemed to many to be a series of interminable disputes with no agreement on the right answers. What exactly was preventing philosophy arriving at truths that were generally acceptable? Is there some flaw in the whole enterprise? Ayer's bold claim was that philosophy was indeed seriously flawed, and in identifying that flaw philosophy could at last be transformed into an altogether more productive activity. This involved a clear account of what the legitimate purpose and method of philosophy is.

Like Hume, Ayer makes a distinction between *analytic* statements that are true by definition, and therefore tautologies that do not depend upon sense experience or empirical evidence for their truth, and *synthetic* statements that are propositions about reality and in principle subject to verification. Ayer goes on to contend that metaphysical statements are neither analytic nor synthetic and are in fact nonsense statements since they cannot in principle be verified. The book has been seen principally as an attack on metaphysics, but it was generally an attempt to diminish the epistemic authority of philosophy in general by demarcating its legitimate aims and objectives.

It was against this background that Collingwood developed his theory of absolute presuppositions. Collingwood's response to Ayer's claim that metaphysical statements are pseudo propositions was to agree, but also to ask, in addition, that if such statements are not propositions, what are they? Ayer gives no answer to the question, whereas Collingwood suggests that they are in fact suppositions (more precisely absolute presuppositions), and that Ayer himself has mistaken suppositions for propositions.[71] Collingwood goes on to argue that underlying the thought of any age is a series of absolute presuppositions upon which every other belief or statement rests. Absolute presuppositions are not propositions and therefore their truth does not come into question. Such absolute presuppositions would be 'God exists', or that everything has a cause in Newtonian mechanics. Positivists maintain that metaphysics is not science, just as in the case of anthropology positivist anthropologists maintain that 'magic' is not science. Both are pseudo sciences in that they formulate unverifiable propositions about empirical reality. In Collingwood's view metaphysics deals with the presuppositions that underpin ordinary science, where what he means by science is a systematic or orderly body of thinking about a specific subject matter.[72]

A fellow Idealist, whose philosophy of history Collingwood admired, was more explicit in applying some such theory to the activity of being a historian. As a mode of experience, or world of ideas, the conclusions historians reach are conditional upon the acceptance of a number of unquestioned postulates: for example, that what historians write about is an accessible past consisting of events, that are somehow connected, and not discrete, random, arbitrary occurrences. Such postulates are constitutive of the activity of being a historian. They belong to the world of ideas that circumscribe the form of knowledge that history purports to attain.[73] F. H. Bradley had said something similar about nature as the subject matter of

---

[71] *EM* 4.

[72] *EM* 4. Ayer did not challenge Collingwood's criticism, but instead later argued that Collingwood's examples of absolute presuppositions and their inferred implications for natural science were not credible. See A. J. Ayer, *Philosophy in the Twentieth Century* (New York: Vintage Books, 1984), esp. 197–205.

[73] See e.g. *Experience and its Modes* (Cambridge: Cambridge University Press, 1933), ch. 3; 'The Activity of Being an Historian', in Michael Oakeshott, *Rationalism in Politics and Other Essays*, ed. Timothy Fuller (Indianapolis: Liberty Press, 1991), 151–83; and *On History and Other Essays* (Oxford: Blackwell, 1983), essays I–III.

natural science. Nature, he maintained, is an ideal construction required by natural science, 'and it is a necessary working fiction'.[74]

What we have, then, is an activity constituted by its postulates. Methodological debates relate to the manner and method by which the requisite knowledge is achieved. The activity is able to tolerate a wide variety of approaches and methods. What postmodernist and poststructuralist theorists do is to confuse or conflate these notionally distinct considerations. They at once question the postulates and ridicule the methods instrumental to achieving what the postulates postulate. History is not, of course, a static activity; it has changed and will continue to change over time. What is currently being asked of it is that it abandon its character and become transformed into something else, on the philosophical ground that the practice of history cannot attain what it aims to achieve, that is, knowledge of the past. Collingwood was quite right when he said that people tend to be ticklish in their absolute presuppositions, and this is why contemporary historians of ideas who adopt a Collingwoodian approach are hostile to the literary challenge in its postmodernist form.

The Importance of Presuppositions: The Role of the Anthropologist

I have already made reference to Harlan's approving use of Rorty's statement about the role of anthropology when attacking the contextualism of Skinner, Pocock, and Dunn. Rorty's point was that it is not enough to teach us how to go native. Disinterested curiosity may be fine for the cultist. What we really want to know is whether a particular people have anything interesting to tell us in relation to our interests and standards.[75] The first point to make is that at least one of the contextualists attacked by Harlan agrees with this statement. Quentin Skinner is one of the three authors who penned the introduction from which it came.

Would Collingwood subscribe to it? If we repeat the mistake of taking re-enactment in a literal sense and hence take Collingwood to be advocating the rediscovery of the past as it really was from a disinterested objectivist stance the following statement may appear

[74] F. H. Bradley, *Appearance and Reality* (Oxford: Clarendon Press, 1930), 434.
[75] Rorty, *Philosophy in History*, 6–7.

at variance with Harlan's and Rorty's views. Collingwood maintains that:

man to his fellow-man is never a mere external object, something to be observed and described, but something to be sympathized with, *to be studied by penetrating into his thoughts and re-enacting those thoughts for oneself.* Anthropology—I refer to cultural, not physical anthropology—*is a historical science, where by calling it historical as opposed to naturalistic I mean that its true method is thus to get inside its object or recreate its object inside itself.* [My emphases][76]

It is certainly the case that Collingwood is much more sensitive to historical understanding than Rorty, but he would not reject Rorty's position without reservation. The purpose of studying history, of which anthropology is a species, is not to satisfy curiosity for its own sake. We study it for self-knowledge. In understanding so-called primitive peoples we find out something about ourselves. In knowing what people are capable of doing, we find out what our potential is for future action. History, Collingwood maintains, 'is man's knowledge of man, not man's knowledge of an external world, history demands, or rather brings about, a peculiar intimacy between the knower and the known'.[77] We are unable to understand that which we are unable to think for ourselves. To posit the so-called 'savage' as other, alien to our own minds, a being whose thought and practices survive only in irrational vestiges, is to deny the possibility of understanding ourselves. The 'primitive' mind, from which our own civilized minds developed, lives on in the historical process of which it is part. Anthropology, understood as a historical science, is imperative to civilized societies because, Collingwood believes, the 'savage' is not something alien but survives in us. Collingwood's view of the role of anthropology, then, is not so much at variance with that of Rorty as Harlan implies, and in this respect does not constitute a form of contextualism.

In *The Principles of Art* Collingwood continues his attack on positivism. Magic in *The Principles of Art* is a form of representational art that is designed to re-evoke certain emotions for their practical value. Magic, he maintains, has become a meaningless term of abuse, reduced to this status by anthropologists who two generations previously embarked upon the scientific study of

---

[76] FT2, fo. 26.   [77] FT3, fo. 20.

civilizations different from their own. The question they asked was what is magic for?[78] Their answer to this question was determined by the prevailing philosophy of positivism that dismissed the emotional nature of human beings, and gave emphasis instead only to those forms of intellectual activity that contributed to the making of natural science. In their prejudice they compared the magical practices of the 'savage' with the scientific practices of civilized people who used scientific knowledge to control nature. Magic and natural science, they maintained, were species of the same genus: 'Thus, they concluded, magic is at bottom simply a special kind of error: it is erroneous natural science. And magical practices are pseudo-scientific practices based on this error.'[79]

It is just as much an issue today as it has been for over a hundred years in anthropology and cultural history. How are we to make sense of, or render intelligible, cultural practices that seem to us distinctly odd? On the question of explaining the death of Captain James Cook at the hands of the Hawaiians in 1779, for example, we have the opposing views of Gananath Obeyesekere and Marshall Sahlins. Sahlins on the one hand accuses Obeyesekere of giving an over-rationalized account in terms of an instrumental rationality alien to the Hawaiians. While on the other hand, Obeyesekere, using the same evidence, accuses Sahlins of using a structural model of history that evokes the irrationalist accounts of primitive societies associated with the likes of Lévy-Bruhl and Freud.[80] The latter is specifically taken to task by Collingwood in chapter 4 of the folktale study for equating his psychotic patients with children and savages. In one of his notebooks on folklore Collingwood exclaims with exasperation: 'Savagery is now a mental disease to be cured by psychoanalysis.'[81]

The key issue is this: should anthropologists, cultural historians, and intellectual historians make truth judgements about the beliefs

---

[78] *PA* 57.   [79] *PA* 58.

[80] Clifford Geertz, *Available Light: Anthropological Reflections on Philosophical Topics* (Princeton: Princeton University Press, 2000), esp. 97–106. Representative arguments are to be found in Gananath Obeyesekere, *The Apotheosis of Captain Cook: European Myth Making* (Princeton: Princeton University Press, 1992), and Marshall Sahlins, *How 'Natives' Think, about Captain Cook, for Example* (Chicago: Chicago University Press, 1995).

[81] R. G. Collingwood, 'English Folklore I–III', notebook I, Bodleian Library Collingwood Papers, dep. 21/1, fo. 83.

of the people they study? Or should questions of explanation be entirely separate from those of truth? When this question is posed by philosophers it generally means this: when historians seek to explain a particular belief should they also take account of whether the belief is true, judged by the standards of our own considered contemporary convictions on the same issue?[82] Charles Taylor argues that it is impossible to bracket questions about the truth-value of a statement from those explaining why people believed what they believed. Judgements have to be made about what stands in need of explanation, about what strikes us as distinctly odd, or unintelligible, and this in itself entails asking if they are true. What he is suggesting is that the self-understanding of the subjects of historical inquiry have to be confronted by the languages of explanation in terms of which we study them.[83]

What Collingwood effectively argues in the folktale manuscript is that the three schools of anthropology he discusses, philological, functional, and psychological, in their different ways, fail correctly to identify what he later came to identify as the absolute presuppositions from which the beliefs of 'primitive' societies arise.[84] In Charles Taylor's terms they fail to confront their languages of explanation with the beliefs of their subjects in an adequate manner. The explanatory languages of all three schools Collingwood considers to be positivist; they assume that their own version of instrumental rationality was also that which their subjects tried, but failed to attain. In the folktale manuscript Collingwood is accusing the anthropologists of making mistakes about the presuppositions that underpin the societies they study. In other words, metaphysics is a necessary part of anthropology as a historical science. The anthropologists criticized by Collingwood fail correctly to identify what was being absolutely presupposed by their subjects. What is absolutely presupposed in magic, for example, are not the absolute presuppositions of natural science that underpin modern utilitarian society. The utilitarian mentality wishes to

[82] Quentin Skinner, 'Interpretation, Rationality and Truth', in *Regarding Method*, 29.

[83] Charles Taylor, 'The Hermeneutics of Conflict', in Tully (ed.), *Meaning and Context*, 218–28.

[84] Collingwood fully formulated the theory of absolute presuppositions in 1939 and published it in *EM* in 1940, shortly after writing the folktale manuscript. The idea is nevertheless implicit in his criticisms of the three schools of anthropology.

deny and suppress the emotions, ridiculing superstitions and primitive survivals from the past in the belief that they are irrational, and lead to what Collingwood calls the corruption of consciousness.

The accusation of irrationality is still levelled by respectable historians at societies that hold beliefs which appear incredible by modern criteria. Emmanuel Le Roy Ladurie, for example, in giving an historical account of the beliefs in magic and witchcraft held by the peasants of Languedoc presupposes that they are manifestly false and in need of explanation. He accuses those who held such beliefs of exhibiting a form of mass delirium. He maintains that their minds were unhinged by savagely sinking into irrational behaviour and by harbouring demonstrably incredible beliefs.[85] In some instances the beliefs are so completely bizarre that Ladurie is at a loss to offer any explanation at all. Take for example, the belief in castration by magic. Fear of having an Aiguillette tied in one's name by a sorcerer casting a spell for impotence was sufficiently widespread in sixteenth- and seventeenth-century France to inspire a whole range of diversionary tactics, including marrying outside of one's own village in secret in order to circumvent a sorcerer tying an Aiguillette during the ceremony. Future bridegrooms began to put coins in their shoes as a precaution against the Aiguillette. The coins were marked and symbolic of hiding the future groom's testicles for safe keeping in his shoes.[86] Ladurie calls the beliefs and associated behaviour a 'collective abnormality', and the people who held the beliefs suitable cases for psychoanalysis.[87] Indeed, he recommends handing the problem over to Freudian psychoanalysis.

Quite a commonplace response to attributing a breakdown in rationality, or collective psychosis, to people who hold beliefs that do not square with our own is to suggest that, once we have reconstructed the context of beliefs, along with their underlying assumptions, then the rationality of the actions becomes apparent.

[85] E. Le Roy Ladurie, *The Peasants of Languedoc*, tr. John Day (London: University of Illinois Press, 1974), 203–8. I elaborate upon an example used in my 'Collingwood and Anthropology as a Philosophical Science', *History of Political Thought*, 23 (2002), 303–25.
[86] Emmanuel Le Roy Ladurie, 'The Aiguillette: Castration by Magic', in *The Mind and Method of the Historian* (Brighton: Harvester Press, 1981), 94–5.
[87] Ibid. 84.

It is suggested that we have no independent criteria by which to pronounce them irrational. One of Michael Oakeshott's disciples, W. H. Greenleaf, argues along these lines. Greenleaf argues that the business of the historian is to understand not what is the truth of the matter, but what people believe to be the truth. In other words, historians of intellectual history should be interested in the way people look at things, and not in the things themselves.[88] The historian must never be satisfied with the apparently contradictory, and instead search for the most rational explanation within the terms of reference of the beliefs that informed the ideas. In other words the sympathetic construction of the context renders apparently irrational beliefs coherent. The historian has to demonstrate why such beliefs as that in the Divine Right of Kings, that may appear absurd on modern criteria, inspired so many supporters of Charles I to go into exile, sacrifice their property and wealth, and even risk their lives for what they believed.[89] Greenleaf goes as far as to maintain that: 'If ways of thinking are recreated sympathetically, then one never refutes but always sustains', however bizarre the beliefs appear.[90]

This is to assume in advance the opposite of what many of the anthropologists thought, that, instead of being irrational, all the actions of so-called 'savages' are rationally explicable. This, however, is a conclusion from which Collingwood would dissent.[91] Collingwood argues that the assumption that actions are done by reasonable agents, in pursuit of reasoned ends, need not commit us to the view that they are rational. What we do have to assume is that human beings have reasons for acting, and that they are just as capable of having bad as good ones. Humans are intermittently and precariously rational, but in so far as they are rational at all they act for reasons.[92] In other words, their thought is criteriological.

[88] W. H. Greenleaf, *Order Empiricism and Politics* (Oxford: Oxford University Press for the University of Hull, 1964), 3–4.

[89] W. H. Greenleaf, 'The Divine Right of Kings', *History Today*, 14 (1964), 642; W. H. Greenleaf, 'James I and the Divine Right of Kings', *Political Studies*, 5 (1957), 38 and 47.

[90] W. H. Greenleaf, 'Hobbes: The Problem of Interpretation', in Maurice Cranston and R. S. Peters (eds.), *Hobbes and Rousseau* (New York: Doubleday, 1972), 28.

[91] Cf. Quentin Skinner, 'A Reply to my Critics', in Tully (ed.), *Meaning and Context*, 244–6.

[92] *PH* 47–9.

While Malinowski, for example, still saw magic in terms of a failure to comprehend nature, he was nevertheless convinced that while 'savages' may not be any more rational than ourselves, they are at least as reasonable.[93]

Collingwood certainly did not think that all magical practices could be rendered rational or even reasonable. Magic was capable of being perverted, and put to uses for which it was not intended, and generating false beliefs that it could not sustain. Magic is perverted when we falsely believe that the expression of emotions instigating actions is equivalent to doing the corresponding action. It is the belief that the benefits resulting from an action can be gained merely by expressing our desire for them. The result is that the relation of the function of magic to action has changed and become deluded. When magic is perverted the criticisms of unscientific folly become justified. Victims of such delusions cease trying to attain their ends by reasonable means, and substitute erroneous attempts to bring them about by magical means. In Collingwood's view people are justifiably criticized for equating magic with pseudo-science, when, for instance, 'they will falsely persuade themselves that they can and must do by magic things which human beings cannot do at all; for example, they will claim the power to make rain, or to bring the sun or moon safely through the crisis of an eclipse, by means of charms and ceremonies'.[94] Collingwood argued that, in failing to re-enact, or re-experience, their subject matter the three types of anthropologists he identified, philological, functional, and psychological, failed to overcome the contrived oppositions between rational and irrational, science and magic. To posit the 'savage' as other, something alien to our minds, and of which only irrational vestiges survive, is to deny the possibility of both understanding ourselves and our subject matter because in us, Collingwood contends, the capacities of the primitive mind, from which our civilized capacities have developed, live on. The explanation for this, of course, is to be found in the discussion of the difference between a historical and a natural process. We repress the 'savage' in us and project our irrational fears upon an artificial construction, which we call the 'savage'

---

[93] Adam Kuper, *Anthropology and Anthropologists: The Modern British School* (London: Routledge, 1989), 25.

[94] FT4, fos. 48–9: Cf. *PA* 63 and 68.

mind. By contrast, in understanding the 'savage' historically we understand the 'savage' within ourselves.[95] While Malinowski was accused of being unconcerned about historical development with his emphasis upon function, and was sometimes derided for his crude utilitarianism, he nevertheless saw the study of 'savage' life as a form of self-understanding: confronting the fundamental motives and passions which impel the actions of 'savages', he argued, is to confront what is essential in ourselves.[96]

Conclusion

I have tried to show that Collingwood, both in the folktale manuscript as elsewhere, is not so much of a 'Collingwoodian' as either 'contextualists' or their critics would like him to be. Both parties dismiss Collingwood's theory of re-enactment because they mistakenly attribute to him an intuitionist theory of knowledge that implies privileged access to other minds and a direct line into the past as it really was. I have tried to show that this is too literal an interpretation, and that on many fundamental issues he is much closer to those who endorse the return of literature than they or the contextualists acknowledge. The past for him is not fixed and finished, and he enthusiastically maintains that each generation must rewrite the past for itself, inspired by changing values and contemporary problems. In defending Collingwood I have suggested that we must go beyond *The Idea of History* and *An Autobiography* in supplementing his view of the activity of being a historian. It is in this extended context that we can fully appreciate Collingwood's philosophy of enchantment, the common element to be found in fairy tales, and his emphasis upon the importance of correctly understanding the place of magic in any society, 'primitive' or 'modern'.

[95] 'Lectures on Moral Philosophy' (1933), Bodleian Library Collingwood Papers, dep. 8, fos. 125–6. He says on fo. 125: 'The forms of rational action have their own emotional colourings. In a sense, each is a peculiar emotion or complex of emotions; but only in the sense that they are emotions of a special kind, proper to rational beings as rational, and constituting the emotional aspect of their rationality.'

[96] Bronislaw Malinowski, *A Diary in the Strict Sense of the Term* (New York: Harcourt, Brace & Wood, 1967), 119.

PART I

ART AND CULTURE

WORDS AND TUNE

What is it that a composer is doing who takes a poem, or a piece of prose, and sets it to music? Or to put the question in another way, what does a passage of prose or verse gain by being set to music? What change has it undergone by being 'composed'?

We may offer a few tentative answers at the outset, which will assist us to understand more precisely the nature and aim of the composer's activity. In the first place, the music ought to be a commentary on the words. It ought to enforce their meaning, to drive home in the listener's mind the true force of phrases whose fullest significance he has, perhaps, never before realized. A well-composed song differs from an ill-composed one in this respect primarily, that in the good song words and music form an inseparable unity, the words as it were generating the music by an apparently inevitable process, and the music in turn reflecting a new light on the words, completing their significance, and reinforcing their emotional import. In a bad song, on the other hand, the music is irrelevant: any other tune, we feel, would have done as well, and this particular tune in no way illuminates the words. It suggests a state of mind which the words do not suggest, and is thus in positive conflict with them; or perhaps—and this is far commoner—it suggests a mood which they do indeed suggest, but a mood which they only bear on the surface, while deeper down they have meanings to which the tune does not penetrate. The business of a composer is to bring out the meaning, and not only the meaning but the deepest and most vital meaning, of the words; in so far as he has not done this he has failed.

This, then, we may take as our first axiom—that the composer must have a thorough and profound apprehension of the meaning of the words he is setting, and that he must somehow express this meaning in his music—if this can be done—and no one will deny that, to some extent, it can—then the value of the resulting song is obvious. The song—and when [2] we say song we include recitative,

Bodleian Library, Collingwood Papers, dep. 25/1. The title is Collingwood's. The date 'September 13th 1918' appears at the end of the essay.

chorale, motet, anthem, cantata, oratorio, opera, and every other form of composition in which words are sung—is an exposition or interpretation of the words; it is a good composition just so far as it is a good interpretation.[1]

But here at the very outset a grotesque corollary threatens us. A good interpretation is a correct interpretation; a correct interpretation is one which says exactly what the writer means. Two conclusions follow: first, that the writer ought to be the best man to set his own words to music; secondly, that there is only one musical setting of words which is really right—namely that which reinforces exactly the meaning which the writer would wish to have reinforced—and all others must be wrong. But, plainly, the first corollary is false; no one is likely to suggest that Wilhelm Müller could have made better tunes to the Schöne Müllerin cycle than Schubert's,[2] or that Mr Gilbert could have scored the *Mikado* better than Mr Sullivan did. And this is surely comprehensible if we remember that the musician's task is after all to express the meaning musically: the writer may best know what the meaning is, but he is not on that account most able to express it in music, a language whose technique he has not mastered. In the same way a landscape-painter, not a gardener, is the man to paint a truthful and accurate picture of a garden. The gardener knows what is there, but he has never learnt to put it down on canvas.

To the second corollary we reply that the meaning is always a meaning to somebody. If half a dozen critics expound a great master, they may all express things which the master consciously put there, and yet none of them need exhaust all he meant. So every actor worthy of the name will reinterpret such a part as Hamlet; and the number of legitimate and in their degree convincing interpretations is certainly large. The interpreter is always aiming at saying 'This is what Shakespeare meant'; but he always

[1] Collaborative practice in musical composition, performance, and reception was to be a theme of the closing stages of *PA*. Collingwood was also to include a detailed analysis of our production of, and reaction to, music in his 'Notes towards a Metaphysic' ('begun Sept. 1933'). See Bodleian Library Collingwood Papers, dep. 18/3, esp. the section on 'Pattern and Quality', fos. 42–53.
[2] A reference to the collaboration between the poet Wilhelm Müller (1794–1827) and Franz Schubert which produced the song cycles 'Die schöne Müllerin' (1823) and 'Die Winterreise' (1827).

actually says, if he rightly understands what he is doing, 'This is what Shakespeare means to me'.

[3] And yet we must admit a certain truth in each corollary. Ideally, if the writer were equally gifted as a musician and as a poet, it does appear that he could give an authoritative setting of his own words which would make it unnecessary for anyone else to repeat the experiment. In ancient Greek literature this appears to have been universal, as it probably is to this day in the region of folk-song. And with regard to the second inference, there certainly might be settings which seemed so right that any successors would be forced to repeat their main features, or, in the attempt at originality, would definitely fall behind their predecessors. I am not sure that an example might not be found in the numerous nineteenth-century resettings of some of Goethe's lyrics. But in general there is latitude enough: there are as many ways of composing 'Blow, blow, thou winter wind'[3] as there are of playing the Emperor Concerto;[4] and there is no inherent reason why any single one of them should not be right.

Now in what way exactly does the composer express the meaning of the words by his music? This is the question which we are trying at present to answer; and there are perhaps three main lines along which the answer may be sought.

First, it is said that a poem or any piece of literature describes a mood or emotion; or a series of changing moods; joy, sorrow, triumph, melancholy, and so forth; and that these moods can be accurately expressed by music. A melancholy poem must not be set to a cheerful tune; a poem indicative of religious joy must not be set (as such poems too often are) to a tune expressive of secular or even Bacchanalian merriment.[5] At first sight this leaves to the composer a hopelessly vague and nebulous task. A hundred different poems express the sorrow of love: are they all therefore to be set to the same tune? Is the composer to represent his task to himself in no more precise terms than to say 'wanted, a tune to express unrequited love'? But granted that unrequited love *can* be expressed by a tune (and the assumption is not by any [4] means an

---

[3] One of the songs from Shakespeare's *As You Like It*, 2. 7.

[4] Beethoven's Piano Concerto No. 5, E flat major. Op. 73.

[5] e.g. the well-known advent hymn 'Lo he comes', set in the English hymn-books to an 18th-cent. drinking song [*Collingwood's interlinear note*. The words of the hymn are by Charles Wesley and John Cennick].

uncontroverted one), it can go further and express the particular
kind of unrequited love which makes this poem different from
other poems of the same genre. The existence of a hundred
poems on one subject shows that the subject has a hundred distinguishable aspects: and therefore, *ex hypothesi*, a hundred different
tunes can be written to express them in musical terminology.

This theory I shall call musico-literary parallelism; meaning
thereby, the view that the same emotions and situations can be
expressed in words and in music just as they could be expressed in
Latin and Greek, and that in the song or opera they are concur-
rently expressed in both as in a parallel Greek and Latin Bible. It
leads directly—granted its initial assumption, the possibility of
effecting the translation from words into music—to the following
difficulty. If the music expresses the same thing as the words, why
drag in words? Why not jettison the human voice? Why duplicate
the whole thing? To sing a song is like acting, say, a play of
Molière in French and having a man in a box shouting out an
English translation all the time. It would merely spoil the effect.
If you know French you don't need it: if you don't know French,
get it acted in an English translation and have done with it. Very
well, apply this to music. The logical result is the abolition of the
choral composition and the substitution of programme music—
instrumental music which purports to be a translation of a poem or
what not. Well and good: but first, if programme music is mere
translation, if César Franck's symphonic poem[6] is related to Victor
Hugo as Pope is related to Homer, it is a mere tour de force, a naïve
and rather childish expression of pleasure at finding that poetry
can be so translated (naïve and childish because we can all read
Hugo and therefore don't need a translation, as some of us do in the
case of Homer), and only justifiable, apparently, when the composer invents his own programmes: and secondly, the printed
explanatory programme is necessarily superfluous. For if you
understand the music you can't need the programme. To print it
for a musical audience is as if the preacher of the Latin sermon in
the University of Oxford should hand round a translation of his
sermon to the congregation.

[6] César Franck (1822–90), *Ce qu'on entend sur la montagne: Poème Symphonique*
(1846). The work was composed in response to a poem by Victor Hugo that
appeared in the collection '*Feuilles d'automne*' of 1831.

This point is worth mentioning because apologists of programme [5] music generally adopt the parallelist theory and,
inconsistently, protest that the programme is necessary. Thus
Mr Ernest Newman in an essay which has become almost a classic,
first argues that the virtue of programme music is that it conveys
'a veracious rendering in tone of an emotion that is as definite as'
the emotion conveyed by non-programme music 'is indefinite';
and goes on to say that a person listening to Tchaikovsky's
Romeo and Juliet would not know, unless he had read it on the
programme, that a certain passage describes the lovers on
the balcony; and that therefore he would lose part of the pleasure
which a hearer who had read the programme would get.[7] These
two statements are clearly contradictory. I do not wish for a moment to depreciate programme music as a form of art: but it is not
by such aid or such defenders that it stands.

But we are not discussing the general theory of programme
music; we are merely considering the specific problem of the
relation between music and words in a vocal composition. And
this the parallelist theory fails to explain; because, granted that
theory, either the words or the music—since both express the same
thing—is otiose. This conclusion might be evaded in various ways.
It might be said, yes, we agree: and we accept the conclusion that
vocal music is an unsatisfactory genre. It is doomed to disappear
before the symphonic poem. It arose because primitive music had
an inadequate technique: and therefore composers had to add titles
or sung words or programmes as children write under a drawing
'this is a cow'. But now that instrumental technique is approaching
perfection we can really describe in music; we can compose a
passage which nobody who listens intelligently can mistake for

---

[7] Ernest Newman, 'Programme Music', in *Musical Studies* (London: Bodley
Head, 1905), 103–86. For Newman's remark on the rendering of emotion by tone
see p. 117, and on the example of *Romeo and Juliet*, pp. 149–50. Cf. also *PA* 148:
'A person who listens to music, instead of merely hearing it, is not only experiencing
noises, pleasant though these may be. He is imaginatively expressing all manner of
visions and motions; the sea, the sky, the stars; the falling of the rain-drops, the
rushing of the wind, the storm, the flow of the brook; the dance, the embrace, the
battle.' Collingwood has a note on this page of *PA* to *Musical Studies*, 109, where
Newman had given several of the same examples to illustrate 'painting' in music.
James Connelly's catalogue of the part of Collingwood's library retained by Mrs
Teresa Smith indicates Collingwood's ownership of Newman's volume, and its
bookplate: 'R. G. Collingwood (Prize for Harmony, Rugby 1908)'.

anything but what we mean it for. Eighteenth-century musicians wrote music which some people might reasonably think solemn and others mournful; but such ambiguity in a modern composition would simply mean that the composer was illiterate. Music has learnt from poetry the necessity of definiteness; and now that it has learnt the lesson it can and will dispense with words. To this one can only reply, but does it? Is there any composer so modern as to write no songs? Plainly not. Is there any evidence that songs are dying out; that they are an archaism? Not a shred. Modern song-writing is as vital, shows developments as bold and characteristic, as any other branch of composition.

Or again, it might be said, poetry and music are indeed parallel **[6]** but parallel with a difference. There are certain emotions which are the proper subject of literature, others which are the proper subject of music; and where the verse-writer can only express that part of a situation which falls within the scope of his art, the composer supplements his work by adding a description of the musical aspect, so to speak, of the same situation. But with this argument, parallelism breaks down; and we need here pursue it no more.

The second type of answer is at first sight less serious. As a lyric evokes pictorial images which might be taken up and illustrated by a painter, so, it is suggested, it may evoke auditory images which can be represented in music. A poem describes a young man sitting beside a stream and soliloquizing as he listens to the nightingale: set to music, it will display the murmur of the stream and the song of the bird. Thus, to take a few out of innumerable instances, Schubert gives us the cock-crow, the growling of dogs and the drone of the hurdy-gurdy in the *Winterreise*; Purcell's chorus chatters with cold in the frost-scene of *King Arthur*;[8] Strauss gives us the bleating of Don Quixote's sheep;[9] and composers have already begun to transcribe the Last Post in setting Rupert Brooke's 'Blow out, you bugles, over the rich Dead!'[10] This I call

---

[8] A reference to the setting by Henry Purcell (1659–95) of Dryden's opera *King Arthur, or The British Worthy* (London: for Jacob Tonson, 1691). The famous 'Frost Scene' (III. iii) has been regarded as one of Purcell's masterpieces.

[9] Richard Georg Strauss (1846–1949). A reference to *Don Quixote . . .* Op. 35. Partitur (Munich: J. Aibl, 1898).

[10] The first line from the third of Brooke's War Sonnets ('The Dead'), originally published in Lascelles Abercrombie's *New Numbers* in Dec 1914. See *Collected*

copying-music—the transcription in the musical score of heard noises. There is no harm in it; one gets much innocent pleasure out of the thing well done; but it takes one a very little way. Plenty of lyrics raise no definite sound-images at all; and in those which do, the sound-image is often the least part of the musician's responsibility. To set 'Piping down the valleys wild' thinking of nothing but a flageolet would be silly: the point of the poem is not the noise made by piping, but the atmosphere of golden sun and infinite cloud-swept sky, suffused by a feeling as of early morning dew.[11] These are not sounds: yet the composer has to get them in somehow.

In short, copying-music is in song-writing a dangerous device. It is often brilliantly done by the greatest song writers, like Schubert; but it is not the key to their greatness. Other great songwriters, like Brahms, out of a sophisticated sense of its danger, consciously avoid it; though of course Brahms offers splendid examples of its use, as in the rocking cradle's irregular bump in *Wiegenlied*, or the pattering drops of the *Regenlied*.

But copying-music is capable of developments. You may copy [7] waves in music either by imitating their sound, which is tolerably easy with a modern orchestra; or by writing a scale figure that rises and falls on the score as waves rise and fall. Now this is strictly not musical copying at all. The sound it makes is not like the sound waves make. The resemblance is between the written notes and the waves as you look at them. If you wrote the music in tonic sol-fa no one could even see the least suggestion of waves in it: and the same if you regarded it as a series of sounds, not as a series of marks on paper. And of course music *is* a series of sounds, properly considered. To take an exactly parallel case, poetry is a series of sounds, and any device which depends for its effect upon the spacing of poetry on a printed page is an unpoetic device. So when George Herbert prints a poem in the shape of an altar or a pair of wings he

Poems of Rupert Brooke: With a Memoir (by Edward Marsh) (London: Sidgwick & Jackson, 1918), 7.

[11] The poem is the introduction to *Songs of Innocence, shewing Two Contrary States of the Human Soul* (1789) by William Blake, and had been the subject of musical settings by Florentia Bernani (1892), Felix Corbett (1889), Sir Arthur Somervell (1894), Bertram Luard Selby (1897), Helen Patterson (1910), and Alfred Jethro Silver (1913).

is playing a game which may be quaint and amusing, but is entirely irrelevant to the import and significance of the poem.[12]

This false development of copying-music I call pseudo-copying. The curious may find abundant examples—to go no further—in the works of John Sebastian Bach, in whose day it was a recognized device. A passage running up or down indicated an ascent or descent; a tune whose notes traced a zig-zag on the stave was held to resemble lightning; and so on to infinity. It is sometimes difficult to distinguish it from genuine copying; thus is the undulating accompaniment-figure in *Gretchen am Spinnrade*[13] an attempt to draw, as it were, a series of circles—a kind of cycloid— on the stave, or to transcribe the sound of a spinning-wheel? I suspect, the former. Psychologists gravely try to justify the crudest kinds of pseudo-copying by maintaining that notes of a high pitch are naturally and universally associated in our minds with elevation in space, and vice versa; a contention which no one need go to the trouble of refuting who knows that the Greeks called that end of the scale the top which we call the bottom.

Pseudo-copying is very definitely out of fashion at present. No competent musician would employ it today; and everyone laughs at the simpler and more obvious forms of it. But like many obsolete practices it holds a disproportionate place in theory: because writers on programme music, strangely enough, seek in it a link between copying-music and music of another kind, namely that which is supposed to describe states of mind; music, that is to say, conceived on the parallelist hypothesis. The argument is that programme music has three stages of simple and logical development: first, copying sounds; secondly, as a natural consequence, copying spatial relations; thirdly, copying emotions **[8]** and states of mind generally. So the case is stated for example in Niecks's standard work on programme music.[14] It is a total misconception; for first, the supposed intermediate stage is no true development but a monstrosity; and secondly, there can be no possible link between the third stage and the first. As well try to develop lan-

[12] A reference to Herbert's 'The Altar' and 'Easter Wings', both printed in *The Temple: Sacred Poems and Private Ejaculations* (Cambridge, 1633).

[13] *Gretchen am Spinnrade* (Gretchen at the spinning wheel) from Goethe's *Faust* (Vienna: Cappi & Diabelli, 1821).

[14] Frederick Niecks, *Programme Music in the Last Four Centuries: A Contribution to the History of Musical Expression* (London: Novello, 1906).

guage out of onomatopoeism, according to the method of the once influential 'Bow-wow school' of philologists, as to develop music out of the mimicry of natural sounds. And yet, as we shall see in the sequel, the copying-theory of music has a certain value. It does at least try to explain how the noises which a musician makes are connected with the things he is talking about; a problem which the parallelist theory totally ignores.

I propose to offer a third answer to the original question. A piece of music consists of an organized system of sounds, related to each other in three ways at least: pitch, duration, and intensity. I omit timbre or tone-quality for the time being for reasons to be explained hereafter. Now a piece of literature is also an organized system of sounds. At first sight it might be said that these sounds are only related in one way, namely by differences of articulation— that is to say, that literature consists simply of vowels and consonants. But this is not so. Duration is also present; the voice dwells for a definite space of time on each sound, and not on all sounds for the same length of time. This is recognized, in a very crude fashion, by the distinction between long and short vowels or long and short syllables. But a little analysis shows that there are not only two lengths of time which the voice may take in enunciating syllables, but several lengths. Secondly, intensity plays an important part in literature; syllables are stressed or unstressed, and stressed in very varying degrees; sometimes one whole sentence receives a heavy stress in almost every syllable, while others have a comparatively feeble stress throughout. And thirdly, pitch is no less important. The speaking voice rises and falls; and the vocal cords, whose function is to create a musical note, are active in the pronunciation of every syllable.

Now these three factors are just as essential to the proper enunciation of language—to the very existence, that is to say, of literature—as articulation. If you take a certain phrase of words, it is notorious that you can alter its emotional colouring, indeed its meaning in the narrowest sense of the word, by altering the stressing of the syllables or the time taken in speaking them. And it is equally true, though less commonly recognized, that you can do so by altering the pitch-outline of the sentence. A rising [9] intonation and a falling intonation on the same words make them mean different things. This is now fully realized by phoneticians, and the modern method of teaching foreign languages lays great stress on intonation—on the proper rising and falling of the voice. If you learn a foreign language from books alone you may, by studying poetry, get some rough idea of the right way to stress it, and of the right duration of syllables; but there is no way (apart from the devices of some modern phoneticians) of learning the right intonation; and it is here that the learner goes most hopelessly astray. Anyone accustomed to hearing foreigners talk English knows, if he happens to have observed, that the pitch-outline of their sentences is the worst part of their talking, and the last thing in which a foreigner acquires accuracy.

But for these three factors literature, as we write it, possesses no notation. There are certain rudimentary attempts at it in most languages; some languages double a consonant (as in Italian) to indicate that the voice dwells on it, others (like Greek) have special symbols for 'long' vowels. Some writers (like H. G. Wells) use, at times, a capital letter to indicate a stress; and the Greek accent is a very interesting case of a rudimentary pitch-notation. Modern punctuation is a device for noting certain features as duration and pitch. But these are exceptions; the rule is for the notation to indicate the articulations only, and to leave the other three factors to tradition and memory. In reading aloud, we extemporize them: in learning a piece by heart as a reciter or actor learns it, we think them out with all possible care, certain that to misrepresent them will mean misrepresenting the meaning of the passage. 'The expression', as we call it, is an integral part of literature; that part of literature which is written down is only a part, incomplete unless our imagination or voice supplies the relations of stress, duration, and pitch which the written word omits.

This operation is by no means a trivial one: upon it depends the right understanding of the literary passage we are considering. Nor is it in all cases an easy one: all the difficulties which an actor or reciter finds in a passage, all the problems which face the reader-aloud, are reducible to this. It may seem an insult to say that all the effects of fire, pathos, or humour, all the resources of eloquence, are strictly composed of articulations *plus* the correct relative pitch, duration, and loudness of the syllables which the speaker utters; but such is the case, and anyone who knows anything about elocution is well aware of it. The mysterious and incalculable must be sought, if anywhere, in the orator's intuition that *this*, and no other, is the scheme of [10] sound-relations which will move his audience in the desired way; but there are no other means by which he can do it, except those we have enumerated. (I still omit timbre, as I said at the outset; this will be considered later.)

Let us now return to music. Here too we have an art consisting of sounds. Qua music, it knows nothing of articulation. But it has its own notation; and this is especially developed in three directions. First, it is a pitch-notation. It is not an exhaustive one; for there are theoretically an infinite number of pitch-distinctions within the octave where the chromatic scale only notes thirteen. And many of these unnoted intervals, we know, are actually played and sung. A piano's F is the same sound whether it functions as the subdominant of C, the submediant of A minor or the leading-note of G♭; but a violinist or a singer forms these three notes at quite distinct pitches. Secondly, it is a time-notation. And in this aspect it is much more perfect; there is no unit of duration which the ordinary music cannot accurately express, though in certain cases the expression would be so complicated (involving perpetual new metronome-marks and other devices) that words like *accelerando*, *rallentando*, or most trustful of all, *rubato*, leave the precise time-values to the discretion of the performer. Thirdly, it is a stress-notation; though this aspect is of comparatively modern introduction and consists in the use partly of bar-lines and partly of marks (sf, >, etc.) other than the notes.

Musical notation thus supplies the precise elements which literary notation lacks for the proper and adequate transcription of spoken language. If a poet or prose-writer wished to write out a passage in such a way that no one could misinterpret his meaning or speak it in a misleading manner, he would have to invent a notation to indicate the relative duration, pitch, and intensity of the sounds whose articulations he can write alphabetically. But such a notation already exists in music; not perfect, it is true, but on the whole much more adequate to these purposes than the English alphabet is adequate to noting the articulations of spoken English.

Here, then, we have the true function of the song-composer. His task is to discover what is the correct way to pronounce a phrase in order to give it the correct meaning, and then to write down this pronunciation in musical notes. Setting a phrase [11] to music means determining the precise stress, pitch, and duration values which will give to it the desired meaning. We use the word 'meaning' in the widest possible sense, to include both grammatical and logical structure on the one hand and (what properly considered is perhaps hardly to be distinguished from these) emotional colouring or atmosphere. All these things *can* be conveyed by means of sound-relations, or literature would not exist; and in a song, which is a collaboration between poet and musician, the poet specializes in perfecting one kind of sound-relation—the articulations—while the musician perfects the system of durations, stresses, and pitches.

But, it will be replied, the poet in composing his verses already, in his voice or his imagination, supplies them with the correct durations, stresses, and pitches: he has done the work of the musician beforehand. The musician, if this is a true account of his function, does no more than to copy down slavishly what he hears. In a sense, yes: and yet he copies it in his own material, as a portrait-painter copies a head. He is working in a definite medium, the medium of the scale as he knows it: he has to work within certain definite technical limitations, like any other artist. The speaking voice may use an infinite subdivision of the octave: the musician has only thirteen semitones, and those only if he uses an entirely chromatic technique. This is the truth underlying an objection which might easily be urged against our theory. It might be said, 'doubtless the musician must be faithful to the spoken word. If he stresses a syllable that ought not to be stressed, dwells on one that ought to be passed over quickly, rises to one on which the voice ought to fall, he is certainly writing bad song-music. But these things are all subsidiary to the main point, which is that he must write a beautiful and expressive tune. And it is the beauty of melody that proves him a musician. If music were what you say, it would never contain melody at all: it would all be a sort of formless recitative. But the essence of music is melody: and the peculiar difficulty of the song-writer's task is that he must keep the balance between beautiful melody on the one hand and right intonation and stressing of the words on the other.'

This dualistic view is a serious error. It is only one stage removed from the worst possible mistake about song-writing—the mistake which looks at words as the mere excuse for a tune, to be maltreated as much as you please so long as the tune comes out pretty. This mistake was characteristic of the great symphonic school of musicians. Obsessed by instrumental methods, they used the voice as an instrument; uneducated men, they cared

nothing for literature and had no fine feeling for its adequate
presentation. Bach sometimes attempted to [12] write with proper
regard for the words, but not very often: his vocal writing is too full
of instrumental passages and pseudo-copying. With Haydn,
Mozart, and Beethoven the attempt was much rarer; Haydn is
the best of the three, Mozart the worst. Schubert really rediscovered the duty of music towards literature, and made a deliberate
and conscious effort to live up to it. Schumann did something to
carry on the principle, though much of his work is much worse
than Schubert's; Brahms now and then tries, but in general his
song-writing is purely instrumental. Thus almost all the great
German composers except Wagner, who saw the principle plainly
enough, and his follower Wolf—a great vocal writer—have written
for the voice on entirely wrong principles, at most doing homage to
the dualistic view which, while regarding abstract melody as the
first aim, admitted that some respect ought to be paid to the words.

The essence of music is certainly melody. But our view of song-
writing does not exclude melody; it does not even exclude highly
formal and decorative melody. It only insists that no melody be
imposed upon the words from without. A well-written poem does
not only scan and rhyme: it also forms a beautiful series of inton-
ation-curves; that is to say it sings its own tune; and it is only a
perfect poem if the tune is a good one. If a writer has no ear for
melody he can no more write a poem than if he has no ear for metre.
Literary critics usually overlook this fact; but it is undeniable.
Now as regards rhythm, some poems have their stresses so arranged as to form a definite system of recurrent stress-groups
which can be represented in music by a fixed dancing or marching
rhythm, quite formal and, in extreme cases, monotonous. Other
poems have a much freer system of rhythms; not at all less highly
or delicately organized, it may be, but organized in a way other
than by the repetition of a stress-formula. So some poems are
written round a repeated intonation-formula, and these will best
be set strophically, to a recurrent tune: in others the intonation-
curves, while still delicately balanced and organized, are not based
on repetitions, and therefore the composer must not write a recurrent melody, but a continuous one whose organization follows the
organization of the intonation-curve. If then a song-composer is
to write beautiful melody he must set words which contain
a beautiful melody: if he sets words whose pitch-curve is

ill-designed and haphazard, he cannot write beautiful melody however hard he tries, unless he falsifies the meaning of the text.

But—and this is the truth underlying the objection—no one will write beautiful tunes unless he is a skilled musician. For the difference [13] between the speaking voice and the singing voice is precisely that the singing voice uses the notes of a conventional scale, just as the painter uses a palette of conventional colours; and to write a tune in a scale one must learn the technique of handling the scale.

We are not trying to offer an account of the origin of music, or to explain how it gets its effects. Herbert Spencer tried to show that music originated by development from excited and rhetorical speech.[15] He was right in seeing that speech and song were really inseparable, but with the usual stupidity of an evolutionary philosopher he tried to use this connexion to show how one had grown out of the other. Song could not have grown out of speech unless it was always *in* speech; and, as we now see, it always was. All speech contains those elements, intonation, pitch, and stress, out of which music is composed: all speech *is* already song, more or less highly organized. And if one philosopher tries to evolve music out of speech, another might equally well try to evolve speech out of music. Both attempts would be futile. The fact rather is that the musical characteristics of speech are an integral and vital part of it: that without them speech has no meaning, for it cannot be spoken: and that disorganization in these elements—e.g. a singsong or monotonous delivery, misplaced stress, and so forth—reduces speech to a minimum of significance. A song-composer, by taking up these elements and organizing them more delicately, must obviously add to the significance of language, bring out unsuspected meanings, subtler or less subtle according to his power of understanding the words and expressing his understanding in the terms of the musical scale.

---

[15] See Herbert Spencer, 'The Origin and Function of Music', *Essays: Scientific, Political, and Speculative* (London: Longman, Brown, Green, Longmans, & Roberts, 1858), 359–84. Spencer notes that: 'the dance-chants of savage tribes are very monotonous; and in virtue of their monotony are much more nearly allied to ordinary speech than are the songs of civilized races', inferring that 'vocal music originally diverged from emotional speech in a gradual, unobtrusive manner' (371–2). Spencer's essay was originally published in *Fraser's Magazine* (Oct 1857), and is again cited in 'Aesthetic Theory and Artistic Practice' (hereafter ATAP), fo. 26, below.

Such is the true function of the song-composer. There is nothing mysterious about it: the nonsense commonly talked about the immaterial, lawless, incalculable nature of music may safely be ignored. The mystery of music is only the mystery of language— the mystery that sounds have meanings.

[14] Note I. *Timbre*. This forms an important element in literature and music; but it occupies a less satisfactory position than the other three. There is no notation for it in ordinary song-writing; but (on the one hand) it is developed with extraordinary subtlety in orchestral music, whose very essence is timbre-relations; and (on the other) it is very carefully inculcated by any good teacher of singing. Attempts to get the exact timbre required out of a voice are frequent in modern choral music, where the voices are required to sing on a certain vowel, with closed lips, etc.

Note II. *Historical*. A detailed history might be written of the principle we have laid down. It can easily be shewn that plain-song attempts to obey it accurately, though in a mechanical and very limited way; that the choral writers of the polyphonic period mostly attended to it with the greatest care, greater in proportion to their magnitude as musicians (thus of the English madrigalists the greater simply write the tune they hear in the words: the inferior write a tune and put the words to it); that with the rise of instrumental music it fell into abeyance, and was on the whole grossly neglected in the eighteenth and early nineteenth century; that the modern Germans still suffer severely from the same neglect; and that it is most carefully cultivated by the modern French composers, and by those of the English who have escaped German influence. Clearly also foreign influence is fatal to its true development; for the German song at best could only copy the intonation of German, and English songs imitated from the German could never represent English intonation. This is why the thesis we have defended may seem a paradox in England, but would appear a truism in France; for England is so far under the domination of German music (which has never really accepted the principle owing to the disastrous influence first of the *choral* and secondly of the symphony) that our song-writers, instead of honestly setting English words, imitate and thereby intensify the vices of the Germans.

OBSERVATIONS ON LANGUAGE

1. Language is not a tool or instrument which we use in order by its use to do things which we could not do without it. It is a mode of conduct, an activity.

1.1. It is therefore a mistake to think of language as an 'invention' or the like, comparing it with fire or other instruments invented at a certain time (or at various times) by men.

1.2. It is a mistake to think of it as having certain properties or powers in itself and apart from the 'using' of it: for since it is an activity, not an instrument, it does not exist save in being 'used'.[1]

2. Significance or meaningfulness, the attribute which is essential to language, is therefore an attribute not of an instrument (as sharpness or heaviness is of a chisel or hammer) but of the linguistic activity, or rather the agent engaged in that activity.

2.1. When language is considered in itself, apart from the activity of 'using' it, and the question raised: does significance belong to *it* or to the *person using* it? The answer must be, the latter: but with this qualification, that the abstraction presupposed by the question is a false one.

2.2. When language considered in itself is divided for the convenience of grammarians into separate words, and the question is then raised, what does this or that separate word mean? There is properly speaking no answer; for (a) since words are never used except in a context, and have no meaning except as used, they have no

---

Bodleian Library, Collingwood Papers, dep. 16/13.

[1] Wittgenstein famously said that "The meaning of a word is in its use in language'. See *Philosophical Investigations*, tr. G. E. M. Anscombe (Oxford: Blackwell, 1978), 20e, para 43. Wittgenstein's ideas were known to some Oxford philosophers, but there is no evidence that Collingwood knew of them, and he may have formulated his ideas on language independently. In *PA* 250, he says: 'One does not first acquire a language and then use it. To possess it and to use it are the same. We only come to possess it by repeatedly and progressively attempting to use it.' In *NL* likewise, Collingwood writes that: 'A word is not a sound or group of sounds . . . ; it is a sound or group of sounds having its own meaning, namely what a person using that word means by making that sound' (41).

meaning except in a context; (b) since it is the speaker, not the word, that means, the nearest we can get to an answer is 'it means whatever people mean [2] when they use it'.

2.2.1. It is possible, however, to define the meaning of a word lexicographically, i.e. by giving a synonym. But (a) by doing this we do not say what the word means, we only say that whatever it does mean is the same as what a certain other word means. (b) Even so, we do not define the meaning of the word, we only generalize about the kinds of occasions on which a speaker uses it. (c) Even so, what we say is never quite true, for no word is quite synonymous with any other (i.e. if we take the totality of occasions on which one of the alleged synonyms is used, it is never true that on all these occasions the other could be used instead without a change of meaning).

3. It is a mistake to say that words 'stand for' things. For to 'stand for', 'represent', and so forth, signify a relation in which one thing A acts or is used as a substitute for another thing B. If we are talking about certain things e.g. stones, our words are in no sense substitutes for the stones.

3.1. From this mistake arises a whole cycle of errors about language, as that words should resemble the 'things for which they stand'. It is possible that such resemblance should exist if the things in question are sounds, but not otherwise; and even in that case the degree of possible resemblance is very slight; if it were at all close, we should be mimicking sounds instead of talking.[2]

[3] 3.1.1. Or such errors as that the order and connexion of words in a sentence does, or may, or should, correspond with the order and connexion of the things about which we are talking. This is impossible, because the separate words are grammatical fictions and the relations between them are therefore grammatical relations (syntactical relations); and nothing can correspond with one set of syntactical relations except another set of syntactical relations.

3.1.1.1. From this error there arises the further error of hypostatizing grammatical relations into metaphysical relations.

4. It is a mistake to say that words 'stand for' thoughts (activities of thinking). Only in so far as a speaker also thinks can his speech (activity of speaking) be significant: if the words he uses 'stood for'

---

[2] Cf. WT above.

thoughts, this would imply that qua speaker he is absolved from the necessity of thinking, which is absurd.

4.1. From this error arise various common fallacies in logic, as, that the grammatical articulation of a sentence somehow corresponds with the logical articulation of the speaker's thought: and from this arise all those errors in logic which may be summed up under the name of logical verbalism.

5. From the discovery that grammatical structure in sentences corresponds neither to the structure of the things spoken of nor to the structure of the thought in the speaker's **[4]** mind there arises, by inference from the mistaken doctrine that there ought to be such correspondence, the theory that language as it actually exists is an imperfect instrument for the expression of thought: and from this again there may arise *either* the search for a language fulfilling this requirement, an artificial 'philosophical language', which is an absurdity, *or* the despair of ever expressing thought in any language, i.e. the refusal to attempt the expression of thought at all, which is fatal to thought itself.

JANE AUSTEN (1921)

Strange influences were abroad in the years 1770 to 1775. The French Revolution was brewing, the Romantic movement was unfolding itself, the whole world was coming to a new dawn: and the spirit of the age produced a generation of geniuses that has no parallel in the records of history. Look at the people whose birth falls in these years. At other times there have been giants on the earth; there were great men in Athens in the fifth century and in Florence in the fifteenth; but if you look through history and mark the birth-year of every man who stands unsurpassed in his own line of work, you will find no period when they fall so close together as in the years of which I am speaking. Here, falling within half a dozen years, are the births of Beethoven, the greatest man who ever wrote music: Turner, the greatest man who ever painted a landscape: Hegel, the supreme philosopher: and—Jane Austen.

I don't mean that to be an anti-climax. There is an art of novel-writing, as there is an art of landscape-painting: and in her own art I dare to maintain that Jane Austen stands supreme. **[2]** I am not forgetting the great pioneers, Boccaccio, Cervantes, and Fielding, or the mighty figures of the nineteenth century, Balzac, Dickens, Henry James or Dostoevsky: with all these in mind I say, humbly but firmly, that Jane Austen is the greatest of them all. It has been said before. And yet people who love and admire her work have been too often browbeaten into an apologetic attitude. She was apologetic about it herself. She wrote disparagingly of the scraps of ivory on which with so fine a brush she produced so small an effect with so great an expenditure of labour.[1] But that was simply Jane's mock-modesty. She dearly loved to pull a reader's leg, and when

Bodleian Library Collingwood Papers, dep. 17/2. The manuscript title is followed by 'Johnson Society', and 'Nov. 27 1921'.
 [1] Letter 134, To Edward Austen (Jane's nephew), Monday, 16 Dec. 1816: 'What should I do with your strong, manly, spirited Sketches, full of Variety and Glow?—How could I possibly join them on to the little bit (two Inches wide) of Ivory on which I work with so fine a Brush, as produces little effect after so much labour.' See *Jane Austen's Letters to her Sister Cassandra and others*, ed. R. W. Chapman, 2 vols. (Oxford: Clarendon Press, 1932), ii. 468–9.

you have produced an obvious masterpiece you can afford to
describe it as a trifle. We know that John Locke referred to the
epoch-making *Essay on Human Understanding* as 'my odd notions'[2] and the world's greatest sonnet-sequence is prefaced by a
dedication giving all the credit for its existence to a person whom
posterity only knows as Mr W. H. Such modesty is well enough in
giants: but it ought not to be echoed by their admirers. And the
admirers of Jane Austen have almost always pitched her claims far
too low. Not all, and not the ablest. Scott knew that she was among
the very greatest of writers: her talent, he wrote plainly, was the
most wonderful he had ever met with.[3] And Archbishop Whately,
who was a very competent man, wrote an article upon her work
some three years [3] after her death in which he maintained that
her power of characterization could only be compared to Shakespeare's. What specially moves the Archbishop's admiration is the
astonishing power, nowhere met with except in Shakespeare and
Jane Austen, of depicting fools.[4] Any writer of ordinary talents, he
remarks, can give you a good description of a sensible man or of a
striking character: but it takes a genius of no ordinary type to paint
a fool who shall yet be a solid human being. Shakespeare does it:
his fools are unsurpassed in their sheer folly, yet Slender, Shallow,
Aguecheek, and the rest are as different from one another and as
living as Richard III and Macbeth and Julius Caesar. And Jane

---

[2] The quotation does not appear in 'The Epistle to the Reader' but it is the
general thrust of what Locke is saying there. Generally speaking he is arguing that
any new ideas at first appear odd and take some time to become accepted. He says
that some of his ideas are 'out of the common road'. See John Locke, *An Essay
Concerning Human Understanding*, ed. Peter H. Nidditch (Oxford: Clarendon Press,
1975), 3.
[3] A near quotation from Scott's journal entry for 14 Mar. 1826. See John Gibson
Lockhart (ed.), *Memoirs of the Life of Sir Walter Scott, Bart*, 7 vols. (Edinburgh:
Robert Cadell, 1837), vi. 264. The comment is prompted by a rereading 'for the
third time at least' of *Pride and Prejudice*.
[4] Richard Whately (1787–1863), Archbishop of Dublin, and author of the
satirical *Historic Doubts Relative to Napoleon Buonaparte* (London: J. Hatchard,
1819) (in refutation of Hume on miracles). The article by Whately referred to, a
review of a new edn. of *Northanger Abbey, and Persuasion*, is in the *Quarterly
Review*, 24 (1821), 352–76. It was reprinted as 'Modern Novels' in Whately's
Miscellaneous Lectures and Reviews (London: Parker & Son, 1861), 282–313, and
is cited by Mary Augusta Austen-Leigh in her *Personal Aspects of Jane Austen*
(London: John Murray, 1920), 97. Collingwood refers again to Whately in FT2,
fo. 8.

Austen does it too: you could never mistake Miss Bates for Mrs
Allen, or Mrs Norris for Mr Collins, after reading a simple sentence of their utterances. So far Archbishop Whately and his
judgement remains as true today as when it was written.[5] Human
silliness is a subject which tests to a quite extraordinary extent the
powers of the dramatic writer: any failure either of intellect or of
temper is at once revealed by the attempt to portray it. Shakespeare
could draw a fool because not only did he know a fool when he saw
one, but he could delight in his folly as a delicious and exquisite
thing, as purely precious as the colour of a primrose or the song of a
[4] nightingale. Meredith couldn't draw a fool really well, though
he tried hard: his intellectualism deprives him of all delight in folly
for its own sake, and he rages at the fool for being foolish—which is
as if some fanatical follower of Peter Bell should tear up the
primrose and stamp on it for being yellow. Even Henry James,
from whom the human heart had no secrets, couldn't draw a fool,
because the springs of pity were always, in his tender soul, ready to
overflow and quench the dry light of reason for which alone folly is
folly at all.[6] To Henry James, human folly is not a laughing matter
but a crying matter: and the same is true of his great contemporary
Thomas Hardy. Between these two extremes, the intellectualism
of a Meredith and the emotionalism of a James, there is a mid-
point of equilibrium, where the intellect is perfectly pitiless in its
clear vision of truth, and the feelings are perfectly fresh in their
ecstatic enjoyment of it. A step to one side or the other destroys this

[5] Whately, 'Modern Novels', *Miscellaneous Lectures and Reviews*, had written of
Jane Austen as having 'a regard to character hardly exceeded even by Shakespeare
himself. Like him, she shows as admirable a discrimination in the characters of fools
as of people of sense; a merit which is far from common . . . it is no fool that can
describe fools well; and many who have succeeded pretty well in painting superior
characters, have failed in giving individuality to those weaker ones, which it is
necessary to introduce in order to give a faithful representation of real life . . .
Slender, and Shallow, and Aguecheek, as Shakespeare has painted them, though
equally fools, resemble one another no more than Richard, and Macbeth, and Julius
Caesar; and Miss Austin's [sic] Mrs. Bennet, Mr. Rushworth, and Miss Bates, are
no more alike than her Darcy, Knightley, and Edmund Bertram' (295–6).
[6] See the Preface to *The Princess Casamassima*, in *Henry James: The Critical
Muse: Selected Literary Criticism*, ed. Roger Gard (London: Penguin Books, 1987),
501–2: 'Verily even, I think, I think, no "story" is possible without its fools—as
most of the fine painters of life, Shakespeare, Cervantes and Balzac, Fielding, Scott,
Thackeray, Dickens, George Meredith, George Eliot, Jane Austen, have abun-
dantly felt.'

harmony: either the intellect dominates and the feelings become atrophied or embittered, or else the feelings dominate and the vision of life is blurred by tears or distorted by desire. The attainment of this perfect poise is the rarest thing in life.[7] Momentarily, perhaps, we can all achieve it, but we do not maintain it. If we did, we could walk unscathed through the world as Blondin crossed Niagara on his tight rope. But there are some people who really do walk through the world like that, and when [5] they are artists their achievement betrays itself in their art. And as a touchstone to reveal its presence, there is nothing so sure as the way in which they depict folly: that is to say, the quality of their laughter. Man has been well defined as a laughing animal: and the difference between a good man and a bad, a sick man and a well, a great man and a small, is nowhere more clearly seen than here. It is not enough, as Meredith's philosophy would have us believe, that a man should laugh. The comic spirit in itself has no special value over and above any other privilege of humanity, such as the possession of four incisors in each jaw. You must discriminate between laughter and laughter: the cracked laughter of the maniac, the boor's guffaw, the vacant giggle of the idiot, the snarl of the misanthrope, and so on. It is by this test that we begin to see the true greatness of Jane Austen.[8] You very seldom find in her works anybody at whom she does not laugh. For her as for Carlyle mankind and womankind too is mostly fools. I do not think she meant us to laugh very much at Mr Knightley, and hardly at all at Anne Elliot and Captain Wentworth: but with those exceptions, is not the whole texture of her work a fabric of laughter through and through? Is there a single character in *Pride and Prejudice*, a single character in *Northanger Abbey*, or a single character but Knightley in *Emma*, that is not conceived in the vein of comedy and treated as

[7] Collingwood seems here to apply to the novelist's treatment of folly what Matthew Arnold had said of the perfect balance necessary to the critic of poetry: 'To handle these matters properly there is needed a poise so perfect that the least overweight in any direction tends to destroy the balance.' See 'Last Words' (1861), 'On Translating Homer IV', *The Complete Prose Works of Matthew Arnold*, i. *On the Classical Tradition*, ed. R. H. Super, 11 vols. (Ann Arbor: University of Michigan Press, 1960), 174.

[8] George Meredith, 'On the Idea of Comedy and of the Uses of the Comic Spirit', *New Quarterly Magazine*, 8 (June–July 1877), 1–40. Meredith had claimed that 'Emma and Mr. Elton might walk straight into a comedy, were the plot arranged for them' (29), and 'the test of true Comedy is that it shall awaken thoughtful laughter' (33).

something of a fool? And yet in spite of that I defy **[6]** anyone to produce a passage in which Jane Austen expresses anything but delight at the folly of the inhabitants of her world. She has been accused of disliking John Thorpe, alone I believe among all her characters: and there is an intensity about her portraiture of that horsey undergraduate that is almost terrible: but on anxious reflexion I do not think Jane Austen hated him. Her observation of his appearance and manners is cool intellect, unclouded by any such passion of annoyance as that which blurs the portrait of Sir Willoughby Patterne.

Her world is a world of fools: and therefore in a sense you might call her a satirist. But nothing could be less true. The satirist is a flagellator, not an artist: the crudity of his metres and the carelessness of his style, traditional since Juvenal and before, reflect (like the tub of Diogenes) a hatred and contempt of his environment, a black and bitter blasphemy against the world's order, which may be good morals or bad, but simply is not art. The satirist lives at the very opposite pole of thought from a serene and delighted aesthetic vision of life like that which Jane Austen enjoyed. That, again, is what distinguishes her from Molière, another artist whose whole work falls into a comic view of life. Molière is a comedian *malgré lui*. He does not really find life funny, but uses a comic form half to conceal and half to express a very deep-lying melancholy and dissatisfaction. Molière's plays are not of a piece with his life: they are an **[7]** escape from it. He wrote to keep his mind off reality. Such a cleavage between life and art does not exist for Jane Austen. For her, art and life are one: her novels are simply her actual world as she sees it. Her imagination illuminates her characters precisely as it illuminated, for her, the people she met in Hampshire or at Bath. The whole of life unrolled itself before her eyes in the form of one of her own books, or an infinite succession of them; and the novels she wrote are only a continuation and partial record of the novel in which she lived. I do not mean that her work was what is nowadays called realistic.[9] When an unimaginative person records

---

[9] Collingwood was to take up the general question of artistic realism in *SM* 63: 'The artist as such does not know what the word reality means; that is to say, he does not perform the act which we call assertion or judgement. His apparent statements are not statements, for they state nothing; they are not expressions, for they express no thought. They do not express his imaginations, for they are his imaginations. What he imagines is simply those fantasies which compose the great work of art.'

the misunderstood facts which he half-sees, he calls it realism: what Jane Austen did was not to write down the way in which she saw her parents and friends behaving, but to see in their behaviour a whole world of subtle meanings and to make that world her home. That places her work in the rank of great art as opposed to minor art. Minor art is a dream, indulged because we can dominate it when we cannot dominate real life: great art is the domination of real life itself by our own understanding of it.[10] The minor novelist invents imaginary old men by compensation because he cannot fathom the soul of his flesh and blood uncles: the great novelist invents them as a direct continuation of his insight into his uncles' characters.

My contention that Jane Austen's unflinching attitude to art is the reflection of an unflinching attitude to life and in no sense a refuge from life is borne out by everything we know of her. [8] Charlotte Brontë complained of her work that it had no sentiment or poetry in it and in her sense of the words she was right.[11] Jane Austen was a healthy, vigorous woman who came of a healthy vigorous family, a family noted for its practical gifts and remarkable for its longevity. There was no sentiment, no airs and graces, in any of them. None of them had any anything the least like an artistic temperament, that gift which makes it so easy for its possessor to be a second-rate artist and so impossible to be a first-rate one. They were neither intellectual nor cultured above the average.

[10] Collingwood was to distinguish in *OPA* between imaginative creation as mere dreaming and dreaming which 'in creating a work of art we are doing with critical care and labour' (22); in *PA*, he identified 'a vulgar misconception, common in the nineteenth century, according to which the artist is a kind of dreamer or daydreamer, constructing in fancy a make-believe world which if it existed would be, at least in his own opinion, a better or more pleasant one than that in which we live' (138).

[11] Letter 341 (264) To G. H. Lewes, 18 Jan. 1848: 'What a strange lecture comes next in your letter! You say I must familiarise my mind with the fact that "Miss Austen is not a poetess, has no 'sentiment' " (you scornfully enclose the word in inverted commas), "no eloquence, none of the ravishing enthusiasm of poetry"; and then you add, I *must* "learn to acknowledge her as *one of the greatest artists, of the greatest painters of human character*, and one of the writers with the nicest sense of means to an end that ever lived." The last point only will I ever acknowledge. Can there be a great artist without poetry?' See *The Shakespeare Head Brontë*, ed. T. J. Wise and J. A. Symington, *The Brontës: their Lives and Friendships and Correspondence in Four Volumes*, ii. *1844–1849* (Oxford: Blackwell, 1932), 180.

Mr Austen had been a fellow of a College in his youth, and had been known in Oxford for his good looks and for his success and popularity in the office of Proctor: he married a daughter[12] of the then Master of Balliol and retired to a country living in Hampshire where his children were born. But these academic connexions, though they show him to have been an educated man, do not prove him anything very remarkable intellectually, in an age when fellows were many and their duties few: it was an age in which Samuel Johnson might still have complained of being fined 2d. for non-attendance at a lecture not worth 1d. Still, it meant that the little Austens grew up with a library in the house and a father whose interests extended to a wider sphere than his pigs and his parish. And you will notice in the novels that it is only the worst kind of men—the Mr Collinses and the John Thorpes— who do not read books as a matter of course and as a pleasure. [9] The children were remarkable, as a family, for their vitality and their practical gifts. Setting aside Jane, and a brother who died young at 50 odd, they all lived to a good old age. Two died at 73, one at 80, and one at 92:[13] the last after a long and distinguished naval career which ended as Admiral of the Fleet. Another brother went into the navy and also reached the rank of admiral: but he was cut short in the prime of life at 73. The careers of these two sailors give us a fair sample of the family character and the family vigour. It is the same vigour that vibrates in the pages of their sister's work. It is true she died early: some illness, we do not know what, carried her off at 40: but it would be a great mistake to fancy on that account that she was anything like an invalid. On the contrary, we know of her as tall, handsome, and active: given to country pursuits and long walks: untiring both in the energy of her body and the vivacity of her mind. There is no sign, in any of the records we have of her, of the morose and retiring habits or the melancholy disposition which we are apt to associate with the pursuit of letters. There is no sign that the great god Pan, in making an artist of her, found it necessary to cut the ties which bound her to the life of the world. She may have been a perfect artist, but she was none the less a perfectly human being.

---

[12] She was actually his niece. The detail is correct in Collingwood's later (undated) lecture on Jane Austen.

[13] Of the two admiral brothers, Charles died at 73 and Francis at 91.

[10] As we should expect from what I have said, she began writing early.[14] A writer in whom the working of the imagination was so direct and spontaneous could hardly have done otherwise. We know that she wrote great quantities of stories in her childhood,[15] and it is interesting in this age of infant prodigies to compare the childish notes of authentic genius with the knack, so often strangely developed in the very young, of turning out well-written stories. Our nurseries are full of Daisy Ashfords:[16] but there is all the difference between the light come and light go of an ordinary childish gift, which melts away at adolescence like the colours of the dawn, and a talent which weathers that crisis and rounds the cape of storms to reach the open sea of mature life.[17] Jane Austen's early work consisted largely of parody or burlesque of the popular literary styles. This is very rare in children. A child does not objectify literary style as a thing by itself: when it writes, it may write imitatively but only because it is unconscious of imitating and because the style of a favourite author has tinged its outlook on life. A child with any literary gift will react to styles with pleasure or distaste: but it will not reflect on this reaction in the way that is implied by parodying a style. In Jane Austen's early burlesques one sees the premonition of a quite exceptional sense of language and of literary form.

[11] This fits in with the almost incredible maturity of her first surviving work. *Pride and Prejudice* has so strong a backing for the title of Jane Austen's masterpiece that it is astonishing to reflect that it was written at the age of 21. For novel-writing is not like lyric poetry, in which the freshness of early youth often achieves a perfection never to be regained by the maturity of riper age. It is an art that requires, in an extraordinary degree, experience both of writing and of living, and the novels of very young people seldom

[14] The following discussion of Jane Austen's early efforts can be compared with other Collingwoodian reflections on creativity in children and primitive peoples in *OPA* and *PA*. Cf. also LPA, fo. 25, below. The vital distinction between the creativity of children and that of primitive man is a leading hypothesis of the folktale MS, esp. FT3.

[15] Struck out in pencil: 'and it would be interesting in this age of infant prodigies if we could rediscover some of them to set beside our Daisy Ashfords for comparison. I suspect that Jane's earliest efforts were not wholly unlike *The Young Visiters*'.

[16] Daisy Ashford wrote *The Young Visiters: Or, Mr. Salteena's Plan* at the age of 9 in 1890. The novel was published by Chatto & Windus in 1919.

[17] Struck out: 'We know only that her early work was already strongly marked by her comic vein, and'. [Ends.]

deserve any higher epithet than promising. But *Pride and Prejudice* is not promise: it is performance. I have not had the time to conduct a statistical inquiry into the question whether any other so obvious a masterpiece in the novel-writer's art has been composed at the age of 21; but I rather doubt it.

Yet on close inspection there are marks of youth in the book. In comparison with *Emma*, it has a certain thinness of texture and here and there a certain lack of coherence. The opening is unsurpassed. The picture of the Bennet family is in the great style, and the characters of its members are worked out with a completeness and solidity that are altogether astonishing. Mr Bennet, I should venture to maintain, is the real hero, the central figure, of the book. Nothing else in it comes quite up to the coherence and decision with which his subtle character is drawn. He is a clever man, witty [12] and studious, with a capacity for affection and a good deal of charm, who has sunk under the influence of a silly wife and a dull country existence into a state of disappointed and apathetic indolence, his wit turned to a sometimes brutal sarcasm and his affection soured into contempt. The way in which this degrading of his character is shown, and the obvious tracing of it back to his living with a woman whom he cannot help despising, is one of the most masterly things in fiction: especially as nothing whatever is said about it by the author, and it emerges solely from the incidents and dialogue. The only person he respects is Elizabeth, who inherits his wit and charm and sarcasm, and might in similar circumstances degenerate into a similar bitterness. Hence—on one of the very rare occasions when Mr Bennet allows himself to be really moved—when he hears that Elizabeth is to marry Mr Darcy though, as he thinks, she dislikes and despises him—he says:

I know your disposition, Lizzy. I know that you could be neither happy nor respectable, unless you truly esteemed your husband; unless you looked up to him as a superior. Your lively talents would place you in the greatest danger in an unequal marriage. You could scarcely escape discredit and misery. My child, let me not have the grief of seeing *you* unable to respect your partner in life. You know not what you are about.[18]

[13] But the serious mood only lasts a minute: and it is the only occasion on which Mr Bennet ever gave himself away. In general

---

[18] *Pride and Prejudice: A Novel in Three Volumes, By the Author of 'Sense and Sensibility'* (London: T. Egerton, 1813), iii, ch. 17, 297–8.

we find him simply giving free reign to his malicious humour, at
the expense of anybody and everybody: a form of self-indulgence
in which he is only allowed to proceed by reason of the deterioration in his character of which I have spoken. This turn of malice,
fostered by the weaknesses of his wife and his younger daughters,
found a singularly happy butt in Mr Collins. Pardon me if I recall
to your minds the introduction of that gentleman into the book.[19]
How well Mr Bennet's hopes were justified by the event we all
know: and his parting shot at the end of everything, when Elizabeth and Mr. Darcy were engaged in spite of all Lady Catherine de
Bourgh could do, was equally characteristic:

> Dear Sir,
> I must trouble you once more for congratulations. Elizabeth will soon be
> the wife of Mr Darcy. Console Lady Catherine as well as you can. But, if
> I were you, I would stand by the nephew: he has more to give. Yours
> sincerely etc.[20]

I would fain linger over Mr Collins. As a fool, he yields to no one,
not even Sir Andrew Aguecheek, to whom he almost deserves to be
related.[21] **[14]** The later parts are not all so good. The change of
scene to Kent and Derbyshire breaks the thread: and the narrative
only recovers its swing when Elizabeth gets back to Hertfordshire.
But once there the plot develops with splendid inevitability and
turns on that consummate scene, the attempted browbeating of
Elizabeth by the formidable dowager.[22]

---

[19] Collingwood cites *Pride and Prejudice*, first with deleted reference 'vol. I,
p. 79–83', and then 'pp. 53–56'.

[20] *Pride and Prejudice* (1813), iii, ch. 18, 311.

[21] Struck out: 'Allow me to give you a passage from his exquisite attempt to court
Elizabeth.' Collingwood refers to *Pride and Prejudice* 'I, pp. 137–140' and 'pp.
94–96' (but deletes the references). In the 3-vol. 1813 edn. of *Pride and Prejudice*,
the courtship scene occurs in vol. i, ch. 19, 243–54. A transition from the discussion
of characters to the topic of narrative is deleted opposite fo. 14: 'I have said that one
supreme mark of Jane Austen's genius was her power of depicting fools: but that,
precious though it is, is not the greatest proof of her art. I think Aristotle says that
the plot of a drama counts for more than its character-drawing; and it is certainly
true that the greatest novelists are those who can tell a story. A second-rate writer
can make his characters come to life, but only the first-rate can put together a story
which moves by its own inner necessity in such a way that the tiniest incident
contributes its whole weight to the'. [Ends.]

[22] *Pride and Prejudice* (1813), iii, ch. 14, 239–57. Collingwood inserts a reference
to *Pride and Prejudice*, '313–318'.

To this scene all the elements of the book contribute. It is the
direct effect of Mr Collins's servile garrulity, fed by a chain of
gossip as inevitable as the law of gravitation: and it is the direct
cause, when reported by Lady Catherine to Darcy, of his seeing
that the moment was favourable for renewing his suit to Elizabeth,
his coming hastily from London, and his being accepted. The
whole thing makes a dénouement of quite exceptional brilliance,
where nothing is wasted and nothing is accidental.[23]

I wish I could say something of all the six great novels, but time
forbids, and I must pick and choose. *Sense and Sensibility* is merely
a new version of an immature work; *Northanger Abbey* is a youthful
frolic, a rag novel, raised to a higher power but still not serious
work; *Mansfield Park* is laboured and lacks spontaneity. And

---

[23] A struck-out section of the lecture—probably cut for reasons of time—then
discusses *Northanger Abbey*: 'I am not going to describe all the immortal six novels.
Sense and Sensibility I shall omit altogether, because it is after all only a new version
of an immature work and does not stand in the first rank: *Mansfield Park*, because it
is an example of a manner sufficiently shown elsewhere: and *Persuasion* because, in
spite of its subtle charm and the very beautiful work it contains, it does show signs
of the illness under which it was written. I pass to that curious [15] and piquant
mixture, *Northanger Abbey*. The special interest here is the relic of Jane Austen's
early habit of writing parodies. The plot of the book, so far as it has a plot, is built
round the figure of Catherine Morland, a Don Quixote in petticoats whose intellect,
naturally feeble, has been so far undermined by a long course of blood and thunder
novels that she looks upon real life as a mask hiding Heaven knows what deeds of
darkness and skeletons in cupboards. She is a country-bred child, taken by friends
at the age of seventeen to stay in Bath. Mrs Allen, her chaperone, is one of Jane
Austen's best silly old women and the unspeakable friends she makes are evidently
drawn from the real life of Bath. [*Northanger Abbey*, 18–21]. With Isabella Thorpe,
one of these exquisite creatures, she discusses literature and life—['23–25']. The
Thorpe family, especially Isabella and the egregious John, took up Catherine very
warmly. ['44–48']. The Tilney brother and sister, however, with their old father
General Tilney, were a superior attraction, and finally invited Catherine to stay
with them at Northanger Abbey. The burlesque business now gets the upper hand,
and Catherine goes into raptures in the search for secret passages, skeletons, and so
forth, a search which leads to various entertaining [16] indiscretions including a
theory that General Tilney murdered his wife. The plot would now begin to peter
out, had not the General been roused by slanders circulated by John Thorpe to
expel Catherine and send her home ignominiously, an act which of course could
only be expiated by Henry's following her hot-foot and proposing marriage to her
out of hand. The plot is slender: it has none of the solid construction of *Pride and
Prejudice*: but the richness and felicity of the rambling detail is unequalled, and the
comparatively bald patches which one sees here and there in the earlier work are
quite absent.'

Persuasion is overcast by the shadow of its author's last illness, which has sadly chilled the vivacity of her writing. There remains *Emma*, which has every merit of the others and none of their defects. It has the vividness, the passion of *Sense and Sensibility*, the rich detail and exuberance of *Northanger Abbey*, and the maturity of *Persuasion*; and its descriptions of festivities even surpass those of *Mansfield Park*. Above all, it has the solidity of structure which I have praised in *Pride and Prejudice*, and it has it in an even higher degree. If there is anything in the old-fashioned idea that the first duty of a story-teller is to tell a story, then *Emma* is one of the prime treasures of literature; for a story so convincing and inevitable has seldom been told.[24]

[16] The book opens, like *Pride and Prejudice*, with a domestic prologue. Emma and her father are discovered in front of their fire discussing the late marriage of their governess.

To them enter Mr Knightley.[25]

The subsequent conversation, as in *Pride and Prejudice*, gives us a perfectly definite dramatic expression of their characters and explains their situations relatively to their neighbours: Mr Weston, Mr Elton the bachelor parson, and the rest. The action begins by Emma's adopting as an intimate friend Harriet Smith, 'the natural daughter of somebody',[26] and [17] a parlour boarder at Mrs Goddard's school: and trying to wean her affections from a farmer, to bestow them more suitably on—say—Mr Elton. Mr Elton however misunderstands the drift of Emma's intentions so far as to fall in love with the wrong girl and propose to Emma herself, in an unforgettable scene.[27]

As a dramatic effect, that is richer and more complex than anything in *Pride and Prejudice*: there are more elements held together, not merely, as in the great scenes of the earlier book, a clash of two personalities. Where *Pride and Prejudice* is modelled in relief, this is modelling in the round.

But Mr Elton very soon consoled himself with the smiles of the rich Augusta Hawkins, of Bristol, whom before long he brought back as his bride. The impression she made is duly recorded.[28]

---

[24] This whole paragraph is inserted opposite fo. 14.
[25] The references given parenthetically by Collingwood at this point are to '5–6'.
[26] *Emma*, i, ch. 3.
[27] Referenced parenthetically by Collingwood as '114–118'.
[28] Referenced parenthetically by Collingwood as '242–245'.

The whole book is rich in detail of this kind: in characters drawn dramatically by their own speeches in a way, I think, never surpassed and very seldom equalled in literature. But I must not weary you by dragging out my analysis further. I only wish to say that *Emma* has a plot of extraordinarily delicate and clear structure. The plot consists of the convergence of Emma's own affections upon **[18]** Mr Knightley through a progressive chain of misunderstandings and éclaircissements: in each case the éclaircissement coming about by a recoil of Emma's own action upon her protégée Harriet Smith. She sets out to shape Harriet's life, in which she fails entirely, for after a series of false starts initiated by Emma, Harriet at last simply reverts to her original farmer love. But in attempting to mould Harriet's destiny Emma moulds her own. By trying to make Harriet marry Elton she draws Elton's attention upon herself and on the rebound he marries Mrs Elton whose vulgar obtuseness shocks Emma into a clearer vision of her own intimacy with Knightley:[29] in the mean time she fancies herself in love with Frank Churchill, but in a half-hearted and frivolous way which leads in fact (this one of the subtlest strokes in all the Austenian psychology) to her putting forward her protégée in her own place and trying to make a match between Harriet and Churchill. But this she does so discreetly that Harriet, mistaking her meaning, obligingly falls in love with—Mr Knightley. And when it comes out that Churchill has all along been engaged to Jane Fairfax, two things happen. First, Emma discovers Harriet's present passion: secondly, Knightley, fearing that Emma loves Churchill, comes as her oldest friend to offer what solace he can. May I trespass on your forbearance to give you a sample of one of these scenes?[30]

[19] This paper has already been too long, and I shall not make it any longer. I only ask your pardon for having made it as long as this: and my apology must be that here in Oxford, where Jane Austen has never lacked a succession of admirers to worship her this side of idolatry, and to agree with my estimate of her as the most perfect of all novelists, it can hardly be possible to praise her too highly or too long.

[29] A reference to 'p. 260' is inserted in square brackets at this point.
[30] The reference given by Collingwood is to '364–368'.

JANE AUSTEN (?1934)

There are times in history when the powers that preside over the
birth of human beings seem bent upon squandering, in a brief riot
of prodigality, all the store of genius which in other ages they
would have frugally spread over centuries. At such times the
portents which we call great men, the bright dynasts that, shining
in the ether of time, bring winter and summer to mortals, appear,
astronomically speaking, in conjunction; grouped in astonishing
constellations, their radiance produces a cumulative effect, and the
single notes sung by the spirits of their several spheres unite in a
harmony whose unique character serves to define once for all the
spirit of the time.

Such a prodigality of genius visited the earth a hundred and fifty
years ago, in what may be called the Napoleonic Age. There were
great men before Napoleon; but the great men of the eighteenth
century were either unrecognized in their day, because the world was
not worthy of them, or else they show a lack of that perfect balance
between the form and the matter of their work which masks a truly
great age. The greatest of them all, John Sebastian Bach, had a
vocabulary and a style only equalled in greatness by the ideas that
he expressed: but his generation was unaware of his greatness. The
men of recognized genius, like Pope, Voltaire, Hume, Gibbon, Kant,
achieved either a perfect form with a trivial content, as in Voltaire
and Pope, or a massive content left in formal chaos, as in Kant or Dr
Johnson. In the most curious case of all, that of Goethe, the two faults
succeed one another in an almost rhythmical alternation.

[2] This lack of equilibrium between form and matter was
overcome by a group of extraordinary people who were all born
within a few years of Napoleon. Napoleon himself, in the world's
eye the most conspicuous of all, because the politician of the group,
the exponent of that architectonic science to which all others
are subordinate, was born in 1769 and stands side by side
with Julius Caesar and Alexander as a person who has perfectly

Bodleian Library Collingwood Papers, dep. 17/3. For evidence relating to the
estimated composition date of this MS see the final footnote.

combined the technique of statecraft and war with a content worthy of the form: a person who knew not only *how*, but *why*, to fight battles. In the following year, 1770, Beethoven was born; and Beethoven stands out as the only person known to us in history who has written music of the first rank whose inspiration has been derived from a general and profound view of human life as a whole. This is why Beethoven's music sounds different from other people's, sounds as if it were not music at all but some urgent and revolutionary gospel preached in a language we do not quite understand. Beethoven is a great musician, but he is also and primarily a great man writing music. The year 1770 also saw the birth of Hegel, the Napoleon of philosophy: the only man since Aristotle who has succeeded in focusing human knowledge into a single field and detecting the rhythm of its universal pulse. Less mighty than these three, but barely below them come Wordsworth and Turner, the great twin interpreters of English scenery, born in 1770 and 1775; Sir Walter Scott, who combined a Wordsworthian insight into peasant life with a romantic view of national history, in 1772; Niebuhr, the founder of modern historical research, in 1776.[1] Beethoven, Hegel, and the men of their generation, as it were in an international partnership, created the nineteenth century; they were the fathers of that age and the grandfathers of our own; and from their work begins everything that, in contradistinction to the old times of the seventeenth and eighteenth centuries, we call modern.

[3] One of the curious things about the modern or post-Napoleonic world is that it has no drama. It has a feeble and artificial reflexion of the drama that belonged to the previous period: Shakespeare and Racine,[2] whose spiritual progeny were active far into the eighteenth century, left no successors in the new age, and today the play is an extinct form of literature. Our few surviving playwrights are either tractarians or novelists, who have made use of the stage as an accidental medium of expression. If anyone doubts this, let him try to discover a single great play written in the nineteenth century. Instead, the nineteenth century

---

[1] Barthold Georg Niebuhr (1776–1831). Collingwood gives his date of birth as 1766. As a specialist in the field, Collingwood would have been familiar with Niebuhr's *Lectures on Roman History*, tr. H. M. Chepmel and F. Demmler, 3 vols. (London: Chatto & Windus, 1875).

[2] The name of 'Corneille' is struck out and 'Racine' substituted.

wrote novels. The novel differs from the play by being, as it were, less epigrammatic: less content to show a single action in a vivid light and a simplified form, and more anxious to delve into the secrets of personality. The play takes a sample of life and concentrates on that: it substitutes an anecdote for a history. The novel protests against the formalism of the play: a deepening interest in human character demands a new and more flexible form, adequate to the new content: and this is why the eighteenth century gradually turned from drama to fiction.

Now the Napoleon of fiction is Jane Austen. Precisely as the orchestral symphony, which before Beethoven is archaic and experimental, struggling to work out a convention for a new form of composition, acquires with Beethoven a finished technique and a content of ideas adequate to its form, so, with Jane Austen, the novel, which had hitherto been a mere succession of experiments towards a new literary form, reaches maturity and [4] discovers a structure adequate to express the novelist's entire experience of life. And very much as all subsequent symphonies have been modelled on the style of Beethoven, so all subsequent novels have been constructed according to the principles of Jane Austen; the most successful ones, in either case, being those in which the author has been most able to live up to his model.

Miss Austen was of the generation of Napoleon; like Turner, she was born in 1775. In passing, I would observe that Charles Lamb was born in the same year, and that Lamb did for the essay what Miss Austen did for the novel: he at once perfected its formal structure and gave it something to say which was precisely adequate to that form, in curious contrast with the sometimes chaotic and sometimes empty essay-style of, say, the *Spectator*. Had the essay been as vital and valuable a literary form as the novel, Lamb would have been as important a figure in history as Miss Austen. But in point of fact the essay had no real future in the nineteenth century, which was not an age of introspection: and the essay is essentially an introspective form.

Genius is not produced *in vacuo*; on the contrary, it never arises except in social surroundings so exquisitely fitted to produce it that its voice seems almost the impersonal voice of these surroundings themselves. Jane Austen grew out of a soil now long ago exhausted, the deep and fertile soil of English middle-class country life. Her father was fellow of an Oxford college when fellows had time to improve their minds, if they wished to improve them, and country livings to support their bodies when, tired of improving their minds, they resolved to marry. The Oxford of Gibbon's [5] undergraduate days and of the succeeding generation was not perfect; in some ways it was worse than the Oxford of today; but it had one great merit: it was an integral part of a social system, a kind of heart which circulated intellectual blood through the whole country. The system of unmarried fellows maintained a constant supply of ex-fellows of Colleges available for country livings, and this made the English country parsonage what it has now ceased to be—the nursery of most of the best talent in England. So when George Austen retired to a living near Basingstoke after marrying a niece of the Master of Balliol,[3] his vicarage became what Henry Crawford in *Mansfield Park* said Thornton Lacey vicarage would be when Edmund Bertram went there—'the residence of a man of education, taste, modern manners, good connections'.[4] At Steventon, close to the Roman road that comes north from Winchester, a family of seven little Austens grew up in surroundings healthy for body and mind, with plenty to read, plenty to do, and a sufficiency of people to talk to. Here among the peaceful curves of the chalk downs Jane Austen, says a critic, had a 'fitting nursing-ground for that delicate genius which in the noise and bustle of town life might easily have been dazed into helpless silence'.[5] I doubt if the critic has lived in a country house with seven healthy children, and I do not see Jane dazed into helpless silence by anything short of a boiler-factory; but Steventon certainly did form her mind, not so much by its rural quiet, whatever that means, as by the very definite atmosphere of self-contained and industrious activity which country life alone can produce. A family of intelligent children in a remote country place must invent its own amusements, and thus acquires a kind of [6] corporate personality which gives each of its members the sense of expressing something wider than himself. Jane Austen's novels are largely made up of gossip: but its

[3] The information here is correct. In JA1 (1921), Collingwood had mistakenly referred to Jane Austen's mother as the 'daughter' of the Master of Balliol.

[4] *Mansfield Park*, ch. 25.

[5] This quotation remains untraced: it does not appear in James Edward Austen-Leigh's *A Memoir of Jane Austen* (London: Richard Bentley & Son, 1871), or in the many other critical accounts of Steventon's influence upon the young Jane Austen appearing from the turn of the century to *c*.1934.

peculiarity is that it is gossip seen from a point of view which raises it to the level of drama: and this faculty of seeing gossip as drama was developed, I conjecture, in the nursery of Steventon Vicarage.

It is somewhat characteristic of the Napoleonic age that we know nothing of Jane Austen's sentimental or inner life. In history she appears simply as a healthy, tall, strapping, handsome woman, keenly interested in everybody's affairs, enjoying life to the full, never at a loss for a repartee and never ailing until she contracted the illness of which she died. The streak of disease or insanity that a later generation loved to find in the pedigree of genius never appeared in the Austen family; her two admiral brothers lived respectively to 75 and 90,[6] and longevity was as characteristic of the family as good looks. The artist of the classical tradition in whom form and content are perfectly balanced is not a romantic figure; he is inclined to eat well and sleep well and to be on good terms with life. It is the artist whose art is one-sided and incapable of floating on an even keel, that provides the biographer with spicy material. About Jane Austen biography has nothing to say, except to relate her visits to friends, her changes of residence, and her unidentified last illness; she went about *incognito*, the greatest living novelist disguised as a very ordinary English lady. A life as dull as that of Shakespeare, or Sophocles, or Virgil, or any of the greatest classical artists.

So much for biography. It remains to speak of her writing. She began early. A talent like hers, with its peculiar balance, could do no otherwise. Many able writers begin writing late; but that is because they are driven into an art whose form does not come natural to them by something which they want to express: the content [7] takes precedence of the form and balance is never achieved. Thus arises the amorphous music of a Wagner or the crudely constructed novels of a William De Morgan.[7] Jane Austen was writing busily in the nursery. Plenty of children do that; it is common form in country nurseries where the children are at all intelligent. Do town-bred children do it? I have never known a case. But though these childish efforts are often surprisingly

[6] See JA1, n 13.
[7] William Frend De Morgan (1839–1917), author of *When Ghost Meets Ghost* (1908), *It Can Never Happen Again* (1909), and *A Likely Story* (1911). De Morgan also illustrated collections of fairy tales by Mary Augusta Morgan. See e.g. *On a Pincushion and Other Fairy Tales* (London: Seeley, Jackson & Halliday, 1876).

clever, they are almost always on the lower side of the line that
divides nature from art. The child tells the story like that because
that is how the story comes into its head: it is an immediate and
unreflective reaction to stimulus, imitative very often of what the
child has read, but imitating quite naïvely, without criticizing what
it imitates.[8] Now the odd thing about Jane Austen's nursery output
is that instead of imitating she parodies. Her heroines languish and
faint not because she imagines real young ladies do so, but because
she regards the languishing and fainting heroine of the romantic
novel as a delightfully funny figure, a figure to be treated ironically. And so we find in *Love and Friendship*[9] the whole apparatus of
the romantic novel—the innocent country-bred heroine, the interesting stranger arriving by night, the elopement, the accident to
the coach, the swoon, and all the rest of it—treated as a joke whose
point is that the author, for all her tender years, is making fun of
the literary methods and conventions of eighteenth-century fiction. I have some curiosity in children's writings, and have seen
many interesting and charming specimens; but I have never found
any other case of a child indulging in sustained and deliberate
parody. This fact alone, if properly understood, would place Jane
Austen by herself as a person who before she put her hair up had
arrived instinctively **[8]** at a conception of literary technique far in
advance of the professional practice of her time. Even so might a
Napoleon playing with tin soldiers have made fun of eighteenth-
century tactics.

Nothing but this extraordinary precocity of judgement, the fruit
of a naturally balanced mind, could have permitted a girl of 20 to
write *Pride and Prejudice*. I am not referring to the wit, or the
character-drawing, or the polished style of that novel: I am referring to its solidity of structure and the absolute harmony between
the story told and the method of telling it. When you travel
through the history of the eighteenth-century novel, and give all
the weight you can to the solidity of Fielding, the satire of Smol-
lett, the humour of Sterne, and the delicacy of Richardson, to reach

[8] Cf. LPA, fo. 23.
[9] Usually cited as *Love and Freindship* (sic) (1790). The parodic tale is told in
epistolary form as a sequence of letters addressed mainly from the narrator, Laura,
to Marianne. See *Love and Freindship and Other Early Works*, with a Preface by
G. K. Chesterton (London: Chatto & Windus, 1922). The work is 'here published
for the first time' (p. ix).

Pride and Prejudice is like coming out of a tunnel: here at last you find somebody who can write, somebody who can lift in one hand all the mass of technical difficulties with which her predecessors have been struggling in vain: and that somebody a village girl of 20.

I am not saying that *Pride and Prejudice* is perfect. It is not: it is hesitating in many places, and a shade thin throughout, when you judge it by the standard of her later work; and above all, it lacks unity. The narrative is broken by episodes connected especially with a defective unity of place: the journey to Derbyshire is out of key, and the key is subsequently never quite recovered. And in the depiction of character there is genuine exaggeration: the vulgarity of the Bennets, the pride of Darcy, the selfishness of the Bingley sisters, and the arrogance of Lady Catherine, are all a little over-drawn, and I cannot acquit Mr Collins of improbability. The author is getting her whole picture a shade out of key in an uneasy anxiety to make each colour tell: every feature is a little exaggerated, and the whole **[9]** in consequence lacks breadth. I should like to read you a passage or two to illustrate this point.[10]

Or take the description of the ball at Netherfield, where Elizabeth thought that 'had her family made an agreement to expose themselves as much as they could during the evening, it would have been impossible for them to play their parts with more spirit, or finer success'.[11] The function of this ball in the story is to make Darcy so disgusted with the Bennet family that he forced Bingley to leave Netherfield in order to escape falling in love with Jane Bennet; but in order to disgust Mr Darcy it was not necessary for Mrs Bennet to misbehave nearly so grossly as she did. At supper, you remember, Mrs Bennet talked to her neighbour Lady Lucas freely, openly, and of nothing else but her expectation that Jane would soon be married to Mr Bingley. Elizabeth, perceiving that she was overheard by Mr Darcy, tried to stop her: but was only scolded for her pains. 'What is Mr Darcy to me, pray, that I should be afraid of him? I am sure we owe him no such particular civility as to be obliged to say nothing *he* may not like to hear.'[12] After this,

---

[10] Collingwood inserts a parenthetical reference to 'pp. 56–60' and to 'Ch. XIII (57–60)' at this point.

[11] *Pride and Prejudice: A Novel in Three Volumes, By the Author of 'Sense and Sensibility'* (London: T. Egerton, 1813), i, ch. 18, 235–6.

[12] *Pride and Prejudice*, i, ch. 18, 230.

one is hardly surprised that the expression on Mr Darcy's face
changed gradually from indignant contempt to a composed and
steady gravity, and that in a few days he had removed his friend
from the neighbourhood of such an intolerable family. But in order
to make his motive for doing so both clear and reasonable, the
author has grossly overdrawn Mrs Bennet's vulgarity and silliness—overdrawn it to such an extent as to damage her own plot,
for one can no longer really believe in Mrs Bennet as the mother of
the refined Jane and the witty Elizabeth. Yet notice, even here,
how the faults are good faults. The overdrawing of character is
done not just [10] idly or wantonly, but as it were diagrammatic-
ally, to emphasize the lines of force which hold the plot together.
And the relation between the members of the Bennet family is
subtle even in its exaggerations: the clever and sensitive Mr Bennet, a little too clever, inclined to relapse into epigram where action
is needed, has married a silly woman for her looks; the eldest
daughter has his refinement and her beauty; the second his wit
and her fine eyes; in the third his bookishness and her silliness have
combined into a kind of dull pedantry, and the two youngest are
simply brainless flirts. Every element in the character of the children is accurately to be accounted for in the parents. Compare that
with the genealogical crudity of Fielding, and you see how the
study of human nature has advanced in half a century.

But what I want especially to lay stress upon in *Pride and
Prejudice* is the texture of the plot. Not a single incident is out
of place or wasted with regard to the development of the story.
Mr Collins's connexion with the Bennets is one reason for Darcy's
disgust with the family: but it is also the reason for Elizabeth's visit
to Mr Collins's rectory, where Darcy, staying with his aunt Lady
Catherine, inevitably meets her again and becomes fatally conscious of her attractions. Her rejection of his courtship is equally
inevitable, and the resulting shock to his pride—as if the beggar
maid had turned down king Cophetua[13]—is a crucial point in the
history of his character and a first lesson in humility: while at the
same time his defence of himself against her accusations plays a

[13] The allusion is to the song 'King Cophetua' (London, 1876) composed by
Charles George Cotsford Dick, with words by Alfred Lord Tennyson. See 'The
Beggar Maid', in *Poems* (1842). Tennyson's poem alludes to Shakespeare's *Romeo
and Juliet*, 2. 1. 13–14. Edward Burne-Jones's painting of *King Cophetua and the
Beggar Maid* was exhibited in 1884.

parallel part in her, so [11] that this unsuccessful piece of love-making has the result of turning both the chief characters into a new path, along two different lines that are bound to meet again because each is now ashamed of himself and respectful towards the other. The story now develops through various backwaters so as to permit this new double tendency to work itself out: and circumstances precipitate it in the most ingenious way. Nothing in the book is more ironically exquisite than the visit of Lady Catherine to Elizabeth, intended to extort from her a promise never to marry Darcy. Lady Catherine takes this step as a result of idle gossip, which, like so much idle gossip, is better founded than it deserves to be; and finds to her surprise that Elizabeth refuses the promise. The irony lies in the fact that this very refusal, coming to the ears of Darcy, is the first thing that gives him the idea of renewing his addresses to Elizabeth, this time successfully. Lady Catherine has thrown them together precisely by the steps she took to keep them apart.

The interview between Lady Catherine and Elizabeth deserves an extract.[14]

This again is exaggerated. The author is too eager to give Elizabeth an annihilating moral victory over Lady Catherine: the old lady is too rude, too stupid, too conceited; the young one too firm, too spirited, too devastatingly ready in repartee. Yet with these faults, the scene is still masterly, as a scene, equal to anything in any earlier novel; and in its structural purpose and effect hardly short of sublime. Yet this masterpiece was not allowed to burst on the astonished gaze of the world: the publisher to whom the author's father offered it refused even to see the MS, and the book was not printed till 1813, four years before the author's [12] death.

I have dwelt on *Pride and Prejudice* because it reveals in such a startling manner the quality of Jane Austen's genius in its first phase. As soon as it was finished, she took up an early work called *Eleanor and Marianne*, written in the Richardsonian style as a sequence of letters, and recast it into the form which she had so triumphantly discovered. *Sense and Sensibility*, which is the name of the rewritten story, is less mature then *Pride and Prejudice*,

---

[14] At this point Collingwood refers parenthetically to '341–347'. The interview appears in *Pride and Prejudice* (1813), iii, ch. 14, 239–57.

though it contains a great deal of brilliant writing. In no book are Miss Austen's powers of satire more congenially employed; but the plot is artificial, and the heroine Marianne is a relic of the pre-Austenian romantic novel—a conventional figure chiefly made up of hypersensitive feelings, who is only restrained from swooning by Miss Austen's unconquerable aversion from that ladylike habit. Yet for good rich pictures of thoroughly human vulgarity *Sense and Sensibility* would be hard to beat. By the time she was 23, Miss Austen had finished her third complete novel, *Northanger Abbey*. Of all her books, *Northanger* is the best fun; it is largely burlesque, partly aimed at the gruesome novels of the *Mystery of Udolpho* school,[15] which were to that age what crime-novels are to this, and partly devoted to a highly ironical description of society at Bath. The idea of taking as heroine an exceedingly ordinary little girl, whose head is so turned by blood and thunder fiction that when invited to stay at Northanger she cannot refrain from believing that her elderly host has murdered his wife, is in the author's happiest style; and the creditable thing is that Catherine Morland continues to be not only a very good joke but a perfectly real character. The handling of the whole thing is **[13]** easier and more effortless than in *Pride and Prejudice*; the author is taking it more in her stride, setting herself a less ambitious task and performing it with far less trouble.

But at this point, in 1798, she stopped writing altogether for a dozen years. *Sense and Sensibility* was published, but *Pride and Prejudice* languished in manuscript and *Northanger*, sold for £10 to a Bath bookseller, had gone no further towards publication and was actually not printed till after Miss Austen's death. I do not think it was the disappointment of literary ambitions that stopped her writing at 23. She had very little of that kind of ambition that requires to be fed on public notice; her early training had rendered her more sensitive to the opinion of her family than to that of the world, and we find her keenly interested in her brothers' opinions of her books but singularly unmoved by fame, when at last that came her way. The reasons for her silence between 1798 and 1811 were domestic. In 1801 her family moved to Bath, and she was thereafter much taken up with care of her parents till 1809, when

---

[15] Ann Radcliffe, *The Mysteries of Udolpho: A Romance*, 2nd edn., 4 vols. (London: G. G. and J. Robinson, 1794).

after her father's death she settled with her mother and sister at Chawton, not far from her first home. It may have been the return to the familiar Hampshire downs that led her to begin writing again; in any case, between 1811 and 1816, she now wrote three other books. The first of this batch, *Mansfield Park*, is regarded by many as her best. To me, such a judgment can only indicate a blindness to all her highest merits. The narrative is brilliantly and firmly drawn, but the plot and characters are not at her highest level. The characters of Fanny Price and Edmund Bertram are praiseworthy but dull; both have admirable principles, warm hearts, and all the domestic virtues, but I [14] cannot help thinking that Miss Austen has depicted them under the quite mistaken idea that, being no longer young, she must now be serious and choose characters whom she will not be forced to laugh at. The result is unfortunate; and the best parts of the book are the most comic, for instance the descriptions of the theatrical rehearsals at Mansfield and of the sordid but jolly Price household at Portsmouth. If anybody seriously thinks *Mansfield Park* up to Jane Austen's standard, let me remind him that all the latter part of the main plot develops off the stage and is merely reported in letters, a clear sign that the author has not a firm enough grasp on the development to place it before our eyes. A Richardson can be forgiven for such weakness; not a Jane Austen.

In the second novel of this series she recovered her form and brilliantly surpassed everything she had yet done. If novels are to be judged as novels, on their strictly literary merits, judged as pieces of construction and not as stimulants to lachrymatory glands or the philanthropic sentiments or the religious consciousness, then there is some ground for arguing that *Emma* is the best novel ever written. It is not its author's most popular work: that is because the average English reader neither knows nor cares when a book is well written, but goes to fiction only for sympathetic characters, and finds that he is not quite sure whether he likes Emma Woodhouse. And the English highbrow is pursued by an even deadlier heresy than the cult of the sympathetic character: I mean the cult of a wide outlook. Miss Austen says nothing about international affairs, nothing about the Napoleonic Wars, nothing about the Industrial Revolution, nothing about slums and millhands and Tom Paine and the Rights of Man: therefore, say the [15] highbrows, she has a narrow middle-class provincial outlook, moves in a commonplace and trivial circle of ideas, and is therefore a far worse writer than Dickens with his warm sympathy for the oppressed or Wells with his profound insight into social and philosophical problems. The long ears and the loud braying of this school of critics may be found wherever cant and claptrap are held in honour: and even people who see that sympathy for the poor and philosophical insight are different from literary genius are sometimes tempted to apologize for a Jane Austen because she doesn't write about larger and more imposing things—to placate the long-eared critics by a half-hearted echo of their braying. Nothing can be less wise or necessary. Grant that Dickens has been chiefly popular not because of his literary merits, but because of his good heart; grant that Scott has been chiefly admired for his worst work, by a public more interested in knights and crusaders than in writing; grant that the Browning Society made its living by wholly ignoring Browning's literary gifts and fastening exclusively on his imaginary philosophy; yet after all this is said and done, Jane Austen is left, a test case of pure literary genius: anyone who admires her must admire her on literary grounds, for with the austerity of the highest genius she makes no other appeal: she has no meretricious arts, she asks nothing from anyone except the appreciation of her purely literary qualities; and if on irrelevant grounds someone chooses to deny these qualities, one can only say in the immortal words of Thomas Ingoldsby: 'No doubt he's a very respectable man, but I can't say much for his taste.'[16]

[16] *Emma* begins in front of the fire in Mr Woodhouse's drawing room on the evening of the governess's wedding.[17] To them enter Mr Knightley.[18] The scene being thus set, the action begins: Emma chooses to take up and befriend Harriet Smith, a pretty parlour-boarder in a neighbouring school, and tries to

---

[16] See Richard Harris Barham, *The Ingoldsby Legends, or, Mirth and Marvels, by Thomas Ingoldsby*, pseud., 2nd ser, 5th edn. (London: Richard Bentley, 1852). From the verses spoken to his driver by the visitor to the ruins in 'Netley Abbey. A Legend of Hampshire': 'Be so good as to say / That a Visitor, whom you drove over one day, / Was exceedingly angry, and very much scandalized, / Finding these beautiful ruins so Vandalized, / And thus of their owner to speak began, / As he ordered you home in haste, "NO DOUBT HE'S A VERY RESPECTABLE MAN, / But—*I can't say much for his taste*"' (117).

[17] Collingwood inserts the reference in parentheses 'E p. 3–4'.

[18] In parentheses 'E 5–6'.

marry her off to the vicar, Mr Elton. But Mr Elton, misunderstanding her manœuvres, concludes that he is to fall in love with
Emma herself, and does so heartily.[19]

Compare this with *Pride and Prejudice*; it has gained immensely
in solidity, in balance, in justice; the parts are played without the
least exaggeration; the author never raises her voice to make her
effects. Or take the scene in which Mrs Elton, whom the vicar has
married on the rebound after being refused by Emma, pays her
first call on the Woodhouses.[20]

In *Emma*, as in *Pride and Prejudice*, the rarest and most brilliant
merit is the construction of the plot, which unfolds itself with
unerring logic and, here as in the earlier work, culminates in a
motive of Sophoclean irony. But here the irony is subtler. The
theme of the book is the settling of Emma's affections on Knightley; and the crucial part in this process is played by Harriet Smith,
Emma's protégée, whom, having failed to marry [17] to Mr Elton,
she next tries to marry to Frank Churchill. This time it is Harriet
who misunderstands, and thinks that she is being encouraged to set
her cap at Knightley. Emma's discovery of this mistake is the
climax of the book.[21]

And now I have left myself no time to speak of *Persuasion*, which
in the eyes of the most devoted Janeites is the greatest book of the
six. The high spirits of the earlier works have here a little abated;
their place is taken by a calm and mellow glow which is rich in
tender comedy and almost wholly devoid of satire. Miss Austen
seems to get fonder and fonder of human beings as she sees more
deeply into them. Where at first she could only triumph over the
impotent arrogance of a Lady Catherine, she now feels more
compassion than anything else for Lady Catherine's successor,
Lady Dalrymple; and no comedy has ever been more free from
malice than *Persuasion*. And here, if I may add a last word, I should
like to point out that however little Miss Austen parades a moral
lesson or a sermon on human affairs, her art, like all great art, draws
its substance from a deeply moral attitude towards life. Those who
fail to see this because she omits to rant about it are only accusing
themselves of blindness. Miss Austen is afraid of nothing: neither
of greatness nor of littleness, wealth nor poverty, happiness nor

---

[19] In parentheses 'E 115–118'.   [20] In parentheses 'E 242–245'.
[21] In parentheses 'E 364–368'.

grief. If she stands up quite cheerfully to the fulminations of Lady Catherine, she faces with equal severity the slums of Portsmouth. Contrast Dickens, who thinks slums loathsome, or Mr Arnold Bennett, who thinks worldly grandeur awe-inspiring. Compared [18] to Miss Austen, Dickens and Arnold Bennett are snobs and sentimentalists, and describe their subject through a mist of distorting emotions. Those who say that her scene is no wider than a middle-class parlour are partly right: her scene is even narrower than that: it is simply the human heart.[22] The problem in all her books is the problem of knowing one's own mind. Every one of her heroines is placed in a situation where a resolute and fearless facing of her own motives is demanded of her. The catastrophes are one and all caused by failure to distinguish one's real thoughts and desires from those which one idly supposes oneself to have; and the happy endings take place invariably by a moral crisis in which these illusions are swept away and the heroine is left face to face with her real self. This crisis, tragic as in *Emma*, or comic as in *Northanger Abbey*, is the turning-point of all the books, whose common theme is thus conversion of the soul, as Plato would call it, from illusion to reality. If that is not good morals, I do not know good morals when I see them; but I am here not to talk morals but to talk literature, and[23] on that I have said enough for your

---

[22] Cf. Ezra Pound: 'People will read Miss Austen because of her knowledge of the human heart, and not solely for her refinement.' See 'The Rev. G. Crabbe, LL.B.', 'The Future' (1917), *Literary Essays of Ezra Pound*, ed. T. S. Eliot (London: Faber & Faber, 1954), 279.

[23] After this, a deleted passage identifies one of the venues for Collingwood's lecture: 'I wander from my subject. It is a subject which I am especially glad to have mentioned in this place, as having thereby, to the best of my poor ability, repaid a debt: for many years ago it was in this college that, as an undergraduate, I listened to a paper on Jane Austen by [William] Warde Fowler, and came away saying to myself: "Oxford is not such a bad place after all: for Jane Austen has lovers here" '. Collingwood's old undergraduate college at Oxford was University, and the University College literary society active at the time was called the Martlets. It seems apparent from the minute books of this society that Collingwood addressed them twice in the 1920s, once as an undergraduate and again as a young Fellow of Pembroke College—on both occasions on Sir Thomas Browne (see Bodleian MS Top. Oxon. D. 95/3). Collingwood returned in June 1936 to give a paper on King Arthur ('Who was King Arthur?', Bodleian Library Collingwood Papers, dep. 23/15). There is no evidence that it was to this society that he offered the paper on Jane Austen of 1921 (University did not have a 'Johnson Society' in the 1920s), or at any later date, and the deletions here indicate a lecture adapted for delivery on different

indulgence. So I will make an end, only observing that it is right to praise Jane Austen in Oxford, for Oxford prides itself on studying and valuing the classics, and there is no English writer more purely representative of the classical spirit in literature than Jane Austen.

occasions and in different places of which only one was a 'Johnson Society'. The McGowin Library at Pembroke College holds no records of Johnson Society meetings between 1913 and May 1923. However the minute books of the Pembroke Beaumont Society, active at the time, do record Collingwood as having read 'a most entertaining paper on Jane Austen' to this society on 11 Feb 1923, and it is clear from the contents of the minute that Collingwood was reading from his dated (1921) draft on this occasion. When records of the Pembroke Johnson Society resume in 1923, the minute books of the Society show that he spoke at least twice on Austen. He was a guest of the Society on 16 Nov 1924 and at the same time, as the contents of the minute suggest, his dated (1921) version of the Jane Austen lecture was before him. A further report of Collingwood having lectured to the Pembroke Johnson Society on Austen appears nearly ten years later in the minutes for 4 Feb 1934. Then, however, it is clear that the meeting heard a version of the lecture whose details seem to correspond with the undated version printed here. All three reports praise Collingwood's reading of quotations from Austen. In 1934 the Secretary to the Society notes that: 'Mr Collingwood read extracts from her work, enjoying himself so much that the society could not help but be charmed. The paper met with an enthusiastic reception.'

THE PHILOSOPHY OF ART

Art, in the sense which we are to discuss it, is not *ars* = τέχνη in general; for that = the producing of results, and the philosophy of that is the philosophy of action at large.[1] We are discussing *fine art*, that is the special case of production where the production is that of *beautiful objects*. But this is an inadequate account of the scope of our inquiry: for a beautiful object may be produced κατὸ συμβεβηκός by ἁ οὡγνόων, and then he is not an artist: whereas to apprehend the beauty of an object is, so far, to be an artist whether or not one turns out any object or so-called *work of art*. Hence *art* means, for us, the activity by which the beautiful as such is apprehended.

About this activity we have three questions to ask.

1. *What is it*, in its most general or abstract nature? (Here we are asking for a Socratic definition of it).
2. *How is it articulated or differentiated—what distinctions emerge within it?* (Here we are asking for an account of all those antitheses, for example between formal and naturalistic art, beauty of **[2]** art and beauty of nature, etc. which make up the body of the life of art: the *dialectic* of art.)

Bodleian Library, Collingwood Papers, dep. 25/2. The title on the outside front cover of a small exercise book reads: 'Philosophy of Art: Outline of Lectures T[rinity] T[erm] 1924' and on the title-page: 'Lectures on the Philosophy of Art, Delivered at noon on Saturdays, T[rinity] T[erm] 1924'. On the inside front cover there is the note: 'These lecture-notes, written during Trinity Term 1924, represent a much abbreviated and systematized version of the notions worked out at Avignon in the spring of 1924 and noted down, in a rough and chaotic form, in the notebook entitled "Rough Notes for a book on the Philosophy of Art" '. The 'book' that the 'Lectures' anticipate is *OPA* of the following year, and they offer a fully detailed plan or draft of that work, which is a filling out with examples and argument of the basic structure and logic of what Collingwood has set forth in LPA. Other elements look towards FT and PA, but go into more detail on several issues relating to the definition of art.
[1] Cf. *PA* 5 where Collingwood differentiates his conception of 'art' from the words used by the Greeks and Romans to denote a 'group of crafts'.

3. *What is its place in life as a whole?* (That is, how is it related in general to other activities in general, for example religion, science, morality?)

No account of art is complete without including these three aspects. They are not really separable, for the view we take about each commits us to some view about the others: but it is necessary to develop each distinctively. Most philosophies of art err by omitting to consider one or even two. Thus Plato (*Republic*) only deals with (3), Kant deals almost exclusively with (1), Croce wholly omits (2), and only deals with (1) and (3). In order to deal with (1) it is necessary to analyse art carefully, but this may be done from the outside, that is without being a trained artist. (2) can only be dealt with by specialized artists, and is elaborately or even excessively prominent in artists' own writings and talkings about art. (3) requires a person who is both an artist and something more, that is a person who understands *from the inside* not only art but religion, science, etc.[2]

---

[2] Opposite fo. 2. '*Note on the origin and point of view of this aesthetic.* The origin is the view of art as imagination and imagination as a non-conceptual, non-logical consciousness—non-logical because pre-logical or infra-logical and hence dialectically primitive—which is common to Plato, Vico, Kant, Hegel, Coleridge, and Croce—to go no further. Croce is the immediate source: but as I work over Croce more and more I find more and more satisfaction in the other statements, especially perhaps Vico. The special programme of this aesthetic is the attempt to overcome Croce's faults. These, as I see them, boil down to the one point that art is for him an *abstract*, not a concrete, concept—the unity of indifference, in which all cows are black. His concept of art contains no germ of self-differentiation, no dialectical principle; hence his ridiculous negation of Nature, Technique, Subject, Meaning, his unintelligent and pigheaded rejection of the didactic theory of art, the theories of mimesis, choice, etc. and the moralistic theory. All these, I contend, spring from real features of art, and my purpose is to elicit these and other implications from the concept of imagination. I take Croce's concept of intuition as my *starting point*, not (like him) for the whole content of aesthetic, and develop out of it an account of the life of art as a whole in which the facts, instead of being told they ought not to exist, are transcendentally deduced. But this deduction cannot be arrested with the close of the gate of aesthetic categories, and hence I go on to do precisely what Croce most hates, viz. deduce a transition from art to science. This again is only the result of treating the concept of art as a concrete concept and trying to get away from the barren and blind abstractness of Croce's aesthetic.' Collingwood engages with Croce's 'identification of intuition and expression' in *SM* 87 ff.

[3] § 1. THE GENERAL NATURE OF ART

Analytic psychology distinguishes three aspects of all psychical life:[3] cognition, conation, emotion (thought, will, feeling). These are inseparable: any activity involves all three. Art therefore qua activity is all three at once: and therefore it has certain *generic* and certain *specific* properties. (Define *per genus et differentiam*.)

a. Art Generically

(i) *qua cognition*: we distinguish in art a subject and an object, a contemplator and thing contemplated: art has an *object*.

(ii) *qua conation*: art is a life of effort or struggle to do something, to realize something not yet realized: art has an *ideal*.

(iii) *qua emotion*: art has a certain aspect of feeling, pleasant and painful at once like all feeling: desire and aversion—art has an *emotional life*. (All this is true of human activity generally.)

β. Art Specifically

a. Qua cognition

The object of art is an object which is not judged to exist. It is indifferent to art whether its object exists or not, for example characters in a novel or play: these are not historical. When they *are* historical, this historicity is irrelevant to their aesthetic value. In other cases there is not even the *appearance* of historicity: for example no one thinks that a symphony is a description of actual **[4]** sounds heard by the composer on some occasion, as one might falsely suppose every novel to be an account of actual occurrences. We for example ask upon whom such and such a character is modelled, assuming that it is modelled on someone historical: but we realize that a fugal subject can't be modelled on anything historical, except in very rare cases.[4]

Now the *not being judged to exist* is not an accident but the essence of the object of art. This object is essentially *imaginary*,

---

[3] Opposite fo. 3: 'This appeal to analytic psychology is of merely didactic importance: its only value is as a rejection of the literally preposterous idea that art is purely theoretic and not at all practical—a faded relic of Schopenhauer'.

[4] For a discussion by Collingwood of the comparison between musical and literary forms of art see WT above.

and art, qua cognition, is imagination. To imagine trivially is to
create trivial art, to imagine greatly is to create great art. Every
work of art, so far as it is a work of art, is something imagined: and
to call a man imaginative is to call him an artist. Imagination does
not mean fancying that which does not exist, for to do this is to be
guided by the distinction between existence and non-existence,
and that means that imagining would be only one kind of thinking.
It means taking up a certain attitude to objects irrespectively of
whether they exist or not. The imagined object may be real: but to
imagine it is to pay no attention to the question whether it is real.[5]
Our thoughts are sometimes true and sometimes **[5]** false: if then
we take all the thoughts that come into our mind and consider them
irrespectively of the distinction between true and false, we are
imagining. Everything we imagine either *is so* or *is not so*: but to
imagine it means refraining from asking which it is.

b. *Qua conation*

So far this looks as if art were the mere uncontrolled floating of
images across the mind: and this is not art but dreaming; and
dreams are not art but the raw material out of which art is made.
Imagining is not merely the refraining from judging whether our
fancies are true or false; it is also the activity of creating these
fancies. Art, if it is a kind of dreaming, is controlled and purposeful
dreaming. The control in question is nothing but the effort to
imagine as imaginatively as possible: that is, to imagine beautifully.
Art is imagination, and goodness in art (beauty) means imagination
done well, that is done according to its own proper law, that is done
imaginatively. A thing is beautiful, in terms of common opinion on
the subject, when it is harmonious, individual, a unity in plurality,
and so on. This just means that it is coherently imagined.[6] As a true

---

[5] Cf. *SM* 60–1: 'The aesthetic experience cares nothing for the reality or unreality
of its object. . . . [I]n imagining an object we are indifferent to its reality or unreality';
OPA 12–13: 'The object, in the case of art, is an imaginary object, not a real object. . . .
To imagine an object is not to commit oneself in thought to its unreality; it is to be
wholly indifferent to its reality. An imaginary object, therefore, is not an unreal object
but an object about which we do not trouble to ask whether it is real or unreal'; *PA* 136:
'Imagination is indifferent to the distinction between the real and the unreal.'

[6] Opposite fo. 5: 'This is not a rejection of the correspondence theory of truth—
only an implied confession that it is meaningless'. Collingwood saw his own logic of
'Question and Answer' (*A* 29–43) as going beyond both the coherence and correspondence theories of truth.

thought means a thought that is thought out and not full of self-contradictory [6] undigested elements, so a beautiful idea is one which is imagined out,[7] one which is imaginatively a whole, free from elements which jar upon the imagination. The achievement of this imaginative unity, harmony, or beauty is the task of art as an activity.[8]

c. Qua emotion[9]

All activity is immediately present to the agent in the form of feeling; in so far as the activity triumphs over obstacles this feeling is pleasant, so far as it breaks down the feeling is painful. The obstacles to activity arise always from the nature of the agent, not his environment: it can only be by his own weakness or misdirection of effort that he can ever fail to conquer his environment and turn it to his purpose. Therefore pleasure is the feeling of our own strength, pain the feeling of our own weakness. Every type of activity has its peculiar type of pleasure and pain: and in art these are the pleasure of the experience of beauty and the pain of ugliness. Whenever we succeed in imagining something coherently *and* harmoniously we have the pleasure of beauty, whenever we fail we have the pain of ugliness. Now we never either succeed or fail absolutely. Every success is purchased at the price of an effort [7] whose intensity is proportionate to our own weakness: we only try because hitherto we have failed, and therefore the effort is itself painful. But no effort is merely painful, for no effort is altogether

---

[7] Cf. *OPA* 22, where Collingwood writes of 'the deliberate attempt to "imagine out" an object'.

[8] Opposite fo. 6: 'NB. The *individuality* of the beautiful object is a self-contained individuality. Contrast the individuality of a historical fact e.g. a century, a revolution, etc. which is a self-transcending individuality. To *think* a thing is to think it in relation to other things: to *imagine* it is to imagine it in isolation. Hence in the last resort we can only think a whole world: nothing short of the whole world is intelligible: but we can imagine isolated objects, and these objects (i.e. individual works of art) are beautiful by their *internal* coherence, but are not *externally* coherent, not imagined as in relation to others. There is therefore no such thing from the artist's point of view as a universe; or rather, each work of art is for him a kind of temporary universe.'

[9] Cf. *OPA* 10: 'cognition, conation, and emotion. This threefold distinction has a very real value, but it becomes a fantastic mythology if it is mistaken for a distinction between three activities which can exist separately, or of which one can predominate over the other, or of which one can undergo modifications without producing corresponding modifications in the other.'

unsuccessful. Hence in the life of art pleasures and pains always
jostle one another and are mixed up in a very curious way. Listening to music, or watching a play, is never fully and deeply pleasant
unless it is also and at the same time agonizingly painful.

This general account of art as imagination is only preliminary and
a starting point rather than a conclusion. It has, however, at least
the merit of cutting out a number of false approaches: for example
(1) the theory of art as giving a kind of transcendental truth:
whereas it really ignores truth and merely imagines, (2) the theory
of art as mere pleasure, or one kind of pleasure, or somehow
specially connected with feeling. [NB. (1) is due to preoccupation
with the highest works of art and failing to see art in its whole
breadth: (2) is due to the dilettante[10] approach to art, looking at
pictures and asking yourself how they make you feel, instead of
painting pictures and asking how it is done.[11]]

§ 2. THE DIALECTIC OF ART

Art=imagination is only the starting point. We have now to see
what that implies, that is what kind of life in detail the life of
imagination must be. This means extracting the implications of
the concept of imagination. [NB. the actual process of thought is
the reverse of this: we are confronted by a mass of empirical facts,
empirically connected with the life of art, and we ask ourselves *why*
they are connected, and find that they are necessary implications of
imagination in general.]
    So far, art=imagination, and the activity of art consists in fram-
ing works of art which, so far as they are harmonious individual
wholes, are beautiful and so far as they fail to achieve this unity are

---

[10] Opposite fo. 7: '* what is especially intended is to strike a blow at all Loafers'
Theories of art—e.g. Schopenhauer, Croce—i.e. theories which regard works of art
as finished products contemplated with hands in pockets, *opus operatum* theories, –
instead of regarding the work of art as an ἐνέργεια, an activity of creating something
through a cycle of dialectical phases. The habit of dabbling in art and talking about
it instead of learning to do it is responsible for such theories.'
[11] Cf. *OPA* 101 ('Suggestions for Further Study'): 'Looking at pictures and
listening to music are inadequate for this purpose [philosophizing about art]: the
student must learn to draw and compose.'

ugly. They exist wholly in the imagination. But it is not essential, in order to imagine, that you should know you are imagining. You may either know it or not know it. In dreams, normally, we do not know it:[12] in the more primitive and childish forms of art we do not know it (hence children's mendacity): the civilized and educated artist does know it from time to time, but he forgets it in the actual course of his work, and to remind him of it may **[9]** easily break the current of his thoughts.

Beauty[13]

The felt quality of the object, that is its beauty, differs according as the artist is or is not aware that he is imagining. If he simply imagines without realizing that he is imagining, his imaginations rise up before him in a mysterious and unexplained way, and their beauty, that is, their aesthetic power or value, seems to be something independent of himself, something which comes from outside and takes possession of his soul without his own cooperation or permission. Beauty that does this is a beauty which appears as overwhelming force, that is to say, it is *sublimity*. The sublime is simply the beautiful seen as power; that is, seen by a mind impressed by it and prostrate before it: it is the beautiful in so far as the beautiful affects us with awe. Now this awe is based on our not recognizing that the sublime object is the mere creature of our own imagination: and therefore it disappears as soon as we recognize this truth.[14] When we discover that the true and only source of sublimity is our own aesthetic imagination, the awe vanishes, we cease to be impressed, we feel suddenly conscious that the thing which overwhelmed us is in reality nothing **[10]** at all, and this revulsion of feeling is *the comic*. Proverbially, the ridiculous is that to which we are taken by one step from the sublime; and philosophers are more or less agreed that in laughter we assert ourselves instead of abasing ourselves. It is noteworthy that we laugh most

---

[12] Cf. *OPA* 22: 'To dream is to imagine, but not to work at imagining; when we dream, we are doing in a lazy and haphazard way the same thing which in creating a work of art we are doing with critical care and labour.'

[13] Ch. 2 of *OPA* is entitled 'The Forms of Beauty'.

[14] Cf. *OPA* 38: 'we become familiar with the object, and familiarity breeds a feeling that the beauty we saw in it was our own work and not due to any real power in the object'.

satisfactorily at things of which we are tempted to be afraid: we joke about God, about sex, about death; we make fun of our superiors and our enemies; in these cases the joke has a real spiritual value, as an indication that we are keeping our spirits, and not allowing ourselves to be paralysed by awe but asserting our own creative freedom.

Laughter destroys sublimity, but out of the ashes of sublimity it raises up the true and perfect *beauty*. Beauty is the aesthetic value of an object no longer regarded as something outside ourselves, but regarded as something unutterably intimate to ourselves, it is born in the secret places of our own heart, its life is our own life, and in enjoying it we are enjoying the activity of our own mind. Beauty in this form, or the intimacy of the object to the subject, is only possible when the first overwhelming power of beauty, revealed as sublimity, has collapsed into laughter: and therefore true beauty is [11] always vibrating between the poles of the sublime and the comic, that is, between the feeling of self-abnegation before an overwhelming aesthetic force and the feeling of self-liberation from this force. This is why works of art which are too unrelievedly grim become things to laugh at, because we have to supply the element of comedy for ourselves when the artist has left it out: and this again is why the greatest works of art are always a kind of web of tragic and comic elements.[15]

Inspiration[16]

Beauty in its full sense, as the synthesis of the sublime and the comic, is only possible to the artist who knows that he is imagining—who has discovered this truth and has got over the shock of the discovery. But when I know that I am imagining, I am doing two things: imagining and knowing. What I imagine is my work of art: what I know is myself as imagining my work of art. I have a conception of my own mind, but I conceive my mind as a merely imagining mind, and nothing more. Yet it is something more, for it is not only a mind that imagines but a mind that thinks of itself as

---

[15] Cf. *OPA* 32: 'The highest beauty somehow contains within itself, as subordinate and contributory elements, both the sublime and the comic, and indeed all other forms of beauty. . . .'

[16] Cf. *OPA*, ch. 3, § 13.

imagining: and therefore my self-knowledge is so far [12] defective
at this stage that I think of myself not as a thinking but only as an
imagining mind. The artist's self-consciousness consists of watching himself at work, as it were from the outside. He, qua thinker,
watches himself qua imaginer: and he sees this process of imagination going on in himself almost as if it were going on in someone
else. In so far as the artist watches himself at work, he thus seems to
watch himself from the outside, without any inner understanding
of how the work is done: and in so far as he actually does the work
of imagining, he only imagines and does not understand the activity of his own imagining.[17] Therefore from both points of view the
artist's activity is a mystery to himself, something that he does
without understanding how he does it. The work certainly gets
itself done in his mind, but since he does not understand how he
does it, it appears to him as though the real agent were an active
force other than himself which makes him its mouthpiece. In a
word, he feels himself *inspired*. This feeling is a permanent and
essential element in the experience of all artists. As soon as an artist
at work turns and looks at himself, he necessarily regards himself
as the vehicle of a force which is dictating his works or somehow
guiding his hand. [13] The words he utters are put into his mouth:
he did not originate them. This universal experience is expressed
sometimes by saying that the artist is inspired by gods, sometimes
by ascribing the origin of art to the unconscious mind; these
explanations are mythological and fantastic statements of the
plain fact that because imagination is only imagination and not
thought it cannot understand its own nature, and regards itself as
something mysterious and non-human. The thinker can understand his own thought because logic is itself thought: but the artist
cannot understand his own imagination, because understanding
and imagination are different. To understand one's own thinking
one need only think: but to understand one's own imagining it is
not enough to imagine. Hence art, to the artist, is always a mystery,
and hence he always feels himself in the grip of a power he does not

---

[17] Cf. *OPA* 47: 'The artist . . . is always doing two things: imagining and knowing that he is imagining. His mind is at it were a twofold object: as imagining, he has
before him the imagined object; as thinking, he has before him his own act of
imagining that object.'

understand; though this power, properly understood, is only his own activity.

Nature[18]

The artist who feels himself inspired feels that the aesthetic activity which goes on in him is not his activity; consequently his correct attitude towards it is not to work hard in the attempt to promote it, but to place himself passively at its disposal. In other words, he [14] must stop trying to imagine freely on his own responsibility, and simply accept whatever is presented to his mind by this power which has taken possession of him. The object now appears as something external, something given; not something invented by the artist's mind, but something imposed upon his mind from outside, whose aesthetic value lies precisely in the fact that it *is* so imposed. An object so conceived is *Nature*: and nature, the beautiful nature of the aesthetic experience, is thus the objective aspect of inspiration. Nature in this sense is not the physical or material nature of science, that is, not a *conceptual* nature: nor yet the nature of common sense, that is, not a *perceptual* nature: it is an aesthetic nature, whose essence is its beauty, that is, its appeal to the aesthetic consciousness. It is not conceived or perceived but imagined: but its peculiarity is that our imagination of it is an inspired or guided imagination, an imagination not controlled by the absolute decisions of our own free choice but by a power which is using us as its vehicle. If this power is called God, then nature in this sense is correctly defined as the art of God.

At first sight this phase in the development of the aesthetic consciousness may seem a mere illusion. Our imagination is our own, and cannot be controlled by any external force; and if it is an illusion [15] to regard our imagination as the working in us of some power not ourselves, it is equally an illusion to regard the object of our imagination as a Nature with a beauty of its own, independent of our own mind. But if this is an illusion, it is a necessary and beneficent illusion, an illusion necessitated by the very nature of

---

[18] Cf. *OPA*, ch. 3, § 15, 'The Beauty of Nature', and § 16, 'The Forms of Natural Beauty'.

imagination itself: that is to say, not altogether an illusion.[19] The
finding of beauty in nature is a mark of highly developed aesthetic
powers. It is not the philistine who finds himself dissatisfied with
his own fancies and turns to nature as to a more satisfying source of
aesthetic pleasure. This turning away from mere imaginations, and
this plunging of the mind into the sea of natural beauty, is a
remedy, instinctively adopted by the aesthetic consciousness, for
its own weakness: it is a process of self-discipline through which
alone the imagination can come to its full powers. Whenever the
imagination is dissatisfied with its own achievements or feels that
they are trivial and commonplace, it turns to nature in order to
enlarge its outlook, in other words to get its teeth into a problem
more worthy of its attention. Essentially Nature is a problem set by
the artist to himself. He approaches a natural object saying to
himself, as it were, 'here is something which you must find beautiful; if you don't find it [16] beautiful, the fault is your own'. The
artist goes to nature in this attitude of humility just because Nature
is by definition the object of a humble aesthetic mood, namely the
mood in which the artist feels himself inspired by a power not his
own.

Nature is that which is a given to the artist and by him accepted
passively: that is to say, it is that in which he gets away from the
capriciousness and freedom of imagination. Therefore the beauty
of nature is a beauty which objects display so far as they show no
trace of human artistry. The mountain and the forest are beautiful
because no human hand carved the one and planted the other; the
flowers on the rock are more beautiful than a rock-garden because
they show no signs of having been put there to look beautiful. If, as
we sometimes do, we ascribe natural beauty to the design of God,
making God a cosmic landscape-gardener, a painter whose canvass
is the sky and whose paints are the colours of the sunset, we here
insist on God's transcendence, his omnipotence, the infinite gulf
between human art with its fretful subjectivity and the art of God
with its unhurried and inevitable triumphs. It is not because it is
art, but because it is God's art and not man's, that we admire it.

[19] Opposite fo. 15: 'it isn't really an illusion at all. It is strictly true that the power
in virtue of which we achieve beauty is a power not merely our own—not the private
property of our empirical selves—but a power coextensive with the universe, which
informs and inspires our empirical personality. The only illusion is to regard this
power as another finite being somehow "outside" our own empirical personality.'

Nature in the ordinary sense is not the only place in which [17] natural beauty is found. Man himself, so far as he is not an artist, is felt as part of nature: and human customs, the human form, even human artefacts, are vehicles of natural beauty when and in so far as they are not designed to be beautiful. The unsophisticated traditional life of a village, with its observations of feasts and fasts, its costumes, its cycle of agricultural and pastoral occupations, is beautiful with a beauty which is at bottom natural beauty. When the villagers dress up to look smart, instead of dressing up because tradition requires it, or when they consciously ornament their cottages with antimacassars and oleographs, the beauty vanishes. They are beautiful so long as they do not try to be beautiful. And further, they are only seen as beautiful by an alien eye. A dweller in the village soon ceases to find it beautiful; for that, he must see it across the gulf which separates the sophisticated spectator from the unsophisticated object. This illustrates the point that this beauty is the beauty of nature, that is, the beauty of an object to a subject distinct and detached from it. This detachment consists in the fact that the object must not be conscious of its own beauty, whereas the subject is conscious of the object's beauty. Wherever [18] this double condition is fulfilled we have the peculiar experience of natural beauty. For the artist recognizes natural beauty as having a quite peculiar flavour or fragrance of its own, something fresh and ethereal like a spring morning, something in the nature of an uncovenanted mercy, an eternal surprise. Natural beauty is the beauty of a perpetual paradox, which consists in the discovery of beauty just where there was no reason to expect it.[20] Hence not only is the unplanted daffodil or the unadorned village girl beautiful, but the undecorated cup and the unarchitected cottage; the unplanned footpath follows a beautiful line across the fields, when the engineered road destroys the forms of

[20] Opposite fo. 18: 'perhaps people who are not artists fail to recognize the distinction between the flavour of natural beauty and artistic beauty, and reduce artistic beauty to a level with natural beauty, or do not see clearly that they do not so reduce it. Similarly Dean Inge says, evidently not disingenuously, that he can't distinguish religion from philosophy: i.e. he reduces philosophy to the intellectual level of religion. So a scientist reduces philosophy to the level of science and thinks it is an affair of hypotheses and experiments. These are mere gaps in the experience of the people in question and do not amount to serious "theories"or "arguments".' The reference is to William Ralph Inge (1860–1954), Dean of St Paul's.

an entire countryside: but even the road, like the locomotive or the battleship, has a kind of natural beauty depending on the fact that its creation, though a free human act, has at any rate been a sternly practical and unimaginative act, untouched by aesthetic consider-ations and planned with a single eye to efficiency. Hence the beauty of the steamship, like the beauty of the cottage, is a kind of natural beauty.

The love of natural beauty is one of the most vital and precious forms of aesthetic activity: and it is a form especially prominent [19] in the present age and perhaps more than elsewhere, in this country. Our love of scenery and our hatred of over-decoration, our sympathy with the simple and unsophisticated forms of human life, and our readiness to see beauty in works designed only to serve the ends of utility, are things into which we at present throw the greater part of the aesthetic energy of our race—a race of perhaps unusual aesthetic gifts. But we are the more bound to recognize the permanent and necessary defects of this form of aesthetic experi-ence.[21] Of all natural beauty it is true that the object which pos-sesses it must be unaware of it, and must show on its face no sign of being affected by any such awareness. The object is therefore spoilt as soon as it becomes conscious of its beauty, that is, as soon as it bears on its face the signs of being regarded as beautiful. The picturesque village is vulgarized by becoming the goal of charabanc excursions; the forest and the mountain are desecrated by being swarmed over by tourists:[22] the innocent village maiden has only to guess that she is thought beautiful in order to lose all

---

[21] Opposite fo. 19: 'Natural beauty is a beauty whose very essence lies in its fragility. Because it is a beauty of surprise or paradox, it is no sooner enjoyed than it begins to fade. All natural beauties are transitory, and this transitoriness is an inevitable consequence of their very nature. The beauty of a cloud-effect on a mountain passes as we watch it: the flower is no sooner in blossom than it begins to die, the bloom of youth on human flesh passes: rude winds do shake the darling buds of May, and summer's lease hath all too short a date. In the sphere of natural beauty, more than anywhere else πάντα ῥεῖ καὶ οὐδὲν μένει—tout passe, tout lasse, tout casse. And it is no consolation to reflect that nature's fertility is inexhaustible and that the beauties we love will be succeeded by others. Death does not lose its sting because flowers blossom on the grave of the dead. But this natural fragility is only one kind of destruction: there is another which is less easy to contemplate with resignation.'

[22] The invasion of the countryside by town-dwellers is lamented more stridently by Collingwood in AM, below.

her natural beauty. Still more is the beautiful object spoilt when anyone tries to improve it, to make it more beautiful. Now the blighting effect of trippers on scenery is wholly due to the fact that the trippers go there because the scenery is beautiful. They are not **[20]** a part of the scenery, like the shepherds and the woodcutters, but spectators of the scenery: and the mood which enjoys natural beauty is a mood in which we want to forget ourselves, the spectators, and absorb ourselves in the object spectated. The presence of the trippers is blighting because it reminds us that we too are trippers, that is, spectators and alien to that which we are contemplating: and this rude reminder of our own subjectivity breaks the spell of natural beauty. The subjectivity of the spectator has intruded upon the object and impaired its pure externality: the freshness and surprise of the natural beauty are therefore dissipated, and the beautiful object is spoilt.[23] Now this spoiling is the inevitable fate of all natural beauty. It is not only a frail and fleeting beauty, but a *spoilable* beauty, and its lovers are always trying to preserve it from contamination. But this they cannot do, for there is one contamination against which they cannot preserve it, the contamination of their own presence. One spectator is already an intruder, and already knows the delicate symphony of natural beauty out of tune. If there are two such spectators, each realizes that the other destroys the beauty of the object. Therefore the lover of natural beauty is always jealous, always trying to keep others away, because these others will destroy the beauty he **[21]** loves. But he is already destroying it himself by his own presence. Thus natural beauty is destroyed by the very enjoyment of it, and therefore this enjoyment is self-frustrating and contradictory.

---

[23] Opposite fo. 20: 'Why don't trippers spoil the beauty of the scenery *for themselves*? The answer is that to some extent they *do*, but that the scenery even thus partly spoilt is still partly unspoilt, and they enjoy the unspoilt parts and are not in a position to deplore the spoilt parts by comparison with the same parts before they were spoilt. Cf. the fact that e.g. the Lakes as found beautiful by the Lake poets simply no longer exist now. Wordsworth would consider it ridiculous to try to preserve the district, in its present state, from further uglification because he would certainly consider that it had already been uglified past recognition. Yet some aspects of it are still preserved, and it is these that the modern resident or writer wants to save.'

The Physical Work of Art (Externalization)

But the lesson of this destruction of natural beauty is that a beauty which man's act can destroy, man's act must have created. Hence we get the recognition that the external object really owes its beauty to the mind of the artist: and the artist can range at will through nature finding beauty whenever he looks for it in a sufficiently imaginative way. But if whatever external object is presented to him can be rendered beautiful by his aesthetic activity, he need not wait till chance brings before him this or that object: he can create objects for himself. These objects are natural objects in so far as they are no mere imaginations but external or given realities: but they are more than merely natural objects, for they are consciously created by the artist himself in order to be beautiful. The artist has now established himself as a creator of beautiful things, and nature itself is his handiwork so far as the external or natural world contains landscapes, buildings, statues, paintings, etc. **[22]** made by his hand. These are, however, highly developed forms of the external work of art. In its pure form, this external work of art is any object whose production is due to the purpose of creating something beautiful, that is, something expressing the aesthetic activity.[24] Thus a child will make meaningless scribbles with a pencil on paper, and these scribbles are to the child a real work of art, because their deliberate production gives the child a genuine aesthetic satisfaction. The satisfaction which people get from stamping rhythmically on the floor or singing in a random and tuneless fashion, the satisfaction which a child gets out of its tin trumpet or a savage out of his tomtom,[25] is of this kind. In all these cases the base activity of externalizing is an end in itself, and the satisfaction which it gives is unaffected by the question whether it is well done or ill done. But this type of satisfaction is definitely childish and savage. The externalization is random and uncontrolled, and mere repetition of it, if that repetition produces any growth or advance in the fastidiousness of the aesthetic

---

[24] Opposite fo. 22 the subheading 'a. The Elementary Work of Art'. Cf. *OPA* 68, 'The Work of Art in its Immaturity'.

[25] Cf. the discussion of early human ritual in FT, where Collingwood condemns psychologists', anthropologists', and folktale scholars' use of 'savage' (and 'primitive') as consciously or unconsciously pejorative, non-descriptive, terms, and where he places them in inverted commas (FT2, fo. 21).

consciousness, creates a disgust with its own primitiveness. The child which at first is content merely to make a noise now begins to care what noise it makes, and [23] is no longer content with merely making marks on paper, but wants to make marks of one kind and not another. This means that the primitive act of externalization comes to realize the need of self-discipline, and this is what is meant in art by *technique*.[26] Learning to draw, learning to sing, and so forth, means learning to draw what you want to draw and sing what you want to sing, not merely to make random marks and noises. Technique is acquired by setting oneself a task of such a kind that failure or success cannot pass unnoticed or be mistaken for each other.[27] Even the random primitive work of art contains already some technique; the child must be able to hold and in a rough way to guide the pencil and so forth: but this technique is an implicit technique, which only becomes explicit when the artist realizes the deficiency of his self-command and sets himself definite tasks by which he can increase it. This command, acquired by technical training, is not merely a muscular control. It is not that the singer merely learns to sing whatever note he likes: it is rather that he learns to discriminate notes more finely, and train not only

[26] Opposite fo. 23 the subheading 'b. Technique'. Cf. *OPA* 69: 'Technique is based on the realization by rudimentary art of its need for self-discipline, which depends on a growing dissatisfaction with bare creation and a desire to develop the power of creating this thing rather than that thing.' Cf. also the section on 'Technique' in *PA* 26–9 where Collingwood famously distinguishes 'art' from 'craft'.

[27] Opposite fo. 23: 'Croce, *Il Ammaestramento tecnico*, in *Problemi*, misses the point of technique with his usual precision. He points out (*a*) that technique is not, as some say, the presupposition of art, because you must be an artist already before beginning technical exercises: (*b*) that technical exercises are simply works of art, but small ones, fragmentary ones, etc. But (*a*) technique, though it presupposes art in a more primitive form, is the presupposition of art in a more advanced form, i.e. it is a means developed by art, in the course of its own self-development, to assist that self-development: (*b*) no one but a fool would judge a technical exercise by the same standard as a work of art. A student's study and a master's fragment are utterly and formally different things; and it is only because all cows are black in Croce's aesthetic that he fails to see the difference.' The reference is apparently to Croce's *Problemi di estetica: E contributi alla storia dell'estetica italiana*, vol. i of *Saggi filosofici*, 14 vols. (Bari: Laterza, 1910–52). Croce has no chapter or section entitled 'Il Ammaestramento tecnico' in *Problemi*. Collingwood may be recalling ch. 3, iii, 'Il padroneggiamento della tecnica', 247–55. A copy of Croce's *Problemi di estetica* is recorded in the Blackwell's Sale Catalogue, no. 496, containing many books from Collingwood's personal library.

his larynx but his ear. Similarly the manual training **[24]** of the draftsman is in reality a training of the eye, by which it learns to see things which it had not seen once.

The tasks by which technique is acquired must be tasks which can be checked. If the learner does his exercise badly he must not be able to plead that he meant to do it so. Hence the ideal to be realized must be already present in a perceptible form, so that it can be compared point by point with the perceptible product. Therefore technique is necessarily and always acquired by copying existent models. These models are not natural objects but works of art. The beginner, in our art-schools, is put into the antiques room: that is, he is put to copy works of art, not to draw from the living model.[28] This is right, because a learner's work is and ought to be an imitation of other people's work. Only the finished artist can paint well from the life; the student must be content if he can paint well from a copy. So the singer at this stage learns to reproduce the style of his master, and so forth. The only merit which the student's work can have at this stage is the merit of faithfully copying its model: and anyone who went round praising or blaming the work of students on any other principle than this **[25]** would show himself a fool, like a teacher who should blame his pupil for being deceived by a misprint in his Latin grammar.[29]

But in copying works of art the student is not doing anything slavish. This labour is itself a creative labour, and in the practice of it the imagination is strengthened and developed. For the student is here learning to handle his materials, to master the methods of his trade: and in this education it is, as we saw, not the hand but the eye that is being trained. The act of imitation is an original and creative act, for the imitation is an imitation of an object which was not itself imitative, and therefore the imitation is really in essence

---

[28] Opposite fo. 24: ' "To try to begin drawing direct from nature, without studying other works of art, would be like trying to begin Latin by reading Cicero, without a grammar or a dictionary." [This quotation is consistent with the teachings on art education of Vernon Blake, but has not been identified.] The beginner, given a pencil and paper and told to draw nature, can have no idea where and how to begin: he must *either* learn the established conventions by which nature is already depicted, *or* invent his own conventions, which untaught people actually do. This necessity of "models" to the learner is a thing everybody knows, but people do not usually know *why* models are necessary.'

[29] Opposite fo. 25 the subheading 'c. The Skilled Work of Art'.

fundamentally other than the object imitated, even if in final appearance indistinguishable from it. The imitator is creating, but creating unawares;[30] and when he has learnt this truth he is no longer an imitator but a creator, no longer an art student but an artist. He has now, through this course of discipline, achieved the self-consciousness of the act of externalization, and is henceforth the skilled creator of works of art: no longer the random creator, but the trained and therefore free creator.[31]

[26] The free work of art is the work which expresses the skilled creativity of the trained artist. Now this is formal art, the art of pure designs or patterns. A pattern is a work of art which refers to itself alone, and depends for its beauty on itself and nothing but itself, involving no explicit reference to anything else. The scribble becomes a controlled line or pattern of lines, the shout becomes a pure sustained note or melody. No art is purely formal, because there are always considerations external to the design itself which restrict it, such as the inherent character of the material which insists upon being handled in this way or that; the shape to be covered, the time at disposal, and so forth. But the skill of the designer turns these limits into positive sources of inspiration: from the artist's opponents they become, as he grows more skilful, his collaborators.[32] A further restriction is that of artistic tradition. To all appearances anyone might invent any pattern: but nothing in all the history of art is more striking than the continuity of patterns and the strength of the hold which tradition always main-

---

[30] Opposite fo. 25: '* This phase of doing something at unawares is the essence of *education*. The function of the teacher is to help his pupil to do what he couldn't do alone—which is a paradox, because if one can do it one can do it, and if one can't one can't: but it is the paradox of all education. The rope doesn't take the weight of a climber, he has to climb for himself; but a better climber can coax him up places that he couldn't get up without the "moral support" of the rope because he doesn't know he could get up them. Similar is the function of *example* in morality, etc.' On the creativity of imitation see FT6, below.

[31] Collingwood adds the subheading 'i. As Formal art' opposite fo. 26, this followed by further subheadings (which we also omit): 'a. the pure pattern', 'β. Limitations of material', 'γ. pattern growing out of material'. This last is further subdivided into '1. Freely' and '2. Subject to tradition as limitation of freedom'. Cf. *OPA*, ch. 4, § 19, 'Formal Art'.

[32] On the collaborative conditions for art see also FT6, 'The Authorship of Fairy Tales', and the closing pages of *PA*.

tains over the designer.[33] Every work of formal art is actually constructed and actually judged by standards derived from tradition. We ask of an arabesque or a sonata not only whether it is beautiful, but also whether it conforms to the standard pattern of arabesques or sonatas. Philosophers who do not see why we do this are in [27] the habit of scolding us for it and calling it a pedantic and anti-aesthetic form of criticism; but the human race is not likely to be intimidated out of the habit because some philosophers do not see the reason for it.[34] The reason lies in the fact that art, because it is not a wholly self-understanding activity but one whose inner nature is always mysterious to itself, is not wholly free, and therefore at every point of its course finds itself in bondage to unsuspected influences. The artist resembles a man whose bondage to a habit is the more complete that he does not suspect the existence of the habit in himself.[35] Art, merely because it is a human activity, is a corporate activity, so if it understood itself it would recognize this. But it does not, and the artist tends to think himself a free and isolated individual. Because he thinks that, he is at the mercy of an unconscious traditionalism; and he only overcomes the power of this traditionalism by recognizing and embracing it, that is, by ceasing to regard himself individualistically and regarding himself as a representative of tradition. The tradition now becomes a developing and dynamic tradition, a law not fixed once for all but reinterpreted and recreated by every fresh member of the school whose law it is.[36] In this way the laws of the sonata are precisely the immanent spirit of the school of sonata writers, and

[33] Opposite fo. 26: 'The apparent freedom of the pattern-designer, seen from his own point of view, and his absolute servitude to tradition, seen from the historian's point of view, form a contrast which reappears in an important way in Ethics. Action which to the agent sounds quite original and spontaneous is seen by a spectator to be hide-bound in convention. Hence the *feeling* of freedom is not a real test of freedom, as Spinoza saw.'

[34] Cf. *OPA* 72.

[35] Opposite fo. 27 at this point the subheading '3. Tradition as dynamic freedom' and his following reflections echo T. S. Eliot's celebrated essay 'Tradition and the Individual Talent' (1919). Collingwood's concept of the creative dynamism of tradition, held in common with Eliot's notion of a tradition constantly recreating itself in the present, pervades alike the thinking of *OPA*, *FT*, and *PA*.

[36] Cf. *OPA* 73: 'in the actual life of an artistic tradition the rules are neither pedantically obeyed nor anarchically flouted, but reinterpreted and created afresh by each new member of the school in whose life the tradition lives'.

this spirit works out its own life in the life of the school. The new member of the school looks at its former productions not as models to be copied but as suggestions to be developed. He does not reproduce them, he lets them germinate in his mind into imaginations. They are a seed which is vivified by the fertility of his mind, and their value to him is merely measured by his ability **[28]** to make use of them.[37]

That is to say, they are to him mere objects, hints given him by some external source, the conversion of which into new works of art has to be effected by his own aesthetic labour.[38] But such hints given from without are by definition nature: and the art which builds itself up by following out hints so given is naturalistic art. Once the work of art which gives the hint is reduced to the position of a mere given fact, any given fact may serve its turn: and thus we get the idea of a special type of art (in the sense of artefact) whose beauty is derived from the beauty of nature.[39] Naturalistic art consists not merely in enjoying nature, but in depicting it.[40] By depicting nature, the artist in a sense overcomes the fragility of natural beauty and fixates it to eternity; the fleeting moment of natural beauty fades and dies, 'But thy eternal summer shall not fade / . . . When in eternal lines to time thou grow'st: / So long as tongue shall speak or eye shall see, / So long lives this, and this gives life to thee.'[41] The natural beauty is copied: but by being copied it is made the artist's own and saved from the wreck of time.

[29] The copying of nature is sometimes mistaken for the whole end and purpose of art. And at other times naturalistic art is represented as one of two great types of art, the other being formal. Both these views are mistaken. There is a more or less implicit element of naturalism in all art, which comes to the surface in some arts more easily than in others: it is seldom far below the surface in

---

[37] Opposite fo. 28 the subheading 'ii. As Naturalistic Art'. Cf. *OPA*, ch. 4, § 20, 'Naturalistic Art'.

[38] Opposite fo. 28: 'i.e. once the mind takes up this independent attitude towards the works of art which serve it as ὁρμαὶ καὶ ἐπιβάσεις for its labour, it is clear that the very same attitude can be taken up towards natural objects'.

[39] Opposite fo. 28 the subheading 'a. copying nature'.

[40] Opposite fo. 28: 'NB. Croce in *Problemi* (*Il Ritratto e la Somiglianza*) asserts that a *portrait* as such is history, and only art in so far as all history is also art. This is an error. The essence of a portrait is that it does not narrate, it copies.' Collingwood refers to *Problemi di estetica* (1910), 256–61.

[41] Shakespeare, 'Sonnet 18'.

painting and sculpture, less obvious in literature and less again in music: but analysis can detect signs of its latent presence even where at first sight it is wholly absent, as in the theriomorphism of formal ornaments and the subtle relation between musical rhythms or melodies and the movements of the body or the succession of natural sounds. But it is never the whole of art. It could at most only be the whole of that aspect of art which we call externalization: and of this the fundamental element is formal beauty.[42] We only copy nature because in nature we find a beauty which is always at bottom formal beauty, and because in copying nature we create a beautiful object, that is, an object which forms a harmonious pattern. Nor is there any distinction between formal and naturalistic art as between two species of art: rather all art as such is formal and nothing but formal, and naturalism is only a means, though a necessary means, to the highest formalism.[43]

[30] The copying of nature, however, is not real copying. Just because nature is so infinitely fertile in beautiful subtleties of design and colour, we cannot copy her: our best attempts at a reproduction of her detail are clumsy caricatures, and the naturalistic painter is at best like a man writing a piano version of an orchestral score.[44] He has to leave out practically everything. Hence naturalistic art, conceived as copying nature, is a vain quest, and the attempt to achieve it frustrates itself by losing itself in the slavish and meticulous elaboration of detail.[45] But if that is

---

[42] Opposite fo. 29: 'NB. Naturalistic externalization, the copying of nature for the sake of copying it, is already found at a very primitive level of consciousness: so much so that Aristotle could claim the existence of a natural human instinct of imitation and made this the very basis of art. It is *not* the basis of art, because it requires a basis of its own: before we imitate a natural object, that object must present itself to us in a striking, that is an aesthetic, manner. A child of 8 months will already imitate a motor-horn with ease and exactitude: but this is because it finds a musical beauty in the sound of the horn. The proverbial imitativeness of children is really naturalistic externalization.'

[43] Opposite fo. 30 the subheading 'β. impossibility of copying nature'.

[44] The parallel is repeated in *OPA* 75.

[45] Opposite fo. 30: 'When the artist exerts himself to the utmost to reproduce the detail of nature, he fails not only because there is always yet further detail that he can't reproduce, but also because this very effort makes his picture look laboured and takes it further and further away from the *effortlessness* which is so characteristic of natural detail. He *forces* us to say "By Jove, that man has sweated at it", whereas nature merely impresses us with her easy prodigality, and reckless overflow of unlimited energy.'

so, to leave out details, though it alters the whole, may alter it for
the better as well as for the worse. If the artist leaves out the
unimportant things and puts in only the essentials, his picture
may improve upon nature.[46] This is called *idealizing* nature: and
this conception is an advance on that of copying nature because the
artist now takes upon himself the responsibility for his own work—
a responsibility which really belongs to him inalienably, whether
he recognizes it or not. But the principles according to which we
idealize nature are at first conceived as principles learnt from
nature herself, the ideal being the normal or universal, into
whose likeness we alter the exceptional. This is the idea of the
beautiful as the *typical* [31] or average.[47] But it breaks down on the
discovery that such a criterion, like any other criterion, can only be
applied by a free and autonomous act of the mind: and therefore
the principles according to which we select and idealize natural fact
are really laid down a priori by the mind. The mind, in the sense of
the absolute activity of imagination, is the only criterion of beauty.
But to make this discovery is to pass beyond the naturalistic art
into imaginative art, and art in which the artist creates works which
are wholly formal, that is, beautiful considered as patterns, and
also naturalistic in the sense that they are not mere patterns but
have a subject, that is, stand in a definite and conscious relation to
other works of art.[48] Thus to call a shaped piece of marble Aphrodite is to confess that it does not stand by itself but refers to other
statues and paintings of the goddess of love, and is concerned with

[46] Opposite fo. 30 the subheading 'γ. idealizing nature' this further sub-divided
into '1. the artist as altering nature' and '2. as altering by reference to nature itself
(the typical)'. Cf. *OPA* 76.

[47] Opposite fo. 31 the subheading '3. as altering nature by an a priori criterion',
this followed on the same page by 'iii. As Imaginative Art' (Cf. *OPA*, ch. 4, § 21,
'Imaginative Art'), 'a. its formal aspect (design)', 'β. its naturalistic aspect (subject)',
and 'γ. the union of these'.

[48] Opposite fo. 31: 'Croce's denial of the *title* and *subject* as necessary moments of
art is a residue of the aesthetic which he is controverting, i.e. the dilemma of form
and matter (controversy between aesthetic of form and aesthetic of content). To say
that artists oughtn't to take trouble about subjects and titles is merely silly, as if one
said that moral agents oughtn't to take trouble about doing good to others: it only
stultifies one's own theory. This goes along with Croce's denial of nature and
naturalism as part of his general denial that art has any dialectic, or rather his
recognition that it *has* a dialectic, combined with a futile attempt to ascribe that
dialectic to non-aesthetic motives, as if these could on his own theory *be* such
motives!'

an aesthetic problem which these other works have bequeathed to the artist. An Aphrodite, qua pattern in marble, is formal: qua shape of a woman, it is naturalistic: qua shape of an ideal woman, it is both these at once, not a mere pattern nor a mere cast of this or that female shape but pattern and woman in one. With this phase of free or imaginative art the act of externalization culminates.

[32] *The Life of Art*

The work of art in its final and perfect form being achieved, it remains to ask what we are to do with it. Ask an artist this, and he will say that it is either sent to an exhibition or turned with its face to the wall; it is published, handed on to others, or else merely suppressed, but in any case the artist henceforth has no further use for it. He may later return to it with admiration for his own genius or disgust for his own incompetence: but at the moment his attitude to the completed work, just so far as it is completed, is one of indifference. He wants now to get to work on something else. But the history of the work of art does not cease here. In being published (which may coincide with its being externalized, as in dancing or singing, or may follow it, as in painting and writing) the work of art comes to the attention of others beside its creator. To these others it appears as something whose purpose is to be beautiful, and therefore they look at it with that same reverence with which the lover of natural beauty looks at nature, with this difference, that whereas nature is not conceived as a product of imagination, the work of art is, and therefore there is a kind of intimacy between the work and its beholder which there is not between nature and her beholder.

[33] In looking at nature, we find it, so to speak, a perpetual miracle that it should be beautiful, and our expectation of beauty is only that kind of faith which looks for miracles: whereas in looking at works of art we expect to find beauty as a matter of course, and are surprised rather when we do not find it than when we do.[49] We

---

[49] Opposite fo. 33: 'The difference, of course, comes out in countless ways. But one way is that a bad work of art *angers* us with a feeling that we have been cheated; we want to stamp and swear and hit people; whereas ugliness in nature, except when due to human perversity, at most makes us vaguely uncomfortable, melancholy and disappointed. Indeed I doubt if nature is ever *ugly* in the sense in which bad art is ugly: nature is either beautiful or not beautiful, art either beautiful or ugly.'

look on the artist as upon a person of semi-divine endowments, a *genius*, who can create works having for us a precious message of beauty. For ourselves we only claim the endowment of *taste*, or the faculty of recognizing a genius when we see one.[50] We cannot create works of great art; we must therefore content ourselves with enjoying the works which great men have produced for us. This is that attitude of genius-worship which creates a class of works called classics and holds them up to itself as embodiments of the aesthetic ideal and unfailing sources of beauty for all time. It is a necessary phase of all aesthetic life: but it is based on something of a confusion. If taste is really so far inferior to genius, it cannot even appreciate the works of genius. Reflexion cannot but show that if I understand a great man it must be because I too am great: for if I were not, his great thoughts would be to me mere gibberish. And hence the worship of the classics is only the mark of an aesthetic spirit **[34]** ignorant of its own strength, which when it realizes its strength necessarily overturns the pedestal on which it has set up its idols. This idolatry is none the less a right and valuable attitude in its place, for only in this way can the aesthetic spirit train itself to see its own strength. Worship of the classics is merely the lack of aesthetic self-confidence, but this lack of self-confidence is right and proper in the immature.[51]

But when the aesthetic spirit begins to discover its own strength, it begins to see that the advance which it has all this time been making was due not to the classics but to its own efforts to understand the classics. This discovery leads to that revolt against the classics which is a necessary and perpetually recurring phase of all healthy aesthetic life. The genius, once sublime, becomes an object of ridicule, and the spirit embarks on a campaign of iconoclasm against its own superstitions.[52] Everything which it has admired it now rejects as worthless, and it rejects these things not for any

---

[50] Opposite fo. 33: 'a. Genius and Taste. The Classics'. Also: 'Croce is of course right in denying an ultimate distinction between genius and taste, but wrong in thinking that the distinction does not deserve any attention whatever. As usual, he gives the dog the name of Merely Empirical because he wants to hang it. It is *not* merely empirical: it arises necessarily at a certain stage of the aesthetic life, which is a necessary and in a sense a permanent stage.'

[51] Opposite fo. 34 the subheading 'b. Revolt against the Classics'.

[52] Cf. *OPA* 84: 'The genius, once sublime, becomes ridiculous, and the aesthetic spirit embarks on a campaign of iconoclasm against its own superstitions' etc.

other reason but merely because it has admired them. The mere fact of a past admiration is, in this phase of revolt, a sufficient reason for rejection. This rejection expresses itself not in the mere indifferent ignoring of the works in question, but in a passionate hatred and [35] contempt. The more a work has previously been loved, the more it is now hated.[53] This is because the movement of revolt is the aesthetic spirit's declaration of independence, and such a declaration is meaningless unless there is something against which independence has to be asserted, that is to say, unless there is a claim over it which the mind still feels as a claim, though a claim to be fought against and denied. In other words, the mind is here revolting against itself, against habits of admiration which by its own effort it has implanted deeply in itself. The movement of revolt is not a movement against an external authority, but a movement against the internal habit of deference to an external authority. This, however, is always ignored by the revolted mind itself. To know it is to have transcended the mere phase of revolt and to have come out the other side of the conflict. The revolted mind thinks that what it is fighting against is just this particular authority—Victorianism, the eighteenth century, medieval art, and so forth—and thinks that all art is more or less good except the art of the particular period, generally the period of the imme-diate past, against which it is in rebellion. The result is that this revolt against the tyranny of tradition or academicism rushes into the assertion of a new and equally tyrannous tradition, an equally narrow academicism; the people whose avowed aim is to be unconventional always worship conventions of their own which are the more crushing for being quite unconscious. Hence revolt frustrates itself and the rebel becomes in his turn a tyrant and the just [36] object of other rebels' hatred. Rebellion as such is the destruction of what exists merely because it exists: and therefore

[53] Opposite fo. 35: 'La Révolte in Jean-Christophe [part 4 of Romain Rolland's novel about a young musician who revolts against German militarism and escapes to Paris (English tr. by Gilbert Cannan, 4 vols. (London: Heinemann, 1910))] is perhaps the locus classicus in literature for a description of this phase: the important thing is to recognize that it is a necessary phase, and not to be stampeded by it. It is the phase of father-beating which "runs in the family" (Eth. Nic. 1149 b 11), and is a permanent feature of all spiritual life: it is this that the psycho-analysts have represented in a distorted form as the Oedipus Complex.'

as soon as it has established itself, that is, affirmed its own existence, it is logically bound to destroy itself. Rebellion is simply the
negative phase which is inherent in all activity: because
activity must, by its very nature, go forward, it must destroy
what it has created and wipe out its past achievement, on pain of
stagnation.[54]

When this phase of rebellion has burnt itself out, in a revolt
against the spirit of revolt itself, what is left behind is not just
nothing but a new frame of mind, namely the attitude of combatants who because they have fought their battle to a finish can be
friends again. We return not to the blind worship of our first
attitude but to a discriminating enjoyment of works of art, which
we can now enjoy the better for being able to praise as equals and to
keep our admiration on this side of idolatry. We now no longer, like
children, call any work of art either good or bad without qualification, but we can discuss each work on its merits and point out its
strong and weak sides impartially.[55]

[37] § 3. THE PLACE OF ART IN THE LIFE OF THE SPIRIT

Art is one of the permanent and necessary forms of all spiritual
activity. Taking art as equivalent to imagination, we have already
seen that imagination is the genus of which knowledge is a species,
the other species being error: and thus to know is always to imagine, though it is not mere imagination. Art is accordingly the
presupposition of all other spiritual activities: it is so to speak the
material out of which they are all made, the primitive stuff of
which they are all developments and differentiations.

---

[54] Opposite fo. 36 the subheading 'c. The discriminating attitude'.

[55] Opposite fo. 36: 'Within this phase all the "pseudoconceptual" predicates of
art have their right place. Nothing could be more gratuitously silly than the dogma
that the critic has, or ought to have, only two words in his vocabulary, "beautiful"
and "ugly", to indicate success and failure. Nor is it any better to try to overcome
this ridiculous false abstraction by claiming *degrees* of beauty and (or) ugliness. It is
necessary to say not *that* a work of art has failed (which is the very triviality and
rudiments of criticism) nor *how much* it has failed (if that means anything) but
in what way it has either failed or succeeded, or both: and this is the only thing that
a competent critic ever tries to do.'

The key to the determination of the place of art in life is this conception of the *primitiveness of art*.[56] Art is the simplest and most naïve of all activities. This is why children are more competent in art than in anything else, and for the same reason the same thing is true of savages.[57] Man in the Reindeer age had little that could be called religion, and still less that could be called science, but he had an art of extraordinary richness and power. In the same way a child, long before it has any grasp of religious or scientific ideas, can throw its whole soul into art and live in a world of imaginations with a success which could never attend any effort to live, at that age, in a world of mathematical and philosophical conceptions. All children, and all barbarians, are by nature sublime poets, as Vico put it. Plato was expressing the same truth when he maintained that the best thing one could do for children was to tell them fairy tales and teach them poetry and songs. Art is the kingdom of the child: and anyone **[38]** who wants to enter that kingdom must enter it as a child. Hence we can say that not only is every child an artist, but every artist is a child.[58] The so-called *artistic temperament* is the necessary psychological condition of all art: but the artistic temperament is the very opposite of the temperament necessary in a grown-up man of the world. The artistic temperament is the child's temperament. Its marks are a certain emotional instability, a tendency to live for the moment, an unreflective and uncalculating selfishness which does not deny but simply ignores the claims of other people to consideration, a blindness to even

---

[56] Opposite fo. 37: 'The error of the Romantic movement, which resulted in all the vicious aestheticism of the nineteenth century, consisted in *misplacing* art in the life of the spirit, denying its primitiveness, and assigning to it a place dialectically above, instead of beneath, the scientific and "common-sense" consciousness. The result was a morbid and vicious worship of art as an especially elevated and mysterious thing. This is clear in Kant, in Hegel, in all the Romantics and right down to the end of the century e.g. in the exaggerated stuff about art in people like Nettleship. The real importance of Croce is that he has decisively revived the doctrine of Plato and Vico which places art at the bottom of the scale of activities of the spirit. Yet even in Croce traces of the Romantic aestheticism remain, e.g. where he too easily adopts Schopenhauer's idea of art as "liberating" the mind from practical interests, and where he assumes a spiritual grade *below* art in the shape of crude emotionality, sensation or the like.'

[57] Cf. *OPA* 15: 'the doctrine of the primitiveness of art is slowly forcing itself upon us as we come to know more of the mental life of children and savages'.

[58] Cf. *SM* 58–9.

one's own real interests when they conflict with the impulse of the moment, an incapacity for thinking and acting in a consistent and businesslike way. In general, it is the temperament of one who does not face facts and imagines instead of thinking.[59]

The artistic temperament has its drawbacks, and these are generally recognized. We all know that artists tend to be moody, impolite, unpractical, and even vicious: precisely as a child is. It is no good blaming the artist for these faults and at the same time expecting him to go on being an artist. They are the price he pays for his artistic work. If you civilize him he ceases to be an artist. The beauty of ballad and folk-song is the outgrowth of a rude and boorish country life, and if you educate the rustic, improve his morals, and teach him to vote intelligently, the spring of ballad and folk-song dries up of itself. The beauty of Greek art and medieval architecture is bound up inseparably with the passionate and cruel nature of the Greeks [39] and the childish superstitions of our medieval forefathers, and you cannot restore the art without restoring the life out of which it grew. And just as the artistic gifts of the child very often fade away when it grows up, so that even great poets often fail, all their life, to equal the poems of their first youth, so the artistic gifts of a society disappear when that society advances in civilization. Civilization is the enemy of art: and that fact cannot be adequately accounted for by denouncing civilization as an evil. Partly it is because art is a primitive thing, a childish thing, a savage thing. But civilization can never destroy art, because man never ceases to be a child and a savage. Childishness and savagery are always breaking out in new forms and hence the death of art is a death of the phoenix: art in this or that form is killed by the advance of civilization, but in a new form it rises up again at every phase of history from its own ashes. But every such resurrection of art has about it something of the character of a resurrection: it is a breaking of solid crusts of habit and tradition, the emergence of something which is crude and startling and as it

[59] Opposite fo. 38: 'The *great* artist in part redeems the faults of the artistic temperament just by having the artistic temperament on a heroic scale, in part corrects them by being more than a mere artist. But to judge of art by the standard of great art is precisely the Romantic error about art. Art must be studied in its entire range or not at all.'

were wilfully childish.[60] All new movements of art have about them a certain air of *fauvisme*.

But the child is essentially a man *in fieri*, and the savage is essentially a struggle towards civilization. If art is the characteristic activity of the child, it is an activity whose aim is to transcend itself. The child's aim in life is to grow up: the aim of art is to grow up into knowledge. Hence art is a *self-education* of the spirit. Education means [40] the pursuit of a certain activity not for what it is but for what it leads to. Art, just because it is primitive, points beyond itself to an activity less primitive, and the pursuit of art inevitably leads the mind beyond art. Thus art is *self-destructive*: it has a dialectic which breaks down its own characteristics and transforms it into something which, ostensibly at least, is its own opposite.

The nature of this dialectic is by now clear. We saw that art could never be mere imagination, but was always imagination on the one hand and the self-knowledge of the imagining mind on the other. The artist is always at once an artist and a critic, an imaginer and a thinker. He remains an artist by cultivating his imagination and repressing his thought: but he is only an artist at all, as opposed to a dreamer, in virtue of this very thought, and any kind of success or competence in art is achieved by thinking, by the mastery of thought over imagination. The artist as such is already self-conscious: his artistic work forces his self-consciousness into ever greater relief: and hence, the further his artistic work goes, the more the question burdens his mind. What am I? He thinks of himself as a mere imaginer: but when he so thinks of himself, he realizes that his imagination is not everything, for it appears to him as an inspired imagination: he and his little works of art appear to himself as a mere point between the immensities of God and Nature.

[41] Thus art itself lands the artist in the problems of religion and philosophy. If he wants to go on being an artist, he can repress these problems and protest that he is practising *art for art's sake*:

---

[60] Opposite fo. 39: 'The Hegelian conception of the death of art is really truer than the Crocean conception of its permanence: for the life of art is a life in death, every phase of which exists by rejecting and stamping out the preceding phase. As natural beauty is perpetually being spoilt but has never *been* spoilt (because as soon as one natural beauty is spoilt another arises) so art as a whole is always dying but never dead, because reborn in the moment of death.'

this frame of mind is a conscious and deliberate clinging to the primitiveness of art and an attempt to resist the dialectic which is sweeping the artist off his feet and hurling him into philosophy. But it is a futile attempt: for the art for art's sake gospel is itself already a philosophy. The dialectic of art is not to be resisted.

This explains why artists have always been regarded as teachers of humanity. Boys have schoolmasters, but young men have poets, says Aristophanes, and the same idea has been repeated over and over again in all ages. Now there is a difficulty here: for if art contains no truths, how can the artist be a teacher? From *Julius Caesar* we learn either bad history or no history; from *Paradise Lost* either bad theology or no theology; from *Back to Methuselah* either bad biology or no biology. Art is really just imagination: therefore it cannot instruct. Hence people have concluded that the 'didactic theory' of art is a mere mistake, or, if we learn anything from art, we learn only to be better artists.

But to reject the 'didactic theory' of art on this ground is to fall into a confusion of thought. There are two senses in which we say that a thing is learnt: first, by doing that thing itself, and secondly, by doing something else which leads on to it. Thus, a person may learn to swim by being thrown into water out of his depth, or by learning the motions of **[42]** swimming in his depth or on dry land. Now all education consists in a training of the learner for facing certain situations which have not yet arisen. This training is always a *preliminary* training, and it is therefore heterogeneous with the activity for which it is a training, and yet has a definite relation to it, namely the relation of leading to it, in other words, the relation of dialectical priority. Now art is not knowledge, for it precisely lacks the *differentia* of knowledge, the distinction between truth and falsehood, and therefore it does not inculcate truths. But it is the dialectical *prius* of knowledge, and it is therefore the presupposition[61] of knowledge: we must learn to imagine before we can learn to know, and in learning to imagine we are training ourselves for the activity of knowing. This is why art is the teacher of humanity. The child's life of imagination is a training for the adult life of thought, and the specialized imagination of the artist is a training for the specialized thought of the scientist. It is only in

---

[61] Collingwood's thinking on this topic is later developed in *EM*. See esp. ch. 4, 'On Presupposing', 21–33.

a society whose artistic life is healthy and vigorous that a healthy and vigorous scientific life can emerge.

But the passage from art to science, by which is here meant deliberate and self-conscious thought, can only take place through the mediation of a third term which is neither wholly art nor wholly thought, but partakes of the nature of both. This is *religion*. [43] The place of religion in the life of the spirit may be defined either as a transition from art to science, or as the antithesis to art which in science is reconciled with its opposite.

(*a*) Religion may be represented as the mythological or symbolic or metaphorical expression of philosophical truth. What it expresses is truth, and so far it is science: but the form in which it represents this truth is a form consisting of imaginative and therefore aesthetic fictions. The doctrines of religion are not literally true but symbolically true: it is not true that God is a father or a judge, or that he is distinguished into three persons, or that he is a potentate who grants our petitions: but in so far as our religion is a true religion what we *mean* by these figures of speech is true.

(*b*) Religion may be represented as the opposite of art because it cares most intensely for precisely the truth of its statements, and because for this reason the religious temperament is the antithesis of the artistic temperament: humble where that is conceited, self-denying where that is selfish, anxious where that is careless, eager to face truth where that is eager to forget it.

Science or self-conscious thought is the completion of the transformation which has already begun when art passes into religion: that is to say, religion still clings to the imaginative mythology which is the special creation [44] of art, while science goes behind this and interests itself not in what is said but solely in what is meant. Or again, science is the synthesis of art and religion because in science the intimacy of the subject and object, which is broken in religion by the transcendence of God and the feeling of an immeasurable gulf between his holiness and our sin, is restored, and the mind feels itself once more in secure and permanent contact with its object. That unification of the self with God which is the task of religion is in science an achieved fact, and the mind here discovers its true nature as the creator not only of imaginary worlds but of the real world.

The life of the spirit is thus a dialectic whose three terms are art, religion, and thought, or the beautiful, the holy, and the true. And the place of art in this life is the place of a foundation and starting-point. All else grows out of it, and is a differentiation of it. The life of the spirit is always and eternally a life of art, and whatever else it may become it becomes only because it is first and always this. Hence the art of savages and children is the mark of their potential civilization and intellectual growth, and the art of adult and civilized man is the proof that the spring of spiritual life in him is a spring that is not yet exhausted.

AESTHETIC THEORY AND ARTISTIC PRACTICE

I

The first object of any inquiry is to find out the truth about something; and the first business of aesthetic theory is to discover the truth about art in general, that is to say, to answer the question, 'what *is* art?'

But although that is agreed, there may be a difference of opinion on a further question. Is there, or is there not, an ulterior purpose as well as this primary purpose? When we have decided what art is, can we then go on to use this knowledge for the improvement of our practice as artists or our taste as judges of art, or can we not?

There is something to be said on both sides of this question. One might think that aesthetic theory is bound to react on artistic practice, because a theory of art will give rules for the artist to follow, and therefore a good theory will lead to better works of art, a bad theory to worse.[1] At the same time, a theory of art will give the ordinary man some idea of what he ought to look for in works of art, and thus lay down rules to help him in judging their merits.

Bodleian Library Collingwood Papers, dep. 25/4. A note on the cover-sheet of the MS reads: "This is the complete form of the paper which was to be delivered, in abbreviated form, as a lecture before the British Institute of Philosophical Studies on March 17, 1931'. The MS is dated 'Feb. 23–28, 1931'. In transcribing this material, the editors have been mindful of the fact that the document was originally a long essay of 44 pages, subsequently cut down for presentation as a talk. The many sentence- and paragraph-length deletions do not therefore always signal a critical rejection of unsatisfactory thoughts, and have generally been silently restored to the main text as it is printed here. The more interesting alternative readings, either as further thoughts, or to contract the argument, are occasionally noted. Numerous other deletions have been silently accepted as part of the process of polishing the hand-written text. For Collingwood's preliminary 'Notes on Aesthetic' towards this paper see Bodleian Library Collingwood Papers, dep. 25/5.

[1] The question of the relationship of theory and practice is later developed in the opening pages of *PA* in terms of 'artist-aestheticians' and 'philosopher-aestheticians', and substantially recalls Collingwood's opposition to Croce's excessive abstractionism (as he sees it) as set out in *LPA*, above.

Or, even if we were inclined to be sceptical about the extent to
which hard and fast rules could be laid down by an aesthetic
theory, we might think that reflexion on artistic practice would in
some way or other clear up our minds about the aims of art and
therefore make us less liable to go off in a wholly wrong direction,
[2] whether in creating works of art or in judging them.

But if there are reasons for thinking that aesthetic theory may
help artistic practice, there are also reasons against it. In a general
way, artists do not pay much attention to philosophical questions;
they often seem uninterested in them or even hostile to them.
Certainly artists are not in the habit of applying to philosophical
experts for a theory of art which shall help them to do their own
business, which, they think, they can do for themselves without
any such assistance. And, on the other hand, it does not appear that
philosophical experts, by turning their attention to the problems of
aesthetic, are enabled to produce works of art, or even noticeably to
improve their own taste in pictures or poetry or music. The creating and appreciating of works of art, and the enjoyment of natural
beauty, seem to go on independently of being philosophized about;
and from this point of view the philosophical theory of art seems to
be a mere description of things which we do whether or not we are
able to describe them, and therefore shall not do any better for
being able to describe them accurately.

These two points of view define the problem which I propose to
discuss. It may be taken as agreed on all hands that aesthetic theory
is a science, in the sense that its first object is simply to arrive at the
truth about art. But there remains a disagreement[2] [3] as to
whether this science is 'normative' or 'descriptive'. A normative
science, according to the traditional use of the term, lays down
rules for the activity which it studies, in other words, describes not
what it is but what it ought to be. A descriptive science takes things
as it finds them, and describes not what they ought to be but what
they are. Both aim at truth; but a normative science has a double
relation to its subject matter: it attempts both to give a true account of it and to help it to realize its own proper nature; a
descriptive science has only the simple relation to its subject

[2] Opposite fo. 2: 'Is aesthetic a normative science or a descriptive one? does it tell
us what art ought to be, or what it is? Is it a guide to artistic practice, or merely an
account of it?'

matter, of attempting to give a true account of it. The difference really turns on this: a normative science assumes that the proper nature of its subject matter is not realized, that there is a difference between what it ought to be and what it is; whereas a descriptive science assumes that its subject matter is already all it ought to be, that its proper nature is realized in the facts as they stand.

I will say at once that I do not think either of these conceptions can give us a satisfactory answer to our question. It might seem perfectly clear that, if we ask whether aesthetic theory can be of use in the practice of art, the answer must be either yes or no; if the answer is yes, aesthetic is a normative science; if no, descriptive. But there are plenty of questions which we must refuse to answer either with a plain yes or with a plain no, in addition [4] to the classical example 'have you left off beating your wife?' Philosophy is full of questions of this type, *des questions mal posées*; and I hope to show that this is one of them. I shall argue that neither the normative nor the descriptive theory of aesthetics is sufficient, and that the truth has some resemblance to both theories. In order to develop this argument, I shall first give some general account of the antithesis between normative and descriptive science, with regard to the philosophical sciences in general, and then I shall take a particular historical case—the case of nineteenth-century art—and analyse it in order to see how aesthetic theory and artistic practice are related in actual fact.

[5] II

In asking whether aesthetic theory can give us help in the practical pursuit of art, we are raising a question which, *mutatis mutandis*, arises about all the philosophical sciences.[3] Does logic improve our thinking? Is ethics any use in solving the problems of conduct? In each case we have a department of human life which is studied by a special philosophical science, and the question is whether the

<hr>

[3] The philosophical basis for an overlap between theory and practice is worked out in various of Collingwood's texts, principally *SM*, *EPM*, *A*, and *NL*. In his view, all philosophical problems arise in the world of practice and return to the world of practice for their solution. See David Boucher, *The Social and Political Thought of R. G. Collingwood* (Cambridge: Cambridge University Press, 1989), 51–7.

pursuit of this special science does or does not assist the doing of
the things which are to be done in the department of life that it
studies.

To an ancient Greek philosopher the question would have
seemed hardly worth raising, so certain was the answer. To him
there was no doubt that these philosophical sciences were a valuable
aid to practice. When Socrates brought down philosophy from
heaven to earth, abandoning astronomy for ethics, his intention
was not only to cease a fruitless inquiry, as he thought it, into
matters which could never be thoroughly understood, and transfer
men's attention to a field where definite and ascertainable knowledge awaited them; he also hoped that men, by studying the principles of their conduct, would learn to conduct themselves
differently, and arrive at practical solutions of their practical problems **[6]** through a theoretical understanding of what these
problems involved. From this belief the Greek philosophers never
departed. It underlay Plato's proposal that philosophers should
become kings and kings philosophers; for this proposal depended
on the principle that the practical pursuit of the good was greatly
helped by a theoretical grasp of its nature. It underlies the whole of
Aristotle's *Ethics*, whose fundamental thesis is that ethical or rather
political theory is of value as a preparation for political life. It
reappears in the later Greek schools, Stoicism and Epicureanism,
where it is an axiom that the practical pursuit of happiness is aided
by, or even impossible without, the possession of philosophical
wisdom. Ethics, for all the Greek philosophers, was more than a
description of 'virtue'; it was a description which enabled the man
who understood it to realize the thing defined; and this faith in the
practical value of ethics had its counterpart in logic, and, so far as
aesthetics had gone, in aesthetics also. Logic appears in Greek
philosophy not only as the science of thought, but also as an organon
of rules for the proper conduct of thought. It is assumed, not indeed
that no one but a logician can think, but that a logician is likely to
think better than a non-logician, because the logician understands
what he is trying to do and knows when it has been successfully
done. In aesthetics, Aristotle put forward a theory of rhetoric and
tragedy which not only described what these things actually were,
but also gave rules showing how they could best be made.

The Greeks in this way inaugurated a long tradition of conceiving the philosophical sciences as normative sciences, **[7]** sciences

laying down rules for the proper performance of various human functions: scientific thought, moral conduct, artistic creation. But in the world of today, although this tradition has left abundant traces of itself, it is no longer dominant. A reaction against it has set in, and an altogether opposite view holds the field.

According to this modern view in its extreme form, the philosophical sciences have no practical value whatever. Their business is to give a true account of certain classes of fact or regions of the real. Logic does not tell us how to think, for 'God has not dealt so sparingly with man as to make him barely a two-legged animal, and leave it to Aristotle to make him rational'; its task is to find out what thinking actually is, and how it actually goes on; or else, if we prefer a more metaphysical and less psychological definition, its task is to study the nature of 'truth', or 'order' or some such character of the real world. Ethics, again, does not tell us how to behave; that is the function of our moral consciousness—our moral sense, or conscience, or practical reason, call it what you will, according to your theory of its nature; the function of ethics is to study and describe this moral consciousness, not to alter or develop it; or else, metaphysically, to give an account of something called 'value'. And aesthetics, in the same way, is the study of an activity that exists and develops and perfects itself unhelped by this **[8]** reflexion on it; the activity of seeing things as beautiful, or discovering or creating beautiful things; the aesthetic activity, whatever precisely we understand that to be. Or we may prefer to define its task as the investigation of beauty as such.[4]

---

[4] Opposite fos. 8 and 9: 'But when you look closely at this theory of philosophical science as merely descriptive, you find that it is never consistently held. The people who are keenest on asserting it always abandon it over one crucial point. They won't, it is true, admit that *good* theory leads to good practice, but they do think *bad* theory leads to bad practice: for example, they think that a man with a bad theory of ethics may be led by it into doing wrong acts, that a man with a false logical theory may allow it to pervert his scientific thinking, and that a man with an erroneous philosophy of art may have his taste spoilt by the theory. I think this is certainly true: but see what it implies. A true theory, refuting the false one, will remove its baneful influence and restore the unsophisticated moral or scientific or aesthetic consciousness to its rightful throne. But if this is admitted [continued opposite fo. 9], it follows that ethics and logic and aesthetic are not descriptive sciences; for in a really descriptive science, like astronomy, error can have no such consequences. Bad astronomy does not derange the movements of the stars.'

I have spoken as if the business of these philosophical sciences were the study of certain activities proper to mind. But that is not the only possible view of them. They may be regarded from a point of view rather metaphysical than psychological. Logic will now appear as the theory of truth, ethics of goodness, and aesthetic of beauty, where truth, goodness, and beauty are the names of objective values or forms of order, wholly independent of the special ways in which we human beings react to them by pursuing the specific activities of science, morality, and art. This way of thinking, which appears in many modern philosophers, is in part a return to the Greek tradition, for these objective values or forms of order are much like the Platonic Forms. The difference is that whereas Plato believed the apprehension of the Forms to be the proper work of philosophy, these modern theories assign the apprehension of truth not to philosophy in the form of logic but to science, the apprehension of goodness not to ethics or moral philosophy but to the moral consciousness, and the apprehension of beauty not to philosophy in the shape of aesthetics, but to the non-philosophical aesthetic consciousness as it exists in the artist. Accordingly, the return to a Platonic or metaphysical point of view, as against a Lockean or psychological, makes no **[9]** difference to the present question. Both the psychological view of philosophy, as the study of the thinking or acting mind, and the metaphysical view of philosophy, as the study of the ultimate nature of the real world, are compatible with the doctrine that the philosophical sciences have a purely theoretical interest, and are completely devoid of practical value.

The view that the philosophical sciences are descriptive, not normative, has therefore no special connexion with modern realism, if modern realism means a reaction against the psychological view of philosophy and an attempt to displace consciousness from the centre of the universe. The traditional view of philosophical thought as normative was already, as I have pointed out, rejected by Locke in the case of logic; in the case of ethics, its rejection was a commonplace from at least the earlier part of the eighteenth century; in the case of aesthetics, the late eighteenth century saw the same process completed, when aestheticians threw Aristotle to the winds and proclaimed the enthronement of genius as absolute monarch of the world of art.

I am not sure whether anybody holds what I have called the modern view quite consistently. Locke himself,[5] though rejecting the conception of logic as a normative science, undertook his analysis of human understanding with the express object of discovering the limits of human knowledge, and so enabling men to avoid wasting time over problems which their minds were powerless to solve.[6] He [10] hoped in this way to aid men in the pursuit of truth by offering them a theory of knowledge; in other words, his theory of knowledge was a normative science, practical, not merely theoretical, in its purpose. Without multiplying instances, I will come down to our own time and quote a living writer.

Moral philosophy does not aim at making men better, but at clearing up our notions of goodness. The goodness of a man without any theory about goodness may be just as good as that of one who has found its correct description. His acts are just as likely to be both right and moral . . . . The theory is nothing but an attempt to describe the facts; and to tamper with them is to poison the wells of truth.

Here moral philosophy appears as purely descriptive. But the consequences of this view are not consistently maintained. The writer qualifies them by making two admissions: first, that reflection upon the moral law is likely to make a man reverence it more; secondly, that false moral philosophies may lead to wrong conduct, and that in this sense a true moral philosophy may lead to right conduct because, exploding the false claim of philosophy to be normative, it replaces the unsophisticated moral consciousness on its rightful throne.[7]

---

[5] * *Essay Concerning Human Understanding*, I, i, §§ 4–7.

[6] Opposite fo. 9: 'Whether we prefer a more psychological view of these sciences, as investigating certain activities of the mind, or a more metaphysical view, as investigating certain objective correlates of these activities, makes no difference: in either case it is possible to regard them as merely descriptive and devoid of anything like a normative value.'

[7] * E. F. Carritt, *The Theory of Morals: An Introduction to Ethical Philosophy* (Oxford: Oxford University Press, 1928), 70–1. So, in his *Theory of Beauty* (1914; 3rd rev. edn. London: Methuen, 1928), Mr. Carritt holds that 'Aesthetics are for aesthetics' sake' (3). [Opposite fo. 10: "This "descriptive," as opposed to normative, view is certainly dominant in modern thought; but it is seldom, if ever, held consistently. Even the people who most definitely assert that moral philosophy aims, not at making us better, but at clearing up our ideas as to what goodness is, will go on to say that such clearing-up of our ideas may make us more sensitive to the

To the question, 'is moral philosophy of value to moral conduct?' this author therefore at first replies, 'no; the first is merely a
[11] description of the second'. But afterwards he replies 'yes; for
bad moral philosophies may claim to be normative and so corrupt
moral conduct, and in these cases a good moral philosophy is a *sine
qua non* of its restoration'. But if bad ethics may lead to bad
conduct, whatever the reason, the relation of ethics to conduct is
not simply that of a description to the thing described. Bad astronomy does not derange the movements of the stars.[8]

That bad theory may lead to bad practice will, I think, be
generally allowed. Epicurus himself was no epicure; but that was
because his simple nature and moral integrity saved him from the
dangers to which, later, his school proverbially succumbed. If a
man is persuaded that all action is right in so far as it promotes one
particular end, he is likely to become on that account less scrupulous about the performance of duties not explicable in terms of that
end. If a man believes that all universal truths are reached by
induction from particular instances, he is likely to be confused
and uncritical in his thinking about truths that cannot be so derived. In these cases there is certainly a connexion of some sort
between bad theory and bad practice; and it does not seem plausible to suggest that the bad theory is simply an *ex post facto*
description of the bad practice. The case of Epicurus suggests the
opposite view, that the bad practice is, sometimes at any rate, a
result of the bad theory.

[12] If bad theory can lead to bad practice, the theory is not
simply a description of the practice. But it is still possible to admit
this, without admitting that good theory, as such, is of use towards
good practice. It may be held that practice is capable of being
corrupted by bad theory, but not capable of being improved by
good. We produce good art because we are good artists, and do
virtuous actions because we are virtuous men; the theory of art or
virtue cannot be a substitute for art or virtue itself, and therefore
these theories cannot help us to produce good art or to do virtuous

claims of duty, and may even, by clearing our minds of a false casuistry, restore us to
the possession of an unsophisticated conscience and so make us better men.']

[8] Opposite fo. 11: 'Clearly, these admissions are fatal to the conception of ethics
as a merely descriptive science. If bad ethics may lead to the corruption of morals,
then [running on to main text] practice is capable of being corrupted . . . '

actions. What they can do is to distract our attention to theoretical questions, and divert our minds from the practical business of art or virtue.

The effect of such a view is that the artist as such ought to eschew philosophy altogether, since it may do him harm and cannot do him good. The same applies to the virtuous man and to the seeker after truth. In none of these three cases can any useful result be expected from philosophy, whether in the form of aesthetic, ethics, or logic; and the guaranteed harmlessness of a good philosophy is no comfort, because not only is it easier to attain no philosophy at all than to attain an altogether true one, but a true one, if it is ever reached, will be reached only at the end of a process of inquiry in whose course we shall doubtless fall into many errors. In short, philosophy on this view is a vice which ought to be suppressed.[9] **[13]** Nothing is gained by leaving it to a special class of professional philosophers, for such a class has no reason to exist, and no man has any reason to enter it. If anyone says that he must become a philosopher in order to satisfy his native thirst for knowledge, he forgets that it is possible to satisfy this thirst in a restricted field where it cannot do harm and may do good, the field of science, or whatever name we give to our knowledge of the objective world.

Thus the view that theory may corrupt practice, but cannot amend it, leads straight to the condemnation of philosophy in general as a vice of the intellect; a view which I mention here not as a curiosity but as an actual opinion widely held among ourselves. There are a great many artists and scientists and practical men who think that philosophy is just that; and although, for my own part,

---

[9] Opposite fo. 12: 'On such a view, philosophy is at best a harmless eccentricity to be indulged in by professional philosophers, though why professional philosophers should exist is hard to say. At worst, it is a vice of the intellect that ought to be altogether suppressed. Both these views are widely held; and they cannot be seriously challenged, as long as those who would wish to challenge them are content to think of the philosophical sciences as merely descriptive, while admitting that they have the peculiarity of being able [opposite fo. 13] to pervert, though not to assist, the activities upon which they reflect. Yet it seems to be a fact that such perversions do occur, and the correct inference would seem to be that the philosophical sciences are not descriptive sciences in the sense in which botany or astronomy or psychology is descriptive. In the search for a better conception of the relation between these sciences and their subject matter, it would perhaps be useful to leave abstract argument.'

I believe this opinion does harm to their art and their science and
their practical virtues, I do not think that we can attack it effectively, or induce them to respect the studies in which we engage,
without revising our whole conception of the relation between
philosophical sciences, such as aesthetic, and the activities, such
as artistic practice, which they make their subject matter.

[14] III

We have found no one to support the view that aesthetic is a
normative science; and we have seen reason to reject the view
that it is a descriptive, because, where a theory is merely a description, bad theory cannot lead to bad practice. But if neither of these
views will hold, what third alternative is there?

It is perhaps time that we left abstract argument[10] on one side for
a little, and looked closer at concrete facts. If we examined a
particular artist's work and compared its characteristic qualities
with the outstanding features of the same man's philosophy of art,
we might get valuable results, provided we could light on a man
who was a good enough artist to justify us in spending time over his
work, and also a good enough philosopher to justify us in taking his
philosophy seriously. Such a man is hard to find. But we might get
equally valuable results if we took a school or movement instead of
a single man. A group of men, sharing many ideas in common, may
contain some individuals worthy of being regarded as their spokesmen in art, others in philosophy. For neither artists nor philosophers produce their work for themselves alone; they rely on a
more or less sympathetic audience, and they desire not so much to
instruct this audience as to put to it more clearly what it is already
thinking and feeling obscurely. If, in a certain country at a certain
time, one man is a popular philosopher and another a popular
artist, we are likely to be right if we assume that their philosophy
and art are [15] in some sense expressions of a single mind. In
trying to judge of the relation between aesthetic theory and artistic

---

[10] Opposite fo. 14: 'In order to get a clearer conception of the relations between
aesthetic theory and artistic practice, it would be well to get our feet planted on the
ground of fact; and for this purpose I propose to ask how the two things were
actually related during a period of history with which we are all more or less
familiar—the central nineteenth century.'

practice, therefore, we shall find it useful to take a single period of history in a country or group of associated countries, and consider the relation between the artistic works and the aesthetic theories there current.

For this purpose I propose to take the nineteenth century, and in particular its central portion, and to remind you of certain features which that period presents in England and to some extent in France. I have no intention of doing anything so ambitious as to describe the whole course of artistic history during that period: I only want to speak of one characteristic quality by which the period as a whole was strongly marked, namely its naturalism.

Nineteenth-century art, taken as a whole, was a naturalistic art. Its chief object was to copy nature. This is plainest in the case of the painters, who all tended, in all their work, to gravitate round the ideal of accurately reproducing natural facts. A vast amount of landscape was painted; and this was no doubt due to the fact that landscape readily lends itself to this kind of treatment: you can sit down in front of a scene and copy it almost as if your canvas were a window, with the scene visible through the glass. The landscape of other periods was adversely criticized, just because it did not aim at this accurate copying of natural scenes. Other branches of painting were equally naturalistic in their principles: portraits, for example, were often painted so as to look like photographs, and [16] even pictures of imaginary scenes were painted with the greatest possible care to make them look like real ones.

The same naturalism pervaded other branches of art. In literature this took various forms: the everyday realism of a Dickens, the scientific observation of a Zola, the archaeological exactitude of Flaubert in *Salambo* are all versions of it, and the formula for them all is that a book should be a slice of life, very much as a landscape is an excerpt from nature. Even music felt the same spell, and painted natural scenes, or imitated actual noises, with increasing skill and concentration. Beethoven's cuckoo is hardly more than a joke, and Schubert's spinning wheel is a decorative pattern merely suggested by the wheel's hum; but Brahms's raindrops are meant as seriously as the bleating of the sheep in Strauss's *Don Quixote*, or the Fire Music itself.[11]

---

[11] Collingwood had referred to 'the pattering drops' of Richard Strauss's *Regenleid* and 'the bleating of Don Quixote's sheep' in WT, fo. 6, above.

This all-pervading naturalism demanded the concentration of
the artist's every thought on the reproduction of the natural object,
or an object compounded—as in some picture of Greek girls on a
marble seat—of natural elements. Every work of art was either a
single study from nature or a mosaic of studies from nature; and in
either case the merit of the work was regarded as lying, first and
foremost, in the success with which nature had been copied.
Drawing, from this point of view, came to mean **[17]** not the
construction of expressive and significant shapes, but the accurate
reproduction of the shapes of natural objects.[12] Description, in
literature, came to mean describing an actual scene or event, or
one so imagined that it might pass for actual; not describing scenes
or events in such a way as to give them a value in relation to a
coherent whole with a formal and expressive character of its own.
This implied the neglect of drawing and description in these other
senses of the words: the sense in which a Renaissance arabesque is
well drawn, or a scene in Dante's *Inferno* well described. It also
implied the neglect of composition or construction, which is only
the same thing on a larger scale; not because these artists had never
heard of composition, for on the contrary they thought much of it
and valued it as highly as they valued drawing; but because they
believed that good composition, like good drawing, was to be
found ready made in nature. Nature's drawing—the line of hill
and tree, cloud and wave, feather and muscle and bone—was
impeccable; contained an inexhaustible store of beauty which
human invention could not rival, and should be proud and content
to use. Nature's composition was no less perfect; the arrangement
of objects, their grouping into patterns, had already been done by
nature as well as it could be done. Beauty did not wait for man's
hand to bring it into existence; it existed, infinitely various and
infinitely rich, in the natural world, and the proper function of the
artist, since he could never hope to improve on nature or to produce work equalling hers in formal perfection, was to go humbly to
her as a pupil, and repeat his lesson syllable by syllable.

   [18] The work produced under the influence of this principle
had many merits, but it had one defect, which proceeded directly

---

[12] Opposite fo. 17: 'The reason for this lay in the belief that nature was always,
not only beautiful, but pre-eminently beautiful; more beautiful than art could ever
be, and a source from which art could borrow all the beauty it needed.'

from the principle itself. This defect may perhaps be described as shapelessness. The work has a way of sprawling or lounging; indulging an inordinate prolixity if inclined to be garrulous, merely fragmentary if it has less to say. Poets wrote amorphously, long works or short works, all equally formless; the long poems might, for all one can tell, have ended much sooner, the short ones might have gone on much longer; and it is characteristic of the time, that the old strict verse-forms for short lyrics fell out of use among the chief poets, to lead a kind of underground life among a certain class of minor poets whose fastidious taste rebelled against the prevailing fashion, though their poetic energy was too slight to make their rebellion effective. To handle an exacting metre with skill and grace; to construct an elaborate pattern of vowels; these are parts of the poet's trade which the major poets of the nineteenth century so completely neglected that one can only suppose they thought them despicable; yet they are no more despicable than is the art, in a musician, of playing a scale so as to make the notes sound, as John Sebastian Bach said, like a 'string of equal pearls'.[13]

The same formless habit made itself felt in painting, with equally unfortunate results. There is an art—Vernon Blake has called our attention to its importance—of placing an object on the canvas, no matter what the object is, and what else there may be on the canvas; it may be the placing of a mere ink-blot on a piece of paper.[14] If a man **[19]** has mastered this art, his ink-blot is already a picture, something worth hanging on a wall and looking at every day. How much more, if there are two or more ink blots; or if, instead of being mere ink-blots, they have a shape and an interest of their own. Blake reproduced a drawing by a Chinese artist of the thirteenth century,[15] representing six fruits on a table;

[13] Philip Spitta, *Johan Sebastian Bach: His Work and Influence on the Music of Germany, 1685–1750*, tr. Clara Bell and J. A. Fuller-Maitland, 3 vols. (London: Novello & Co., 1884), iii. 36, notes: that when Bach played, 'everything came out with a perfect clearness, and a pearly roundness and purity'.

[14] Collingwood refers to Blake in *PA* 145, admired his work, and visited him in the South of France. Peter Johnson, *The Correspondence of R. G. Collingwood: An Illustrated Guide* (Swansea: R. G. Collingwood Society, 1998), 10, notes that Blake wrote to Collingwood asking him for comments on and corrections to his book *Relation in Art: Being a Suggested Scheme of Art Criticism* (London: Oxford University Press, Humphrey Milford, 1925).

[15] Six Plaquemines by Mou-hsi (dated about AD 1250). In *Drawing for Children and Others* (London: Humphrey Milford, Oxford University Press, 1927), fig. 15.

the table was not drawn at all, and the fruits were reduced to mere patches of colour each with a couple of lines for a stalk and a leaf; there is practically nothing in the drawing at all except the placing of these coloured patches on the sheet of paper, but this is done with such skill that the result is a masterpiece. 'Perhaps', says Blake in his note on the drawing,

you think it is easy to do something like this. Well, I can tell you that nothing is more difficult; this is the reduction of all art to its most simple form. Notice . . . how the fruits seem to be resting on the surface, *which is not drawn at all*, and yet which we feel to be there. Notice how the top of the paper does not seem to be empty . . . in spite of the fruits being down at the bottom of the paper. This is because the pattern is exquisitely arranged with regard to the shape of the paper.

And he goes on, explaining what he means by the difficulty of such a feat: 'Mou-hsi has given himself no chance of making a mistake which should not be seen. That is why the great critics of the east admire such pictures as this so much. All the difficulties of art are observed and vanquished in such a drawing.'[16]

[20] Now, the great fault of nineteenth-century painting is precisely its deficiency in the qualities which Vernon Blake is here expounding. Painters did not realize that the problem of placing an object on the canvas was the central problem of their art, and a problem which came up anew every time they laid on a new touch of paint. Trusting to nature to settle the shapes and arrangements of their subject, they were scarcely more sensitive to this problem than the photographic camera itself. I say 'scarcely' more sensitive, because I am of course aware that the painters of whom I am speaking did to some extent compose their pictures; they very seldom painted a subject just as the camera might have photographed it; they put in a foreground from one source and an object in the middle distance from another, and so on. But, in taking these liberties with nature, they moved within so narrow a margin of license that they never faced the necessity of making themselves responsible, to themselves and their audience, for what they were doing. The completed picture still claimed to be a scene taken from nature, and whatever modifications of nature were included in it were included, as it were, surreptitiously, and not intended to be known for what they really were. The artist's

---

[16] * *Drawing for Children and Others*, 36.

freedom to compose his subject was a freedom which he dared not openly claim, and exercised only in matters where it could pass unnoticed. Consequently those qualities in his work which demanded a confident and skilled use of this freedom were not achieved, or achieved only in a low degree. The placing of objects on the canvas was either [21] neglected, as a thing not worth thinking about, or else it was disposed of by the mechanical application of a few crude and elementary rules—so crude that a Whistler, by breaking them, could appear a bold innovator in composition.[17]

The same insensitiveness to the placing of objects on the canvas reappeared with regard to another aspect of the same matter—the shapes of the objects themselves. These shapes were taken over ready-made from nature, in obedience to the doctrine that nature's shapes were more beautiful than any that art could invent; and the result was that painters left off asking themselves what the shapes of things ought to be, and contented themselves with asking what their shapes in nature were. The result was good observation but bad design. The business of a shape, in a picture, is to have meaning, and a meaning that helps to make up the meaning of the picture. The curves of the wind-blown cloak in Botticelli's *Venus* are almost as full of meaning as the forward tilt and poise of the wind-blown goddess herself; but there is no guarantee that any instantaneous photographs of a fluttering cloak would reveal so significant a group of lines, and there is much reason to think that no photograph of a female model on a floating shell could ever reproduce that tilt and that poise.[18] The ability to think out groups of lines having this kind of significance is what I call design; and this is the ability which became atrophied in the naturalistic artists of the nineteenth century, until at [22] last their works sprawled and lounged over their canvases in a kind of creeping paralysis where no single line or mass was of value because it stood just where it did, and had just the shape it had.

---

[17] Opposite fo. 21: 'just as Swinburne's crude and clumsy sound-patterns could please a generation whose ear was starved for lack of formal qualities in its verse'.

[18] Struck out in pencil from 'there is no guarantee . . . ' to this point but restored here. Collingwood's pencilled amendment reads: 'no amount of observation, even assisted by instantaneous photographs, would have sufficed to determine the way in which the curves should go'.

This endemic disease did not, of course, affect all artists of the time in an equal degree. I am describing the symptoms; and if there were artists who showed them only to a small or venial extext,[19] that does not invalidate the general description, which I believe will be accepted by anyone who now looks back on the period as a whole. And I want also to point out that the disease was not due to external influences, it was a home-grown product. A curious proof of this lies in the word 'Pre-Raphaelite'. The English Pre-Raphaelite painters came forward ostensibly as pupils and followers of the Italian primitives. Now, if there is one thing that we of today notice more than another in the Italian primitives, it is their design—their faculty of making lines and masses intensely significant. If there is anything that can be learnt from study of the primitives, we should say that it is the importance of scrupulous and relentless design. The kind of thing which most of us have carried away from the primitives in last year's Italian exhibition[20] is the pattern of the rocks of Lorenzo's St Benedict, or the gesture of the tree in the little *Noli Me Tangere* ascribed to Giotto. The Pre-Raphaelites saw many paintings of this kind, but this element in them was completely hidden from their eyes. Even after looking at Giotto and Masaccio, it never occurred to them that designing [23] his picture was the prime duty of an artist.

The lack of design or construction, which I have called the endemic disease of nineteenth-century art, was not due to the lack of good models. Good models were known, but they were studied from a point of view which deprived them of their power to cure this particular disease. We have, then, to inquire into the nature and origin of this point of view. It cannot be dismissed as mere bad taste; what we have to explain is not bad art as such, but a particular kind of bad art, an art defective in one particular quality. The essence of this point of view is what I have called naturalism. By naturalism I mean not simply the habit of enjoying natural beauty, but something more: the habit of regarding artistic beauty as a transcript of natural beauty. Art and nature are not placed side by side as different repositories of beauty, or repositories of differ-

---

[19] * [Edward] Burne-Jones [1833–1898] was an artist who tried to design his pictures instead of merely copying them from nature. He was therefore not popular. [Collingwood's marginal note.]

[20] *Exhibition of Italian Art 1200–1900* (London: Royal Academy of Arts, 1930).

ent kinds of beauty: nature is regarded as having a monopoly of
beauty, and the beauty of art is regarded as a loan upon the
inexhaustible store of nature. Artists who took up this naturalistic
attitude towards their work began by trusting nature to do the
designing of their own works of art; they ended by having their
faculty of design so atrophied that the difference between good
design and bad design meant little or nothing to them, and the
difference between good drawing and bad drawing meant simply
the difference between accurate and inaccurate copying of nature.

Now, this naturalism is a philosophy of art. It is the theory that
the function of art is to copy nature, and that, by copying nature,
art comes to participate in the beauty that is ready-made in nature.
[24] And this theory of art implies a theory of beauty, according to
which beauty is an inherent property of nature as such, whether
because it results necessarily from the physical structure of the
natural world, or because it arises from nature's being the handiwork of a divine or transcendental mind.

Were the artists of the nineteenth century consciously possessed
of such a theory? For answer, we need only to look at Browning, to
whom, I confess, I have already alluded in speaking of the garrulous prolixity, the lounging and sprawling formlessness, of the best
nineteenth-century poets. Browning has expressed this theory
more than once. He puts it into the mouth of 'Fra Lippo Lippi'
(*Men and Women*, 1855):[21]

> Paint these
> Just as they are, careless what comes of it . . .
> God's works—paint any one, and count it crime
> To let a truth slip. Don't object, 'His works
> Are here already—nature is complete:
> Suppose you reproduce her—(which you can't)
> There's no advantage! you must beat her, then.'
> For, don't you mark, we're made so that we love
> First when we see them painted, things we have passed
> Perhaps a hundred times nor cared to see;
> And so they are better, painted—better to us,
> Which is the same thing.

Here beauty, as the visible signature of God in his handiwork—a
theory familiar from Hegel and Ruskin—exists ready-made

---

[21] 2 vols. (London: Chapman & Hall, 1855), i. 50.

everywhere in nature: art, in copying nature, achieves beauty [25] by the accuracy of its transcript, and thus the beauty of nature is, in Hegel's words, 'born again of the spirit',[22] brought nearer to man and given to him for a fuller and more intimate enjoyment. This is precisely the naturalistic aesthetic which we have found put into practice by the nineteenth-century artists. Elsewhere Browning actually goes to the length of attributing this aesthetic to the Italian primitives as a whole. Greek art, he explains, had represented an ideal—'you saw yourself as you wished you were, as you might have been, as you cannot be'; the primitives, rebelling against this, resolved to 'paint man, *man*'—to represent nature—human nature—just as it is (*Old Pictures in Florence*, in *Men and Women*, 1855).[23] In this attribution of a naturalistic purpose to early Italian painting we see the whole of 'Pre-Raphaelitism' in germ.

Another leading artist who deliberately expressed the same view in his writings, though with more emphasis on practice than on theory, was Sir Gilbert Scott the architect, who in 1857—two years after Browning's *Men and Women*—published his *Remarks on Secular and Domestic Architecture*, in which he contends that 'an implicit and unconditional falling back on' nature must be 'the great, all pervading characteristic of the future style', and pushes this principle to the length of advocating the decoration of interiors with sky-blue ceilings and walls in various shades of greens.[24]

[26] As a theoretical counterpart to the practical architect, we may recall Herbert Spencer's essay on the 'Origin and Function of Music', published in the same year, and maintaining that 'vari-

---

[22] John 3: 3–7: 'We are born again of the spirit, we have the greater one living in us, we have been set free from the law of sin and death.' Collingwood appears to be remembering the biblical quotation to which Hegel alludes. Hegel actually says 'aus dem Geiste geborene und wieder geborene' or (literally) 'born and born again from the spirit'. In his translation of Hegel's *Introductory Lectures on Aesthetics* (1886; London: Penguin Books, 1993), Bernard Bosanquet renders it: 'For the beauty of art is the beauty that is born—born again, that is—of the mind' (ch. 1, § II, 4, and Commentary, 98).

[23] The quotations from 'Old Pictures in Florence' appear in *Men and Women*, ii. 36; 39. The emphasis is Collingwood's.

[24] * Quoted by Miss Joan Evans, *Pattern: A Study of Ornament in Western Europe from 1180 to 1900*, 2 vols. (Oxford: Clarendon Press, 1931), ii. 155, 194. Miss Evans's chapters on 'The Return to Nature' and 'The Age of Theory' are extremely rich in material bearing on my subject. [Collingwood had taken detailed notes from Evans in his 'Notes on Aesthetic'.]

ations of voice are the physiological results of variations of feeling'
and that song is a natural development of these variations.[25] Here
music exists as it were ready-made in nature, in the shape of
sounds artlessly produced, and significant because proceeding directly from the feelings they express: and the musician's business is
to draw upon this store of natural music.[26]

But all these expressions of the naturalistic aesthetic fall short of
Ruskin's. In *Modern Painters*, beginning in 1843, he built up an
elaborate and detailed account of the principles of art—primarily
the art of landscape painting, but implicitly of art as a whole—
whose central thought was the conception of nature as the original
repository of all beauty, and of art as achieving beauty just so far as
it remained faithful to the task of transcribing nature. In this
conception, all distinction between formal and naturalistic art
vanished. Formal elements in beauty were recognized freely
enough: much of Ruskin's best work was devoted to analysing
the decorative qualities of mountains, clouds, and so forth; but
these were regarded as possessed of beauty only because they were
part of nature. A line discovered in nature, like the curve of a bird's
wing, was thereby authorized to be used as beautiful by the artist;
any line not to be found in nature must be banished from the best
art, which will always use 'the forms of nature, not the spirals and
zigzags of children **[27]** and savages'.[27]

[25] Herbert Spencer, 'The Origin and Function of Music', *Essays: Scientific, Political, and Speculative* (London: Longman, Brown, Green, Longmans, & Roberts, 1858), 363.

[26] Cf. WT, fo. 13, above.

[27] * *Stones of Venice*, vol. I, ch. ii. [Collingwood's style of citation retained. In FT, Collingwood was decisively to reject the kind of artistic primitivism which conflates the work of 'children and savages', arguing that human societies do not have a childhood. The quotation Collingwood refers to here is not found at the location cited in *The Works of John Ruskin*, ed. E. T. Cook and Alexander Wedderburn, 39 vols. (London: George Allen, 1903–12), and does not appear in the 3-vol. edn. of *The Stones of Venice* (London: Smith, Elder & Co., 1851), nor in the 2-vol. (revised) 3rd edn. (Orpington, Kent: George Allen, 1884). Ruskin does, however, write of Indian art in *The Two Paths* (1858), Lecture 1, *Works*, xvi. 265: 'To all the facts and forms of nature it [Indian art] wilfully and resolutely opposes itself: it will not draw a man, but an eight-armed monster; it will not draw a flower, but only a spiral or a zigzag.' The beautiful natural curve of a bird's wing is discussed in *Modern Painters*, *Works*, vi. 246–7. It is possible that Collingwood was excerpting a general sense of the Ruskinian aesthetic at this point.]

$$\text{IV}^{28}$$

In all this, Ruskin is very far from attempting to describe, in a generalized way, the traditional practice of artists. On the contrary, his principles bring him into sharp and conscious opposition with a great deal in that practice. His condemnation of 'spirals and zig-zags' leads him explicitly to denounce the Greek fiet or maeander, the guilloche, and a great part of the traditional decorative *répertoire*, as inaesthetic. The main thesis of *Modern Painters* is that the classical schools of landscape painting were producing what was properly not art at all. If he was describing any actual art, it was the art of Turner. But if we ask whether the general account which Ruskin gives of the principles of art[29] is a better description of Turner or of the art of the succeeding generation, the right answer undoubtedly is the latter. Turner was by no means a purely naturalistic painter. He went to nature for his *répertoire* of forms, just as his contemporary Wordsworth went to the common speech of every day for his poetic vocabulary. But both artists were deeply rooted in the technical traditions of the eighteenth century. The generation to which they belonged—the Romantic generation—worked on the basis of a magnificently fertile, but unstable, compromise between two methods: the formal 'classical' methods of Pope and Claude and Haydn, and the naturalistic methods which were expounded by Ruskin in the 1840s and **[28]** did not actually take entire control of artistic practice until somewhat later. A reader who tried to reconstruct Turner's work from Ruskin's pages, without ever having seen a Turner drawing for himself, would construct something with far too much Corot in it, and far too little Claude.[30]

[28] Section heading inserted in pencil, and apparently retrospectively, at this point.

[29] Collingwood's use of the phrase 'the principles of art' will suggest the measure in which *PA* was conceived as a response to, and correction of, Ruskin.

[30] Opposite fo. 28: 'In fact, as Mr Christopher Hussey has shown, Turner closes one period and Ruskin opens the next: Turner belongs to what Mr Hussey calls the *picturesque* school, whereas Ruskin belongs to the school of 'minute imitation' of nature; and it is a fascinating task—though I have no time for it this evening—to show how Ruskin's attempt to base his theories on an examination of Turner's practice breaks down because over and over again, Turner offends against Ruskin's fundamental principles and adopts a practice far more consonant with the principles of Alison. Alison, towards the end of the eighteenth century, expounded a view

As an illustration of this, I may refer to Ruskin's chapter on 'Turnerian Topography'.[31] The crux of this chapter is the fact that Turner will not paint places 'just as they are'; instead of giving us a photographically naturalistic study of a scene, he gives way to 'an entirely imperative dream'; 'he can see, and do, no otherwise than as the dream directs'.[32] Now, what the dream directs him to do is to alter the proportions of his scene—Ruskin is analysing his drawing of the Pass of Faido, on the southern approach to the St Gothard—so as to bring it 'up to the general majesty of the higher forms of the Alps';[33] a rock five-hundred feet high is exaggerated to one thousand, the mountains in the background are enlarged and brought forward so as to impend menacingly over the valley, now reduced to a precipitous gorge, and the road is altered so as to make it more sensational and perilous. These liberties taken with the actual scene are, in reality, altogether alien from the spirit of Ruskin's aesthetic, just as they are from the practice of Ruskin himself as a landscape artist. On the strict naturalistic theory, Turner ought not to have taken them. But seeing that he did, and that he produced a fine romantic landscape by doing so, Ruskin offers a justification of them. Turner, he says, was combining the **[29a]** scene as he saw it with impressions derived from his journey, earlier on the same day, through the higher mountains. This 'mental chemistry', which Ruskin confesses to be 'utterly inexplicable',[34] is certainly inexplicable on the naturalistic theory of art, for it contradicts the fundamental principle of that theory. It is more consistent with earlier theories, such as that of Alison; but over a crucial matter like this there is a radical divergence between Turner's practice and Ruskin's theory, Turner's practice harmonizing with the theories of the late eighteenth century, and Ruskin's theories with the practice of the middle and late nineteenth.[35]

according to which the great merit of landscape lies.' [Ends.] A pencilled '30' suggests where the main text resumes.

[31] In parentheses: '*Modern Painters*, IV, ii'. See *Modern Painters*, iv, 'containing Part V: Of Mountain Beauty', *Works*, vi. 27–47.

[32] Ruskin, *Works*, vi. 38.   [33] Ibid. 37.   [34] Ibid. 41.

[35] * I am glad to be able to quote Mr Christopher Hussey in my support on this point. In *The Picturesque: Studies in a Point of View* (London and New York: Putnam, 1927) he makes his list of 'the most eminently picturesque English painters' culminate in Girtin, Turner, and Constable: 'Turner's painting comprehends and glorifies all the ideals of the picturesque' (272). It is [29b (ult.)] clear that picturesque art as understood by Mr Hussey is a very different thing from the

Whence, then, did Ruskin and his contemporaries derive this naturalistic theory of art? Not, we have seen, from a study of existing works of art: it was not a description of past achievements, but a manifesto for the future. Nor did they derive it from the works of earlier aesthetic theorists. Ruskin, for example, had read Alison's *Nature and Principles of Taste* (1790) and Dr Thomas Brown's *Lectures on the Philosophy of the Human Mind* (delivered 1810–20).[36] These works contain no hint of his special theory: on the contrary, Alison expounds a view according to which the great merit of landscape lies **[30a]** precisely in 'beating' nature—to quote Browning's word—because the artist is free to select and compose, and so to give 'both greater extent and greater unity to his composition'. 'It is not now a simple copy which we see, nor is our Emotion limited to the cold pleasure which arises from the perception of accurate Imitation.' '[T]he object of painting is no sooner discovered, than the unity of expression is felt to be the great secret of its power; the superiority which it at last assumes over the scenery of Nature, is found to arise in one important respect, from the greater purity and simplicity which its composition can attain.'[37] Thomas Brown has little to say of art, but much of beauty; and he nowhere betrays any thought that nature enjoys a monopoly of it. On the contrary, he follows the eighteenth-century tradition which regards both nature and art as beautiful, each in its own right.

The naturalistic movement in art, led, I think we may now say, by Ruskin as an aesthetic theorist, and followed by the practising artists of the middle and later nineteenth century, came into being through the breakdown of this equilibrium between nature and art. Can we trace any premonitions of this breakdown before Ruskin?

---

naturalistic art which, inaugurated by *Modern Painters*, followed it. Mr Hussey's conception of Turner as closing a period seems to me substantially just: and his references to Ruskin (e.g. on his p. 216) show that, like myself, he regards Ruskin as opening the next, that of 'minute imitation'. [The material from 'scene as he saw it' in the main text to 'culminate' in the note stuck over unreadable original.]

[36] See Thomas Brown, MD, *Lectures on the Philosophy of the Human Mind*, 4 vols. (Edinburgh: James Ballantyne, 1820).

[37] * Archibald Alison, *Nature and Principles of Taste* (Dublin, 1790), 'Essay I: Of the Nature of the Emotions of Sublimity and Beauty', 77, 79, 80–1.

None, I think, in the region of artistic practice; few even in that of aesthetic theory.[38] But there is no scarcity of them in [31] the general philosophical thought of the period. When Rousseau, in *Émile*, laid it down that '[t]out est bien sortant des mains de l'Auteur des choses, tout dégénère entre les mains de l'homme',[39] he stated a principle which, if applied to aesthetic, would have led directly to *Modern Painters*. This principle consists in the perfection of nature as contrasted with the imperfection of man, and therefore the duty of man to look towards nature, and nowhere else, in his search for perfection. This view of nature was widespread in the eighteenth century, from Voltaire's doctrine that bad taste is 'ne pas sentir la belle nature'[40] to Wordsworth's famous advice to close up the 'barren leaves' of Science and Art, and receive the love of Nature.[41] It was not a mere expression of pleasure in the beauty of *natura naturata*, and it cannot be sufficiently accounted for by calling it a mystical and half-religious feeling for *natura naturans*. It goes back to the early part of the century, when Hume argued that truth concerning nature was reached not by reasoning—'our line is too short to fathom such immense abysses'[42]—but by following an instinct implanted in

[38] * I ignore isolated cases, like that, mentioned by Miss Evans, of John Harris, who as early as 1709 tried to reduce poetry, music, and painting to imitation of nature. [30b (ult.)] And in such a context it would be equally irrelevant to quote Reynolds, who said that the best pictures 'are but faint and feeble' in comparison with the splendours of Nature, but refrained from pressing the inference that artistic beauty was a mere borrowing from natural.

[39] Jean-Jacques Rousseau, *Émile ou de l'éducation* (1762; Paris: Garnier Frères, 1904), 'Livre Premier', 1.

[40] In 'Section Première' of Voltaire's 'Goût', *Œuvres complètes de Voltaire*, 52 vols. (Paris: Garnier Frères, 1843–85), xix, *Dictionnaire Philosophique*, iii (1879), 274.

[41] The final stanza of 'The Tables Turned; An Evening Scene, on the Same Subject' (1798), ll. 29–32: 'Enough of Science and of Art; / Close up these barren leaves; / Come forth, and bring with you a heart / That watches and receives.' See *The Poetical Works of William Wordsworth*, ed. E. de Selincourt and Helen Darbishire, 4 vols. (Oxford: Clarendon Press, 1940–7), 57.

[42] There is no footnote on fo. 31, but an explanatory aside appears on fo. 32, given over in its entirety as follows: '* Hume's words (*Inquiry Concerning Human Understanding*, § 7), though primarily referring to the "theory of the universal energy and operation of the Supreme Being", accurately express his view concerning the nature of scientific knowledge about the physical world; for it is of this knowledge that he says (*Inquiry*, cit., § 5: *Works* (1826), iv. 53–4) that custom and

man by nature herself; and when Shaftesbury contended that
virtue was not the offspring of egotism out of calculation, but lay
in the following of our natural and spontaneous affections towards
benevolence. The English philosophy of the early eighteenth century had consisted in the main of an attack upon the pretensions of
human reason; this would have been a merely negative position
and[43] **[32, 33]** led nowhere, but for the fact that nature gained
what reason lost. What prevented Hume from being a mere sceptic
was his conviction that the ideas which had been implanted in us
by nature were thereby guaranteed as trustworthy, whereas ideas
that had been thought out by ourselves could have no such guarantee.

This philosophical conception already overthrows the equilibrium between art and nature, and places nature in a prerogative
position. Nature contains, ready-made, the perfection at which
man is aiming: whatever perfection he attains must be one borrowed from nature. This conception, as applied to aesthetic, gives,
not the equilibrium between art and nature which we find in
eighteenth-century artistic practice, but the naturalistic art of the
nineteenth century. In the generation of Hume the idea was fully
developed as a conception of general philosophy; in aesthetic, it
rises to the surface from time to time, but for the most part it is
working underground, deepening and strengthening the sense of
nature's beauty and sublimity, but without calling for any drastic

not reasoning is "the great guide of human life", and explains this (ibid. 66) by
stating that *nature* "has implanted in us an instinct which carries forward the
thought in a correspondent course to that which she has established among external
objects", i.e. nature (*naturans*) has arranged a pre-established harmony between the
course of nature (*naturata*) and that of our thoughts. I do not forget Spinoza's
natura sive Deus or Bacon's *homo naturae minister et interpres*; but neither Spinoza
nor Bacon used the conception of nature as Hume used it, as a means of giving back
to man what the destructive criticism of his rational faculties had taken away: and
this (*mutatis mutandis*) is the precise point of the Ruskinian aesthetic. For Shaftesbury's "natural sense of right and wrong", see his *Inquiry Concerning Virtue*, I, iii,
Selby-Bigge, *British Moralists*, I, 18–19. So Hutcheson writes of "practical dis-
positions to Virtue implanted in our nature" and of our "instinct to benevolence";
and Butler's examination of the term "nature" in the Pauline "by nature a law to
themselves" and the Stoic "following nature", in the Second and Third Sermons, is
classical for this line of thought.' [Collingwood's style of citation retained.]

[43] The sense of the main text carries over from fo. 31 to fo. 33 to make way for the
page-length note on fo. 32.

revolution in the methods of art; finally, in the early nineteenth century, it appears as a more or less systematic philosophy of art, based on the principle that all beauty is natural beauty, and that art has nothing to do except to transcribe nature. In the light of this principle, the ability to copy shapes and colours from nature must necessarily be regarded as the chief or the whole of artistic ability; the power accurately to describe some actual event will tend to be identified with literary [34] power. Those results will, in fact, follow which actually occurred in the nineteenth century, whose peculiar practice in the arts is thus the consequence of an aesthetic theory derived from general philosophical views already current early in the eighteenth.[44]

As I have said something about the rise of nineteenth-century naturalistic art and its relation to its predecessor, the art of the Romantic period, I shall perhaps be expected to complete the frame of my picture by saying something about its relation to the artistic movement which followed. The naturalistic movement spent its force towards the end of the nineteenth century, and, before that time, elements of a very different kind had already made their appearance. In painting, the crucial point seems to me to be the figure of Cézanne, who turned his back on naturalism and on the impressionism which was, for the most part, only a new phase of naturalism, and insisted on the idea of a picture as something constructed, something not found in nature by the artist and transferred to his canvas, but something built up on the canvas itself by an artist fully conscious of all that is implied in the term composition. Cézanne may stand as the inventor of modern pictorial art, which is altogether dominated by the same idea. Modern artists are always told, by people whose taste lingers in the nineteenth century, that they 'cannot draw'. This means that they cannot accurately [35] reproduce the shapes of natural objects. It is assumed that they cannot do this because it is assumed that this is what all painters are trying to do, and it is seen that these painters

[44] Opposite fo. 34: 'I think I could show, in the same way if I had time, that the great movement of modern art, since the end of the 19th century, represents the working out of ideas first clearly expressed in philosophy a generation earlier. That revolt against naturalism and positivism and the worship of natural fact which, in philosophy, gave us English idealism and French spiritualism in the 70s and 80s, gave us, in art, Cézanne and all his offspring—the painters for whom drawing means, not copying natural objects, but designing a picture.'

are not actually doing it. If the truth comes out that they are not even trying to do it, the case against them is still blacker: they are deliberately producing what is ugly. And some artists, still unconsciously dominated by the theory that nature alone is beautiful, and that art must copy nature or not be beautiful, foolishly embrace this consequence, and admit that their works are not intended to be beautiful—a disgraceful surrender to an unworthy antagonist. The right answer would have been, that drawing is not copying; that the ability to draw is the ability to set down the lines one wishes to set down, and that drawing *par excellence* means setting down lines that are worth setting down because they are significant, or expressive, or beautiful. And, with this answer, the war may be pushed into the enemy's country by arguing that many a well-trained nineteenth-century painter could not draw. I name no names, but there were plenty who would draw a particular line not because they wished to draw it, still less because it was worth drawing, but because they happened to see it in front of them. If that is drawing, the ability *not* to draw is a possession to be jealously guarded by everyone who wishes to be an artist. The modern artist, then, in that sense of the word drawing, will not draw. He wants not to copy, but to design.

[36] This modern movement in art began during the last quarter of the nineteenth century; and about the same time, or rather earlier, a new movement was making itself felt in philosophy. In the middle of the century the dominating philosophy had been a naturalistic positivism—a worship of 'natural facts'—which accurately expressed the spirit of the naturalistic art of the age. The Romantic period had conceived an idealistic philosophy of nature according to which 'we receive but what we give'.[45] In the materialism and positivism of the succeeding period, this conception had been rejected; or rather, it had fallen apart into two elements. That we receive from nature, was still believed; that we give to her, was denied. Now, in the last quarter of the century, there arose in England and France a new school of philosophy, in revolt against naturalism and materialism and positivism, asserting the freedom of mind to create an orderly life of its own and a world in which to dwell. The generation which, in France, produced Cézanne, pro-

---

[45] 'O Lady! we receive but what we give, / And in our life alone does nature live.' Samuel Taylor Coleridge, 'Dejection: An Ode' (1802), stanza iv, ll. 47-8.

duced Lachelier and Renouvier, and prepared the way for Bou-
troux and Blondel, Poincaré and Bergson, the philosophers of
action and freedom. At the same time, Green and Caird, Bradley
and Bosanquet,[46] were attacking naturalism in England, and it was
their generation that produced the central literary figure of modern
England, Thomas Hardy, the novelist who turned his back on
naturalism and conceived life as a drama[47] **[37, 38]** whose actors
are spiritual forces working within the mind of man. The art of
Hardy, like that of Cézanne, is an art that can no longer be described in terms of nature and the copying of nature. In order to
describe it, we must appeal to the conception of the artist as
constructing in his imagination an object whose purpose is to be
significant or expressive, and which achieves that purpose just so
far as it is genuinely constructed in the imagination—an intuition
and therefore an expression. These are the ideas round which all
modern aesthetic revolves.[48] When they are clearly grasped, the
gain will be both theoretical and practical. Theoretical, in that the
'mental chemistry' which Ruskin found 'utterly inexplicable'[49]
will become, with all such constructive elements in art, perfectly
intelligible. Practical, in that the residue of naturalism which is still
strong both in Hardy and in Cézanne—the local colour, the dialect,
the oranges and bottles and rocks—will no longer be needed as a
fixed point round which the work of art may crystallize out. It is
not my business to say how this will happen. As Monsieur Bergson

[46] Fo. 37 in its entirety a note to fo. 36: '* These names may perhaps suggest a
merely academic movement, and one confined almost exclusively to Oxford. That
would be a false suggestion. Balfour, neither a professional philosopher nor an
Oxford man, was one of the foremost leaders of the movement, and the inventor
of the term "naturalism". One of the most effective contributions to it was written
by a very unacademic person, Edward Carpenter. On the whole, this English
movement was noticeably poor in aesthetic. Bosanquet's *History of Aesthetic* (London: Allen & Unwin, 1892) shows a remarkable absence of rigour and grasp in the
treatment of theoretical problems. Oscar Wilde's aphorisms, many of which ring
true in spite of their deliberately frivolous pose, may be joined with a few observations of Thomas Hardy (e.g. in the Preface to *Tess*) as slight indications of the
aesthetic implied by the revolt against naturalism.'
[47] The sense carries over to fo. 38.
[48] Opposite fo. 38: 'and they are the ideas of modern idealistic philosophy
translated into terms of aesthetic'. The relationship between this modern aesthetic
and Collingwood's conception of 're-enactment' in history is clear at this point.
[49] Ruskin, *Works*, vi. 41.

remarked, a good many years ago, 'if I knew what the literature of the future would be like, my faith, I should go and write it'.[50]

[39] v[51]

To summarize the results of our historical inquiry: we have found that the principles of naturalistic art, as practised in nineteenth-century England, are expressed in the form of an aesthetic theory by Ruskin in *Modern Painters* as early as 1843. This theory cannot have been derived, inductively or otherwise, from a study of the works of art in question, for it preceded them in time. Regarded as a description, it applies with reasonable accuracy to these future works; Ruskin himself recognized that, when the Pre-Raphaelites began to paint. It was derived from a study of Turner, but it was not a description of Turner's practice, it was a manifesto for new developments based on that practice; a description, not of anything actual, but of an ideal as yet unrealized.

But the sources of the Ruskinian aesthetic are not confined to Turner. Ruskin's Nature is Wordsworth's Nature, and through Wordsworth the conception is derived from roots lying deep in the mind of the eighteenth century: the same roots which nourished the thoughts of Ruskin's contemporaries who knew nothing about Turner. This conception of Nature had already given rise to theories of knowledge and of ethics; finally, towards the middle of the nineteenth century, it presented itself in the form of an aesthetic, and from that moment artists began to conform their practice to it, for good or evil, with a new precision and a new consciousness of what they were doing.

[40] In this, they were not obeying any set of rules given to them by philosophers. We have travelled a long way from the conception of aesthetics as a normative science. But we have at any rate, I think, seen reason to abandon the idea of aesthetic, or any other philosophical science, as an *ex post facto* generalized description of a group of facts existing independently of the being described.

[50] * Monsieur Bergson made this remark at Oxford in 1920. I do not know if he has printed it anywhere, but it is too good to lose.

[51] Section heading 'IV' deleted at the top of fo. 39 and replaced by 'VI'. We have substituted what appears to be the correct heading.

Aesthetic is not a simple statement of what art actually is or has been. It is a statement of what art is, when it is really art; just as logic is a description not merely of how we actually think, but of how we think when we are really thinking. And this means that aesthetic tries to discover not merely what art is, but what art ought to be. This again is true of all philosophical sciences; Plato was right, for instance, when in his inquiry concerning the nature of the state he attempted—whether successfully or not is another question—to describe, not any actual state, but the ideal state.

The business of aesthetic, then, is to determine the ideal of art, the goal towards which artistic production is directed. If anyone has this ideal already before his own mind; if, in other words, he knows—or thinks he knows—what artists are trying to do; then he has a philosophy of art—or thinks he has.

If the producing of poems or pictures were an unconscious process, like digestion or respiration, it would be possible to produce them without knowing what one was trying to do. But the effort involved by artistic work is an effort not[52] [41] muscular but mental. Trying to write a poem is an effort in the same sense in which trying to recall a name is an effort; in either case we are trying to do something with our minds, something whose fruit, if it succeeds in bearing fruit, will be consciously present to our minds. A man cannot be trying to write a poem, unless he knows that he is doing so. If there are premonitory symptoms of a poem's inward growth—and no doubt there are—the obscure motions and

---

[52] Opposite fo. 40: 'Philosophers as such have neither the right nor the duty of teaching artists their business. But, on the other hand, they cannot confine themselves to merely describing how artists actually behave. If we must give up the normative theory of aesthetic, we must equally give up the descriptive. What then is the truth? The truth I believe is that we must stop thinking of art as if it were the private preserve of a clique of professional artists, and of philosophy as the preserve of professional philosophers. So conceived, the relation between them becomes unintelligible. Plainly, the philosopher [opposite fo. 41] as a man skilled in philosophy but inexperienced in art, if he has not the right to dictate to the artist, equally has not the information necessary to describe him. Art and philosophy are no doubt professions, but they are also something more: they are universal human interests, and the artist or philosopher has an audience only because he can appeal to the artist or the philosopher in every man. Now, an artist when he is, say, writing a poem, is trying to do something with his mind: and he must know what he is trying to do or he could not be, in that sense, trying to do it. He must know what a poem is, or rather, what a poem ought to be: and this knowledge is a philosophy of art. A philosophy of art must.' [Ends.]

sufferings which these involve cannot yet be described as an attempt to write the poem. That attempt only begins when the poet has recognized these symptoms for what they are, and has set himself consciously to complete the process whose beginning has come upon him thus unawares.

But the knowledge that he is trying to write a poem implies the knowledge of what a poem is; or rather, since the poem is not yet written, of what a poem should be. This knowledge is a philosophy of art, and such a philosophy must therefore preside over the birth of every work of art—unless indeed there are works of art which the artist lets fall inadvertently, without suspecting it, as Monsieur Jourdain spoke prose. Setting aside these possible by-blows, every work of art is conceived through the agency of some theory, and is fashioned according to the dictates of some theory, concerning the nature of art as such. No doubt the theory changes; continued experience in artistic work is very likely to change it; but because theories change as experience changes, it does not follow that the theory is a mere description of the experience. It would be **[42]** truer to describe the experience as an attempt to put the theory into practice.

There is thus a reciprocal relation between aesthetic theory and artistic practice. To suppose that an aesthetic can be worked out *in vacuo*, apart from all experience of actual artistic work, and then used as a normative science laying down once for all a code of rules that art must obey if it is to be genuine art, is to suppose an absurdity. If that is all that is meant by the conception of aesthetic as a normative science, the conception is a chimera. But the conception of aesthetic as a descriptive science, following after the facts and merely noting their characteristic features, is no less chimerical. The true relation between aesthetic theory and artistic practice would seem, rather, to be of such a kind that neither can exist in isolation from the other. Art cannot exist without a theory of art, because unless the artist has such a theory in his own mind— unless, for example, he can set before himself the end of producing a picture as like nature as he is able to make it—he does not know what he is trying to do, and therefore is not trying to do anything. For this reason it is useless, and worse than useless, for professional philosophers to advise professional artists to leave aesthetic theory alone and get ahead with their own business, the making of pictures or what not, leaving philosophy to the philosophers. The advice is useless because the artists can never take it, and it is worse [43] than useless because it shows the philosophers to be bad philosophers.

The theory of art cannot exist without art, not because it merely describes art, as entomology cannot exist without insects, but because it is an organic element within the process by which works of art come into being, and it cannot exist except as an element in that process. No doubt, a particular theory of art may be extracted from its place in such a process and isolated for expert scrutiny. It is right and necessary that this should be done; and here the artist is wrong if he tells the philosopher to keep his hands off aesthetic theory, because that is his business, not the philosopher's, and the theory that serves him in the creation of his own works of art is thereby justified. The artist is wrong because a theory is a theory, and must stand or fall by its merits as such; and to say 'my theory is justified by its fruits' is to expose oneself to the retort 'if your theory was a better theory, your pictures might be better pictures'.

But to separate the artist from the philosopher in this way, and set them at loggerheads, is to create trouble. Much of our difficulty over the whole problem of normative sciences is due to the fact that philosophy is supposed to be incarnate in certain eccentric, ridiculous, and vaguely disquieting persons called philosophers. It is these persons who, since they possess [44 (ult.)] philosophy, possess the normative rights which belong to the philosophical sciences; and people who are interested in science, or morals, or art, naturally resent being ordered about and told how to conduct their own affairs by these shadowy figures. And it is equally natural that professional philosophers should hasten to reassure them by insisting that they personally make no such claim and, on the contrary, regard philosophy not as normative but merely as descriptive. Both parties are frighted by false fire. Art and philosophy may be professions, but they are more than that; they are universal human interests, and this is indeed the only reason why the professional artist or the professional philosopher has an audience. He speaks, not to his fellow-professionals, but to the artist or the philosopher in all men.

The philosophy of art, then, may be a department of study to the professional philosopher, but to the artist it is a matter of life and death. The philosopher may neglect aesthetic, but the artist cannot; he must decide what art is, or he cannot pursue it. If he decides wrong, he will pursue it wrong. This is the purpose or function of aesthetic theory in its relation to artistic practice. The artist, as a rational being, must know what he is doing, or he cannot do it. In so far as he is an artist, his knowledge of what he is doing is his philosophy of art.[53]

[53] Opposite (and on the reverse of) fo. 44: 'It seems to me therefore that the philosophy of art is not a system of thoughts which philosophers think about artists: it is a system of thoughts which artists think about themselves in so far as they are able to philosophize, and philosophers think about themselves in so far as they are interested in art. In either case, its purpose is the same. The mind, in its intellectual function, is trying to understand itself in its aesthetic function. The art about which we philosophize is not a ready-made fact, it is something which we are trying to do, and by understanding what we are trying to do we come to be able to do it better. The philosophy [last fo.] of art is therefore not a description of what aesthetic facts are, nor yet an attempt to force them into being what they are not: it is the attempt of art itself to understand itself and, through understanding itself, to become itself. This is why artists, even if they care little about philosophy in general, cannot help caring about the philosophy of art. For there is no escape from the dilemma: either an artist does not know what he is doing, or else he has a philosophy of art, an aesthetic theory expressing the principles by which he tries to guide his artistic practice.'

PART II

TALES OF ENCHANTMENT

Thorstein finds Thurston-water.

FAIRY TALES

Everything men have made can be used as evidence for their history; but in order so to use it, we must find out how to interpret it. For a long time, it seemed impossible to use anything effectively as historical evidence, except written documents attesting the occurrence of certain events. During the nineteenth century, archaeologists learnt to use very ancient implements as evidence for periods of history which have left no written memorials. The result has been a vast enlargement of historical knowledge. Similar enlargements will perhaps be made in the future. The purpose of this book[1] is to consider the possibility of one such enlargement, by suggesting how fairy tales may be used as historical evidence.

In calling a story a fairy tale, we are in effect ascribing to it two essential characteristics. As regards its form, we imply that it is a traditional story, handed down by oral transmission[2] from the past. As regards its content, we imply that it is, not indeed necessarily about fairies, but about faëry, féerie, fays' work, or enchantment: that its subject matter consists in a general way of elements arising out of the idea of magic. In this chapter I shall make a few preliminary remarks about these two elements in the idea of a fairy tale.[3] **[2]** In calling these stories traditional, we do not mean simply that their authorship has been forgotten. We mean that they

---

Bodleian Library Collingwood Papers, dep. 21/4. The document, written in ink on one side of 21 sheets of lined paper, is untitled except for the section/chapter designation 'I'.

[1] What follows was clearly intended as a book. A passage paralleling this opening appears as a pasted over section at the end of FT3.

[2] Much of what Collingwood describes as characteristic of oral transmission also appears to cover the tradition of tales handed down through written transmission via literature.

[3] After the first paragraph Collingwood has stuck a piece of paper over part of the original. The original reads: 'The word fairy tale is well enough established in English to convey my meaning to any reader who knows the language. The stories which go by that name are not all about the quasi-human beings called fairies; but

constitute a social institution carefully preserved by the people, like the traditional arts of agriculture, or the handicrafts of everyday life in a peasant society. This traditional character is well attested. Gervase of Tilbury tells us that in thirteenth-century England fairy tales were told round the fire of an evening in every gentleman's house. He gives an example of one, which shows how like these medieval fairy tales were to those which have been collected in recent times. It is about an ancient hill-fort, Wandelbury on the Gogmagog Hills, where if you rode into the earthworks at night and shouted a challenge, an armed man would ride to meet you and engage you in combat. This theme of the Warden and the Challenge is one of the regular themes of European fairy tales.

The same custom flourished in the Scottish Highlands as late as the nineteenth century. Early in that century, the household in a Highland farm gathered round the fire and told stories. If a guest was present, the rule was that the host told the first story, to break the ice, and the guest then told stories 'until daylight'. These stories were not inventions of the teller; they were traditional; and it was a point of honour to abide by the tradition. If a teller departed from the established form, someone present would break in with a protest. The interrupter would then tell the story in his own way, and the company would thrash the matter out among them, and decide who was right.

To call a story traditional is to imply that it has been handed down by a custom of this kind. Where such [3] customs exist and are taken seriously, a story might be kept alive, changed perhaps in details but substantially the same, for a very long space of time. There has been much argument about a mysterious thing called folk-memory, by which traditions, with or without considerable garbling, have been thus preserved. The most interesting British example is perhaps that of the 'fairy hill' at Mold in Flintshire, where it was said that a ghost in golden armour used to ride of nights round the hill; and when it was opened in 1833 there was found in it a burial of the later Bronze Age, richly furnished with amber beads and other things, among them a golden breastplate

they can be roughly identified by two tests—First, they are traditional: they come down to us from an earlier stage of our history, and their authorship is unknown. This may seem an unscientific criterion: someone, it may be urged, must have invented each one of them, and the fact that we do not know'. [Ends.]

for a pony, which is now in the British Museum.[+] The 'folk-memory' which preserved a record of that chieftain's burial for nearer three than two thousand years can easily be explained by reference to such a custom of story-telling; it cannot be explained otherwise, except on psychological hypotheses from which a scientific mind would shrink.

This example, with others of the same kind, may encourage us to believe that the fairy tales we possess may well have come down to us, in some cases, from a like or an even greater antiquity. If our study of them gives us ground to think that certain themes embedded in them are several thousand years old, there is no a priori reason to reject such a conclusion as absurd.

At the same time, it is unlikely that they have come down to us, over such a space of years, unaltered. Where a story is handed down from mouth to mouth, however conscientiously successive tellers try to keep it from changing, change it must. Any alteration in the structure, customs, and beliefs of the society that tells it will tend to be reflected in the story itself; for a story so handed down, like the language in which it is told, is a living [4] thing, organically

---

[1] * Edwin Sidney Hartland, *Ethnographical Survey of the United Kingdom*, 6; Robert Eric Mortimer Wheeler, *Prehistoric and Roman Wales* (Oxford: Clarendon Press, 1925), 176. [The relevant passage by Wheeler reads: 'Finally, the gold horse-peytrel found in 1833 at Mold in Flintshire is perhaps the most famous discovery of pre-historic gold-work in Britain. The discovery was made by workmen levelling a cairn which was said locally to be haunted by a man in golden armour. The peytrel appears to have lain in a cist-grave with an inhumation burial, and to have been accompanied by a large number of amber beads and the remains of coarse cloth which had formed a fringe to the peytrel. Traces of iron are also said to have been noticed, but are only vaguely recorded. Elsewhere in the cairn was found (and destroyed) an urn containing burnt bones.' Reference is made parenthetically in this passage to Fig. 67 where a British Museum photograph of the peytrel is reproduced. After 'golden armour' a note appears giving two references, one of which is to 'E. Sidney Hartland, *Ethnographic Survey of the United Kingdom*, p. 6'; this is precisely the reference in Collingwood's MS, and he may well have simply noted it in passing from this source. While Hartland was a prolific writer on folktales and anthropology—he was the editor of *English Fairy and Other Folk Tales*, and had written a 'Report on Folk-Tale Research in 1889' for *F-L* 1/1 (Mar. 1890), 107–70—we have not been able to trace the particular title referred to. At the end of the passage quoted from Wheeler, a second footnote adds: 'The various accounts are collected in Roy. Com. Anc. Mons., Flints. Invent., p. 193.' Collingwood was a close friend of Wheeler and letters from Collingwood to Wheeler are to be found in the National Museum of Wales, Cardiff, where Wheeler was Keeper of Archaeology, 1920, and Director, 1924.]

connected with the social life in which it plays a part: and no living thing can be altogether unchanging.

It follows from this explanation of the term traditional, that the various versions of what is essentially one and the same story cannot be regarded as corruptions of a single original version, whose points of difference from each other are devoid of interest. The tradition which conserves a story of this kind alters it by the same right by which it conserves it. The story continues to be told only because people still find in it something that satisfies their needs as narrators and audiences; it is told in a modified form because the modification better satisfies those same needs. There is here no question of authenticity *versus* corruption. As Cecil Sharp demonstrated in the parallel case of folk-song, every variant has an equal right to be considered authentic.[5]

Subject to these inevitable modifications, our knowledge of the history of European peoples, and in particular of those of the British Isles, gives us no reason to doubt the possibility that a story collected in the nineteenth century may have been continuously told ever since the Bronze Age or even the Neolithic; for by now it is a recognized fact that the peasant population of the British Isles, in spite of invasions and conquests, has in the main preserved its continuity for as long as that; but we shall expect that, in its nineteenth-century form, it will bear many traces of the later history of the society which has preserved it. To take an archaeological parallel, its antiquity will not be like the antiquity of a flint implement picked up from a gravel-bed; it will be like [5] the antiquity of a site upon which men have lived from very ancient times to the present day; and in order to interpret it we must not be content to classify it as the prehistorian classifies flint implements, we must excavate it, as it were: we must try to strip off the layers of modern and recent occupation, and so reach the earliest stratum.

The methods to be used in this kind of excavation will resemble those used by the archaeologist, differing only in that they are here applied, not to the relics of what is called material civilization, such as pots and knives, but to the relics of custom and belief. In order

---

[5] See Cecil James Sharp (1859–1924), *English Folk Song: Some Conclusions* (London: Novello & Co., 1907), esp. ch. 2, 'Origin', where Sharp argues that changes in folk-songs from one singer to the next 'are not corruptions in varying degree of one original': 'They are the changes which, in the mass, engender growth and development' (11).

to use them at all, we must first accept the two principles that the themes found in fairy tales are organically connected with the customs and beliefs of the people who originated them, and that customs and beliefs are things which have a history. It is only fair to warn the reader that these two principles, however unobjectionable they may seem, will not be accepted everywhere. It is held by many psychologists that fairy-tale themes have their origin in 'the unconscious', and symbolize certain inward dramas that go on everywhere and always in the human mind. If that is so, they clearly cannot be used as historical evidence; for the same theme might spring up spontaneously in any part of the world at any date. In the next chapter I shall have more to say about this psychological approach to our subject. For the present I will only say that the facts are against it. Many fairy-tale themes are widely diffused; but not more widely than the types of weapons or agricultural and household implements; and not more widely than the forms of social life to which, on the view I am here putting forward, tales and implements are alike organic.

Archaeology, helped by comparative ethnology, is coming to realize that the [6] old classification of Stone, Bronze and Iron Ages, however useful it may be up to a point, gives a superficial view of the earliest developments of human life. These changes in the materials out of which the more durable implements were made have not necessarily accompanied profound modifications in human life as a whole. It is therefore becoming usual to distinguish, first and foremost, food-gathering civilizations, which were undoubtedly the earliest, from agricultural or cultivating civilizations, which in most countries have followed them. In this country the change appears to have taken place in the Neolithic age. Allowing a round half-million years for the total antiquity of man, the origins of agriculture in this country go back about four thousand years—less than one hundredth of the whole—and in the Near East some thousands more. It is easy to imagine, and here again comparative ethnology gives confirmation, that the traditional tales of food-gathering peoples will differ from those of agricultural peoples. The rise of urban civilization, with its accumulation of wealth and power in certain densely populated areas, began in the Near East even before agriculture had spread to our islands; and here again the change in customs would naturally carry with it a change in beliefs and a change in the kind of tales that were told.

New developments in social and political organization might have a similar effect; but of this we must not be too confident, because developments of this kind, which seem so important to the historian, do not as a rule greatly impress the mind of the people. A more important influence is likely to be that of new inventions. To the average medieval household, the advent of the spinning-wheel was a far more significant revolution than the signing of Magna Carta. Lastly in this brief list, it is obvious that [7] a change in religion will tend to affect the repertory of story-themes: thus in many European fairy tales we find a Christian stratum which can sometimes be stripped off to reveal underlying ideas of a very different kind.

The proposal to use fairy tales as evidence for the history of custom and belief is open to an objection which in the eyes of many students has appeared fatal. If all such tales had originated in the place where they are now told, they would doubtless, when interpreted on the above principles, give information about the history of human society in that place. But if that hypothesis cannot be maintained; if it is likely or even possible that many of them have originated elsewhere, and have reached their present home by a process of diffusion; then they cannot be so used. Suppose, for example, that a story-theme depending on a peculiar type of magical practice is found in England; and suppose that this theme was originally Indian, and reached England in the Middle Ages: it would follow, according to the method described above, that the practice in question once existed in India, but not that it ever existed in England. If this objection is sound (and it is certainly plausible) the historical interpretation of fairy tales cannot begin until we have settled the question where each of the themes we propose to discuss had its origin.

Today, in spite of long and arduous work on this subject, it remains a very obscure one. To begin with, students are not agreed as to how far similarity in thematic material necessarily implies diffusion from a common source, and how far similar themes might grow up independently in different [8] places. In a general and abstract way, there is an opposition between two a priori doctrines: the doctrine that similarities in human custom and belief are due to independent invention, and the doctrine that they are due to diffusion. It is possible to argue in defence of each doctrine, but I will not waste the reader's time by doing so; for this abstract opposition is not actually of much importance. Everyone would now agree that both doctrines are half-truths: that, in the abstract, diffusion and independent invention are both theoretically possible, and that in a concrete case the choice between them has to be made on the evidence available. The question thus becomes one of evidence; and we have to ask what kind of evidence is needed, and how it is to be used.

One possible criterion is that of simplicity. A very simple story might be invented over and over again; but the more complex it is, the less likely it is to have been invented more than once. Thus, it has been pointed out that the comic stories or 'drolls' which figure so largely in folklore are generally based on plots of extreme simplicity and obviousness, whereas fairy tales proper have much more complicated plots; and it is inferred that similar drolls have sprung up independently in many different countries, whereas each fairy tale has been invented once, by some unknown author in some definite place, and has then travelled into the various places in which it has been found.[6] But this criterion, though it applies to the complex plot of a whole story, cannot be applied to the separate themes used in that plot; for these themes are often in themselves very simple, and are used over and over again in different stories. Thus, *Tom Tit Tot* reappears in Germany as *Rumpelstilzchen* **[9]** and these two stories are so much alike that they can hardly have been invented independently; but each of them uses themes that occur in other stories; for example, the lazy girl whose success is due to a combination of luck and mother-wit, the fairy helper who performs a task that is impossible (either simply or to someone, as Aristotle would say), and the magical power of names. Whoever invented the story known to us as *Tom Tit Tot* and *Rumpelstilzchen* found those themes ready to his hand; and it is the origin of the themes, not the origin of the story, which concerns us in this inquiry.

Another possible criterion, which overcomes this objection because it applies even better to themes than to complete stories, is that of distribution. If you plot on a map all the known bronze implements of a certain type, their distribution may (in favourable cases) give you evidence that they were made in a certain district,

---

[6] * This is the view of [Collingwood's incomplete footnote].

where they lie thickest on the ground, and travelled thence into certain others along definite lines of trade. The plotting of fairy-tale themes on the map may give results of the same type. But the analogy is imperfect. If a bronze axe made in Britain is traded to Spain and lost there, it has undergone no change in transit; when found again, it is in every respect just like the British-found axes of the class to which it belongs. But story themes cannot be moved about bodily in this way. Every reappearance of such a theme involves a retelling of it; retelling, especially under different social conditions, will in time lead to modification; and consequently we may be sure that a theme which travels far will change in travelling, and that the tracing of its source by means of a distribution-map will therefore be a precarious and somewhat arbitrary business, much inferior in scientific cogency to the archaeological reasoning from which its method is [10] borrowed. If we set out to plot the distribution of a theme, what exactly are we plotting? By progressive abstraction, the name-magic theme in *Tom Tit Tot* may be classified as (*a*) the escape of a woman from the power of a fairy who has done her spinning through its inadvertently revealing its name to her husband, (*b*) the escape of a human being from the power of a helpful but malicious fairy through discovering its name, (*c*) human power over supernatural beings through knowledge of their names, (*d*) power depending on knowledge of names.[7] If it is classified as (*d*), the theme reappears, for example, in Mr Yeats's story of the Irishwoman who concealed her name from the fairies which infested her house;[8] if as (*c*) it reappears in the religious practice represented by Horace's phrase *Matutine pater, seu 'Iane' libentius audis*,[9] and in the revelation to Abraham of the Name of God;[10] and so forth. If you abstract far enough, you

---

[7] In *NL*, 93, Collingwood writes that: 'There is a type of fairy-tale in which a human being gets into the power of a demon, and escapes by learning the demon's name and pronouncing it when challenged (Edward Clodd, *Tom Tit Tot*, is a comparative study of the type).'

[8] W. B. Yeats (1865–1939) published a compilation, *Fairy and Folktales of the Irish Peasantry* in 1888, and a second, *Irish Fairy Tales* in 1892. A personal collection of tales appeared as *The Celtic Twilight* in 1893.

[9] The apostrophe of the dawn, Horace, *Satires*, 2. 6. 20: 'O Father of the dawn, or Janus, if so thou hearest'.

[10] Genesis 17.

get an element reappearing in[11] the phrase 'you have the advantage of me', used in speaking to someone who knows your name when you do not know his. The feeling that to know someone's name gives you a kind of advantage in dealing with him is a feeling which exists wherever names exist, and its widespread occurrence can hardly be due to diffusion unless the practice of nomenclature itself is due to diffusion. Story-themes based on that feeling might therefore arise independently all over the world; and the question how elaborate they must be, in order that we should infer a single origin, is a question of degree which can never be scientifically settled.

It seems that the question whether a given similarity in story-themes is due to diffusion or to independent invention is one which cannot be objectively settled by appeal to evidence; and we are thus led to reconsider the terms of the original antithesis. It is an antithesis which applies very well, as we have seen, to [11] artefacts like bronze axes. If you find an artefact in a certain place, you are entitled to say that it was either made there or made somewhere else and brought there. It even applies to plays or poems or symphonies or songs or the like. The works of Aeschylus or Dante on my shelves, the works of Beethoven or Hugo Wolf performed in the Town Hall, are in a sense imports, even though the books were printed and the performances given here in Oxford. But this is because these works of art are not traditional: they exist (ideally, at any rate) in an authoritative form, any departure from which is a corruption. But the relation between *Tom Tit Tot* and *Rumpelstilzchen* is not the relation between an original and a corruption, or between two corruptions of the same original. Neither is a corruption. Each is authoritative. The English and German story-telling traditions which respectively modified their common stock of themes into those two stories were thus independent inventive forces, in so far as they invented the differences between the stories, and also connected by a link to which, if we like, we may give the name of diffusion, in so far as they were not creating the two stories out of nothing but were using a common stock of themes.

---

[11] Underneath a piece of paper reads: 'such stories as that by R. L. Stevenson of the American who spent a long railway-journey'. [Ends.] The anecdote had been recalled by Andrew Lang in his presidential 'Address to the Folk-Lore Society, session 1889–90', *F-L* 1/1 (Mar. 1890), 9.

Diffusion and independent invention are thus not alternatives; they are elements existing together in the tradition of story-telling and in every other tradition. For the problem does not affect fairy tales alone; it affects all parts of human civilization. Most countries have been originally peopled, and from time to time recruited, by immigrants from outside, bringing their own civilization with them and modifying it to suit the conditions of their new home. The cultural history of a country like Britain can on no hypothesis be treated as a history enacted solely on British soil. And if **[12]** we do not shrink from tracing the origins of our history in some cases to the Low German coastlands, in some cases to the ancient country of the Celts, in some to the Thuringian or Spanish home of the Beaker folk, and so forth, we need not shrink from tracing it in part to countries which have contributed nothing to the biological pedigree of the English people, but have none the less contributed ideas to the historical pedigree of English culture.

For cultural borrowings such as those insisted upon by the diffusionist theory imply not only the power to lend but also the power to borrow: that is, they imply that whatever was borrowed was something capable of incorporation in the existing culture of the borrowers. There must be some kind of organic relation between a given culture and the elements which it borrows from elsewhere; a relation such that the offered loan is welcomed as satisfying a need that is actually felt when the borrowing takes place. Otherwise there would be no borrowing. The incorporation of what is borrowed into the culture of the borrowers always implies a certain modification adapting it to its new context; as thus adapted, it becomes a new and original thing, the product of that culture's spontaneous energy and the expression of its peculiar needs.

When, therefore, it is said that one culture may borrow from another some element altogether foreign to its own life, an element detached from its original culture-complex and thus, by the time it has been borrowed, having the character of a mere survival, from which therefore no historical inferences can be drawn, this is only half the truth. Even survivals are cultural facts, and must stand in organic relation to the culture in which they are found: there must, in other words, be a reason why they survive. If we find in England a story-theme borrowed in the Middle Ages **[13]** from India and testifying to a peculiar magical practice, this does not prove that the practice in question ever existed on English soil; but it does prove that the practice existed in a country (whether India or some other) to which Britain is indebted for certain elements in its cultural tradition, and which therefore figures among its cultural ancestors; it proves that the cultural mind of Britain, at the time when that theme was borrowed, needed it in order to express some idea of its own, just as the Anglo-Saxon kings borrowed the Greek title *basileus*, to express their own conception of their kingly office, or as medieval French and English artists borrowed the Oriental motives [motifs] which they incorporated into Gothic art. To rule such an Indian story-theme out of the history of English culture because it was borrowed would be like ruling out Christianity, Greek philosophy, French Gothic, or the Italian madrigal. A history of culture composed on that principle, if the principle were consistently applied, would contain nothing whatever.

Nor does it greatly matter, to the historian of English culture as such, where the borrowed material came from. What primarily matters is the use to which it was put. That certain stories were used by Shakespeare as plots for his plays, and that out of them he wrote plays of a certain kind, which constitute a great part of our literary heritage, is important for the historian of English letters; the history of these stories before Shakespeare got hold of them, in so far as they were not already current in England, concerns the historian not of English literature but of European literature in general. Thus, to the student of English fairy tales, it is not a matter of primary importance to discover whether a given theme [14] is derived from India or Persia or Greece. The crucial fact for him is the fact that it was adopted by English narrators and accepted by English audiences as something capable of being incorporated into the traditional story-telling of the English people.[12]

So much for the first point in our definition, the implications of the term traditional. It is time to consider the second point: the

---

[12] Cf. T. S. Eliot, 'Tradition and the Individual Talent' (1919): '[Tradition] involves, in the first place, the historical sense ... a perception, not only of the pastness of the past, but of its presence; the historical sense compels a man to write not merely with his own generation in his bones, but with a feeling that the whole of the literature of Europe from Homer and within it the whole of the literature of his own country has a simultaneous existence and composes a simultaneous order.' *Selected Essays* (London: Faber & Faber, 1932), 14.

definition of the subject matter of fairy tales in the term magic. In a later chapter[13] we shall have to consider the meaning of this term in some detail. For the present, it is enough to say that the word indicates a characteristic common to themes of very various kinds—fairies, dwarfs, giants; animals that turn into men and vice versa; clothes or weapons or other properties which make their user invisible or invincible or in some other way successful by the mere possession of them; methods of overcoming an enemy by uttering a secret form of words or doing a secret action or finding out where he keeps his life or power; and so forth. Each of these things may be described, from the point of view of our scientific conception of nature, as unnatural and indeed supernatural, since these things do not merely lie outside the laws of nature as known to us, they override those laws. But in saying this we are describing the magical from our own point of view, not from that of the persons who originally told the stories. The peculiar effect which these magical themes produces in us is due to the fact that in hearing such stories we are liberated, by a temporary make-believe, from our normal scientific conception of nature. We feel this liberation as a relief, because we feel the scientific conception of nature a burdensome inheritance, though no doubt a precious one. As long as the laws of nature hold good, there is no hope of realizing our wishes except [15] by discovering those laws and obeying them: *natura non vincitur nisi parendo*. The world of fairy tales thus appears to us as a world where wishes can be realized in another way. By contrast, it seems as if in that world we could get what we want by merely wanting it. Hence we think of it as a world where wishes come true, or (in psychological language) fairy tales have for us the peculiar fascination of wish-fulfilment fantasies.

But this is only how they appear to us. It does not follow that they appeared in the same light to the people who originally told them. On the contrary, when we look more closely at them we find that the land of fairy tales has laws of its own, no less exigent than the laws of nature. You can destroy a giant, it is true, without overcoming him in fair fight or even infecting his water-supply with bacteria, if you can get at the egg in which he keeps his heart; but before you can do that you must, by your own unstudied

---

[13] FT4 on 'Magic'.

courtesy, lay an obligation upon the otter, the hawk, and the other beasts which alone can help you to find it. As if to make this principle clear, there are many stories whose main theme is the contrast between the reward of courtesy or courage or intelligence and the punishment of their opposites: stories in which there are two protagonists, one achieving success through the practice of these virtues, the other setting out in the misguided conviction that success is to be had by merely wishing for it, and failing ignominiously because these virtues are lacking.

Magic, then, if we are to use that word for this supernatural element in fairy tales, is a very different thing from mere wish-fulfilment. It is a system of beliefs and practices with definite laws of its own; and those who accepted it, and told these stories to illustrate its principles, took these laws [16] no less seriously than we take the laws of natural science. The sense of relief which we experience in looking into their world is based on a romantic illusion. Because it is a world in which the laws of our world do not hold, we fancy it a world in which there are no laws at all, a world where we could get all we desire by simply desiring it. It is the same illusion that makes people sigh for this or that past age of history, fancying it a tract of time in which they would be free from the grinding necessities of modern life, and not realizing that it had necessities of its own, just as onerous to people who lived under them.[14]

The laws of the fairy-tale country, in so far as they are based on what we call magic, are certainly very different from the laws of natural science. It has been held that they are a kind of caricature of these laws; that magic, broadly speaking, is a kind of pseudo-science, believed in by people who are, or were, too stupid to discover genuine scientific laws. This is a romantic illusion of the opposite kind. We shall have to examine it more closely in the sequel.[15] For the present, it is enough to say that, thanks to

[14] Struck out: 'In using fairy tales as historical evidence, we must first of all get rid of this romantic illusion, which is a characteristic not of the stories themselves but of our own first superficial view of them. It may seem odd to us that they should regard success in life as due to courtesy and courage and ready wit, instead of the possession of money and powerful friends and the habit of driving hard bargains with those we employ; but if that is the belief which we find them to express, we must conclude that it was a belief held by those who invented them.'

[15] See especially FT3, 'Three Methods of Approach', below.

the work of ethnologists, we know a good deal about the daily life
of peoples among whom magical beliefs like those recorded in fairy
tales are current; and [17] we know that these peoples are very far
from being stupid or devoid of scientific knowledge. They have
enough biology to breed cattle; enough botany to grow crops;
enough astronomy to work out an agricultural calendar; enough
mineralogy and chemistry to prospect for ores, to smelt copper and
tin, and to alloy them into bronze, or to mine and smelt and forge
iron, or to find and work clay and fire it into pottery; enough
physic to use medicinal herbs, and enough surgery to perform
operations, sometimes delicate ones, with flint knives and deer-
sinews; enough engineering to construct a plough or a boat; and so
forth. All these operations may be, and often are, accompanied by
magic; but they are not performed by magic; they are performed
by technical skill based, as all technical skill must be based, on
scientific intelligence.

All this must be born in mind when we try to use fairy tales as
historical evidence.[16] A theme contained in such a story is a fragment of ancient custom or belief, very much as a stone implement
is a fragment of ancient technical skill. In each case the historian
uses the fragment by reconstructing in his mind the life and
thought of the people who have left him this sample of their
work. The archaeologist is helped in this attempt by the ethnolo-
gist, who may be able to point out similar implements now used in
a particular way by this or that primitive society. The student of
fairy tales must avail himself of the same kind of help. When he
finds a theme testifying to a belief in magic, he must not reconstruct the experience of the people who originated it by assuming
in them an attitude towards magic like that which he recognizes in
himself: that would be like arguing that palaeolithic man made
hand-axes for display in a museum. He must find out what part
is played by magical beliefs and practices among living [18] societies in which these things are not survivals but an essential part of
everyday life.

But when that is done the work of historical reconstruction is
still incomplete. All historical knowledge involves the recreation in

[16] The clear suggestion here is that fairy tales can be used as means to the end of
gaining historical information about the world from which they came—as distinct
from the history of the literary, pre-literary, or para-literary 'text' of the tale itself.

the historian's mind of the past experience which he is trying to study. If magic were a form of belief or custom peculiar to primitive peoples and absolutely foreign to the mind of civilized man, the civilized historian could never understand it. He could at most collect and classify examples of it, as the archaeologist may collect and classify implements (or what he supposes to be implements) whose purpose he cannot divine. In doing this he is no doubt showing himself an archaeologist; but he is not yet being a historian, any more than a man who collects and arranges inscriptions in an unknown tongue is a historian. The material is only being prepared for future interpretation. It is not yet being interpreted. To be interpreted, the inscriptions must be read; the implements must be understood in the light of some human purpose. When he has interpreted them, the scholar can see why the inscriptions were written, and the archaeologist can see why the implements were made: these things fall into place in a particular historical context of human life and thought.

The central problem, for anyone who wishes to use fairy tales as historical material, lies here. The common characteristic of such tales is their magical character. To understand them means understanding magic: understanding why people behaved in the ways for which we use magic as a general term. Now, if magical behaviour is irrational behaviour, this cannot be done. If, without being downright irrational, it is a mode of behaviour entirely foreign to ourselves, we at least cannot do it. In order to understand [19] fairy tales, therefore, we must give an account of magic which will show that in its essence it is a thing familiar to ourselves, not as a spectacle, but as an experience: something which we habitually do, something which plays a part in our social and personal life, not as a mere survival of savagery, but as an essential feature of civilization. If we can do this, we shall have reached a point of view from which, in principle at least, the magical elements in fairy tales become comprehensible; and we can go on to the strictly historical question which of them can be understood, not only abstractly and in principle, but in detail, as manifestations of a particular historical stage of human development.

There are, therefore, certain preliminaries to be gone through before we can proceed to the study of fairy tales in detail. What I am here proposing is in effect a new kind of archaeology. Like all archaeology, it aims at reconstructing the past of mankind from the

evidence of things he has made which are still with us. But whereas
archaeology in the ordinary sense studies the fragments of his
industry and manufacture, this new kind studies fragments of
his customs and beliefs handed down in traditional stories. So far
as it is a new enterprise, the first thing to do is to establish the
methods on which it is to work. Fairy tales have been actively and
profitably studied for more than a hundred years, but never in
quite the way I am here proposing. One part of the study, and a
very important part, is the mere collection and classification of
them, resulting in the recognition of standard themes appearing
more or less frequently, but stopping short of interpretation. Interpretation began, more than a century ago, with the work of the
German philological school which regarded them as 'myths' **[20]**
describing natural phenomena in poetic or metaphorical language.
A second line of interpretation, which no doubt came far closer to
the truth, was that of the anthropological folklorists in the late
nineteenth century. According to this view, they were organically
connected with certain magical rituals practised by primitive societies. In principle, I believe this school to have been right; but they
failed to reach a genuine interpretation because they failed to reach
a satisfactory conception of magic, and therefore a surd[17] was left
in their solution of the problem. A third attempt, deliberately
directed to resolving this surd, has been that of twentieth-century
psychologists, who have sought to show that the magical element
in fairy tales is a symbolic expression, not of the natural phenomena surrounding man, but of the wishes within him. Inasmuch
as wish-symbols are not peculiar to the savage, but are universal
features of human life, this is a step in the right direction; but here
too the solution breaks down, this time because of a tendency
to subsume all the special features of fairy-tale material, not
under the historical conception of determinate phases in human
development, but under the pathological conception of mental
derangement.

   In the next chapter I shall discuss these three attempts, after
which, having learnt something from each in turn, we shall be free
to sketch the principles of what I call the historical method. After
that, the central problem, the nature of magic, will be ready for

---

[17] An irrational element.

attack; and then the conclusions of these preliminary studies can be applied to the interpretation of particular fairy-tale themes.

The reader must not expect too much. Unlike science, history can never be a closed system. It cannot lay down universal rules for the explanation of [21] an entire class of phenomena. It can only deal with its objects of study one by one, and can never cover them all with sweeping generalizations. Here and there, it can find an interpretation for this or that piece of evidence. But its successes are only partial and fragmentary. The historian's field is at best only chequered with light; by degrees it reaches back first into twilight and then into darkness; and on either side of the strip partially illuminated by knowledge is a tract whose investigation must be left to others. Even within his chosen field there is an infinity of problems that he cannot deal with, and an infinity of potential evidence which the mere shortness of life and limits of endurance forbid him to interpret. He must practise humility and be content with very little. If his methods prove good, others can extend their use.

In the concluding chapters I shall therefore confine my study to fairy tales found in the British Isles, and among these to certain classes of theme which I think I know how to interpret.[18] Illustrative material I shall use wherever I think needful, and from whatever sources are most helpful; but my task is interpretation, not comparison, and the piling-up of parallels—an easy business in these days of classified folklore indexes—is a method of impressing readers which does not advance the inquiry I have undertaken.

---

[18] This sentence seems to confirm the unfinished state in which Collingwood's book on fairy tales was set aside, and that more material than was written up or has survived was intended. There is, however, a substantial treatment of *Cinderella* in what the editors have designated ch. 5, or FT5, below.

2

THREE METHODS OF APPROACH:
PHILOLOGICAL, FUNCTIONAL,
PSYCHOLOGICAL

According to the programme laid down in the preceding chapter, our first task is to consider the methods of approaching our problem used by the philologists, the functional anthropologists, and the psychologists. This will mean studying the history of three movements of thought, the first dated roughly 1810–70, the second 1870–1910, the third 1900–20.[1] We need not here discuss either the rise or the development of these movements in detail. It will be enough to fix our attention on what may be called their high lights: for the first, Grimm and Max Müller; for the second, Tylor and Sir James Frazer; for the third Freud and Jung.

A reader may ask why I say nothing of the controversies and inquiries which are occupying the minds of anthropologists today: the diffusionist controversy, for example, or the attempt to blend the functional and psychological methods into a new synthesis. If I ignore these, it is not because I doubt their importance. It is because the cross-currents of a 'critical period', as the present age of anthropological studies has been called by Mr T. K. Penniman in his recent book, *A Hundred Years of Anthropology*,[2] are of

---

Bodleian Library Collingwood Papers, dep. 21/5. The chapter title, numbered 'II', is Collingwood's.

[1] This periodization is Collingwood's own; by closing the last period off in 1920, he is clearly distancing his own commentary from these past movements of thought. As he explains in the subsequent paragraph, he wishes explicitly to associate himself with more recent and critical developments in anthropology.

[2] Thomas Kenneth Penniman, *A Hundred Years of Anthropology* (London: Duckworth, 1935). Penniman had divided the history of anthropology into 'The Formulary Period: Anthropology before 1835', 'The Convergent Period: c. 1835–1859', 'The Constructive Period: 1859–1900', and 'The Critical Period: 1900–1935', followed by a chapter on 'The Future' (itself replaced in the 2nd, rev.

interest not for what they have achieved but for what may come of them; in other words, they are hardly yet appropriate subject matter for historical criticism. What I have to say is rather a contribution to the work of this critical period than an estimate of it.

Fairy tales had been collected, written up, and otherwise noticed in various countries and at various times before the nineteenth century; but it was not until then that they became the subject matter of anything that could be called a science.[3] The fact that they did so then was due to the work of Jacob Grimm, who with his brother collected a great number of them in Germany [2] (printed in 1812) and in 1835 published his great work on German Mythology.[4] This undertaking arose directly out of the romantic

edn. of 1952 with a new one entitled 'Anthropology since 1935'). In the present chapter Collingwood uses Penniman's book as a general guide, though without detailed reference. Penniman had defined anthropology broadly as 'the Science of Man', dividing it into physical and cultural branches. Social anthropology was a division of cultural anthropology, along with archaeology and technology (13–15). Penniman's scheme for summarizing the history of anthropology into the four major periods drew on suggestions by R. R. Marett put forward in 'The Growth and Tendency of Anthropology and Ethnological Studies', Plenary Address in the *Proceedings of the International Congress of Anthropological and Ethnological Studies* (London: Royal Anthropological Institute, 1934), 39–53; summarized in *Man*, 162 (1934), 141–2. Marett had identified the current 'period of criticism' as beginning with the recognition of Mendel's genetic discoveries ('Growth and Tendency', 51), along with the increasing specialization of the branches of anthropology and the need to find a new synthesis between evolutionary, diffusionist, functional, and psychological approaches. See *Hundred Years*, 21–2.

[3] In a footnote to *PA* 72, Collingwood records that 'By 1893, 140 "fairy tales" had been collected in England; few others have been found since. In 1870–90, France and Italy yielded over 1,000 each.' For an authoritative modern survey of the development of the process of collecting and translating tales from Oriental, Italian, French, and German traditions see Jack Zipes, 'Cross-Cultural Connections and the Contamination of the Classical Fairy Tale', in Zipes (ed.), *The Great Fairy Tale Tradition: From Straparola and Basile to the Brothers Grimm* (New York and London: Norton & Co., 2001), 845–69.

[4] *Kinder- und Hausmärchen: Gesammelt durch die Bruder Grimm* (Berlin: Realschulbuchhandlung, 1812; vol. ii, 1815). A revised and expanded 7th edn. of the tales was published in Göttingen in 1857, and a translation entitled *German Popular Stories* had been published by Edgar Taylor (London: C. Baldwin, 1823). For modern edns., see *The Complete Grimm's Fairy Tales* (London: Routledge & Kegan Paul, 1975), and *The Complete Fairy Tales of the Brothers Grimm*, tr. Jack Zipes, 3rd edn. (New York: Bantam Books, 2003).

nationalism that swept over Germany at the beginning of the nineteenth century and awakened the interest of her people in the ancient Germanic civilization out of which their own had sprung. The whole of Grimm's work was inspired and coloured by a romantic passion for this primitive Germanic culture, conceived in its relation to modern Germany as a beloved mother, long lost but now at last in process of rediscovery; and in itself conceived as the childhood of the German nation, so that the emotion which in one aspect appeared as the child's love for its parent appeared in the other aspect as the yearning for a vanished youth. These romantic mixtures of emotion seem today a trifle absurd; but at the time they represented a perfectly genuine attitude towards a remote and newly discovered national past. In our own time they are of interest chiefly because (as we shall see) the metaphorical phrases in which they found expression continue to encumber the ground of anthropological discussion, dead blocks of verbiage from which all meaning has flown.

The tales which Grimm collected and published were valued chiefly as a legacy from this romantic past. They had been invented then, and in now enjoying them we were directly communing with the mind of our own nation in youth. We longed to find ourselves back in those great days of our national dawning; and behold, with the discovery of these tales our wish is granted, for through them we can make our own that very experience of life and the world which presided over their birth. Thus our national fairy tales are actual surviving fragments of our national youth, and by steeping ourselves in them we live that youth over again.

[3] This romantic and emotional attitude had at least one advantage. It gave an incentive to collect stories, to publish them with the minimum of editorial writing-up, so as to provide a relatively uncorrupt text, and to analyse them with all the resources of contemporary scholarship.[5] The more strongly the great romantics

[5] For an account of the Grimms' writing up of the tales, and the introduction of distinctively literary and poetic characteristics in successive editions, see Siegfried Neumann, 'The Brothers Grimm as Collectors and Editors of German Folktales', *The Reception of Grimms' Fairy Tales: Responses, Reactions, Revisions*, ed. Donald Haase (Detroit: Wayne State University Press, 1993), 24–40; repr. in Zipes, *Great Fairy Tale Tradition*, 969–80. See also the more sceptical account of John M. Ellis, *One Fairy Story Too Many: The Brothers Grimm and their Tales* (Chicago and London: University of Chicago Press, 1983).

felt about a subject, the harder and the more scientifically they worked at it; and thus out of the romantic *Schwärmerei* about fairy tales there grew up the first attempt to create a science of folklore.

For our purpose, there is no need to follow the development of that attempt in detail. Its main lines were already worked out with tolerable completeness by Jacob Grimm; and if to an English reader it seems to culminate in the work of Max Müller, that is due not so much to Müller's originality or superiority to the rest of his school, as to the fact that when he migrated to England he introduced its common doctrines into this country. Hence it is convenient to choose, as an expression of the school's views, his essay on 'Comparative Mythology', published in 1856.[6]

The unity of the Germanic languages had been demonstrated by Grimm himself, using the method of comparative grammatical study and showing that there were certain constant phonetic relations between a given word in one Germanic language and the kindred word in another. By the middle of the century this circle of kindred languages had been widened so as to include others beside the Germanic: it now embraced all the languages of Europe except Basque, and many of western Asia and India. Hence, where Grimm had painted a romantic picture of the primitive Germanic people, Müller substituted one of the primitive Aryans; for that was the name he coined [4] to denote the imaginary race whose linguistic birthright was the Indo-European (or, as he called it, Aryan) language. Assuming, like Grimm, that common language means common blood, he conceived the bold but unfounded idea that all the Aryan-speaking peoples were descended from one original stock; and just as Grimm had used the German fairy tales as evidence for the way in which the ancient Germans lived and thought, so Müller reconstructed the life and mind of this primitive Aryan people from evidence of two kinds: the myths common to all their descendants, and the words similarly common. Whenever the same fairy tale was found in Sanskrit, Greek, and

---

[6] The essay is printed in Friedrich Max Müller, *Essays on Mythology, Traditions, and Customs,* in *Chips from a German Workshop,* 2 vols. (London: Longmans, Green & Co., 1867), ii. 1–143. Cf. Müller's *Lectures on the Origin and Growth of Religion,* Hibbert Lectures, 1878 (London, 1878; Routledge/Thoemmes Press, 1997). A commentary by E. E. Evans-Pritchard on Müller's theories (very similar in tone to Collingwood's) may be found in his *Theories of Primitive Religion* (Oxford, Clarendon Press, 1965), esp. 20–3.

Icelandic, it was (he argued) derived from a common source in the
mythological possessions of the original Aryans: by such arguments one could show what stories they told. Whenever etymo-
logically kindred words were found in languages thus widely
scattered, they were in the same way derived from a word in the
original Aryan vocabulary: and if you know what words a people
uses, you know a good deal about its habits and institutions.

It would be unfair to judge this conception by the standards of
modern historical thought. Today, thanks to the work of innumerable anthropologists, we know that between race (or in general
human biology) and language (or in general human culture) there
is no constant relation. Thanks to the progress of historical
methods, we should dismiss the idea of an ancient civilization for
which no archaeological evidence can be produced as a baseless
fancy. For our present purpose, it is more important to understand
why the philological school indulged in fancies of this particular
kind. The reason is to be found in the romantic tradition. In the
strong but confused emotions of the romantic period, no distinction was made between [5] the passion with which a civilized
people clings to its own civilization and resists its destruction or
contamination by another's, and the passion with which parents
love their children and children their parents. Thus the motives
which underlay the national uprising of the Germans in the defence of their freedom and culture against Napoleonic aggression
were confused with the motives underlying the solidarity of a
family; and the fiction of a Germanic race, in which every member
was related to every other by blood, grew up under the influence
of this confusion, as an aetiological myth to explain the fact of
German patriotism.

The racial myth thus became an orthodox and central doctrine
of romantic thought. In enlarging the Germanic myth into an
Aryan myth, Müller was working out the logic of the idea quite
correctly; but the emotional impulse from which it drew its
strength evaporated in the process; for whereas there was such a
thing as German patriotism, there was and is no such thing as a
common patriotism of Aryan-speaking peoples. The recent history
of the Aryan myth illustrates this fact. The principles of romantic
thought are still very much alive in Germany; but in order to be of
use for political purposes the Aryan myth has undergone a strange
reinterpretation, contracting itself again into a Germanic myth on

the ground that the Germans are the only true representatives of the original Aryan stock. Before we reach the end of this chapter, we shall find that the romantic tradition, with its confusion between race and culture and its tendency to project images derived from emotional sources upon the blank screen of the unknown past, so as to create a pseudo-historical mythology, has left its mark not only on Nazi politics but upon the psychological theories of central Europe.[7]

[6] Max Müller found the most ancient documents of Indo-European literature in the Sanskrit books of India. These were the earliest monuments of Aryan thought, nearest therefore to the original source, and thus peculiarly valuable as giving the clue to the interpretation of the rest. He observed that many of the themes which Grimm had discovered in Germanic fairy tales reappeared in Sanskrit literature. In their Sanskrit form, he thought he could find evidence of a process of symbolism by which the ancient myth-makers had expounded in poetical form their observation of the events attending the sun's daily path through the sky: the dawn, the high noon, sunset, and night. Here too he was influenced by the romantic tradition: for one powerful element in that tradition was the nature-poetry which in England is especially represented by Wordsworth, and the poetic nature-philosophy of such German writers as Schelling. There is no doubt that this romantic view of nature coloured his reading of the Sanskrit texts and made him over-emphasize everything he found there which could be regarded as evidence of nature-mythology: a method of interpretation which was not peculiarly his own, for Grimm had used it already.

Apart from such romantic preconceptions, it is surprising to see how weak is the evidence on which his case nominally rested. For example, he finds in the Rigveda the well-known fairy-tale theme of Cupid and Psyche, that is, of the wife who is forbidden to see her husband on pain of separation. In the Sanskrit version, which he quotes at length, Urvasi loves Pururavas, but may not see him

---

[7] In the closing passage of *A*, Collingwood reflects on the triumph of irrationalism instigated by 'the propagandists of a coming Fascism' (167), and in the final chapter of *NL* on the plunge into barbarism by Germany in the 1930s. For more recent commentary, cf. 'The Fight over Fairy-Tale Discourse: Family, Friction, and Socialization in the Weimar Republic and Nazi Germany', ch. 6 of Zipes, *Fairy Tales and Art of Subversion*, 134–69.

naked. Her sisters, wishing to break up the marriage, devise a trick to make Pururavas spring naked out of bed, and at the same time send a flash of lightning. Urvasi sees Pururavas naked, [7] and vanishes. Now, in the whole of the long passage quoted, there is only one word which even Müller's determination can twist into evidence of solar mythology. The separated lovers meet again: he asks her to come back to him: but she replies, 'I am gone for ever, like the first of the dawns; I am hard to be caught, like the wind.' The word dawn is quite enough. It 'shows a strange glimmering of the old myth in the mind of the poet',[8] and forthwith the story is explained. Urvasi is the dawn, which vanishes when she sees the naked sun; a conclusion which is reinforced by quotations from Wordsworth, Tennyson, and Homer.

Such are the preconceptions and the arguments out of which Müller built up his theory of the 'primitive Aryan sun-myth'. Once formed—and, as we have seen, the determining element in that process was not the evidence but the preconceptions—the theory was verified by going through the whole corpus of Indo-European fairy tales in search of themes which could be translated into terms of solar mythology. The task was a disgracefully easy one. Adepts of the school had only to learn a few ready-made formulae, and at once they became able to turn the handle of the machine and produce sun-myths out of the spout.

It soon became evident that what you put into the hopper made no difference. An anonymous *jeu d'esprit* demonstrated, by a perfectly fair use of the method, that Müller himself was a sun-myth and that every detail of his career proved it. His name—Müller, *mjolnir*, Thor's hammer—his eastern origin and journey to the west, from Germany to England, his unsuccessful struggle for the Boden chair of Sanskrit (*Boden* of course is *earth*) with a certain Monier-Williams who turns out to be mysteriously identical with his own father the poet [8] Willhelm Müller and is therefore the darkness out of which the sun comes and into which it departs again, his marriage with Miss Grenfell, 'the nymph Greenfield'— the marriage of heaven and earth—and his final election to a fellowship at All Souls, joining the company of the blessed dead: all these are worked up with a wealth of corroborative and illustrative detail into an argument which stands supreme in the field of

---

[8] 'Comparative Mythology', *Chips*, ii. 104.

scientific parody, far outclassing its only serious rival, Whately's *Historic Doubts concerning the Existence of Napoleon Bonaparte.*[9]

What is wrong with the method, however, is in fact not that it turns every fairy tale into a sun-myth; it might conceivably be true that all fairy tales really are sun-myths; not even that it can be used to turn history into sun-myths; it might be true that all history is a blend of fact and fiction, and that the fictitious parts are all derived from solar mythology; but that it treats its evidence dishonestly. Everything that can be twisted into a support for the theory is emphasized; everything else is not explained away, it is simply ignored. This is how the enlightened man accuses savages of thinking; no other supposition, we are told, will explain the belief in magic. Here is a case where the method is actually used, and used not by savages, but by a learned **[9]** scholar thinking about savages. It creates an uncomfortable suspicion that the alleged irrationality of the savage is only an introjection of the civilized man's irrationality when he thinks about savages. Shutting his eyes to most of the facts, he finds himself in a world of shadows, a phantasmagoria in which almost anything can be almost anything else, a twilight in which all cats are grey. He mistakes this darkness of his own making for a darkness enveloping the mental world of the savage; as Müller himself puts it on occasion, the mythology is incoherent and careless of consistency; whereas, for the savage himself, the details which the scholar ignores are the life and soul of the story and things which no teller is allowed to misrepresent.

This brings us to the crucial question why mythology should exist at all. If the primitive Aryan was so deeply interested in the daily cycle of light and darkness, why was he not content to describe it in plain Aryan? Why did he wrap it up in this maze of

[9] * R. F. Littledale [Collingwood adds a question mark since Littledale does not appear among the list of contributors], 'The Oxford Solar Myth', in *Kottabos* (Trinity College Dublin) (5 Nov. 1870), 145–54; repr. in Friedrich Max Müller, *Comparative Mythology: An Essay*, ed. A. Smythe Palmer (London: Routledge, n.d. [actually 1909]), pp. xxxi–xlvii, where the essay is attributed to Littledale. As an example of the essay's exuberant detail, I would mention the admirable footnote [on p. 152 of the original or p. xliii of the reprinted text] proving that the Oxford and Cambridge boat-race is a mythological description of a storm at sea, conceived as a battle between the dark blue sea and the light blue sky. [Collingwood's reference to Whately is to Archbishop Richard Whately's satirical *Historic Doubts Relative to Napolean Buonaparte* (London: J. Hatchard, 1819). Cf. n. 4 to JA1 fos. 2–3.]

riddles? Müller answers this question by postulating in the remote past a Mythological or Mythopoeic Age, coming after the origin of language and before the creation of political society, religion, and poetry.[10] This, of course, is simply the romantic fiction of the 'childhood of the race' over again. But Müller is less romantic than his predecessors in his view of what this age was like, or at least romantic after another fashion. Irrational and often repulsive as its products are, it must have been a period of 'temporary insanity', when 'violent revolutions . . . broke the regularity of the early strata of thought, and convulsed the human mind, like volcanoes and earthquakes arising from some unknown cause, below the surface of history'.[11]

Working out this idea, he explains mythology as a 'disease of language'. In the original Aryan language there was no neuter gender. Every substantive [10] was either masculine or feminine. But these are indications of sex. Therefore, by a confusion of thought, the primitive Aryan when he talked of the sun and moon, dawn and evening, day and night (which, it is assumed, were the things he chiefly talked about), fancied himself to be talking about men and women, and embroidered this fancy into myth. So terrific a misunderstanding about the nature of the language it had invented for its own use can hardly be accounted for except on the theory that the primitive Aryan race, having invented the primitive Aryan language, proceeded to go mad.[12]

Here the romantic substitution of myth for history has travelled full circle. Beginning with the assumption that fairy tales are a legacy from the past, and forming a romantic picture of that past as the childhood of the race, it has piled myth upon myth and come ultimately to the conclusion that the age which created myths was

---

[10] 'It is a period in the history of the human mind, perhaps the most difficult to understand, and the most likely to shake our faith in the regular progress of the human intellect. We can form a tolerably clear idea of the origin of language, of the gradual formation of grammar, and the unavoidable divergence of dialects and languages. We can understand, again, the earliest concentration of political societies, the establishment of laws and customs, and the first beginnings of religion and poetry. But between the two there is a gulf which it seems impossible to bridge over.' See 'Comparative Mythology', Chips, ii. 10.

[11] 'Comparative Mythology', Chips, ii. 11, 13.

[12] This is of course ridiculing Müller, and nothing to do with Collingwood's serious treatment of 'madness', a theme explored at length in MGM, included in Part III below.

an age when people thought so confusedly that there was nothing
for it but to call them insane. Yet an age which created myths so
startling as these could hardly justify its belief that the age of myth-
making was over. And once more, the unpleasant question arises: if
the pseudo-history thus projected upon the blank screen of the past
is a history of mental confusion, where does the confusion arise?
Has not the modern myth-maker created in these huge and sinister
imaginings a symbolic picture of the unreason at work in himself?

While Müller was still at work, a totally different approach to the
same problem was being explored by others. The origins of this
approach need not concern us here; it will be enough if we study its
maturity, in the empirical school of anthropological research which
developed chiefly in England, the home of empirical science and
empiricist philosophy.

[11] The great master of this school, which may be called the
functional school, is by common consent Sir Edward Tylor, who
published his chief work, *Primitive Culture*, in 1871 (I shall quote
from the third edition of 1891).[13] By his time the foundations of
prehistoric archaeology had been firmly laid, and it was well
known that close analogies existed between the material culture
of 'backward races' still living, and that of our own remote ancestors. Tylor, quoting with approval the remark of Dr Johnson that
'one set of savages is like another',[14] a remark whose truth, he
observed, is confirmed by inspection of any ethnological museum,
proposed 'to treat mankind as homogeneous in nature, though

[13] Sir Edward B. Tylor, *Primitive Culture: Researches into the Development of
Mythology, Philosophy, Religion, Language, Art and Custom*, 3rd revised edn. 2 vols.
(London: John Murray, 1891). Collingwood's use of the phrase 'functional school'
to refer to Tylor and Frazer will look odd to a modern student, who will associate
this term rather with the fieldworking methods of Malinowski and the generation
taught by him. Those today labelled 'functionalists' focused on living communities
and emphasized resonance and connection in the present, sometimes specifically
rejecting any need for historical reconstruction or evolutionary explanation. Nevertheless they shared, perhaps, with their armchair predecessors more of a holistic
approach to the materials of folktale and culture than was recognized at the time,
especially by comparison with the antiquarians and linguists. Cf. Evans-Pritchard's
commentary on Tylor, in his *Theories of Primitive Religion* (Oxford: Clarendon
Press, 1965), esp. 124–7.
[14] Tylor, *Primitive Culture*, i. 6. Johnson was commenting on Captain Cook's
Voyages to the South Seas at the time. See James Boswell, *Life of Johnson*, ed.
George Birkbeck Hill and L. F. Powell, 6 vols. (Oxford: Clarendon Press, 1934),
iv. 308. Collingwood's own reference is parenthetical.

placed in different grades of civilization';[15] that is, to assume that
in a general way human nature has everywhere and always dis-
played the same laws, though with different cultural material to
work upon. He distinguishes three cultural stages in an ascending
scale: savagery, barbarism, and civilization.

His chief concern is with savagery; and he begins by urging that
it is wholly wrong to identify it with folly or depravity. 'Few who
will give their minds to master the general principles of savage
religion', he writes,

will ever again think it ridiculous . . . . Far from its beliefs and practices
being a rubbish-heap of miscellaneous folly, they are consistent and logical
in so high a degree as to begin, as soon as even roughly classified, to display
the principles of their formation and development; and these principles
prove to be essentially rational, though working in a mental condition of
intense and inveterate ignorance.[16]

Here we find the first principle of the new method admirably
stated, in a formal caution against the doctrine of the insane savage.
And [12] it is his fidelity to this principle, even more than the
width and variety of his learning, that makes Tylor's book the great
work that it is.

In order to justify this principle, a kind of Copernican revolution
was needed in the anthropologist's conception of his own relation
to his materials. The weirdness and irrationality which we find in
these materials must be due, not to what they are in themselves,
but to the relation in which we stand to them. This is the meaning
of the doctrine which Tylor next proceeds to expound, his doctrine
of survivals. Civilized peoples have developed out of savage ones;
and civilization contains many elements which, taken at their face
value, are condemned as irrational and described as superstitions;
but it would be better to drop that word and describe them as
survivals, for they are things whose proper home and meaning
must be sought in the context of an earlier civilization. With this
clue he examines children's games, proverbs, riddles, and certain
customs which, from a modern point of view, are meaningless.

Meaningless customs must be survivals[; . . .] they had a practical, or at
least ceremonial, intention when and where they first arose, but are now
fallen into absurdity from having been carried on into a new state of

---

[15] Tylor, *Primitive Culture*, i. 7.
[16] Ibid. i. 22–3. Collingwood's own reference is parenthetical.

society, where their original sense has been discarded. Of course, new customs introduced in particular ages may be ridiculous or wicked, but as a rule they have discernible motives. Explanations of this kind, by recourse to some forgotten meaning, seem on the whole to account best for obscure customs which some have set down to mere outbreaks of spontaneous folly.[17]

The second main principle of his method is the comparative principle. When we come across a fact that demands explanation, the way to explain it is to discover similar facts, and arrange these side by side. So arranged, they form a class of facts exhibiting a characteristic of our subject matter, in this case primitive culture. This is the inductive method of naturalistic science, here applied to mankind, in spite of certain objections and scruples, because human nature is constant and therefore a proper object of scientific [13] inquiry.

In the present book I am concerned to maintain that this principle is faulty and to propose a better one. I must therefore pause to show that even so great a man as Tylor was led astray by his use of it.

In the first place, his justification of it is confused. If there is a thing called human nature, which is constant however culture may vary, and if the justification of the naturalistic method is this constancy, the naturalistic method applies properly not to the cultural phenomena in human life, but only to those phenomena which arise, independently of cultural differences, from human nature itself. The argument used does not justify its extension to cultural phenomena, but rather bends in the reverse direction; it suggests that in order to explain these phenomena another method must be used. The constants in human life, if there are such things, must be derived from the unalterable laws of human nature, and can be explained (in the naturalistic or inductive sense of that word) by showing that they appear everywhere and always; but the variables—and on his own showing cultural facts are all variables—must be explained otherwise: namely, by taking a particular culture as a unit, and studying each fact in it, not in its relation of similarity with analogous facts in other cultures, but in its relation of organic connexion with different facts in the same culture.

[17] Ibid. i. 94.

In actual practice, the results he obtains from the method are far from conclusive. As an example, let us consider his treatment of magic. Why, he asks, should savages believe that you can injure a man by doing something to his nail-cuttings? Here is his answer.

'Man, as yet in a low intellectual condition, having come to associate in thought those things which he found by experience to be connected in fact, [14] proceeded erroneously to invent this action, and to conclude that association in thought must involve similar connexion in reality.'[18] The association of ideas which leads us, on seeing a man's nail-cuttings, to think of the man himself, leads the savage to suppose that a real bond unites the things thus ideally joined, so that injury to nail-cuttings will injure the man.

It will be observed that the theory turns on the 'low intellectual development' of the savage: that is, it bases magic on an endemic and inveterate error, not a mere ignorance, but an illogicality in thought. This is a breach of the principle that folly must not be invoked as the explanation of savage customs.

Even waiving this objection, the theory is doubly at fault: confused in itself, and inadequate to the facts. The associationist philosophy on which it is based, the doctrine that we take ideal connexions for real ones, was invented by Hume to explain, not magic, but science. Hume discovered that the idea of causation, upon which science depends, is not derived from experience, but from the habit of taking relations between our ideas of things, notably those of succession and contiguity, for causal relations between the things themselves. Tylor is here accepting the associationist theory of knowledge, but illegitimately using it, not as a description of science, but as a condemnation of magic. Yet, according to that theory itself, if it applies to magic, magic is thereby shown to stand intellectually on a level with science.

Apart from this, however, the description does not fit the facts. What the savage is doing is not to argue from an ideal connexion to a real one, but to argue from one kind of connexion, whether ideal or real, to another kind. The savage has the idea that a man's nail-cuttings are parts of himself that have been separated [15] from himself. This is what in fact they are; and if the 'savage' in some way or other argues from this relation between his idea of a man and his idea of that man's nail-cuttings to a corresponding relation

---

[18] Tylor, *Primitive Culture*, i. 116.

between the things themselves, he commits no logical fallacy. He is only doing what we all do whenever we assume (as we commonly say) that 'our ideas correspond to the facts'. What the savage really does, or is supposed to do, is something very different from this: namely to believe that the relation between a separated part of a man's body and that body itself somehow entails the further relation which is expressed by saying that damage to the separated part of a body will cause damage to the body. This belief is doubtless a very odd one. It is queer arguing to say 'this thing is a cut-off piece of So-and-so's body, therefore by damaging it I can damage So-and-so'. But you cannot explain this argument by subsuming it under the general conception of assuming that one's ideas correspond to the facts. It is the idea itself that needs explaining.

How the idea is to be explained we shall consider in a later chapter.[19] Tylor himself, not content (it would seem) with this purely formal or logical attempt to explain it, put forward what is in effect a second, quite different, explanation, contained implicitly in his theory of animism. This theory forms the main body of his book, and is set forth as the sequel to his chapters on mythology. These chapters, in spite of their enormous learning and fine imaginative sympathy, fail to achieve any definite result. Tylor classifies fairy tales into groups: myths of earth, of sky, of sun, moon, and stars, of rainbow and thunder, of waterfall and sandstorm, and so forth. He rejects Max Müller's theory that these myths are based on accidents of language, but follows him in regarding their main function as being to provide an imaginative description **[16]** of natural phenomena, a kind of poetical science of nature. What makes it imaginative or poetical is, according to him as according to Müller, the habit of personifying natural forces and things; but instead of deriving this habit from a misunderstanding of language he derives it from what he believes a fundamental feature of the primitive mind, namely animism: the conception of all things as living, a universal anthropomorphism.

According to this theory, the savage has no idea of causal connexion or natural law. Finding (or believing himself to find) that his own actions are the outcome of choice, that he does what he chooses to do and does it because he wants to do it, he argues that the events which he perceives in the world around him, not only

---

[19] FT4, 'Magic'.

those of other men but those of animals, plants, stones, meteors and heavenly bodies, proceed from the same principles of desire and choice: that, for example, the river rises because it wants to rise, whether benevolently, to fertilize his land with its silt, or maliciously, to sweep away his house. The next step in the savage's supposed process of thought is to argue that, when he wishes to control the actions of another human being, he does so or tries to do so by methods based on the assumption that this other, like himself, is a free agent, choosing to do what he wishes to do: to control his actions, therefore, one must command, argue, placate, threaten, or promise. These, then, will be the means by which to control the forces of nature. The result will be various kinds of magical practice: so that, on this theory, magic will be applied animism, or the technical side of a system of ideas whose theoretical side is the animistic conception of nature.

This conception of magic as the 'technique of animism' was not explicitly worked out by Tylor, but it is easily reached from his own position, and has [17] become almost the orthodoxy of the anthropological school that is proud to regard him as its founder. Its implicit acceptance by Sir James Frazer has left its mark on almost every page of his writings; and Dr Marett has developed out of it a theory as to the difference between magic and religion.[20] Magic, on this theory, is the attempt to control the actions of natural things by command, cajolery, and threats. At some great crisis in the development of the human mind it was discovered that these methods were vain; man found that the spirits of the natural world were not to be bullied or coerced. So man—or at least the more progressive and intelligent men—learned a new humility; set aside the pretence of magical power, and took up towards the spirits an attitude of supplication. Prayer replaced spell, and magic gave place to religion.

---

[20] R. R. Marett, *The Threshold of Religion*, 2nd edn. (London: Methuen, 1914), esp. ch. 2, 'From Spell to Prayer', 29–72. Cf. also his *Anthropology*, rev. edn. (London: Thornton Butterworth, 1914), ch. 8. Marett had proposed a 'pre-animistic' stage to religion, where conceptions of the world and things in it were infused with an emotional power, preceding the intellectual application of the 'techniques of animism' to manipulate the environment, that is, the stage of magic, itself leading to religion, where humankind recognizes its humble position in the face of the powers that move the world. Marett's inaugural lecture was entitled 'The Birth of Humility' and is included in *The Threshold of Religion*.

Before such developments of the animistic theory of magic are criticized, it is necessary to criticize that theory itself. It may tolerably well fit certain kinds of magic, those which already stand in very close relation to practices we ordinarily call religious, such as charms and spells, magical sacrifices, and so forth. These are comparatively easy to explain animistically. But in other kinds of example the explanation is hardly plausible. If, in the hope of bringing rain, we make a noise imitating thunder, it is far from natural to argue that we do this in order to arouse the weather-god to a sense of his responsibilities, or make him wish to show us how much better he can do it himself. It is much more reasonable to say that, since thunder and rain generally go together, we are producing the thunder in order that the rain may follow. On that view, magic would be not an embryonic form of religion but an embryonic form of science. And in fact there has been a tendency [18] since Tylor's day for theories of magic to divide themselves into two classes, one bringing it under the general category of science, the other under that of religion.

Even the original animistic theory has not been exempt from criticism. However much we may admit that savages often attribute something like human life, consciousness, and volition to inanimate things, as well as to beasts and plants, there are difficulties in the way of asserting that this is an article of doctrine as a general principle of savage philosophy. For, in the first place, granted that the savage does this, we still want to know why he does it. To say that he is stupid and ignorant is not enough. Stupidity and ignorance, invoked as causes, may explain (if we think the explanation a good one) why mistakes in general should be made; they can never explain why one particular mistake should be made out of all the infinity of possible mistakes. Besides, Tylor himself has warned us not to be content with explanations of that kind.

Moreover, the savage is not a consistent animist. Engaged in smelting copper, for example, he does not command the copper to melt; he treats it quite scientifically, raising it to the right temperature by means of a furnace and bellows. We cannot logically explain this by saying that he is too stupid to be a consistent animist; for we have no reason, apart from what he does and says, to think him an animist at all. So far as he does not behave like one, he is not one.

Further, he does not attribute a quasi-human soul to all things, but only to some; he treats certain special trees as having souls, but not others; evidently, then, these special trees have souls for some special [19] reason, not because of a philosophical doctrine attributing souls to everything. In a general way, the truth seems to be that the things which have souls are things with which he comes into contact as partners, friendly or hostile, willing or unwilling, in his own labour, and more particularly in the ritual which accompanies that labour. We plough the earth; annexed to that action are certain ritual practices which may be described as magicking the earth; and out of these practices there seems to grow the conception of the earth as endowed with a quasi-human soul. When magic is called the technique of animism, it is conceived as a system of practice logically deduced from the animistic conception of nature, somewhat as aseptic surgery is deduced from the bacterial conception of disease. There is some ground for thinking, and many anthropologists have thought, that this puts the cart before the horse: that animism is rather a rationalization of magic, a theory invented partly by anthropologists and partly by the savages themselves to explain practices which in fact are logically prior to it and can exist in its absence. In themselves, these practices require no theoretical basis whatever.

[20] The great service of Tylor to his successors, so far as mythology was concerned, consisted not in what he did but in what he made possible. It consisted in opening up a new line of approach to the whole subject, very different from that which he followed in his own chapters directly dealing with it. We have seen how he interpreted the 'superstitions' of modern civilization as survivals from an earlier culture whose context, if we could discover it, would explain their meaning. His followers applied this same method to the study of myths. The original impulse came from Mannhardt, who found among the popular customs of modern Europe extensive survivals of an ancient ritual designed to promote by magical means the fertility of the soil. It was soon recognized that certain classes of myth or fairy tale were not, as even Tylor had supposed, metaphorical descriptions of natural processes, but more or less literal, though often garbled, accounts of this ritual itself and statements of its purpose. The persons figuring in such stories were, according to this view, not personified representations of the earth, the corn, the rain, and so forth but

actual human beings, dramatically representing these things in the ritual.

This discovery made it possible to approach mythology from an entirely new angle and in a far more scientific spirit. It was henceforth assumed as an axiom that a given myth was no mere flight of poetic fancy, but stood in the closest relation with the customs of the people among whom it originated: the custom being in fact logically prior to the myth, as the fact of which the myth gave a description. English writers, realizing the intimate connexion between this new principle of mythology and the lessons they had already learnt from Tylor, took it up with enthusiasm; and, to ignore a host of less important works, the chief result was Sir James Frazer's monumental book *The Golden Bough*.[21]

[21] The new angle of approach to mythology may be defined as the functional approach. The new school of anthropologists refused to select one aspect or product of primitive life, such as the myth or fairy tale, and treat it by itself. They took the view that the culture of a given people at a given stage in its development is a single whole, in which every element is connected with every other. Hence, when studying a given myth found in a given culture, they made it their primary object to ask, not, 'What similar myths have been found elsewhere?' but, 'how is this myth organically connected with the culture in which we find it?'[22]

---

[21] James G. Frazer's project *The Golden Bough: A Study in Magic and Religion* began with a two-volume set of books published by Macmillan in London in 1890. This was itself revised, and many further volumes added in a long sequence, culminating in *Aftermath: A Supplement to the Golden Bough* (London: Macmillan, 1936). A modern 12-vol. set is edited by George Stocking (Harmondsworth: Penguin, 1996). An abridged edn. was published in 1922 (London: Macmillan) and has been republished several times since. Evans-Pritchard's comments on Frazer may be found in his *Theories of Primitive Religion*, 27–9. The Collingwood of *PA* is much more outspoken in his condemnation of Tylor's influence: 'The fact that . . . [Tylor's theory] is still taught in our own time by Sir James Frazer (*The Golden Bough*, passim) has been a disaster to contemporary anthropology and all the studies connected with it' (58 n.).

[22] In this paragraph, Collingwood appears to be looking beyond his comments on Frazer and his contemporaries, even anticipating Bronislaw Malinowski as a key figure among the 'new school of anthropologists'. His comments closely follow Malinowski's 'Myth in Primitive Psychology' (1926), reprinted in a collection of his essays *Magic, Science and Religion: And Other Essays* (London: Souvenir Press, 1974), 93–148.

This did not involve ceasing to look for parallels to it in other cultures; but it gave these parallels a new significance. Instead of being important only for their resemblances, they could now become important for their differences also: because the differences as well as the resemblances could be treated as functions of the different, but yet similar, cultures in which the parallel myths were found. But it did involve ceasing to think of myths as expressions of a 'savage philosophy' which could be conceived as something separable from savage life as a whole. Indeed, it made the whole idea of such a 'savage philosophy' out of date. The increasingly detailed study of 'primitive' life made it increasingly plain that the 'savage' is a practical man, systematic in his methods of getting food, of ordering his private affairs, and of arranging for the government of his commonwealth. It might be difficult or impossible to follow his abstract thoughts, but his customs were found to be meticulously logical and precise. It became a rule of sound anthropological method to begin by studying his actions.

Working on this rule, they found that an important part of all primitive life is ritual. The savage is at least as anxious for success in hunting and fishing and [22] agriculture as any civilized man; but he appears to think that in addition to what we should call practical means towards achieving this success it is necessary to practise ritual means also. He will not hunt or fish or plough without performing ceremonies intended to bring about some indispensable part of the total result. If he ploughs and sows, he has a ploughing and sowing ritual without which he apparently does not think the seed will grow. It is not that he thinks the ritual efficacious by itself; he would never expect to get a crop simply by performing the ritual, without ploughing and sowing at all; nor does he suppose that the ritual will make good any mistakes he makes in the ploughing and sowing. The practical or technical side of the work must be properly done; but the ritual side of it must be done as well. And this is not peculiar to savages. A servant-girl in my father's house, when I was a boy, would never light a fire or put on a kettle without saying to it 'burn up fire', or 'boil up kettle'. Without that ritual, she would not have expected the fire to burn or the kettle to boil. But, simple country lass though she was, and deplorably superstitious, she would have laughed at you had you suggested that the charm would act if the fire was clumsily laid or the kettle unskilfully placed upon it. And this is what the anthropologists found among 'savages'.

They found, too, that the rituals actually used stood in a close relation to the fairy tales told. One might say that a ritual proved, in many cases at least, to be an acted fairy tale, and a fairy tale a described ritual. Now, they argued, the ritual differs from the practical or technical side of an act, such as ploughing, in that there is not any real reason for it. If the savage asks himself 'why do I plough?' he can answer that this is a good way of turning up the ground without the labour of hoeing it or [23] using a digging-stick; and that is a perfectly rational answer. To anyone who asked him that question, he might reply by telling a story which would be a fragment of history. 'Our ancestors used a digging-stick, so my grandfather told me; but one day a very clever man thought of making a huge digging-stick and harnessing a pair of cows to it, and we have all done so ever since.' But if he begins his ploughing with a dance in which an old woman is knocked down by a devil with a blackened face and raised up by a doctor, as in the traditional English Plough Monday play, and is asked why he does that, we know that he cannot give any real reason, for we know that there is no real reason; civilized people have discovered by experiment that ploughing is just as efficacious without it. He will therefore have to invent a reason, which will be modelled on the kind of reason he gives for ploughing at all. It will therefore be a story about someone who was killed and brought back to life. This will be a fairy tale. Thus the fairy tale is (to use the term invented by this school) an aetiological myth; a cock-and-bull story, in plain English, invented to give a fictitious explanation of the ritual.

This method of approach has proved extraordinarily fruitful. It has been found possible to trace a close connexion, in a large number of cases, between the rituals and the fairy tales of this or that people. The connexion is not merely a general or vague connexion; it is not established by overlooking the details; it extends into the details themselves. But as work went forward it was found necessary to abandon the original conception of the aetiological myth. It was found that myth and ritual were not related as consequent to antecedent, but were coexistent parts of a single indivisible whole. The ritual is not carried out dumbly; it is accompanied by a description of what is being done. This description is itself part of the ritual: it is solemnly spoken or chanted, [24] and the acted part of the ritual would not be complete without it. You may equally say that a ritual is performed and simultaneously described in a myth, or that a myth is ceremonially recited and acted at the same time.

The work of this school, culminating in Frazer's *Golden Bough*, has for the first time, and permanently, set the study of fairy tales on the path of scientific progress. But if its principles had been altogether satisfactory, there would have been no need to write this book. In three ways, these principles were defective.

First, Frazer's method involves the assumption that similarities between customs or myths indicate substantial identities. If a custom or myth found among one people reminds the student of one which he finds among another, he is justified in assuming that the two things are one and the same. For example, in an essay on 'Some Popular Superstitions of the Ancients'[23] he observes that Pythagoras warned his disciples not to point their fingers at the stars. Why, he asks, should this strange rule be laid down? To explain it, he collects similar things from elsewhere. There is a German superstition to the same effect, and those who hold it explain it by saying that it would put out the eyes of the angels, and that the finger would drop off: you can prevent it from dropping off by biting it. But why bite it? The Ojibway Indians, he continues, supply the answer. They say that if you point your finger at the moon, the moon will be angry and bite off the finger. 'The reason, therefore, why a German bites his finger is to make the star believe that he is himself biting off the offending finger, and that thus the star is saved the trouble of doing so.'

Here the assumption is that one and the same superstition holds among the Ojibways, the Germans, and the ancient Greeks; and that what Pythagoras meant by his rule can be explained by appeal to the other two cases. But what **[25]** is there to justify that assumption? How do we know that the three superstitions do not spring from different sources, and that the resemblance between them is not merely superficial? The comparative anatomy of the animal and vegetable kingdoms is full of such things: cases where two animal or plant species exhibit resemblances which on closer study prove to be misleading: fins that turn out to be modified fore-legs, petals which are parts not of the corolla but of the calyx, and so forth. Only a general study of the entire culture of one

[23] * *F-L* 12 (June 1890), 145–71. Reprinted in *Garnered Sheaves: Essays, Addresses, and Reviews* (London: Macmillan, 1931), 128–50; quotation at p. 134.

people can justify the assumption that a feature in it which is superficially parallel to a feature in another culture is structurally parallel.

Moreover, the conclusion as stated by Frazer himself, which he gives as part of the superstition and indeed as its motive, is not contained anywhere in his material. It is his own invention. And his reason for stating it is his implicit belief in the conception of magic as the technique of animism. Granted that the German and Ojibway superstitions really are the same, the Ojibway belief that the moon will bite off the finger might be an animistic gloss on a custom which, as originally existing, had no such implication. In his explanation of the German superstition, Frazer is not checking the animistic theory of magic by the facts, he is reconstructing the facts so as to make them conform with the theory.

Lastly, there is something defective in the spirit in which the whole subject is approached. In the preface to one of his volumes, Frazer describes his great work as a record of the long tragedy of human folly and suffering.[24] Such words show that he approaches his subject matter as a thing external to himself and the civilization which he feels as his own: without any attempt to work himself into the spirit of it and to recreate in his own mind the experiences whose outward expression he is studying. This may **[26]** be the right method in natural science; but that is because in natural science man is working to understand and control the external world of things around him. In anthropological science man is trying to understand man; and to man his fellow-man is never a mere external object, something to be observed and described, but something to be sympathized with, to be studied by penetrating into his thoughts and re-enacting those thoughts for oneself. Anthropology—I refer to cultural, not physical, anthropology—is a historical science, where by calling it historical as opposed to

---

[24] Preface to *The Golden Bough: Balder the Beautiful* (London: Macmillan, 1913), p. vi. Cf. also the later formulation: 'When I first put pen to paper to write *The Golden Bough* I had no conception of the magnitude of the voyage on which I was embarking; I thought only to explain a single rule of an ancient Italian priesthood. But insensibly I was led on . . . into indicting what I cannot but regard as a dark, a tragic chronicle of human error and folly, of fruitless endeavour, wasted time, and blighted hopes.' See James G. Frazer, Preface to *Aftermath: A Supplement to the Golden Bough*, pp. v–vi. The Preface is dated 13 Aug. 1936, that is, shortly before Collingwood began to prepare MGM and his study of folktale.

naturalistic I mean that its true method is thus to get inside its object or recreate its object inside itself.

Anyone can see this if he considers, for example, the historical study of early mathematics. Greek geometry, and Egyptian geometry even more, is a crude and primitive thing compared with the geometry of our own day; but if we are to study it historically (and there is no other way of studying it) we must examine its documents until we find ourselves able to think again for ourselves the thoughts of those early geometers. There is no difference of principle between this and any other case in which an attempt is made to study the early history of human ideas. The universal rule in every such case is to reconstruct for oneself and in oneself the ideas whose history one is trying to study. If one cannot do this, one may speak with the tongues of men and of angels, but the result is not anthropology.

Taken as a whole, Frazer's work is a study of magic. As a collection of crude facts conveniently arranged to the reader's hand, that work is beyond praise. But as a piece of scientific theory, it is built round a framework of ideas which are radically unsound. Magic is defined as the pseudo- [27] science of the savage: a false form of that same thing whose true form, natural science, is possessed by our wiser and happier selves. The essential character of magic, Frazer thinks, is that it proposes to itself exactly the task which science proposes to itself, namely to understand and control the forces of nature; that it uses exactly the methods which science uses, namely observation, hypothesis, and experiment; but that it uses these methods wrongly instead of rightly, and hence arrives systematically at false conclusions, arguing that causal connections exist where in fact there are none.

The issue here is so important that no veneration for a great scholar must prevent us from pushing it home. I shall therefore take courage to say things which, I fear, will offend readers in whom the veneration for Sir James Frazer is as lively a feeling as it is in myself.

First, this theory of magic offends against the principle laid down by Tylor, when he made his memorable statement about the beliefs and practices of savage religion being no rubbish-heap of miscellaneous folly, but consistent and logical in a high degree. If Tylor was right here, any conception of magic which reduces it to a long tragedy of human folly stands self-condemned.

Secondly, as Frazer has repeatedly told us, his work is based not on personal acquaintance with its material, but on a second-hand knowledge through printed books. A study of that kind is peculiarly liable to fundamental misunderstandings. As he himself, with the humility of a true scholar, wrote to Sir Baldwin Spencer: 'Books like mine, merely speculative, will be superseded sooner or later (the sooner the better for the sake of truth) by better indications based on fuller knowledge.'[25]

[28] Thirdly, the fundamental ideas of this theory are hopelessly confused. The product of an age when natural science was on all hands regarded as the one and only genuine form of knowledge, it started with the prejudice, common to most men of the time, that every system of ideas must be an attempt, successful or unsuccessful, at a system of natural science. If any system of ideas was found which resisted explanation on these terms, the inference was not that the method of explanation was at fault, but that the system of ideas in question was exceptionally bad science.

But to describe something as pseudo-science implies two statements about it: first, that it is not science (not science proper, successful or scientific science), secondly, that it is something else, offering itself as science or mistaken for science. In the case of magic, what is this other thing which is not science? Its characteristics are not merely negative: they are not sufficiently defined by calling it not science. It has certain positive and constant features of its own, and these follow, not from its failure to be something else, but from its success in being itself.

The description of magic as pseudo-science betrays a further confusion. To call magic pseudo-science implies that it is mistaken for science. But who mistakes it for science? Not the savage: for magic is (on the theory) all the science he has or conceives. If I mistake one thing for another, I must have a conception of that other. If magic is mistaken for science, it must be so mistaken by someone who knows what science is or might be. Clearly, then, the error implied in calling magic pseudo-science is an error on the

---

[25] * Letter of 13 July 1898, Spencer's *Scientific Correspondence with Sir J. G. Frazer and Others* (Oxford: Clarendon Press, 1932), 22. [T. K. Penniman, who with Marett had edited the *Correspondence*, had quoted the same remark from Frazer's letter to Spencer in *Hundred Years*, 313.]

part of the modern scientifically trained anthropologist. It is he, and not the savage, who has taken magic for that which it is not.

[29] Anthropology since Frazer has shown hopeful signs of improving both upon his method and upon his spirit; but as yet these advances have produced little effect on the public mind. Meanwhile, a third attempt has been made to create a science of fairy tales, which has achieved great notoriety.

By now it is clear that fairy tales cannot be considered except in relation to the whole culture in which they arise. I shall therefore consider what this new school of thought has to say about that culture as a whole, not about fairy tales alone.

The work of the anthropologists has not escaped the attention of the psychologists; and here in particular I refer to the greatest of modern psychologists, Sigmund Freud. In his book on *Totem and Taboo*[26] he has given an outline account of the 'primitive' or 'savage' mind from the point of view of psycho-analysis. His work in psychology is so enormously important, and its effect on the whole science of psychology has been so gigantic—almost every living psychologist being by now either a disciple of his

[26] Freud's *Totem and Taboo* was first published as a series of four articles in *Imago* (Vienna) between 1912 and 1913 under the title 'Über einige Übereinstimmungen im Seelenleben der Wilder und der Neurotiker' (On Some Points of Agreement between the Mental Lives of Savages and Neurotics). Here, Collingwood seems to be using the text of *Totem and Taboo: Resemblances between the Psychic Lives of Savages and Neurotics*, tr. A. A. Brill (London: Kegan Paul, Trench, Trubner, 1919). In an unpublished set of notes dated 'Dec 1933' and headed 'Outline of a Theory of Primitive Mind' (Bodleian Library Collingwood Papers, dep. 16/8), Collingwood had begun by 'Accepting the genuineness and significance of the discoveries made of late, especially by Freud, concerning the primitive mind, but [. . . was] unable without doing violence to scientific decency to accept the mythology invoked to explain them'. He noted that 'I have . . . banished the terms Unconscious, Censorship, Superego; I have made no reference to sex, whose central place in the Freudian ideology is altogether accidental' (fo. 1). Collingwood returns to a trenchant critique of Freud's paralleling of 'savage' mentality and neurosis, citing Brill's 'Authorized English Translation' in ch. 4 ('Art as Magic') of *PA* 62. And in *EM* 118, he notes that 'It would not take long to expose the tissue of errors and confusions that underlies, for example, Freud's *Totem and Taboo*.' Collingwood's quotations in the present MS seem to be taken from Brill's version, which is also the translation mentioned in his reading notes, 'English Folklore I', Bodleian Library Collingwood Papers, dep. 21/1, fo. 78. Collingwood's notes on *Totem and Taboo* are particularly extensive and anticipate the sequence of topics in the chapter. Cf. Evans-Pritchard on Freud's use of anthropology, *Theories of Primitive Religion*, 40–3.

own, or the disciple of a school derived from his, or at least profoundly influenced by his ideas—that this book and other writings more or less derived from it have created a new school of thought about primitive life. It is impossible here to review the work of this school as a whole. I shall confine myself to discussing this one book of Freud's, and one of Jung's.

It is the strength of Freud that he is a specialist: a specialist in mental disease. It is from this point of view that he has approached the problems of anthropology. He explains that in reading of savage ideas and customs he has found himself reminded of things already familiar from his experience of neurotics; and he has followed this up by a course of reading which, as can be seen from his [30] references, is both wide and deep. Far too original and adventurous a thinker to content himself with a few obvious textbooks and articles in encyclopaedias, he has studied many of the chief works of modern anthropology, and he has made himself familiar with the chief periodicals.

His book consists of four chapters, respectively dealing with exogamy, taboo, magic, and totemism. I will review these in turn.

The first chapter is called 'The Savage's Dread of Incest'. Its general thesis is that savages suffer from so acute a dread of incest, and in consequence are so intensely anxious to prevent it, that 'their whole social organization seems to serve this object or to have been brought into relation with its attainment'.[27] The expedient which they have devised as means to this end is the system of social organization by totem clans.[28]

---

[27] *Totem and Taboo*, 3.

[28] The word 'totem' is first recorded as used by a North American Ojibwa speaker in 1791; it came to fill a significant place in anthropology as scholars struggled to account for the widespread phenomenon whereby human groups distinguished themselves by reference to natural species, especially animals. In important work by figures such as Robertson Smith and Durkheim, 'totemic' groupings were the elemental forms of religious association, and 'totemism' was widely discussed as a stage in the evolution of religion as such. See William Robertson Smith, *Lectures on the Religion of the Semites* (Edinburgh: Adam and Charles Black, 1889) and Emile Durkheim, *The Elementary Forms of Religious Life* (1912), tr. Karen E. Fields (New York: Free Press, 1995). Lévi-Strauss undermined the whole idea that 'totemism' was a particular religious system, or a special phenomenon of any kind. He emphasized the universal capacity of human beings to classify, distinguish, and recombine categories in nature and in the human world, as the very foundation of reason, art, and science. See Claude Lévi-Strauss, *Totemism*

It is difficult to embark on the chapter without a word of protest at the approach indicated by its title. The whole chapter is about 'The Savage'. But there is no such person as The Savage. Every civilization is called uncivilized by every other; and when we have agreed to extend the term civilized to a group of peoples (with ourselves, of course, in the centre) whose civilization is a good deal like our own, we use the word savage as a general name for others outside that charmed circle. But there is not necessarily anything common to these except their unlikeness to ourselves. To discuss the psychology of the 'savage' is like discussing the psychology of the 'foreigner', as when we argue whether he has or has not a sense of fair play. The term savage has no scientific meaning; it has only an emotional meaning, of which more must be said in the next chapter.

But for the present this need not greatly matter. For the purposes of Freud's chapter it is possible to define savage societies as those which have a system of totem-clans. The argument, then, is that where these [31] exist they are evidence of a peculiar and overwhelming dread of incest, because they have been created as a safeguard against it. Incest here (though Freud does not explain the point) clearly means incest in the normal sense of the word: sexual relations between persons closely related by blood. It is an idea which presupposes the idea of the family and of kin-relationship.

These ideas are in fact present in every human society known to us; and in every society there are rules (as there are in our own) against marriage or sexual relations between persons thus related in certain determinate ways. These rules, in some civilizations like our own, are the only limitations imposed by society on its members' freedom to select partners. But the odd fact is that in certain societies a second set of rules is, as it were, superimposed on them. These are the rules of totemistic exogamy, according to which sexual relations between members of the same totem-clan are forbidden.

(1962; Harmondsworth: Penguin, 1969). Ironically, today's extension of moral arguments towards the rest of the animal kingdom has led to what has been labelled a new kind of totemism. See e.g. R. G. Willis (ed.), *Signifying Animals: Human Meaning in the Natural World* (London: Unwin Hyman, 1990), esp. 6–7.

Freud seems, on encountering this fact, to have argued as follows. 'The savage evidently does not consider himself sufficiently
protected against incest by rules based on his table of kindred and
affinity. He has found it necessary to reinforce these rules by
devising another set, expressed in terms of the totem-clan. The
necessity for this reinforcement can only have arisen, on sound
psychological principles, out of an excessive dread of incest, con-
ditioned by an excessive temptation to commit it.' I say he seems to
have argued thus, because the argument is never stated: but no
careful reader, I think, can doubt that it is implied.

This argument is in the familiar hypothetical form in which
scientific theories **[32]** are commonly stated. A theory is pro-
pounded to explain a certain group of facts; if the facts really are
what they would be, were the theory true, the theory is acceptable,
and remains so until reason is found for rejecting it—for example,
until a fact is found which is different from what it would be if the
theory were true.

In order that the argument should be even partially valid, the
exogamous limitations on marriage must reinforce the limitations
based on kinship: that is to say, the two kinds of rule must forbid
the same kinds of unions. In order that it should be wholly valid, it
is further necessary that all totemistic clan-systems should be
exogamous: for the theory is an attempt to explain the motive
leading to the introduction of such systems in general.

The second condition is notoriously unfulfilled. Among the
Arunta of central Australia, totem-clans are not exogamous.[29]
There is no evidence that they ever were. In fact, there are signs
that in the past they were endogamous. And most students have
regarded the Arunta as the most primitive people known to us, in
which case they ought surely to reveal the nature of totemism in its
purest shape. Freud is aware of this fatal exception to his rule, but
he tries to disqualify it by adopting the view that the Arunta are not
really primitive but exhibit totemistic society in a decaying and
evanescent form; a view which certain other writers had already

---

[29] Freud is likely to have relied on Baldwin Spencer and F. J. Gillen, *The Native
Tribes of Central Australia* (London: Macmillan, 1899), and *The Northern Tribes of
Central Australia* (London: Macmillan, 1904). Collingwood himself is likely to have
been aware of their later 2-vol. work dedicated to the Arunta, *The Arunta: A Study
of a Stone Age People* (London: Macmillan, 1927). The complexities of totemic
organization are presented in chs. 2–5.

taken before him, and for the same reason, namely that the facts of Arunta society were fatal to their own theories of totemism.[30] But actually, the question whether the Arunta are primitive or not has nothing to do with the point at issue. To look for a primitive example of totemism in order to discover from it what [33] totemism in its purest form most essentially is, means abandoning all historical and evolutionary ideas in favour of belief in a kind of anthropological Garden of Eden. The true nature of an institution is shown not in its beginnings but in its developments. If anyone wishes to define totemism so as to exclude the Arunta, he may do so; but he should do it openly and not shelter himself behind dubious metaphysics.

The first condition also is unfulfilled. Exogamy forbids sexual relations between members of the same clan. Where descent is matrilinear, the children being of the same clan as their mother, exogamy forbids a man to marry his sister, his mother, or his maternal aunt, but leaves him free to marry his sister-in-law, his mother-in-law, or his daughter.[31] Where descent is patrilinear, it forbids him to marry his sister or daughter or brother's daughter, but leaves him free to marry his mother, sister-in-law, or sister's daughter, and even his mother-in-law unless she happens to belong to the same clan as his father. The only point at which both systems coincide with the kindred-rules against incest is in forbidding brother–sister unions; whereas they both concur in permitting (apart from the case stated above) the union between a man and his mother-in-law, upon which as a matter of fact most primitive peoples look with quite peculiar horror.

The facts are thus quite different from what, on Freud's theory, they ought to be. To his credit, he does not get over this by the easy expedient of arguing that the savages who invented exogamy were too stupid to realize its uselessness for their purpose. He modifies the theory, or rather abandons it, and tells us that exogamy is designed not as a safeguard against incest in general but as a safeguard against the incestuous desires of the son.

[30] *Totem and Taboo*, 192–3: 'The Aruntas seem . . . to be the most developed of the Australian tribes and to represent rather a dissolution stage of totemism than its beginning.' The 'other writers' referred to by Freud are Durkheim and Lang.

[31] The case for the central significance of matrilineal descent in the evolution of human society had been made by Edwin Sidney Hartland in *Primitive Society: The Beginnings of the Family and the Reckoning of Descent* (London: Methuen, 1921).

[34] But even this will not fit the facts. The chief incestuous desire of the son, as Freud has told us over and over again, is his desire for union with his mother; and this is forbidden only by matrilineal exogamy, not by patrilinear. In order to meet this difficulty he changes the meaning of the term incest, making it refer not to close kinship within the family, but to membership of the same totem-clan; for the mutual obligations of clan-members may 'supersede consanguineous relationship', inasmuch as 'the role of the totem as ancestor is taken very seriously'.[32] Now, even granted the truth of the doctrine that the totem is conceived as ancestor (and it is a doctrine which anthropologists have in fact long abandoned), this would make havoc of the whole theory. For the theory that totemism is a device to reinforce the rules against incest implies that incest is understood in the normal sense as incest within the family. If incest is to mean not family-incest but totem-incest, the clan-system cannot be a device to ensure protection against this: for, apart from the clan-system, there is no such thing; the danger to be averted does not exist.

By the time the theory has reached this point it has become simple nonsense. The thesis is that savages, like ourselves, find it necessary to have rules against incest; but in view of their bestial lusts have to reinforce these rules by an additional system of safeguards. On examination, it turns out that these safeguards

---

[32] *Totem and Taboo*, 49. The original of the latter reads: 'the role of the totem (the animal) as ancestor is taken very seriously'. In his reading notes, 'English Folklore I', Bodleian Library Collingwood Papers, dep. 21 / 1, fos. 79–81, Collingwood had quoted this remark, summarizing Freud's argument with the comment that 'even the most distant grades of relationship are an absolute obstacle to sexual relations', and outlining his objections thus: 'So the savage has "an unusually high grade of incest dread ... combined with the peculiarity, which we do not very well understand, of substituting the totem relationship for the real blood relationship." This is an inconceivable muddle. If the savage *really* believes in the totem ancestor, as Freud wrongly thinks, he believes that totem relationship *is* real blood relationship and acts accordingly. All through, he muddles his mind by using *incest* to imply relationship *as we know it*, and then wondering (*a*) why the Australian is so frightened of this (*b*) why he is so confused about it as to mix up real relationship with totem relationship. He thinks that (i) First there is the temptation to incest (ii) then the exogamic clan system as a "protection" against it, forgetting that it is only the clan system that lays down what incest is! When he says (15) that these savages are more subject to temptations than we are and hence require more extensive protection against it [sic] it is as if he said A is more tempted to get drunk than B, and *hence*, whereas B won't drink alcohol, A won't drink lemonade or milk.'

protect them not against incest but against other dangers which become dangers only through the existence of the safeguards. This is like saying that Brown and Jones are both tempted to alcoholism; that Brown, to avoid this danger, becomes a teetotaller; but that Jones, because his temptation is stronger, keeps rigidly clear of anything in a screw-topped bottle.

[35] The second chapter deals with taboo.[33] Now, taboo is a convenient term; it serves the anthropologist as a label under which to collect all sorts of avoidances and prohibitions many of which are curious and interesting in themselves. But although taboos in particular may be interesting, taboo in general is not; and anyone who attempted to construct a theory of taboo as such would expose himself to the ridicule of Bergson for thinking about 'les étiquettes collées sur les choses'[34] instead of the things themselves. This is because a taboo properly means a prohibition or refusal, irrespective of what is prohibited and why. A chief will put a taboo on the luggage of white explorers, to prevent his people from stealing it. Pigs may be taboo because they are ear-marked to be eaten at a tribal feast. A savage who uses the word would equally call it observing a taboo when we refuse to eat soup in which somebody has spat, or when we refuse to allow people with scarlet fever to travel by train; when we take a glove off to shake hands, or when we sterilize a dressing before applying it to a wound. No single theory of prohibition or avoidance will cover all these cases.

---

[33] 'Taboo' was introduced into general English usage, from the Polynesian word *tabu*, by Captain Cook in 1784. It has served anthropology well, but mainly as a topic for debate over the question of the universality and meaning of the phenomenon it supposedly signifies, that is, the existence or placing of a special ban on some action or object. A study of lasting value on this question by Steiner has recently been reissued. See Franz Steiner, *Taboo* (1956), vol. i of *Franz Steiner: Selected Writings*, ed. Jeremy Adler and Richard Fardon (Oxford: Berghahn, 1999).

[34] Possibly a recollection of Henri Bergson's 'Enfin, pour tout dire, nous ne voyons pas les choses mêmes; nous nous bornons, le plus souvent, à lire des étiquettes collées sur elles' from *Le Rire: Essai sur la Signification du Comique* (first published in book form 1900, with a 43rd edn., Paris: Libraire Félix Alcan, 1935); in *Œuvres*, ed. André Robinet and Henri Gouhier (Paris: Presses Universitaires de France, 1959), 460. Translated as: 'In short, we do not see the actual things themselves; in most cases we confine ourselves to reading the labels affixed to them'. See *Laughter: An Essay on the Meaning of the Comic*, tr. Cloudesley Brereton and Fred Rothwell (1911; London: Macmillan & Co., 1935), 153. This translation appears among the volumes listed in Blackwell's Sale Catalogue, no. 496, of Collingwood's personal library.

In order to define his subject matter, Freud takes a taboo to mean a prohibition or avoidance 'whose origin is unmotivated';[35] that is, which serves no purpose or springs from no psychological ground. He is thus dividing avoidances or prohibitions in general into two species: one being rational, that is, for which reasons exist and can be given, the other irrational, or those for which no reason can be given because there is none. His problem is to discover why prohibitions of this second class are nevertheless insisted upon. The problem, by the terms in which it is stated, is insoluble. No wonder he says that the term taboo 'express[es] a fragment of psychic life which really is not comprehensible [36] to us'.[36]

Nevertheless, he tries to comprehend it. As an example of it, he quotes the case of a Maori chief who would not blow the fire because his sacred breath would infect the fire and the food cooked upon it, so that the eater would die.[37] Now, he points out, there is a class of persons in our own society, namely compulsion-neurotics, who create taboos for themselves. He gives an instance. A woman patient refused to allow into her house a thing bought in a street whose name was the name of a former friend with whom she had quarrelled; but she had repressed this connexion of ideas and replaced it with a rationalization. In what are called phobias, the horror-stricken refusal to do a suggested action conceals a powerful desire to do it. This situation has arisen out of a prohibition in childhood to do something that the child wants to do. In obedience to the prohibition it has repressed the desire; but in later years the emotional tone of its refusal to do the same act betrays the surviving strength of the repressed but not eradicated desire.

Now, Freud continues, we must study taboo as if it were of the same nature as the compulsive prohibitions shown by our patients.[38] The phrase is curious. It seems as if Freud were anxious,

---

[35] *Totem and Taboo*, 45: 'The first and most striking correspondence between the compulsion prohibitions of neurotics and taboo lies in the fact that the origin of these prohibitions is just as unmotivated and enigmatic.'

[36] Ibid. 37.   [37] Ibid. 47.

[38] Ibid. 52. In his reading notes, 'English Folklore I', Bodleian Library Collingwood Papers, dep, 21 / 1, fo. 83, Collingwood comments on Freud's thought on prohibition in childhood, and he complains angrily of *Totem and Taboo* (52): 'we must now study taboo as if it were of the same motive as the compulsive prohibitions of our patients [why? The savage is *not* your patient! This is a new attitude towards the native: not the "damn nigger" attitude but the "lunatic" attitude. Savagery is now a mental disease to be cured by psychoanalysis!]'

on the one hand, to remind himself that a taboo is not a neurosis and that the savage who observes it is a sane member of society; but anxious, on the other hand, to assimilate this action to the actions of a neurotic. Why should we study taboo 'as if it were' a neurosis, if it is not one? Is it because Freud, as a specialist in neurosis, can treat it on no other hypothesis? Or is it because he, as a psychologist, genuinely thinks that the phenomena of primitive life may perhaps be capable of explanation as symptoms of insanity? For Frazer's long tragedy of human folly is he [37] proposing to substitute a long tragedy of mental derangement?

On this hypothesis he attempts to explain certain taboos as the result of prohibitions, enforced by an older generation, of actions for which there was a strong desire: the desire therefore repressed, but still persisting. Why should the person of the Maori chief be thus charged with taboo? Because in his elevated position he arouses envy. Other classes of persons are taboo because, for example, their helplessness incites our aggressiveness in one form or another: they are standing temptations. 'Therefore these persons are taboo, for one must not yield to the temptations which they offer.'[39] But why should one not yield? Because one has been prohibited in childhood. Thus we have the genesis of taboo set forth in its completeness. Childish desire: parental prohibition: result, taboo. But of the two preconditions required by this analysis for the genesis of the taboo, one is simply the taboo itself: for the parental prohibition just is the taboo.

Freud may be aware that he has effected nothing more than a *generatio aequivoca*, deriving the thing from itself; at any rate, some motive which he does not explain induces him to make a fresh start. Why, he asks, should we not give free rein to our envious aggressiveness against a chief? The taboos which hold us back are nominally, for the conscious mind, a means of guarding him from harm as a person valuable to the commonwealth (if so, one observes, they are no longer unmotivated and are therefore in his sense not taboos); but really, for the unconscious, they are restrictions not on our activity but on his, and thus expressions of our envy; they are our revenge on him for being a chief. This hidden

---

[39] *Totem and Taboo*, 56. The sentence in Brill's translation reads: "Therefore all these persons and all these conditions are taboo, for one must not yield to the temptations which they offer.'

hatred of the chief is of course our old friend the Oedipus complex, the child's hatred of his father; compatible no doubt **[38]** with the tenderest love, and (as analysis shows) generally underlying such love.

But this revelation of 'the savage's' unconscious can only be effected by psycho-analysis. Does Freud mean us to believe that he can psycho-analyse the savage on the strength of a general impression gained from reading books about him? What judgement would be passed on such a pretension by the Freud of *Vier Krankheitsgeschichten*, the Freud who analyses a single patient month after month with unflagging individual attention, and even then is not ashamed to give the case up as one beyond his powers? What would he have said to a patient or colleague who professed to analyse Dora's unconscious on the strength of mere descriptions written by Herr and Frau K.?[40] The real Freud, the endlessly resourceful psychologist of the consulting-room, whom we all revere as a man and a scientist, is hardly recognizable in this armchair student of savages in the abstract.

Yet, after all, it is the real Freud who writes. The conclusions arrived at are tacitly withdrawn. In the last pages of the chapter, he pulls himself together and reminds himself that taboo is not a neurosis; the savage is not a madman but a sane and useful member of a genuine human society. The neurotic shuns the real world of human life: taboo is a social formation and assists the savage to play his part in his own world.[41] So the whole argument of the chapter is wiped out. Even the initial definition of taboo is abandoned; for a prohibition that assists to maintain a balanced and healthy human life can no longer be called unmotivated. All that is left of the chapter is **[39]** the impression, sure to be left on the mind of a hasty disciple, that his master meant seriously the confused arguments and false analogies which in fact he has withdrawn.

---

[40] See J. Breuer and Sigmund Freud, *Studien über Hysterie* (Vienna: Franz Deuticke, 1895); and 'Fragment of an Analysis of a Case of Hysteria' (1905), in *Selected Papers on Hysteria and Other Psychoneuroses*, 3rd enlarged edn., authorized tr. by A. A. Brill (New York and Washington: Nervous and Mental Disease Publishing Co., 1920).

[41] Ibid. 92: 'In one way the neuroses show a striking and far-reaching correspondence with the great social productions of art, religion and philosophy, while again they seem like distortions of them.'

In the third chapter, on magic,[42] the tone abruptly changes. Hesitation and diffidence vanish; Freud now seems sure of his ability to explain the facts. The foundation of all magic, he says, is the omnipotence of the wish. 'Primitive man had great confidence in the power of his wishes. At bottom everything which he accomplished by magic must have been done solely because he wanted it.'[43] This is a difficult passage, because it is difficult to see the meaning of the words 'at bottom'. If we ignore them, the statement is flatly untrue. It is precisely because the savage knows that he cannot get what he wants by merely wishing for it, that he uses elaborate and stereotyped rituals for securing it. If 'at bottom' means 'when we ignore the differences', the statement may be true; no doubt, if savages did think they could get what they wanted by merely wishing for it, and therefore did not practise magic but merely wished, they would be showing great confidence in the power of their wishes. But then there would be no magic.

However, it seems that there are people who have this odd idea. Freud quotes a case from among his own patients: a compulsion-neurotic who, as a symptom of his neurosis, believed in what he called 'the omnipotence of thought'.[44] He believed that if he thought of a man, the man was thereby conveyed to the spot; that if he wished death to a man, the man died; and so on.[45] Such a neurotic, Freud evidently thinks, conceives himself as a magician: and, to make the parallel complete (very necessary, because the ritual which is essential to magic is absent from the neurosis as thus far described), neurotics of [40] this kind invent 'protective formulae' of speech or action which ward off the results of their omnipotent thought and are the 'counterpart' of magical rites and incantations.[46] But they are not counterparts; their function is not analogous but opposite. The magician performs his rites and utters his spells because otherwise his wish will be impotent; the

---

[42] 'Animism, Magic and the Omnipotence of Thought'.

[43] *Totem and Taboo*, 139. The Brill translation reads 'by magic means'.

[44] Ibid. 143.

[45] Freud does not in fact mention the neurotic actually wishing death to a man but only swearing at him and then hearing that he had died. Ibid. The detail is more accurately recalled by Collingwood in *PA* 63.

[46] *Totem and Taboo*, 146: 'The protective formulae of the compulsion neurosis also have a counterpart in the incantations of magic.'

neurotic described does these things because otherwise the wish will be effective.

As the author does nothing towards correcting this fundamental error, the rest of the chapter is of no great interest. Throughout, he has been deceived by a superficial and purely negative resemblance. The magician and the neurotic are alike in this, that each conceives himself as able to produce certain results in the absence of what may be called orthodox scientific means. But there the resemblance ends. On a closer scrutiny the two cases are not similar but sharply dissimilar, and a savage who acted as Freud's patient acted would be thought by his fellow-savages not a magician but an idiot. Once more, we trace the tendency to conceive savage life as a tissue of mental derangements, and to support this conception by ignoring the facts.

Finally, we come to the chapter on totemism, whose origin Freud now sets out to explain. Anthropologists whom he has read have already warned him that totemism is not so much a fact as a hypothesis by which we attempt to understand various groups of social institutions,[47] but he proceeds to analyse it as if it were a single perfectly definite thing, what medical science would call an 'entity'. The explanation he finds in the neurotic phenomenon of 'phobia'.

Children, he points out, as a rule feel themselves to be on excellent [41] terms with their animal neighbours; but sometimes this feeling breaks down in a special case and they develop a phobia of, for example, horses, dogs, cats, birds, or the like. Where analysed, this turns out to be fear of the father. It is an Oedipus feeling displaced upon the animal; and, as one would expect, compatible with love and admiration for the animal and even identification with it. Now these (says Freud) are characteristic traits of totemism. He sees that this explanation of totemism requires the equation of totem with father or, in general, ancestor. He seems conscious that students deny this equation, because he continues 'psycho-analysis warns us . . . to emphasize this very point'.[48] If

---

[47] * E. S. Hartland, one of the shrewdest of anthropologists, in 'Totemism and Some Recent Discoveries' [Presidential Address to the FLS], *F-L* 11 / 1 (Mar. 1900), 58 ff; a periodical familiar to Freud. A. C. Haddon in an important review of *The Golden Bough*, *F-L* 12 / 2 (June 1901), 232, observes that different things which we lump together as totemism may be different in origin.

[48] *Totem and Taboo*, 219. Collingwood omits 'very' from his quotation.

the reported facts of totemistic belief are incompatible with its explanation from the Oedipus complex, *tant pis pour les faits*. Science has travelled far since Newton set aside his theory of universal gravitation because the moon's distance from the earth, as calculated by the astronomers, failed by a fraction to satisfy his formula.

This analysis reaches its climax in a passage, deeply charged with emotion, in which Freud offers his own account of the origin of totemism. Human society began in the form of a patriarchal horde ruled by a savage and lustful father who monopolized the women of the horde. The sons, goaded to fury by the demon of their Oedipus complex, one day joined forces, slew and ate the father (for these savages were of course cannibals), and put an end to the father-horde. They accomplished their desired identification with the father by eating him, and thus each acquired a part of his strength. The totem feast discovered by Robertson Smith would be the repetition and commemoration of this memorable, criminal act with which so many things began: social organization, moral restrictions, and religion.[49] For the victors then, to **[42]** appease their sense of guilt, created the two fundamental taboos: you must not kill the totem, that is the father, and you must not take the liberated women, the members of your totem clan.

If we can free ourselves for a moment from the eloquent force of this passage, we shall notice many things about it. First, that we asked for history and are given a myth. In method and aim, it is a revival of the long exploded doctrine of the Social Contract, the imaginary act by which man lifted himself from a state of nature into a state of civil society. The fact that Darwin toyed with some such an idea of a primitive patriarchal horde is no justification.[50] Darwin was a great naturalist, but he lived and wrote before social anthropology had begun. Secondly, this primitive horde is conceived as a patriarchal family, both polygamous and incestuous. On Freud's own showing, the latter characteristic indicates that the father himself had no Oedipus complex, and therefore never himself had a father. Thirdly, it is assumed, in defiance of what anthropologists report, that a totem is essentially an ancestor or

---

[49] Freud cites William Robertson Smith, *The Religion of the Semites* (1889 and 1894), 2nd edn. (London, 1907).

[50] The main source is Darwin's 'Secondary Sexual Characteristics of Man, Continued', ch. 20 of *The Descent of Man, and Selection in Relation to Sex* (London: Murray, 1871).

rather (for one stands in no immediate family-relationship to one's ancestor) a father.

Further analysis is hardly necessary. The whole myth is a projection of the modern, European and Near Eastern, conception of the patriarchal family, as seen through the eyes of a son hideously tortured by an Oedipus complex, seeing his father as a horribly magnified and uncreated being bestially greedy of women, an ogre to be butchered and devoured if only the poor worm could get the necessary help from his brothers—a projection of all this into the earliest phase of human history, about which in reality we know nothing.

[43] In conclusion, there are two remarks to be made. First, Freud is throughout, in spite of inconsistencies and misgivings, assimilating the phenomena of 'savage' life to the phenomena of neurosis. Emotionally this assimilation has a valid basis; it expresses the contempt and horror with which our civilization looks upon those different from itself; and the identification of those who belong to them with the insane is a very natural wish-fantasy for reassuring our own civilization as to its sanity and excellence. But intellectually, the assimilation is justifiable only on one condition: namely, by being verified. If by psycho-analysis it is found possible to remove the characteristic marks of 'savagery' from the minds of this, that, and the other human being, and to produce the patients at the end of the treatment clothed and in the right minds of good Europeans, then so far the initial postulate will be made good. Till that has been done, it is a mere tissue of speculations, to be judged by the cogency of the arguments advanced in support of it. Of these, so far as I can see, there is not one that stands examination.

Secondly, it may be said that so great a psychologist as Freud has a right to be listened to when he discusses the psychology of savage life; a right, indeed, to be listened to in silence, except by those who think themselves his equals in psychological work. To this I reply that as a psychologist I admire Freud only on this side of idolatry, but that what I admire in him is the untiring earnestness with which, face to face with his patients, he wrings from them secrets whose genuineness is vouched for either by their corroboration or by their restoration to health. When he departs from that method he must be judged like other men.

[44] There has grown up something like a Freudian school of folklore-study, whose members spend their time tracking down

sexual symbolism in myth and fairy tale.[51] It is not an exacting pastime. In order to become a qualified master of it, one has only to learn a few easy formulae, and apply them mechanically to any material that one comes across. It is also a perfectly safe amusement, for there is no way in which these 'analyses' can be checked. It serves the double purpose of shocking the shockable, and proving to one's fellow-devotees one's own unshockableness; so that, as an exhibitionist ritual, it has great attractions. Scientifically, it is on a level with the sun-myth hunt of the old philological school, and psychologists have not been wanting who have demonstrated that the two things are one and the same: for the sun, like everything else, is a sexual symbol.

In this country, where the work of the anthropological school has definitively criticized the sun-mythologists not only as regards their conclusions but as regards their methods, the revival of these methods by this new psychological school presents a curiously anachronistic appearance. One feels as if Max Müller had come to life again, having forgotten nothing but his scholarship and learnt nothing but a smattering of psycho-analysis.

With certain Freudians or post-Freudians, this kind of study reaches a higher level. This is especially the case with Jung, whose book *The Psychology of the Unconscious* (Eng. tr. 1918)[52] contains much material bearing on the subject.

---

[51] Stuck-over: 'Of the minor Freudians I shall say nothing except that, in their tedious game of hunting sexual symbolism in ceremonial and fairy tale, they have sunk to the level of the justly forgotten followers of Max Müller. No more is gained by tracking down sexual symbols than by tracking down sun-myths. It is merely an exhibitionist ritual designed to convince its devotees of each others' freedom from false shame. It has added nothing to our understanding of folklore, and it is not even an intellectual gymnastic requiring skill and determination; you have only to learn two or three easy tricks, and you are a qualified master of it. With certain Freudians or post-Freudians, the study of fairy tales reaches a higher level. This is especially the case with Jung, whose book *The Psychology of the Unconscious* (Eng. tr. 1918) contains much material on this subject. The first thing a reader notices with regard to Jung's general attitude towards "myths" is that the years have rolled back to about 1870. The approach to the problem is at bottom that of Max Müller with a dash of psycho-analysis to bring it up to date. Fairy tales are conceived as symbolic ways of expressing the "folk-mind's".' [Ends.]

[52] Collingwood is presumably referring to Beatrice M. Hinkle's 1916 English translation of the *Psychology of the Unconscious: A Study of the Transformations and Symbolisms of the Libido* (New York: Moffat, Yard & Co.). Collingwood's interest in Jung was long-standing. He reviewed Jung's *Psychological Types or the Psychology*

The first thing an English reader notices is that, so far as method is concerned, the years have rolled back to about 1860. There is no hint that a functional [45] approach to the problem has even been invented. Myths or fairy tales are conceived exactly as by Grimm and Müller, as symbolic ways of expressing what is in the 'mind' of the 'folk'. Only the question what it is that finds this expression has been modified. According to the old philologists, it was the primeval folk-mind's apprehension of natural facts. According to this new psychology, it is that *plus* its intimate wishes. We see that the old philological theories, in spite of their explosion by the English school, have been accepted *en bloc*; and merely supplemented by the addition of a psycho-analytic appendix. Jung's book is full of etymological passages vividly recalling the days of Max Müller. As with Müller, too, the myth of today is a relic of a former mythopoeic age, an age of corporate childhood. Jung quotes with approval a remark of Abraham: 'the myth is a *sustained, still-remaining* fragment from the infantile soul-life of the people, and the dream is the myth of the individual'.[53]

This equation of myth and dream is fundamental for Jung's treatment. It seems plausible so long as we attend merely to the content of the two things—the themes and incidents which form their subject matter. As soon as we think of their form, that which makes a dream a dream and a tale a tale, the plausibility vanishes. A fairy tale is something closely related to the whole objective social order in which it exists. It is handed down with meticulous care from generation to generation: its plot arises out of the daily life of the people to whom it belongs: it is, as the anthropologists have shown, the translation into words of a solemn and obligatory ritual. A dream is the visitant of a night, never to be dreamed again: not conserved and renewed in any re-enactment, and not dramatically represented.

[46] It may be said: All this only expresses in detail what has been already admitted by saying that the dream is an individual

---

of *Individuation*, tr. H. Godwin Baynes, International Library of Psychology, Philosophy and Scientific Method (London, 1923) in the *Oxford Magazine*, 41 (1922–3), 425–6, reprinted in *Collingwood Studies*, 1 (1994), *The Life and Thought of R. G. Collingwood*, 188–90.

[53] *Psychology of the Unconscious*, 29. Jung cites Karl Abraham's 'Dream and Myth' (Vienna: Deuticke, 1909). See *Selected Papers of Karl Abraham*, ed. Ernest Jones (London: Hogarth, 1927).

formation, the myth a social one: the myth a dream of the people, the dream a myth of the individual.

This would not be true. The distinction between the fleeting subjectivity of a dream and the objective permanence of a myth is a quite different thing from the distinction between the individual and the people. If we wanted a genuine example of a myth of the individual, we might take Sir Thomas Browne's confession that he celebrates his nativity not on the anniversary of his birth but on that of his baptism.[54] If we want an example of a dream of the people, we shall inquire in vain: dreaming is not a corporate activity. The nearest we shall come to it is by taking such mass-hallucinations as occur, for instance, in time of war, when the people of one belligerent nation fancy every member of another a devil incarnate. For these are like dreams in this way at least, that we awake from them and wonder how we could ever have taken them for real.

Although, however, there can be no scientific motive for assimilating two things so different as myth and dream, there is a perfectly good emotional motive. The psychologists are experts (all honour to them) in explaining dreams. Confronted with fairy tales, they say to themselves 'if these things were dreams, we could explain them too, and thus extend our empire by the annexation of a vast new territory. So far as their subject matter goes, they are certainly rather like dreams. Such and such incidents in them can be paralleled by similar incidents in dreams. Of course, fairy tales are public, and dreams are private; but do not let us think too much about that; let us assume **[47]** that there is a thing called the folk-mind, and that fairy tales are simply the dreams of this peculiar type of mind. Then we can proceed to our work of annexation with a good conscience.'

[54] Sir Thomas Browne (1605–82), *Religio Medici* (London: for Andrew Crooke, 1643; repr. London: Everyman's Library, 1906), 50: 'Now, besides this literal and positive kind of death, there are others whereof Divines make mention, and those, I think, not meerly Metaphorical, as mortification, dying unto sin and the World. Therefore, I say, every man hath a double Horoscope, one of his humanity, his birth; another of his Christianity, his baptism; and from this do I compute or calculate my Nativity, not reckoning those *Horae combustae* and odd days, or esteeming my self any thing, before I was my Saviours, and inrolled in the Register of CHRIST.'

As if to betray a lingering uneasiness, they provide themselves with a second and incompatible line of defence. The sentence quoted from Abraham shows them both, side by side. Instead of the distinction between individual and corporate mind we may borrow from the old romantics the distinction between adult and childish mind, and postulate a past age in which the people was in its infancy and consequently endowed with a mythopoeic faculty. But this is going further and faring worse. To speak of the infancy of a people is to talk nonsense. Anthropologists have found no infantile peoples; historians have no evidence that they ever existed. The whole idea is, in fact, a myth; and when such fantasies can still pass current, why should we suppose that the age of myth-making is past?

From what has already been said, it will appear that the two characteristics of Jung's thought are the tendency to suppress distinctions like that between myth and dream, so as falsely to simplify problems, and the tendency to create pseudo-history so as to give fictitious explanations of origins. Further study shows how powerful these tendencies are. Some myths, he tells us, are myths of capture. The stories of Proserpina, Deianira, and Europa are examples. They are explained by saying that 'the capture of women was something general in the lawless prehistoric times'.[55] Two comments are called for. First, these three stories are based on three radically different themes. Proserpina is the Sleeping Beauty, the vegetation-spirit who, as daughter of Mother Earth, awakens from her underground prison in the spring. [48] Europa is Beauty and the Beast, the girl with the lover disguised in animal shape. Deianira is the Wicked Stepmother, the woman who is cruelly punished for her crimes. Secondly, what times is he referring to? The La Tène period or the Hallstatt? The Bronze Age, late, middle, or early? The Neolithic? The Maglemose or the Mas d'Azil? And what is his evidence that the period in question was a lawless one? It would be interesting to know, because, so far, the evidence has not been revealed to anthropologists and prehistorians, who have found many societies with many kinds of law, but never a lawless one.

It is plain that in such passages we are being regaled with a pseudo-history in which the writer's desires and fears are projected

[55] *Psychology of the Unconscious*, 32.

on the blank screen of a past which to him is absolutely unknown. Why has he unconsciously twisted a vegetation-myth, a shape-changing myth, and a punishment myth into examples of the institution formerly imagined by anthropologists and called marriage by capture? There is evidently some unconscious force at work in his mind, creating this fantasy. Here, if you like, in this bogus history of an age when rape was universal, we have a myth of the individual, on its way to become the myth of a sect.

In a later passage, Jung observes that the Dioscuri are phallic symbols because the *pileus* which they wear is a pointed head-dress.[56] **[49]** The note on this sentence reads as follows.

Compare the coronation above. Feather, a symbol of power. Feather crown, a crown of rays, halo. Crowning, as such, is an identification with the sun. For example, the spiked crown upon the Roman coins made its appearance at the time when the Caesars were identified with *Sol invictus* ('Solis invicti comes'). The halo is the same, that is to say, an image of the sun, just as is the tonsure.[57]

Setting aside the exclamatory opening of this note, one comes at last to a professed statement of fact. What is the actual fact? Roman emperors are represented as wearing the radiate crown in posthumous portraits, that is, after their deification, from the first; but the living portrait so decorated begins with Nero and was used rarely by Titus and increasingly by Domitian; Trajan allowed it on the senatorial coinage; Hadrian hardly ever permitted it; but thereafter it is a regular though exceptional feature, until after the middle of the third century, when it suddenly becomes extremely common, almost ousting other head-dresses. Certainly this radiate crown indicates identification with the sun-god. But not with Sol Invictus; that particular form of sun-worship is a third-century introduction. And the title *Solis invicti comes* is in fact hardly ever

[56] *Psychology of the Unconscious*, 133: 'The two sun heroes, the Dioscuri, stand in relation to the Cabiri; they also wear the remarkable pointed head-covering (Pileus) which is peculiar to these mysterious gods, and which is perpetuated from that time on as a secret mark of identification.'

[57] Collingwood has 'just like'. The words from the note quoted here by Collingwood actually come from *Psychology of the Unconscious*, 500 n. 16. This is in fact n. 16 to a sentence in part 1, ch. 4 'The Song of the Moth', 97, and is the chapter which precedes mention of the Dioscuri. The latter location, 'Aspects of the Libido', part 2, ch. 1, 133, also refers the reader to n. 16. Collingwood appears to have slipped a chapter in looking up the notes.

used by or of any emperor: never by a good many such as Diocle-
tian, Carausius, and the Gallic emperors, whose heads are almost
always shown adorned with the radiate crown.

But what do these details matter? We are at once told that the
halo and the tonsure are 'the same' as the radiate crown; we have
already been [50] informed that 'crowning, as such, is an identification with the sun'. Evidently a crown of whatever sort signifies
exactly the same thing as a radiate one. Perhaps even the laurel
wreath of the Roman imperator, the conqueror's badge which
Julius Caesar habitually wore although he refused the royal diadem, is the same thing again. Radiate crown, diadem, laurel
wreath, feather crown, tonsure (whether Celtic or Roman), Sam-
son's hair, top hat, academic mortar-board, bishop's mitre, papal
tiara, baby's bonnet, are evidently all the same thing and all interchangeable. They all identify the wearer with the sun; they all
symbolize power.

There is a grain of truth in all this. It does seem to be the case
that all headgear can in some sense be described as a power-
symbol. But there are many kinds of power: spiritual and temporal,
emotional and intellectual, and many grades of each. The reason
why Jung would, no doubt, be quite unimpressed by my criticism
of his statement about the radiate crown and the title *Solis invicti
comes* (if indeed it is a statement at all, and not merely a free
association) is that he cares no more for these distinctions than he
does for the distinction between myth and dream.

Jung's ground of difference from the Freudian school is that
they are too much absorbed in the study of sex. For Jung, the
importance of sex is not the fact that it is sex, but that it is one kind
of vital impulse or energy. This vital energy, which he calls libido,
is for him the fundamental thing, the only one that really matters in
psychology. Every psychic activity is one form of it; everything in
which anyone is interested is a symbol of it. The reason why the
sun is centrally important in religious symbolism (for he follows
Max Müller's school in believing this to be the case) is that the [51]
sun is conceived as a gigantic source of power, and is therefore a
universal libido-symbol.[58]

This modification of Freud might seem an improvement, since
it is able to bring into the psychologist's net all those things which

---

[58] *Psychology of the Unconscious*, 99–105, 127–9.

resist analysis into sexual terms. If they are of any interest or importance at all, they are charged with libido (the two phrases are in fact synonymous) and thus stand as libido-symbols. At the same time it might seem an improvement on Max Müller: for if any symbolism appears in fairy tales which resists interpretation in terms of sun-mythology, it will not resist interpretation as libido-symbolism. The mere fact that it figures there at all shows that some interest is taken in it, and thus convicts it of being a libido symbol.

In point of fact, it is not an improvement: it is a degradation. To identify something as a sexual symbol or a sun-myth may not be saying much, when the denotation of those terms has become so vast and the connotation so microscopic; but it is saying something. The cats are all grey, but they are still cats. But to call it a power-symbol, now that everything is a power-symbol, is to call it nothing at all. The difference between any one kind of headgear and any other is left out; the difference between headgear and phallus is left out; the difference between the residue of that process and the sun is left out; the difference between that again and water, vegetation, and so forth is left out; and when the reader turns round and asks 'then what is the difference between a river and a post and a tonsure?' he gets the reply 'oh, those are merely transformations of the libido'. And if he asks what transforms it, and in particular why it should be transformed now in this way and now in that, **[52]** the oracle is dumb.

It would be easy to go through the book I have mentioned, making a collection of egregious historical blunders. As a single example: 'That the monks have again invented cowls seems of no slight importance'.[59] The innuendo here is that the monk's vow of chastity is compensated for by inventing for himself a phallic head-dress. The author does not seem to know that the monk's cowl is merely the hood of ordinary medieval garb, and that this again is the standard head-dress of the ancient Celtic and Germanic world, as described in the Icelandic sagas or depicted in the Romano-British statuette of a ploughman from Piercebridge. But no such

---

[59] This is n. 17 to part 2, ch. 1, 'Aspects of the Libido'. The note is on p. 509 and refers to the statement that 'Attis (the elder brother of Christ) wears the pointed cap, just as does Mithra. It has also become traditional for our present-day chthonian infantile gods . . . ' (133).

criticism would interest the author or his disciples; for this blur-
ring of every detail, to him, is not a defect but a merit. It is the
essence of his method. It is by thus shutting his eyes to the concrete
reality of the facts that he finds his way into the gloom of his own
theories. In the same way, contemporaries noticed that criticism
never produced the slightest effect on Max Müller, who at the very
end of his life cheerfully affirmed that nothing said against his sun-
myth theory had shaken his belief in it. You can put facts
before a theorist's eyes, but you cannot make him open them;
and when he has trained himself to keep them shut, you shout at
him in vain.

3

THE HISTORICAL METHOD

Three methods of approach to our problem have now been tried and found wanting. But the time spent in working them out has not been wasted; nor has the time which we have spent in examining them. Each has left behind it a legacy of permanent value; although, by an irony common enough in the history of human affairs, the lesson that each has taught us is in some respects the exact opposite of the doctrine it was trying to teach.

The philological school, taking one great group of languages, the Indo-European, has shown that the same fairy-tale themes are found in them all. Now, unity of language is a cultural unity; the inference therefore is that identity in culture corresponds with identity in fairy-tale motives, and that this double identity overrides all differences of race. Actually, the Indo-European civilizations studied by the philologists were (as they well knew) agricultural civilizations; so that we can restate their conclusions, replacing their falsely biological expressions by cultural or historical ones, if we say that the philologists' work created a presumption that the common stock of Aryan myths were somehow organic to the life of an agricultural society. Of course, to become logically valid, this induction should be checked by negative instances, showing that non-agricultural societies have fairy-tale themes of a different kind; but this the material in the philologists' hands did not enable them to say.

The functional anthropologists cleared up this point. They showed that there is a connexion between the mythology of any given society and its magic; and a connexion between its magic and the way it provides itself with food, arranges its political affairs, and so forth. For the vague conception of nature-myths they substituted the precise conception of aetiological myths arising out of agricultural fertility-ritual. For the false conception of

Bodleian Library Collingwood Papers, dep. 21/6. The chapter title, prefixed by 'III', is Collingwood's.

culture as a function of race they substituted [2] the true conception of culture as an autonomous historical reality. But they failed
to grasp the psychological significance of magic, and were therefore left with a false view both of ritual and of myth, as expressions
of human stupidity; and they also failed to grasp the dynamic and
self-differentiating nature, the truly historical nature, of civilization
in all its different forms, thus replacing the historical study of culture
by a merely classificatory study, so that the functional school of
anthropological science came to be opposed to the historical school.

The psychologists have tried to break down this classificatory
scheme and substitute a genuinely dynamic one, by representing
savagery, with all its characteristics of magic, myth-making, and so
forth, not as a form of life totally other than civilization and
therefore, from the point of view of civilized man, a thing to be
studied from outside, a mere spectacle for his contemplation, but
as an element contained within civilization itself, and transcended
by the higher elements which make it civilized. As the child, with
his infantile fears and passions, is contained within the adult man,
but contained there as a transcended element which reasserts itself
only when the balance of adult life breaks down into neurosis, so
the primitive life of the savage is contained within the life of
civilized peoples, who achieve and maintain their civilization precisely by solving the psychological problems which it presents, but
which the mere savage cannot solve. This is a profound and important doctrine. Properly developed, it has in it the germs of a
complete answer to the main questions of anthropology. But the
fruits of this conception are thrown away by a false development.
A man reverting to the mental condition of infancy is certainly
neurotic. It does not follow that the infant [3] as such is neurotic.
On the contrary, the distinction between mental health and mental
disease is one which applies to children no less than to adults: the
child as such is no more a pervert or a neurotic than the adult.
Similarly, a civilized society that breaks out in symptoms of savagery may be described as collectively insane; but it does not follow
that there is any true parallel between the characteristics of savage
life as such and those of insanity.[1] The Freudian assimilation of

---

[1] These themes are dealt with variously in *MGM* (Part III), 'Fascism and
Nazism', *Philosophy*, 15 (1940), 168–76, and *NL*. Collingwood's most sustained
discussion is found in *NL*, where he gives a particular cast to the common distinctions between savagery, barbarism, and civilization. He takes barbarism to be a

savage beliefs and customs to those of his own neurotic patients might be of value if the former were used by him to throw light on the latter; used, as he uses it, the other way round, it is profoundly misleading.

So far as they are involved in systematic and methodical error, all these three schools err in the same way. Their common mistake is to deal with an historical problem by naturalistic methods. For the problem is at bottom historical. It is a mere accident (though in some ways a fortunate one) that the different peoples now living exhibit different grades of civilization, so that actual examples of civilizations more primitive than our own can be studied empirically. The essence of the problem lies in the fact that our own civilization has come to be what it is by development out of a more primitive one. The reason why anthropology is an important study for civilized men is not, as might have been thought in the heyday of imperialism, because civilized men have to rule over savages and must learn, therefore, to understand them. It is because the civilized man contains a savage within him, in the special sense in which any historical present contains within itself its own past, and must therefore study this savage—not savages in the abstract, but the savage that **[4]** he himself in this sense is—for the same reason for which all history is studied, namely to make possible a rational human life in the present day. The problem of anthropology is a special case of the problem of self-knowledge; and history is the only way in which man can know himself. And this special case is of especial urgency at the present time, when the question what civilization is, and what it is trying to be, is raised on all sides and is fraught with the gravest issues in immediate practice.

To such a problem naturalist methods cannot be applied without falsifying it and foregoing all hope of a true solution. Naturalistic methods, those which are adapted to the study of the natural world which is man's environment, cannot be used in the study by man of himself. To himself, man can never be an assemblage of phenomena to be observed and classified and studied inductively. To find the

revolt against civilization, a repression of mental maturity that is susceptible to the herd instinct. Barbarism is irrational and therefore akin to mental illness. It is a denial of responsibility for one's own actions.

truth about himself he must look, not around him, but within him; and what he finds when he looks within him is his own history.

The three methods described in the last chapter are all in essence naturalistic. Each of them treats its subject matter as something to be contemplated from without, something external to the thinker, something that is not himself but something else. To the philologists, the mythopoeic age was far removed from themselves in time, and still further removed in spirit. Its products were totally unlike anything that the philologist could imagine himself producing. To him, therefore, they were mere brute facts, and Müller described quite correctly the spirit in which he studied them when he explained that the science of language was for him simply a natural science. The functional anthropologists stood directly in the tradition [5] of empirical naturalistic science. They conceived their subject matter not as a past age, but as a present fact or body of facts; but these were not facts about themselves or their own civilization; they were facts about 'primitive peoples', and these peoples were contemplated by the anthropologist from across the whole width of the gulf that separated savagery from civilization, or the savage survivals in civilized countries from the scientific point of view achieved by the educated élite in those countries. The psychologists also stand committed to the method of naturalistic science; in their case the gulf is that which separates the psychologist himself from the person whose mind he is studying, a gulf which with Freud is widened into that between the sane and scientific psychiatrist and the neurotic and deluded patient.

In the preceding chapter a good deal has been said concerning the tendency, visible in all three schools, to slur over details, emphasize similarities at the expense of diversities, and thus reduce to a spurious uniformity things which may well be essentially different. This procedure is legitimate and necessary in natural science; it is simply the abstraction which, there, is the first rule of method. Natural science frames generalizations which apply to all cases of the same type; so long as a case falls under that type, the differences which mark it off from others in its class do not matter; if they do, they can be similarly dealt with by further generalizations. History does not work in terms of classes, types, and generalities. Its business is with the individual. Hence, when naturalistic methods are applied to a historical subject matter, the necessary ignoring of detail becomes a neglect of essentials; it becomes unscholarliness, failure to distinguish accurately what the object is to which attention is directed. This lack of exhaustiveness [6] in the study of detail is, in the case of a historical subject matter, the one deadly sin, like the lack of accuracy in measuring, weighing, or mathematical thinking, in a scientific. Its inevitable consequence is arbitrariness in distinguishing the details that are important from those that are not; which means that the student, instead of genuinely getting his conclusions out of his evidence, twists the evidence into support for preconceived conclusions, putting himself at the mercy of his own unconscious desire to interpret the material in this way instead of that. Thus naturalistic methods, instead of yielding historical knowledge, yield a pseudo-history which is merely a magnified projection of the would-be historian's desires upon the blank screen of the unknown past.

What will be the general common character of the images thus formed? That depends upon the emotional attitude of the student towards his subject matter. But *ex-hypothesi* he has no real knowledge of his subject matter; the emotions that determine his conclusions are therefore emotions concerned with himself. Now, the civilized man studying savagery regards himself as the representative of rational living and rational thinking. What he is studying, conceived as savagery, is the opposite of this. It therefore presents itself to his mind as a coagulated mass of unreasonable behaviour and illogical thought. We have already seen that naturalistic methods lead to the conception of the savage mind as groaning beneath a load of mythopoeic insanity (Müller), folly (Frazer), or neurosis (Freud). These conceptions do not rest on evidence; they are read into the evidence, and rest on the false assumption, implicit in the naturalistic method, that subject and object are external to each other and that each is the other's opposite; an assumption made explicit [7] at the very beginning of modern scientific history when Descartes, expounding the presuppositions of physics, distinguished mind as thinking and unextended from matter as extended and unthinking.

But in historical knowledge, where the object is the subject's own past, this opposition has a peculiar emotional significance. The savage is not outside us; he is inside us. Conceiving ourselves as rational and civilized people, which is what we want to be, we are aware within ourselves of savage and irrational elements, parts of ourselves which we would willingly disown. Hating these things in ourselves, and hating ourselves for harbouring them, we throw them in fancy away from us into the picture we form of other people. Thus we create the mythical figure of the savage, no actual historical person but an allegorical symbol of everything which we fear and dislike, attributing to him all the desires in ourselves which we condemn as beastly and all the thoughts which we despise as irrational. This abstract idea of the 'savage' or 'Primitive Man', however, is not merely an object of our hatred and contempt. It has also a kind of horrid fascination. Because these beastly desires and irrational thoughts are actually present in ourselves, we wish to indulge them, though our ideal of ourselves as reasonable and civilized men will not allow us to do so; our idea of the savage is therefore a wish-fulfilment fantasy in which these repressed wishes are given license for imaginary gratification.

The fundamental difficulty of anthropological study lies here. It is not an intellectual difficulty but an emotional one. If we could contemplate the life and mind of the savage without horror, we should not find them hard to understand. This is why the anthropological ideas of people with experience of field-work are so much better than those of the merely book-learned. It is not that through personal acquaintance with the facts they **[8]** are better informed on points of detail; it is rather that, in human contact with human beings, they have learned that there is no such thing as the abstract savage, there are only men and women, living their own lives in their own way and (surprisingly, perhaps, at first) living them as decently and rationally as ourselves.[2]

To sum up: the naturalistic method contains two pitfalls. First, it ignores detail in order to generalize; secondly, the generalizations which it fabricates tend to be mere expressions of emotion, not conclusions from evidence. Both these dangers must be guarded against by the maxims of a sounder method.

Such a method, therefore, will be based on two rules, which may be called the maxim of Spinoza and the maxim of Bishop Butler.

---

[2] Struck out: 'And this, again, is why the functional school of anthropology is so much sounder in its general approach to the subject than either the philological or the psychological; for they are primarily dependent on book-learning, while it takes its stand mainly on actual acquaintance with the peoples whose customs it sets out to describe.' Though not made explicit, Collingwood's reference here is less to Tylor and Frazer (who depended on the ethnographic reports of others) than to his contemporaries such as Malinowski, Seligman, and Evans-Pritchard.

The maxim of Spinoza[3] is neither to condemn nor to deride the feelings and actions of men, but to understand them. It might seem a truism that this rule must be obeyed by all students of human custom and belief; but that is not so. Many people who claim to be students of human nature think that by condemning others they are proving their own superior virtue, and in deriding them their own superior wisdom; or rather, they do not think about it at all, but act as if they thought thus, because of a devil inside them that can only be appeased by this self-glorification at the expense of others. Here the professed study of human nature is simply a pretence for gratifying *odium humani generis*.

That is an extreme case. But cases less extreme are hardly less dangerous; if **[9]** only because they are likelier to go unnoticed. Obedience to Spinoza's maxim would mean that every phrase and every statement which imply in the student a contempt for the belief or custom he is describing; every hint of ridicule or disparagement in his account of the facts or in the theory which he invents or accepts to explain them; every trace of patronage or superciliousness towards the people whose mind he is studying; all this must go. And this not simply as a point of good manners, though that is a point that might well be made; but as a point of scientific method, as schoolboys misconstruing Horace are told (to their surprise) that Horace was a sensible man and did not write nonsense.

The adoption of this maxim will have a considerable effect on the vocabulary of the science. The word savages, with all its synonyms, natives, primitives, and so forth, will go, because it is not a term of description but a term of contempt. It does not stand for any definite type or grade of civilization, it lumps together all those types and grades which we consider hopelessly inferior to our own. Terms like magic and taboo will follow, if they are intended (as they usually are) to imply that the beliefs and practices so named are due to ignorance and stupidity. They will remain in use only if, from being terms of contempt, they can be made into descriptive terms, applied to customs whose specific character can

---

[3] 'I have striven not to laugh at human actions, not to weep at them, nor to hate them, but to understand them.' Baruch Spinoza, *Tractatus Theologico-Politicus* (1670; Gebhardt edn., 1925), tr. Samuel Shirley (New York: E. J. Brill, 1989), I, iv.

be explained without disparagement and in a properly scientific spirit. This purge will be welcomed by serious anthropologists, because it will set them free to investigate the facts—details of social organization, ceremonial and so forth—without the need to be constantly sticking upon them labels of whose irrelevance they are not unaware. Tylor himself led the way when he proposed to drop the disparaging term superstition as applied to certain customs and beliefs found in our own civilization, and to substitute the descriptive term survival.[4]

[10] The inferences and logical constructions of anthropology will undergo a like purge. It will be an absolute rule not to foist upon any custom an explanation which makes fools of the people who observe it; not even to accept such an explanation from their own lips. Here the anthropologist will only be recollecting the commonplaces of other sciences. If the literary scholar makes nonsense of a passage, he assumes first that he has mistranslated the text, and then that the text is corrupt. If the scientist finds atoms or bacteria behaving oddly, he first checks his observations, and then revises his expectations, that is, his conception of the laws governing their behaviour. He knows that all science would be at an end if he allowed himself to say 'these atoms or bacteria have gone mad'. If anthropology is to be a science, it must adopt the methodological rules of science in general.

These rules, so far as they are rules of scientific method, are not mere rules of manners or morals; they are indispensable means to arriving at the truth. The anthropologist, like every kind of scientist, is sure to find in his researches a great deal that is perplexing. If he is to understand it, he must approach it in the belief that it is intelligible. To account for a custom or belief by appeal to human folly or perversity is to give up the attempt to understand it; for these things are not *verae causae*, they are only an oblique way of saying that we have found no *vera causa* and do not intend to go on looking for one. Suppose it true that people behave in a certain way because they are fools: still, it cannot be because they are fools in general, it must be because they are a special kind of fool. It is not the madness that is the *vera causa* of their conduct, it is the method in the madness. And when we have discerned the method, calling it madness is a matter of taste.

---

[4] Tylor, *Primitive Culture*, e.g. i. 16 ff., 70 ff.

[11] At the same time, obedience to these rules involves a certain moral discipline. Our temptation to deride and condemn what we call savages instead of understanding them arises from an emotion of fear, aroused by the contemplation of things which awake within us an echo that alarms and disturbs us. If our own minds were free, as we fancy they are, from all traces of what we call savagery, we could study it in others without passion. The source of our loathing and derision is a secret voice within us whispering 'that art thou'. Consequently the adoption of Spinoza's maxim is not only a point of scientific method, it is a moral discipline for the whole man, for the whole of our civilization. We must learn to face the savage within us if we are to understand the savage outside us. The savage within us must not be stamped down out of sight. He too, by the same Spinozistic rule, must be neither condemned nor derided, but understood. Just as the savages around us, when thus understood, cease to appear as savages and become human beings, courteous and friendly and honourable and worthy of admiration for their virtues and of love for their humanity, so the savage within us, on the same terms, will become no longer a thing of horror but a friend and helper: no savage, but the heart and root of our own civilization.

[12] The maxim of Bishop Butler[5] is that every thing is what it is, and not another thing. To accept this as a rule of method is formally to recognize that our study is historical, not naturalistic, in character. It means recognizing that the subject matter about which we are thinking consists of facts taken as facts, not of facts taken merely as instances. Thus, if someone wished to construct a naturalistic sociology in which it was proved (for example) that wars had always had the same kind of cause, such as an economic one, he would take the Peloponnesian war, the Crusades, the War of the Spanish Succession, and the Napoleonic wars, and point out certain common characteristics in them all. These common characteristics would be what interested him. Other characteristics, peculiar to one of these but not found in the rest, he would ignore; and thus, in his treatment of wars, the differences

---

[5] 'Things and actions are what they are, and the consequences of them will be what they will be. Why then should we desire to be deceived?', *Fifteen Sermons Preached at the Rolls Chapel* (London: J. and J. Knapton, 1726), N. 7, 16. Bishop Joseph Butler was successively bishop of Bristol and Durham.

between different wars would disappear, and any one war would figure merely as an example of sociological generalizations equally exemplified by any other. For the historian, these ignored peculiarities would be important for the same reason which makes them unimportant to the naturalistic sociologist: namely because they are peculiarities, and thus reveal the special historical characteristics which make one period of history different from all others.

In the philological school, the ignoring of differences is a matter of principle whenever fairy tales are interpreted. For Max Müller, Tithonus, like all other mythical heroes, is the sun, and to that extent is interchangeable with any other mythical hero. Whatever story is substituted for that of Tithonus in the discussion, the result will be the same. What we are aiming at by adopting the historical method (I do not say that we shall often achieve it) is a type of interpretation which will explain why the people who originally told the [13] story of Tithonus told that story and not a different one.[6] The details in the story which make Müller accuse it of being 'careless about contradictions, or ready to solve them sometimes by the most atrocious expedients'[7] will be, on this method, features indicating the history of the story itself in its origin and its subsequent telling and retelling. The psychologists have here followed the philologists' example, but have immensely exaggerated it. We have already seen how, in their hands, everything becomes some other thing: savagery becomes mental derangement, magic and taboo become different kinds of neurosis, totemism becomes an Oedipus complex, Europa becomes Deianira and Deianira becomes Proserpina, and so forth. Even the functional anthropologists, whose closer attention to the facts has saved them from the worst of this confusion, have tended to think of the savage's mind as a strangely illogical world where things are not themselves but turn irresponsibly into other things. The *reductio ad absurdum* of this projection is when learned books are written

---

[6] Greek legend has it that Tithonus was a beautiful Trojan granted life by the goddess Eos (Aurora). He had neglected to ask for youth and vigour and grew old and decrepit. He begged to be allowed to die but Eos could not consent to it. Instead she turned him into a grasshopper.

[7] 'Comparative Mythology', *Chips from a German Workshop*, ii. 84.

about the Primitive Mind, explaining at length that in this pre-logical realm anything can be anything else.[8]

If 'the savage' really thought in this pre-logical way, he could never have mastered, as he has done, the principles of hunting and fishing, agriculture and stock-farming, metallurgy and carpentry; he could never have devised his elaborate languages and social systems; he could never even have preserved and handed down the traditional stories and rituals upon which this accusation of illogicality is based. It cannot be replied that the savage thinks clearly enough when he is thinking about practical matters such as his food-supply, his weapons, and the principles of his family and tribal life, but allows a free rein to [14] his illogicality when he thinks about supernatural beings. For these supposedly illogical fancies are about precisely those practical matters: his plough and his spear, and his mother-in-law.

The identification or rather confusion of one thing with another is not actually present in the 'savage' mind at all. The anthropologist does not find it in his material. He reads it into his material. Using a naturalistic method which depends upon overlooking distinctions, he distorts the facts which he is studying so as to make them conform with the method, and thus ascribes to the 'savage' an illogicality which is altogether his own.

Christ and Mithras, says Jung, are identical. They are the same as Adonis, Attis, and Osiris. But in the third century, when Christianity and Mithraism were living side by side in the Roman world, no one thought of Christ and Mithras as the same. They were different gods with different liturgies, different theologies, different worshippers. To accept one was to reject the other. Everyone knew that in some ways they were alike; had they not been alike, they could not have been rivals. But nobody mistook their resem-

[8] Collingwood clearly has in mind the work of the French armchair anthropologist Lucien Lévy-Bruhl, productive of some notoriety among English scholars when translated into English: for example, *Primitive Mentality* (1922; London: George Allen & Unwin, 1923). Lévy-Bruhl introduced the term 'pre-logical' and other key terms such as 'participation', 'mystic perceptions', and 'confusion' in his first book; see *How Natives Think* (1910; London: George Allen & Unwin, 1926), 76–80. Several books by Lévy-Bruhl were in Collingwood's possession (see Blackwell's Sale Catalogue, no. 496). Lévy-Bruhl delivered the Herbert Spencer Lecture, 'La Mentalité primitive', in Oxford in 1931, an occasion which Collingwood might well have noted. For Evans-Pritchard's commentary on his ideas, see ch. 4 of *Theories of Primitive Religion*, 78–99.

blance for identity. It was reserved for Jung to do that; and he does it by neglecting those details in which their difference consists. Even Frazer seems to think that Adonis is Attis, and Attis Osiris. They are much alike, as he has shown; they are all vegetation-gods worshipped in agricultural rituals, and in so far as agriculture in one country resembles agriculture in another (to whatever cause those resemblances are due, whether to imitation or to independent discoveries) the agricultural rituals and vegetation-gods of these countries will show similar likeness; yet each god is himself and not his neighbour, though the relation between them may be so close as seriously to exercise **[15]** the minds of their respective worshippers when they become aware of each other's worship. If, as a result of such theological speculation, they end by identifying Jupiter with Zeus, or Mars with Cocidius, this is not due to the confusions of a pre-logical thought which cannot see differences; it is because they see that two things which are in some sense different may yet in some sense be the same. And the logical or metaphysical problem of the relation between identity and difference cannot be disposed of by ascribing it to confused or pre-logical thinking.[9]

One example of this supposedly confused identification is that of the priest-king with the god. Wherever fertility-rituals exist, it would seem, they take a dramatic form, and the chief actor impersonates the god. In some sense he 'is' the god: in the sense in which Sir John Martin-Harvey[10] 'is' Hamlet, but not in the sense in which Hamlet 'is' the Prince of Denmark. The difference between the two cases is that in the case of a priest-king the drama is not performed and then set aside. Sir John Martin-Harvey stops 'being' Hamlet when the play is over. For a priest-king the play is never over. His whole life is a sacred ritual; he is 'being' the god all the time, from the coronation ceremony which casts him for the part until his death. 'There is something shocking to our ideas', say the anthropologists, 'in this identification of a man with a god'. By Spinoza's rule, the sense of shock ought to be a warning. If we disregard it, a breach of Spinoza's rule leads to a breach of Butler's.

[9] The problem of identity and difference, or unity in diversity, was addressed by most of the Idealists. The classic statement is to be found in F. H. Bradley, *Appearance and Reality* (Oxford: Clarendon Press, 1930).
[10] Sir John Martin-Harvey (1863–1944), the actor-manager who produced *Hamlet* in 1904.

The savage is perfectly able to distinguish the human 'person' of the priest-king from the divine 'persona', the god whom he 'impersonates'; though very likely he could not explain it with such metaphysical skill as a Catholic theologian expounding the distinction between the bread of the Host and [16] the body of Christ; but if he could, how many anthropologists could follow the argument? And how many playgoers, if asked by an anthropologist to distinguish between Sir John Martin-Harvey and Hamlet, could do it in such a way as to clear themselves of an accusation of 'primitive mentality'?

Another case of alleged confusion concerns the relation between the god and the things in which or through which he works. Almost every religion accuses almost every other of idolatry, that is, of identifying the god with the god's vehicle. Even in countries where a vernacular theological literature exists, accessible to everyone, people can be found who confuse reverence for sacred objects with worship of those objects, and use their own confusion as a stick with which to beat their fellow-countrymen's religion. Where such a confusion is on the whole somewhat admired as a mark of enlightenment, there is no wonder that it should be extended to the case of savages, who cannot defend themselves. But there is no more reason for it in the one case than in the other. If a man regards as divine the power in his stone axe which enables it to cut down trees, or the power in wheat which enables it to rise out of a seed in the ground and grow new grains of life-giving food, it is not that he mistakes the stone of the axe or the tissues of the plant for a god. Still less is it that he 'has no idea of natural causation', and thinks that these things are not material objects but merely visible spirits. In making and mending his tools, and in tending and reaping his crops, he treats them as the material objects which they are; but he distinguishes their physical bodies from the powers that reside in them, and these powers he thinks divine. If we, in the stupidity of our vulgar materialism, have forgotten how to make that distinction, the confusion is ours, not his.

[17] A third alleged confusion is that between the different ways in which the same power works. The savage is well aware of the kinship between the processes of growth and reproduction in the animal and vegetable world respectively.[11] He knows that fertility

---

[11] In this and the following paragraph Collingwood is clearly referring to Frazer's *Golden Bough*.

in corn and fertility in man are the same thing. Consequently the priest-king 'is' the fertility-god in two different senses: not only as representing that god in a lifelong dramatic performance, but also *in propria persona* as a man and thus a vehicle of the vital and reproductive power. There is a relation between these two things. Temporally and logically, being a man is the presupposition of being a king. If the king's bodily strength and virile energy fail, he is no longer fit to be a king. It is not enough that after such failure he should continue to perform the ritual, for he would then be performing it under false pretences.

Every act of the community, in what we call primitive societies, has its ritual aspect, and cannot be conceived as done without it. If the king, the leader in all the essential ceremonies, becomes disqualified for playing that part, the ceremonies are no longer being properly conducted and the acts with which they are connected are thus, not so much automatically frustrated, as deprived of their proper ritual accompaniment and therefore less likely to be successful. Thus arises the belief that the king's failure in health and strength entails the general barrenness of the land.

This belief has actually been found in a great many countries. Stated in that immediate shape—the ideas of the king's health and the land's fertility being directly brought into relation without any connecting links—it looks absurd, and the hasty student is tempted to explain it as a confusion of primitive thought, as if the king's health was in some mysterious way identical with the fertility of the soil. We feel inclined to say that the savage has mistaken the generic identity of these two things for a numerical identity between them.

[18] But the presence of a strange belief is a signal to look more closely at the facts. The belief is part and parcel of a certain way of life, and examination of that way of life will explain the belief.

We are dealing with a society in which the degree of mechanization is small. In a house that is cleaned by electricity, ill-health in the housewife would produce no visible effect on the carpets. But if everything has to be swept and beaten and dusted by hand, a visitor might judge of the housewife's health by simply using her eyes. So on a farm worked by the labour of a single man, or even by others under his supervision, poor crops, weeds, and broken fences would give the visitor some ground for saying 'I can see he is not the man he was'. Where ritual is an essential part of life, defect or even suspicion of defect in the ritual will take the heart out of labour; and conversely, such defect will be tolerated only by people whose vigour and discipline have become weak in ways that are likely to affect all their work. There is an old saying that meat and mass never hindered man: the morning ritual like the morning meal does not steal energy from the day's work, it adds conviction to it. With us, shaving is a morning ritual; and it would not be fanciful to connect omission of the morning shave with a tendency to slovenly work during the day.

If this is true, apart from all magic and superstition, about a single man and a single household, it is true of a community. No one would expect a great business to thrive equally whether the head of it was well or ill. In a small community where the priest-king is a genuine head, a change in his health such as would make his subjects cease to respect him will lead to a slackening of all communal activities. Thus the belief that the king's ill-health causes the land to become waste,[12] though it seems a silly superstition when stated thus baldly, becomes a reasonable enough generalization when considered in terms of the social structure and customs of the people who believe it.[13]

[19] Round this idea of the waste land, others have crystallized which are doubtless in many cases mistaken. If it is said, for example, that rain will not fall when the king's virility fails, we can reject the statement, not as a superstition, but as an error: a scientific mistake, a piece of bad meteorology. But it may be possible to see how it arose. A whisper goes round that the king is growing feeble. His subjects become disheartened, and their cultivation suffers. When the crops fail, since nobody likes to blame himself, it is said (and perhaps truly) that with a better rainfall they would have succeeded. So the loss of confidence in the king is connected with the crops' failure not through the true middle term, the slackness of his subjects, but through a fictitious one, shortage of rain.

---

[12] A key theme of *The Golden Bough*; see esp. the 2-vol. *Adonis, Attis, Osiris: Studies in the History of Oriental Religion*, 3rd edn. (London: Macmillan, 1914).

[13] Struck out: 'the function of officers is not so much command as leadership. It is the men who win battles; and to say that a battle was lost through the cowardice of the officers might therefore seem absurd; but it is the business of a good officer to hearten and steady the men by his example, to show himself a man whom other men will follow.'

This example, perhaps, makes it clear why attention to detail is so important. Without understanding the structure of a 'primitive' agricultural society, we could never understand the myth of the waste land. That myth is a function of agricultural ritual, and when regarded in its proper social setting is seen to be no idle superstition but a shrewd observation of important facts.

This may serve as a clue to the right method of interpreting all such things. The method is to reconstruct, from all the evidence at our disposal, the social structure in which they grew up. It is thus a historical method: [20] one proceeding not by abstraction and generalization, but by the reconstruction of fact in all its detail.

The two rules laid down above are closely connected with this notion of historical method. Butler's rule points to the distinction between history and natural or naturalistic science: for science in that specialized sense proceeds by leaving out certain details and thus arriving at abstractions concerning which generalization is possible; history attempts to use every detail of its material in the reconstruction of concrete facts. So far as the philologists, anthropologists, and psychologists have deliberately adopted the method of ignoring details and identifying things that are different, they have been trying to adapt the methods of natural science to the study of man. All such attempts must fail, for the simple reason that man is man and not merely nature, thinker and not merely object thought about, the user of powers and not merely the powers used. The only way in which man's thought and actions can become the object of human knowledge is through the methods of history.

Spinoza's rule points in the same direction. Because history is man's knowledge of man, not man's knowledge of an external world, history demands, or rather brings about, a peculiar intimacy in the relation between knower and known. The historian can only understand a thought by thinking it over again for himself. If there is any type of thinking which for any reason he is unable to do for himself, he cannot thus rethink it and cannot understand it historically. Consequently it is impossible for him to understand magic, superstition, and so on if he himself has no inner experience of these thought-forms. He is on the horns of a dilemma. Either [21] these things are only phenomena outside him, in which case they must be to him for ever unintelligible; or they are a part of his own experience, and therefore not the peculiar thought-form of other people called savages but thought-forms of his own. He has therefore to stop pretending that the subject matter of his study is the life of societies inferior to his own; he has to face the fact that the distinction between savage and civilized man is a fiction designed to flatter his vanity. But he must go further. The historian cannot study what he despises. If his study of it is effective, he reconstructs it within his own mind and it becomes a prized possession. What he began by thinking peculiar to savages, and now finds inside himself, must therefore be regarded not with hatred and contempt as irrational or perverse, but as something worth having, something of which the recognition increases instead of impairing his self-respect and self-confidence.[14]

This will no doubt seem a paradox. We have grown so accustomed to hearing it said that the minds of savages work quite differently from our own, that it has become an accepted dogma, and we have created a whole vocabulary of technical terms— magic, taboo, mana, totem, and so forth—which we use in describing the categories of this savage mentality. If this dogma were true, the experience of savages would be so radically unlike our own that we could never hope to understand it. But it is not true. Such terms are not categories of savage thought; they are concepts of anthropological science, classifications under which we conveniently group certain kinds of customs and beliefs. The fact that the words are in some cases borrowed from 'primitive' languages does not alter the case; it is the anthropologist who decides how he shall use them.

Before we proceed to our central problem, therefore, it would be well to challenge this dogma, and to show that the facts which we classify under these terms are facts of a kind with which we are quite familiar in ourselves. The most important of these terms is magic. We must therefore ask what magic is.

---

[14] Stuck over: 'The purpose of this book is to apply historical method to the study of fairy tales. I shall try to show how they arose, how they developed, and how they reached their present form. They did not arise in a fabulous mythopoeic age or Childhood of the Race, for they were not created ready-made. They arose as a natural and inevitable function of certain historical conditions. But in this original state they were not fairy tales. Their transmutation into fairy tales was the work of time, or rather of history. This process again is one which I shall endeavour to trace. To give a preliminary notion of the method, I may say that it means treating a fairy tale in the kind of way in which an archaeologist treats an ancient site. I shall excavate it, clearing away the traces of recent occupation.'

4

MAGIC

We began by defining fairy tales as traditional stories about all sorts of magic. In order to understand them, therefore, we must understand the nature of magic. This cannot be done by offering any formal definition of the term; for, as we have seen, it is merely a convenient label by which we designate a variety of beliefs and customs found among savages. What we need to understand is these beliefs and customs, not the label we stick upon them. Or rather, that is what we must do if we wish to understand the minds of savages; to understand the label would be to investigate the minds of anthropologists.

In order to understand the beliefs and customs, we should do well to fix our attention on one kind at a time. I therefore propose to begin by considering a well-known type of magical practice to which I have already referred: the practices connected with hair-cuttings and nail-clippings, round which Tylor built up his classical theory of magic as pseudo-science.[1]

The practices are of various kinds, obviously dependent on one central idea. It is thought that an enemy skilled in magic, if he gets possession of such jetsam from my person, can damage me by damaging it; and therefore, to prevent this from happening, I conceal or destroy it myself. The injury to myself is not conceived (as on Tylor's theory it must be) as due simply to the destruction of these things; if it had been, my own precautionary destruction of them would be a kind of suicide.[2] It is due to their magical destruction: a destruction accompanied by magical formulas and

Bodleian Library Collingwood Papers, dep. 21/7. The title, with the prefix 'IV', is Collingwood's.

[1] Tylor, *Primitive Culture*, i. 112–16. Collingwood recurs to this example of the 'savage's' supposed sense of a mystical connection between his nail-clippings and his own body in his chapter on 'Art as Magic', *PA* 59–60, where he is equally derisory.

[2] *PA* 60: 'if he believed this, he would regard his own destruction of his nail-clippings as suicide'.

designed to injure me in a specifically magical way. And the materials used in this magical destruction need not be severed parts of my person. An article of my clothing, or an image of myself in clay or wax, will equally serve the purposes of the same idea.

[2] What is the source of this idea? The rationalistic psychology by which students like Tylor and Frazer have sought to analyse it as a quasi-scientific idea, based on intellectual principles, has clearly failed to explain it; marking that failure by a *reductio ad absurdum* in which unreason takes the place of reason as the principle of interpretation. Perhaps we shall do better if we seek the source of the idea not in the savage's intellect, but in his emotions. And since we can understand what goes on in the savage's mind only in so far as we can experience the same thing in our own, we must find our clue in emotions to whose reality we can testify in our own persons.[3]

We all have a feeling—not an intellectual idea, but an emotional one—of an intimate connexion between ourselves and the things which we have made. These things are felt as parts of ourselves, in the sense that an injury to them is felt as an injury to us. If a picture I have drawn, or a letter I have written, or some trifling thing, useful or useless, which I have made, is destroyed by accident, my sense of loss bears no relation to the intrinsic value or merit of what has been destroyed; it is like a wound or blow to myself, as if the destroyed thing had been a deposit or outpost of my personality in

---

[3] Collingwood here turns to the emotional dimension of the human mind as he finds it expressed in the otherwise puzzling accounts of magical practices provided by the anthropologists and folklorists. As Dray and van der Dussen have suggested in their Editors' Introduction to *PH* (p. xxv), this emphasis should serve significantly to modify and complicate perceptions of the place of emotion in Collingwood's descriptions of history as a history of 'thought' (e.g. as derived from *A* and *IH*). Knox's editing gave the impression that only purposive rational thought qualified as subject matter for history. In *IH* Collingwood says that all history is the history of thought, but in *PH* this is significantly qualified: 'All history is the history of thought. This includes the history of emotions so far as these emotions are essentially related to the thoughts in question' (77). The importance of emotions in history and how they are related to the folktale MS, to *PA*, and *PH*, has been explored by David Boucher in 'The *Principles of History* and the Cosmology Conclusion to *The Idea of Nature*', *Collingwood Studies*, 2 (1995), *Perspectives*, 140–74; and 'The Significance of the *Principles of History*', *Journal of the History of Ideas*, 58, 2 (1997), 309–30. In his last book, *NL*, Collingwood also treats the interconnection of thought and emotion as fundamental to human action and thus to history.

the world around me. And if the destruction was malicious, the sense of injury is more severe, as a deliberate blow is harder to bear than an accidental one.

The same feeling unites us with things which, although we have not made them, have acquired a similar status by use. A man's well-worn clothes are to him objects of unreasoning affection; to part from them, even when they are quite unpresentable and hardly serviceable, is a wrench which he feels almost like a bodily injury. Nor does this feeling arise from the memories of [3] long usage; its objects may be things which he has in no sense used, but which he has deliberately adopted in order to place them in this relation to himself. A child will often in this sense adopt a particular tree or star, or some place which he visits in the course of his walks. These facts are not survivals, for (unlike genuine survivals, such as a traditional children's game) they do not depend for their existence on a continuous tradition; they are emotional facts which arise spontaneously in the mind of each one of us, even though he may not know of their existence in others.

These connexions between ourselves and the things which (in this specifically emotional sense) may be called 'ours' are important not only to ourselves but to those who love or hate us. A lover will cherish whatever stands in this peculiar relation to his mistress: her glove, her handkerchief, her letters, and so forth. The destruction of any such relic by a third party he will resent as an injury to the lady and an affront to himself. The same will apply to her photograph or other likeness, even though it may not be very like. Hatred for someone, again, will direct itself in the same way upon these outposts of his personality. The jilted lover will destroy his lady's photograph not on the cold calculation that it has no further place among his possessions, but with a destructive rage that shows how the photograph is bearing the brunt of his resentment against its original. I have heard a philosopher confess a desire to dance upon a book whose doctrines he disapproved of; not, clearly, because he thought this would refute the doctrines or induce others to reject them, but because the hostile and aggressive impulses which he felt towards the author directed themselves quite spontaneously upon his book.

The same emotional connexion makes us reluctant to destroy things which [4] stand in this relation to ourselves, except in fits of self-hatred or despondency, like those which cause a child to break its favourite toys. Hence the impulse to hoard our manuscripts, drawings, old clothes, broken watches, and all manner of things which, coolly considered, are rubbish. But where the sense of connexion is strong we would much rather destroy these things ourselves, giving them as it were Christian burial, than allow them to fall into the careless and perhaps malicious hands of others. We have the same feeling about the relics of a dead person whom we have loved. When we consider these feelings in ourselves, it is not difficult to see why some peoples have broken a dead man's sword, killed his horse, or even burnt his wife at his grave. Such practices need rest on no theory of placating the dead in their anger or furnishing them in their penury; they have a direct emotional basis independent of any such doctrine, though if we fail to understand this basis we may easily foist upon them a rationalization in terms of this or that theory concerning ghosts and the ghost-world. When after the death of George V his yacht *Britannia* was scuttled at sea, the act was not based on a custom of destroying favourite possessions on their owner's death, for we have no such custom. It was not based on a theory that our king needed the ghost of his yacht in the world to which he had gone, for we hold no such theory. Still less was it based on that theory *plus* our fear that he would be angry with us if we neglected to supply his need; though such acts, when we observe them in other civilizations, are habitually taken as evidence for fear of the dead. Its motive was directly and straightforwardly emotional. It expressed our feeling that a thing so intimately belonging to King George as this, so much a part of himself, ought never to belong to anyone else; and that the appearance of the *Britannia* on the second-hand yacht-market would be an insult to his memory.

[5] Emotions of this kind have been felt *semper, ubique, ab omnibus*. Different civilizations have to some extent differed in the choice of objects for them. Among ourselves photographs play a conspicuous part; locks of hair less than formerly, but they are not even yet wholly out of date. I have not discovered any such significance in nail-cuttings, except in those semi-obsolete customs which have so far lost their hold upon our minds as to have acquired the name of superstitions.

This is the foundation of the type of magic we are now considering. The fundamental idea throughout this type of beliefs and customs is the idea of certain material objects as what I have

called outposts or deposits of one's personality in the external
world: an idea which arises spontaneously, without any theoretical
or intellectual basis, from our emotional nature. Granted this
feeling, various types of situation will arise in which it finds expression.

First, a person who feels a relation of this peculiar kind between
himself and a certain thing will act towards that thing in certain
ways. He will cherish it, protecting it from accidental damage and
still more from malicious damage; he will feel that if it should be so
damaged some injury, undefined perhaps but none the less genuinely feared, will follow to himself. If it must be destroyed, he will
prefer to destroy it himself, or arrange that it shall be destroyed by
some friendly person acting as his agent. The injury to himself
which he fears is in reality an emotional injury, a kind of mortification or shock to his feelings. One might suppose him foolish to
think this a real injury. But psychologists have demonstrated (if
any one ever doubted it) that it may be a very real injury indeed:
depriving a man of that self-confidence without which none of his
enterprises can succeed, and that respect for himself, felt by others,
without which he cannot lead or control them; and often producing
as a symptom **[6]** some physiological disturbance hardly different
from the symptoms of organic disease.

Secondly, some other person, aware of this relation and hostile
to the person it concerns, may use it in order to express his hatred.
If I feel my yacht as part of myself, and if you hate me, and are
aware of that feeling, you can express your hatred of me by throwing stones at my yacht. In so far as your hatred craves expression,
and is relieved by being expressed, damaging the yacht will genuinely relieve your feelings. If all you want to do is to release your
hatred, an attack on the yacht will give you the same kind of
satisfaction as an attack on my person. A further development of
this case is where the thing on which you wreak your hatred is a
thing which you feel as emotionally connected with me, though
I have no such feeling perhaps because I am ignorant of its existence. You might, for example, destroy a photograph of me which
you had taken surreptitiously; or a clay or wax image of me which
you had made secretly for the express purpose of destroying it.
Here the act is essentially an expression or release of hostile emotion, which is satisfied by being directed upon an object emotionally connected with the hostility's proper object.

So far, the act is a mere expression of emotion, which may do good to the agent in so far as his emotion obtains release, but can do no harm to the victim. This is well on the way to becoming magic, but it is not yet magic fully fledged, just because the emotion is thus 'earthed'. Such acts become genuinely magical only when performed in a society where a third situation exists, combining the first and second. In this situation, the established habits of society, based on the emotional facts already described, are such that the victim knows or fears that the agent is acting in this way, and consequently sustains injury in the shape of mortification and whatever consequences that implies. He loses confidence in himself, forfeits the respect **[7]** of others, and may develop the symptoms of disease. Thus arises the complete magic act; not a mere harmless release of emotion, but an actual assault upon the victim. The agent's belief that he is really injuring his victim, which in the second case is a self-deception based on the fact that he feels his hatred to be discharged and thus feels very much as he would have felt if he had injured his victim, is in this third case well founded: because the victim is emotionally vulnerable, the injury he sustains is a genuine one.

It is on this principle that the well-known fairy-tale motive [motif] of the 'external soul' must be explained.[4] Stories are very common in which the soul or life of a person (generally a giant, or witch, or someone whom, being very strong or very clever, one would hesitate to attack openly) is contained not in his body but somewhere else, hidden where enemies cannot reach it. One discovers the hiding-place, and by destroying the thing hidden there, an egg or the like, destroys the giant. This is simply an extreme case of the same magical practice. The hair, or nail-cuttings, or wax effigy, are just such an 'external soul'; but the point of the extreme case is that we have a person whom these commonplace magics will not harm: there is only one thing in his external world with which his personality is thus linked; and, until we have discovered that, no assault upon him can injure him.

[8] Other well-known themes are to be explained in the same way; for example, the theme which has been called the life-index.

---

[4] See Frazer, *The Golden Bough: A Study in Magic and Religion*, 3rd edn., 12 vols. (London: Macmillan & Co., 1907–15), part 7, 2 vols., *Balder the Beautiful: The Fire-Festivals of Europe and the Doctrine of the External Soul*.

A boy setting out on his travels gives his brother a knife. So long as all goes well with him, the knife will be clean and bright. If it becomes rusty, that will mean that he is dead. Rust, as Socrates observes in the *Republic*[5] is the 'natural evil' of iron: the special corruption to which it is liable, and which, if it goes far enough, will destroy it. The knife, as the traveller's own knife, or even as a knife deliberately 'adopted' into this relation, is emotionally connected with himself, so that injury to the knife is felt as injury to him, the knife's 'death' is felt as his death.

This group of beliefs and practices depends on no theory. It is not the application in daily life of a scientific doctrine, whether true or false. Its basis is emotional. I believe that this is true not of one type of magic only, but of all magic. In the hope of persuading the reader to take this hypothesis seriously, I will broaden the basis of my induction by turning to another group of customs, namely those connected with the fear of ghosts. I have said that certain practices relating to the dead, which are sometimes explained as due to fear of them, are due to a quite different cause. But I do not mean to deny the existence of that fear. On the contrary, I am convinced that it is very real and very common. In order to keep close to the facts and not lose myself in vague generalities, I shall consider it in one special case, that of the jealous ghost.

[9] All over the world, it is customary for widows to fear the jealousy of their dead husbands if they should marry again. This fear is rationalized into the logical consequence of a theory: and the theory must be that the dead husband still exists in the shape of a ghost, preserving in that shape his sexual desires and powers, looking upon the widow as still his mate and resenting any transference of her affections to another. Thus arises the superstition of the 'haunted widow', which has been discussed by E. S. Hartland in one of his scholarly essays.[6] From Iceland to Delagoa Bay, from Kamchatka through China and India and Europe to British Columbia, the same cycle of ideas has been traced. Any attempt to explain this distribution on diffusionist principles would be a *reductio ad absurdum* of the principles themselves. There must be

---

[5] * Plato, *Republic* 10. 609A.

[6] * [Parenthetical note] Hartland, *Ritual and Belief: Studies in the History of Religion* (London: Williams & Norgate, 1914), 194–234. ['The Haunted Widow' is Hartland's chapter title.]

a spontaneous cause producing ideas of the same kind in the most widely differing races and civilizations. According to the hypothesis with which we are experimenting in this chapter, the cause should be sought in a certain complex of emotions: these emotions will be those arising out of a certain type of situation. What precisely is this situation?

The ghostly husband as such is not necessarily an object of terror. In Chinese versions, the relation between the widow and her husband's ghost may be entirely happy; and as a rule this seems to be the case so long as the widow remains faithful and refuses to marry again. The terror which is so often the dominant note in such stories is not a terror of ghosts as such; it is a terror of what they may do to a surviving mate in revenge for infidelity. [10] But this terror does not arise from any general principle as to the inviolability or indissolubility of the marriage tie. Strange though this may appear to us, the ghost's jealousy is feared even where divorce is easy, and where no objection is made to a wife's taking a temporary partner during her husband's absence from home. Among many peoples the same situation occurs as between a widower and the ghost of his dead wife; though this is not so common as the other.

These terrors are a special case of our general relation to the dead, or rather to those of them with whom we have, during life, been in a close and affectionate relation. Our feelings towards all such are curiously complex. First, their death has broken off that relation, and thus baulked of expression the emotions which it served to discharge; consequently we have a painful sense of being crippled, overloaded with emotions which henceforth we shall not be able to express. This is the feeling which we describe as 'missing' the dead, or *desiderium*. Secondly, we cannot overcome this feeling by allowing the emotions in question to become atrophied; for they are emotions necessary to our own healthy and effective life. We must not spend the rest of our years weeping at a tomb, or living upon it when the desire to weep has left us; we must find new channels through which these emotions can flow, by contracting new human relationships. Thirdly, the feeling that our hearts are buried with the dead and the feeling that they are, after all, not buried there but must seek a new home elsewhere, inevitable though each of them is, are in mutual conflict. In so far as we act on the second (which we must do, in so far as we truly survive the death of those dear to us) we outrage the first, and thus create in ourselves a sense of guilt towards [11] the dead. This sense of guilt is in reality a conflict in the emotions which we feel towards the dead. We want them back and do not want them back; thence arises a peculiar perplexity and distress. This distress is no doubt reinforced by that bitterest ingredient in the cup of *desiderium*, the memory of our own unkindnesses towards the dead while they lived: in other words, by the knowledge that our love was never pure love, but was adulterated with elements of fear and cruelty. But these memories are not the essential ground of our distress. In all life we take the rough with the smooth, and learn to forgive ourselves our trespasses against those we love, as we forgive them their trespasses against us. It is not because she used to scold her husband that the widow fears his ghost. She knows that he took the nagging with the kisses, as part and parcel of married life. His ghostly wrath visits her not because she nagged him in the past but because she now nags someone else. Our guilt towards the dead is not our past unkindness to them, but the fact that we are going on living when they are dead.

In the special case of a dead husband or wife, this conflict is peculiarly violent. The relation to a parent is one which exists ready-made from birth; it is not of our making, and we can never break it: consequently we tend to accept it with the same acquiescence with which we accept other facts not under our control. Owing to the difference in age, we accept along with it the fact that it is likely to be ended one day by the parent's death, so that this probability is inherent in it from the beginning. Since our filial emotions can never be genuinely transferred to another object, the sense of guilt arising from such a transference does not occur, or occurs only in a mild and manageable form. The relation to a friend is one which is made, and must be maintained, by our own efforts; in so far as it exists between equals in age, its destruction by death is felt as an outrage and the transference of our affection to another friend is accompanied by a sense of guilt: but this is mitigated by the fact that the relation itself, however real, is emotionally somewhat simple and superficial, so that an injury [12] to it produces less profound and complicated emotional disturbances. But the relation to one's mate (not merely a sexual partner, but the partner in a whole *consortium vitae*, including the propagation of children) is like the relation to one's parents in that it roots itself very deeply into every part of one's emotional nature, and like the relation to one's friend in that it is between equals in age, and freely undertaken so that it has to be maintained by one's own efforts. An injury to such a relation has all the gravity of injuries to these other two, but without their respective mitigations. The only way in which it can be terminated without arousing an extreme sense of guilt is by the free consent of both parties, that is, by divorce. But when it ends in the death of one partner, there is nothing to assuage the survivor's guilt-sense.

The two sexes are here not on an equal footing. In every society known to us, marriage bulks larger in the emotional life of a woman than in that of a man. Hence in a general way the guilt-sense of a widow is more acute than that of a widower, and more exacting in the measures needed for its alleviation. The extreme case, in which the conflict can be ended only by death, has in many societies given rise to institutions in which widows are killed at their husband's funeral, but I know of none in which the converse custom exists.

It is in these emotional facts that we must seek the explanation of events like those which Hartland quotes as having taken place in Iceland in 1606. A certain Ivar Eyjulfsson being drowned at sea, his widow Herdis was courted a year or two later by one Sturla Gottskalkson, and on her father's advice agreed to marry him. By the time of the betrothal she [13] already suffered from an ulcer in the foot, and it now became worse. Her husband's ghost visited her in bed, and she struggled to protect herself against his advances. Another ulcer sloughed away half her tongue. The visits of the ghost became more frequent and more menacing. It interrupted the marriage-ceremony, and its persecution frustrated every attempt to consummate the marriage. After vain appeal to a magician, Herdis perished in the collapse of her bed-place, and it was believed that the ghost had strangled her. All the essential features of the story are explicable as due to the widow's intolerable sense of guilt.[7]

What is the magician's function in this and similar stories? Not the otiose one of protecting Herdis against a non-existent visitor, nor the fraudulent one of claiming to protect her against a danger which actually he cannot avert; but the legitimate and valuable one

---

[7] * Hartland, *Ritual and Belief*, 205–8; from Conrad von Maurer, *Isländische Volkssagen der Gegenwart* (Leipzig and Munich [printed], 1860).

of solving her emotional conflict by means of an appropriate ritual, and thus banishing at once the hallucinations and the pathological symptoms to which this conflict gave rise. He is protecting her against her own emotional vulnerability, which in this case is exploited, not by the malevolence of an enemy but by her own guilt-sense.

This, we may conclude, is the general function of those almost infinitely various magics which serve, in one way or another, to protect human beings against the ghosts that haunt them. Either these magics placate the ghosts, and thus turn them from enemies into friends; or they disarm them, robbing them of the power to carry out their hostile intentions; or they banish them from human presence and send them back to the world of shades, their proper home. In the first case, the sense of guilt towards the [14] dead is effectively discharged, so that the living can now think of them without fear. In the second case, it is not discharged, but reduced to manageable proportions, so as no longer to make ordinary life impossible. In the third, which is the least satisfactory of the three, the hallucinations arising out of it are dissipated and shown to be the illusions that they are; but this is mere treatment of symptoms; there is no security that they will not return. If some charms, such as the sign of the cross, are more effective, this is because the cross symbolizes a complete relief from our sense of guilt, standing as it does for the belief that God himself has borne the burden of our sins.

So far, we have been considering magical customs found in relatively primitive societies, but not existing among ourselves. It is true that here and there survivals or re-emergences of them do exist. For example, in 1912 a divorce was granted at Macon, Georgia, to the second husband of a widow whose first husband's ghost haunted the couple so pertinaciously that they could no longer live together.[8] Ghost-stories are common enough in our civilization to convince us that the psychological causes which produce them are still operative there. But among ourselves they are the exception rather than the rule. This can only be due to some special feature of our civilization. What can this feature be?

If magic in general is an expression of emotion, and grows up naturally and inevitably from its emotional roots, its disappearance

---

[8] * *Daily Chronicle* (17 Feb. 1912), *apud* Hartland, *Ritual and Belief*, 209.

in a given society would seem to indicate that, in that society, emotional vulnerability has been (partially at least) overcome by the deliberate cultivation of a thick-skinned or insensitive attitude towards emotion itself.

[15] This is actually the way in which our civilization has suppressed magic. After a long and hideous experiment in suppressing it by force, by burning witches, we came to see that burning witches meant believing in them, and that their victims' belief in them, what I have called emotional vulnerability, was the source of their power. So we changed our own attitude towards them: replaced persecution by ridicule, and gradually developed a whole system of education and social life based on the principle that magic was not a crime but a folly, whose success depended on a like folly in its victims.

This hard-headed or thick-skinned or rationalistic attitude towards life, which our civilization invented in the seventeenth century, worked out in the eighteenth, and applied to all aspects of human affairs in the nineteenth, is the dominant factor in modern civilization. The best single-word name for it is utilitarianism. Our civilization prides itself on being sensible, rational, businesslike; and all these are names for the same characteristic, namely the habit of justifying every act, every custom, every institution, by showing its utility. The doctrine that utility is the only kind of value that a thing can have is called utilitarianism; and it is obvious to anyone who reflects on the general character of our civilization that it is, characteristically, a utilitarian civilization. We justify the state as a means to the protection of life and property against crime; the armed forces of the state, as a means to protect these against foreign aggression; the church, as a means of inculcating sound morality; mechanized industry as a means of increasing wealth or saving labour; sport as a means of getting exercise and preserving health; clothes as a protection against the weather and a safeguard against the passions that are aroused by nudity; cleanliness as a protection against germs; and so forth.

This utilitarianism is more than a principle; it is an obsession. Whatever cannot be justified in this way our civilization tends on the whole to suppress. In general, it discountenances emotion and the expression of emotion; in particular it distrusts art and religion as things not altogether respectable. To live within the scheme of modern European-American civilization involves doing a certain

[16] violence to one's emotional nature, treating emotion as a thing that must be repressed, a hostile force within us whose outbreaks are feared as destructive of civilized life.[9] We have already had occasion to observe that our horror of savages is really a horror of something within ourselves which 'the savage' (that is, any civilization other than our own) symbolizes. We are now finding reason to think that this thing is emotion: for magic, which sums up all that we dislike in savage life, is beginning to reveal itself as the systematic and organized expression of emotion.

Accustomed as we are to explaining our own institutions on the utilitarian principle, we naïvely extend it without misgiving to those of other people. Opening *The Golden Bough* at random, in chapter viii of *Adonis, Attis, Osiris*, I read: 'When the earth quakes in some parts of Celebes, it is said that all the inhabitants of a village will rush out of their houses and grub up grass by handfuls in order to attract the attention of the earth-spirit, who, feeling his hair thus torn out by the roots, will be painfully conscious that there are still people above ground.'[10] Here a custom whose nature is obviously magical is explained in utilitarian terms. Such an explanation is called by psychologists a rationalization. It does not affect my point whether the rationalization was invented by the anthropologist who recorded the custom, or by the villagers themselves in answer to leading questions demanding an explanation of that kind, or even (as in the case previously mentioned) by Sir James Frazer himself; my point is that our anthropologists, looking at savage life from the point of view of the utilitarian obsession, require for this custom an explanation of this kind, and, having got it, are satisfied.

---

[9] Collingwood expresses very similar sentiments about the emotional decay of modern civilization as he responds to T. S. Eliot's *The Waste Land* in the concluding pages of *PA*. For the links between this emotional impoverishment and the mechanization of art, see *AM* below.

[10] Collingwood is referring to ch. 8 of book 1 (Adonis) of *Adonis, Attis, Osiris: Studies in the History of Oriental Religion* (London: Macmillan, 1906), 110. In 2 vols., *Adonis, Attis, Osiris* became part 4 of the 3rd edn. of Frazer's *The Golden Bough* (1907–15). In his 'Notes on *The Waste Land*' (1922), T. S. Eliot refers to these two volumes as a source of references to vegetation ceremonies in his poem and of his general debt to *The Golden Bough*, esp. i. 200. See Eliot, *Collected Poems 1909–1962* (London: Faber & Faber, 1970), 80. (Eliot's *Collected Poems 1909–1935* was first published in 1936.)

We, with our superior scientific equipment, know that pulling up the grass [17] cannot stop the earthquake. These poor savages, who do it because they think it can, are thus acting under a delusion. Owing to a scientific error, they are doing an act as a means to a certain end, when in fact it cannot further that end. Generalize this example, and you get what has become the ortho-dox definition of magic as pseudo-science. This definition of magic is the result of examining customs, whose true basis is emotional, through the spectacles of the utilitarian obsession.

[18] But if this definition is wrong; if magical practices are not utilitarian activities based on scientific theories whether true or false, but spontaneous expressions of emotion whose utility, so far as they have any utility, lies in the fact that they resolve emotional conflicts in the agent and so readjust him to the practical life for which these conflicts render him unfitted; then a new problem arises about our own civilization. We pride ourselves on always acting from utilitarian motives or scientific theories; but that very pride should warn us that this belief about ourselves may perhaps be unjustified. We may be conceiving our own civilization not as it actually is, but as, with our utilitarian obsession, we should like it to be. We think that our rationalism has done away with magic because that is what we want to think; but is it true?

The question has a double importance. For the conduct of our own lives and the right ordering of our own societies, it is import-ant that we should not live under illusions about the nature of our own civilization; but that is not the point with which we are here concerned. We are concerned to understand the mind of the 'sav-age', with its furniture of magical ideas; and we have already seen that unless we can sympathize with these ideas, by recognizing their kinship with certain elements in our own experience, we cannot hope to understand them. If we are to understand the 'savage' mind, we must dispel our rationalistic conception not only of savage culture but of our own, and find among ourselves practices which fall under the conception of magic as we have now defined it.

Such practices can easily be found in our traditional religion. But these will not serve our turn, because it may be argued that this religion itself is [19] a survival from a more primitive age, and that the more advanced spirits among ourselves have already learnt to do without it. As I do not wish to argue this point and evoke the passions which are sure, when it is argued, to confuse the issue, I shall choose my ground elsewhere, and seek for magical significance (in the sense defined above) in social customs that are generally accepted as elements in what we call civilized life.

As I write, the lunch-bell rings. Before going into the dining-room, I wash my hands. What is my motive? I am conforming with an established custom; but what is the nature of this custom? On utilitarian principles, there must be some end to which it is the means. What is this end? I cannot say that I wash my hands in order to avoid being scolded for not doing so. That would be to argue in a circle. Those who scolded me would scold because they thought I had omitted something of importance, and what we are asking is why it is thought important. I may suggest, then, that it is done in the interests of health, to keep noxious bacteria out of my food. But I have no idea what bacteria these could be, and in any case I am well aware that washing does not make my hands bacteriologically clean. Reflexion soon shows me that there is no ulterior end in view, and that really the washing of hands before meals belongs to that class of acts which are concerned with the decencies and civilities of life: a class of acts whose basis is emotional, and to which utilitarian explanations cannot be applied.

If I tried to think out this idea more explicitly, I should reflect that the essence of the civility in question is a feeling that impels me to remove all traces of my labour before I enter the ceremonial atmosphere of a civilized meal. For the [20] meal is not a mere taking of food. It is also a social ceremony for which one prepares oneself by a ceremonial ablution symbolizing the dismissal from one's mind of work and its preoccupations. I might express this feeling in a metaphorical way (the only way in which it can be expressed in words; the literal expression of it is by the ceremony of washing) by saying that somehow or other I feel the spirit of work sticking to my hands, and I must not bring it in to lunch with me, because its presence would spoil the social atmosphere of the meal.

What this really comes to is that washing my hands expresses quite naturally the feelings with which I go from the atmosphere of a morning's work to the atmosphere of a family lunch. But suppose I had said all this in answer to an anthropologist, suffering from a strong utility-obsession, who had asked me why I washed my hands. For him, the word 'why?' has one meaning and only one: namely, 'as a means to what end?' The only appropriate meaning, 'as an expression of what feeling?', is thus ruled out, and he stands committed to misunderstanding me. My careful (and, I flatter myself, rather good) explanation of my feelings will thus appear to him as a confession that I believe in the existence of certain invisible but quasi-material beings which infest my study and fasten upon my hands as I write; and that, since they would make the food go bad if I brought them into the dining-room, I remove them first by washing.

Moreover, if I were not on my guard against the utilitarian obsession, if I thought the anthropologist a disinterested searcher after truth with no axe to grind, I might accept his version of my explanation as roughly corresponding with what I actually felt, though doubting whether it described my feelings with all the **[21]** metaphysical subtlety that they deserved. I might even, if very skilfully cross-questioned, invent his version on my own account, and thus be my own accuser in the damning indictment he was building up against me.

This example does not stand alone. It is easy to prove that our customs are full of magic. And since there is no better way of showing what magic is, I shall enlarge a little on this point before going back to the practices, which we commonly call magical, found in other civilizations. In this way we shall be following the sound scientific method of arguing from the known to the unknown.

It is part of our English social custom that a man should wear his hat out of doors and take it off in the house. To wear it in the house is felt as uncivil; to walk abroad without it is in some subtle way undignified. The hat, as such, is felt to be a badge of dignity, and inspires a certain awe: and special kinds of hats are the badge of special kinds of dignity. Hats may no doubt be also protective against sun and rain; but this does not account for the way in which we feel about the wearing of them. The special dignity which belongs to such headgear as the crown, the mitre, the cardinal's hat, the priestly biretta, the top hat, the footballer's cap, the hat of the Spanish grandee, is only a development of the dignity which belongs to the hat in general, quite irrespective of utilities which it may or may not possess.[11]

---

[11] In this passage Collingwood is echoing A. M. Hocart's discussion of clothing, specifically headgear, in *The Progress of Man: A Short Survey of his Evolution, his Customs and his Works* (London: Methuen, 1933), ch. 8, esp. 89–91.

Our motive for wearing a hat is a purely emotional one. A man wearing a hat feels himself somehow strengthened by it. It gives **[22]** him a feeling of assurance, a sense of security. He feels that it protects him in a critical or hostile atmosphere. That is why he puts it on when he walks out, not knowing whom he will meet, but must take it off in the friendly atmosphere of the house, or when he meets someone in whose presence it would be insulting to put himself on the defensive. Anyone able to analyse his feelings can verify this for himself. But such a person, cross-examined by an obsessed utilitarian, might easily be forced into maintaining that the hat, as such and by itself, possessed a magical power of protecting him against his enemies; and that his wearing of it and removing of it were utilitarian acts designed to gain this protection or, by laying it aside, to show confidence in his companions. No such conception is really implied. It is not that there is magic in the hat as a separate thing. It is rather that he feels himself-hatted and himself-uncovered as two different states of himself, like himself smiling and himself frowning.

These feelings are to some extent observable in all human beings. But they are developed in different ways by different peoples. Frenchmen, I have observed, feel no need to take their hats off in the house. One might infer that Frenchmen have no manners, but that would be a false inference. We should infer rather that to some extent they feel differently about hats from ourselves. The question might then be raised: do they wear their hats in the house because of this different feeling, or do they feel differently because of their different customs? There is no answer to this question. The feeling and the custom are not two separate things which can be related as cause and effect. There is only one thing. The custom is the outward **[23]** side of it, the feeling the inward side.

Wearing a hat is only one special case of wearing clothes. When we ask ourselves why we wear clothes, the utilitarian principle concealed in the question comes out in the reply that we do it for protection against the weather. In certain extreme cases this might be true: the case of very cold climates, and the case of pale-skinned persons in very hot ones. But in temperate climates people need no such protection; if they catch cold when they take their clothes off, it is because they have grown accustomed to wearing them; and on the whole their habit of wearing them is bad rather than good for health. A second rationalization is that clothes are demanded by modesty. This comes nearer to covering the facts, because it would explain why we object to nudity even when the weather is such that it can do no possible harm to the health of its votaries. But modesty is the result of clothes, not clothes of modesty: plenty of peoples go about naked without feeling shocked. There is also the opposite theory, that we wear clothes because nudity is not exciting enough, so that the habit is the mark of what Bergson calls an 'aphrodisiac civilization'.[12]

The first theory is right to this extent: that clothes give us a feeling of security or of being protected against something. The second is right, in that the absence of such protection causes, not fear of rain or cold or bodily injury, but a kind of purely emotional injury; a shock to our finer feelings, not our bodily senses. The third is right, in that feeling clothed is not an emotionally negative thing but an emotionally [24] positive thing. There is doubtless a certain exhilaration about having one's clothes off; psychologists ascribe it to exhibitionism; but we put them on, not in order to deny ourselves and others that exhilaration, but to enjoy one of a different kind. But this exhilaration is not the same thing as sexual excitement. A fourth theory meets all these points by suggesting that the real function of clothes is ornament. But this will not do when one thinks how far many clothes are from being ornamental, and how tolerant we are of ugliness, how intolerant of nudity.

Anthropologists know the answer, or rather their own version of the answer. Clothes are magic. Their function is to protect the wearer against evil influences; the evil eye, and so forth. If civilized people are more obsessed than any savage by the necessity of wearing them, that is because the civilized man has democratically extended to all men and all occasions the extreme of magical over-

---

[12] Cf. Hocart, *Progress of Man*, 85: 'It is now generally agreed that clothing produces shame, and not shame clothing.... The art of alluring concealment has been carried very far by us, as by all people in what Bergson calls an "aphrodisiac" state of civilization.' The original reads: 'Toute notre civilization est aphrodisiaque', from Bergson's 'Les Deux Sources de la morale et de la religion' (1932), in *Œuvres*, 1232. Translated as 'Sex-appeal is the keynote of our whole civilization.' See R. Ashley Audra and Cloudesley Brereton, with the assistance of W. Horsfall Carter, *The Two Sources of Morality and Religion* (London: Macmillan & Co., 1935), 261. Struck out: 'This too is a mere rationalization, an oblique self-flattery for people who, in a rather dull life, like to believe that they are going the pace'.

4. MAGIC 213

clothing which among 'savages' is reserved for the greatest men on the greatest occasions. I will try to express this in my own way.

The wearing of clothes gives one a feeling of security or self-confidence. To take off one's clothes in public is to 'give oneself away', to 'make an exhibition of oneself', that is, to forfeit one's dignity. It makes one ridiculous or contemptible. This is a universal human feeling, to be traced, I think, in every civilization. How far and in what ways it is allowed to develop into a principle governing social life depends on the extent and manner and kind of occasion on which people feel it necessary to stand on their dignity. People who generally go naked wear clothes on state occasions when they wish to feel and look impressive. The central figure in a ceremony, the bride or the king or the [25] priest, wears extra clothes. With us, it is a principle that men keep up their dignity before women and women before men; but men or women separately will strip in each other's presence, though the first time he does it is a sad shock to a little boy's dignity and an occasion of ridicule to his school fellows. The public removal of his trousers is a traditional method, in some societies, of humiliating an offender. There is no question of sexual modesty here: the little boy simply feels that he is making a fool of himself: the debagged undergraduate, that he is being made a fool of. The Cupid-and-Psyche[13] theme in our fairy tales must come down from a culture in which keeping up one's dignity in this way was thought necessary as between husband and wife.

A special example is the wearing of shoes. They are ugly, uncomfortable, and bad for the feet, and people who wear them walk and run worse than people who do not. No other civilization has worn them consistently and universally, as ours does.[14] We wear them simply for dignity's sake, as in other civilizations kings and exalted people wear them though other people go barefoot.

On special occasions, when we permit ourselves to relax a great part of this dignity, we allow ourselves a greater or less degree of public undressing. But the custom of our civilization is that on such occasions we draw the line at our sexual parts. These are also

[13] Apuleius's *Cupid and Psyche* of the 2nd cent. was revived in La Fontaine's version of 1669.

[14] Cf. Hocart, *Progress of Man*, 91: 'It is impossible to account for the continuous use of shoes on purely utilitarian grounds ... shoes appear to have begun as a ritual necessity which spread.'

the first parts to be clothed when a people habitually naked takes by degrees to clothing itself. The reason is that we feel these parts, as the seat of our reproductive powers, to be specially bound up with our self-respect.

Under the influence of the utilitarian obsession, these feelings may easily be twisted into pseudo-science. If a naked savage wears a single ornament which makes him feel clothed, we call it an amulet to attract the evil eye, a kind of magical lightning-conductor. The wearing of shoes becomes a kind of insulation to prevent the wearer's *mana* from leaking out into the [26] ground.[15] But, apart from a desire to flatter our own vanity, there is no reason to ascribe to the savage these strange caricatures of our physical science. All we need ascribe to him is the feelings which we can recognize in ourselves.

The reason why our civilization insists with so peculiar an emphasis on the wearing of clothes is to be sought in the facts of cultural psychology. It must surely be connected with an altogether exceptional fear of ridicule and contempt, an abnormal craving for self-reassurance and desire to protect one's dignity. As compared with the people we call savages, it is well known that we laugh very seldom, and are very intolerant of being laughed at. The suggestion that our elaborate clothing is a mechanism to achieve self-confidence is borne out by examining certain other characteristics of our culture.

One of these is our passion for tools and machinery. The rationalization of this is of course obvious: we want these things in order to save labour and to increase wealth. But closer scrutiny may lead to doubts. Why does a woman want an electric vacuum cleaner? Not necessarily because she lacks the strength to do her own housework; not necessarily because the machine enables her to get through it quicker and spend the time saved on loftier or more agreeable pursuits. On the contrary, one of the oddest things about modern machinery is that it creates large quantities of leisure which no one knows how to use, and produces goods in excess of

---

[15] *Mana* is a Melanesian word first discussed by the missionary-ethnographer R. H. Codrington. See *The Melanesians* (Oxford: Oxford University Press, 1891), esp. 118; it was adopted as a term of general currency for the innate power of things and people by R. R. Marett, a notion which he maintained had pre-dated animism or other forms of explicit religious representation. See Marett, 'The Conception of Mana', ch. 4 of *The Threshold of Religion*, 99–121.

what can be distributed and consumed. In spite of these consequences we cherish and develop it for the same reason for which a
housewife wants a Hoover. It makes us feel grand: the possession
and direction of all this power gives us a sense of our own dignity.

The dignity we get by using machines is a good deal like the **[27]**
dignity we get by wearing clothes. The machine or tool has a very
curious relation to our personality. It is rather like a kind of extra
limb, an extension of ourselves, adding to our specialized abilities
or, in the case of a power-driven machine, increasing our bodily
strength. But it is not quite this, for it is not a part of us but
something outside us, something that does by itself what we
could not do at all, or does the same kind of work that we might
do, but does it better and more powerfully. The experience of
using tools or machines is emotionally a quite peculiar one, very
different from the experience of using our own strength. The
feeling of satisfaction which we get from walking fast uphill or
knocking a man down is a feeling due to the consciousness of doing
something for ourselves. The satisfaction we get from using a tool
or a machine is due to the consciousness that we are making
something else, which is stronger and cleverer than ourselves, do
it for us. Anyone who can remember the joy of using a very fine
tool for the first time, his first experience of a really sharp chisel, or
a perfectly balanced sailing yacht, or an adding machine, will know
what I mean. He will remember feeling that the tool is alive with a
power and intelligence of its own, and that what it does is not his
own doing, but is 'done by magic'.

There may be readers who will say 'No doubt people do feel like
that; but the feeling is an illusion, for actually the tool is under our
control.' Yes; the tool is under our control; and the more perfectly
we control it the more vivid the feeling is. In fact, the whole
essence of the feeling is our consciousness of controlling this
thing which has a life of its own, but a life obedient to our hand.
As for the feeling being an illusion, I do not know how that can be.
It is something we directly experience in ourselves, like a feeling of
warmth or happiness. It is simply the feeling of using a tool. If the
reader continues 'nevertheless the illusion is there; it **[28]** lies, not
in the feeling, but in a certain theory about the feeling, namely the
belief that the tool is alive', he is merely cavilling at a word. If,
instead of referring to the tool's life, I had referred to its function
of converting one kind of motion into another, he might have

understood me. For a carpenter or a yachtsman, it is good enough
to say that the thing 'comes to life in your hands'; and I shall stick
to that phrase.

To feel a tool or machine come to life in your hands is a glorious
feeling. That is not an exclamation, it is a description; I am trying
to state what kind of feeling it is. It is a feeling of power, but not a
mere feeling of power; it is something more than that; it is the
feeling of glory in awakening and controlling a power which is not
your own, and is greater than your own. If you were asked what it
is like, you might say 'it is like being able to make thunderstorms or
move mountains by just saying "Let it be so"; it is like being God.'
That is, of course, putting it strongly; but by putting things
strongly you can often describe them more accurately, by showing
what their peculiar quality would be like if it were magnified
x diameters. The wielding of tools and the controlling of machines
gives us this glorious or godlike feeling because the work which we
do through them is not done by our own strength and skill. These
are, as it were, kept intact behind the battle. The task that is
accomplished is one against which our own muscles are never
pitted. Tools protect us against the recalcitrance and hostility of
inanimate things in the same kind of way in which clothes protect
us against the hostility and criticism of our fellow-men. The
housewife values her Hoover not only for utilitarian reasons, but
also because it gives her this feeling of protection; like a familiar
spirit, it saves her from exposing her personal forces in the struggle
against dirt.

This experience is something quite distinct from the experience of increasing [29] or cheapening production. It is not a
utilitarian experience at all. It is to be had in combination with
utilitarian activities, as in using the Hoover; or apart from them, as
in the glory of notching the table-edge with your first knife or
touching eighty in your new car. In the second case, it is the motive
of many things in modern life: the habit of turning on the wireless,
whatever kind of noise comes out of it; the delight in tearing over
the face of the land in fast cars, no matter where you get to; the
desire to scrap one's old machines and install bigger and better
ones, irrespective of whether one can afford the cost or sell the
output; and the fact, often verified, that 'if you make enough guns
they will go off of themselves'. But since, with our utilitarian
obsession, we cannot rationalize this delight except by calling it a

desire to increase production (or, in a phrase significantly charged
with emotion, 'speed it up'), the glory of machinery for its own
sake is apt to become a demon, darkly working in the unconscious
recesses of our minds and breeding overproduction and bank-
ruptcy and slaughter on the highway and the battlefield. It has
these ill effects because we will not face it. We repress it as something that will not fit into our utilitarian picture of ourselves. So we
drive it into 'the unconscious', and it becomes a thing of evil.

In the cult of machinery for its own sake we see the deliberate
detachment of this experience from all considerations of utility.
Probably there has always been a tendency towards this detachment: the existence of such a tendency in archaic societies is
attested by the toy boats, 'magic' or 'votive' weapons, 'sacred'
ploughs and so forth, whose explanation is conventionally found
in the superstition and folly of the savage. But perhaps [30] the
impulse to withdraw machines from utilitarian work, for the sheer
sense of glory in the use of them, and the kindred impulse to
conceal this desire behind a mask of sham utilitarianism, has
never been so strong as it is today. If this is the case, the reason
may be that we lack that self-confidence which is fostered by doing
things for ourselves, but is to some extent weakened by every new
tool that we invent. As we come to rely more and more on our
machines, the glory of using them becomes a drug whose magic
conceals from us the fact that, behind this façade of machinery, we
ourselves are sorry examples of the human kind. In driving a fast
car we fancy ourselves strong, and in tuning the wireless we fancy
ourselves clever; but this is self-deception, and we know it. It is our
refuge against our self-disgust at bleached and undeveloped bodies, and minds choked with smatterings of useless information. It is
this abnormal lack of self-confidence which leads our civilization
both to insist upon clothes and to worship machinery.[16]

The use of human labour, hired or servile, gives the same kind of
feeling as the use of tools; for, as Aristotle puts it, the slave is a
living tool. And this feeling underlies our conviction that having
servants to do your work is grand, doing it for yourself undignified.
It underlies the fascination of 'business', which is not (as the
utilitarian rationalization pretends) a means to getting rich, but a

[16] Collingwood conducts a sustained polemic against the mechanical element in
civilization in AM, below.

way of achieving power over other men. It underlies the desire for political power and victory in war. Where power over men is inordinately desired, one may be sure that those who desire it are driven by fear of their own weakness, and ready to go to any length in the search for a delusive reassurance. But men are harder to control than machines, having wills of their own; so, whereas the feebler souls among ourselves [31] forget their self-dissatisfaction in the cult of machinery, the stronger do it by becoming kings of business, political bosses, or dictators. But here again, as in the desire for clothes and tools, the impulse in itself is universal and healthy. It is only when it is disowned by a world of obsessed utilitarians that it becomes a madness.

The same self-confidence is procured, in a slightly different way, by means of sport. Why does a man play golf for exercise, but use a motor-car to reach the course? If (as he will doubtless tell us) it is because golf is better exercise than walking, why does he not stay at home and dig in the garden? His preference for golf over digging is not utilitarian. Digging in the garden is a menial occupation, slightly ridiculous, like running for a train. He therefore deputes the first to a gardener and the second to a motor-car; and then, having done this systematically with all kinds of real work, discovers that his body needs exercise. He therefore invents a form of bodily labour which serves as a further protection to his tottering self-esteem because the tasks involved in it are fictitious ones, which need be no harder than he wants them to be. Sport protects a man's dignity because in it he is never in naked contact with real difficulties, never under compulsion to use the utmost of his strength and skill. However hard the tasks he has set himself, there is no need for him to carry them out. Even in hunting big game, or climbing terrible mountains, he is like a child playing at savages, who knows that there is tea at home. Sport, like the use of tools, is a thing of universal human value; but the making of it into a kind of religion, concealed behind the utilitarian cult of exercise, is one mark of a society that is losing its nerve.

This analysis of things familiar in ourselves may give a clue to understanding certain things in 'savages'. It is well known [32] that they regard all new inventions, all new accretions of power, as having what we commonly call a magical side. The plough is not only an engine, well adapted to its purpose; it is a focus of ritual, charged with *mana*. To the civilized anthropologist, this plough-

worship is an odd fact. It seems to imply either that the savage
ascribes the plough's efficacy not to its mechanical qualities but to
its magical ones, which is absurd, or that he thinks of it as having,
not the one kind of efficiency which it really possesses, but two
kinds, one mechanical and the other magical. If the anthropologist
would analyse his wife's attitude towards the Hoover, he would be
able to clear up this puzzle. The plough, like the Hoover, can
be looked at in either of two ways. It is an engine or tool, to be
understood mechanically; and it is also a kind of servant monster, a
cross between a slave and a god: like a slave in its absolute obedience to his will, like a god in being able to do things that no mere
man could do. A sociologist may say that it is merely a development of the digging-stick, but from the cultivator's point of view it
is nothing of the kind. The digging-stick has to be driven downwards to pierce the earth and levered up to turn it, by sheer
strength and skill. The plough pierces and turns the earth by
its own weight and shape, when simply moved forward by the
animal that pulls it. It does not save labour in the utilitarian
sense of increasing the cultivator's output for a given amount of
digging. It takes the digging off his hands altogether. Having a
plough, he no longer needs to pit his own strength against the soil's
stubbornness.

This is why the possession of a plough is more than merely
useful; it is glorious. The plough bestows a double blessing, once
in utility and once in this feeling of glory. This is the source of the
'savage's' so-called magical attitude towards [33] his tools. In
one sense it is an unscientific attitude; it is non-scientific, just
like the boy's glory in possessing a watch, or the woman's in
possessing a Hoover, or the man's in possessing a powerful car.
But it is not anti-scientific; it does not imply failure to understand
the mechanical principles on which the tool works. On the contrary,
savages who did not thus understand their tools could neither make
them nor use them. The sense of glory in the use of tools does
certainly disappear when we begin worrying about their scientific
aspect—valve-clearances and spark-gaps and so forth—but it is
only increased by a scientific understanding of the whole machine
triumphantly carrying out its function. The better a savage understands his plough, the more keenly he feels the joy of using it.

The ritual which we find savages performing in connexion with
their use of all tools—axes, hunting-gear, ploughs, boats, weapons,

and so forth—is their way of expressing this feeling of glory. Like all joy, it demands expression; and since he does not suffer from the utility-complex, the savage sees no reason why he should not express it, although the expression has no utilitarian value. He dances and sings his joy. As he does not worship machinery for its own sake, but because he needs it, the joy does not wear off. It renews itself with every using of the tool. Thus it comes about that whenever he ploughs or sows or reaps, whenever he takes his fish-spear to the river or his axe to the woods, whenever he takes his sword and club and goes out to war, he sings and dances to celebrate the prowess of his implements, and the glory which he finds in mastering that prowess for his own ends.

[34] Now imagine that a group of cultivators is seen by a curious observer dancing and singing their joy in the sense of power given them by such a marvellous invention as the plough, and asked why they do it. In the first place, such a question would seem wholly unintelligible. If you come to think of it, the boot is on the other leg: such people would be very right to ask you or me why we do not similarly express our joy in the electric light or the Underground Railway. The asking of the question, as it were, puts them in the wrong. It implies the assumption that normal people get no 'kick' at all out of owning a boat or a rabbiting-plane, or, if they do, bottle up their feelings for fear of being laughed at. It is 'civilization', not 'savagery', that takes explaining. But once they have got down to the very queer job of explaining what is so obvious to so unintelligent a stranger, they will no doubt try to tell him what [35] I, in my own way, have been trying to explain. They will say that the tool in question works of itself, has in its own right a power of producing certain determinate effects. This is literal truth, as I have shown; and if, instead, they had used the stranger's own jargon and said that it converted a forward movement into a downward one, he would have understood. As it is, he writes in his notebook 'These people attribute a soul to inanimate objects: animism.' They go on to explain that, although this power belongs to the instrument and not to themselves, they can direct it. He writes down 'this soul is, however, controlled by their own soul: magic as the technique of animism'. Next, they say that this ritual is somehow intimately connected with the fact that they are con-scious of their control over the instrument. So he writes: 'this control, by which they make the plough's soul do what they

want, is effected by means of a magic ritual, whose purpose is to strengthen their own *mana* to the point of forcing the plough to obey it'. Then they say that, although the plough has this queer power in it, it cannot use it of itself; the power is latent until they bring it out of its hut and, after the usual dances and songs, start ploughing with it. 'The ritual dance', he writes, 'is ultimately designed to confer on the plough the magical powers attributed to it. This seems inconsistent with animism; but on this point my informants were very confused and self-contradictory.' Finally he asks them what would happen if they tried ploughing without the usual ritual. They say that they don't know because they never tried; and anyhow they would never dream of doing such a thing. He writes: 'they have no conception of experiment or scientific method, and none of natural causation. They perform the ritual quite irrationally, under a sense of blind compulsion probably to be explained on the analogy of the compulsion-neurosis.'

[36] In this dialogue I have no doubt exaggerated the savages' power to give an accurate and coherent account of their ideas and institutions. Probably, confused by the incomprehensible nature of the original question, they lose all memory of what they actually do and think, and answer more or less at random, quite justifying the anthropologist's worst suspicions about their intellects. A fireman was asked what exactly he did when the fire alarm rang. He replied 'I don't know; but if it rang I should know fast enough.' What I have tried to show by my dialogue is that, even if the savages gave completely true answers to the anthropologist, he would look at these answers from the standpoint of our utilitarian obsession, and therefore describe what he heard in terms of animism and a host of other ideas which need not on that account be attributed to savages at all.

We have now passed in review three groups of magical customs: those connected with the 'external soul', those connected with ritual ablutions, and those arising out of the use of tools. In every case we have found that the magical practice has its basis in emotions which are universally human and can be verified as existing, and even sometimes as giving rise to definite customs, in and among ourselves. We have found that such customs depend on no scientific or pseudo-scientific theory; that is an illusion which arises from a mistaken attempt to understand them in utilitarian terms; their emotional basis sufficiently accounts for them by itself. Before leaving this subject, however, it would be well to consider a fourth group of magical practices or beliefs, namely those which anthropologists call taboos. For when anthropologists describe a prohibition or a refusal as a taboo, they mean that it is a prohibition or a refusal with a magical sanction. Taboo is thus a special case of magic, and any theory of magic should be called upon to explain it.

[37] Take a case where pigs are taboo because they are reserved to be eaten at a tribal feast. A hungry tribesman encountering a pig at large, without witnesses, is very conscious of a desire to kill and eat it; but he refrains, not through fear of the law, since there is no one to accuse him, nor yet through what we should call a moral scruple, since the pig is taboo only because a taboo has been put upon it, and moral scruples do not arise in that way; but through fear of the magical sanction to which breach of the taboo would expose him.

If our analysis of magic is correct, this sanction must be describable in terms of emotion; and if our method of approach is correct, the emotions concerned must be discoverable in ourselves and may perhaps be found at the basis of certain customs existing in our own society. These customs will be in the nature of prohibitions or refusals; and negatively they will have two characteristics: their sanction will not be a legal sanction, involving prosecution and punishment by the officers of the law, and it will not be a moral sanction, consisting in the idea that to break the custom is to do something inherently wrong.

A young man going in for an examination where he is instructed to wear black clothes, if the weather is hot, may very well wish that he could go in flannels. But he will not do this, because he knows that if he did he would be denied entrance to the examination-room. Here is a legal sanction; none the less legal for depending, not on the law of the land, but on the law of his university; and none the less legal for the fact that the only penalty is loss of the right to sit, thus clothed, for the examination.

The same young man, invited to a dinner-party, is told to wear a [38] dinner-jacket; and once more, although he would be more comfortable in flannels, he obeys. Suppose we ask him, what is the sanction of this rule? What ill consequences does he fear, if he should go in flannels? He would find this a rather difficult question to answer. He knows that he would not be handed over to the police, or beaten, or otherwise maltreated. He has no reason to think that he would be turned away from the door. If once he got in, he is pretty sure that no one would scold him, or make the smallest reference in conversation to his dress. But there would be an almost intolerable atmosphere of disapproval; and being a sensitive young man he would feel the oppression of this atmosphere like a thundercloud on his spirits. He would be most uncomfortable in his inside; very likely his dinner would disagree with him and he would suffer agonies of indigestion and a sleepless night; and for years afterwards he would feel quite unwell whenever he thought of his experience.

There is no question here of moral delinquency. If that were the case, his sufferings would be less had the thing been an accident; had he, for example, been decoyed into the middle of the dinner-party in his flannels by a false message that the dinner-party had been cancelled and replaced by an informal party at which ordinary clothes would be worn. But the fact that he had broken the rule innocently would here make no difference to his consciousness of having broken it, and all the painful emotions therein implied.

For we must observe that the discomfort and so forth which are the penalty of his act are not in the ordinary sense consequences of the act. They are the emotions attendant on his consciousness of having done it. There is between the act and the penalty no intermediate link which might break; no avenging hand [39] which in mercy might withhold or lessen the blow. It is his own feelings that punish him for having broken a ceremonial rule whose essence (for we have seen that such ceremonial clothes are magic) is that it expresses feeling.

A thick-skinned and brutish young man might argue himself out of this penalty, on the ground that though he had shocked the party he had done them no harm and they had done none to him: he had not been kicked down the front steps, he had not been sent away hungry, and he had not received a challenge from the host to fight a duel. But a young man like that would be, as we say, little better than a savage.

The difficulty which we find in understanding taboo is chiefly due to the attitude expressed in those words. We like to think that refinement of feeling is a product of civilization, and that savages (proverbially people who have no manners, and whose customs are beastly) are defective in it. Beastliness of customs is a matter of taste; but the actual people whom we call savages are as sensitive to good or bad manners as ourselves. Indeed, they are more so. Our own civilization, with its elaborate legal system, has tended to harden the distinction between ill conduct that is punishable at law and that which is not, with the result that we attach, as a rule, exaggerated importance to the former and ridiculously little to the latter. Travellers going no further afield than Spain or Crete can vouch for the fact that the standard of manners is never so high, and the rules of courtesy are never so punctiliously observed, in our law-ruled countries as they are in places where the man to whom you are talking carries a knife. In proportion as the king's writ is less effective, the distinction between crime and discourtesy tends to vanish, and increasing importance is attached to those emotional sanctions which, in all societies, attend what we call a breach of good manners.

[40] The anthropologist, explaining our example in terms of magic conceived as pseudo-science, will say that the young man has offended against the *mana* of his host, and that this *mana* will avenge itself by sending a demon to lacerate his interior. But this is only a metaphorical and picturesque way of describing a very simple emotional reaction. If we find it hard to connect the case of an ill-dressed young man with the case of a pig-stealing Polynesian, the reason is either that we cannot bring ourselves to think of a Polynesian as possessed of what we call nice feelings; or that we have not enough psychological knowledge to understand the devastating effects which a purely emotional shock may produce; or that we understand the Polynesian's situation in his society so ill that we do not see why stealing a pig should produce in him the kind of effects which the wrong kind of evening tie, as we know, produces in us.

The 'savage' of whom we are thinking lives in a society whose judicial system is, compared with ours, elementary. If such a society is to be well-ordered, there must be some method of securing obedience both to universal law and to particular *ad hoc* decree without relying on the ubiquity of the policeman. The material for such a method lies ready to hand in the idea of good manners, with its emotional sanction. And there is no need to intensify this idea by devices of statecraft or priestcraft. As we have seen, it is already stronger in such a society than among ourselves, precisely because it has not been paralysed by the development of a tentacular legal system, which is one aspect of our deliberately rationalistic, thick-skinned attitude towards life. Thus the general form of a taboo-system for regulating human conduct, which even in our own law-ridden civilization retains its validity over several large parts [41] of life, applies over larger and larger areas according as the society in question is in a legal sense more and more primitive: a conclusion which follows at once, if we grant the premiss that the savage's emotional nature is very much like our own, and that where we differ from him is not in our feelings but in our institutions.

Granted the general form of a taboo-system, that is, a system of prohibitions with purely emotional sanctions, as something always and everywhere found in every human society, different societies will differ from each other in two ways.

First, they will differ in the extent to which this system covers the various sides of social activity, the area of this extent diminishing as law develops, and shifting its position as this or that department of activity comes under the purview of law or is withdrawn from it. To take an example of the latter type, the disappearance of the ecclesiastical courts in England has handed over to the reign of taboo the sexual offences with which, while those courts existed, they had the power to deal: and this has given many English people the odd idea that there is an essential and eternal connexion between taboo and sexual ethics. Again, the repeal of the prohibition laws in the United States has had the same effect there with regard to drunkenness.

Secondly, the particular content which a given society puts into this general form—the particular kinds of action on which it places a taboo prohibition—may vary almost infinitely. There is no need to illustrate this in detail. It is enough to say that, once we recognize the ubiquity and necessity of taboo as a social institution, the corporate wisdom of a society may very well be judged from a study of its taboos, directed to answering the question whether they are well adapted to giving it the fullest and healthiest life that can be had in the conditions in which that society is obliged to live.

[42] The general conception of magic as the expression of emotion gives rise to a further problem which must now be considered. The expression of emotion as such is the essential business of art; and therefore the result of our analysis is not only to withdraw magic from its association with science, but also to bring it into relation with art.

That such a relation exists, and is a close one, is well known. It is a commonplace that primitive art, such as that of the palaeolithic cave-man, appears to have a magical motive. It is a commonplace that, in the higher civilizations, those developments of art which we generally regard as supreme in their kind—Greek drama and sculpture, medieval architecture, Renaissance painting—have generally had a close connection with religious beliefs and practices. It is a commonplace, again, that the utilitarian obsession is equally hostile to art and to religion, and that a civilization suffering from it tends to suppress both these things. We are thus familiar with the idea that the fortunes of art and religion, or of art and magic (since magic and religion, whatever may be the precise distinction between them, are again very intimately connected), are somehow bound up together. The reason for this close connexion, we can now see, is that art and magic are to this extent the same thing, that each is essentially the expression of emotion. We must therefore ask: is magic simply identical with art, and if not, what is the difference between them?[17]

All magic is art, but all art is not magic. There is no magic without some kind of artistic work—song, dance, drawing, or modelling,—which serves as its vehicle. In order to satisfy the needs of the magician, however, it is not necessary that these should be a very high kind of art; magic verses may be a poor sort of [43] doggerel, the clay image may be, from a sculptor's point of view, contemptible, and so forth. Thus, though there is a magical motive for producing works of art, there is none for producing good works of art: and when these are actually produced for magical purposes, their high artistic quality is due to a specifically aesthetic impulse and tradition, not to a magical.[18] There is no reason to suppose the paint-smudged pebbles of the Aurignac period less efficacious or satisfying, in their religious or magical aspect, than the exquisite drawings of the earlier cave-men. And since high artistic quality is not demanded by the magical and religious impulse, but only by a specifically aesthetic one, its

---

[17] Collingwood is later to discuss this distinction in *PA*, ch. 4, 'Art as Magic', 57–77.

[18] Cf. *PA* 69: 'When magical art reaches a high aesthetic level, this is because the society to which it belongs ... demands of it an aesthetic excellence quite other than the very modest degree of competence which would enable it to fulfil its magical function.'

attainment is regarded, by persons whose attention is strongly focused on magical or religious interests, as a mark of dispersed energy and divided allegiance. This is why, as we can see for ourselves by merely looking about us, it is on the whole preferred that the art which serves the cause of religion, patriotism, or social ceremony should be rather bad art.

Magic is thus a special modification of art: that is, a special way of expressing emotion. The war-dance, with its accompaniment of song, which is the magical prelude to the act of fighting, is obviously a work of art: its function is to express the somewhat complicated but quite definite emotions characteristic of a people about to engage in war.[19] Now, it is an observation as old as Aristotle that when we express our emotions of pity and terror by watching a tragic drama, we experience what he called a catharsis of these emotions. By expressing them, objectifying them into something we can contemplate, we ease ourselves of their burden: the emotion works itself off into the work of art, finding thus a way of discharging itself which is, so to speak, an alternative to the normal discharge through practical activity. If we **[44]** discharged all our emotions in this way, life would come to an end for lack of emotional motive power;[20] but when we are (as a Greek poet puts it) sick with longing for what cannot be had, we experience an emotion which no practical activity can discharge; and by easing ourselves of it through artistic expression we enable ourselves to turn away from the unattainable object and take up again the thread of practical life. The poet who wrote

> Christ! that my love were in my arms
> And I in my bed again,[21]

was not vainly indulging a desire for what he could not have; he was facing the fact of his desire, hammering it into a poem, and thus conquering it.

---

[19] Cf. *PA* 66: 'A tribe which dances a war-dance before going to fight its neighbours is working up its warlike emotions.'

[20] Cf. *PA*, esp. 'Conclusion', 325–36.

[21] 'Westron winde, when will thou blow, The smalle raine downe can raine? Christ if my love were in my armes, And I in my bed againe.' See *Medieval English Lyrics: A Critical Anthology*, ed. R. T. Davies (London: Faber & Faber, 1963), 291. Davies dates the lines as earlier 16th cent.

It is here that magic differs from art proper. The war-dance does not effect a catharsis of the warlike emotions: on the contrary, it crystallizes them as emotions, and confirms the dancers' resolution to discharge them through the channel of action. It is essential to genuine magic that the emotion it expresses should not be discharged by the mere expression of it. The distinction between magic and art proper thus turns on the question: how can an emotion be expressed without effecting a catharsis of it?

An emotion may be considered in either of two ways. It may be considered in itself, as a peculiar and self-contained experience; or it may be considered in its relation to practical life, as a motive for acting in a particular manner. Neither is an arbitrary or false way of considering it, for any emotion actually is both these things. And it is possible to study it in either aspect without necessarily considering the other. I may attend to my actual feelings in a given situation without considering the direction in which they tend to make me act; or I may attend to the way in which they lead me to act, without closely considering what in themselves they are.

[45] The business of art is to apprehend and express an emotion considered in itself. The artist (or rather, every man in so far as he is an artist) expresses his feelings as self-contained experiences: the question which interests him is what these experiences are, and his construction or enjoyment of a work of art is the creation or discovery of a form of expression which serves to answer that question. That is why the greatest triumphs of art are achieved in the expression of feelings for which practical life provides no outlet: longings that are doomed to frustration, or rebellion against the tragedy and futility of life itself. But for their expression in art, feelings of this kind would have perforce to be disowned and repressed for the sake of effective action; as so repressed, they would become a source of hidden weakness and discouragement, sapping the foundations of all our activity; and hence Aristotle was right to see in tragedy a therapeutic agent for promoting a sane and healthy practical life.

The business of magic is to apprehend and express an emotion considered as a motive for action. The ritual prelude to the work of agriculture or hunting or war expresses the feelings with which that work is undertaken. These feelings are expressed not as pure experiences, not simply because they are the feelings we discover in ourselves on a certain type of occasion (had that been the case, a

war-dance might very well have expressed our fear of wounds and
death); but as the motives instigating us to act in a certain type of
way: thus the war-dance expresses our hope of victory, and so
forth.

Hence, in spite of their close connexion, there is always a certain
hostility between art and magic. To the artist, magic seems dis-
honest; because it expresses, not all that we feel, but only those
parts of it which are selected for emphasis [46] because they
instigate to this particular form of action: the war-dance hypocritically conceals our cowardice, the funeral lamentation our relief at
parting with persons who have burdened and oppressed us, the
marriage rejoicing our fear of entanglements and responsibilities.
To the devotee of magic, art seems immoral; for it emphasizes not
only the feelings which are right and proper, and help us to build
up a satisfactory life, but equally those on which we must not act,
and which it would be better if we did not experience. Each is right
in its own way, and each has its necessary place in life. But confusion arises when the two are not kept distinct: when, to take a
modern instance, a lyrical and tragic poet like Mr T. S. Eliot is
reproved by his contemporaries for not devoting his art to the great
aim of furthering the regeneration of society by a communist
revolution; in other words, for practising poetry when he might
be practising magic, and writing verses which can never be sung to
accompany a war-dance.[22]

A further problem of the same kind is presented by the relation
between magic and religion. At certain relatively primitive stages
of civilization, the two are hardly, if at all, distinguishable. And
what is recognized in those stages of civilization as magic is redis-
coverable in higher stages as a magical element inseparable from all
religion. For the rationalist, this is a slur on religion as such; but
not for us, because we have seen by now that magic is a permanent
form of human experience, and pervades the secular part of our
lives no less than the religious. Hence, in analysing the higher
stages of civilization, a distinction between magic and religion is
indispensable.

---

[22] Collingwood defends Eliot on similar grounds in *PA*: 'To readers who want
not amusement or magic, but poetry, and who want to know what poetry can be, if it
is to be neither of these things, *The Waste Land* supplies an answer' (335).

In the early days of anthropology, when students brought up in the atmo- [47] sphere of Christianity began to study the life of relatively primitive peoples, their inquiry into the religion of these peoples took the form of asking what beliefs they held concerning God. In some cases, they got no answer to this question, and reported that they had found a people without any religion at all. Later, it began to be thought that the question had been wrongly asked, and that the right method was not to inquire for creeds but to watch ceremonies. Now ceremonies, as social customs practised for their emotional expressiveness, are magic: and hence the new principle amounted to this: that among so-called savages magic is the only religion we can find. This too has undergone a certain modification in recent years, and it is now held that creeds are not so rare among primitive peoples as we used to think.

From these considerations it would appear that when we distinguish religion from magic we imply that religion has, or is, a creed, a doctrine concerning a god or gods; something of philosophical import, claiming to be true and demanding expression in a form of words which is either the germ or the summary of a system of theology. In magic pure and simple, based as it is on emotion, nothing of the sort is present. Magic as such is no more theology than it is science; no more bad theology than it is bad science. Nor is it a kind of anti-theology, a thing which sound theology ought to expel from the body of believers. If there is a Christian or a Muslim theology, there will also be certain emotions aroused by its acceptance, and these will find expression in a Christian or Muslim ritual which is the magical side of these respective religions. There is no need for the rationalist to gloat over this conclusion or for the believer to shrink from [48] it. For the result of our inquiries in this chapter has been that the term magic, from being a term of reproach, has become a term of description: it no longer implies that the thing so denominated is foolish or in any way discreditable, it expresses scientifically the nature of that thing and assigns to it a permanent and necessary place in every department of human life.

There remains, however, a grain of truth in the bitter remark that a history of magic is a history of human folly and suffering, beyond the sense in which it is a mere reflexion of the truth that all human history is the history of these things: the sense in which, as Hegel has put it, history is a vast shambles in which the happiness of peoples, the virtue of individuals, and the wisdom of princes have again and again been mercilessly done to death.[23] For magic, which in itself is nothing but the expression of those emotions on which we propose to act, is liable to a special perversion; and it is this perversion of magic to which, when we speak of magic, we sometimes exclusively refer.

The perversion of magic is the false belief that when we have expressed the emotions instigating a certain course of action we have as good as done the corresponding action itself: the belief that the fruits of action can be enjoyed by means of merely expressing our desire for them. The effect of this illusion is to change the function of magic in its relation to action. From being a prelude to action, it becomes a substitute for it. When such a perversion has taken place, everything that has been said about the unscientific folly of magical practices is justified. For, first, the people who are affected by it cease, so far as they really are its victims, trying to realize their ends by reasonable means, and substitute the absurd attempt to bring them about by **[49]** magical ones, thus justifying the description of magic as a kind of pseudo-science; for example, instead of fighting their enemies they will make spells against them, and instead of curing diseases they will try to charm them away. And, secondly, they will falsely persuade themselves that they can and must do by magic things which human beings cannot do at all; for example, they will claim the power to make rain, or to bring the sun or moon safely through the crisis of an eclipse, by means of charms and ceremonies. Such perversions, whose folly is not hard to recognize when we study them in societies other than our own, play a great part in the history of magic; as great, indeed, as the part played by scientific and philosophical errors in the history of science and philosophy. But they are perversions of magic, not magic itself; and it is our business to see how they arise.

The general principle of their origin is easily stated. A magical custom is misunderstood by the people who practise it, and thus believed to have a function which it cannot really have. For example, the true function of the war-dance is to hearten the warriors; to consolidate their hope of victory and their will to fight. Actually, it thus plays an important part in preparing for their

---

[23] G. W. F. Hegel, *Lectures on the Philosophy of History*, tr. J. Sibree (London, 1988).

success in the field. And in so far as the heightened morale thus achieved will appear on the battlefield as equivalent to a lowered morale on the part of their enemies, it is easy, and subject to the necessary qualification not false, to say that the war-dance weakens the enemies' will to fight, or even that it destroys the efficacy of their weapons. The qualification, of course, is that the relation between the dance and these effects is not an immediate one: it comes about only through the improvement in one's own morale as shown on the field of battle. But the qualification is easily over-looked. Even today, medical [50] men do not always find it easy to distinguish the beneficial effects of a treatment which directly attacks the disease from those of one which increases the patient's confidence in his power of recovery. It is the rule, rather than the exception, that success in human affairs depends on the co-operation of several factors, some of which are under human control while others are not. Thus, in agriculture, a good crop depends partly on the cultivator's skill and labour, partly on the fertility of his seed, partly on rainfall. If his agricultural magic heartens him to cultivate more energetically and conscientiously, it will certainly in general improve his chances of success; but failure to analyse the various factors needed for that success may lead him to fancy that its effect is to make the seed fertile or to make the rain fall. At a certain stage of reflexion, when he has not accurately distinguished these factors, he may believe that his magic indifferently affects all three. At a further stage, becoming aware that it affects only himself, he might think it wise to invent other forms of magic affecting the other two.

This is the sense in which magic can be described as the tech-nique of animism. As we have already seen, there is one case in which mere magic, without any further activity to which it might be the prelude, can achieve results. This is where the emotions expressed by the magic impinge, as it were, directly on human beings. No one whose feelings are at all sensitive can avoid being depressed in spirits by the malice or hostility of his fellow-men, especially when they are his neighbours or tribesmen, and when their malice is deliberately and formally expressed. The magical ritual which expresses this malice is thus already, as I have explained above, an assault upon the reputation, the self-confidence, and even the health of its [51] victim. A person who knows this, and whose grasp upon the general principles of physics and chemistry is weak (although he may well understand their application in certain familiar types of case), might easily imagine that the seed which comes to life in his own or his neighbour's field, or the tool which comes to life in his own or his neighbour's hand, is amenable to the same treatment, and can be heartened to do its work by one magical ritual, or discouraged from doing it by another. By a natural encroachment of the same illusion, it may be applied to things over which man has no control whatever: rain and sunshine, drought and flood, the stability of the earth, and the stars in their courses.

These perversions arise from misconceiving the relation between magic and the objects on which it is directed. Another type arises from misconceiving its relation to the person who performs it. As we have seen, magic consolidates our emotions regarded as springs of action; art, by effecting a catharsis of them, 'earths' them. But the distinction between art and magic is a fine one. If it is overlooked, the would-be magician runs a danger of discharging, through an act of aesthetic creation, the feelings which ought to remain alive as motives to practical action. A man who is cursing his enemy might, if he was not careful, end by composing a poetical invective against him and thereby discharging his hostility. In so far as the victim suffers in his feelings, that might not matter; but if he cursed the river that flooded his farm so satisfyingly that he no longer felt any need to build an embankment, the expression of his emotions would have over-reached itself and he would have found a refuge (as psychologists put it) from an intractable reality in a wish-fulfilment fantasy. Just as misconceiving the objective function of [52] magic perverts it into the pseudo-science of Tylor's theory, so misconceiving its subjective function perverts it into the imaginative wish-fulfilment which Freud has so well described. These false theories of magic, whose falsity I have shown above, can thus be explained, on the theory here expounded, as descriptions of alternative perversions to which magic is liable.

The disastrous effects of this double perversion have been so often and so eloquently described that there is no need to detail them here. What is perhaps worth saying is that, if they had ever completely dominated the human mind, human life itself would have come to an end in an orgy of misdirected activity. But in the most primitive societies the mere pressure of practical needs has kept men relatively sane. The primitive warrior dances and fights;

he does not dance instead of fighting. The primitive cultivator practises his agricultural magic, but does not allow it to distract his attention from the work of agriculture. In such societies, these perversions seem to flourish only where they can do little harm: in man's conception of his relation to those things over which he has no control. And in that limited sphere it may even be true that his delusions serve a useful purpose, as giving him courage to live in a world where courage is needed if one is to live at all. It is in the higher civilizations, where inherited scientific knowledge has eased the immediate shock of man against his natural environment, that these perversions especially run riot, as in the witchcraft of modern India or seventeenth-century Europe. And this is why anthropological science, when it tries to study magic, has so constantly mistaken the perversion of magic for magic itself.

5

EXCAVATING *CINDERELLA* AND *KING LEAR*

Few stories are so well or widely known as *Cinderella*. Moreover, we are fortunate in possessing a collection of 345 variants of it, abstracted and arranged by the late Miss Marian Roalfe Cox;[1] and for the purposes of this chapter I shall treat this as my material, without attempting to supplement it by adding variants discovered since it was published. If the reader is disposed to blame me for this omission, I would remind him that completeness in such collections of material is unattainable, and that if 345 versions do not give a sufficient sample of the whole to form the basis of a tolerably secure inductive study, then the very idea of an inductive study is an illusion.

Miss Cox divided her variants into three classes. The first, or *Cinderella* proper, is the story of a girl who is ill-treated (almost invariably by her stepmother) and receives magical help, generally from an animal, which enables her to attend some gathering where she is seen by an eligible young man. He loves her, and following her homewards picks up a shoe which she has let fall; by means of this he recognizes her and marries her.

The second class is called *Catskin*. Here the heroine leaves home in order to escape from her father, who has fallen in love with her. After various adventures, in the course of which she commonly becomes a servant in a great house, she attends a gathering as in

Bodleian Library Collingwood Papers, dep. 21/10. The chapter title in this case is the editors', not Collingwood's. The MS essay is untitled.

[1] * *Cinderella: Three Hundred and Forty-Five Variants of Cinderella, Catskin, and Cap o' Rushes, abstracted and tabulated, with a discussion of Medieval Analogues and Notes*, with an Introduction by Andrew Lang, by Marian Roalfe Cox (London: David Nutt, for the FLS, 1893). [Essays on the *Cinderella* narrative were published in the same year by Alfred Nutt, 'Cinderella and Britain', *F-L* 4/2 (June 1893), 133–41; Joseph Jacobs, 'Cinderella in Britain', *F-L* 4/3 (Sept 1893), 269–84; Andrew Lang, 'Cinderella and the Diffusion of Tales', *F-L* 4/4 (Dec. 1893), 423–33.]

Cinderella proper; but is ultimately recognized by means of food which she cooks for her lover.

The third class is called *Cap o' Rushes*. It resembles *Catskin* except in the opening: for here the girl is driven from home by her father, **[2]** who is angry with her for not expressing her love for him in what he thinks a warm enough manner. As a rule, when he asks her how much she loves him, she replies that she loves him like salt. The story ends, after she has won her husband, with a saltless meal designed to convince the father of the value of salt.

Beside these three classes, of which Miss Cox has given respectively 131, 64, and 26 versions,[2] she adds two other classes: one of 83 'indeterminate' variants, inclining to one or another of the main types, and one of 23 'hero-tales'[3] where a similar story is told about a boy instead of a girl.

These stories are found all over Europe; in Asia (where the most significant are three in India, two in Annam and one in Japan), in Africa (only four, including one in Mauritius) and in America (one in Martinique, one in Brazil, one in Chile). It is easy to see in them all a wish-fulfilment fantasy of a very natural type; the neglected and persecuted girl, who when given her chance turns out a dazzling beauty and makes a splendid marriage. Fantasies of that kind must have grown up wherever girls have been, or have imagined themselves to be, misunderstood by their families. But this will not account for the origin of the story. It would prove at once too much and too little. If it were the sufficient cause of the story's origin, the distribution would surely be far wider; and if it were the sole cause, the details in the different versions could never show such elaborate similarities. No such theory will explain, for example, why practically all the *Cinderellas* culminate in recognition by means of a dropped shoe, and practically all the *Catskins* in recognition by means of food. The more closely we examine the details, the more impossible it becomes to believe that these **[3]** stories have grown up independently, from similar psychological causes. Nor can we

---

[2] Including abstracts found in the appendix and in a section on 'Additional Variants' at the end of the volume (533–5), Cox actually lists 134 abstracts of 'A: Cinderella', 78 of 'B: Catskin', and 23 of 'C: Cap o' Rushes'. The 'Additional Variants' include three of 'Cinderella' and 'two Irish stories'.

[3] A footnote is indicated here but not supplied. Cox lists 82 variants in 'D', the 'Indeterminate' category. Collingwood's tally of Cox's 'hero tales' appears to be correct.

explain the similarity on the anthropological method, by regarding the stories, wherever they are found, as descriptions of a widespread ritual. There is no ritual known to us, to which they in any way correspond. We are forced to accept the hypothesis of diffusion.

The entire series of *Cinderella*-stories in the wider sense, including all Miss Cox's subdivisions, thus forms an excellent subject matter for investigation by the methods of the Finnish school.[+] I shall not weary the reader with a complete exposition of such a study, but I will indicate a few of the results to which it leads.

The three main classes are so interrelated that we are compelled to think of them as derived from a common original. Their distribution shows that this original had its home either in Europe or in Asia; for the versions found in other continents are easily explained by diffusion from one or other of those two. If we examine the Asiatic versions, we shall soon find that those from India and Annam have the best claim to be regarded as most nearly representing the original. No. 25 (I use Miss Cox's numbers throughout), from Bombay, tells of a heroine ill-treated by her stepmother. She is nourished by a cow which gives her milk; the stepmother accordingly resolves to kill it. The cow tells her that all will be well, but that she must on no account eat its flesh. The cow is killed and the heroine collects its bones and skin and buries them. The prince is about to choose a bride; the heroine is not allowed to compete, but is left at home to cook while her stepsister goes to the palace. The cow now comes to life and gives her dresses and gold clogs. She goes to the palace, and drops one of the [4] clogs; the prince picks it up, traces her, and marries her. The stepmother and stepsister are punished.

But for local colour in details, this would almost pass for an ordinary European *Cinderella*. But before deciding that it is a European story strayed to India, we must look at the other Indian variants. Here is one from Madras (235).

The heroine is a magic girl from whose lips precious stones fall when she speaks, and her soul is contained in a necklace she wore

---

[+] This is the first occasion on which Collingwood has mentioned the Finnish school and may be one reason to think that he had not settled the order of material for his study when he set it aside. Collingwood recalls the work of the Finnish school in a footnote to fo. 14 of FT6 'The Authorship of Fairy Tales', below.

from birth.[5] She loses a shoe in the jungle, and a hunting prince finds it, traces her, and marries her. His first wife hates her, and steals the necklace, so that she dies; but in the night she comes to life again. One night she bears a son, and thereafter revives in the tomb at night and suckles him. The prince, one night, hears the baby cry and discovers the truth.

Another variant (307) has been collected among the Salsette Christians of Bombay. A seventh daughter is magically born to a mendicant, from a blister on his thumb. The parents expose all seven girls in the forest; they find a house with seven vacant rooms, and the heroine's room contains magic dresses and gold shoes. They go to church, where the heroine loses a shoe and the prince falls in love with her and ultimately marries her. She bears a son; her sisters bury the child alive and tell the husband she has borne a stone. This happens three times, after which the heroine is disgraced and imprisoned, but restored and avenged.

The two versions from Annam (68, 69) are much alike, and we need only summarize the second and fuller variant. The heroine and her foster-sister hold a fishing-competition to decide which is the elder. [5] The foster-sister steals the heroine's fish until she has only one left, which she makes into a pet. While she is watching the goats her foster-sister kills and eats it; she buries its bones and they turn into gold shoes. A crow carries off one of these and drops it at the palace, where the king finds it and invites everyone to come and try it on as a marriage test. The rightful owner is not allowed to go; her foster-mother and foster-sister keep her at home working on two tasks, disentangling thread and sorting out a mixed mass of grain; she must do these before she may go to the palace. Ants and birds come and do the work for her; she goes, and the shoe fits her. But the foster-mother begs the king to let her come home for a few days. They make her climb a palm tree and cut it down, and she falls into a lake and turns into a golden turtle. As she has disappeared, the foster-sister marries the king instead. He finds the gold turtle and makes a pet of it, but his wife kills and eats it. Its carapace turns into a bamboo shoot. She eats that; its rind turns into a bird. She eats that; its feathers turn into a tree which bears a gourd-like fruit supposed to resemble a woman in shape. An old

---

[5] Cf. Frazer, *The Golden Bough*, part 7, *Balder the Beautiful: The Fire-Festivals of Europe and the Doctrine of the External Soul.*

woman finds the fruit and takes it home. While she is out, the girl emerges from the fruit and prepares a beautiful meal. Next time, the old woman hides and discovers the girl, who persuades her to ask the king to dinner. He recognizes the dishes his lost bride used to cook, and they are reunited. The foster-sister plunges into boiling water in the hope of becoming as beautiful as the heroine, and perishes miserably.

The chief interest of these variants lies in the sequel which they append to the shoe-recognition story. In 235 the bride is made away with, [6] but returns to suckle her child. This is an incident which appears in some European *Cinderellas*. In Russia (101, 95) an ogress changes the bride into a reindeer, which comes to suckle the child by night. In another Russian variant (228) the step-mother changes her into a goose, which does the same thing. In Poland (242) the stepmother kills and buries the bride, and the stepsister impersonates her, but her ghost comes back to nurse her child.

In the Salsette version (307) the bride is disgraced through being accused of unnatural births. In a French variant (232) she is accused of having given birth to puppies, by the same kind of trick and with the same result.

The Annam story (69) is more complicated. First, the bride is thrown into the water; then she is transformed successively into a number of different things; then she lives inside a fruit; then she is recognized by the food she cooks; and lastly her rival is boiled to death. All these motives [motifs] reappear in the West, but they appear separately. (*a*) In Armenia (8) the bride is drowned by her step-relations. In Tiree (27) she is pushed into a loch and seized by a monster; the same thing happens in Ireland (29). In Albania (50) she is put in a chest and flung into the river. In Lorraine (233) she is thrown into the river. (*b*) Successive transformations as part of a *Cinderella*-sequel are found in Russia (95), where the reindeer-mother turns into a spinning-wheel, a washing-vat, a spindle, and so forth, which her husband breaks until at last she reappears in her human form; the same kind of thing happens in the Russian version (228) where she first reappears as a goose; and again in a Polish variant (242). Altogether, these post-nuptial persecutions occur in eighteen European variants, grouped in the East and North: Russia, [7] Poland, the Balkans, Scandinavia, and Iceland account for twelve of them; two are Celtic; and the four others come from Italy, Germany, and eastern France. Their home is surely in the East; and their European distribution illustrates a truth which Strzygowski[6] and other historians of art have already taught us: namely that the east, north and north-west of Europe are more open to Asiatic influences than the centre, south, and south-west.

(c) The heroine's hiding place inside a fruit has produced some very curious developments both in Europe and in the far East. A Japanese tale (277) has a poor but beautiful heroine whose dying mother places on her head a wooden bowl. A rich young man, peeping beneath the bowl, sees her features and falls in love with her. At first she refuses to marry him, but she is persuaded by a dream in which her mother bids her do so. At the marriage-feast the bowl, which she has tried in vain to remove, bursts asunder, and all are dazzled by her beauty. This is surely the motive [motif] of the girl hidden in a wooden integument, derived from something like the Annamese story, and curiously like certain European *Catskins*. For although the type-variant of *Catskin* is that of the girl disguised in an animal-skin, in no less than twenty-eight of the sixty-four variants she is concealed or disguised in something made of wood: a gourd, a pumpkin, a wooden top, a hollow wooden figure, a dress made of laths or boards, a box, a boat, or a hollow tree; and in several cases the hero discovers her by peeping inside it, as in the Japanese story. The box version is the commonest of these; possibly because it seems the most rational, possibly through the influence of the Danae legend; but it cannot be derived from that legend. Such a pedigree could never **[8]** have produced the variants in which the only resemblance of the integument to a box is the fact that it is made of wood. Derivation from an original resembling the Annamese story will explain them all.

(d) The death of the stepsister by boiling occurs seven times in Europe; always in Italy (7, 24, 34, 148, 229, 237, 241). But it has also left traces elsewhere. Sometimes (e.g. 239, Italy) the stepsister is put into a tub; sometimes (101, 102) thrown into a flaming pit, or (8^7) burnt.

In these cases, the European variants develop scraps of thematic material (to borrow a phrase from the musician) which in the

---

[6] Josef Strzygowski (1862–1941).
[7] Collingwood leaves a space for more numbers here.

Annamese story coexist in a single whole. The order of derivation is clear. The Annamese version can hardly have been compiled by a learned folklorist out of elements taken from this and that European story; the European stories represent alternative selections from some original more or less resembling the Annamese. And we can already see that the magical and mysterious elements appealed more to the Slavs, Scandinavians, and Celts, the brutal and cruel human elements more to the Italians.

This original must have contained, as the Annamese story contains them, both the essential *Cinderella* and its sequel of persecution. I will not try, as a thoroughgoing disciple of the Finnish school would, to reconstruct this original in all its detail; I will merely give a rough outline of what I must suppose its contents to have been.

The heroine is oppressed by her stepmother (or foster-mother) in the interests of the elder woman's own child. She is befriended by a helpful animal, probably a cow which gives her milk. [9] Her stepmother, in spite, kills the cow and impiously (if the story is Indian, as I suppose) cooks and eats it; the heroine of course taking no part in the meal, but collecting and burying the victim's bones. Next comes the prince's choice of a bride. To prevent the heroine from competing, the stepmother makes work for her, setting her two outrageous tasks: disentangling a skein and sorting scrambled seed. To reward her for her piety, birds and insects do the work for her, and the cow gives her dress and shoes in which she goes to the gathering. The prince falls in love with her, but she cannot wait; she must be home before her oppressors; she flees, dropping a shoe. The prince searches for the shoe's owner, finds her, and marries her. But while he is away her stepmother and stepsister (who have come to live in her new home) conspire against her. They throw her into the water; the powers that befriend her turn her into one thing after another, to rescue her from her murderers, and allow her to come back in her own shape to suckle her child. The stepsister marries the prince, and calumniates his vanished wife, who is now hidden inside a fruit; but she emerges from this, makes herself known to her husband by cooking him the food she used to give him, and is reunited to him. The stepsister perishes in a magic bath in which she hoped to become beautiful enough to defeat her rival in fair fight.

It has been observed before now[8] that where the Indian mind loves to heap a profusion of themes together into a single story, the European selects one theme, or a small number of themes, and develops its implications. Such a story, transported to Europe, would accordingly tend to become two stories, dividing at the marriage, a fit close for a single tale. **[10]** The first half gives us *Cinderella*; the second, worked out in alternative ways, gives *Catskin* and *Cap o' Rushes*. The division, however, is not inevitable. In the east and north,[9] it is sometimes not made at all, and we get the Russian, Finnish, Scandinavian and Celtic variants in which both parts are present; capable at times of yielding a wonderfully dramatic and complete story like the Hebridean (27), or the Irish (29) which Jacobs[10] has reprinted in *Celtic Fairy Tales* (*Fair, Brown and Trembling*).[11] But in the drier and more logical thought of the south the division is normal.

When it is made, *Cinderella* is a simple matter. The story is complete in itself, and demands no modification. But it generally gets it; and chiefly in two ways: one a degradation, the other a genuine and original development.

The European *Cinderellas* almost always misunderstand the function of the tasks. In the original these had a special purpose. Work has to be made for the oppressed heroine, to keep her away from the gathering at which the prince is to choose his bride. The

---

[8] * Kaarle Leopold Krohn, *Übersicht über einige Resultate der Märchenforschung*, FF Communications, ed. for the Folklore Fellows by Walter Anderson, Johannes Bolte, Kaarle Krohn, Knut Liestøl, C. W. von Sydow, and Archer Taylor, 34/96, Suomalainen Tiedeakatemia, Academia Scientiarum Fennica (Helsinki, 1931). [A further part of what is probably the same note is entered on a separate slip of paper tipped in between fos. 9 and 10. Again, we supply fuller bibliographical details.]
* Jan de Vries, *Die Märchen von Klugen Rätsellösern eine Vergleichende Untersuchung*, FF Communications, 24/73 (Helsinki, 1928). Krohn, commenting on this observation (*Übersicht*, 170–1), objects that the supposedly Indian confusion of themes is found whenever oral tradition is stronger than literary. But this is not to deny the alleged fact: it is to suggest a possible reason for it.

[9] This phrase, and the foregoing two sentences, inserted at the top of fo. 10, appear to replace the final two sentences (which Collingwood has forgotten to delete) of fo. 9: 'The first story gives us *Cinderella*; the second gives us both *Catskin* and *Cap o' Rushes*. This division, however, is not invariable. In the north, it is sometimes not made at all.'

[10] Joseph Jacobs was on the editorial committee (and acting editor) of *F-L* in 1889–90, then editor in 1890–1.

[11] *Celtic Fairy Tales*, ed. Joseph Jacobs (London: D. Nutt, 1892).

tasks are therefore not part of her ordinary work: they are specially
devised, and devised for that special occasion. As we have seen,
they are of two kinds: disentangling thread, and sorting mixed
grain. Where they have not altogether disappeared from the European variants, they tend to fall apart into these two separate classes,
and the first is converted into the familiar daily task of spinning.
This occurs ten times in Italy, thrice in Serbia, twice in Poland,
once in Portugal, and once in Lithuania. In every case it has lost its
original connexion with the plot of the story and appears as a mere
part of the ordinary labour imposed on the heroine. The grain-
sorting task, which is very variously defined (it may, for example,
turn into the recovery of spilt milk from the stove, or the cooking a
dinner from one pea and one grain of rice, or the like), occurs ten
times in South-East and Central Europe, ten in Russia and Finland, eight in Scandinavia, [11] four times in the north-west, once
in France and twice in Spain; and sometimes, as in the original, it is
a condition of her attendance at the gathering, sometimes a pretext
for keeping her away; and sometimes (most often) it is mentioned
in the context of the gathering but without the relation between the
two things being explained. Once more, the east and north of
Europe are more sensitive to oriental influence than the south.
But in three-quarters of the European *Cinderellas* the tasks have
disappeared altogether, evidently because the European tradition
has failed to grasp that particular point in the original plot.

The other modification is more interesting, because it shows
what elements in European custom and belief were superadded
to the stock of ideas expressed in the original. In the original, the
magical helper was an animal; a sacred or divine animal, no doubt;
but there is no suggestion that it was anything else. But in the
European versions a strong tendency is at work to identify this
animal with the heroine's dead mother. In eight variants we are
explicitly told that the mother was transformed into the helping
beast, and then killed. In three, the mother herself is killed, eaten
by the villains, and piously buried by the heroine, afterwards
giving her magical help. In a dozen others, the magic help comes
not from the grave of a dead animal but from the mother's grave.

Moreover, there is an equally strong tendency to introduce into
this episode the idea of a soul-tree, the tree which grows on a grave
(especially the grave of a murdered person) and in some mysterious
way represents the person himself. We have nearly a score of cases

where the mother's soul-tree is the medium through which she helps her child, and about ten others in which it stands in a like relation to the helping animal, beside [12] another score in which (having, one supposes, lost its connexion with the dead) it figures simply as a magic tree.

The dead mother may pass through another transformation. She may appear as a fairy, a saint, an angel, or the Blessed Virgin; or, in a shape more purely human, an old woman, a nurse, governess, god-mother, or witch; or, with what is probably a change of sex (for I do not think the two sexes can be referred to distinct original themes) a strange man, an uncle, a priest or confessor, or even the Pope.

Of these various mother-apparitions, it is noteworthy that those which have a magical or mysterious character come oftenest in the east and north of Europe; those lacking such character, in the south. The soul-tree never appears in Italy, the magic tree hardly ever; here, as in other particulars, the Italian variants are humanistic and rationalistic. The French are in this respect second to the Italian; then come the Spanish. It is among the Slavs and Scandinavians and Celts that the frankly magical ideas are most constantly and most openly expressed.

When *Cinderella* proper has been separated from its sequel, the sequel as a separate story is far less easy to manage. Doubtless, this is why we have in Europe 131 *Cinderellas* and only 90 *Catskins* and *Caps o' Rushes* together. The source of the difficulty is the fact that the sequel lacks an opening, and one has to be provided. The situation with which it opens in the original is, as we saw, the happily married bride who has fallen again into the power of her enemies. Why, the narrator has to ask himself, should this happen?

[13] If the current theory of transmission is correct, these In-dian stories were reaching Europe mostly in the tenth and eleventh centuries. By that time there was already a European tradition of romantic story-telling, in which it was usual for a story to have what we still call a love-interest, and to end in a marriage. The *Cinderella*-sequel, exposed to the influence of that tradition, would undergo a first modification by marrying the heroine at the end and having her a maid at the beginning. Instead, therefore, of starting with a wife calumniated by her enemies to her husband, it would start with a girl calumniated to her family, and in particu-lar to her father. Thus we get the first incident in the story: the father's injustice towards his daughter.

Of this we have two forms: *Cap o' Rushes* or *King Lear*, where the father is angry because the daughter's declaration of love fails to satisfy him, and *Catskin*, where the daughter flees from the enamoured father. The latter is the commoner; but it would be rash to suppose it the original of which the alternative is a bowdlerized version. The legends of Christian saints are full of violence offered to chastity, and the situation of a virgin threatened by such violence is a commonplace of medieval romance. If the violence is incestuous, the heroine's situation is all the more dreadful and all the more romantic. The opening of *Catskin* is most easily explained, not as a relic of some unknown (and to an anthropologist inconceivable) custom of father–daughter marriage, but as the work of medieval story-tellers piling on the agony. The original, upon which this fresh agony was piled, might certainly have been the *Lear* story; which, without such reinforcement, is so lacking in plausibility that Shakespeare, to [14] make it conceivable, had to postulate a lunatic father. But in both versions the narrators found their plot troublesome. The incestuous father has to be, not exactly whitewashed, but made credible, by a deathbed promise to his wife that he will only marry a woman exactly like her, or one whom her ring or the like will fit, or by advice from his councillors or reassurance from a bishop or a dispensation from the Pope; the irascible Lear-type has lost his credibility in order to point a moral and adorn a tale which in effect has become an apologue on the sin of anger.

But now arises a further difficulty. The original version of this tale ends with a recognition through food. The person recognized is of course the heroine; but who recognizes her? It might be merely the father. In that case the whole *Cap o' Rushes* story is nothing more than this: the girl who talks about salt goes into hiding, persuades the cook to prepare a saltless meal, and is reconciled to her penitent sire (214, from Italy). But that is very bald, and lacks love-interest. Let the heroine go right away, meet a prince, and captivate him; let him meet her again (perhaps in his own mother's kitchen) but fail to penetrate her disguise; then let her cook him the food of recognition (perhaps by dropping in it the ring he gave her at the dance) and we can proceed at once to the wedding-bells and the saltless feast at which her father, the guest of honour, bursts into tears as he remembers his injustice to his lost daughter: and so to a touching reconciliation.

This is precisely the plot of the English *Cap o' Rushes* (219, Suffolk) and may be regarded as the standard formula. The chief variations are in the heroine's disguise. Sometimes it is a wooden integument (hollow **[15]** tree, box, candlestick) sometimes an animal's skin or old woman's skin taken off a corpse—a curious idea to which we must return later—or a softened form of the latter, the garb of an old woman, servant, or peasant. Sometimes, as in *King Lear*, the father becomes an outcast to emphasize the generosity of his daughter's forgiveness. Sometimes the magic dress or the lost shoe is borrowed from *Cinderella* to fill out the story of her meeting with the prince. But even at its best, as anyone can see from Shakespeare, it is a lame plot. The real problem, set by the opening, is a problem in the relation between father and daughter. The love-interest breaks across this problem with a disturbing note. The European story-teller, taking over from the East a plot which turned on the tribulations of a faithful wife (a subject which has never bulked large in European literature) has tried to reconstruct it so as to deal with two problems that interest him more: the intricacies of a father–daughter relation, which have given European writers a subject ever since the Greeks wrote of Iphigenia and Electra, and the romantic love-story which begins with the speech of Aristophanes in Plato's *Symposium*, yields its first harvest in the hands of the late Greek novelists, and has dominated the European imagination ever since the eleventh century.[12]

The interest of these stories lies not in this ambiguous plot but in their details: and particularly in that strange disguise, the old woman's skin (215, 217, Italy; 218, Germany). This must be connected with the heroine's habit, in other branches of the *Cinderella* cycle, of wearing as a disguise the skin of the helping beast which we have already seen cause to identify with her mother.

In the *Catskin* type the father–daughter problem, having become too acute for solution, is simply left unsolved, except in two cases (148, 200; Italian) where the father pursues the heroine and ends in boiling oil or the like; and in a very few where he attends the wedding and is forgiven. The love-interest, once the heroine has got away, takes charge, and in consequence **[16]** the *Cinderella* material is much more uniformly and unscrupulously borrowed. All that remains, to prove that we are still dealing with the original

---

[12] * C. S. Lewis, *The Allegory of Love* (Oxford: Clarendon Press, 1936), ch. 1.

sequel, is the often-recurring wooden dress and the almost invariable food-recognition. But once more, there is an interesting detail
in the shape of an animal-disguise alternative to the wooden
covering. In the English chapbook *Catskin*, for example,[13] the
heroine disguises herself in a catskin dress and afterwards, except
when in her ball-dresses, behaves in such a way as to show that she
really is a cat; for example, she shakes her ears when the cook
throws water over her. Just as, in several *Cinderellas*, the mother
is both a human being and a cow or ewe ('in them old days', as an
Irish narrator put it, 'a sheep might be your mother') so, by a
similar and doubtless hereditary magical power, the daughter is
both a human being and a cat. In a Danish story (39) the helping
animal is a cat: to reward the heroine for feeding her, it sloughs off
its skin for her to wear as a disguise. In one from Finland (109) the
cow-mother gives the heroine her cowskin; in one from Sweden
(117) the helping animal is a bear, which the heroine has to kill
with her own hands, so as to wear its skin. In one of Grimm's
stories (37) the mother becomes a bird; her daughter hides successively in a pear-tree and in the dovecot; originally, one must
suppose, in the shape of a bird. Finally, in two or three stories
(18, Italy; 89, 90, Portugal), the heroine, for no assigned reason, is
nicknamed 'cat' by her step-relations.

Identifications of the dead mother with a helping animal, and
identifications of her daughter with an animal of her species,
whether explicit or con- [17] cealed beneath such artifices as the
old-woman skin disguise, are thus too common in the European
tradition to be accidental. Just as the soul-tree references correspond with a European superstition as old as Virgil, so these shape-
changing motives [motifs] correspond with the ancient, but not yet
extinct, belief in werewolves (the mother is in one case actually a

---

[13] Collingwood's in-text parenthetical note reads: 'not in Cox; but cf. Jacobs'
More English Fairy Tales, no. 83'. Joseph Jacobs published his edn. of *English Fairy
Tales* in 1890, and the sequel *More English Fairy Tales* in 1893. This was Collingwood's favourite book of fairy tales. He was particularly fond of the Hobyahs and
inscribed the verse tale on the flyleaf of his copy of the (undated) Routledge edn. of
Hobbes's *Leviathan*: "The next night the Hobyahs came again and said: / Hobyah!
Hobyah! Hobyah! / Tear down the Hempstalks! / Eat up the old man and woman! /
and carry off the little girl.' The lines appear in *More English Fairy Tales*, 118–24,
and remind Collingwood of p. 121 of the Routledge edn. (p. 94 of original edn.).

wolf[14]) and in the power of witches to turn themselves into cats, hares, and other animals. If we ask why the European narrators were not content to keep the helpful cow of the Indian story, but insisted upon cats, wolves, and so forth, the answer is to be sought in these ancient European beliefs, twisting the story into conformity with themselves.

We must turn to the problem of date. All the material contained in Miss Cox's book was collected and written down before 1893; about nine-tenths of it in the nineteenth century; a little in the seventeenth and a handful in the sixteenth. It is certain that most of it had taken its final shape in the mouth of the people before the end of the seventeenth. In 1697 Perrault published his *Cendrillon*, in which he jettisoned the helping animal (as became an enlightened subject of the Roi Soleil) and substituted a fairy godmother.[15] His book became enormously popular, and if any literary influence during the next two centuries could have affected the spoken tradition we should have found, especially in France, a great crop of fairy-godmother *Cinderellas*. In point of fact, Miss Cox's book contains hardly any stories in which such a character appears. The only case in which the Perrault *Cendrillon* has entered into the folk-tradition is no. 55, a Russian story from Kazan, obviously based on Perrault. In no. 3, from the Riviera, there is a fairy godmother, but she is identical with the wicked stepmother. A fairy godmother also appears in nos. 145, 190, and 191, but these belong to the *Catskin* type, and are popular copies of another Perrault story, *Peau d'Ane*. When these few scattered echoes are compared with the vast bulk of the extant *Cinderella*-stories, one cannot but be impressed by the smallness of Perrault's influence upon the [18] popular tradition.[16]

---

[14] Collingwood leaves a space at this point to insert a number.

[15] Charles Perrault, *Histoires ou contes du temps passé* (Paris, 1698). The collection contained eight prose tales in total: *Cinderella, Sleeping Beauty, Little Red Riding Hood, Blue Beard, The Fairies, Puss in Boots, Ricky of the Tuft* and *Little Tom Thumb*. It was translated into English by Robert Samber in 1729 as *Histories, or Tales of Past Times, By M. Perrault.*

[16] * It has been thought that the glass shoe is another innovation of Perrault. Whether this is so does not seem certain; at any rate, the suggestion that *verre* in Perrault (or his printers or reprinters) is an alteration of the obsolete *vair*, fur, is open to the objection that no Cinderella known to us ever danced in so odd a footgear as fur slippers. But if it is so, Perrault's influence is traceable in Scotland

On the other hand, the *Cinderella* story forms no part of pre-medieval European literature or (so far as we know it) folklore. The theme of recognition by a shoe which a bird has carried off is known from ancient Egypt; both Strabo (xvii, p. 808) and Aeolus (*Var. Hist.* xiii, 33) tell us that while the celebrated Rhodope was bathing an eagle carried off one of her sandals and dropped it in the lap of the king, who sought its owner out and married her; but although this proves that the theme of recognition through a shoe stolen by a bird, found in the two Annamese stories, was known in Egypt before the birth of Christ, it does not prove that the complete *Cinderella* story was known there. It rather reminds us that it is important in studying fairy tales to distinguish the history of individual themes from the history of the stories in which we find them embedded.[17]

[19] The first clear trace of *Cinderella* in Europe is in Geoffrey of Monmouth, who towards the middle of the twelfth century told the story of King Lear very much as Shakespeare gives it. He claimed to be using ancient Celtic material, but, though that may have been true in a sense, he was certainly combining it with material from elsewhere, and he cannot be used as evidence that *Cap o' Rushes* belongs to the Celtic folklore of the Dark Ages. Most likely his story is simply what, on the face of it, it seems to be: a recension of the sequel to the original Eastern *Cinderella*. In order that such a recension should have been made by the time he heard it, the main story must have been in circulation for some time previously, so that it must have begun to acclimatize itself by the tenth or at latest eleventh century. Our European variants were

(4, 152), Catalonia (72), Chile (21) and perhaps the Netherlands (224, crystal shoes). See Cox, *Cinderella*, 507–8.

[17] * Friedrich von der Leyen (ed.), *Das Märchen* (1911), insists on this distinction. [Collingwood probably refers to Friedrich von der Leyen's *Die Märchen der Weltliteratur* (Jena, 1912–17).] Kaarle Krohn, *Leitfaden der vergleichenden Märchenforschung*, FF Communications, 2/13 (Helsinki, 1913), 11, contends that the themes out of which stories are built up are very much older than the stories themselves. [This paper is actually by Antti Aarne, who refers to Krohn and is correctly cited in Collingwood's note to fo. 14 of FT6 below. Jack Zipes, *The Oxford Companion to Fairy Tales* (Oxford: Oxford University Press, 2000), gives the publication date for von der Leyen's *Das Märchen* as 1917, as does Collingwood in FT6. '1911' is the date attributed to the work in a footnote to Aarne's *Leitfaden*, 14.]

therefore composed (if that is the right word) at different times between the tenth century and the seventeenth.

The ideas which European narrators put into them were therefore ideas current in Europe during those centuries; not as mere inert 'survivals', but as ideas strongly enough held to influence the structure of stories passing from mouth to mouth and to impose upon them a significance which they did not originally possess.

The most important of these ideas is the identity of the mother with the helpful animal. This implies that a human being may be an animal and vice versa; and not merely an animal but a helpful animal, protecting and guiding its own human kindred. It further implies that the human kindred thus protected are themselves, in virtue of their relation to this animal, animals of the same species. All this is apparent from our analysis of the incidents in the fairy tales. It shows that [20] among the people in whose mouth those stories took shape there existed a system of beliefs about the relation between animals and human beings, far more complex and definite than the familiar notion that a witch may turn into a cat or a hare: a system of which the werewolf, the witch-cat, and so forth are presumably fragmentary relics. The belief seems to be that a girl may have (for example) a cat-mother who after her death as a woman can return as a cat to look after her; and that the girl herself is, as it were, a hereditary cat, and can turn into a cat in order to escape from persecution.

Beliefs of this kind carry us into a world of ideas very familiar to anthropologists under the general name of totemism. The name covers a large variety of things not all, perhaps, capable of reduction to species of a single genus, or identifiable by possessing a definite number of fixed and invariable characteristics; but the same admission could be made about many other general terms like religion or civilization; and it serves as a warning, not against using the word, but against forcing it into the mould of a rigid definition. It would certainly be correct to describe as totemistic a society in which the belief described above was generally held and became the basis of a social organization. In such a society there would be clans, each of which stood in the described relation to a certain species of animal (not that animals are the only possible kind of totem, though they are probably the commonest); and if descent were reckoned through the mother, a daughter, or for that matter a son, would inherit the mother's totem. If the mother's totem is a cat, the daughter's will be a cat.

A helpful beast is not necessarily a totem; not even if it is a hereditary [21] helper in certain families. The belief that human beings can change into beasts, as witches into cats, is not necessarily a totemistic belief. But where these two ideas are found together, where a certain group of persons related by blood at once regard animals of a certain kind as their natural hereditary friends, and also regard themselves as members of that animal species and vice versa, there it can hardly be denied that totemism exists. For the totem is a kind of god belonging specifically to the clan whose totem it is. As god, it is the special helper and protector of that clan's members, both individually and collectively. But, as god, it is worshipped in a peculiar ritual; and since the object of all religion is to bring about the identification of the worshipper with the god he worships, the ritual of totemism is in essence an identification of the clansman with the totem of his clan. This ritual, in a general way, takes the form of dramatic dances in which the dancers act the part of their own totem. If you meet a stranger and wish to know what his totem is, you ask him, 'what do you dance?' and he will reply 'we dance reindeer'. This does not mean simply 'we dance in honour of the reindeer', or 'we dance in imitation of reindeer', it means both these, and something more: it also means 'we dance ourselves into reindeer'. In a clan which dances thus, each member of the clan is as it were an honorary reindeer, and every reindeer is an honorary member of the clan.

For a reindeer-man to kill and eat a reindeer is therefore murder and cannibalism. But although for this reason reindeer-men are forbidden to kill or eat reindeer in the ordinary course of hunting, there are [22] special occasions on which they are obliged to do so: namely the totem-feasts at which this further and more drastic method of identifying oneself with the totem animal is put into practice. Once more, a mere taboo on eating a certain animal is not necessarily totemistic. From the prohibition in Leviticus 11, 7 it does not follow that the pig was a totem among the Hebrews.[18] But if, in addition to observing this taboo, they had eaten pig's flesh on certain solemn occasions, regarded the pig as a divine or divinely

---

[18] 'And the swine, though he divide the hoof, and be clovenfooted, yet he cheweth not the cud; he *is* unclean unto you.'

appointed helper, and believed that they could turn into pigs and vice versa, the conclusion would have been irresistible.

In the original *Cinderella*, we have supposed that the heroine was forbidden to join her step-relatives in their impious feast on the body of the slain cow. That is not totemism, it is merely taboo, and its purpose in the plot is to explain why she was favoured in the sequel by the divine powers whose wrath was visited on them. But when in the European versions we find the helpful animal after its death magically supplying her with food ('feel in my right ear' is the usual formula) a suspicion arises—it can be no more than a suspicion—that the incident may possibly be a relic of the totem feast, just as the heroine's disguise in the animal's skin may be a relic of the totem dance.

Attempts have often been made to find relics of totemism in European folklore. Salomon Reinach[19] thought that a modern survival of totemism existed in the bears which are still kept at Berne, and supported the suggestion by pointing out that in the Roman period a bear-goddess Artio was worshipped close by. But a bear-goddess is not necessarily a bear totem. The late **[23]** Sir Laurence Gomme thought that the British superstitions about metamorphosis into cats, hares, magpies, and so forth were relics of a time when these were totem animals. But, as Andrew Lang pointed out in a presidential address to the Folk Lore Society,[20] ideas which are parts of totemism when organized in a certain way do not prove totemism when they are found in isolation. These excesses have led to a wise caution about falling into similar errors, and some temerity is needed if the phrase 'survivals of totemism' is to be used at all today; nevertheless, it is the writer's opinion, on the evidence discussed above, that during the Middle Ages, when the European *Cinderella* stories took shape, there were relics of

[19] * Salomon Reinach, *Orpheus: Histoire générale des religions* (Paris, 1909), ch. 1, § 36. Reinach (1858–1932) was a historian of classical art and an archaeologist who became Director of the Musée des Antiquités in 1902 and professor at the École du Louvre.

[20] * *F-L* 1/1 (Mar. 1890), 4–15. So Charlotte Burne, Presidential Address, 'The Value of European Folklore in the History of Culture', *F-L* 21/1 (30 Mar. 1910), 14–41, argued that rituals like the Horn Dance at Abbots Bromley, where the dancers disguise themselves as stags, or the Quantock squirrel-hunting on Good Friday, are not survivals of totemism or hunting-magic but relics of medieval or even later customs symbolically claiming certain rights granted by charter or the like.

totemistic beliefs and of magical practices based on them, garbled no doubt but recognizable, existing in most parts of Europe and specially in the east, north, and north-west.

Before deciding that such a view is inherently absurd, it would be well to reflect that totemism, like other systems of custom and belief, has a certain connexion with the economic life of the people among whom it exists. The classical examples of it have been found among food-gathering peoples; and although it may, and often does, survive the adoption of agriculture, its natural home is in a food-gathering civilization. For though all religions are at bottom attempts to [24] solve one and the same problem, the problem of establishing a sound relation between man and the power that works in and behind the world he inhabits, this problem is never a purely 'metaphysical' one, in the sense of being divorced from his immediate practical interests. The god that satisfies his hunger and thirst after righteousness and eternal life is also the god that gives him his daily bread. The prayer for daily bread is the cultivator's prayer, because bread is what he eats; the food-gatherer prays for daily fish or fowl, with nuts and berries in due season. His god, therefore, is not the god that makes the corn grow, but the god that brings fish to his spear and game to his traps.

But when the question arises how to conceive this god, the answer can only be given, whether by savage or by civilized man, in symbolic terms; and the vocabulary of the symbolism is inevitably determined by the way in which the god reveals his presence in his gifts. To put this in other language, the objects upon which man habitually concentrates his emotions and thoughts become thereby charged with a significance which makes them his natural source for a religious symbolism. The cultivator's god is not an unknown power that gives him corn; in the corn that it gives him, this power reveals to him its own nature; for in giving corn it gives itself, and in that sense the corn and the god are identical. The seasonal growth and life and death of the corn are thus a seasonal growth and life and death of the god. The bread which is made of the grain and becomes the food of man is the body of the god, given for man. The new growth of the seed is the god's resurrection to a new cycle of life.

[25] If this is how the cultivator conceives the god whom he worships, the hunter conceives him analogously, in his own way. The animals which he hunts, upon which as the source of his

livelihood his thoughts and emotions are focused, become to him not merely gifts sent by the god, but symbols and vehicles of the divine nature. To the hunter or fisherman, his game or his fish is not an enemy to be destroyed. His emotions towards it are not hostility, hatred, or cruelty. Every real hunter loves what he hunts, rejoices in its beauty, and admires its intelligence. In over-civilized men, occasional hunting may be little more than an outlet for aggressive emotions; but among habitual hunters, and especially among those for whom hunting is the means to livelihood, there is invariably a strong admixture of tender emotion, love and respect and gratitude, towards their quarry. The quarry is a helpful friend, whose help can only be given through a death which in the eyes of the hunter is both a tragedy and a triumph. This feeling, universal among people in whom hunting and fishing are normal activities (all such people understand how it was that William Rufus 'loved the tall deer as though he were their father'), is stronger in proportion as the technique of hunting is more primitive; for in proportion as that is the case, success in hunting demands a kind of co-operation on the part of the quarry, which must swim to the net or walk into the trap of its own free will, almost as if it offered itself a willing sacrifice to the slayer. And in so far as the quarry is a symbol or vehicle of deity, the hunter's god is not a god that drives the beast into the trap, it is a god that in its shape as beast walks into the trap to die for its human worshippers.

[26] These ideas about God find their reflection in man's ideas about himself. To the cultivator, the life and death and resurrection of the corn are a symbol not only of divine existence but of human as well. As a tender plant from the darkness of the soil, so man issues from his mother's womb; as a flower of the field, so he flourishes; and when he tries to assure himself of a future life, the thought to which he clings is the thought of his own seed-corn, which is not quickened unless it die. These symbols of humanity, which have become so integral a part of our own heritage, are the natural symbols of an agricultural civilization. To a hunting civilization they would have no meaning. The hunter thinks of himself as a wanderer beset with perils, like the beasts of his own chase; born, like them, into a community of his own kind, in which a sufficiency of births, like a sufficiency of births among his quarry, is the object of his anxious care; living like them under the law and custom of his tribe; and dying perhaps—who knows?—like them to

feed another life which will be his own life in a new shape. And these thoughts he will express not in philosophical prose, but in a ritual which he devises and performs about as blindly, and about as intelligently, as I write these sentences: not knowing why I write them or whether anyone will read them, not even sure that I am making my thought clear to myself or to anyone else, but knowing that there is in me something that craves expression and knowing that, if I am to express it at all, I must express it through that pen-driving ritual which is the custom of my tribe.

This is not offered as a theory of totemism. It is offered only by way of prolegomena to the study of totemism, a rough description of the motives [motifs] underlying any totemistic religion and social order. It is based on the assumption that totemism in its primary or fundamental shape is a **[27]** kind of animal-worship which grows naturally out of the emotional experience of a hunting people and its attitude towards the quarry that it hunts. On this assumption, some at least of the known features of totemism are easy to explain. Of the others, some (notably the specialization through which the various sections of a totemistic society have different totems) must be explained on different principles, per-haps through the analogy between the division of human society into interrelated groups and the division of the animal kingdom into species;[21] some (notably the kindred specialization through which members of a clan are forbidden, except on certain solemn occasions, to kill or eat their own totem) must be explained partly as an extension of that same analogy, partly perhaps by the preva-lence of tragedy over triumph in the death of the beloved quarry: a prevalence humanly possible only if the food-supply can be otherwise assured.

If there is anything in these suggestions (and they are offered in all humility by one whose knowledge of totemistic societies is derived entirely from books), it follows that in Northern Europe the religious ideas and social structure of the people must have been in some sense totemistic during all the long period of time which ended in the Neolithic Age with the introduction of agri-culture. Even after that, the same system must long have survived;

---

[21] * Cf. Frazer's notion that in a totemistic society the various clans each concen-trate upon one type of food-supply, so that the whole is a co-operative society for the magical maintenance of the food-supply in general.

for the agricultural revolution of the Neolithic age was not accomplished at a blow: like all such revolutions, it must have been a slow
[28] and gradual process, so that even in the Bronze Age, or later
still, the totemistic habit of thought and structure of society pre-
dominated in regions where agriculture had scarcely taken root,
and had not wholly died out among the peoples which had most
completely adopted it. The great age of European totemism, always using that word in its most general sense, must have been the
Palaeolithic; and that is the age to which belong the monuments
that seem most clearly to demand a totemistic interpretation.

The Palaeolithic is commonly divided into three parts, the so-
called Lower, Middle, and Upper. In the Upper or latest of these
ages, man was no longer the almost ape-like creature represented
by the bones from Piltdown or Neanderthal; he was physically very
much like ourselves. The human type, as we know it, was established. The Upper Palaeolithic begins with the widespread Aurig-
nacian culture, and culminates in the Magdalenian, which is
almost confined to France and northern Spain. To this belong
the best part of the sculptures and cave-paintings which for half a
century and more have excited the admiration of all students by
their brilliant realistic portraiture of animals. Although by their
style these works recall and indeed rival those of our own artists, it
is clear that they were not made with the same kind of intention.
Magdalenian cave-paintings were not meant as decorations of the
caves in which men lived; they often occur only in the remotest
inner recesses of caverns, impossible for habitation but very appropriate for secret ceremonies; and it has often been pointed out
by way of comparison that central Australian tribes perform totemistic ceremonies before animal-pictures similarly painted on
rocks in places to which access by women, children, and uninitiated men is strictly [29] forbidden.[22]

Among these Palaeolithic drawings and painting are some which
appear to represent men disguised in animal masks. These are
supposed to depict the worshippers in the cult, as distinct from

[22] * Joseph Déchelette, *Manuel d'archéologie préhistorique, celtique et galloromaine*, 11 vols. (Paris, 1908–[24]), i. 268–71, still fairly represents the general
opinion of archaeologists as to the magical purpose of Magdalenian art. Cf.
V. Gordon Childe, *Man Makes Himself*, Library of Science and Culture, 5 (London:
Watts & Co., 1936), 69–71.

other human figures which mingle with the animal-figures and no doubt represent hunters.

These works of art do not, of course, prove that the Magdalenian tribes of France and Spain had a totemistic organization and cult in all respects like those of the Arunta or any other modern people known to anthropologists. But they do, unless the opinion of archaeologists about their magical purpose is entirely mistaken, prove that these tribes had an elaborate system of ritual which was connected with the fact that they lived by hunting certain animals and served to express their desire that these animals should be fruitful and multiply, and should fall a sufficiently easy prey to their hunters. In such a ritual the fundamental features of totemism, as described above, are plainly recognizable.

The artistic genius of the Magdalenian civilization has thus given us means of satisfying ourselves that there was, in this one phase of Palaeolithic culture, a totemistic religion in the sense above defined. Evidence exists that cults of the same general kind went on after this artistic movement had died away. As late as the Neolithic and copper ages, paintings[23] were being **[30]** made in Spanish caves and rock-shelters which are conventionalized derivatives of the Magdalenian, and therefore presumably designed for the same purpose. With the Bronze Age, derivatives still further conventionalized are found still further afield, including the cup-and-ring markings on rocks and stone monuments in the British Isles.[24] If these trace their pedigree back, as they seem to do, to the Magdalenian cave-paintings, it is probable that they were associated with rituals of similar derivation: that is, with a religion where the new agricultural symbolism had not yet altogether supplanted the totemistic.

Even if the Bronze Age cup-and-ring marks testify to a survival of totemistic ideas and practices, they certainly do not indicate a strictly and purely totemistic state of society. They coexist not only with a well-established agriculture, which by itself is evidence for the existence of agricultural rites and ceremonies, but also with

---

[23] * The Abbé Henri Breuil and Miles Crawford Burkitt, *Rock Paintings of Southern Andalusia: A Description of a Neolithic and Copper Age Art Group* (Oxford: Clarendon Press, 1929).

[24] * For the connexion of British cup-and-ring marks with Spain (Galicia) see V. Gordon Childe, *The Bronze Age* (Cambridge: Cambridge University Press, 1930), 150, 164–6.

religious monuments of an altogether non-totemistic kind. The Neolithic Age had already introduced the long barrow, which is a communal burial-place implying by its huge proportions and elaborate architecture a well-developed cult of the dead; in the Bronze Age the communal vault gave way to individual tombs, but these again were so large and so elaborate that they testify to a further development of the same cult. Even the great stone circles of which Avebury and Stonehenge are the best examples are now regarded by many archaeologists as specialized developments of the Early Bronze Age disk-barrow[25] which would make them at once tombs and temples, places where [31] the cult of the dead was practised on a vast scale; and this cult of the dead seems to be a fairly constant feature of agricultural civilization. Yet it is the British Bronze Age that has left us cup-and-ring markings, sometimes actually on the stones of megalithic monuments. The ritual practised at such monuments may therefore have contained relics of totemism, and these relics must have been tolerated and even fostered by the official opinion of the community; but they were doubtless garbled and confused.

Terms like Neolithic or Bronze Age denote types of culture, not periods of time. In the Eastern Mediterranean, in Egypt and Mesopotamia, the Neolithic revolution had set in by about 5000 BC. In Britain it did not make itself felt until 2500 BC or even later. By 3000 BC the Mesopotamian Bronze Age was well established;[26] in Britain, bronze begins to appear in very small quantities only after 2000, the Bronze Age drew gradually to a close during the last millennium before Christ, and in out-of-the-way parts of the country civilization was still in many ways of a Bronze Age character when the Romans came. If, therefore, the Bronze Age culture in Britain retained lingering and garbled elements of totemism in

[25] * O. G. S. Crawford and Alexander Keiller, *Wessex from the Air* (Oxford: Clarendon Press, 1928), 213. For the view that megalithic structures in general imply a cult of the dead, cf. V. Gordon Childe, *The Dawn of European Civilization* (London: Kegan Paul & Co., 1925), 284–5. [Collingwood's personal letters to Crawford of 1940 and 1941 are available in the Bodleian Library, Bodl. MS. Crawford 3, fo. 205, and Bodl. MS Crawford 4. Crawford and Keiller's *Wessex from the Air* and the work of the Ordnance Survey had been recommended by Penniman, *Hundred Years*, 336, and Collingwood refers to these sources in his paper of 8 July 1936, 'Mayborough and King Arthur's Round Table', Bodleian Library Collingwood Papers, dep. 23/16.]

[26] * For these dates see Childe, *Man Makes Himself*, 49, 50, 133.

its official religion, it is not at all impossible that they should have
continued to exist, no doubt still further garbled and still more
fragmentary, as elements of popular superstition down to the
Middle Ages. For we know that medieval Christianity was full of
more or less Christianized fragments of pagan custom and belief
which became tolerated and recognized features of its own life; we
know, too, that in addition to these there also survived others,
never effectively Christianized, which the Church would have
suppressed if it [32] could, but could not. For the most part,
these relics of paganism were no doubt relics of the agricultural
religions that came in first with the Neolithic revolution; but to all
the northern fringes of Europe the principle applies which Sir
Cyril Fox[27] has formulated as especially distinguishing the outer
or 'highland zone' of Britain from the inner, Continent-facing,
'lowland zone': that whereas in the lowland zone new cultures
tend to be imposed, in the highland zone they tend to be absorbed,
thus giving the highland zone a continuity of cultural character and
a tendency to preserve or even to reassert old-established ways of
living and thinking side by side with the new ways that have come
in from the Continent. Early Christian missionaries like St Patrick
certainly worked hard at destroying the sacred places and rituals of
pagan belief; but to suppose that this resulted in their complete
disappearance would involve the same kind of error as supposing
that the Saxons made a clean sweep of the British inhabitants
whom they found in possession of the soil. To take a concrete
example from Fox: 'The Bronze Age custom of depositing white
quartz stones on the burial place is carried on in south-west Wales
to the present day.'[28]

---

[27] * *The Personality of Britain: Its Influence on Inhabitant and Invader in Prehistoric and Early Historic Times*, 2nd edn. (Cardiff: National Museum of Wales,
1933), 77.
[28] Ibid. 33.

6

THE AUTHORSHIP OF FAIRY
TALES

In those civilized countries where fairy tales still exist as a living institution, they form part of a cultural unity which contains also a variety of songs, dances, dramatic performances, festivals, beliefs, and so forth, to which the collective name of folklore[1] is given. This name, invented in 1846 by an English antiquary, W. J. Thoms, to replace the older term 'Popular Antiquities',[2] was originally designed to express a certain theory as to the nature of the thing so designated. That theory is no longer tenable, and the term has consequently given rise to much confused thinking. The source of this confusion is an ambiguity in the word folk, which may mean either *populus*, the entire body of a nation or community, or *plebs*, its lower orders. According to the first sense, folklore should mean the ideas of the community at large, as distinct from those of its individual members; according to the second, it should mean the ideas peculiar to its lower social strata.

The Old English word *folc* has the first meaning only: a body of persons, *du monde* as the French have it, and in particular the body

---

Bodleian Library, Collingwood Papers, dep. 21/9. The (restored) title is Collingwood's, though it has been struck out and replaced by 'Folklore and folk-tale' at the head of the MS. MR counts this section as amongst the final pages of FT which are 'in disarray' (MR 239). We have elevated the pages to chapter status on account of the coherence and connectedness of the arguments, and their value as a conclusion.

[1] Collingwood actually writes 'folk-lore' (with a hyphen) in this instance, a usage which was common in the 19th century. We have standardized the term in conformity with his other uses.

[2] Under the pseudonym of 'Ambrose Merton, Gent., FRS', W. J. Thoms revised and amended a volume of *Gammer G's Famous Histories of Sir Guy of Warwick, Sir Bevis of Hampton, Tom Hickathrift, Friar Bacon, Robin Hood, and the King and the Cobbler* (Westminster: Joseph Cundall, 1846), and a second volume in the same year entitled *Gammer G.'s Pleasant Stories of Patient Grissel, the Princess Rosetta, and Robin Goodfellow, and ballads of the Beggar's Daughter, the Babes in the Wood, and Fair Rosamond.*

of persons that together make up a community having a common name like Englishmen.[3]

In Old and Middle English there is no suggestion that the gentlefolk were any less a part of the folk than the simple. There are, however, Old English usages in which the word *folc* refers to laymen, as opposed to clerics. The illuminism of the eighteenth century, with its distinction between the enlightened or educated man and the ignorant (and therefore superstitious) vulgar, tended to reassert this opposition in a somewhat new sense; we see one result in Blackstone's curious misunderstanding of the Old English term folkland, as meaning land held by servile tenure.[4] Hence, in the nineteenth century, [2] the word folk had become definitely ambiguous. It was used in a simple and colloquial way for persons of whatever kind; but it was also used in a pseudo-archaic and artificial way for the lower orders, the simple and uneducated. And when it was discovered that in European countries these uneducated people had a traditional culture of their own, including fairy tales as one part of itself, the word folklore was coined to convey the suggestion of an antithesis between this culture of the uncultured and the culture properly so-called of the educated classes.

The Romantic movement, to which the discovery of this lower culture was due, began as a reaction against eighteenth-century illuminism; and, like all reactions, it carried in its heart more than a mere relic of the principles against which it was in revolt.[5] The two movements agreed in making a sharp distinction between the enlightened or educated man and the unenlightened or uneducated. The enlightened man, having gone through a discipline designed to free his intellect from the power of authority and prejudice, studied the opinions of others as expounded in the

[3] * Joseph Bosworth and Thomas Northcote Toller, *Anglo-Saxon Dictionary*, 2 vols. (Oxford: Clarendon Press, 1882–1921), s.v. *folc* and derivatives: and in particular the corresponding articles in Toller's *Supplement*.

[4] See Sir William Blackstone, *Commentaries on the Laws of England*, 4 vols. (Oxford: Clarendon Press, 1765–9), ii. 91–2, where 'folkland' is defined as land 'held by no assurance in writing, but distributed among the common folk or people at the pleasure of the lord, and resumed at his discretion. . . . Under the Saxon government there were . . . a sort of people in a condition of downright servitude, used and employed in the most servile works. . . . These seem to have been those who held what was called folk-land, from which they were removeable at the lord's pleasure.'

[5] Cf. ATAP, fos. 20–5, above.

world's literature, and arrived by the use of reason at his own conclusions. The unenlightened man, never having learnt to disentangle his reason from the tentacles of authority, never thought for himself at all, but simply believed what he was told. The Illuminists, taking their stand on Descartes's famous manifesto,[6] pinned their faith to the enlightened thought of the [3] unprejudiced individual. The Romantics, having discovered that the individual by himself is a very feeble thing and that his supposed enlightenment is very often only a prejudice in favour of his own prejudices, swung to the other extreme and decided that the constructive forces in human history are to be found precisely in those traditional and therefore corporate ways of thinking and acting which the Illuminist had regarded as a mere brake on the wheel of progress.

The conception expressed by the term folklore arose out of this Romantic doctrine. Folklore meant something not invented by original and individual thinkers, like *Paradise Lost*, or the *Essay on Human Understanding*, or *Tom Jones*, or the *Jupiter* Symphony, but something handed down from mouth to mouth among people whose uneducated condition made them incapable of original creation. Yet this very fact gave it a peculiar value and importance. For, in the first place, because it was invented by no individual, it expressed a corporate experience in which the eccentricities and errors of individual thought were cancelled out: it thus achieved a profundity and universality which no individual thinker, whatever his genius, could emulate.[7] And, in the second place, because it was not the work of individual creators, but was the heirloom of tradition, it came down to us unaltered from the remotest antiquity, from the very infancy of the human race; it enshrined the ideas about himself and the world which man enjoyed before the shades of the prison-house closed about him; and therefore in studying it we were studying the documents of our own original and essential human nature, uncomplicated and uncontaminated by the many

---

[6] * *Discours de la méthode pour bien conduire sa raison et chercher la vérité dans les sciences* (Leiden, 1637). [Collingwood is extremely critical of 'illuminism' in *EM* 231, 246–7, and 252.]

[7] In this conception of the folktale as an exemplar of creative collaboration, Collingwood appears to prepare the way for an attack on aesthetic individualism in the closing part of *PA*. See 'The Artist and the Community', esp. § 7, 'Collaboration between Artists', 318–20.

inventions that separate [4] civilized man from the days of his innocence.

Superficial criticism of these conceptions is easy. The Illuminist view may be reasserted, by arguing that civilization is what gives man his value, and that his condition, before he had it, was not one of innocence but one of bestiality; so that the relics of that state are only relics of an inhuman savagery, best ignored. That is an effective debating point against the Romantic advocates of folklore study, but it is no more; for it accepts the premises of their argument, and admits their main contention that folklore is a body of immemorially ancient ideas, passively received and handed on by a tradition which, just because it is mere tradition, can create nothing. A second line of argument is a shade less superficial. Because the tradition which enshrines folklore is a mere tradition, the property of unenlightened people who have no creative power, the ideas which it contains must have been derived from elsewhere. They must therefore have been borrowed from the creations of the educated classes. Folklore, in other words, is a diluted and degraded form of literature, in which motives and elements originally created by the educated have been picked up and used, without any creative energy, by the uneducated.[8]

But here again the original antithesis between the creative culture of an educated and enlightened élite, and the merely traditional and therefore uncreative culture of the lower classes, is left uncriticized.

Because the temper of our own age is on the whole anti-Romantic, views of this sort are in fashion. To criticize assumptions is at best a severe logical exercise; to accept them when they also flatter one's own [5] vanity is not only easy but pleasant. The student of folklore is conscious of himself as an educated man, and tempted to be proud of the possessions that distinguish him from the illiterate. To the educated man as such, there is no pleasanter kind of self-flattery than the doctrine that folklore, the one cultural possession of the illiterate, is merely their perversion of what his own class has bestowed upon them. Whether this doctrine is true or not is a question which cannot profitably be discussed until

[8] * This view has been recently stated by Charles B. Lewis, 'The Part of the Folk in the Making of Folklore', F-L 46 (1935), 37–75.

the presuppositions on which it rests have been examined. These presuppositions are contained in the conception expressed by the term folklore; and unless they are sound, the question how the thing so designated has arisen is a meaningless question. These presuppositions are (1) that there is a distinction between an educated élite and an uneducated vulgar mass, each with a culture of its own. (2) That the culture of the élite consists of original works created by individual thinkers, artists, etc. (3) That the culture of the vulgar consists of traditional ideas handed down without alteration and passively received by each generation from the last. Let us consider these in turn. **[6]**

(1) The idea of folklore as the culture of an uneducated class, distinct from an educated, implies a society divided into these two classes, and is valid only where that division exists. That division is not a permanent reality. It was an ideal of eighteenth-century illuminism, partially realized in the nineteenth century. It implies that the educated class has a culture based on reading and writing, an individualistic morality, and a scientific conception of the world: while the uneducated has a culture based on oral tradition, a customary morality, and a religious (or, as it is called from the scientific point of view, a superstitious or magical) conception of the world. This is a situation which to some extent exists in modern European-American society, but it is peculiar to that society. In the Middle Ages there was a distinction between literate and illiterate classes; but the literate classes did not think of the world in a scientific as opposed to a religious manner. As late as the sixteenth and seventeenth centuries, when Queen Elizabeth and James I, both highly educated and scholarly persons, employed official astrologers and wrote about witchcraft, education and belief in magic were not incompatible. To us, witchcraft is 'folklore' in the sense that it belongs not to the written culture of the educated classes but to the oral tradition of the vulgar. But it was not folklore in that sense when James I wrote [his *Daemonologie*][9]

[9] Collingwood leaves a gap at this point, suggesting a title is to be added. James's writings included a *Daemonologie*, and Elizabeth's *A Book of Devotions*. There are also references to witches and witchcraft in James's letters. See G. P. V. Akrigg (ed.), *Letters of King James VI and I* (Berkeley: University of California Press, 1984). See also *Elizabeth I: Collected Works*, ed. Leah S. Marcus, Janel Mueller, and Mary Beth Rose (Chicago and London: University of Chicago Press, 2000).

or when Glanvill published his *Saducismus Triumphatus.*[10] In what we call a savage society, there is no such thing as folklore; the distinction between educated and uneducated does not exist; no one is literate, but every adult member has received such education as the society can provide. Hence, when Sir James Frazer wrote his great work on *Folklore in the Old Testament,*[11] the title was a misnomer. The beliefs about the mandrake which are implied in Genesis, 30, would be folklore if they existed in modern Europe, for they could only exist there as part of the oral [7] tradition of the uneducated; but they were not folklore among the ancient Hebrews, where the distinction implied by that name did not exist. The same applies to all the innumerable books about the folklore of this or that primitive people. The beliefs and customs which these books describe may have been well observed and accurately recorded; but in order that facts should become the foundation of a science something more is needed; the science must have its fundamental conceptions clearly thought out, and be capable of using them as a guide in the collection, arrangement, and interpretation of these facts; and in all these respects the conception of folklore is worse than useless.

(2) The conception of an original work of science or art, created in its entirety by a single man, is a mere fiction. We owe it to Descartes, who undertook in his own philosophical system to give us an example of such a thing: but actually that system contained large elements of medieval scholasticism, Renaissance Platonism, and so forth, which he found ready-made in the philosophical tradition to which he was heir, and incorporated in his own work as he saw fit. His contemporary Shakespeare took his plots from all manner of sources, and his dramatic technique from Marlowe and other predecessors. Voltaire, the high priest of illuminism, borrowed his philosophical method from Locke; Gibbon his general point of view from Voltaire, his historical method from Mabillon and others; and so forth. The absolutely unprejudiced thinker, the original creator who makes an absolutely new work of art, is no actual human being; he is an imaginary creature, like the purely

---

[10] Joseph Glanvill (or Glanvil) (1636–80) had defended the belief in witchcraft in *Saducismus Triumphans: Or the Full and Plain Evidence Concerning Witches and Apparitions* (London, 1681).

[11] 3 vols. (London: Macmillan, 1918).

economic man of the early economists. Every actual thinker, every actual artist, works by adding his quota to a **[8]** tradition, a common stock of ideas already current.[12]

(3) Equally fictitious is the conception of a purely traditional culture consisting of ideas passively received by one generation from the last. When Sir Walter Scott confessed himself unable to retell a story without giving it a new hat and stick, he was not talking as a man of education. He was talking as a story-teller, and any story-teller could make the same confession, or the same boast.[13] The human mind may be receptive, but receptivity is not passivity: it is an effort of active thought. An old story retold always to some extent acquires a new colouring from the mind of the teller and the life of his environment. If he is a skilful and imaginative narrator, these changes will turn the story, to that extent, into something both new and good; if the opposite, changes will still come about, but they will result in weakening the structure of the story by impoverishing its incidents.

To distinguish the folktale as a traditional narrative, passively transmitted by a process from which creative imagination is absent, from the literary story as the creation of an individual artist, is therefore to deal in shadows, and to frustrate in advance any attempt to construct a rational theory of fairy tales. The folktale and the literary tale are in this respect on the same footing. Each of them uses traditional themes and handles them by traditional methods; in each, the teller or writer modifies both the themes and the methods in the course of his work, sometimes for the better, sometimes for the worse; in neither case does he leave them exactly as he found them.

From these reflexions it would seem that the accepted distinction between folktales and literary stories must be abandoned, and that each alike **[9]** is simply a work of art: the supposed distinction between them turning out on analysis to be merely a distinction

---

[12] Cf. *PA* 319: 'If we look candidly at the history of art, or even the little of it that we happen to know, we shall see that collaboration between artists has always been the rule. I refer especially to that kind of collaboration in which one artist grafts his own work upon that of another, or (if you wish to be abusive) plagiarizes another's for incorporation in his own.'

[13] The remark is quoted by Thomas Huxley in his review of Darwin's *Origin of the Species* for *Macmillan's Magazine* (1859), 147, and again in 'Agnosticism' (1889), *The Major Prose Works of Thomas Henry Huxley*, ed. Alan P. Barr (Athens, Ga., and London: University of Georgia Press), 261.

between two aspects—traditionality and originality, or receptiveness and creativeness—both of which are present in all works of art
and indeed in all human products.

But although this would be true, it would not be the whole truth.
There is a distinction, and an important one, between the folktale
and the literary story. In order to grasp this distinction, let us begin
by recalling an old theory concerning the authorship of folktales,
advanced by some of the Romantics and fallen long since into
discredit. These maintained that the folktale, like the folk-song
and folk-dance, was peculiarly the property of the folk, not in the
sense of *plebs* but in the sense of *populus*: the community, not the
lower orders of the community. They thought that these things
were actually composed by the community: not by an individual
artist, but by a gathering of persons corporately extemporizing a
story or song or dance. It was a suggestion easily ridiculed. How,
asked the scoffers, were we to conceive this communal act of
composition? What inspiration, descending upon a group of savages squatting round a fire, caused them to invent and declaim in
unison the story of *Tom Tit Tot* or the ballad of *Binnorie*?

As a matter of fact, the thing is not so impossible as these critics
imagined. The Bach family, a prolific tribe which included large
numbers of professional musicians and traced their musical tradition back to the time of Luther,

exhibited a clannish attachment to each other. They could not all live in
the same locality. But it was their habit to meet once a year at a time and
place arranged beforehand. . . . On these [10] occasions music was their
sole recreation. . . . Best of all they liked to extemporize a chorus out of
popular songs, comic or jocular, weaving them into a harmonious
whole. . . . They called this hotch-potch a 'Quodlibet', laughed uproari-
ously over it, and raised equally hearty and irrepressible laughter in all
who listened to it.[14]

And persons less talented than the Bachs can testify to the ease
with which dramatic performances, for example, can be extempor-
ized by a group of willing actors.

But although this method of composition is quite possible, there
is nothing in what we know of the institution of story-telling

[14] * Johann Nikolaus Forkel, *Johann Sebastian Bach: His Life, Art, and Work*, tr.
Charles Sandford Terry (London: Constable & Co., 1920), 7–8. The authenticity of
the statement, coming as it does from Carl Philipp Emmanuel Bach, is beyond
question. [Collingwood has changed the ending of the quotation to 'in all who
listened to it' from 'in their audience'.]

among modern peasants or medieval gentry, in Eastern courts or by savage camp-fires, to suggest that it was the way in which our folktales actually originated. In spite of this, the theory of folk-authorship suggests an idea which is worth developing.

If a folk-song is sung in a modern drawing-room, the singer is careful to sing it exactly as it is printed in the book. The printed version is the authentic version, and he is no more entitled to depart from it than he would be entitled to alter a phrase of *Die Beiden Grenadiere*; or a reciter to alter a line of *Lycidas*; or a producer to give *Hamlet* a happy ending. A rendering which differs from the authentic version is a corruption. The business of the performer is to give a faithful rendering, that is to say, one which corresponds with the authentic text. These three conceptions—authentic text, faithful rendering, corruption—between them serve to determine the status of the performer under ordinary modern [11] conditions. But these conceptions not only presuppose the invention of writing and of musical notation; they also presuppose a widespread ability to read, and a widespread accessibility of the written or printed book or score. In an illiterate society, or even a society predominantly illiterate, they would have no meaning. If we rid our minds of the peculiar conditions imposed on recitation, acting, and musical performance by the existence of printed books (I say printed, because no amount of manuscript literature can make the authentic text widely enough accessible) we shall see that, apart from these conditions, the performer would be perfectly entitled to introduce modifications into the literary or musical works which he was performing; and that, since no question of authenticity could arise, the question whether these modifications became part of the received tradition would depend solely on their merits, as these were judged by the audience.

It is true that the well-trained memory and habitual conservatism of an illiterate society act as a brake on such innovations. A man of South Uist told J. F. Campbell that his versions of stories known to them both were good for nothing; 'Huch!' said he, 'thou hast not got them right at all!'[15] For all that, innovations are made;

---

[15] * John Francis Campbell, *Popular Tales of the West Highlands*, 2nd edn. 4 vols. (No place of publication: Gardner, 1890), i, p. xxii. [The title-page to each volume indicates that the tales are 'orally collected'. They are printed in Gaelic and preceded by Campbell's English translation.]

and this is the way in which variant versions of songs and stories come into existence. If two versions of a folk-song air differ, as they may, only in one note, one of them must almost certainly have arisen through altering the other; but neither is the authentic version, neither a corruption of it. The alteration must have been made either because some singer preferred it to the original, [12] or because he forgot how the original went at that point, and could think of no way to fill the gap that pleased him so well. In either case, the new version is a measure of his abilities as a composer. Similarly, one version of a story may differ from another by the alteration of some incident, or by putting in or leaving out an incident or block of incidents. Each is now as authentic as the other. If the person who made the alteration was a good story-teller, the new version will be better than the old; if a bad story-teller, it will be worse. There are lame and weak versions of common stories, to be explained as the work of bad story-tellers who have misunderstood or forgotten something they have heard; there are also, here and there, exceptionally good ones, testifying to the work of gifted or experienced tellers who have improved on their original.

In an illiterate or predominantly illiterate society, the performer's function is thus very different from what it is among ourselves. Instead of being responsible only for reproducing a fixed and authentic text, he is responsible for the text as well, in the sense that it is his business to improve upon his original in whatever way he thinks fit, subject to the demands made upon him by his audience. Any successful alteration (which need not be, in any absolute sense, an improvement; it may be a change for the worse, provided that this particular worse is one which his audience likes) will create a new variant by imposing itself on the memory of his hearers. The composer and performer are thus no longer two distinct persons: the performer is a co-creator, and the version which he performs is his version not in the sense that it is the version he has learnt, but in the sense that it is the version which, by altering at discretion, he has made to be as he likes it, or as he thinks his audience will like it. His story is a traditional story; but the tradition is not merely reproductive, it is creative.

[13] If these alterations, introduced by story-tellers where the invention of writing has not perpetuated an authentic version or where printing has not widely disseminated it, can account for the

differences which we find between the variants of one and the same story; and if such alterations may be changes for the better or for the worse, and make the stories longer or shorter, according to the lights and tastes of tellers and their audiences; the same kind of process will serve to explain how folktales came into existence. All we have to assume at the start is a variety of such themes as, according to anthropologists, are found pretty well all over the world: themes each of which is a story in embryo, and capable of being combined with others into a relatively long and organized narrative. It is said that long and elaborately organized stories like those of the European peoples are comparatively rare; that they are found in Asia and Europe, and to some extent in Africa and America, but that elsewhere the stories which people tell are either short and epigrammatic—anecdotes rather than novels or epics— or else, as among the decadent Bushmen,[16] rambling and incoherent. It is a reasonable supposition that the remote ancestors of the Asiatic and European peoples, like other savages, told such jocular and other anecdotes. By some enrichment of their imaginative and intellectual powers, such as must in any case have underlain their rise in civilization, they would begin to demand a gradual development of these earliest story-fragments, filling out details, explaining how the initial situation arose, adding sequels, and so forth. Thus would arise, out of the primitive story-theme, the elaborately organized story. Such a movement, like all [14] advances in civilization, probably began in one place and spread thence to neighbouring countries. Where and when it began we do not know; but the likeliest places for it are the oldest cradles of civilization, Mesopotamia, Egypt, and northern India; and of these three, the third is perhaps the strongest claimant. At any rate, it is in India that the art of story-telling reached the highest perfection, at a date long before any achievement at all comparable had arisen elsewhere. In Europe story-telling, like agriculture and metal-working and other elements of civilization, was probably not a native and independent invention, but was brought in from the East.

Thus the tradition which both conserves and alters stories— alters them both for better and for worse—is quite capable of

[16] * Cf. W. H. I. Bleek and Lucy C. Lloyd, *Specimens of Bushman Folklore* (London: G. Allen & Co., 1911 [Collingwood gives 1921]), for examples.

having created them in the first instance. We need not, to explain their existence, revive the old fable of a mythopoeic age, the golden age of fairy-tale-telling, when the stories we know were invented by an almost superhuman race of story-makers, their subsequent history having been one of careful conservation and of alteration, where alteration has happened, for the worse.[17]

[15] Tradition, thus understood, is no mere passive reception of a ready-made idea transmitted from generation to generation. It is a creative process, in which the transmitter is more than a medium through which the story conserves itself (or, if it be a distorting medium, fails to conserve itself and suffers degradation); he is a sharer in the work of invention.[18] This is the only conception of tradition which will fit the known facts of human history; if the science of folklore has failed to attain it, that may partly serve to explain why the science of folklore occupies so unsatisfactory a place among the historical sciences. How else could we understand the tradition of agricultural operations, or of chipping and grinding

***

[17] * This appears to be the doctrine of the Finnish school, for whose learning I have unbounded admiration, but whose ideas on questions of principle I sometimes find hard to follow. For they hold, not only that every story is a definite entity created once for all at a definite time and place (Antti Aarne, *Leitfaden der vergleichenden Märchenforschung*, FF Communications, 2/13 (Helsinki, 1913), 12), which seems intended to exclude their gradual growth by development and accretion from the original and simple themes whose existence and [15] great antiquity the school admits (ibid. 11), but also that, the more logical the structure of a given version is, the nearer it stands to this original. (Archer Taylor, *The Black Ox: A Study in the History of a Folktale*, FF Communications, 23/1/70 (Helsinki, 1927), 6). [Taylor writes that in assigning normal or primitive form to a tale, 'one will give more weight to a trait vouched for by well preserved, carefully told narratives and less weight to a trait found only in narratives which are fragmentary or otherwise known to be corrupt and contaminated'.] This is a kind of Garden-of-Eden doctrine which seems to me more than questionable. For the view that our ancestors had short stories before they had long ones, cf. e.g. Friedrich von der Leyen, *Das Märchen* (1917). [Collingwood seems to be referring once again to von der Leyen's *Die Märchen der Weltliteratur* (Jena, 1912–17).]

[18] Cf. LPA, fo. 27, on 'Tradition as dynamic freedom'. Collingwood had here defined 'tradition' as 'developing and dynamic', 'a law not fixed once and for all but reinterpreted and recreated by every fresh member of the school whose law it is'; cf. also *OPA* 35, where he writes that: 'conservation is only sustained creation, and that activity whose first fulguration is pure sublimity must continue to be freshly active at every point of its course'. The conception of 'tradition' within human society is further explored in other contexts in relation to Collingwood's idea of history. See e.g., the extracts from 'Notes towards a Metaphysic', *PH* 119–39.

stone implements, or of building houses, or of making weapons? The various types of primitive house are not scattered and imperfect relics of a few perfect house-patterns once invented and thereafter more or less successfully copied. These types of house have been developed and differentiated from the crudest and most primitive beginnings by the age-long work of the human mind, each generation at once conserving and, where it felt the need, modifying the designs of the last. There is no mystery about the way in which man, by this corporate and sustained effort, has invented such things as the plough and the boat and the axe. These inventions have [16] been the work not of one man but of whole communities, not at sudden moments of corporate inspiration but in a long and gradual process of patient consideration and reconsideration.

Nor has the savage copied his stone axe and his dug-out boat from the steel implements and clinker-built craft of civilized man. To suggest such a thing would be to betray the most monstrous misconception of the whole course of human history. But it would not be more absurd than to suggest that the folktale and the folk-song are, in general, relics of literary works, filtered down to the level of the common people and there, losing touch with their authentic originals, degraded to a traditional mode of existence. Such degradations have no doubt happened, as human races have here and there parted with their civilization and sunk into savagery; but to regard such reversals of the normal historical sequence as themselves normal is to forget all the principles of sound historical study and expose the would-be science of folklore to the ridicule of all historians.[19]

This corporate and creative tradition is the normal method by which man acquires every element, material or spiritual, in his culture. In the case of music, poetry, and narrative it has given us the folk-song, the folk-dance, the ballad, and the traditional story.

[19] * Mr C. B. Lewis, in the paper quoted above, attempts to derive all the May-time vegetation-festivals of Western Europe from the Roman imperial cult of Cybele and Attis. This is a typical case of what I am objecting to. I do not claim expert knowledge of vegetation-rituals, but as a specialist in the Romanization of the Western Provinces, I have no hesitation in saying that the suggestion is as baseless as Miss Jessie L. Weston's similar attempt (*From Ritual to Romance* (Cambridge: Cambridge University Press, 1920), chs. 10, 12) to derive the Grail legend from the same source *plus* Mithraism.

[17] When these are called folk-art or traditional art, the only meaning that can be legitimately attached to the qualifying words is this conception of a creative tradition in which the functions of composer and performer are not divided, as in our own literature and music, but are combined in a single person, or rather in a succession of single persons who are at once the performers and co-creators of each work.

The contrast in this respect between illiterate and literate societies, however, must not be exaggerated. The modern poet or musician can publish an authentic text, but no more. He cannot publish those details of emphasis, intonation and so forth which are essential parts of the poem or sonata in its concrete reality as actually performed. The dramatist supplements his text with stage directions, and the musician with 'expression-marks', but these are hints rather than unambiguous commands; and in all other respects the producer and actor, the reciter, and the executant are in the same situation in which the folk-singer or teller of folktales is with regard to the text itself.[20] He plays his part in a creative tradition of 'interpretation'; and his place in that tradition is an important matter for his reputation as a performer. If we could trace in detail the history of this tradition among actors of Shakespeare or players of Chopin, we should find a state of things closely analogous to what we find in the variants of folk-song or fairy tale.

For the printed text of a literary or musical work is not the work itself. It is not even a complete indication of the composer's or writer's intention as to what the work should be. It only indicates certain elements in that intention, namely those which our literary or musical notation, so far as it has yet developed, permits him to record. With regard to [18] the other elements our own music and literature are still in the condition of folk-art.

Even with regard to the text, our situation is not quite so different from that of the folk-artist as one might suppose. Sir George Henschel, in singing *Die Beiden Grenadiere*, used to embroider the accompaniment of the last page with inventions of his own, admirably effective, but not Schumann's. Good conductors will

---

[20] Collingwood is harsher on the use of stage directions in plays and of expression marks in musical scores in *PA* 327–8. He is especially critical of George Bernard Shaw on this count, while 'the same tendency is to be seen at work in most plays of the later nineteenth century; and it is just as conspicuous in music' (327).

interpolate new inner parts into the somewhat bald polyphony of
the slow movement of the Second Brandenburg Concerto.
Mozart's wind parts, added to the score of Handel's *Messiah*,
have become traditional. On the other side of the account, all
producers cut Shakespeare, and there was a time when they used
to stick bits out of one play into another, as conductors once used to
replace the slow movement of Beethoven's seventh symphony with
that of the second. Liberties of this sort are out of fashion nowadays, yet they are still taken, especially on the stage; and so
judicious a scholar as Mr John Sparrow has argued for their
extension, pleading that there are many passages in the corpus of
English poetry where alterations might be improvements.[21] These
are signs that our modern idea as to the relation between the artist
or writer and the performer, according to which the latter is the
former's humble slave, doing what he is told and never venturing
to disregard jot or tittle of the sacred text, or aspiring in however
small a degree to the position of co-creator, is exaggerated and
impracticable; and that we need to be reminded of another idea,
the idea which rules in all illiterate societies, according to which
the creation of music and literature is the work, not of a separate
[19] class of composers and writers, but of their performers acting
in collaboration with their audiences.

Be that as it may, this is the manner in which folktales were
composed. Before leaving the subject, it may be well to point out
two consequences.

First, there is no sense in asking whether the music, stories, and
verses which have been composed in this way are better or worse
than those which have been composed in our modern fashion. It is
a question that has been hotly debated. Some have exhausted the
vocabulary of admiration over the achievements of folk-song and
folk-poetry; even going so far as to suggest that their 'folk' quality
gave them a native superiority over the products of sophisticated
art. That is sentimentalism, resting insecurely on a basis of contempt. We are so proud of being educated that we expect the art of

[21] Collingwood indicates an intended footnote here but does not supply it. John
Hanbury Angus Sparrow (1906–76) was a prolific critic of often pungent views;
Collingwood may have in mind his *Sense and Poetry: Essays on the Place of Meaning
in Contemporary Verse* (London: Constable, 1934). Sparrow later became Warden
of All Souls College (1954–76).

illiterate persons to be, for that reason, bad; we find that it is not; and in our astonishment we judge it more highly than it really deserves. In reaction against this sentimentalism we look at these works more coolly,[22] and find that we had deceived ourselves; and we rush to the opposite conclusion that our original prejudice was right and that only 'educated' people can produce really good art. The fact is that traditional art, like all art, is good, bad, or indifferent according to the temper and skill of the people who have made it. Some folk-tunes and fairy tales are very good; others very bad; most of them a fair average in merit, like the output of our [21] own printing presses. If they seldom rise so high and seldom fall so low as these latter, that is because they stand in closer relation to their audience, on which they rely for their perpetuation; and this tends to reduce them to an average level satisfactory to the demands of that audience.

A second consequence is that there is no such thing as folk-sculpture, folk-painting, folk-architecture, folk-embroidery, or the like, in the sense in which there is folk-literature or folk-music. We do no doubt talk of these things, but we use the phrase in a different sense: a sense which would be better expressed by speaking of peasant arts. The special character of the folk-song or folktale arises out of the fact that it has been handed down from mouth to mouth, altered to suit the varying demands and capacities of the singer or teller and his audience. Its *esse* is its *fieri*; its *fieri* is the tradition of those in whose mouth it lives. But a village woodworker who carves an oak chest, or a village lover who carves a stay-busk for his girl, is producing something that lasts, something which we today can see pretty much as he left it; its being is the material being of a piece of wood, not the impalpable being of a tale which survives only because it is retold. Between him and the anonymous master-mason who carved a roof-boss at Westminster, or Michelangelo who left us the Medici tomb, there is no

---

[22] * 'When a ballad is set in a collection alongside the best of Herrick, Gray, Landor, Browning—to name four poets opposite as the poles and to say nothing of such masterpieces as Spenser's *Epithalamion* or Milton's *Lycidas*—it is the ballad that not only suffers by the apposition but suffers to a surprising degree; so that I have sometimes been forced to reconsider my affection, and ask, "Are these ballads really [as] beautiful as they have always appeared to me?"' Sir Arthur Quiller Couch (ed.), *The Oxford Book of Ballads* (Oxford: Clarendon Press, 1910), p. xvi. [This footnote actually appears on fo. 20 and is the only text on that sheet.]

difference of principle, only the difference between a little artist and a big one. In the sense in which *Tom Tit Tot* is 'traditional', a peasant's carving or weaving is no more traditional than the Sistine Madonna or the B Minor Mass.

ADDENDA TO THE FOLKTALE MANUSCRIPT

MODERN SCIENCE A DEVELOPMENT OF THAT RITUAL
WE MISCALL MAGICAL

In the spirit of their work, all three [existing approaches to the study of early societies][1] share the same vice: that of lumping their subject matter into the category of 'primitive' or 'savage' mind. They have all assumed that, ultimately, their problem was to expound the nature of this thing and the laws of its working. By doing this, they have committed themselves to the absurd task of giving a scientific account of a non-existent subject matter. 'Primitive' strictly means original or initial; and the primitive mind means the form in which man's mind existed at the beginning of human history. But when and where did human history begin, and what documents have we as evidence for how the first men thought? These are questions which mean nothing. Before the earliest Palaeolithic period, which has left us implements showing certain facts—very few—about the minds of those who made and used them, it is suspected that there was a long period when men made 'eoliths'. But it is not certain that eoliths were made by man at all. If they were, the men who made them were not primitive; they had acquired a tradition of craftsmanship and a kind of civilization. And doubtless, before they lived, there were still earlier men, who made nothing whatever that has come down to us. Let us be frank. We know nothing whatever about the minds of any human beings, until human beings had lived on the earth

---

The heading is the editors'. These Addenda bring together two MS fragments on fairy tales from the Bodleian Library Collingwood Papers, dep. 21/8 (11 fos.) and dep. 21/11 (7 fos.). The title of dep. 21/8, 'Modern Science a Development...', was originally inserted at the top of fo. 2 by Collingwood. The first few pages of the fragment may be read as a draft version of the opening of FT3, 'The Historical Method' (above), where Collingwood is working through the same set of ideas, though he has also written 'to concluding chapter' at the top of fo. 2.

[1] Presumably referring to the "Three Methods of Approach: Philological, Functional, Psychological' of FT2.

for thousands of years. There are no beginnings in history. As we trace it back, it vanishes in the darkness long before we reach its beginning.

But those who talk about primitive mind do not mean what they say. What they are trying to describe is the mind of people who are 'savage' or 'uncivilized'. But the depth of their [. . .]² **[2]** the faith in nature which is the root of science is not demonstrable, any more than its correlative, the faith in reason. This double faith, attaching itself to the idea of mechanism, that is, of action as mediated by a tool or machine at once connecting and separating the agent and what he acts on, is science. Attaching itself to the idea of action as unmediated, going direct and without any intervening tool from agent to patient, it is religion. The fundamental faith itself is nothing but man's consciousness of himself as living and acting. Its decay would be the mental death or madness of man. No man can possess it except in both of these two forms. If he ceased to know that he acts immediately, without any intervening tool, as mind on his own body and as the unity of mind and body upon his environment, all his activities would be cut off at the source. If he ceased to know that he can act on one thing through the mediation of another thing, he would lose all the special powers of thought and action which make him stronger than the other brutes.

What we call primitive man does not lack science. He understands enough of mechanics, of chemistry, of biology, to plough and fish and throw spears, to light fires and bake pots, and to sow seed and breed animals. Astronomy gives him his agricultural calendar. Medicine and surgery enable him to find useful herbs and to conduct a good many surgical operations. All these sciences he has studied in the only way in which science can be studied, by means of hypothesis and experiment; and it is an ungrateful vanity in ourselves to forget that in all these matters we are his heirs, and live on the knowledge he has acquired.

[3] But all these ways of working with tools are specialized ways of working without them. Man digs with a plough or a hoe or a stick because he has first dug with his bare hands. He hunts with weapons because he once hunted unarmed. He judges the sowing-

---

² There is a discontinuity between fos. 1 and 2 which suggests these sheets were part of an early draft.

time by the stars because he once judged it by guesswork. And however far he goes on the road of mechanization, he must still have a strong enough faith in his immediate activity to assure him that he can handle the tools he has invented and make them do what he wants. No throwing-stick will help the faltering arm to throw a straight spear; no pharmacopoeia will direct the treatment when the physician's eye and ear and hand fail him. Behind all his array of scientific tools, man is still the same naked animal. If he needed valour and wisdom to face nature unarmed, he needs them all the more if he is to use these tools without destroying himself.

Civilized man, when he takes it upon himself to despise the savage, forgets this. He mistakes the superiority of his tools for a superiority in himself. He forgets that unless his immediate action, his power to make his tools do what he wants them [to do], has advanced in proportion to the advance of his tools themselves, he is sacrificing all the ends of life in his elaboration of means to procure them. Even now, he seems to be cowering in the midst of his machinery, helplessly looking on while it works of itself, like the sorcerer's apprentice who raised the Devil. A mechanized civilization, developing its ingenuity at the expense of its wisdom, and its faith in tools at the expense of its faith in the naked hand, may admire itself; it can hardly expect admiration from those whom it calls savages.

[4] What we call magic or religion, therefore (for attempts to distinguish the two things will always continue to break down as they have broken down in the past) is not an unsuccessful attempt at science. It is the expression and development of man's faith in his immediate action and the immediate action of other persons and things on himself. Our mechanized civilization has decided to suppress it in the mistaken belief that it can be replaced by science. The effect of this on ourselves has been very complex. First, we have fabricated an altogether mistaken idea of our own civilization. We flatter ourselves that it is everywhere based on scientific knowledge, whereas at every point it is riddled with magic. Secondly, we have come to despise as our intellectual inferiors those who still take magic or religion seriously. Thirdly, because in spite of our self-satisfaction we are dimly aware of the magical motives that control much of our own action, we despise ourselves too: our self-contempt being as groundless as our self-satisfaction.

The first error leads us to the absurd hope that, merely by becoming more and more scientific, we shall rise to greater and greater heights of wealth and happiness; as a man going blind might buy bigger and bigger telescopes.

The second error leads us to oppress and exploit and massacre all races whose civilization is less scientific than our own, and to set up as a new religion the worship of mechanized violence.

The third error, most fatal of all, leads us to despair of the future of our own civilization, and to acquiesce in its folly and savagery as things that cannot be mended.

All these things are bound up with that misunderstanding and contempt towards the 'savage' mind which are expressed in Frazer's definition of magic.

[5] THE STUDY OF FAIRY TALES[3]

It is difficult for a civilization to study itself. In a community of people who all think and act in certain well-defined ways, these customs and beliefs are not likely to arouse anyone's curiosity. No one finds himself confronted by them as by something that offers a problem to his understanding and a challenge to his thought. They are not things to study; they are, rather, the spectacles through which other things are studied.

Gervase of Tilbury tells us that in thirteenth-century England fairy tales were told round the fire of an evening in every gentleman's house. He gives us an example of one, which shows how like these medieval fairy tales were to those which we know today. It is about an ancient hill-fort—Wandelbury, on the Gogmagog hills—where if you rode your horse into the earthworks at night and shouted a challenge, an armed man would appear and engage you in combat. This theme of the Warden and the Challenge, as we shall find in the sequel, is one of the fundamental motives of our fairy tales.[4]

---

[3] Collingwood's title (struck out).

[4] This and the previous paragraph are struck out and the note 'to last chapter' is inserted at the head of the fo. above the title. A slightly modified version of this paragraph is in fact worked into FT1, fo. 2.

While the telling of such stories remained a normal practice in all classes of society, there was no more incentive to think about it, to ask what it meant and what good it was, than there is nowadays to ask the same questions about cricket. The thing was an accepted institution; what would need investigation, rather, would be the fact (if such fact should be discovered) that there were people who lived without it. This state of things was reflected in the literature of the age, in Boccacio and Chaucer; transposed into an appropriate key, it entered the monasteries and produced the *Gesta Romanorum*; and there are signs that it survived the close of the Middle Ages and lasted into the time of Elizabeth.[5]

[6] Between 1600 and 1800 this ancient institution disappeared. Its disappearance, like many another social revolution, took place so silently that one can hardly now recover the history of it. But the upshot of that history is well known. By the nineteenth century, these same fairy tales had become 'folk-lore'. The practice of telling them, in other words, had died out from among the educated classes, the gentry and those who had modelled their lives on the example of the gentry: but it survived in what, from the point of view of that class, is an alien and underground world, the world of the 'lower classes'. To be more precise, it survived not in the lower classes as such but in the peasantry, or agricultural lower class. The industrial proletariat of the towns had lost it almost as completely as the gentry themselves. On the other hand, the servants of the gentry, being mostly peasants by birth and training, still have it; and by their agency it is introduced into the nurseries of the educated class.

[7] In the Highlands it was the minister and the schoolmaster who, coming as apostles of education and enlightenment, destroyed this custom. The peasantry, now the sole trustees of what had once been a universal institution, recognized that if they were to keep it alive they must protect it against these powers, and that their only means of doing so was to keep their own counsel. Thus by degrees the ancient stories became, as it were, the property of a secret society from which educated persons were automatically excluded. It was only their children, as yet uncontaminated by education, who could be admitted to a kind of honorary membership; and hence the children's nurse figures in the history of folklore study as the main channel through which

---

[5] This paragraph is struck out in pencil.

the traditional stories filtered through into the educated class. The proverbial secretiveness of the peasant is a thing of modern growth; he has developed it in the course of a long warfare in defence of those ancient beliefs and customs which were once shared by the whole of society.

At the same time, the educated classes became aware that among their own neighbours there existed a mass of beliefs and customs widely differing from their own. Having lost the fairy tales themselves, they rediscovered them **[8]** as something belonging to the peasantry. Because these things were no longer part and parcel of their own culture, they aroused their curiosity and struck them as things deserving of study. Or rather, they struck a few intelligent and open-minded people in this way; to the majority of the educated class, their interest was swamped by the aversion which they aroused as symptoms of rustic stupidity. The cultural breach between the educated man and the peasant operated both ways. It placed the peasant's folklore over against the educated man, as something objective and therefore able to be studied scientifically; at the same time it made the educated man regard this folklore as a thing only fit for his inferiors, the uneducated and ignorant rabble. Intellectually he might be curious about it; emotionally he was repelled by it as typical of that unenlightened state of existence out of which, by dint of education, he had painfully climbed.

This double attitude towards its subject matter created the atmosphere in which the study of fairy tales grew up. Those who pursued it, though intellectually strong in the enjoyment of a good conscience, as studying a very real class of human facts, were emotionally always on the defensive: apologetic towards the rest of the educated class, who regarded the tales of peasants and children as silly, irrational, and therefore undeserving of scientific attention, and apologetic even towards themselves, as feeling that their own condescension to these follies was a trifle undignified. The greatest masterpiece of scientific folklore contains a formal apology for 'the long tragedy of human folly and suffering' which the writer has inflicted on his readers;[6] and to this day, the study

---

[6] * Sir James Frazer, Preface, *The Golden Bough: Balder the Beautiful*, i, p. vi. Tylor knew better: see *Primitive Culture: Researches into the Development of Mythology, Philosophy, Religion, Language, Art and Custom*, 3rd rev. edn., 2 vols. (London: John Murray, 1891), i. 22–3.

which forms the subject matter of the present [9] volume[7] is regarded as a thing lacking the dignity and respectability of a true science. The source of this contempt is not a judgement on the intellectual worth of the study itself or on the human importance of its subject matter; it is an emotional prejudice against the subject matter itself, as the characteristic expression of an attitude towards life not only different from our own but inferior to it, proper only to those infra-rational minds which Locke, the father of modern enlightenment, lumped together as children, idiots, and savages.

In the sequel, I shall be obliged to examine both the grounds and the consequences of this prejudice more closely. For the present, I confine myself to the effect which it had on the scientific study of folklore. In two ways this effect was damaging. First, the open contempt of the enlightened class for fairy tales and everything for which they stood made it difficult to collect the necessary material, and as time went on tended to stamp it out altogether. The collector of fairy tales and folklore found it hard, and increasingly hard, to win the confidence of the people from whom he wished to collect them; he also found that, when he had done so, he was faced with the fact that the things he wished to study were vanishing under his very eyes. With the spread of education, and especially when the effects of the Education Act of 1870 began to be felt, the process which had already turned the gentry away from their old fairy tales began to involve the peasantry too.[8] The enlightenment which filtered down to the 'lower classes' through the medium of the village school and the newspaper was no doubt a mere shadow of the thing to which Voltaire had devoted an apostolic life; but its general principles were the same; and its effect upon the secret society (as I have called it) which held in trust the national tradition of folklore [10] was to break it up from within. By the beginning of the present century it had become almost hopeless to inquire among the peasantry of England for fairy tales and folksongs, except from the very oldest members, the survivors of the generation that had grown up before education became universal.

---

[7] From this we can infer that Collingwood thought of this section, or a revised version of it, as an integral part of his book.

[8] In *PA*, Collingwood criticizes the 1870 Education Act for slowly destroying the values of rural life by imposing on the countryman an education modelled on the city-dweller (101–2).

Secondly, the same cause hindered, and still hinders, the development of sound methods within the science itself. The rise of
natural science in the seventeenth century owes more than is
generally recognized to the previous establishment of a very definite emotional attitude towards nature herself. Long before Gali-
leo began his work, people had accustomed themselves to look
upon nature as divine, either (in the orthodox Christian sense) as
God's handiwork, or in the sense of Renaissance pantheism as
actually identical with God. And for a Christian civilization the
idea that nature is divine implies that it is rational; that, even where
one cannot see the principles on which it works, one can apprehend
by faith that there are such principles, and that in searching for
them one is at least not chasing an *ignis fatuus*. On this emotional
attitude towards nature the whole fabric of natural science is built.

But where the subject matter of a science was regarded as a mere
record of childishness and idiocy, the very foundations of its
method were wanting. Consequently there is little wonder if the
science of fairy tales has lacked the nerve and the incentive to make
itself genuinely scientific, and if, when it has tried to do so, the
attempt has been at best half-hearted. But however unsuccessful
these attempts have been, we must know something about them if
we are to improve on them.

The first thing to be done was to collect a body of raw material to
work upon. And the first collection of this kind was made by the
brothers Grimm in [11] 1819. Before that, we have only prettified
literary versions like those of Perrault at the end of the seventeenth
century in France and of Musäus (1782) in Germany, and, further
back, the Italian collections of Straparola (1560) and Basile (1634–
6).[9] The work of the Grimms arose directly out of the romantic
nationalism that swept over Germany at the beginning of the

<hr/>

[9] Jacob and Wilhelm Grimm, *Kinder- und Hausmärchen, Gesammelt durch die
Bruder Grimm*, 2 vols. (Berlin: Realschulbuchhandlung, 1812–15); Charles Per-
rault, *Histoires ou contes du temps passé* (Paris, 1698); Johann Karl August Musäus,
Volksmärchen der Deutschen, 5 vols. (Gotha: Ettinger, 1782–87); Giovan Francesco
Straparola, *Le piacevoli notti* ('The Pleasant Nights), 2 vols. (1550/3), tr. W. G.
Waters as *The Facetious Nights* (London: Society of Bibliophiles, 1898); Giambat-
tista Basile, *Lo Cunto de li cunti overo la trattenemiento de' Peccerille, de Gian Alessio
Abbatutis*, 5 vols. (Naples: Ottavio Beltrano, 1634–6), tr. N. M. Penzer, *The
Pentamerone of Giambattista Basile*, 2 vols. (London: John Lane and the Bodley
Head, 1932).

nineteenth century and awakened the interest of Germans in ancient Germanic civilization as the root out of which their own had
sprung. That work was scientific in the sense that the tales were
published with the minimum of editing and writing-up, so as to
give a relatively uncorrupt text of the collected material; and also
in the sense that the Grimms subjected this material to analysis,
pointing out the various themes which recurred in different
stories.

DIFFUSION AND INDEPENDENT ORIGIN OF FAIRY TALES[10]

Those who study fairy tales are agreed that very simple and obvious themes might arise independently in different countries; but
that in certain cases, where the resemblance is of a more complex
kind, it is necessary to think of the stories as one and the same,
invented once and propagated by diffusion. Thus, it is easy to
believe that stories describing an escape by flight from a powerful
enemy should have been invented quite independently any number of times; but if the escape is effected by throwing down small
things which grow by magic into huge obstacles, we begin to
wonder whether independent origin is possible; and if the objects
are three in number and consist of a twig that becomes a forest, a
stone that becomes a mountain, and a little water that becomes
a river or sea, we are forced to suppose that diffusion has been at
work.

In a general way, the division is no doubt justified; but the
question where to draw the line is difficult to answer. If mere
complexity is the criterion, how complex must an incident or
block of incidents be, in order that independent origin should be
inconceivable? If singularity or strangeness is the criterion, an
incident which seems strange to people who live in one way may
seem obvious to people who live in another. For example, the
Cupid and Psyche theme, in which a bride loses her husband
because she breaks the rule forbidding her to see him, seems very

---

[10] Bodleian Library Collingwood Papers, dep. 21/11. The title is the editors'.
The item is referred to in Ruth A. Burchnall's *Catalogue of the Papers of Robin
George Collingwood, 1889–1943* (Oxford: Bodleian Library, 1994), as an 'Untitled
manuscript concerning the problem of diffusion versus the independent origin of
folk tales'.

strange to us, but the kind of taboo on which it turns is a common-place in many primitive societies; and, where taboos of that kind exist, [2] stories based on that theme might arise independently. Moreover, there is no such thing as an absolutely simple theme. Any theme contains in itself a variety of ideas and is thus complex; and the structure of the theme itself dictates to some extent the way in which it will develop when a story-teller's imagination plays round it. Human stupidity exists wherever there are men; stories describing and ridiculing it are told wherever there are stories. To imagine that these are all derived from some one *Urmärchen* about a fool would itself be a fine piece of folly. Whenever there are fools, malicious neighbours have conspired at times to expose their folly; and the widespread story-theme of a conspiracy to deceive a fool need not have been diffused from any one centre. But such a theme is already a story in germ. One conspirator tells the fool a thumping lie; the fool disbelieves it, and they agree to refer the question to the first man they meet; he, of course, is in the plot, and the fool ends by being convinced. There are many stories based on this idea; the question to what extent they are derived from a common source must depend not on the logic of the idea itself but on the detail of the stories.

The greatest discoveries and inventions are those which, once they have been made, seem so obvious that those who receive them can hardly believe they have not made them for themselves. An invention which has spread by diffusion in these conditions is so thoroughly at home in the countries of its adoption that it fits into the ideas and customs of those countries like a thing of native [3] growth. This is as true of stories as of anything else; and hence arises the paradox which makes it so difficult to ascertain the truth about their diffusion. The paradox is this: the same facts which, if a story had reached a certain place by diffusion, would have caused its adoption there, would have caused its independent origin there, if it had originated independently. For a story would not have been adopted by a certain people, had it not appealed to them in the first instance as something which 'all had felt, but none so well express'd';[11] that is to say, as something not only tolerated but demanded by their character and temperament and the state of

---

[11] An allusion to Alexander Pope's *An Essay on Criticism* (1711), l. 298: 'What oft was *Thought*, but ne'er so well *Exprest*'.

culture at which they have arrived. But these are precisely the conditions under which they might have invented the story for themselves. For adoption in the case of stories is not like the adoption of exotic material objects like top hats or breechloading firearms; it implies retelling, and retelling implies a certain amount of remodelling, which will bring the story, whatever its source, into line with the artistic abilities and tastes of its new possessors. If a subtle and elaborate story is thus adopted by a people whose abilities are unequal to appreciating its subtleties, it will soon lose them in passing from mouth to mouth, and acquire a literary form suitable to the genius of that people.

This assimilation will affect the content of the story as well as its form. In the first stages of its adoption, it will very likely contain exotic elements; but as the process of assimilation goes forward these will disappear, and the whole setting and colouring will be brought into line with the conditions of life in the country where the story is [4] undergoing naturalization. As J. F. Campbell observes concerning Highland stories which he believes to have been taken over in recent times from the *Arabian Nights*, 'these contain the incidents embodied in stories in the Arabian Nights, but the whole machinery and decoration, manners and customs, are now as completely West Highland as if the tales had grown there. But for a camel which appears', he continues, noting a single point in which assimilation has been incomplete, 'I would almost give up my opinion, and adopt that of MacLean, who holds that even these are pure tradition, that is, independent local inventions.'[12] The conservation of an oral tradition may no doubt act as a brake on this process, and cause narrators to retain as part of a story camels, lions, and other beasts not to be found where the story is told; but in order that this force should operate, the story must first become part and parcel of the tradition that is to conserve it; and this does not happen until a good deal of assimilation has already taken place.

[12] * John Francis Campbell, *Popular Tales of the West Highlands*, 2nd edn., 4 vols. (No place of publication: Gardner, 1890), i, p. xlii.

PART III

THE MODERN UNEASE

ART AND THE MACHINE

One of the points in which our civilization is not wholly sane is in its attitude towards art. There has never been a time when so much trouble was taken to introduce people at large to the best works of art; but the results of all this effort are disappointing in the extreme. We sometimes comfort ourselves in a back-handed kind of way by saying that the English people are an inartistic race.

Collingwood had originally entered the title "Taste and the Machine' at the head of the first fo. (written on the opposite side of Pembroke College notepaper), but crossed out the first word and replaced it with 'Art'. The MS (Bodleian Library Collingwood Papers, dep. 25/8) is undated, but a date of c.1926 is proposed by Taylor, *Bibliography*, who also suggests that much of the essay is a version of Collingwood's 'The Place of Art in Education', *Hibbert Journal*, 24 (1925–6), 434–48, reprinted in *Essays in the Philosophy of Art by R. G. Collingwood*, ed. Alan Donagan (Bloomington: Indiana University Press, 1964), 187–207. The suggestion is repeated by Christopher Dreisbach, *R. G. Collingwood: A Bibliographic Checklist* (Bowling Green, Ohio: The Philosophy Documentation Center, Bowling Green State University, 1993). However, the *Hibbert Journal* article actually concentrates much more on the role of education and art, while 'Art and the Machine' (as its title suggests), focuses emphatically on the mechanical reproduction of art and its degrading consequences for culture and civilization. Collingwood recommends a practical education in art of all kinds as a remedy for this decline. In addition to these considerations, a later date of composition than 1926 may be considered if we take seriously what Collingwood does not say. The first talking picture, *The Jazz Singer* starring Al Jolson, was previewed on 6 Oct 1927. Collingwood does not complain of a lack of sound when he talks of film (AM, fos. 8–9 below), only of the purpose for the audience, the provision of an emotional kick, and of the inability of film to convey the presence of the actor. In fact, the radio and the cinema are described as vehicles for conveying noises that produce emotional stimuli. In *PH* 69–74, Collingwood was later to complain that the purpose of biography was to titillate and play upon the reader's emotions. (See also *IH* 304.) AM also recalls very closely the discussion in ch. 5 of *PA* of art as amusement or entertainment: ' "Why", one hears it asked, "should not the popular entertainment of the cinema, like the Renaissance popular entertainment of the theatre, produce a new form of great art?" The answer is simple. In the Renaissance theatre collaboration between author and actors on the one hand, and audience on the other, was a lively reality. In the cinema it is impossible' (323). Such connections might seem to make it more likely that AM was written nearer the time Collingwood wrote the folktale MS.

Applied to the countrymen of Shakespeare and Chaucer, Purcell and Christopher Wren, the statement is obviously false: and those who make it are perhaps not prepared to explain what art is, that a race could be without part or lot in it. This, however, seems to be true, that somehow we have got into an inartistic streak in the history of our nation. That is a fact which we might regard with indifference if we understood nothing about the nature of art and its necessity to the development of a healthy mental life. We also complain that modern life is drab and uninteresting, and drives people to unwholesome emotional stimulants in the attempt to relieve their boredom; and the two things are more closely connected, perhaps, than we generally recognize.

But what then? say some. We live in a machine-made age. In such an age, can art flourish? No.[1] Let us then eat and drink, and find what consolation we can for the dullness of our existence.

Here we come near to the heart of our problem. We must try to get still nearer, by inquiring further into the relation between art and machinery. Let it be understood that no one denies the beauty of machines, or of machine-made things well designed, like engines and motor-cars; but these, though beautiful, are not works of art. A work of art is something which is only made in order that it may be beautiful.[2]

Let us consider, then, the case of machine-made works of art: and especially, since in the days of the camera, the gramophone, and the wireless these especially concern us, works of art mechanically reproduced.

[2] There is no hostility between works of art and mechanical reproduction as such. A coin or a medallion, a woodcut or a page of printing, is in no way disfigured by being mechanically multiplied. On the other hand, a photograph of a painting or statue, or the reproduction of a musical performance by wireless or gramophone, does disfigure the original, in such a way as to make the proper

---

[1] Collingwood in this paper addresses from a different point of view very much the same question as Walter Benjamin in 'L'Œuvre d'art à l'époque de sa reproduction mécanisée', *Zeitschrift für Sozialforschung*, 51 (1936), 40–63. See 'The Work of Art in the Age of Mechanical Reproduction', *Illuminations*, ed. Hannah Arendt, tr. Harry Zorn (London: Pimlico, 1999), 211–44.

[2] The distinction between the definition of beauty and of the nature of art is made in *PA*, esp. 15–36.

appreciation of it impossible save to an expert, and difficult even to him.

In the case of a painting, the photograph omits the colour. But the colour is an essential part of the original. Even if the colours are reduced to their lowest terms, as for example in a monochrome drawing in sepia or Indian ink, the exact colour-relation between the pigment, with subtle colour-differences where it is laid on thicker or thinner, and the ground on which it is laid, is part of the drawing, and may have been for the artist a very important part. But you cannot omit any of the things which the artist has deliberately put into his work without in some way upsetting the balance and effect of the whole; and it was only to produce that balance and effect that the work was originally done. Again, the relation between the lightness and darkness of various parts is an essential element in a painting; and unless you can get absolutely panchromatic photography, that is always more or less falsified in every photograph. The size of a painting, once more, is an element in its design; no artist would plan or execute a work six inches by four in exactly the same manner as one twelve feet by eight. The mere reduction in size causes a photograph to misrepresent a painting.

Photographs of paintings and other works of art have their uses; they are extremely useful to the student, the teacher, and in general to persons who use them for investigating certain selected aspects of these works: the aspects which a photograph can represent. But there is one purpose for which they are quite [3] useless. They cannot convey the general effect or significance of the works to persons who have no direct knowledge of the originals. An expert can no doubt reconstruct the original in his mind from a photograph, as an anatomist can reconstruct a dog from a single bone. But to offer the photograph to an uneducated man and expect him to find in it the admirable qualities of the original is like giving him the bone and expecting him to make friends with the dog. A humble and diffident man will no doubt persuade himself that he sees what he is told to see; a sincere and courageous man will confess that he sees nothing—nothing, anyhow, to justify the fuss that is made about Rembrandt or whoever it may be.

The same applies to mechanical reproductions of music. A musical performer has to play in time and in tune, but he has also to produce exactly the right quality of sound at exactly the right degree of loudness and softness. Mechanical reproduction can now give us a fair approximation to the quality of musical sounds—we can tell an oboe from a flute, and so on—but can no more represent it with an accuracy comparable to that aimed at by the executant than colour-photography can reproduce the delicate colour-distinctions made by a first-rate painter. As regards loudness and softness, our reproduction is simply chaotic. Instead of having these regulated by the performer, the listener regulates them for himself by changing a needle or turning a knob. That is to say, unless he is already a person of highly educated taste, he does not know how to get out of his machine a noise even approximately like that which the performer is making.

What we get out of these machines, therefore, is not music itself but a photograph of music: useful and instructive to listeners [4] who are already expert, but quite useless for the purpose of giving the uneducated a true representation of the general effect or significance of what they are hearing.

These criticisms may seem exaggerated. Surely, it will be said, the photograph and the wireless can give at least a partial, rough, and approximate representation of the original: and surely that will give the beginner some idea of what the original is really like—as much as he is able to take in.

Nothing could be more mistaken. A work of art has to be grasped as a whole, and as it actually is: as the painter painted it, or as the musician plays it. If in a given work there is too much for the beginner to take in, he should be offered, not a mutilation or caricature of it, but something easier. Snobbery apart, there is no reason why beginners in music should listen to the Choral Symphony or the B Minor Mass, or beginners in the appreciation of painting should look at the Bacchus and Ariadne or the Origin of the Milky Way. But if they are introduced to these things, they ought to be at least given a chance of seeing what Titian and Tintoretto (or the cleaners) have left us, and hearing what Beethoven and Bach, or Sir Henry Wood, meant us to hear. As it is, ninety-nine listeners in a hundred, when a classical concert begins, switch over to another station where they can hear dance-music. And the same proportion would rather look at a magazine-cover with a succulent young lady on it than at a photograph of the Botticelli Venus.

In this they are quite right. These mechanical reproductions destroy the effect of the original in proportion as that effect depends on delicacies of colour, form, texture, scale, and the like which they cannot catch. Works expressly designed for such reproduction, like magazine-cover drawings and the playing [5] of a dance-band, lose in reproduction nothing that matters, and therefore come through as they were meant to be seen and heard. And of other works, it is just the coarser and cruder, the less delicate and sensitive, that come through best. Thus mechanical reproduction acts as a filter which strains out the best works of art, and lets through, not exactly the worst, but those whose merits are consistent with a certain blatancy and harshness never found in really good art.

The promoters and popularizers of mechanical reproduction expected it to result in a general spread of artistic education. It seemed obvious to them that really good art had only to be seen and heard in order to be admired, and that by means of such reproduction it could be seen and heard by everybody and therefore admired by everybody. Half a century ago, this result was expected of prints and photographs from the Old Masters; nowadays the same result is expected from the gramophone and the wireless. The first of these expectations has long ago proved vain. Anyone can buy postcards of famous pictures for a penny or two; but no one buys them except the few who know the pictures at first hand and use the postcards to refresh their memory. The second expectation has had, by now, a fair trial and has proved just as futile. Unfortunately, it is not hard to discover what sorts of noise people prefer to hear from their machines; a hotel lounge, a summer evening on the river, and a walk down a few streets will give a fair cross-section of the popular taste. It would be hypocrisy to pretend that such a cross-section includes any appreciable trace of the music which those who have taken trouble to understand music know to be the best.

The reason why such false hopes were entertained is simple. It came from the expert's inability to put himself in the position of the beginner. The expert so easily goes behind [6] the photograph to the picture, behind the wireless or gramophone to the concert-room, that he does not know he is doing it. He looks at a pattern of printer's ink on a postcard, and imagination transports him to the Uffizi, where he stands in awe before an opalescent radiance of colour. He hears a needle scratching on a vulcanite disk, and his trained ear catches the liquid texture of a Mozart quartet. But these things, like the Emperor's new clothes, are supplied by his imagination, and it takes a candid ignoramus to play the child and blurt out the fact that the Emperor has nothing on at all.

Mechanical reproduction, as a means of bringing great art to the general public, has failed, as it was doomed to fail from the start. But its failure has had positive results as well as negative. It has acted as a corrupting influence, debasing the taste which it failed to elevate. Because the highbrow did not distinguish between the real work of art and its machine-made counterpart, thinking he saw in the reproduction what was only in the original, the lowbrow obediently follows his premises, but reverses the conclusion and infers that because the reproduction is visibly worthless the original is worthless too. Having been trained to judge Botticelli from postcards and Mozart from the wireless, he not only forms a false opinion of what Botticelli and Mozart are like, but carries this false opinion with him, in the shape of a prejudice, against the time when he sees or hears them in the original. When that happens, instead of saying 'they have deceived me with their miserable machines; the thing itself is lovely', he will see nothing in the original except what he saw in the mechanical reproduction, and he will conclude that all 'great art' is a fraud. I state this as a future peril; but to a great extent it is already a present fact. The cleavage between a so-called highbrow minority, which enjoys good art and is publicly despised for doing so, and a frankly philistine majority which regards that enjoyment as a contemptible form of self-deception, not only exists but tends to become deeper. It is not with indifference, [7] but with loathing, that the hotel guest rushes to turn off the wireless when he hears the sound of classical music. Art, from being a mystery to the uninitiated, is becoming a thing that he knows—or thinks he knows—and hates. No great stretch of imagination is needed to think how, in times of violence, the owner of classical gramophone records or reproductions of the Old Masters might find them drawing upon his head the fury of a mob, nominally because the possession of such things betrayed an unpopular attitude in politics, but really because they stamped him as a highbrow.

This failure to educate the people in art, with its result in the hatred of good art as such, is a disaster to our civilization. If it were only a question of appreciating Old Masters and classical music and Greek sculpture, it would not greatly matter. These tastes may with some plausibility be written down as luxuries of the idle rich; at any rate it is true that Pheidias and Titian and Mozart all worked under the patronage of the great. If the elimination of the idle rich is part of our programme for the future, as with many it is, works of art composed for idle rich in the past may perhaps be allowed to fall into oblivion. May it not be that fashions and standards in art are changing; and that a social revolution is going on under our eyes which has already overthrown the old canons of taste, and is proceeding to establish new ones capable perhaps in time of producing results equal to the great works of old, though very different in their character? In order to answer this question we must first ask another: namely, whether the people who consume the mechanized art of today, the cinema and the dance-music and so forth, really do enjoy them at all, in the sense in which works of art are enjoyed; or whether their attitude towards these things is of an altogether different kind.[3]

The enjoyment of a work of art differs from the excitement produced by a physical or emotional stimulus in the fact that it does not wear off. It is not dulled by repetition. A middle- **[8]** aged reader of poetry, reading *Lycidas* for the fiftieth time, probably enjoys it more keenly than when first he read it at 12. Any work of art is in this sense a permanent possession of the person who enjoys it. He may grow out of sympathy with it, and so lose his enjoyment; but that is a result, not of repeated hearing or seeing, but of development in his own mental organization.

Compare this with the public attitude towards a film or a popular song. To judge by box-office figures and the sale of gramophone records, one would say that there was great enjoyment of these things; at any rate, vast numbers of people will pay to see and hear them. But no one would go to see a film fifty times over; and a popular song, even the most successful, commonly enjoys a life of not more than six or eight months. The cinema or mechanized theatre, through the vulgarity and crudeness which are the result of its mechanization, is not enjoyed, in the sense in which a work of art is enjoyed, at all. Those who pay for a seat there are paying for an experience which has nothing in common with the experience of

---

[3] On the proletarianization of art by mechanized reproduction see Benjamin, 'Age of Mechanical Reproduction'. The second half of this paragraph is written on a separate slip and stuck firmly over the original, now largely illegible.

the concert-goer. What they are paying for is not aesthetic enjoyment but sensuous and emotional stimulation. They regard the
film not as a work of art but as a form of 'dope'. The ordinary
attitude towards dance-music, popular songs, and novels is the
same. The reason why all these are popular is that everyday life
in the present world is so dull and drab that emotional stimulation
has become a commodity on sale in the market, and an immense
trade has grown up in what may be called pseudo-art, things
superficially resembling works of art but in reality having a quite
different function and related to genuine art as intoxicating drink is
related to nourishment. Whereas the reader of a poem enjoys the
poem itself, that is, derives pleasure from the objective contemplation of its structure and effect, the audience at a film enjoys, not
the film, but the emotional 'kick' which it gets out of [9] the film.
Next time, it must have a different film, in order to get from it
another experience of the same kind.[4]

The mechanized art of the wireless and the cinema is thus in its
essence not art at all; it is 'dope' or emotional stimulus. Real music
cannot be reproduced on the wireless; the subtleties on which it
depends are lost there, although the musically educated can supply
them from memory and imagination. But noises conveying emotional stimulus can be reproduced quite successfully; the crooner
and the saxophone, whose only aim is to arouse a certain type of
emotional response, lose none of their power to do so. Similarly,
real acting cannot be represented on the screen; it requires the
bodily presence of the actor in personal touch with his audience.
But crude emotional responses, especially those concerned with
the simple and primitive emotions of sexual desire and bodily fear,
can be excited by its means without difficulty.

The habit of taking these emotional drugs is not only leading
people to rely on them increasingly as part of their daily life, it is
also bringing other forms of art into conformity with these models.
There is today a vast consumption of literature, partly in the shape
of what are called novels, partly in the contents of the daily and
other press, whether these are openly fictitious or are offered to the
public as statements of fact. The modern novel is in no sense the
lineal descendant of *Don Quixote*, *Tom Jones*, or *Pride and Preju-*

---

[4] Collingwood unfortunately gives no concrete examples of contemporary
cinema which would allow these propositions to be tested.

dice.[5] It is not a work of art. It is a form of dope;[6] its intention is to arouse certain emotions, and its popularity depends on the reader's finding that the emotions it excites in him are pleasant. No attention is paid to its literary quality. All that the reader notices is the incidents and characters, which he treats as if he encountered them in real life. He likes or dislikes a character not according as the character is well- or ill-depicted, but according as he would like or dislike such a person if he actually met him. In order to facilitate this process, there is one character paradoxically known as the [10] hero, with whom the reader is invited to identify himself, so that the appropriate emotional responses are all prepared for him in advance, in the person of that character. As in the case of the films, the chief emotions prescribed are those connected with sexual desire, and bodily fear: stories of love and crime being almost the only kinds of dope demanded by the novel-reading public.

A people thus drug-sodden in its mental life, systematically replacing all forms of art by corresponding forms of emotional excitement, has naturally lost its power of creating or enjoying art in any form whatever. Instead of displaying, as Englishmen of all generations down to the middle of the nineteenth century did display, an impeccable taste in the architecture of their houses, we find ourselves now struggling in vain with a dead weight of architectural ugliness that has no precedent in the world's history. Instead of furnishing our houses and clothing our bodies with a proper pride in achieving a dignified and beautiful appearance, we alternate between vulgar ostentation, squalid utilitarianism, self-conscious aestheticism, and antiquarian pedantry. The great tradition of English poetry has been divided between the despised highbrows and the purveyors of metrical dope.

The first thing to do with a situation like this is to understand it, so far as we can, historically. First, then, we must note that the general decay of good taste in this country happened long before the present outburst of mechanized pseudo-art. The decay of taste was in full blast half a century ago, and began even earlier; the

[5] Cf. JA1, fo. 2.

[6] In his review of Myron F. Brightfield's *The Issue in Literary Criticism* (1932), in *Philosophy*, 12 (1937), 114–16, Collingwood summarized Brightfield's view of literature 'as a form of dope', but added that: 'And so most modern literature is. But it is disquieting to find an able and accomplished professor arguing that its dope-value is the only value it can have' (116).

mechanized pseudo-art, as a phenomenon affecting the entire people, is a thing of the last ten or twenty years. This would seem to show that the pseudo-art has not, by a kind of Gresham's Law, driven out good art; on the contrary, its coming was due to the dearth of good art; and in fact its growth has coincided with a revival, slender but genuine, of better taste in architecture, music, and poetry.

[11] The decay of taste roughly corresponds with the decline of English agriculture and the predominance of industrial interests in the country. The traditional life of the agricultural population, upper and lower classes alike, was an aesthetically rich one. The gentry, as we can see from the design and contents of their houses, were people of taste: they built well and they employed good artists. The peasantry were enormously rich in folk-song and dance, and their craftsmanship was as admirable in taste as it was in solidity. If proof of these statements is needed, it can easily be had. The houses are still with us; their contents can be traced in the galleries of England and America; Cecil Sharp and others have collected what, early in this century, were left of the folk-songs;[7] and here and there museums are beginning to show the kind of things which a middle-aged man, country-bred, can remember the village joiner and blacksmith making when he was a boy.[8]

Side by side with the agricultural life of the country, strangely out of touch with it, and gathering momentum as the eighteenth century gave place to the nineteenth and the nineteenth went on its way, was another life: that of industry. The story of the relations between these two, in its economic and political aspects, is familiar. Here we are concerned with its aesthetic aspect.

From the first, those who devoted their lives to the service of machines were an inartistic race. They cut themselves off from the artistic traditions of the countryside. They gave themselves up, with a kind of religious asceticism, to the cult of utility. In their daily life they cultivated a Puritanical or Quakerish plainness. In their devotions, they attended places of worship (for they were mostly Nonconformists) barer of architectural grace than any

---

[7] Cf. above FT1, fo. 4, for reference to Cecil Sharp's 1907 volume *English Folk-Songs: Some Conclusions*.

[8] The annihilation of rural life by industrialization is also the theme of the whole third section of MGM (1936), below; this also may add weight to the suggestion that the present piece was written in the mid-1930s.

barn. The houses they built for their workmen were consciously designed for cheapness, but unconsciously (since cheapness alone will not produce ugliness) they expressed the same repudiation of beauty. Thus grew up the drab and squalid environment of the English industrial proletariat: an environment from which even the richest [12] manufacturers hardly escaped. When, towards the middle of the nineteenth century, Disraeli wrote that England was divided into two nations, the rich and the poor, he might with greater truth have called attention to the division between the land and the factory.[9] For in the industrial world the division between rich and poor, by the law of 'clogs to clogs', was shifting and impermanent, but the grimly utilitarian and inartistic character of life was universal.

About the same time, men of taste and artistic education began to discover that, in this respect, England was in a desperate condition. Strangely, in an age when the arts of agricultural life were still thriving, they overlooked the very existence of these things. Looking at England, all they could see was industrialism, and in their judgement of its inartistic character they were not at fault. They set themselves to carry out the artistic regeneration of the English people; and in that attempt they crippled themselves by a long string of mistakes.

First, they failed to see that, on its agricultural side, England was still a richly artistic nation and offered, under their very hands, a starting point for a genuinely home-grown artistic development. Instead of beginning there, they drew their own artistic culture from abroad, and tried to interest their countrymen in French cathedrals and Italian paintings. Thus they began the work of aesthetic education at the wrong end. Instead of contenting themselves with humble beginnings, the materials for which lay ready to hand, they filled their heads with masterpieces and rhapsodized about these over the heads of their audiences, thus creating the gulf of misunderstanding that today separates the highbrow from the common herd.[10]

---

[9] See Benjamin Disraeli, earl of Beaconsfield, *Sybil; or, The Two Nations*, 3 vols. (London: Henry Colburn, 1845).

[10] The last two sentences, from 'began the work . . . ' are written on a separate slip and stuck firmly over the original version, now illegible. The false cultural division referred to here is a prominent theme of FT above.

Then, seeing that the industrial spirit was the force against which they were fighting, they jumped to the conclusion that machines were the enemy of art and that artistic work and hand-work were one and the same thing. This was a tilting at windmills whose only fruit was the revival, here and there, of obsolete industrial methods.

[13] Lastly, by a compensating error in the opposite direction, while they denounced machinery where it was useful, they praised it where it was harmful. Ruskin acclaimed photography as able to beat the artist on his own ground, in depicting architecture or landscape.[11] Thus the door was opened to all the subsequent developments of mechanized art.[12]

Now that the victory of industrial life over agricultural is complete, even to the extent of carrying the war into the enemy's camp and carrying the mechanized dope of cinema and wireless into every village, we are left with the question what to do next. This total rejection of art is a thing in which we cannot acquiesce, because (contrary to the usual opinion, which is based on a confusion between art and emotional dope) no mind can be sanely rational without possessing an artistic basis for its rationality.[13] An inartistic civilization is, to that extent, an insane civilization, melancholy mad.[14] The very drabness of its life drives it, in the search for relief, to the more furious madness of addiction to drugs.

---

[11] In a letter to W. H. Harrison of 12 Aug 1846, Ruskin writes: 'My drawings are truth to the very letter—too literal, perhaps; so says my father, so says not the Daguerreotype, for it beats me grievously.' See *Modern Painters*, i, ch. 3, *Works*, iii. 210 n.

[12] Collingwood distrusted the camera to capture the detail of Roman inscriptions. He hand-drew thousands of inscriptions for his project on the Roman Inscriptions in Britain, and these have been posthumously published. See the W. P. Wright papers in the Ashmolean Library, Oxford.

[13] This, again, is a theme taken up in *PA* 217–21, where the suppression of emotion, which is equivalent to the suppression of art, is said to lead to a corruption of consciousness, and hence a precarious foundation upon which to build rationality.

[14] Cf. Charles Dickens's description of 'Coketown' in *Hard Times*, book 1, ch. 5: 'It was a town of machinery and tall chimneys, out of which interminable serpents of smoke trailed themselves for ever and ever, and never got uncoiled. It had a black canal in it, and a river that ran purple with ill-smelling dye, and vast piles of building full of windows where there was a rattling and a trembling all day long, and where the piston of the steam-engine worked monotonously up and down, like the head of an elephant in a state of melancholy madness'; and book 2, ch. 1 where

It is useless to begin at the end, by improving the cinema, the wireless, and so forth. The reason why these things are popular is that people need dope; 'improve' them—which means cutting off the dope-supply—and people will desert them and seek their dope elsewhere.

The only hope is to begin with that part of the people which is not yet sodden with drugs: the children. The problem is an educational one.

The question is how to give the children an education in art. The first step towards this is to make a gigantic bonfire of the Old Master reproductions, photographs of sculpture and architecture, and all such mechanized art, that still adorn classroom walls, and with them all the little editions of Shakespeare and other classics, the books on musical appreciation, the gramophone records, and in short every aid for introducing children to the accredited works of great art. [14] I have explained the reason for this in every case except that of Shakespeare. I would allow children to see Shakespeare on the stage and to act him for themselves (children's performances of Shakespeare are extraordinarily good; naturally so, indeed, for the plays of that time were written to be acted by children) but never to have him expounded to them, line by line and word by word, at a pace which by destroying the run of the original, the thrust and parry of its dialogue and the flow of its speeches, reduces the living body of his English to the stinking corpse which has made so many victims of the method hate him for the rest of their days.

The second step is to teach them that art is not a thing to be placed on a pedestal and reverently stared at, but an activity, universal and pleasurable, for themselves. To that end we must choose arts for emphasis which stand close to daily life; above all, the arts of language: literature spoken and written. The child must learn to speak; not to repeat the words of others but to utter its own thoughts well and clearly, and to write in the same spirit. What it

the inhabitants of the mills, who, 'wasting with heat', 'toiled languidly in the desert', and where 'no temperature made the melancholy mad elephants more mad than sane'. See *Hard Times for these Times* (1854), ed. David Craig (Harmondsworth: Penguin, 1969), 65, 146. In A. E. Housman's 'Terence, this is stupid stuff', Terence's friends accuse the young poet of killing them with his poetry 'before their time / Moping melancholy mad'. 'A Shropshire Lad' (1896), lxii, *Collected Poems of A. E. Housman*, ed. Christopher Ricks (London: Allen Lane, 1988), 89.

reads, and what (equally important) the teacher reads aloud to it, must be chosen not for being a classic but for being good meat for its young mind: strong, nourishing, not too difficult. Then the arts of bodily gesture: dancing and rhythmical movement. Then drawing, of which handwriting is properly a branch; the child drawing for itself, the teacher drawing with it, and helping it to draw with brush and pen and pencil whatever it wants to draw. Modelling, especially in a good messy medium, is even more important than drawing. The general aim is that the child should become able to speak its mind, to utter itself clearly and accurately in every medium that it handles. I shall be told that a child is too young as yet to have anything in its mind worth uttering; [15] but to the child itself, its thoughts are as important as yours are to you; and more important, because the child is not old enough to know that what it thinks urgent now will one day be forgotten. If a child once realizes the possibilities of its body as a means of expressing what is in its mind, it will have won its latchkey into the house of art. It need no longer experience that boredom of school which is the proper introduction to a drab life and the first lesson of a future drug-addict. A child so trained will need no dope, for it will be able to do something better with its emotions than to stimulate them artificially. It will be able to express them, and so to understand the expressions of other people.[15] Thus its training in art will qualify it to live in a world of reality, facing intelligently the facts of its own and other people's lives.

What? it will be said: would you deprive children of the privilege of studying the great works of classical art? No; I would do the opposite. Instead of forcing caricatures of these works upon them, with the result that they come to hate them, I would train them to speak and draw and model until they are able to see what speech and drawing and modelling are for: and then I will trust them to discover for themselves that Shakespeare and Titian and Pheidias are talking to them in their own language. Children so trained may or may not turn out great artists; they may or may not turn out learned scholars; but they will begin life sane.

[15] For Collingwood on art as expression see *PA* 105–21.

MAN GOES MAD

A generation ago, many thoughtful persons believed not only in the reality of progress, a change visibly (they supposed) taking place in the world by which men were growing wiser, their institutions better, and the entire condition of their lives more enviable; but also in the constancy of the direction in which this change developed; a rectilinear progress, in which a certain kind of advance would be followed by a further advance of the same kind. To take a crude example which may serve to fix the idea by caricaturing it: if the size of an Atlantic liner doubled itself in the last twenty years, it might be expected to double itself again in the next twenty. By thus extrapolating processes of change which (it was believed) would go on in the future as they had gone on in the past, clever men were able to paint exciting pictures of the world as it would appear in the not very distant future.

Since then we have lived through a revolution in human thought: a revolution not so much caused, as precipitated and symbolized, by the war of 1914–18. To the generation that has passed through that experience, those old forecasts of man's future, and the whole system of ideas on which they rested, seem strangely perverse. For they all assumed that the road which nineteenth-century man was treading led uphill to infinity: whereas we have now seen that it led to the brink of a precipice. Over that brink millions of highly civilized men marched, in the course of a few years, to destruction; and now the whole civilized world trembles upon its edge, doubtful whether to continue the mass-suicide, to retrace its steps, or to find means of staying where it is.

Bodleian Library Collingwood Papers, dep. 24/4. The document is marked 'Rough MS. begun 30 Aug. 36'. There is a detailed, highly critical, and extremely intemperate consideration of this essay by Maurice Cowling in *Religion and Public Doctrine in Modern England* (Cambridge: Cambridge University Press, 1980). For a more recent and sympathetic account of the essay see James Connelly, *Metaphysics, Method and Politics: The Political Philosophy of R.G. Collingwood* (Exeter and Charlottesville, Va.: Imprint Academic, 2003), ch. 7, esp. 285–7.

The purpose of this essay is to set down what to the writer seem the chief features of the situation. And here at the beginning it [2] must be said that there will be no attempt to propound a remedy in the sense of a political, economic, or other programme such as has been or might be adopted by a party or sect or class. It will be contended in the following pages that what we are now witnessing is not a minor ailment of our civilization, for which remedial drugs might be prescribed, nor yet a major crisis in its health such as might call for extreme measures medical or surgical; but its death. It will be important to ask what exact meanings such a metaphor should convey: what a civilization is, what its death is, and how that death is related to the lives of the persons who have enjoyed it. From the answers to these questions will emerge an answer to the further question, how persons whose civilization is dying can or should behave, while the event so described is going on. But questions of this kind—philosophical questions, let us call them— fail to awaken interest, and rightly so, until the urgency of discuss- ing them has been established. I shall therefore begin with an attempt to describe those features in the modern world which make it appear to so many observers that modern civilization is destroying itself, or that modern man (in the words of my title) is going or has gone mad. If the reader follows me here, on the question of fact, he may go on to follow me in thinking that an inquiry into the causes and curability of this madness is worth undertaking.

[3] I. THE MARKS OF MADNESS

If a man of great intelligence, great bodily strength, and great mental energy, were found working out elaborate schemes for the betterment of his own condition, and throwing all his powers into their realization; and if it were seen, even by himself, that these schemes when realized involved his own impoverishment, misery, and ultimate destruction, and yet he was unable to stop inventing them and carrying them out, psychological medicine would call him the prey of a neurosis, and ordinary people would call him mad.

That is the condition of civilized man today. I will try to justify this statement by considering various branches of his activity and showing how the general character of self-frustration is evident in them all.

The most flagrant example is that of warfare and its instruments. In mere scale, as judged by the size of armies engaged in battles, the ravages of war as a parasite on civilized life, have increased vastly in the last few centuries. From hundreds in the Middle Ages, the size of armies went up to thousands in the seventeenth century, tens of thousands in the Napoleonic wars, and hundreds of thousands today. As the populations of European nations rose in arithmetic proportion, the percentage of their manhood liable to destruction on the battlefield rose in geometric; the process culminating in the theory, widely preached today, that the armed force of a nation is the nation itself in arms. The conception of armies as protecting non-combatants has by now all but disappeared. In modern warfare there are no non-combatants. War as a means to peace, armed force as a safeguard for the peaceful activities of the nation, these are obsolete notions. The modern nation is in the condition of a man who spends every penny that his safe contains in making it burglar-proof. Modern war is the mutual attempt to burgle these formidable but empty safes. And so obvious has their emptiness become, that a new motive for war has to be invented and fostered by the modern [4] national spirit: no longer greed but fear. In a modern war, no one stands to gain; but every combatant loses, and the defeated nation loses most: it loses the very thing that makes it a nation, namely its power to make war; and therefore any nation, to avoid this ultimate impoverishment, has the right to attack any other of which it is afraid, before it is itself attacked at a time favourable to its enemy.

This resolution of the nation into a fighting machine and of national life into warfare, with the resulting disappearance of that peaceful life for whose protection the instruments of warfare were once thought to exist, has hitherto hardly dawned upon the English consciousness. Like many movements in the history of European thought, it has reached its logical conclusion on the Continent while England is still working with the idea of an older generation. In this country we still think of armaments as a means to conserving that peace in which we can live our national life as we conceive it. But this conception is beginning to break down. Already we complain of the burden of armaments, and find ourselves (somewhat to our indignation) involved in an international competition

for the strongest forces which, we clearly see, is absorbing a disproportionate part of the national income; less and less of our
wealth is inside the safe, more and more is represented by the
safe itself. That, at least, is how we think of the situation, and we
quite ingenuously repeat our invitations to a mutual feast of dis-
armament; but what is really happening is that we too are being
drawn into the whirlpool of militarization, and compelled to serve
in deed a deity whom in words we repudiate, the deity whose
religion it is that war, from being a means to peace, should become
an end in itself.

We conceal this fact from ourselves by pretending that our
instruments of war are intended not to be used, but to be held as
a threat against aggressors: pretending that we mean to preserve
peace not by fighting, and through warfare securing the kind
of peace we want, but by being able and ready to fight. [5] That
is as much as to say that we rely on threats which we do not mean to
carry out. If so, our policy is at the mercy of the first nation that
calls our bluff. But if we really mean to fight in certain contingencies—if our threats are more than bluff—our instruments of war
are meant for use, and not for show, and we deceive ourselves and
possibly our neighbours by pretending otherwise.

Nor is it possible to possess instruments of war, to preserve their
efficiency and to render them formidable, without using them.
Manœuvres and target-practice may be as important as we like,
but as a training-ground for men and an experimental field for
testing material they cannot for a moment compare with actual
warfare. And this is well known to every naval and military man,
however much it may suit politicians to forget or deny it. The man
who handles the machine knows that it is made to be used; and
whatever he as a moral agent thinks about the ethics of warfare, he
as a soldier or sailor or airman wants to see his weapons in action.
In the long run, this demand of the machine to be used—or, to put
it less metaphorically, this demand of the man behind the machine
to be allowed to use his machine—is a force on the side of warfare
that, so long as instruments of war exist, will be stronger than any
force on the side of peace. For the logic of the demand is irresistible. On the theory, the machine exists not in order that we may
fight, but in order that we may be able to fight if we are driven to it.
But to fight, here, must mean to fight successfully or victoriously.
The machine, then, exists to give us victory over our enemies,

should enemies appear. But how are we to know what our machine will do for us in such contingencies? Only by experience of what it actually does. We have no way of estimating the potential performance of our machine except in the light of its actual performance: and this must be its performance in warfare.

[6] When we look at the facts, and see how for example the late Victorian battleship was based on the naval actions of the American civil war and that of the Great War on the battle of Tsushima, we can no longer take seriously the conception of armaments as keepers of the peace: it becomes clear that such a conception is grossly self-contradictory. To keep the peace, armaments must be effective: to be effective, they must be designed on the basis of searching experiments, and only war can provide those experiments. War, actual war, is thus the presupposition of there being armaments. Frequent, destructive, and hotly contested war is the presupposition of there being highly efficient armaments. If there were a long period in which armed nations were at peace with one another, the first nation that felt uneasy at the obsolescence of its weapons must provoke a war in order to get the needful experience for bringing them up to date.

What is to be done with such a situation: as a matter of practical politics? Any nation that allowed its armaments to become weak would, in the present state of the world, be destroyed by its neighbours, without doing anything for the cause of peace. A League of Nations cannot solve the problem without facing the alternative of either becoming itself a belligerent, using armaments of its own or the forces put at its disposal by its constituent members, or else confining itself to diplomatic weapons and expressions of disapproval against aggressors. In the first alternative, some wars may be averted; but war as such remains a reality. In the second, it will soon be found that disapproval is powerless against aggression, and those who intend to make war at their own time and in their own way will join in such expressions of opinion when it suits them and laugh at them when the time comes to throw off the mask. I am not raising the question whether, at the present moment, more temporary good can be done by supporting the League of Nations or by some other policy: I am only urging that, on a longer view, no such policy can do away with war.

[7] War is the ultimate end of the modern state. All the forces that go to make up the modern state combine to drive its activity in

the direction of warfare. On the other hand, war is rapidly becoming more and more destructive, and has now reached a point in its development where it cannot be waged at all, on any considerable scale, without involving the destruction of civilization over the entire field of conflict. The first of these truths is consciously grasped by the militarists of today and in particular by the autocracies that have in some countries grown up on the ruins of nineteenth-century liberalism. The second is realized by the pacifists, who are strongest in those countries where liberalism still survives. The militarists accuse the pacifists of feeding upon illusions and failing to see the inevitability of war; the pacifists accuse the militarists of failing to see that war, if it is allowed to go on, must destroy civilization. The first accusation is well founded. It is a fact that the traditional politics which in England is called democracy, and on the Continent liberalism, is here out of date. It thinks of war as an instrument which statesmen are free to use or not to use in pursuit of their ends, whereas it is in reality a monster which, having invoked it, they now cannot exorcise. What began as a means to an end beyond itself has lost that character: it has become a thing that must be used, whatever comes of it. The militarist sees this, and the pacifist does not: so far the militarist has the clearer vision. But, the pacifist retorts, the militarist could not be a militarist if he realized that war and civilization are incompatible. Is this really so certain? Much that has happened in militarist countries within the last few years suggests that in those countries what we call civilization is no longer valued. Freedom of thought and speech, personal liberty, and many other features of what we should call civilized life, have been deliberately repudiated with the avowed aim of rendering the nation a more docile and responsive fighting-machine. For the militarist, the incompatibility of civilization and war is only a nail in the coffin of civilization. The only corporate activity which he recognizes as desirable in a nation is warfare itself.

[8] But this conception of national life, so logically thought-out and so publicly preached by militarist nations today, is madness. War is no more a complete life for the community than fever is a complete life for the organism. Economically considered, war is a destruction of wealth: a destruction of actual wealth, and even more important, a destruction of potential wealth. There must be wealth in order that there may be war; but if war is the end of a

nation's life, its wealth exists and is created not in order to be consumed but in order to be destroyed. There must be towns, not to be inhabited but to be bombed; farms, not to be cultivated but to be burnt; children, not to grow to maturity but to be killed on the battlefield. And a suspicion arises that the holocaust of modern war is the safety-valve of an economic system where production, pursued as an end in itself and getting out of touch with consumption, has loaded the world with unwanted goods. But this cannot be the explanation, for if these goods were unwanted their destruction, like that of a target in gunnery practice, would not be an act of war. The militarist must value his children and his property, or the Moloch to whom he sacrifices them would not be appeased. The sacrifice is the self-torture of an insane civilization.

Politically considered, war may be called the continuation of policy or the breakdown of policy: the two formulae mean the same thing; namely that when persuasion fails, recourse is had to violence.[1] In order that there should be a war, there must first be a policy: some constructive plan of national life which statesmen are trying to put into practice. War comes about when in the way of this policy obstacles arise which cannot be otherwise overcome. It is of the essence of war that it should thus presuppose policy: every war is directed towards 'aims' or 'objectives', to be realized through its instrumentality. War cannot, therefore, be its own end: the policy of a nation cannot be simply to make war. A war waged for the realization of no end beyond itself, and beyond all war as such, would not be a war, but a very expensive, cruel, and insane form of sport, a sport whose suppression would be a legitimate war-aim of every civilized state.

[9] Alike economically and politically, therefore, the militarism which is so deeply rooted in our modern political system is a form of insanity. To represent war as the ultimate and highest end of the state is to misconceive both the relation between war and wealth,

---

[1] This is an allusion to Karl von Clausewitz's (1780–1831) famous dictum: 'War is nothing but the continuation of politics with the admixture of other means.' More usually it is rendered: 'War is the continuation of politics by other means.' In his notes for the revision of *On War*, dated July 1827, Clausewitz says: '*War is nothing but the continuation of policy with other means*. If this is firmly kept in mind throughout it will greatly facilitate the study of the subject and the whole will be easier to analyze' [emphasis in the original]. See Clausewitz, *On War*, ed. and tr. Michael Howard and Peter Paret (Princeton: Princeton University Press, 1984), 69.

and the relation between war and policy. The inference might seem to be that the militarist nations are a kind of mad dogs, to be set upon and exterminated by all sane members of society. And this inference would be just if the spirit of militarism were a national characteristic. But it is a historical phenomenon; and the sources of its growth are present everywhere in the modern world. Its essence is the doctrine that war, which is in fact an instrument of policy, is an end in itself. That doctrine has already been so widely accepted that those who do not consciously embrace it are finding themselves compelled to act as if they did; and this compulsion comes not from the fact that others around them are preaching and practising it and must be imitated—there is no compulsion on a sane man to imitate a lunatic neighbour—but from the fact that the doctrine in question is one application of a general principle which has been adopted throughout our civilization as the first maxim of wisdom. This principle is the rule: 'take care of the means, and the ends will take care of themselves'. Obedience to this rule is the method in the madness of modern civilization. We take infinite pains to provide ourselves with means by which all sorts of ends might be achieved. We then omit to consider what ends we shall achieve by their help; and treat the mere utilization of the means, no matter what result comes of it, as if that were a sufficient end and the reward of our labours. How this method works in other cases than that of war will be considered hereafter; but in that case the thing is plain.

Warfare, the organized warfare of states as distinct from mere personal violence, is not a primitive human institution. It was invented at a relatively high stage of civilization, and was invented as a cheap and easy way of acquiring riches. For a strong and active barbarian tribe, it is easier to win cattle, slaves, and grain by raiding the possessions of a neighbour tribe than by cultivation and purchase. In such wars much wealth changes hands, little is destroyed: what is [10] destroyed can be easily replaced; and what is diverted into forging the instruments of war need be no very large percentage of the whole. To economic ends, political ends may be added: domination may be desired for its own sake, and wars of conquest, as distinct from wars of exploitation, may be fought. Or a war may be waged for religious motives, the glory of God, not the glory of man, being the prize. The destructiveness of economic or acquisitive warfare is limited by the need to make a profit out of it; hence the conqueror is not willing to spend more than he is likely to get, nor is he likely to bleed his victims to the point of exhaustion. Warfare of this kind may in fact lead to a sort of symbiosis of an industrious people with a warlike one: the warlike plundering the industrious, but careful not to destroy their productive power, and willing to protect them against being plundered by another. Political warfare is crueller and more destructive: but even here a limit is set to its destructiveness by the fact that a conqueror would, in general, rather rule over a tolerably prosperous people than over a wilderness. Religious warfare is the cruellest of all, because the issues at stake being purely spiritual there is no care for material welfare, or even for the life of the body: the very existence of infidels is unpleasing to God and their complete destruction is meritorious. Since the seventeenth century, all wars between civilized peoples have tended to be at bottom wars of religion, the cultural ideals for which people nowadays mostly profess to fight being in the nature of religious principles, however little they may associate themselves with deities and temples. Not only do they resemble religious wars in being fought for spiritual ideals, they resemble them in their absolute ruthlessness and in the fact that they recognize no limit to their destructiveness of life or property. Thus in their general character they resemble religious wars: but they differ from religious wars in that they set before themselves no definite aim, and therefore have no definite criterion of victory or defeat. In a seventeenth-century religious war there was a definite question to be settled by fighting: the question, for [11] example, whether a certain country should worship God according to the Roman or Lutheran form. The settlement of that question terminated the war. In a modern war like that of 1914–18, both parties are aware that they are fighting for spiritual principles, not for economic gains; but neither side is capable of stating what these principles are, with enough precision to enable themselves or a third party to decide at some given moment, that the war is over and that this or that side has won. The aims of the belligerents are swamped in the task of fighting, and the war is over when one side is unwilling to fight any longer. This is as much to say that, in spite of the vaguely religious or quasi-religious character of modern warfare, it is not truly religious, for, so far from having a religious motive, it has no motive at all. It is notorious that in a modern war there are no victors. The reason for this is now clear. In order that someone may win a war, the war must be about something: there must be aims on both sides, and a question to be settled by fighting. In modern war, there are no such conditions. There are, therefore, no victors and no vanquished: only combatants seared alike by the furnace they have conspired to light, all exhausted, though exhausted in varying degrees.

War has always been a parasitic growth in the flesh of civilization. Recourse to warfare has always been an attempt to get something for nothing, to short-circuit the slow processes of honest economic production, political construction, or religious teaching. Dishonesty and parasitism have always existed in the world and, no doubt, will always exist. But the continued life of an organism acting as host to a parasite depends on its solvency in the daily balance-sheet of existence. When the parasitic growth drains more out of its host than the organism can afford to give it, the host dies. Down to the nineteenth century, the wastage of war, though growing in bulk, had kept [12] within such limits that the vital energies of civilization could repair it. In the twentieth, this balance has been reversed. Today, war is a bottomless pit into which all the material and spiritual wealth of the world is draining away.

This is not merely a question of quantities. It is not simply that modern war is, as regards its scale, more destructive than ever before. Had that been all, its ravages might have been met by an increase in the powers of production; and the reality of such an increase is one of the most obvious facts about the modern world. But no hope can be built upon this fact: because (to continue the metaphor) the parasitic growth has now become malignant. In other words, the vast increase in the scale and destructiveness of modern warfare is an outward symptom of a change in the spirit of warfare and in the way in which war is conceived by mankind. Formerly, wars were waged on a small scale partly because science had not yet invented sufficiently destructive weapons, and the power of the state had not yet developed to a point at which all the forces of society could be focused on the battlefield: but partly also because a system of principles prevailed in the civilized world which, though it never abolished war entirely, kept it within bounds by assigning to it the position of a mere instrument of policy.

Machiavelli says much of war, but is careful to insist that it is always subordinate to the nobler art which he calls statecraft;[2] and

---

[2] See Niccolò Machiavelli, *The Prince*, ed. Quentin Skinner and Russell Price (Cambridge: Cambridge University Press, 1988).

Hobbes, though he holds that war is the natural condition of mankind and that sovereigns are always, in their relations with each other, at least potentially in that condition, holds also that the first law of nature and first business of human wisdom is to seek peace and ensue it.[3] Not until the nineteenth century do we [13] find the opinion beginning to be held that war is the highest function of the state. For Hegel,[4] war is a necessary consequence of the fact that states are individuals, externally related to one another. So long as they claim sovereignty, those discords which cannot but arise between finite individuals as such, can be resolved only through war.[5] And because sound morality and sound politics alike are based on recognizing things as they are and accepting their consequences, willingness to engage in war is the expression of a people's moral health in its indifference towards personal wealth and security, and victorious warfare is a means of uniting a people, overcoming its dissensions, and confirming the internal

---

[3] Cf. Thomas Hobbes, *Leviathan, or the Matter, Forme, and Power of a Common-Wealth Ecclesiasticall and Civill* (London: for Andrew Crooke, 1651): 'during the time men live without a common Power to keep them all in awe, they are in that condition which is called Warre; and such a warre, as is of every man, against every man' (62); 'yet in all times, Kings, and Persons of Soveraigne authority, because of their Independency, are in continuall jealousies, and in the state and posture of Gladiators; having their weapons pointing, and their eyes fixed on one another' (63); '*That every man, ought to endeavour Peace, as farre as he has hope of obtaining it; and when he cannot obtain it, that he may seek, and use, all helps, and advantages of Warre*. The first branch of which Rule, containeth the first, and Fundamental Law of Nature; which is, *to seek Peace, and follow it*' (64).

[4] Struck out: 'willingness to engage in war is the expression of the moral health of peoples in their indifference to personal wealth and security; and victory in war is a means of uniting a people, overcoming its internal differences, and re-establishing the internal prestige of its government. (*Philosophy of Right*, § 324). War is for him the inevitable corollary'. Hegel's *Naturrecht und Staatswissenschaft im Grundrisse* was tr. by S. W. Dyde as *Hegel's Philosophy of Right* (London: G. Bell & Sons, 1896), and by Collingwood's pupil, T. M. Knox (Oxford: Clarendon Press 1942). The standard modern translation is *Elements of the Philosophy of Right*, ed. Allen W. Wood, tr. H. B. Nisbet (Cambridge: Cambridge University Press, 1991). Collingwood is here overstating Hegel's position. War, for Hegel, is much less of a war because European states comprise a family in which constraints operate (§ 338–9). See David Boucher, *Theories of International Relations from Thucydides to the Present* (Oxford: Oxford University Press, 1998), ch. 14.

[5] Collingwood inserts the parenthetical reference to Hegel's § 334 at this point, which begins: 'Consequently, if no agreement can be reached between particular wills, conflicts between states can be settled only by *war*.' See *Elements of the Philosophy of Right*.

prestige of its government.[6] Following Hegel's lead in their various ways, the revolutionary socialists preached the inevitability of a class-war, conceiving classes as individual entities in an economic world as Hegel had conceived states as individual entities in a political; the naturalists taught that the evolution of higher forms of life had proceeded and must proceed through a struggle for existence; and a school of political thinkers rose to a position of dominance in Germany with the gospel of war as the true end of the state and the means both of moral regeneration and political progress.[7]

All these doctrines, taken in their practical sense as exhortations to the pursuit of war as something intrinsically valuable, are sophistical. All alike are based on confusing the general notion of conflict or struggle with that special kind of conflict [14] or struggle which is properly called by the name of war. It is certainly true that there can be no life, whether organic life or spiritual life (moral or economic or political), without a constant overcoming of obstacles; and that these obstacles very often exist through the action of other living beings, pursuing in their own way ends similar to one's own. In that case the overcoming of difficulties becomes a victory over opponents. But there are many kinds of victory, beside that which is won by means of bullets and bayonets and poison gas; and a philosophical demonstration of the necessity of conflict for life itself has no bearing on the necessity of conflict waged by those peculiar means.

Confusions like this do not happen without a cause. The underlying motive of this confusion is the recognition of a hard fact, whose reality cannot be cancelled by removing the confusion of thought: the fact that war has got out of hand and, from being an instrument of policy, has become what psychologists call a compulsion, something that we do blindly and madly. Why has this happened? Not merely because science has put into our hands

[6] Collingwood inserts the parenthetical reference to Hegel, § 324, at this point.

[7] Here Collingwood echoes a view that did not go uncontested. He is alluding to the views expressed in J. K. Bluntschli, *The Theory of the State*, 3rd edn. (Oxford: Clarendon Press, 1888); Heinrich von Treitschke, *Politics* (London: Constable, 1916); and Friedrich von Bernhardi, *Germany and the Next War* (London: Arnold, 1914).

engines of destruction which we cannot prevent ourselves from
using, though that is true; but, at bottom, as Hegel saw, because of
our political system, with its double insistence on the individuality
and sovereignty of the state. Militarism is sovereignty conceived in
terms of individuality: the absolute and unlimited power of the
state in all that affects its own concerns, combined with its merely
external relation to all other states.

This conception of the state is not new. What is new is the power
which modern science has given to us of working out its implications in practice. [15] In working out those implications with the
resources of modern science, we have brought ourselves to the
position I have tried to describe: the position of a civilization able
scientifically to destroy itself, and unable to hold its hand from
doing so.

Were it possible to divest ourselves of the scientific knowledge
that we now possess, and to return in that respect to the condition
of the seventeenth or eighteenth century, the instruments of this
corporate suicide would fall from our hands. But it is not possible;
and if it were, the underlying motive would remain, and we should
resume the old search for weapons to carry it into effect. If the
clock could be put back, its hands would in time return to their
present position.

On the other hand, it is clear that no further growth of scientific
knowledge will improve our situation. Its development up to
the present time has put new powers at our disposal, but has
not taught us to use them wisely. Further development will give
us further powers, but the wise use of them is a different thing
from the possession of them, and is what science itself cannot
teach us.

The only remedy is to revise our conception of the state. Any
proposal for such revision will at once encounter the objection that
the root of war is a combative instinct inherent in human nature.
This, once more, is sophistry. Conflict, I repeat, is a condition of
all life: but conflict and war are not the same thing, and the
combative instinct, if there is such an instinct, no more entails
the national use of battleships and bombing aeroplanes than it
entails the private use of rapiers and daggers in the street. We
must turn, then, from the consideration of modern war to the
consideration of modern politics.

318   THE MODERN UNEASE

[16] II. THE ATTACK ON LIBERALISM[8]

The plainest political fact of our times is the widespread collapse of
what I shall call, using the word in its Continental sense, liberalism.[9] The essence of this conception is, or was, the idea of a
community as governing itself by fostering the free expression of
all political opinions that take shape within it, and finding some
means of reducing this multiplicity of opinions to a unity. How this
is to be effected, is a secondary matter. One method is to assume
that the political opinions held in the community fall into two main
groups; to use this division as the basis for a distinction between
two parties; to form a parliament whose members are elected by
constituencies; and finally to form a government consisting of
members of that party which has a majority in parliament. What
makes such a system liberal is none of this machinery, but the
principle that political decisions shall be made solely by persons
who have heard, or at least had every opportunity to hear, both
types of opinion about them. A constituency elects its member
after hearing both candidates express their views on current issues;
parliament, as the sovereign body, acts after a debate in which
chosen spokesmen on both sides take part.

This is, of course, not the only possible system that is liberal in
character. No necessary connexion exists between liberal principles and territorial constituencies, or majority votes, or even
parliamentary representation. The one essential of liberalism is
the dialectical solution of all political problems: that is, their solution through the statement of opposing views and their free discussion until, beneath this opposition, their supporters have
discovered some common ground on which to act.[10]

---

[8] Subheading supplied by the editors.

[9] Collingwood had translated Guido de Ruggiero's *The History of European
Liberalism* (London: Oxford University Press, 1927).

[10] Cf. Collingwood's brief MS note headed 'The Breakdown of Liberalism'
(n.d.) where he defines the liberal idea 'that in addition to α, which is the particular
good of A, and β the particular good of B, there is also a general or common good,
the welfare (i.e. the existence) of the society A + B. This ... is to A more important
than α, and to B more important than β, because it is the presupposition of both:
whatever A or B is to get, he must get as a member of the society A + B, and hence
his first and foremost desire is the desire that this society may continue to exist.' See
Bodleian Library Collingwood Papers, dep. 24/7, fo. 2.

[17] The outward characteristic of all liberalism is the fact that it permits the free expression of opinion, no matter what the opinion may be, on all political questions. This attitude is not toleration; it is not the acquiescence in an evil whose suppression would be a greater evil; it is not a mere permission but an active fostering of free speech, as the basis of all healthy political life. Behind this outward characteristic lies an equally characteristic theory. It is implied that political activity and political education are inseparable, if not identical; that no politician is so expert that he should be allowed to govern without being exposed to the criticism of his fellow experts, none such a beginner or ignoramus that his opinion is valueless to the community. This again implies that politics is a normal form of human activity, one which can be shared very widely among mankind and ought, for the sake of the best human life, to be shared as widely as possible. Political activity is conceived as something that circulates freely through the community and draws vigour from this free circulation: good governments receiving additional strength from the enlightened and co-operative criticism of their subjects, so that, the more widely political experience and political thought are diffused, the better the government is likely to be. Thus the aim of a liberal system is not simply to solve the political problems of the community as they arise, but to act as a constant school of political experience for the entire body politic, training new leaders and training the rest to co-operate with them in their task.

[18] This conception of political life has been gradually worked out in Europe and America during the last three centuries. It is not a monopoly of any one nation. Perhaps the chief contributions to it, both in theory and in practice, have been made in France, England, and the United States; but it can be properly understood only as a corporate effort on the part of our civilization as a whole; and it is certainly one of the greatest achievements of that civilization. But to call it an achievement is hardly accurate, for it is not and never has been a finished product; as a theory, it has never been authoritatively and finally stated, and as a form of political practice it has never been worked out in all its implications. It has been, not so much something done, as something in the doing: a course of action to which our civilization has committed itself, realizing that the developments to which it will lead are not wholly foreseen.

There are certain conditions under which alone liberalism can flourish. It is not the best method of government for a people at war or in a state of emergency: for then silence and discipline are demanded of the subject, bold and resolute command of the ruler. It is not the best method for a people internally rotten with crime and violence: there, a strong executive is the first thing needed; force must be met by force. These restrictions, however, do not amount to criticisms of liberalism on its own ground. It professes to be a political method, that is, a method by which a community desiring a solution for its own political problems can find one. War is not part of politics, but the negation of politics, a parasitic growth upon political life. To say of a political system that it will not work under conditions of war is only to repeat that it is a political system. Similarly crime is a parasitic growth on [19] the social structure. Society, it has been said, lives on the assumption that murder will not be committed, and for murder one may read crime in general. A community can only live a genuinely political life when crime is, not indeed abolished, but so far kept in check that for ordinary purposes it may be ignored.

Liberalism, then, requires for its success only one condition: namely that the civilization which adopts it shall as a whole and on the whole be resolved to live in peace and not at war, by honest labour and not by crime.[11] It might seem, therefore, that liberalism is a mere utopianism, based on a blindly optimistic view of human nature. But this is not the case. A liberal government is still a government, and like every government must enforce law and suppress crime. Because it sets out to hear every political opinion, it is not committed to the dogma that every human being under its rule has such opinions.

At the present time, liberalism is undergoing attack from two sides at once, by two opposite parties and for two opposite reasons. First, there is the attack from the right. Here the complaint is that liberalism talks instead of acting. Instead of taking up definite problems and fitting them with definite solutions, it spends time collecting opinions about them. What it lacks is efficiency.

---

[11] The following sentence is then deleted: 'For, when it invites the free expression of all political views, it assumes that those who accept the invitation will use it as an opportunity for expressing political views, not as an opportunity for acts of violence.'

The remedy is to suppress parties, parliament, and all the apparatus of a political dialectic, and to entrust the work of government to an expert, exempt from criticism and endowed with power to command, who shall invent his own solutions for all problems as they arise and impose them upon an obedient community.

The ground on which this doctrine rests betrays a genuine and absolute opposition to liberalism. The situation is [20] represented as one of emergency. In emergencies, the method of liberalism is no longer valid. But what we are considering here is no temporary suspension of *habeas corpus* and the freedom of the press, it is a permanent declaration of a state of emergency. Naturally, this form of government is adopted most thoroughly in militaristic countries. Regarding war as the true end of the state, they have proclaimed martial law as a substitute for government, and reject liberalism not because it is politically unsound, but because it is political. The first French Republic fought for liberty and the rights of man; these gangster-governments suppress liberty and deny the rights of man, in order that they may fight.

But this attack on liberalism is gaining ground elsewhere than in countries avowedly militaristic. It is a poison that is permeating the whole of our civilization. A generation has elapsed since Lord Rosebery wrote upon his banner the ominous word 'efficiency'. During that generation there has been a ceaseless movement away from liberal principles in the direction of government by 'orders' originating in the offices of the Civil Service, and parliamentary government, with all that it stands for, has fallen increasingly into discredit. Today, members of all parties and shades of opinion may be heard expressing contempt for it as an outworn system, and demanding a more efficient and expeditious method of conducting public business. Even this country, the home of the parliamentary system, is visibly sliding towards authoritarian government.

This jettison of the liberal principles which our civilization so long and painfully acquired—a jettison conscious and violent in Germany and Italy, careless and almost absent-minded in our own country—is political madness. However much so-called liberal governments have failed in acting up to [21] their principles, those principles themselves are the most precious possession that man has ever acquired in the field of politics. The conception of political life as permeating the whole community, of government as the political education of the people, is the only alternative to anarchy on the one hand and the rule of brute force on the other. The work of government is difficult enough in any case; it is only rendered possible if rulers can appeal, over the heads of criminals, to a body of public opinion sufficiently educated in politics to understand the wisdom of their acts. Authoritarian government, scorning the dialectic of political life in the name of efficiency, and imposing ready-made solutions on a passive people, is deliberately cutting off the branch on which it sits by de-educating its own subjects, creating round itself an atmosphere of ignorance and stupidity which ultimately will make its own work impossible, and make impossible even the rise of a better form of political life. Those enslaved populations, when the memories of a long liberal tradition have died out of their minds, will be no longer able to restore sound government. They will be able only to throw up one gangster government after another. So easy is it to destroy a fabric that has been centuries in the building.

The other attack on liberalism, from the left, complains in effect that liberalism, as it has actually existed, is not genuinely liberal at all, but hypocritically preaches what it does not practice. Behind a façade of liberal principles, the reality of political life has been a predatory system by which capitalists have plundered wage-earners. What is proudly described as the free contract of labour is a forced sale in which the vendor accepts a starvation wage; what is called the free expression of political opinion is a squabble between various sections of the exploiter class, which conspire to silence the exploited. Within the existing political system, there-fore, the exploited class can hope **[22]** for no redress. Its only remedy is to make open war on its oppressors, take political power into its own hands, establish a dictatorship of the proletariat as an emergency measure, and so bring about the existence of a classless society.

In one sense this programme is not an attack on liberalism but a vindication of it. The principles on which it is based are those of liberalism itself; and in so far as its analysis of historical fact is correct, it must carry conviction to anyone who is genuinely liberal in principle and not merely a partisan of the outward forms in which past liberalism has expressed itself. The correctness of this analysis has been demonstrated by the sequel. The attack on lib-eralism from the right has actually been the reaction of privileged classes to this challenge from the left. They have been confronted with a dilemma. The socialist has accused them of using liberal professions as a mask for exploitation. 'If you are liberal, as you claim to be,' he has argued, 'you will confess to exploiting us, and reform your social and economic system. If you cling to your privileges, you can no longer hold them in the name of liberalism: you must retain them, if at all, by brute force.' The attack upon liberalism from the right represents a realization by the privileged classes of the fact that this dilemma cannot be escaped; they have, to that extent, chosen the second alternative and dropped the mask of liberal principle to take up the weapons of class-war.

But the socialist programme as I have stated it, though liberal in principle, is anti-liberal in method. Its method is that of the class-war and the dictatorship. Class-war is war, and the time is past when war could be waged as a predatory measure, in order to seize property or power held by another. That is the old conception of war, which, as we saw in the last chapter [section], no longer applies to the conditions of the modern world. There, war means not the transference of property from the vanquished to the victor, but its destruction; not the seizure of political power, but the disintegration [23] of the social structure on whose soundness the very existence of political power depends. In so far as socialists imagine the coming revolution as a war by which the proletariat shall take possession of what is now enjoyed by its oppressors, they are deluding themselves; the fabric of wealth and government would perish in the war. The only way of avoiding this result would be to ensure, by careful preparation in advance, that there shall be no war, that the revolution shall be accomplished without resistance. But as opinion in the privileged class hardens, reinforced by hope of aid from militaristic states outside, this possibility becomes more and more remote. The socialist revolution in Russia took the world by surprise; but the civil war that rages in Spain as I write, in which the aggressors have been not the socialists but their opponents, shows that socialism cannot expect another walk-over.

I have spoken of class-war as if it entered into the socialist programme as a project for a future undertaking; but no socialist will accept this description of it. I shall be reminded that the class-war is not something in the future, but something that exists here and now, and has existed for generations: a conflict, therefore, which there is no escaping, but one which must be fought out to a finish. I have already shown the confusion upon which this doctrine rests: the confusion between the general idea of conflict or struggle, and the special form of struggle which is properly called war. Healthy political life, like all life, is conflict: but this conflict is political so long as it is dialectical, that is, carried on by parties which desire to find an agreement beyond or behind their differences. War is non-dialectical: a belligerent desires not to agree with his enemy but to silence him. A class-conflict within the limits of a liberal political system is dialectical: one carried on in the shape of class-war is non-dialectical. The ordinary socialist conception of class-war is equivocal, slipping unawares from one of these meanings to the other.

[24] Dictatorship, again, no matter who wields it, means the imposition of ready-made political solutions on a passive people, and is the negation of liberal principles in political method. Orthodox socialism recognizes this, and regards the dictatorship of the proletariat as a brief emergency measure, to be dropped before it has brought about (as it must, if it continues) the political corruption of the whole community. But it is a dangerous matter to surrender principles for the sake of expediency. Only in so far as a people has no liberalism in its bones, can a dictatorship flourish in it for however short a time; and every day of that time means a further weakening of all liberal principle throughout the body politic. In Russia, accustomed as it was to Tsarist rule, the dictatorship of Lenin meant only the replacement of one autocracy by another; but in England, or France, or the United States a socialist dictatorship could be accepted only at the cost of an irremediable outrage to the deepest feelings of the people, a loss of that political self-respect which is the root and safeguard of all their healthy public life.

[25] The fact is that socialism, in the Marxian form in which alone it is a vital force in the world today, carries along with it too much dead weight in the shape of relics from the age in which it was born. From the age of enlightened despotism it inherited the idea of a wise ruler imposing on the people his will for their good: a socialist dictator, placed upon the throne by a successful war, and inaugurating an age when production shall be organized and wealth distributed in the general interest. From the utopianism of the eighteenth century, which found perhaps its last expression

in Kant's essay on *Universal History*,[12] it inherited its dualism between a period of revolution and crisis, and a period when all conflict shall be at an end, the happy millennium of a classless society. From the romanticism of Hegel it inherited the idea of war—not war in general, but class-war—as a glorious consummation of political activity, the same idea which has maddened the brains of the militarists.

All these ideas are obsolete: they have been exploded once for all by that very liberalism against which they are now used as weapons. Enlightened despotism as a political ideal has yielded to the conception of a people as governing itself by a dialectic of political opinion. The dualism between a time of troubles and a millennium lying beyond it has yielded to the conception of conflict as a necessary element in all life and (as yet) not destroying its peace. The conception of war as at once glorious in itself and necessary to the achievement of human ends has yielded to the conception of war as distinct from conflict in general, as something anti-political and, so far as it is merely war, merely evil. In all these three ways socialism, in spite of its affiliation to Hegel's dialectic, shows itself radically un-dialectical, and it is liberalism that has proved the true heir of the dialectical method. To use a socialist phrase, they are undigested lumps of bourgeois ideology in the stomach of socialist thought.

[26] If the abandonment of all attempt to live by liberal principles is madness, why has this madness come upon us? It is easy to blame the mad themselves: to argue that the left has abandoned liberalism because the working classes are resolved to seize property and power from their oppressors, and are too ill-instructed (their own leaders being blind leaders of the blind) to know that what they want to get must be destroyed in their attempts to get it, or else too much the slaves of envy and hatred to care, even though that should happen: to argue that the right has abandoned liberalism because the privileged classes are resolved to hold what they have, even though they and it must perish in defending it. Nothing is gained by blame: something perhaps, by trying to understand.

---

[12] Immanuel Kant, *Allgemeine Naturgeschichte und Theorie des Himmels*, tr. Stanley L. Jaki as *Universal Natural History and the Theory of the Heavens* (Edinburgh: Scottish University Press, 1981).

Liberalism, during the period of its growth and greatness, entirely transformed the inner political life of those countries where it took root. But it never applied itself seriously to the task of reforming their international relations. A statesman of the late nineteenth century, reading the narrative of the massacre of St Bartholomew[13] or the treatment of the Dutch by Alva, would feel that he was reading of events in another world. It had become impossible for subjects of any civilized country to be so used by their government. But if he read of international events in the sixteenth and seventeenth centuries—the wars, the alliances, the treaties—he would recognize little or no change in the practice of his own age, as compared with that of which Hobbes wrote that 'Kings, and persons of Soveraigne authority, because of their Independency, are in continuall jealousies, and in the state and posture of Gladiators; having their weapons pointing, and their eyes fixed on one another; that is, their Forts, Garrisons, and Guns upon the Frontiers of their Kingdomes; and continuall Spyes upon their neighbours.'[14] What change there had been, was for the worse: weapons more destructive, wars more expensive, and national hatreds (a thing hardly known in the [27] seventeenth century) smouldering everywhere. The liberal state of the nineteenth century conceived itself as an individual among individuals, in that false sense of individuality which makes it synonymous with mutual exclusiveness, and denies that between one individual and another there may be organic relations such that the welfare of each is necessary to that of the other. The liberal government which 'trusted the people' hated and feared peoples other than its own. It was this unnatural union of internal liberalism with external illiberalism that led by way of international anarchy to the militarism of today.

If liberalism failed to affect international relations, it failed also in certain ways to affect the inner life of communities. A division was made, both in practice and in theoretical writings, between the

[13] In 1572. See *A Warning peece for London, being a True Relation of the Bloody Massacre of the Protestants in Paris, by the Papists and Cavileers ... Wherein you may take notice of the Barbarous and Bloody Religion of the Papists* (London: for Joseph Hunscott, 1642).

[14] Hobbes, *Leviathan*, 63. We have corrected this quotation against the 1651 edn. of *Leviathan*.

public affairs of the community as a whole and the private affairs of its members. It was held that, whereas a man's political opinions were of interest to the government, whose business it was to elicit them for its own guidance, his private actions, so long as he did nothing illegal, were his own concern. In practice, this meant that his life as a 'business' man was under no kind of control by the state, so that the economic life of the community was an anarchy as complete as international politics. This was tolerable in theory only because of the extraordinary doctrine, learnt from Adam Smith, that free pursuit of individual interest best subserved the interest of all; in practice it was soon found wholly intolerable, and the misery of the weaker, to which it gave rise, was the source of modern socialism.

The two attacks that are now being delivered on liberalism are thus the result of no misunderstanding or perversity; they are the result of a double failure, by the accredited representatives of liberalism in the nineteenth century, to apply their principles to regions where the application was urgently needed. The militarism and the revolutionary socialism which threaten to destroy civilization today are a just punishment for its crimes in the years of its greatness. They spring, not from weakness or falsity in the principles of **[28]** liberalism itself, but from the failure of our grandfathers to put those principles consistently into practice. Where these attacks show symptoms of insanity is the fact that they are directed, not against the incomplete application of liberal principles, but against those principles themselves. For three hundred years, civilized man has been working out a liberal system of political method, applying it, bit by bit, to the various parts of his corporate life. Now, because the application has not proved exhaustive, because there are still some regions unreclaimed by this method, it seems that man has decided no longer to use it, but to throw it away as an ill-tempered child throws away a toy, to give up the attempt at living a political life, and to live in future the life of a gunman, the life of violence and lawlessness, the life which Hobbes, thinking he described the remote past only, and not the future, called solitary, poor, nasty, brutish, and short.[15]

---

[15] Ibid. 62.

[29] III. THE DESTRUCTION OF THE COUNTRYSIDE

When God first made man (so the old story tells us) he gave him a garden to live in; a plot of land, well watered and fertile, to till and tend, to live on its fruits and love as his home. And the first commandment God laid upon man, says the story, was to dress that garden and keep it.

Today, the learned have pushed man's history a stage further back. Behind the earliest cultivators, we can descry the dawning civilizations of food-gatherers. But the story still has a meaning for us. Our own forefathers have lived for a hundred generations and more upon the fruits of the earth. Every advance that we have made in civilization since the Neolithic age has been made upon that basis. Every new discovery in the arts of life, every new addition to our thoughts and imaginings, every new movement in the organization of our societies, has been new growth in a tree of human life whose roots are struck in the soil. At bottom, European civilization, with all its offshoots in America and elsewhere, is an agricultural civilization.

As a matter of economics, this is a commonplace. Everyone knows that, with a few exceptions such as the eating of fish and game and blackberries, wherein we inherit the tradition of the food-gathering societies, our daily meals come from the soil; and that, if eating is the basis of life, agriculture is the basis of our civilization. But I do not mean to discuss economics. There is another aspect of this truth which is less familiar, but not less important.

If man outrages his body by refusing to eat, he dies. If he outrages his mind by injuring the foundations of his emotional life, he goes mad. So far as man is merely a member of the human species, the roots of his emotional life are to be found in his feelings concerning his own body and personality and his relation to his mother, his possible and actual mates, and the other beings with whom, no matter to what type of society he belongs, he comes into necessary contact. Injury to these [30] fundamentally and generally human emotions is the profoundest injury of which the human mind is susceptible. If grave enough, it can make the sufferer cease, in any true sense, to be a man at all. This, therefore, is the region to which curative psychology has rightly turned its chief attention.

But man, whenever we meet him, is more than the bare abstract of human nature. In some shape or other, he possesses a civilization. This consists of a traditional way of life, acquired through a historical process in which the later developments are specialized outgrowths from the earlier. A civilization, in order to be real, must have, as we might say, three dimensions. It must have complexity, or an elaborate system of responses to various situations, such as the need for nourishment, the need for human intimacies, the need for protection against enemies. It must have continuity, or identity with itself in its own past: each element in its structure must have grown out of something that was previously there.[16] And it must have vitality: those to whom it belongs must possess it in the true sense of the word, grasp it and treasure it and believe in it, and refuse to part with it except in exchange for some new civilization which they can recognize as its legitimate continuation and heir.

To these three dimensions of civilization correspond three dimensions of mental life. Its complexity is a function of intelligence, the wit or skill by which man, like other animals, invents his responses to new situations. Its continuity is a function of memory, the self-conscious knowledge of one's own present as the outgrowth of one's past. Its vitality is a function of emotion. If any of these failed, civilization would perish. If intelligence failed, man would lose his power of adaptation and human societies would grow static and rigid like those of bees and ants. If memory failed, he would lose his power of comparing what he is with what he has been and what he might be, and instead [31] of being the master of his responses he would become their slave. If emotion failed, the whole fabric of his civilization would crumble in his hands to dust and vanity, and he would sink back into the condition of a human brute.

Changes in civilization seem, in fact, to have been due often enough to the dying-away of certain emotions.[17] For centuries, people have cared intensely about some one thing, and then it seems that they have ceased to care about that, and have begun to

---

[16] Cf. Collingwood's statement of what he terms the 'Law of Primitive Survivals' in *NL* 65.
[17] Cf. *FT*, particularly the treatment of emotion in FT3 and FT4 on 'The Historical Method' and 'Magic' above.

care about something else. European civilization in the Middle Ages owed its special character to the fact that men cared greatly about God, how to think of him and to manage their relations with him. The difference between medieval and modern civilization consists chiefly in the fact that modern man, from the seventeenth century onwards, came to care less and less about God and more and more about nature, how to understand it and use its powers for his own ends.

The food-gathering men of the Palaeolithic and Mesolithic cultures must, so far as they were civilized in their own peculiar ways, have had their emotions strongly centred upon the search for food in its various forms. By studying the mind of those food-gathering tribes that still exist, we can see how these emotions must have focused themselves upon edible beasts and plants, and crystallized into the shape of totemistic cults which governed man's whole life. With the origin of agriculture, a re-orientation must have taken place in all this emotional tract, and instead of feeling deeply about edible grubs man began to feel deeply about corn, the implements of his labour and the seasons governing the growth of crops. But primarily, his emotions learned to focus themselves upon the land itself, the divine mother from whose body he drew his nourishment. And this filial worship of the land—not the abstract earth, but his own land, the garden that he dressed and kept—was not abolished, but only transformed, when he learnt to think of it not as divine in its own right but as given to him by a God who had made it. That [32] is the point in emotional development which is recorded for us in the first two chapters of Genesis.

The sanity of man, as man, depends on the health of his funda-mentally human emotions. The sanity of man as civilized depends upon the health in him of the emotions fundamental to his type of civilization. A Greek of the time of Socrates in whom the emotions attaching him to his city had become confused or feeble might have been sane, as a man; but as a Greek he would have been mad; and in the sanest men of the time, like Socrates himself, these emotions ran strong and clear, and Socrates died happy because he was true to them: for the life of the city, as Aristotle has taught us, was the contribution that the Greeks made to civilization.

Our own civilization, as we have seen, is fundamentally agricul-tural. Its vitality therefore depends on the health of our emotions regarding the land.[18] The question I am raising in this chapter is whether these emotions are in health or not. Of course, our civilization is not merely agricultural; it is much else besides; it is commercial, industrial, scientific, and so forth; and in order that we should possess it in its fullness we must feel strongly concerning all these developments of it. But that from which they have developed is not something past and dead, which we can now afford to ignore; it is the living root on whose life their life depends; and to care for them, without any longer caring for it, would be like caring for our furniture and clothes while ceasing to care for our own bodies, or caring for victory in a scientific debate without caring for the truth.

The love of our country, therefore, its hills and valleys, rivers and fields and woods, is not an aesthetic enjoyment of the 'beauties of nature'. Indeed, our country as it stands is not a product of nature; it is a garden kept and dressed by generations of men, whose whole character and aspect have been moulded by their labour. Nor is it a patriotic pride in our nation's history as written upon the face of the earth; [33] it is something far deeper and more primitive than that, something into which national pride and national rivalries do not enter. It is an experience neither aesthetic nor political, but in the deepest sense religious.

It may be called the worship of our land as *terra mater*, Demeter, our divine mother; it may be called the love of the land God has given us for our home; whatever it is called, it is a thing of religion, our share in the primitive religion of the earth-goddess and the corn-god, the religion of all agricultural civilizations. And upon

---

[18] Collingwood was here echoing a familiar theme, and one particularly pertinent to the circle of his acquaintances in the Lake District. It is a theme that permeates the liberalism of Adam Smith and John Stuart Mill, but Collingwood is more likely to have had first-hand experience of it through his father's association with the ideas of Ruskin, William Morris, and Wordsworth. The Lake District was, for example, the venue for a three-day manhunt, which was established in 1897 and would comprise an array of journalists, politicians, many of them New Liberals, and academic dons. They would group themselves into 'hares' and 'hounds' pursuing each other over the countryside until dark when they would reassemble and sing songs around a camp-fire. There was a general belief among romantics and New Liberals, including C. F. G. Masterman, that there was something spiritually uplifting about nature that satisfied an emotional need that the town could not. See e.g. Avner Offer, *Property and Politics 1870–1914* (Cambridge: Cambridge University Press, 1981), esp. ch. 20, 'Romantic Residues'.

the vitality of this religious feeling depends the vitality of our civilization as a whole.

Until the nineteenth century, this feeling for the land was strong and general. Proof of this is to be found, not so much in the literature of the time (where it is, as a rule, rather taken for granted than expressed), as in the way in which the land was actually treated. The spirit of this treatment has left very legible monuments in the buildings that were put up in each generation. The country-houses of England, large and small, erected from the sixteenth century to the nineteenth, are designed with an instinctive sympathy for their surroundings which can bear comparison with that of a Greek temple. Like Greek temples, they are conceived as ornaments of the country; beautifully wrought jewels placed on hill-sides or by rivers, in sites at once healthy for occupation and suitable for showing off their beauty, while they in turn enhance the beauty of the landscape. From the Tudor period, when conditions of life in the country became peaceful, down to the earlier years of Queen Victoria, through all variations in architectural style, we find a constant succession of buildings which always in this way at once adorn and are adorned by their surroundings. This effect was not produced accidentally. It was the result of a loving care for the country, and a desire to do right by it whenever a new building was [34] put up or an old one altered.

Many crimes have been laid at the door of the Industrial Revolution; but in a direct and immediate sense the ruin of the English countryside cannot be included among them. The scarring of its surface with mines, and the building of mills, were not in themselves fatal to it. Both mine and mill have a dignity of their own, not wholly discordant with the spirit of the country to which, after all, they belong no less intimately than barn and dovecote and oast-house. But nevertheless, our present outrages can trace their pedigree back to the beginnings of the machine age. A new and sinister influence began to creep into English domestic architecture through the growth of cheap and ugly houses for the new industrial proletariat, and whole towns thus built began to spring up in manufacturing districts. With the coming of railways, too, men began to tolerate the defacement of the country by the hard lines and the mechanical curves of permanent ways drawn across its face. Gradually there grew up an antagonism between industry and agriculture as two rivals for political patronage. With the repeal of the Corn Laws, the first serious blow was struck at an agricultural life which was still the most advanced and prosperous in Europe; with the agricultural depression of the late nineteenth century, beginning in the 1870s and intensified in the 1890s, the wealth of the countryside was destroyed and its life frozen into immobility. By 1897 rents had so shrunk that owners were no longer receiving the value of the interest upon the sum which it would cost to replace their farm-buildings and fences. Economically speaking, the countryside was ruined. Its ruin was a perfectly deliberate act of national policy, brought about by successive governments in which industrial interests had acquired the ascendancy. As it expressed its will through Parliament, the nation had ceased to care about the land.

The rest of the story is soon told. By the turn of the century, the motor-car was beginning to put traffic once more on the derelict roads, and the country was being discovered [35] by the town-dwellers. A movement began which has gathered momentum down to the present day, and has not yet reached its peak: the invasion of the country by petrol-driven hordes from the towns. These invaders are moved partly by the growing desire of all classes to escape at all costs and in any direction from the frightful thing that a modern town has become; partly by the discovery that the English countryside, with its age-long life of dignified labour and ceaseless adornment, is a thing of rare beauty: one of the loveliest of our national possessions. If that life had still been going on, the invasion could have been absorbed by the countryside. The demand for weekend cottages, homes for retired businessmen, and 'dormitory' suburbs for those working in the towns, could have been met by a flood of new buildings in the living tradition of country architecture, and these new buildings would have been as much an adornment to the countryside as the old buildings which we still justly admire. But the countryside was dead. Its economic ruin had killed its crafts and its traditions of design and workmanship. When the invaders brought money into it again and demanded in return cottages and houses and hotels and shops, these things had to be supplied from the towns themselves. The architecture of the town, as corrupted by the housing tradition of the industrial revolution, began to spread over the face of the country. The speed-tracks of railways were echoed by the speed-tracks of arterial roads. Those parts of the country that lay

nearest to the large towns were made loathsome by the disease of
these new growths, and the country-seekers were driven further
and further afield, always travelling faster and always pushing the
edges of the devastated area further over the face of the land.
Today, those parts of the country which are, as we call it, 'unspoilt'
by this leprosy are shrinking under our eyes.

The horror with which this process is watched [36] even by
those who are foremost in promoting it has led to a movement for
protecting the 'amenities' of the countryside and saving what is left
of them from destruction. But what are the implications of this
proposal? To preserve the amenities of any given district means, in
plain English, to restrict as far as possible the destruction of old
buildings there and the erection of new ones, the construction of
new roads, and so forth: in other words, to conserve the aspect of
that region in a frozen immobility. The reason why this is desired
is that any new building put up in that district is assumed (and in
the main rightly assumed) to mean a blot on its character and a
defacement of its beauty. But no such assumption was made by our
forefathers. On the contrary, they could build what they liked,
confident that it would only be a further adornment to the land.
Why have we lost this confidence? It is not because we lack well-
trained architects, and clients anxious to preserve the beauties
among which they desire to live. It is because we no longer feel
towards the country as towards a garden in which God has put us
to dress and keep it: we no longer have that religious sense of a
loving union with its soil. Those who wish to preserve its amenities
are as far from having this sense as those who recklessly destroy
them. The speculative builder looks upon it as something to exploit for his own advantage; his enemy, its would-be preserver,
looks upon it as an object of aesthetic enjoyment, a museum
exhibit. It is hard to say which of them is remoter in spirit from
the old religion of earth and seasons and crops, over whose dead
body they are quarrelling.

Once this is realized, we may perhaps admit that there is right on
both sides. We have made our towns into things from which escape
is absolutely necessary; we cannot, therefore, deny town-dwellers
the benefit of country air and country scenery, even if the arterial
road, the charabanc, and the bungalow [37] are the price we must
pay. We have killed the agricultural civilization of our fathers, and,
with our habitual respect for dead civilizations, the least we can do

is to preserve its choicer relics as museum exhibits, carefully grouted and shored up against collapse, as the Office of Works preserves the relics of a castle or an abbey. That whole villages should become parts of a vast national museum is neither impossible nor unreasonable.

But a difficulty stands in the way of accepting this double proposal. The thing which it is proposed to divide into a town-dwellers' playground and a museum exhibit is the dead body of our own agricultural life. If it is true that agriculture is the root of our entire civilization, we cannot do that: not because our bodies will starve, but because the emotional foundations of our civilized life will perish. The horror with which we contemplate the deface-ment of the countryside may be unreasoning, but it is not unrea-sonable. It is the blind working in us of a conviction that our country, with its landscape enriched by centuries of human labour and care, is a thing that we cannot afford to lose, and must some-how keep alive, rescued both from the speculative builder and from the museum-curator. The sense of futility with which, des-pite our love of ships and engines and motor-cars we often find ourselves oppressed when considering the triumphs of our indus-trial civilization, is a sign that at its roots our culture lacks vitality. Instinctively, we turn to the country when we seek for a renewal of emotional power, as Antaeus in the fable derived fresh strength from touching the earth: in walking and camping and field sports we try not so much to exercise our bodies as to refresh our minds. But these are only drugs for a jaded civilization. The earth whose contact would heal us is no mere playing-field. [38] It is the fruitful, life-giving soil from which in the sweat of our brow we win our bread: not a weekly cheque to be exchanged for bread, but the bread itself, the actual nourishment of our life. Industry, if it consciously nourishes itself from roots in agriculture, is well. Cut off from those roots, it is a kind of madness which may endure for a time in a feverish and restless consciousness, but can have no lasting vitality. Of this we are beginning to be aware; we know that our civilization has in it a sickness of the mind, a morbid craving for excitement, a hyperaesthesia of emotion, for which it offers no cure. There is a cure, if only we could get it: the deep, primitive, almost unconscious emotion of the man who, wrestling with the earth, sees the labour of his hands and is satisfied.

BIBLIOGRAPHY OF WORKS CITED

1. PUBLISHED WORKS BY COLLINGWOOD CITED IN EDITORIAL
APPARATUS

'Aesthetic', in R. J. S. McDowall (ed), *The Mind* (London: Longmans & Co., 1927), 214–44.
The Archaeology of Roman Britain (London: Methuen, 1930).
An Autobiography (London: Oxford University Press, 1939).
An Essay on Metaphysics (Oxford: Clarendon Press, 1940; rev. edn. 1998).
An Essay on Philosophical Method (Oxford: Clarendon Press, 1933).
Essays in the Philosophy of Art by R. G. Collingwood, ed. Alan Donagan (Bloomington: Indiana University Press, 1964).
'King Arthur's Round Table and Mayborough: A Report of the Excursion', *Transactions of the Cumberland and Westmorland Antiquarian and Archaeological Society*, NS 37 (1937), 190–1.
'King Arthur's Round Table: Interim Report on the Excavations of 1937', *Transactions of the Cumberland and Westmorland Antiquarian and Archaeological Society*, NS 38 (1938), 1–31.
The History of European Liberalism, Guido de Ruggiero, tr. R. G. Collingwood (London: Oxford University Press, 1927).
The New Leviathan (Oxford: Clarendon Press, 1942; rev. edn. 1992).
Outlines of a Philosophy of Art (Oxford: Clarendon Press, 1925).
'The Place of Art in Education', *Hibbert Journal*, 24 (1925–6), 434–48.
The Principles of Art (Oxford: Clarendon Press, 1938).
The Principles of History, ed. W. H. Dray and W. J. van der Dussen (Oxford: Clarendon Press, 1999).
Religion and Philosophy (London: Macmillan & Co., 1916).
Review of Carl Gustav Jung's *Psychological Types or the Psychology of Individuation*, tr. H. Godwin Baynes, International Library of Psychology, Philosophy and Scientific Method (London, 1923), in the *Oxford Magazine*, 41 (1922–3), 425–6. Reprinted in *Collingwood Studies*, I (1994), *The Life and Thought of R. G. Collingwood*, 188–90.
Review of Myron F. Brightfield's *The Issue in Literary Criticism* (1932), in *Philosophy*, 12 (1937), 114–16.
Roman Britain (Oxford: Oxford University Press, 1932).
Roman Britain and the English Settlements, with John N. L. Myers, vol. i of *The Oxford History of England*, ed. G. N. Clark (1936), 2nd edn. (Oxford: Clarendon Press, 1937).

The Roman Inscriptions of Britain (Oxford: Clarendon Press, 1965). Completed by R. P. Wright. (Vol. ii, ed. S. S. Frere, Margaret Roxan, and R. S. O. Tomlin, 1990.)

Speculum Mentis or, the Map of Knowledge (Oxford: Clarendon Press, 1924).

'Two Roman Mountain-Roads', *Transactions of the Cumberland and Westmorland Antiquarian and Archaeologial Society*, NS 37 (1937), 1–12.

2*a*. COLLINGWOOD'S 'FOLKTALE MANUSCRIPT'

Note: items in this section are not in alphabetical order, but are listed according to the numerical order of the box and item referred to in Ruth A. Burchnall's *Catalogue of the Papers of Robin George Collingwood (1889–1943)* (1994) for the Bodleian Library Collingwood Papers. In both sections 2*a* and 2*b*, as indicated in square brackets against certain entries, we have adopted Burchnall's expanded or descriptive title wherever this seems to clarify the contents of the manuscript. Titles are otherwise those entered by Collingwood on the manuscripts themselves.

'English Folklore I–III' (n.d.), Bodleian Library Collingwood Papers, dep. 21/1–3. [Collingwood's reading notes on folklore.]

'I' ['Fairy Tales A'] (n.d.), Bodleian Library Collingwood Papers, dep. 21/4.

'II. Three Methods of Approach: Philological, Functional, Psychological' (n.d.), Bodleian Library Collingwood Papers, dep. 21/5.

'III. The Historical Method' (n.d.), Bodleian Library Collingwood Papers, dep. 21/6.

'IV. Magic' (n.d.), Bodleian Library Collingwood Papers, dep. 21/7.

'Modern Science a Development of that Ritual We Miscall Magical' (n.d.), Bodleian Library Collingwood Papers; dep. 21/8.

'The Authorship of Fairy Tales' (n.d.), [title struck out and retitled 'Folklore and Folktale'], Bodleian Library, Collingwood Papers, dep. 21/9.

'Cinderella' (n.d.), [no title given], Bodleian Library Collingwood Papers, dep. 21/10.

'Untitled manuscript concerning the problem of diffusion versus the independent origin of folk tales' (n.d.), [Burchnall], Bodleian Library Collingwood Papers, dep. 21/11.

'Table of survey, possibly of the incidence of various folk tales in different countries' (n.d.), [Burchnall], Bodleian Library Collingwood Papers, dep. 21/12. [Not reproduced here.]

'Notes from Edwin Hartland's Presidential Address to the Folklore Society in 1900' (n.d.), [Burchnall], Bodleian Library Collingwood Papers, dep. 21/13. [Not reproduced here.]

2*b*. OTHER UNPUBLISHED MANUSCRIPTS BY COLLINGWOOD PRINTED
HERE, AND/OR CITED IN EDITORIAL APPARATUS

'Aesthetic Theory and Artistic Practice' (23–28 February, 1931), ['the complete form of the paper which was to be delivered, in abbreviated form, as a lecture before the British Institute of Philosophical Studies on March 17, 1931'], Bodleian Library Collingwood Papers, dep. 25/4.

'Art and the Machine' (n.d.), Bodleian Library Collingwood Papers, dep. 25/8.

'The Breakdown of Liberalism' (n.d.), Bodleian Library Collingwood Papers, dep. 24/7.

'C[umberland] & W[estmorland] Brit[ish] Sett[lement]s' (n.d.), Bodleian Library Collingwood Papers, dep. 23/26.

'The Devil in Literature—An Essay upon the Mythology of the Evil One . . . Read before "Etanos" 1908', Bodleian Library Collingwood Papers, dep. 1/1.

'Excavations at King Arthur's Round Table, Eamont Bridge, Westmorland July 1937', Bodleian Library Collingwood Papers, dep. 23/23.

'Fragments of Early Drafts of *The New Leviathan* (1942), n.d., [*c*.1939–40]', [Burchnall], Bodleian Library Collingwood Papers, dep. 24/12.

'The Good, the Right, and the Useful—Exeter College Dialectical Society, March 3, 1930', [Burchnall], Bodleian Library Collingwood Papers, dep. 6/5.

'Goodness, Rightness, Utility—Lectures delivered in H[ilary] T[erm] 1940 . . . written Dec. 1939–Feb. 1940', [Burchnall], Bodleian Library Collingwood Papers, dep. 9.

'Ground plan of "King Arthur's Round Table 1937"', [Burchnall], Bodleian Library Collingwood Papers, dep. 23/18.

'"Human Nature and Human History"—March 1936. First draft of paper rewritten May 1936 and sent up for publication by the British Academy', Bodleian Library Collingwood Papers, dep. 12/11.

'Jane Austen' (n.d., ?.1934), Bodleian Library Collingwood Papers, dep. 17/3.

'Jane Austen—Johnson Society Nov. 27. 1921', Bodleian Library Collingwood Papers, dep. 17/2.

'Lectures on Moral Philosophy—1933', Bodleian Library Collingwood Papers, dep. 8.

Letter to the Folk Lore Society, 15 May 1937, and other papers, FLS Archives, 'FLS Corres.' boxes for 1937 and 1938; see also 'Minutes of Evening and General Meetings, 1936–59'.

Letters to O. G. S. Crawford, Bodleian Library, Bodl. MS. Crawford 3, fo. 205, and Bodl. MS Crawford 4. [Copies MS.Facs.c.148, fos. 42–6.]

'Man Goes Mad—Rough MS. Begun 30 Aug. 36', Bodleian Library Collingwood Papers, dep. 24/4.

'"Mayborough & King Arthur's Round Table", a paper read 8 July 1936', Bodleian Library Collingwood Papers, dep. 23/16.

'"Method and Metaphysics"—Paper read before the Jowett Society, 19 June 1935', Bodleian Library Collingwood Papers, dep. 19/3.

'Notes towards a Metaphysic' ('begun Sept. 1933'). Bodleian Library Collingwood Papers, dep. 18/3.

'Round Table Notebook 2. Parallel sites & illustrative material', Bodleian Library Collingwood Papers, dep. 23/24.

'Observations on Language' (n.d.), Bodleian Library Collingwood Papers, dep. 16/13.

'Outline of "Lectures on the Philosophy of Art Delivered . . . T[rinity] T[erm] 1924", with an accompanying letter from "E. F. C.", possibly Edgar Carritt, July 1924', [Burchnall], Bodleian Library Collingwood Papers, dep. 25/2.

'"Outline of a Theory of Primitive Mind", Dec. 1933', Bodleian Library Collingwood Papers, dep. 16/8.

'"Who was King Arthur?" (paper to the *Martlets*, Univ. Coll. Oxon., June 1936)', Bodleian Library Collingwood Papers, dep. 23/15.

'"Words and Tune", an essay written Sept. 1918', [Burchnall], Bodleian Library Collingwood Papers, dep. 25/1.

3. WORKS CITED OR ALLUDED TO BY COLLINGWOOD IN THE MANUSCRIPTS

Note: except where Collingwood supplies the full details in his own note, it is not usually practical to ascertain the edition of a work that Collingwood refers or may allude to. Publication details in this section of the Bibliography should in such cases be taken as indicating editions that could have been available to Collingwood, though to assist readers with access to relevant contextual materials, the section also lists some readily accessible recent editions and/or translations. Broad references by Collingwood to whole authors or works in the main text of the manuscripts, e.g. 'Molière', or to classics or well-known works substantially discussed by Collingwood, such as *Emma*, or *Pride and Prejudice*, are not recorded in this list; nor are passing allusions or references to major authors such as Shakespeare, available in any number of editions at any time and not usefully specifiable here.

AARNE, ANTTI, *Leitfaden der vergleichenden Märchenforschung*, FF Communications, 2/13 (Helsinki, 1913).

ABRAHAM, KARL, *Selected Papers of Karl Abraham*, ed. Ernest Jones, tr. Douglas Bryan and Alix Strachey (London: Hogarth, 1927).

ALISON, ARCHIBALD, *Nature and Principles of Taste* (Dublin, 1790).

ASHFORD, DAISY, *The Young Visiters: Or, Mr. Salteena's Plan* (London: Chatto & Windus, 1919).

AUSTEN, JANE, *Jane Austen's Letters to her Sister Cassandra and others*, ed. R. W. Chapman, 2 vols. (Oxford: Clarendon Press, 1932).

—— *Love and Freindship* (sic) (1790), *Love & Freindship and Other Early Works*, with a Preface by G. K. Chesterton (London: Chatto & Windus, 1922).

BARHAM, RICHARD HARRIS, *The Ingoldsby Legends, or, Mirth and Marvels, by Thomas Ingoldsby*, pseud., 2nd ser., 5th edn. (London: Richard Bentley, 1852).

BASILE, GIAMBATTISTA, *Lo Cunto de li cunti overo la trattenemiento de' Peccerille, de Gian Alessio Abbatutis*, 5 vols. (Naples: Ottavio Beltrano, 1634–6), tr. N. M. Penzer, *The Pentamerone of Giambattista Basile*, 2 vols. (London: John Lane and the Bodley Head, 1932).

BEETHOVEN, LUDWIG VAN, Piano Concerto No. 5, E flat major. Op. 73.

BERGSON, HENRI, 'Les Deux Sources de la morale et de la religion' (1932), tr. R. Ashley Audra and Cloudesley Brereton, with the assistance of W. Horsfall Carter, *The Two Sources of Morality and Religion* (London: Macmillan & Co., 1935).

—— *Laughter: An Essay on the Meaning of the Comic*, tr. Cloudesley Brereton and Fred Rothwell (1911; London: Macmillan & Co., 1935).

—— *Le Rire: Essai sur la signification du comique* (first published in book form 1900, with a 43rd edn. Paris: Librarie Félix Alcan, 1935).

BERNHARDI, FRIEDRICH VON. *Germany and the Next War* (London: Arnold, 1914).

BLACKSTONE, SIR WILLIAM, *Commentaries on the Laws of England*, 4 vols. (Oxford: Clarendon Press, 1765–9).

BLAKE, VERNON, *Drawing for Children and Others* (London: Humphrey Milford, Oxford University Press, 1927).

BLAKE, WILLIAM, *Songs of Innocence and of Experience, Shewing Two Contrary States of the Human Soul* (London, 1789).

BLEEK, W. H. I., and LUCY C. LLOYD, *Specimens of Bushman Folklore* (London: G. Allen & Co., 1911).

BLUNTSCHLI, J. K., *The Theory of the State*, 3rd edn. (Oxford: Clarendon Press, 1888).

BOSWELL, JAMES, *Life of Johnson*, ed. George Birkbeck Hill and L. F. Powell, 6 vols. (Oxford: Clarendon Press, 1934).

BREUER, JOSEF, and SIGMUND FREUD, *Studien über Hysterie* (Vienna: Franz Deuticke, 1895).

BREUIL, ABBÉ HENRI, and MILES CRAWFORD BURKITT, *Rock Paintings of Southern Andalusia: A Description of a Neolithic and Copper Age Art Group* (Oxford: Clarendon Press, 1929).

BRONTË, CHARLOTTE, *The Shakespeare Head Brontë*, ed. T. J. Wise and J. A. Symington, *The Brontës: Their Lives and Friendships and Correspondence in Four Volumes*, ii. *1844–1849* (Oxford: Blackwell, 1932).

BROOKE, RUPERT, *Collected Poems of Rupert Brooke: With a Memoir* (by Edward Marsh) (London: Sidgwick & Jackson, 1918).

BROWN, THOMAS, M. D., *Lectures on the Philosophy of the Human Mind*, 4 vols. (Edinburgh: James Ballantyne, 1820).

BROWNE, SIR THOMAS, *Religio Medici* (London: for Andrew Crooke, 1643; London: Everyman's Library, 1906).

BROWNING, ROBERT, *Men and Women*, 2 vols. (London: Chapman & Hall, 1855).

BURNE, CHARLOTTE, Presidential Address, 'The Value of European Folklore in the History of Culture', *F-L* 21/1 (30 Mar. 1910), 14–41.

BUTLER, BISHOP JOSEPH, *Fifteen Sermons Preached at the Rolls Chapel* (London: J. and J. Knapton, 1726).

CAMPBELL, JOHN FRANCIS, *Popular Tales of the West Highlands*, 2nd edn., 4 vols. (No place of publication: Gardner, 1890).

CARRITT, EDGAR F., *Theory of Beauty* (1914; 3rd rev. edn. London: Methuen, 1928).

—— *The Theory of Morals: An Introduction to Ethical Philosophy* (Oxford: Oxford University Press, 1928).

CHILDE, V. GORDON, *The Bronze Age* (Cambridge: Cambridge University Press, 1930).

—— *The Dawn of European Civilization* (London: Kegan Paul & Co., 1925).

—— *Man Makes Himself*, Library of Science and Culture, 5 (London: Watts & Co., 1936).

CLAUSEWITZ, CARL VON, *On War*, ed. and tr. Michael Howard and Peter Paret (Princeton: Princeton University Press, 1984).

COX, MARIAN ROALFE, *Cinderella: Three Hundred and Forty-Five Variants of Cinderella, Catskin, and Cap o' Rushes, abstracted and tabulated, with a discussion of Medieval Analogues and Notes*, with an Introduction by Andrew Lang (London: David Nutt, for the FLS, 1893).

CRAWFORD, O. G. S., and ALEXANDER KEILLER, *Wessex from the Air* (Oxford: Clarendon Press, 1928).

CROCE, BENEDETTO, *Problemi di estetica: E contributi alla storia dell'estetica italiana*, vol. i of *Saggi filosofici*, 14 vols. (Bari: Laterza, 1910–52).

Daily Chronicle (17 Feb. 1912).

DE VRIES, JAN, *Die Märchen von Klugen Rätsellösern eine Vergleichende Untersuchung*, FF Communications, 24/73 (Helsinki, 1928).

DÉCHELETTE, JOSEPH, *Manuel d' Archéologie préhistorique, celtique et galloromaine*, 11 vols. (Paris, 1908–24).

DESCARTES, RENÉ, *Discours de la méthode pour bien conduire sa raison et chercher la vérité dans les sciences* (Leiden, 1637).

DICK, CHARLES GEORGE COTSFORD, 'King Cophetua', with words by Alfred Lord Tennyson (London, 1876).

DISRAELI, BENJAMIN DISRAELI, earl of Beaconsfield, *Sybil; or, The Two Nations*, 3 vols. (London: Henry Colburn, 1845).

EVANS, JOAN, *Pattern: A Study of Ornament in Western Europe from 1180 to 1900*, 2 vols. (Oxford: Clarendon Press, 1931).

FORKEL, JOHANN NIKOLAUS, *Johann Sebastian Bach: His Life, Art, and Work*, tr. Charles Sandford Terry (London: Constable & Co., 1920).

FOX, SIR CYRIL, *The Personality of Britain: Its Influence on Inhabitant and Invader in Prehistoric and Early Historic Times*, 2nd edn. (Cardiff: National Museum of Wales, 1933).

FRANCK, CÉSAR, *Ce qu'on entend sur la montagne: Poème symphonique* (1846).

FRAZER, SIR JAMES G., *Adonis, Attis, Osiris: Studies in the History of Oriental Religion*, 2 vols. (London: Macmillan, 1906), part 4 of the 3rd edn. of *The Golden Bough*, 12 vols. (London: Macmillan, 1907–15).

—— *Aftermath: A Supplement to the Golden Bough* (London: Macmillan, 1936).

—— *Folklore in the Old Testament*, 3 vols. (London: Macmillan, 1918).

—— *The Golden Bough: A Study in Magic and Religion*, 2 vols. (London: Macmillan, 1890).

—— *The Golden Bough: A Study in Magic and Religion*, 3rd edn., 12 vols. (London: Macmillan, 1907–15).

—— 'Some Popular Superstitions of the Ancients', *F-L* 1/2 (June 1890), 145–71. Reprinted in *Garnered Sheaves: Essays, Addresses, and Reviews* (London: Macmillan, 1931), 128–50.

FREUD, SIGMUND, 'Fragment of an Analysis of a Case of Hysteria' (1905).

—— *Totem and Taboo: Resemblances Between the Psychic Lives of Savages and Neurotics*, tr. A. A. Brill (London: Kegan Paul, Trench, Trubner, 1919).

GLANVILL (or GLANVIL), JOSEPH, *Saducismus Triumphans: Or the Full and Plain Evidence Concerning Witches and Apparitions* (London, 1681).

GOETHE, JOHANN WOLFGANG VON, *Faust* (Wein: Cappi & Diabelli, 1821).

GRIMM, JACOB, and WILHELM, *Kinder-und Hausmärchen, Gesammelt durch die Bruder Grimm*, 2 vols. (Berlin: Realschulbuchhandlung, 1812–15).

HADDON, A. C., Review of Sir James Frazer, *The Golden Bough*, *F-L* 12/2 (June 1901), 230–3.

HARTLAND, EDWIN SIDNEY, *Ritual and Belief: Studies in the History of Religion* (London: Williams & Norgate, 1914).

—— 'Totemism and Some Recent Discoveries' [Presidential Address to the FLS], *F-L* 11/1 (Mar. 1900), 52–80.

HEGEL, GEORG WILHELM FRIEDRICH, *Introductory Lectures on Aesthetics*, tr. Bernard Bosanquet (1886), ed. Michael Inwood (London: Penguin Books, 1993).

HERBERT, GEORGE, *The Temple: Sacred Poems and Private Ejaculations* (Cambridge, 1633).

HOBBES, THOMAS, *Leviathan, or the Matter, Forme, & Power of a Common-Wealth Ecclesiastical and Civill* (London: for Andrew Crooke, 1651).

HOCART, ARTHUR MAURICE, *The Progress of Man: A Short Survey of his Evolution, his Customs and his Works* (London: Methuen, 1933).

HUME, DAVID, *Inquiry Concerning Human Understanding*, vol. iv of *The Philosophical Works of David Hume, including all the Essays*, 4 vols. (Edinburgh, 1826).

HUSSEY, CHRISTOPHER, *The Picturesque: Studies in a Point of View* (London and New York: Putnam, 1927).

JACOBS, JOSEPH (ed.), *Celtic Fairy Tales* (London: D. Nutt, 1892).

—— (ed.), *English Fairy Tales* (London: D. Nutt, 1890).

—— (ed.), *More English Fairy Tales* (London: D. Nutt, 1893).

JAMES, HENRY, Preface to *The Princess Casamassima*, in *Henry James: The Critical Muse: Selected Literary Criticism*, ed. Roger Gard (London: Penguin Books, 1987).

JUNG, CARL GUSTAV, *The Psychology of the Unconscious: A Study of the Transformations and Symbolisms of the Libido*, tr. Beatrice M. Hinkle (New York: Moffat, Yard & Co., 1916).

KANT, IMMANUEL, *Allgemeine Naturgeschichte und Theorie des Himmels* (1798), tr. Stanley L. Jaki as *Universal Natural History and the Theory of the Heavens* (Edinburgh: Scottish University Press, 1981).

KROHN, KAARLE LEOPOLD, *Leitfaden der vergleichenden Märchenforschung*, FF Communications, 2/13 (Helsinki, 1913). [The author of the paper appears to be Antti Aarne.]

—— *Übersicht über einige Resultate der Märchenforschung*, FF Communications, ed. for the Folklore Fellows by Walter Anderson, Johannes Bolte, Kaarle Krohn, Knut Liestøl, C. W. von Sydow, and Archer Taylor, 34/96, Suomalainen Tiedeakatemia, Academia Scientiarum Fennica (Helsinki, 1931).

LÉVY-BRUHL, LUCIEN, *How Natives Think* (1910; London: George Allen & Unwin, 1926).

LÉVY-BRUHL, LUCIEN, *Primitive Mentality* (1922; London: George Allen & Unwin, 1923).

LEWIS, C. S., *The Allegory of Love* (Oxford: Clarendon Press, 1936).

LEWIS, CHARLES B., 'The Part of the Folk in the Making of Folklore', *F-L* 46 (1935), 37–75.

LEYEN, FRIEDRICH VON DER (ed.), *Das Märchen* (1911?). [Probably von der Leyen's *Die Märchen der Weltliteratur* (Jena, 1912–17).]

LITTLEDALE, R. F., 'The Oxford Solar Myth', in *Kottabos* (Trinity College Dublin), 5 (Nov. 1870), 145–54; reprinted in Friedrich Max Müller, *Comparative Mythology: An Essay*, ed. A. Smythe Palmer (London: Routledge, n.d. [actually 1909]), pp. xxxi–xlvii.

LOCKE, JOHN, *Essay Concerning Human Understanding* (1689), ed. Peter H. Nidditch (Oxford: Clarendon Press, 1975).

MACHIAVELLI, NICCOLÒ, *The Prince*, ed. Quentin Skinner and Russell Price (Cambridge: Cambridge University Press, 1988).

MAURER, CONRAD VON, *Isländische Volkssagen der Gegenwart* (Munich, 1860).

MEREDITH, GEORGE, 'On the Idea of Comedy and of the Uses of the Comic Spirit', *New Quarterly Magazine*, 8 (June–July 1877), 1–40.

MERTON, AMBROSE, pseud. [W. J. Thoms], *Gammer G's Famous Histories of Sir Guy of Warwick, Sir Bevis of Hampton, Tom Hickathrift, Friar Bacon, Robin Hood, and the King and the Cobbler* (Westminster: Joseph Cundall, 1846).

—— *Gammer G.'s Pleasant Stories of Patient Grissel, the Princess Rosetta, & Robin Goodfellow, and ballads of the Beggar's Daughter, the Babes in the Wood, and Fair Rosamond* (Westminster: Joseph Cundall, 1846).

MÜLLER, FRIEDRICH MAX, *Comparative Mythology: An Essay*, ed. A. Smythe Palmer (London: Routledge, n.d. [actually 1909]).

—— *Essays on Mythology, Traditions, and Customs*, in *Chips from a German Workshop*, 2 vols. (London: Longmans, Green & Co., 1867).

MÜLLER, WILHELM, and FRANZ SCHUBERT, 'Die schöne Müllerin' (1823).

—— 'Die Winterreise' (1827).

MUSÄUS, JOHANN KARL August, *Volksmärchen der Deutschen*, 5 vols. (Gotha: Ettinger, 1782–87).

NEWMAN, ERNEST, 'Programme Music', in *Musical Studies* (London: Bodley Head, 1905), 103–86.

NIEBUHR, BARTHOLD GEORG, *Lectures on Roman History*, tr. H. M. Chepmel and F. Demmler, 3 vols. (London: Chatto & Windus, 1875).

NIECKS, FREDERICK, *Programme Music in the Last Four Centuries: A Contribution to the History of Musical Expression* (London: Novello, 1906).

PENNIMAN, THOMAS KENNETH, *A Hundred Years of Anthropology* (London: Duckworth, 1935).

PERRAULT, CHARLES, *Histoires ou contes du temps passé* (Paris, 1698), tr. Robert Samber as *Histories, or Tales of Past Times, By M. Perrault* ([London], 1729).

PURCELL, HENRY, setting of John Dryden's *King Arthur, or The British Worthy* (London: for Jacob Tonson, 1691).

QUILLER COUCH, SIR ARTHUR (ed.), *The Oxford Book of Ballads* (Oxford: Clarendon Press, 1910).

RADCLIFFE, ANN, *The Mysteries of Udolpho: A Romance*, 2nd edn., 4 vols. (London: G. G. and J. Robinson, 1794).

ROLLAND, ROMAIN, *Jean-Christophe*, tr. Gilbert Cannan, 4 vols. (London: Heinemann, 1910).

ROUSSEAU, JEAN-JACQUES, *Émile ou de l'éducation* (1762; Paris: Garnier Frères, 1904).

REINACH, SALOMON, *Orpheus: Histoire générale des religions* (Paris, 1909).

RUSKIN, JOHN, *The Works of John Ruskin*, ed. E. T. Cook and Alexander Wedderburn, 39 vols. (London: George Allen, 1903–12).

SCOTT, SIR GILBERT, *Remarks on Secular and Domestic Architecture* (London: John Murray, 1857).

SCOTT, SIR WALTER, *Memoirs of the Life of Sir Walter Scott, Bart*, ed. John Gibson Lockhart, 7 vols. (Edinburgh: Robert Cadell, 1837).

SELBY-BIGGE, L. A. (ed.), *British Moralists, being selections from writers principally of the eighteenth century*, 2 vols. (Oxford: Clarendon Press, 1897).

SHAFTESBURY, 3rd earl of, Anthony Ashley Cooper, *An Inquiry concerning Virtue, in two discourses* (London, 1699).

SHARP, CECIL JAMES, *English Folk-Song: Some Conclusions* (London: Novello & Co., 1907).

SPARROW, JOHN HANBURG ANGUS, *Sense and Poetry: Essays on the Place of Meaning in Contemporary Verse* (London: Constable, 1934).

SPENCER, HERBERT, 'The Origin and Function of Music', *Essays: Scientific, Political, and Speculative* (London: Longman, Brown, Green, Longmans, & Roberts, 1858), 359–84.

SPENCER, SIR WALTER BALDWIN, *Scientific Correspondence with Sir J. G. Frazer and Others*, ed. R. R. Marett and T. K. Penniman (Oxford: Clarendon Press, 1932).

SPINOZA, BARUCH, *Tractatus Theologico-Politicus* (1670; Gebhardt edn., 1925), tr. Samuel Shirley (New York: E. J. Brill, 1989).

STRAPAROLA, GIOVANNI FRANCESCO, *Le piacevoli Notti* (*The Pleasant Nights*), 2 lib. (1550–5), tr. W. G. Waters as *The Facetious Nights*, 2 vols. (London: Society of Bibliophiles, 1898).

STRAUSS, RICHARD GEORG, *Don Quixote . . . Op. 35. Partitur* (Munich: J. Aibl, 1898).

TAYLOR, ARCHER, *The Black Ox: A Study in the History of a Folktale*, FF Communications, 23/1/70 (Helsinki, 1927).

TREITSCHKE, HEINRICH VON, *Politics* (London: Constable, 1916).

TYLOR, SIR EDWARD B., *Primitive Culture: Researches into the Development of Mythology, Philosophy, Religion, Language, Art and Custom*, 3rd rev. edn. 2 vols. (London: John Murray, 1891).

VOLTAIRE, 'Goût', *Œuvres Complètes de Voltaire*, 52 vols. (Paris: Garnier Frères, 1843–85), xix, *Dictionnaire Philosophique*, iii (1879), 270–84.

A Warning peece for London, being a True Relation of the Bloody Massacre of the Protestants in Paris, by the Papists and Cavileers . . . Wherein you may take notice of the Barbarous and Bloody Religion of the Papists (London: for Joseph Hunscott, 1642).

WESTON, JESSIE L., *From Ritual to Romance* (Cambridge: Cambridge University Press, 1920).

WHATELY, RICHARD, *Historic Doubts Relative to Napoleon Buonaparte* (London: J. Hatchard, 1819).

—— 'Modern Novels' (review of *Northanger Abbey, and Persuasion*) in *Miscellaneous Lectures and Reviews* (London: Parker & Son, 1861), 282–313.

WHEELER, ROBERT ERIC MORTIMER, *Prehistoric and Roman Wales* (Oxford: Clarendon Press, 1925).

YEATS, W. B., *Fairy and Folktales of the Irish Peasantry* (London: W. Scott, 1888).

—— *Irish Fairy Tales* (London: T. Fisher Unwin, 1892).

—— *The Celtic Twilight: Men and Women, Dhouls and Faeries* (London: Lawrence & Bullen, 1893).

4. FURTHER WORKS AND SECONDARY SOURCES CITED IN ADDITIONAL EDITORIAL MATERIAL

AKGRIGG, G. P. V. (ed.), *Letters of King James VI and I* (Berkeley: University of California Press, 1984).

ALCOFF, LINDA MARTIN (ed.), *Epistemology: The Big Questions* (Oxford: Blackwell, 1998).

ALLEN, N. J., *Categories and Classifications: Maussian Reflections on the Social* (Oxford and New York: Berghahn, 2000).

ANDERSON, GRAHAM, *Fairy Tale in the Ancient World* (London: Routledge, 2000).

APPLEBY, JOYCE, 'One Good Turn Deserves Another: Moving beyond the Linguistic: A Response to David Harlan', *American Historical Review*, 94 (1989), 1326–36.

ARNOLD, MATTHEW, 'Last Words' (1861), 'On Translating Homer', *On the Classical Tradition*, ed. R. H. Super, vol. i of *The Complete Prose Works of Matthew Arnold*, 11 vols. (Ann Arbor: University of Michigan Press, 1960–77), 97–216.

ASAD, TALAL, *Genealogies of Religion: Disciplines and Reasons of Power in Christianity and Islam* (Baltimore and London: Johns Hopkins University Press, 1993).

AUSTEN-LEIGH, JAMES EDWARD, *A Memoir of Jane Austen. Second edition, to which is added Lady Susan, and fragments of two other unfinished tales by Miss Austen* (London: Richard Bentley & Son, 1871).

AUSTEN-LEIGH, MARY AUGUSTA, *Personal Aspects of Jane Austen* (London: John Murray, 1920).

AYER, A. J., *Language, Truth and Logic*, with an Introduction by Ben Rogers (1936; London: Penguin, 2001).

—— *Philosophy in the Twentieth Century* (New York: Vintage Books, 1984).

BANKS, MARCUS, and HOWARD MORPHY (eds.), *Rethinking Visual Anthropology* (New Haven and London: Yale University Press, 1997).

BARTHES, ROLAND, 'The Death of the Author' ('La Mort de l'auteur' (1968)), in *Image Music Text*, tr. Stephen Heath (London: Harper Collins, 1977), 142–8.

BEIDELMAN, T. O., *E. E. Evans-Pritchard: A Bibliography* (London: Tavistock, 1974).

BENJAMIN, WALTER, 'L'Œuvre d'art à l'époque de sa reproduction mécanisée', *Zeitschrift für Sozialforschung*, 5/1 (1936), 40–63, tr. as 'The Work of Art in the Age of Mechanical Reproduction', *Illuminations*, ed. Hannah Arendt, tr. Harry Zorn (London: Pimlico, 1999), 211–44.

BERGSON, HENRI, *Œuvres*, ed. André Robinet and Henri Gouhier (Paris: Presses Universitaires de France, 1959).

BLAKE, VERNON, *Relation in Art: Being a Suggested Scheme of Art Criticism* (Oxford: Clarendon Press, 1925).

BOSANQUET, BERNARD, *History of Aesthetic* (London: Allen & Unwin, 1892).

BOSWORTH, JOSEPH, and THOMAS NORTHCOTE TOLLER, *Anglo-Saxon Dictionary*, 2 vols. (Oxford: Clarendon Press, 1882–1921).

BOUCHER, DAVID, 'Collingwood and Anthropology as a Philosophical Science', *History of Political Thought*, 23 (2002), 303–25.

—— 'New Histories of Political Thought for Old', *Political Studies*, 31 (1983), 112–21.

—— 'The *Principles of History* and the Cosmology Conclusion to *The Idea of Nature*', *Collingwood Studies*, 2 (1995), *Perspectives*, 140–74.

BOUCHER, DAVID, 'The Significance of the *Principles of History*', *Journal of the History of Ideas*, 58/2 (1997), 309–30.

—— *The Social and Political Thought of R. G. Collingwood* (Cambridge: Cambridge University Press, 1989).

—— *Theories of International Relations from Thucydides to the Present* (Oxford: Oxford University Press, 1998).

BRADLEY, A. C., *Oxford Lectures on Poetry* (London: Macmillan, 1909).

BRADLEY, F. H., *Appearance and Reality* (Oxford: Clarendon Press, 1930).

BURCHNALL, RUTH A., *Catalogue of the Papers of Robin George Collingwood (1889–1943)* (Oxford: Bodleian Library, 1994).

BUXTON, DUDLEY, *Custom is King: Essays Presented to R. R. Marett* (London: Hutchinson, 1936).

CHOMSKY, NOAM, *Cartesian Linguistics* (New York and London: Harper Row, 1966).

CODRINGTON, R. H., *The Melanesians* (Oxford: Oxford University Press, 1891).

COLLINGWOOD, KATE F., Letter of 28 Feb. 1944 to Kenneth Sisam, Archives, Oxford University Press, OP 2395/17613.

COLLINI, STEFAN and BERNARD WILLIAMS, 'Collingwood, R. G. (1889–1943), philosopher and historian', *Dictionary of National Biography* (Oxford: Oxford University Press, 2004).

CONNELLY, JAMES, 'Aesthetic and the Mind', *Collingwood Studies*, 3 (1996), *Letters from Iceland and Other Essays*, 194–215.

—— *Metaphyics, Method and Politics: The Political Philosophy of R. G. Collingwood* (Exeter and Charlottesville, Va.: Imprint Academic, 2003).

—— 'Natural Science, History and Christianity: The Origins of Collingwood's Later Metaphysics', *Collingwood Studies*, 4 (1998), *Variations: Themes from the Manuscripts*, 101–32.

—— and TARIQ MODOOD (eds.), *Philosophy, History and Civilization: Interdisciplinary Perspectives on R. G. Collingwood* (Cardiff: University of Wales Press, 1995).

COWLING, MAURICE, *Religion and Public Doctrine in Modern England* (Cambridge: Cambridge University Press, 1980).

CRANE, R. S., *The Idea of the Humanities and Other Essays*, 2 vols. (Chicago: University of Chicago Press, 1968).

CROCE, BENEDETTO, *Theory and History of Historiography*, tr. Douglas Ainslie (London: Harrap, 1921).

DALY, MARTIN, and MARGO WILSON, *The Truth about Cinderella: A Darwinian View of Parental Love* (London: Weidenfeld & Nicolson, 1998).

DAVIES, R. T. (ed.), *Medieval English Lyrics: A Critical Anthology* (London: Faber & Faber, 1963).

DICKENS, CHARLES, *Hard Times for these Times* (1854), ed. David Craig (Harmondsworth: Penguin, 1969).

DOUGLAS, MARY, *Purity and Danger: An Analysis of Concepts of Pollution and Taboo* (London: Routledge & Kegan Paul, 1966).

DOWNIE, R. ANGUS, *Frazer and 'The Golden Bough'* (London: Gollancz, 1970).

DRAY, W. H., *History as Re-Enactment: R. G. Collingwood's Idea of History* (Oxford: Clarendon Press, 1995).

DREISBACH, CHRISTOPHER, R. G. *Collingwood: A Bibliographic Checklist* (Bowling Green, Ohio: The Philosophy Documentation Center, Bowling Green State University, 1993).

DUNDES, ALAN, *Cinderella: A Casebook* (Madison: University of Wisconsin Press, 1982).

DURKHEIM, ÉMILE, *The Elementary Forms of Religious Life* (1912), tr. Karen E. Fields (New York: Free Press, 1995).

ELIAS, NORBERT, *The Civilizing Process* (New York: Urizen, 1978).

ELIOT, T. S., *Collected Poems 1909–1962* (London: Faber & Faber, 1970).

—— *On Poetry and Poets* (London: Faber & Faber, 1957).

—— *Selected Essays* (London: Faber & Faber, 1932).

Elizabeth I: Collected Works, ed. Leah S. Marcus, Janel Mueller, and Mary Beth Rose (Chicago and London: University of Chicago Press, 2000).

ELLIS, JOHN M., *One Fairy Story Too Many: The Brothers Grimm and their Tales* (Chicago and London: University of Chicago Press, 1983).

EMMET, DOROTHY, *Function, Purpose and Powers: Some Concepts in the Study of Individuals and Societies* (London: Macmillan, 1958).

—— *Rules, Roles and Relations* (London: Macmillan, 1963).

EMPSON, WILLIAM, *The Structure of Complex Words* (Chatto & Windus, 1951).

EVANS-PRITCHARD, E. E., 'Genesis of a Social Anthropologist: An Autobiographical Note', *The New Diffusionist*, 3/10 (1973), 17–23.

—— *A History of Anthropological Thought*, ed. A. Singer (London: Faber & Faber, 1981).

—— 'The Intellectualist (English) Interpretation of Magic', *Bulletin of the Faculty of Arts*, University of Cairo, 1/2 (1933), 1–21.

—— 'Lévy-Bruhl's Theory of Primitive Mentality', *Bulletin of the Faculty of Arts*, University of Cairo, 2/2 (1934), 1–26, reprinted in *Journal of the Anthropological Society of Oxford*, 1 (1970), 39–60.

—— Review of *Roman Britain* by R. G. Collingwood, new enlarged edn. (Oxford: Clarendon Press, 1932), in *Man*, 32 (Sept. 1932), 220–1.

—— 'Science and Sentiment: An Exposition and Criticism of the Writings of Pareto', *Bulletin of the Faculty of Arts*, University of Cairo, 3/2 (1936), 163–92.

—— *Theories of Primitive Religion* (Oxford: Clarendon Press, 1965).

EVANS-PRITCHARD, E. E., *Witchcraft, Oracles, and Magic among the Azande* (Oxford: Clarendon Press, 1937).
—— *The Zande Trickster*, Oxford Library of African Literature (Oxford: Clarendon Press, 1967).
FELL, ALBERT P., 'R. G. Collingwood and the Hermeneutical Tradition', *International Studies in Philosophy*, 23/3 (1991), 1–12.
Folk Lore Society Archives, 'FLS Corres.' Boxes for 1935, 1937, 1938.
Folk Lore Society Archives, 'Minutes of Evening and General Meetings, 1936–59'.
FOUCAULT, MICHEL, *The Archaeology of Knowledge* (London: Routledge, 1972).
—— *The Foucault Reader*, ed. Paul Rabinow (London: Penguin, 1984).
FRAZER, SIR JAMES G., *The Golden Bough: A Study in Magic and Religion*, ed. George Stocking, 12 vols. (Harmondsworth: Penguin, 1996).
—— *The Golden Bough: A Study in Magic and Religion*, abridged edn. (London: Macmillan, 1922).
GADAMER, HANS-GEORG, *Truth and Method* (1960), tr. Joel Weinsheimer and Donald G. Marshall, 2nd rev. edn. (London: Sheed & Ward, 1989).
GARDINER, PATRICK, *The Nature of Historical Explanation* (1952; London: Oxford University Press, 1961).
GEERTZ, CLIFFORD, *Available Light: Anthropological Reflections on Philosophical Topics* (Princeton: Princeton University Press, 2000).
GELL, ALFRED, *Art and Agency: An Anthropological Theory* (Oxford: Clarendon Press, 1998).
GOMME, SIR GEORGE LAURENCE, *Folklore as an Historical Science* (London: Methuen, 1908).
GREENLEAF, W. H., 'James I and the Divine Right of Kings', *Political Studies*, 5 (1957), 36–48.
—— 'The Divine Right of Kings', *History Today*, 14 (1964), 642–50.
—— *Order, Empiricism and Politics* (Oxford: Oxford University Press for the University of Hull, 1964).
—— 'Hobbes: The Problem of Interpretation' in *Hobbes and Rousseau*, ed. Maurice Cranston and R. S. Peters (New York: Doubleday, 1972), 5–36.
GRIMM, JACOB, and WILHELM GRIMM, *The Complete Fairy Tales of the Brothers Grimm*, tr. Jack Zipes, 3rd edn. (New York: Bantam Books, 2003).
—— and —— *The Complete Grimm's Fairy Tales* (London: Routledge & Kegan Paul, 1975).
GUISTI, SONIA, 'Collingwood's Unpublished Writings on Folklore', *Storia, antropologia e scienze de linguaggio*, 8/3 (1993), 23–41.
HARLAN, DAVID, 'Intellectual History and the Return of History', *American Historical Review*, 94 (1989), 581–609.

—— 'Reply to David Hollinger', *American Historical Review*, 94 (1989), 622–6.

HARTLAND, EDWIN SIDNEY (ed.), *English Fairy and Other Folktales* (London: Walter Scott, 1890).

—— *Primitive Society: The Beginnings of the Family and the Reckoning of Descent* (London: Methuen, 1921).

—— 'Report on Folk-Tale Research in 1889', *F-L* 1/1 (Mar. 1890), 107–17.

HEGEL, GEORG WILHELM FRIEDRICH, *Elements of the Philosophy of Right*, ed. Allen W. Wood, tr. H. B. Nisbet (Cambridge: Cambridge University Press, 1991).

—— *Hegel's Philosophy of Right*, tr. S. W. Dyde (London: G. Bell & Sons, 1896).

—— *Hegel's Philosophy of Right*, tr. T. M. Knox (Oxford: Clarendon Press, 1942).

—— *Naturrecht und Staatswissenschaft im Grundrisse (Grundlinia de Philosophie der Rechts)* (Berlin, 1821).

HELGEBY, STEIN, and GRACE SIMPSON, 'King Arthur's Round Table and Collingwood's Archaeology', *Collingwood Studies*, 2 (1995), 1–11.

HOBART, MARK, 'Summer Days and Salad Days: The Coming of Age of Anthropology', in Ladislav Holy (ed.), *Comparative Anthropology* (Oxford: Blackwell, 1987), 22–51.

HOLLINGER, DAVID A., 'The Return of the Prodigal: The Persistence of Historical Knowing', *American Historical Review*, 94 (1989), 610–21.

HOLLIS, MARTIN, 'Say it with Flowers', in James Tully (ed.), *Meaning and Context: Quentin Skinner and his Critics* (Cambridge: Polity Press, 1988), 135–46.

HOUSMAN, A. E., *Collected Poems of A.E. Housman*, ed. Christopher Ricks (London: Allen Lane, 1988).

HUXLEY, THOMAS, 'Agnosticism' (1889), *The Major Prose Works of Thomas Henry Huxley*, ed. Alan P. Barr (Athens, Ga., and London: University of Georgia Press), 253–82.

—— Review of Charles Darwin's *Origin of the Species*, *Macmillan's Magazine* (1859), 142–8.

JACOBS, JOSEPH, 'Cinderella in Britain', *F-L* 4/3 (Sept. 1893), 269–84.

JAMES, WENDY, *The Ceremonial Animal: A New Portrait of Anthropology* (Oxford: Oxford University Press, 2003).

—— 'Tales of Enchantment: Collingwood, Anthropology, and the "Fairy Tales" Manuscripts', *Collingwood Studies*, 4 (1998), *Variations: Themes from the Manuscripts*, 133–56.

JAUSS, HANS ROBERT, 'Literary History as a Challenge to Literary Theory', *Toward an Aesthetic of Reception*, tr. Timothy Bahti (Minneapolis: University of Minnesota Press, 1982), 3–45.

JENKINS, KEITH, *On What is History?* (London: Routledge, 1995).

JOHNSON, DOUGLAS H., 'W. G. Collingwood and the Beginnings of *The Idea of History*', *Collingwood Studies*, 1 (1994), *The Life and Thought of R. G. Collingwood*, 1–26.

JOHNSON, PETER (ed.), *The Correspondence of R. G. Collingwood: An Illustrated Guide* (Swansea: R. G. Collingwood Society, 1998).

KEANE, JOHN, 'More Theses on the Philosophy of History', in James Tully (ed.), *Meaning and Context: Quentin Skinner and his Critics* (Cambridge: Polity Press, 1988), 204–17.

KNOX, T. M., 'R. G. Collingwood', *Dictionary of National Biography 1941–1950*, ed. L. G. Wickham Legg and E. T. Williams (Oxford: Oxford University Press, 1959), 168–70.

KRAPPE, A. H., *The Science of Folk-Lore* (London: Methuen, 1930).

KUPER, ADAM, *Anthropology and Anthropologists: The Modern British School* (London: Routledge, 1989).

LADURIE, EMMANUEL LE ROY, *The Mind and Method of the Historian* (Brighton: Harvester Press, 1981).

—— *The Peasants of Languedoc*, tr. John Day (London: University of Illinois Press, 1974).

LANG, ANDREW, 'Address to the Folk-Lore Society, session 1889–1890', *F-L* 1/1 (Mar. 1890), 4–15.

—— 'Cinderella and the Diffusion of Tales', *F-L* 4/4 (Dec. 1893), 423–33.

LAWRENCE, D. H., *Phoenix: The Posthumous Papers of D. H. Lawrence*, ed. Edward D. McDonald (London: Heinemann, 1936).

—— *Phoenix II: Uncollected, Unpublished and Other Prose Works by D. H. Lawrence*, ed. Warren Roberts and Harry T. Moore (London: Heinemann, 1968).

—— *Studies in Classic American Literature* (1924), ed. Ezra Greenspan, Lindeth Vasey, and John Worthen, *The Cambridge Edition of the Works of D. H. Lawrence* (Cambridge: Cambridge University Press, 2003).

LEAVIS, F. R., and DENYS THOMPSON, *Culture and Environment: The Training of Critical Awareness* (London: Chatto & Windus, 1933).

—— *Revaluation: Tradition and Development in English Poetry* (London: Chatto & Windus, 1936).

—— *The Great Tradition* (London: Chatto & Windus, 1948).

—— *The Living Principle: 'English' as a Discipline of Thought* (London: Chatto & Windus, 1975).

LEVENSON, JOSEPH R., *Confucian China and its Modern Fate*, 3 vols. (London: Routledge & Kegan Paul, 1958–65).

LÉVI-STRAUSS, CLAUDE, *The Raw and the Cooked: Introduction to a Science of Mythology*, i (1964), tr. J. and D. Weightman (London: Jonathan Cape, 1970).

—— 'The Story of Asdiwal', *Structural Anthropology*, ii (1973) (London: Allen Lane, 1977), 146–97.

—— 'The Structural Study of Myth' in *Structural Anthropology*, i (1958) (London: Allen Lane, 1963), 206–31.

—— *Totemism* (1962; Harmondsworth: Penguin, 1969).

LEWIS, C. S., *Of Other Worlds: Essays and Stories*, ed. Walter Hooper (London: Geoffrey Bles, 1966).

LIENHARDT, GODFREY, 'Edward Tylor (1832–1917)', in Timothy Raison (ed.), *The Founding Fathers of Social Science*, a series from *New Society* (Harmondsworth: Penguin, 1969), 84–91.

LÜTHI, MAX, *The Fairytale as Art Form and Portrait of Man* (Bloomington: Indiana University Press, 1984).

MALINOWSKI, BRONISLAW, *A Diary in the Strict Sense of the Term* (New York: Harcourt, Brace & Wood, 1967).

—— 'Myth in Primitive Psychology' (1926), reprinted in *Magic, Science and Religion: And Other Essays* (London: Souvenir Press, 1974), 93–148.

—— *Sex and Repression in Savage Society* (London: Kegan Paul, 1927).

—— *The Sexual Life of Savages in North-West Melanesia* (London: Kegan Paul, 1927).

MARETT, R. R., *Anthropology*, rev. edn. (London: Thornton Butterworth, 1914).

—— *Faith, Hope, and Charity in Primitive Religion* (Oxford: Clarendon Press, 1932).

—— 'The Growth and Tendency of Anthropology and Ethnological Studies', Plenary Address in the *Proceedings of the International Congress of Anthropological and Ethnological Studies* (London: Royal Anthropological Institute, 1934), 39–53. Summarized in *Man*, 34/162 (1934), 141–2.

—— *A Jerseyman at Oxford* (London: Oxford University Press, 1941).

—— Letter of 11 Feb. 1935, Archives, Oxford University Press, LB 7652.

—— *The Threshold of Religion* (1909), 2nd edn. (London: Methuen, 1914).

MARTIN, REX, *Historical Explanation: Re-enactment and Practical Inference* (Ithaca, NY: Cornell University Press, 1977).

MAUSS, MARCEL, with H. HUBERT, *A General Theory of Magic* (1904), tr. Robert Brain (London: Cohen & West, 1972).

MEEK, C. K., *Law and Authority in a Nigerian Tribe* (Oxford: Clarendon Press, 1937).

—— *The Northern Tribes of Nigeria* (Oxford: Clarendon Press, 1925).

MEI, HUANG, *Transforming the Cinderella Dream: From Francis Burney to Charlotte Brontë* (New Brunswick, NJ, and London: Rutgers University Press, 1990).

METZGERAND, MICHAEL M., and KATHARINA MOMMSEN (eds.), *Fairy Tales as Ways of Knowing: Essays on Marchen in Psychology, Society, and Literature* (Berne and Las Vegas: P. Lang, 1981).

MINK, LOUIS O., *Mind, History and Dialectic* (Bloomington: Indiana University Press, 1969).

Minute Books of the Beaumont Society (Pembroke College, Oxford), McGowin Library, Pembroke College.

Minute Books of the Johnson Society (Pembroke College, Oxford), McGowin Library, Pembroke College.

Minute Books of the Martlets (University College, Oxford), Bodleian MS Top. Oxon. D. 95/3.

MORGAN, MARY AUGUSTA, *On a Pincushion and Other Fairy Tales* (London: Seeley, Jackson & Halliday, 1876).

MÜLLER, FRIEDRICH MAX, *Lectures on the Origin and Growth of Religion*, Hibbert Lectures, 1878 (London, 1878; Routledge/Thoemmes Press, 1997).

MURRAY, M., *The Witch-Cult in Western Europe* (Oxford: Clarendon Press, 1921).

NEUMANN, SIEGFRIED, 'The Brothers Grimm as Collectors and Editors of German Folktales', in Donald Haase (ed.), *The Reception of Grimms' Fairy Tales: Responses, Reactions, Revisions* (Detroit: Wayne State University Press, 1993), 24–40.

NUTT, ALFRED, 'Cinderella and Britain', *F-L*, 4/2 (June 1893), 133–41.

—— Presidential Address on 'The Fairy Mythology of English Literature: Its Origin and Nature', *F-L*, 8/1 (Mar. 1897), 29–53.

OAKESHOTT, MICHAEL JOSEPH, *Experience and its Modes* (Cambridge: Cambridge University Press, 1933).

—— *On History and Other Essays* (Oxford: Blackwell, 1983).

—— *Rationalism in Politics and Other Essays*, ed. Timothy Fuller (Indianapolis: Liberty Press, 1991).

OBEYESEKERE, GANANATH, *The Apotheosis of Captain Cook: European Myth Making* (Princeton: Princeton University Press, 1992).

OFFER, AVNER, *Property and Politics 1870–1914* (Cambridge: Cambridge University Press, 1981).

ONG, WALTER J., *Orality and Literacy: Technologizing of the Word* (London and New York: Routledge, 1982).

ORR, LINDA, 'The Revenge of Literature: A History of History', *Studies in Historical Change*, ed. Ralph Cohen (Charlottesville, Va., and London: University of Virginia Press, 1992), 84–108.

PARKER, CHRISTOPHER, *The English Idea of History from Coleridge to Collingwood* (Aldershot: Ashgate, 2000).

PATRICK, JAMES, 'Fighting in the Daylight: The Penultimate Collingwood', *Collingwood Studies*, 2 (1995), *Perspectives*, 73–88.

PERKINS, DAVID, *Is Literary History Possible?* (Baltimore and London: Johns Hopkins University Press, 1992).

POPE, ALEXANDER, 'An Essay on Criticism' (1711), in *The Twickenham Edition of the Poems of Alexander Pope*, i. *Pastoral Poetry and An Essay on Criticism*, ed. E. Audra and Aubrey Williams (London: Methuen, 1961), 197–326.

POPPER, KARL, *Unended Quest: An Intellectual Biography* (London: Routledge, 1992).

POUND, EZRA, 'The Rev. G. Crabbe, LL.B.', 'The Future' (1917), *Literary Essays of Ezra Pound*, ed. T. S. Eliot (London: Faber & Faber, 1954), 276–9.

PROPP, VLADIMIR, *Morphology of the Folktale*, ed. Louis Wagner and Alan Dundes, tr. Laurence Scott, 2nd rev. edn. (Austin: University of Texas Press, 1958).

RADCLIFFE-BROWN, A. R., 'On Social Structure', Presidential Address to the Royal Anthropological Institute, 1940, *Journal of the Royal Anthropological Institute*, 70 (1940), 1–12; reprinted as ch. 10 in *Structure and Function in Primitive Society, Essays and Addresses* (London: Cohen & West, 1952), 188–204.

RATTRAY, R. S., *Ashanti Law and Constitution* (Oxford: Clarendon Press, 1929).

—— *The Tribes of the Ashanti Hinterland* (Oxford: Clarendon Press, 1932).

RÉE, JONATHAN, 'Life after Life', Review of new edns. of *EM*, *NL* and *PH*, *London Review of Books* (20 Jan. 2000), 9–11.

RICOEUR, PAUL, *Hermeneutics and the Human Sciences*, ed. and tr. John B. Thompson (Cambridge: Cambridge University Press, 1981).

—— *Interpretation Theory: Discourse and the Surplus of Meaning* (Fort Worth, Tex.: The Texas Christian University Press, 1976).

—— *Temps et Récit*, 3 vols. (Paris: Editions du Seuil, 1983–5).

ROBINSON, IAN, *The English Prophets: A Critical Defence of English Criticism* (Denton: Edgeways, 2001).

RORTY, RICHARD, J. B. SCHNEEWIND, and QUENTIN SKINNER (eds.), *Philosophy in History: Essays on the Historiography of Philosophy* (Cambridge: Cambridge University Press, 1984).

RUBINOFF, LIONEL, *Collingwood and the Reform of Metaphysic* (Toronto: University of Toronto Press, 1970).

RUDZIK, MAUREEN E., 'Folklore and History: An Analysis of an Unpublished Manuscript by R. G. Collingwood', Ph.D. thesis (University of Toronto, 1990).

RUSKIN, JOHN, 'Fairy Stories' (1868), *The Works of John Ruskin*, ed. E. T. Cook and Alexander Wedderburn, 39 vols. (London: George Allen, 1903–12), xix. 232–9.

RUSKIN, JOHN, Introduction to *German Popular Stories*, ed. Edgar Taylor (London: John Camden Hotten, 1869), pp. v–xiv.

—— *The Stones of Venice*, 3 vols. (London: Smith, Elder & Co., 1851).

—— *The Stones of Venice*, 3rd rev. edn., 2 vols. (Orpington, Kent: George Allen, 1884).

RUSSELL, BERTRAND, *The Problems of Philosophy* (1912; Oxford: Oxford University Press, 1974).

SAHLINS, MARSHALL, *How 'Natives' Think, about Captain Cook, for Example* (Chicago: Chicago University Press, 1995).

SAID, EDWARD, *Orientalism: Western Conceptions of the Orient* (London: Routledge & Kegan Paul, 1978).

SELDEN, RAMAN, *Criticism and Objectivity* (London: Allen & Unwin, 1984).

SHARP, CECIL JAMES, *English Folk-Song: Some Conclusions* (London: Novello & Co., 1907).

SISAM, KENNETH, Letter of 24 Feb. 1944 to Mrs Kate F. Collingwood, Archives, Oxford University Press, OP 2395/17613.

SKINNER, QUENTIN, 'A Reply to my Critics', in James Tully (ed.), *Meaning and Context: Quentin Skinner and his Critics* (Cambridge: Polity Press, 1988), 231–88.

—— 'The Rise of, Challenge to and Prospects for a Collingwoodian Approach to the History of Political Thought', in Dario Castliglione and Iain Hampsher-Monk (eds.), *The History of Political Thought in National Context* (Cambridge: Cambridge University Press, 2001), 175–88.

—— 'Some Problems in the Analysis of Political Thought and Action', in James Tully (ed.), *Meaning and Context: Quentin Skinner and his Critics* (Cambridge: Polity Press, 1988), 97–118.

—— *Visions of Politics*, i. *Regarding Method* (Cambridge: Cambridge University Press, 2002).

SMALLWOOD, PHILIP, 'From Illusion to Reality: R. G. Collingwood and the Fictional Art of Jane Austen', *Collingwood Studies*, 4 (1998), *Themes from the Manuscripts*, 71–100.

—— 'Historical Re-Enactment, Literary Transmission, and the Value of R. G. Collingwood', *Translation and Literature*, 9/1 (2000), 3–24.

—— ' "The True Creative Mind": R. G. Collingwood's Critical Humanism', *British Journal of Aesthetics*, 41/3 (July 2001), 293–311.

SMITH, TERESA, 'R. G. Collingwood: "This Ring of Thought": Notes on Early Influences', *Collingwood Studies*, 1 (1994), *The Life and Thought of R. G. Collingwood*, 27–43.

SMITH, WILLIAM ROBERTSON, *Lectures on the Religion of the Semites* (Edinburgh: Adam and Charles Black, 1889).

SOUTHAM, B. C. (ed.), *Jane Austen: The Critical Heritage, ii. 1870–1940* (London and New York: Routledge & Kegan Paul, 1987).

SPENCER, SIR BALDWIN, and F. J. GILLEN, *The Arunta: A Study of a Stone Age People*, 2 vols. (London: Macmillan, 1927).

—— *The Native Tribes of Central Australia* (London: Macmillan, 1899).

—— *The Northern Tribes of Central Australia* (London: Macmillan, 1904).

SPITTA, PHILIP, *Johan Sebastian Bach: His Work and Influence on the Music of Germany, 1685–1750*, tr. Clara Bell and J. A. Fuller-Maitland, 3 vols. (London: Novello & Co., 1884).

STEINER, FRANZ BAERMANN, *Franz Steiner: Selected Writings*, ed. Jeremy Adler and Richard Fardon, 2 vols. (Oxford: Berghahn, 1999).

STREET, BRIAN V., *The Savage in Literature: Representations of 'Primitive' Society in English Fiction 1858–1920* (London: Routledge & Kegan Paul, 1975).

TAYLOR, CHARLES, 'The Hermeneutics of Conflict', in James Tully (ed.), *Meaning and Context: Quentin Skinner and his Critics* (Cambridge: Polity Press, 1988), 218–28.

TAYLOR, DONALD S., 'A Bibliography of the Publications and Manuscripts of R. G. Collingwood', *History and Theory*, 24/4 (1985), 218–28.

—— *R.G. Collingwood: A Bibliography* (New York and London: Garland Publishing, 1988).

THOM, PAUL, 'The Intepretation of Music in Performance', *British Journal of Aesthetics*, 43/2 (April 2003), 126–37.

THOMAS, KEITH, *Religion and the Decline of Magic* (Harmondsworth: Penguin, 1972).

TUCK, RICHARD, 'History', in Robert E. Goodin and Philip Pettit (eds.), *A Companion to Contemporary Political Philosophy* (Oxford: Blackwell, 1993), 72–89.

TULLY, JAMES, 'The Pen is a Mighty Sword', in James Tully (ed.), *Meaning and Context: Quentin Skinner and his Critics* (Cambridge: Polity Press, 1988), 7–25.

VAN DER DUSSEN, W. J., *History as a Science: The Philosophy of R. G. Collingwood* (The Hague: Martinus Nijhoff, 1981).

WALZER, MICHAEL, *Exodus and Revolution* (New York: HarperCollins, 1985).

WATSON, GEORGE, *The Literary Critics: A Study of English Descriptive Criticism* (London: Chatto & Windus, 1964).

WHITE, HAYDEN, 'Interpretation in History' (1972), in *Tropics of Discourse: Essays in Cultural Criticism* (Baltimore: Johns Hopkins University Press, 1978), 51–80.

WILLIAMS, F. E., *Orokaiva Society* (Oxford: Clarendon Press, 1930).

WILLIS, R. G., *Signifying Animals: Human Meaning in the Natural World* (London: Allen & Unwin, 1990).

WITTGENSTEIN, LUDWIG, *Philosophical Investigations*, tr. G. E. M. Anscombe (Oxford: Blackwell, 1978).

—— 'Remarks on Frazer's *Golden Bough*', in James Klagge and Alfred Nordmann (eds.), *Philosophical Occasions 1912–1951* (Indianapolis and Cambridge: Hackett, 1993), 115–55.

WOKLER, ROBERT, 'The Professoriate of Political Thought in England since 1914: A Tale of Three Chairs', in Dario Castiglione and Iain Hampsher-Monk (eds.), *The History of Political Thought in National Context* (Cambridge: Cambridge University Press, 2001), 134–58.

WORDSWORTH, WILLIAM, *The Poetical Works of William Wordsworth*, ed. E. de Selincourt and Helen Darbishire, 4 vols. (Oxford: Clarendon Press, 1940–7).

ZIPES, JACK, 'Cross-Cultural Connections and the Contamination of the Classical Fairy Tale', in J. Zipes (ed.), *The Great Fairy Tale Tradition: From Straparola and Basile to the Brothers Grimm* (New York and London: Norton & Co., 2001), 845–69.

—— *Fairy Tale as Myth: Myth as Fairy Tale* (Lexington: University Press of Kentucky, 1994).

—— *Fairy Tales and the Art of Subversion: The Classical Genre for Children and the Process of Civilization* (1983; New York: Routledge, 1991).

—— (ed.), *The Oxford Companion to Fairy Tales* (Oxford: Oxford University Press, 2000).

INDEX

Avebury stone circle lvi, 258
Ayer, A. J. cvii, cix, cx–cxi
Azande
  Zande folktales lxxxvii
  reasoning about witchcraft lxiii,
    lxxxiii, lxxxviii
  Azande lxxxi, lxxxiii,
    lxxxvii–lxxxviii

Bach family 267
Bach, John Sebastian 10, 15, 34,
    93, 274
Back to Methuselah (Shaw) 78
Bacon, Francis 104 n. 42
Balfour, Henry lxix n. 38, 107 n.
    46
Bali xc–xci
Balkans: Cinderella-stories 239
Balzac, Honoré de 21
barbarism xxviii, xlix, lxi, 152 n.
    7, 179 n., 312
  according to Tylor 142
Barraclough, Geoffrey ci
Barthes, Roland xliii
Basile, Giambattista xxvii, 284
Beaumont Society, Pembroke
    College 48 n. 23
Beauty and the Beast 173
beauty 49, 52–3, 54, 55–6
  as felt quality 55
  formal 69–71
  in nature li, 58–62, 68–9, 92
  man-made li
Beethoven, Ludwig van 15, 21,
    35, 36, 91, 274
Bennett, Arnold 47
Bergson, Henri 107–8, 162,
    212
Blackstone, Sir William 261
Blake, Vernon 65 n. 28, 93–4
Blake, William xxix
Boccaccio, Giovanni 21, 281
Bodleian Library xiv

Bombay: Cinderella-stories 237,
    238
Bosanquet, Bernard 98 n. 22,
    107
Botticelli, Sandro: Venus 95
Bradley, F. H. cxi–cxii
Brahms, Johannes 9, 15, 91
Brazil: Cinderella-stories 236
Britannia (George V's yacht) 198
British Museum 117
Brontë, Charlotte 26
Bronze Age lvi, lxii, lxxxvi,
    116–18, 256, 258–9
Brooke, Rupert 8
Brown, Thomas 102
Browne, Sir Thomas 172
Browning Society 45
Browning, Robert 97–8, 102
Burne-Jones, Edward 96 n. 19
Butler, Bishop Joseph 104 n. 42,
    183, 186–7, 189, 193
Butterfield, Herbert xcvii
Buxton, Dudley lxix n. 38

Cambridge School xciii n. 3, xcvii
camera, see photographs
Campbell, J. F. 268, 287
Cap o' Rushes-stories lxxxv, 236,
    242, 244, 245, 246, 249
capitalism 322
Carlyle, Thomas 24
Carpenter, Edward 107 n. 46
Carr, E. H. xcvi
Carritt, E. F. 87 n. 7
Catskin-stories lxxxiv–lxxxv,
    235–6, 240, 242, 244, 245,
    246, 247, 248
causation 144–6, 154, 190, 221
Celebes 207
Celts: Cinderella-stories 239, 241,
    242, 244
Central Europe: Cinderella-
    stories 243

364 INDEX

war the destruction of wealth and
production 310–14
Education Act (1870) 283
education 28, 37–9, 64–6, 77–8
role of art in 303–4
educated élite 263, 281–2
Egypt 270
and *Cinderella*-stories 249
Electra 246
Eliot, T. S. xxix, xxxviii, xli, xlviii,
lxvi, lxxx, 67 n. 35, 125 n. 12,
207 n. 10, 229
The Waste Land xxvii, xxxix; *see
also* 'waste-land'
Elizabeth I 264
Elton, Geoffrey xcvi, ci
Emma 24, 29, 32–3, 44–6, 47
Emmet, Dorothy lxviii–lxix
emotion:
anthropology of lxxxviii–xc
in art and the history of art lii,
51, 53–4
emotional attitude towards
nature 284
emotional foundations of
civilization 335
emotional life central to
history xli, liv, lxi, lxxv,
lxxxiv
in the life of hunters and
cultivators 253–5
emotional injury 196–201
and language xc, 11–14
in D. H. Lawrence xxix
and use of machines or
tools 214–20
emotion rather than intellect the
key to understanding
magic 196–201
emotional aridity of modern
life lxxx, 292
emotional stimulation of modern
mechanized art 298–9

in music 5–8
emotional nature of human
beings cxiv, 197–207, 221,
225, 328–9
neglect or suppression of cix,
cxvi
Romantic xxx
and thought xxxxix, xc
Emperor Concerto (Beethoven) 5
empirical science,
empiricism xxxix, lxxx, cvi,
cvii, cvx–xi, 141
school of anthropological
research 141, 185; *see also*
fieldwork
Empson, William xliv n. 78
enchantment xxiv, xxv, liv, lxxvi,
lxxxvii, cxix, 115
and disenchantment liv
lost lxiii
England: *Catskin*-stories 247
enlightenment, *see* illuminism
Epicureanism 84
Epicurus 88
Essay on Metaphysics
(Collingwood) lxx, cix
Essay on Philosophical Method
(Collingwood) xliv, lix, c,
cviii–cix
ethics 84–6, 88
etiquette 209–14, 222–3
Europa xxxi–xxxii, 173, 187
Europe: *Cinderella*-stories 236,
237, 239, 240–1, 242, 243,
249, 252–3
Evans, Joan 98 n. 24,
103 n. 38
Evans-Pritchard, E. E. lxvii, lxix,
lxx, lxxxii, lxxxvii–lxxxviii,
lxxxix–xc
review of *Roman Britain* lxx
*Witchcraft, Oracles, and Magic
among the Azande* lxxii, lxxxiii

Lightning Source UK Ltd.
Milton Keynes UK
UKOW01n0405181016

285535UK00010B/162/P